Political Analysis
& Public Policy

Political Analysis & Public Policy: An Introduction to Political Science

Joyce M. Mitchell

William C. Mitchell

University of Oregon

Rand McNally & Company · Chicago

Preface:
Hopes and Dreams

Recent years have marked a behavioral revolution in political science and such rapid innovations among the social sciences that most, if not all, of the conventional introductory political science texts are now seriously impaired as introductions. These many extensive changes have posed basic conceptual problems for political scientists both in terms of their inquiries and the substance of their teaching.

As a consequence, many political scientists have wondered what should be taught and some of us have even experimented with varying degrees of success. We have both experimented, independently, in teaching introductory courses for majors and surveys for non-majors. This textbook is a product of our experiences and collaboration.

Unlike the physical sciences and economics, political science has not been a cumulative discipline with work progressing in difficulty from the introductory course through intermediate levels to advanced analyses in graduate school. We hope that this introductory volume will be the first of such an attempt at an integrated series of texts on politics and political analysis. More advanced volumes will lead the student further into the technical analysis of progressively more difficult problems until at the end, hopefully, he is equipped to be a professional political analyst.

For the present we are only interested in *introducing* students to political problems and their solutions. This means: basic questions are presented, some possible answers are hypothesized, and a sampling of the facts are made available for developing explanations. Technical definitions and concepts are minimized as are the actual tools of research. Most students will have little need for them until they know what questions they want answered and the difference between seeking answers and asserting them. At the beginning we hope to enlist interest by showing relevance and illustrating how some sense can be made of the apparent confusion of politics. We hope in the process to develop the student's respect for reasoning with some care and precision about public affairs. Subsequent volumes will assume these things and proceed to more technical analysis and to the promising directions of more intensive inquiry.

We believe that students want and deserve introductions that demand a higher level of thinking; introduce them to more or less current research and theory in the field; have a point of view and not just factual summaries of quickly outmoded data; indicate matters about which we know little; provide encouragement to formulate their own theories and tests of propositions; and, convey some of the excitement that political scientists experience in their own work. Teachers of political science ought to also show relationships among the other social sciences and their own discipline. We believe all these things can be accomplished if only we do not underestimate the capacities of students, most of whom now seem far brighter and better trained than we were at equivalent stages in our own educations. We also believe that textbooks are still highly useful if properly written and taught. We hope that ours is a good book in that it accomplishes these objectives.

Like all producers, we like to engage in some product differentiation in the hope that it will prove more profitable. Mention should be made, therefore, of a number of somewhat atypical features of the book. First, we have chosen to concentrate upon nation-states as the primary unit of analysis but not on institutional description as is generally the case in textbooks. The primary concern is with collective political processes and outcomes; institutional facts are treated as settings and therefore are partial explanations of these same processes and outcomes. The nation-state was selected because it is, in fact, the dominant political unit in the world, not because it is the only one. Our propositions should, we hope, have some relevance to other units such as general associations, trade unions, churches, universities, businesses. Secondly, we have placed considerable emphasis upon individual actors but have used both normative and causal approaches to explaining their choices and behavior. We have, however, in our adoption of normative theory reduced reliance upon purely deductive approaches, just as our use of behavioral explanations makes no presumption of strict causality. Subsequent volumes will rely far more on such formal tools of analysis as causal and deductive models.

As for the content of this particular book, we can only state that it attempts to acquaint the reader with a wide but selective range of facts of political life and some normative advice on judging political systems and policies, and on being more effective politically. Furthermore, the two major parts of the book (analytical and normative) are based upon recent developments including systems analysis, the behavioral orientation, public finance, welfare economics and decision and conflict theory. These diverse but highly complementary approaches and data are integrated in terms of an analysis which emphasizes political actors interacting through various processes and deciding upon collective decisions or public policies which are binding upon all members of national systems. Special public problems are regarded as basic to all systems; they include resource mobilization and allocation, distribution of benefits, allocation of burdens, division of labor, control activities and adaptation to meet uncertain conditions. Part 1, Analytics: Problems and Outcomes, attempts to show the student how to think about such matters, presents some actual data or findings on policy outcomes in each decision area and explains or presents alternative explanations.

In Part 2, Politics and Welfare, we shift our analytical focus from that of fact to that of normative or prescriptive advice. We believe that political scientists can and ought to offer policy advice to citizen and politician, alike, on the politically relevant aspects of public issues. We believe that certain criteria can be advanced for judging the processes and outcomes of political systems. We also believe that the citizen and politician ought to have more explicit decision rules or norms to consult or examine in their efforts at becoming more effective participants. Presumably, most persons wish to achieve better allocations of societal as well as their own resources; better distributions of benefits in society; more equitable allocations of costs or burdens; better and more efficient divisions of labor and control systems; better adaptive capacities for handling change in an uncertain world. Strangely, political science has not seen fit to offer such advice, at least in systematic terms in the more recent decades of the discipline. Consequently, we have had to derive much of our advice and decision rules from elsewhere—public finance, welfare economics and in current ideological writings, for example. Our advice is apt to prove controversial; we hope that instructors and students will make the most of this opportunity to consider and test that advice. Only from explicit debate and thought will better rules and policies be formulated.

As to be expected in a text, we have not produced new information but have called attention to somewhat strange facts from other disciplines and we have done so in an unconventional manner. Such novelties will, we hope, induce greater attention and consideration among political scientists, if not all students. We have footnoted very sparingly, not to persuade readers of our originality but in recognition of student indifference to such academic niceties. The general ideas are all 'in the air' and parentage is well-known, but in the case of specific data or findings we have indicated the sources and bestowed appropriate credits. Teachers will note that occasionally we have inserted partially empty 'tables' into the discussion. Such tables may be viewed as exercises for the students and illustrations of incomplete knowledge. Why should we pretend that we know all that should be known?

We have also included a variety of newspaper items, mostly headlines, to suggest to the skeptical student that the problems we discuss are realities and not arbitrary constructions of some idle professor's dream world. Unhappily, we have not achieved 'balance' in these clippings; most refer to the United States and the western world but there are enough to convey the notion that these things happen elsewhere. At the conclusion of each chapter we have also included a brief reference essay pointing to some seminal sources or discussions of important ideas, and some open issues the venturing student may want to pursue further. Finally, we have appended to each chapter some problems for both analytical and normative purposes. Some of these problems have been 'tested' in actual classes at a number of institutions. Some have proven more successful than others in varying contexts. Many have even proven to be highly interesting to students and some have resulted in term papers that are superior to a good many articles we have read in the journals. In any case, instructors ought to find them challenging aids in teaching. Occasionally we have begun each term or new part of a course by reading some of the more relevant types of questions to the class. The relevance of the subsequent discussions seems to be improved. One unanticipated consequence has been that students readily decide whether they are interested in such matters or feel capable of the tasks before them.

Given the highly unsettled condition of political science, decisions about the nature of a beginning textbook have been most difficult to make. Any number of approaches are currently feasible; which will succeed most in pleasing the professor and/or students cannot be predicted with much assurance. The next few years should witness a proliferation of competing introductory texts. Of course, we hope that ours will take the market by storm, but in any case something better will emerge from all the creative activity now taking place in the study of politics. Our bet is that the present influence of sociology and psychology on political scientists will diminish somewhat and that economics and theories of choice will bring additional perspectives and tools of analysis. This book reflects that judgment and prediction.

Finally, our fondest hope is that this book will assist in the rapidly evolving maturity of political science as a rigorous theoretical discipline with a core and theory more systematic and challenging than has heretofore been the case. The sooner that occurs the sooner this book will suffer obsolescence, a fate we anticipate with mingled pride for having participated in its own creative destruction.

We were aided and encouraged in crucial and very helpful ways in many stages of this collective enterprise. To begin with, the ambition or courage to undertake the project was inspired in large part by the example and kind words of the late Morton Grodzins, whom we had come to admire greatly for his contributions toward reviving public policy as a central focus of political inquiry. We turned to Rand McNally to publish this work because of his fine editorship of the political series of that publishing company. We owe a great deal to the initiative of John Applegath and Jack Carr, then with Rand McNally, for helping us initially. We wish to thank many at Rand McNally for their patience during the many stages and revisions of the manuscript, especially Marianne Clark for her warm support of the earlier product, Jan Miller and Martha Urban for their assistance through production and Larry Malley for his very perceptive guidance.

We are especially grateful for the very detailed and careful suggestions given to one of the several drafts by Robert Dahl. Without those comments we would have inflicted many more errors of logic and evidence than those—very few hopefully—which have slipped through. We also wish to thank William Riker for his encouraging appraisal of the book's overall approach. The final draft profited immensely from the careful reading and suggestions of Ralph Miner; we appreciate his regard for the sensibilities of prospective readers and only wish we could have followed his perceptive critique closer.

To our good fortune, the manuscript received most efficient typing and reproduction services, from Hildegarde Teilheit at the Center for Advanced Study in the Behavioral Sciences, from Bea Read, Betty Solberg and Margaret Pluid of Eugene, Oregon, and from Barbara Frazier at the University of Oregon. Only with their most intelligent handling of the manuscript have we been able to meet the inevitable deadlines.

A very special debt of gratitude goes to the Center for Advanced Study in the Behavioral Sciences for a fellowship that enabled a year's full devotion to this enterprise and for many accommodations and services which were so ideally suited to aiding and abetting the scholar. Our thanks especially to Preston Cutler and Jane Kielsmeier for their gracious supervision of all these comforts and stimulants.

And, last of all, a confession: In the trials of producing this manuscript we learned at first hand of the intricacies in collective political processes and problems discussed in the pages ahead. One problem, the allocation of responsibilities, had to be confronted quite clearly. We each admit the common tendency to wish for the more favorable balance of better over worse contributions, but in a rare moment of political awareness we found that collective responsibility had actually come about. We have tried to treat many ideas and values, others as well as our own, but we alone take full responsibility for the selection and presentation. As to the ultimate distributive outcomes, we only hope we have furthered the interests of all in doing so.

Joyce M. Mitchell

William C. Mitchell

September, 1968
Eugene, Oregon

Contents

Part 2 Politics and Welfare

Part I
Analytics:
Problems and
Outcomes

New High in Oregon

Welfare Totals

Farmers Face Los

$58.2 Million

Eugene Register-Guard, Oct. 1, 1967, Eugene, Oregon

If Federal Aid Enc

Arizona Republic, March 20, 1967, Phoenix, Arizona

The New York Times, June 9, 1967, New York, New York

Congress Urged to Curl

WITHHOLDING TAX
LOW IN SOVIET

Rising Rates of Inter

The New York Times, May 20, 1968, New York, New York

alian Faction

icks Leaders

The Oregonian,
June 6, 1968,
Portland, Oregon

Dependants Can Cut Income
Levy to Almost Nothing

The New York Times, April 24, 1967,
New York, New York

REGIME IN ATHENS

BANS MINISKIRTS

Army Ch

eizes Re

Yugoslavia To Satisfy
Some Student Demands

The Oregonian, June 6, 1968, Portland, Oregon

The Oregonian, Oct. 29, 1963,
Portland, Oregon

The New York Times, Oct. 5, 1967, New York, New York

EDERAL SPENDING

ITS 142.2-BILLION

RIDGES FINDS LAG
LABOR'S POWER

Colombian President Goes on T
Scores Rich Who Evade Ta

The Oregonian, Feb. 24, 1966, Portland, Oregon

Ghana Coup

cord Figure Tops Fiscal
ear '65 by $15.8-Billion

The New York Times,
July 6, 1966,
New York, New York

lls Dockers Its Political
Influence Is at New Low

The New York Times, April 3, 1967,
New York, New York

7th Upheaval
In 4 Mon

The New York Times, Dec. 29, 1966,
New York, New York

Negro Youths Rip Down M
They Resented in St. Peter

New York Needs a New Constitution

The New York Times, Feb. 13, 1967, New York, New York

Chapter 1

Basic Problems of Politics

Most readers of a daily newspaper might readily conclude that headlines and stories about congressional fights, presidential speeches, civil demonstrations, revolutions in distant lands, the building of a new public low-cost housing project, and announcements of candidacy for public office are 'political' stories or 'politics.' By implicit American definitions of politics these readers are probably correct; something about each of these incidents seems political to most of us.

But pointing to objects or events and assigning a label or designation to them does not really answer the question of how to identify an entire class of objects or events. Unless we wish to beg the question of defining politics, we must be more precise in specifying the standards or implicit criteria by which we decided that each of the above news events was political. The history of political thought has suggested that the great thinkers, at least, have not always agreed upon the most appropriate criteria and therefore differed about what was or should be considered political or politically relevant. We need not detail this great debate except to point out that some have considered politics to be the study of government, some the study of power, and still others the 'authoritative allocation of scarce values.'

You may ask: Why be concerned over these scholarly definitional quibbles; why not just go ahead and study that which everyone regards as political? This common sense response might be all right except that definitions of subject-matter have consequences not simply for the teacher and

researcher but for the student and his society as well. In the case of the
political scientists the demarcation of subject-matter helps to determine
which areas are pursued in their research and how they will analyze their
problems. If a political scientist thinks of politics as the study of formal
government and laws, he will not study the activity of ordinary citizens;
if the researcher thinks that politics is the analysis of power he will probably
study more than governments, he will study power wherever it is mani-
fested, including fraternities, trade unions, churches, business firms. Thus,
definitions include and exclude various items. With respect to the student
we can quickly see some of the consequences. For example, the courses that
are included in a college catalogue are dependent upon current conceptions of politics and political science. At one time, political science departments offered many more courses of formal law than they do today; on the
other hand, we now find more courses on such matters as political behavior
and scientific methods. Voting behavior, for example, is now a major field
of inquiry whereas twenty-five years ago it was not. Or, today, the student
is offered courses on nations that once were not studied at all. Political scientists even offer courses on military or national security problems, i.e., on
strategy and policies. Research courses are offered on the construction of
questionnaires, interviewing, statistical analyses, mathematical model-
building, experimental design and simulation procedures among many
other esoteric practices for learning about man and his political life. The
fact that these techniques are currently taught and used in research is partly
dependent upon the fact that political scientists have come to define the
study of politics in a different way.

One consequence of this change toward the more scientific affects
the student: He is required not only to learn different and probably more
facts but also to become competent in assessing the use of sophisticated
methods and the data they produce. When we read statistical tables we
must know how they were constructed, from what, why and what they
mean. Whereas once we read histories and commentaries on politics, today
we also read charts, tables and even equations. So the definition of what is
political has enormous consequences for the political scientist and the student. But, what are we to regard as political?

The Basic Questions:
Issues in Collective Decision-Making

If we were carefully to survey the literature of political science, we
would undoubtedly note a profusion of inquiries and studies, but we might
also note that certain rather set questions continually reappear to fascinate
and trouble the political scientist. We might note, in the first place, that
much of political science is about *collective decision-making* or the *making*

of public policies for an entire society. Thus, political science has been greatly concerned with the nation-state and formal governments. The general question is how can we best describe and explain what goes on within a nation-state and its government? How can we account for the policies they pursue? Which policies are adopted? Which are excluded? How were these policies selected? Who participated in their selection or choice?

Political scientists also ask more detailed questions about policy-making; for example, most political scientists are intensely concerned with policy-making from the perspective of what Harold Lasswell termed *"who gets what, when, how?"* from governmental policies, elections, revolutions, formal institutions and informal practices. We often read in the newspapers that a certain aircraft concern 'wins' a governmental contract while another does not. Each day we read that interest groups are struggling over proposed measures which either provide subsidies or levy new taxes on some groups. Each day we read that some men win public office and others are defeated. We read that some government is toppled by a *coup d'etat* and another takes its place. Or, we read that a certain section of town will be rezoned while others will not. In each of these cases we may observe that some men will have their wishes realized while others will not. We may also observe that some acquire more than others and some pay more taxes than others. This problem or set of problems may be termed the *distributive* question since something of value is being distributed or divided among various claimants. As conservatives frequently and unhappily note, the United States Government is distributing more of the national product while the private economy appears to distribute proportionately less. Whether this is a good or bad trend is important for each citizen to decide, but it is not our immediate problem; it will be in Part 2.

Before governments and political systems can distribute the *goods* of life they must decide what will be produced in the way of benefits. Economists label these goods as *public goods and services,* meaning they are produced or distributed as a result of public or collective decisions rather than private decisions. We shall refer to the product of the political system variously as public goods and services, *public or collective goals* and *benefits, rules,* or *controls.* One may conveniently think of governments as being productive much as one thinks of the private economy as productive, i.e., both mobilize and transform resources into goods and services, benefits or goals having utility and providing satisfaction for people. Governments do not so much manufacture these goods as they authorize private persons or public officials to see that they are produced or brought about. In socialist societies, of course, governmental agencies also produce many more goods so there are fewer goods produced in the private sphere.

We are often prone to forget the goods and services that our governments provide because they are simply taken for granted. Perhaps a few illustrations will remind us of the range of such goods and their importance in maintaining a society. First, one might note that many people receive *money incomes* from their governments in the form of veteran's compensation, welfare maintenance, old-age security, agricultural subsidies and, of course, payment for work done for the government itself. Others may receive actual *material goods* such as surplus commodities. Still more of us receive a great many *services* from the government at cost or free. For example, governments in every society establish and regulate a money supply, provide defense against external threats, maintain some semblance of public order and safety, provide an adjudication service (court system) to handle disputes among citizens, establish and maintain a system of weights and measures, service business and others with regular information on weather, business conditions, etc. Certain facilities and opportunities are also provided by most governments for all or some members of society that advance their private individual satisfactions and aspirations. Education is such a primary responsibility. Protecting the civil rights of, say, American Negroes is in effect providing some opportunities for a disadvantaged minority, not adequately maintained by private effort and institutions. In a related sense, governments also produce *rules* and *regulations* governing the behavior of citizens and enterprises, which indeed may limit or expand their opportunities and activities. Still another type of public goods is the 'symbolic action' of a government or political actor. The recognition or attention which various groups attain in a society may be a partial consequence of symbolic gestures on the part of governmental officials and politicians. When an American President invites labor or business leaders or even poets to the White House he grants a form of recognition not bestowed upon those who are uninvited. Ceremonies honoring individuals, groups, or organizations are an integral aspect of political life and systems. Status is distributed in every society and governments are a primary supplier of social status.

What is produced or distributed by public policies must be generated somewhere. Analogous to the economy, one can think of two processes governments will be engaged in to produce their supply of goods. They must *mobilize resources* to engage in collective efforts, and must *allocate those resources* to the various goods desired. The resources which governments mobilize are both material and nonmaterial. The most familiar form is money, of course, extracted from citizens in the form of taxes, tariffs, fees or fines of some sort. Material resources such as land, facilities, buildings and supplies may be directly acquired by governments through compulsory processes (eminent domain, expropriation, conquest, etc.) or less forceful means (purchase, contract, treaty or even voluntary appeals). Governments need manpower as well and again there are both compulsory and more voluntary means of acquiring it, from drafts and forced labor, to paid and unpaid voluntary services. Considering the incentives which get people to give their labor for political purposes brings us to nonmaterial questions. How do their loyalties, ambitions, fears and desires for benefits draw them into the political realm? Political leaders and governments will spend much time encouraging commitments and providing incentives, and many activities in the system will make the task easier by developing sentiments of patriotism, loyalty, obligation, obedience and deference on the part of the citizenry.

Much as with factory production, these resources must be allocated to the various tasks and purposes of the political system, and one might think typically of government budgeting as the major means by which this is done. However, unlike a factory product, the goals of government and the things it could produce are far more complex, to the point of being inter-related, sometimes contradictory, and almost always incapable of complete attainment. This problem has inspired age-old debates about freedom vs. order, 'guns or butter,' conservation or distribution and so forth. Many of the 'rules of the game' of politics have to do with ways of resolving these issues, for example, by bargaining, competition, legal procedures, or voting. Budget agencies alone seldom make the big decisions because the question of relative allocations to the various goals of politics and government is the focal point of most political effort. Considering this, the production and distribution of political and governmental goods are costly in two important ways. In the first sense, they are costly because resources employed to produce them normally cannot be employed to provide private goods or other public goods. *The real cost of every good is an alternative good which is sacrificed.* National resources spent on war are not being devoted to welfare or highways. Further, these goods are costly because they entail the regulation or control of some members of society. Thus, protecting the rights of one man generally involves restraining the rights of another man. If laborers are to engage in collective bargaining, management must accord recognition and deal with unions even if it is against their preference. If a black citizen is to have the right to be served in a restaurant, white waitresses are required to serve them. One citizen's right is usually another's obligation. Because of these costs political action and public policies are often bitterly contended. Frequently one man's gain is another's resource and cost.

As just observed, the benefits of government are costly. Resources must be mobilized and transformed into more valued and useful goods. Time, energy, skill, etc., must be consumed. This being so, *whose* resources will be used and to what extent becomes a crucial question. The *distribution of costs* is a prime problem in the political process. Most often we confront it in the form of taxation and revenue problems. Who will pay how much of the tax bill, under what conditions, for what purposes? How efficiently are they collected and employed by the authorities? How ample is the resource base with which the government works? Every government faces a continual shortage of resources and since they generally have alternative uses the demand for them is apt to be greater than the supplies.

Since the money governments collect in the form of taxes and fees could be used for a great, indeed, infinite variety of purposes, citizens may become highly passionate over the uses of their resources or money. The individual citizen—even in a democracy—can seldom directly determine how his tax money will be spent, i.e., which public goods will be produced and in what quantities. We shall consider this fact in detail in Chapters 2 and 3. For the moment we emphasize the notion that resources have multiple uses and the cost of using a resource in one public program may entail the sacrifice of other programs or private spending. Let us provide a concrete set of illustrations. The cost of the Vietnam war exceeded $20 billion during 1966. This sum of $20 billion might have been used for any of the following purchases by the American citizenry:

1. It could—each month—finance the complete seven-year training of almost 70,000 scientists.

2. It could—each month—double the resources of the Agency for International Development for a full year's economic programs in 38 foreign countries.

3. It could—each month—create three Rockefeller Foundations.

4. It could—each month—pay the full year's cost of state and local police in all 50 states.

5. It could—every year—provide a 10 per cent salary increase for every U.S. public-school teacher.

6. It could—every year—double the social security benefits paid to 20 million Americans.

7. One modern bomber could buy 1 billion bushels of wheat or double the huge education budget of the state of New York.[1]

Some of the so-called underdeveloped or newly-developing nations have serious deficiencies in their resource bases making the achievement of modernization extremely difficult and time consuming. On the other hand, most of the Western democracies have been able to mobilize great amounts of capital resources thereby making the achievement of countless social investments and benefits possible. The newly-developing states have difficulty in providing such commonplace western benefits as a stable monetary system, order and safety, elementary communications and transportation facilities, not to mention such other advancements as social security, education, cultural values and health. The importance of the resource base and the efficiency of the mobilization process cannot be overestimated in a world which values modernization and affluence. Whereas nineteenth-

---

[1] Emmett John Hughes, "A Remembered Reckoning," *Newsweek* (July 11, 1966), p. 17.

century democracies relied more upon purely selfish marketplace economies to mobilize resources, today we witness these same nations and most others relying to a far greater extent upon collective or public decision-making to make the necessary choices in resource allocation and mobilization.

The mobilization of resources for societal goals obviously entails decisions, choices and policies concerning the allocation of resources and such allocations in turn entail an allocation of costs among the citizens.

If governments allocate resources between public and private uses, allocate resources among various public goods and distribute benefits among the citizenry, we can readily appreciate their need for the use of some sorts of *controls*. The making and implementation of public policy on allocation and distribution problems requires the use of power and influence. Programs of action do not administer themselves; they are administered and enforced by persons with authority to compel appropriate behavior. Any study of politics which attempted to ignore this basic fact of life would tell us very little, indeed, about the workings of any kind of political system and government. Political philosophers and political scientists have long recognized this basic character of government. Consequently many maintain that politics, political systems and governments are distinguished from other social institutions by the fact that they exercise ultimate authority and power over citizens. Governments do exercise ultimate sanctions as well as many lesser but more frequently employed ones. A basic question about a political system, therefore, relates to the use of controls. *We want to know who controls whom, with regard to what, how and with what effectiveness.* Why regulation or control is necessary is dealt with in Chapter 6 as are other questions relating to control.

Material allocation, distribution and regulation are not the only problems and processes one finds in political systems and societies. One need not be too perceptive to note that many issues in many lands are really not over these matters at all but over something we may term *symbolic* issues and problems. More specifically, we mean those problems which involve the emotional significance of the society and the identities, status, rights and obligations which members are expected to have or owe the society and its political institutions. Questions of membership, loyalty and one's rights are the chief forms such problems assume. We cannot make much headway in understanding politics if we do not pay attention to the means whereby the institutions are maintained and respected, the ways in which status is conferred by governments and, in general, the non-economic dimensions of political life. Citizens do not, as we shall see, spend all or even a great portion of their time rationally considering the allocation of resources, the distribution of material benefits and costs, either as social problems or as personal problems. Many become activated in political life only by the emergence of great symbolic issues, the moral and emotional symbolism of their societal existence, group affiliations and chances in life. The pageantry of politics, expressiveness of leaders, the struggle over social and political recognition are the fabric of politics for most men. So we must attempt to unravel these extraordinary elements of political life. That we do in Chapters 4 and 7.

The several decisional dilemmas we have mentioned are not resolved by edicts handed down by some other-world deity but by people interacting in and through a political process or system of processes. If we are to understand fully how and why choices are made we must also pay some attention to the people who make the decisions or public policies. This may entail knowing about many citizens or just a few, depending on the society we study. Even in the most decentralized of systems we will observe that relatively few men make most of the policies, most of the time. This being the case, we must have knowledge about these men, who they are and how they were selected, in other words, the *political division of labor*. Decision-makers or policy-makers will be the focus of Chapter 8 as it has been a focal point of much of the political-science tradition. Some of the more fascinating and occasionally morbid research in political science has been done on leaders, leadership and their decision-making. We hope our presentation will be more fascinating than morbid. We also hope it will be less anecdotal and more systematic than the biographies of great leaders would have it. However that may be, the recruitment of leaders is a prime task of all political systems. Important as leadership recruitment is, we believe that it is but an aspect of the much broader question of 'assigning' citizens to all the roles which constitute a political system. Polities have many activities to perform, many services to acquire; 'matching' citizens and political roles and tasks is therefore a prime problem of political life.

One need not be very astute to observe that life today is not quite what it was fifty, a hundred, or a thousand years ago. Politics may, in terms of certain broad generalizations, be essentially similar but the precise manner in which it is conducted and the institutions which govern it are not the same. A vital part of the political scientist's work must include a consideration of this simple fact. He will want to know *what has changed, how it has changed, at what rates, in what directions and why*; likewise, he will want to explain why some systems do not change as rapidly. In a world of dramatic changes such as the present century such questions are urgent and their answers imperative. Political scientists are meeting the challenges by conducting such studies and doing so all over the world. Put another way, political scientists want knowledge about how societies have altered their production and distribution of public goods, how they have changed in their allocation of resources and costs, how controls have varied. And, of course, given the time dimension, they may wish to make predictions about the future. Will the Soviet Union and the United States develop similar means of answering these questions? Will democracy succeed in the newly-developing states? The ubiquity of change presents an exciting problem for political science. Problems of *adaptation and stabilization* will be reviewed in Chapter 7.

Political Issues and Decisions

Social problems and choices have been presented here as political necessities confronting every social system. Such necessities do not, however, present themselves to people as carefully defined lists of subjects, choice alternatives, or likely outcomes; most of daily political life presents itself in a far more confused and uncertain fashion to both leaders and followers. Seldom do we find a pure and distinct problem in the allocation of resources without an intermingling of the other choice dilemmas we have noted. Likewise, there is no such thing as a purely distributive, or regulatory, or symbolic issue or problem. The issues that arise consist more or less of all these choices or simultaneous consequences of choices. That is what makes political life so complex, difficult to understand and fascinating.

We must, therefore, proceed to simplify these complexities and that we attempt by breaking down complex issues and systems into component parts and processes such as allocation, distribution, regulation, symbolism. In short, we arbitrarily draw lines over our confused phenomena in order to point out salient features of more limited areas for more intense examination. Suppose that we imagine an issue of politics or a choice situation as requiring some attention and action for a period of time. Figure 1-1 summarizes the many aspects or sub-problems of a major issue. Any given issue may entail one or more of these sub-problems and may do so in varying combinations and ratios of significance.

Some citizens and politicians will be more concerned with one aspect of some issue while others will be oblivious to that phase but intensely in-

Figure 1-1

Dimensions of Political Decisions and Processes

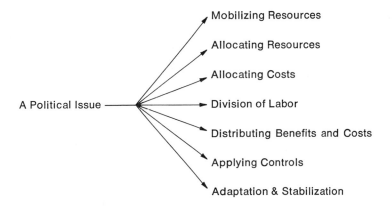

terested in still another dimension. Thus, one citizen may oppose the
Vietnam war because it costs too much, while another ignores money costs
but worries about winning it militarily. The fact that men are not equally
concerned over the same aspects of similar issues has important consequences in the operations of a political system; such consequences are reserved for more detailed treatment in Chapters 9 and 10.

Summarizing the discussion we can list the following sets of political
choices which will confront citizens or politicians. These choices also provide
substantive questions for political study.

1. mobilization of resources:
   a) from private citizens and groups
   b) from operations abroad
   c) from internal governmental operations

2. allocation of resources:
   a) between private, mixed and public uses
   b) among public uses

3. distribution of benefits:
   a) material goods
   b) symbolic goods: identities, statuses, morality

4. distribution of burdens or costs

5. rules and controls

6. division of labor

7. adaptation and stabilization

Providing answers to these problems is the practical work of citizens
and politicians in particular. Finding out what men have done in the past,
are doing in the present and may do in the future is the work of the political scientist. What choices men ought to make respecting all these decisions
is the work of all men for we are all affected by the choices. The work of the
citizen, the politician and the political scientist will never be terminated
for the problems and choices are universal necessities. Perhaps, one day,
you will provide some answers as a student of politics; in any event, you will
participate in the great collective dilemmas and decisions as a citizen.

Decision Processes and Political Systems

The general decisional choices or public policies that governments
must make are universal but the ways in which they are made are not. Public policies may be made in innumerable ways, by innumerable rules but
whatever the rules or institutions it is clear to the political scientist that

various processes do develop in each society for mobilizing and allocating resources, distributing costs and benefits, regulating behavior, etc. These ways of deciding and implementing policies assume certain characteristics which can be observed and once observed enable calculations about future behavior in the relevant processes. If these ways of politics become somewhat regularized or institutionalized we may usefully think of them as constituting a 'system,' a political system or 'polity' in which the many members interact in somewhat consistent, identifiable or familiar ways to meet the problems of collective choice. While there are countless means of depicting political systems in diagrammatic terms we think the following presentation affords a clear, simple and useful device for conceptualizing the complexities of real-life systems.

A number of features of political systems, as depicted in Figure 1-2, will interest us throughout the book. Of course, our conceptualization will become more intricate as we proceed, but for the present consider these basic elements of the diagram:

1. How complex is the division of labor in the system?

2. What processes are employed to transform the contributions of citizens (support, demands, resources) into valued activities and products of government?

3. How are the contributions of citizens made to the government? In short, how are supports given and demands made?

4. How are the contributions of government provided to the citizens?

5. At what levels are the many contributions and activities maintained, i.e., how much support is shown the government? How many demands are made? How many resources are available to the government? How many controls are employed? What sorts of public goods and services are made available? In what quantities and quality?

6. How institutionalized or accepted are the several processes? And how many or who takes part in them?

7. How effective, satisfying and efficient is the system?

8. Who gets what from the operations of the system and its policies?

9. Who among the citizenry pays how much of the resource needs?

10. Who is controlled, and in what ways?

11. Who supports the system? Who does not?

Our conception of the political system is one which emphasizes certain things such as interdependence, exchanges, collective decision-making and

Figure 1-2
The Political System

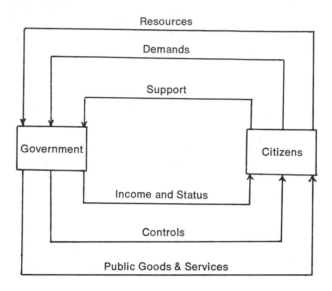

complexity. Furthermore, we tend to view polities as necessities of human life, i.e., we cannot imagine a society without a political system or set of roles and institutions which perform the needed tasks. This functional viewpoint does not, however, prevent us from also seeing political systems as being less than perfect enterprises which often fail to perform very well, and which can and do change by willful effort or inadvertence. Citizens may not derive satisfactions of the kinds they prefer, in the amounts they desire. Systems may be ineffective, inefficient, slow to meet problems and issues, or positively harmful to their subjects. In Part 2 we consider such matters and offer advice for making political systems more effective means of implementing what we regard as good in life.

Some Useful Tools for Analysis: Basic Axioms of Politics

The demanding tasks we have set for ourselves and readers cannot easily be tackled without tools of analysis, so we have thoughtfully included a few. Given the complexity of the approach and the often oblique quality of political life it becomes necessary to simplify. This can be partially accomplished by making use of certain simplifying assumptions or postulates about the subject we are considering—political behavior. So we will advance a number of assumptions or postulates which we believe are highly useful bases on which to find answers to our questions. These postulates are embarrassingly obvious, yet we find that they are seldom made explicit and when they are made explicit they bring forth considerable objection. Most of these postulates are standard 'givens' in social theory, and several have been used by such respected political thinkers as Plato, Aristotle, Machiavelli, Locke, Hobbes, Mosca, Pareto and such modern ones as Lasswell, Downs and Dahl.

Whether these particular points or our way of stating them are useful will be decided by you and other readers. We do make a plea, however; please do not reject any outright until you have completed the book. We also suggest that you judge these postulates not as true or false but as more or less useful in generating ideas about behavior and explaining or accounting for whatever patterns may be detected. And if you find these postulates unattractive you must replace them. What will you use? However you view the matter, here is our set of postulates:

1. A major unit of analysis must be the individual.

2. Each person seeks a multitude of goods (public, private; material, symbolic).

3. Each person would prefer more to fewer or less of such goods.

4. There is a limit to the satisfactions afforded by any one good.

5. Persons place different valuations on goods.

6. All choices and behavior entail costs in the use of resources.

7. Choices are constrained by the values and possibilities of the goods desired.

8. In societies both resources and choices are affected by the preferences and behavior of others.

9. The future is uncertain.

10. The resources of society are scarce or limited and have alternative uses.

11. The resources of power are limited and have alternative uses.

12. The institutions of society enable and regulate the making of interdependent collective choices.

A major unit of analysis must be the individual. The postulate concerning the individual needs to be stated baldly because we sometimes forget that social and political systems are constituted of individuals acting in various roles or capacities. We cannot fully grasp what goes on unless we are able to understand the individual and his identity in the system. While the individual decision-maker is hardly the only unit of analysis it is difficult to imagine a study which does not consider him as an individual. In some systems or situations, to be sure, the autonomous individual can play a much more crucial role in shaping the action of the political system than in others, but in all systems he is a fact of life and must be seen as such. People do make choices which have consequences for themselves and others; they act in relationship to other people. As a result political science devotes much time to unravelling their decisions, behavior and political consequences. As might be expected, some individuals and their decisions are more crucial, far-reaching and significant than others; such individuals are often termed members of the 'elite' or 'power-holders'; but they could also be heroes, leaders or martyrs out of the common ranks. We devote a good portion of this book to such crucial actors, their perceptions, decisions and actions. But, even the lowliest citizen, however inactive politically, is a fact of life for some elites; as such his perceptions and social behavior are also important and particularly so in democracies. So serious attention will be focused upon the individual in politics, and his effects upon others.

Each person seeks a multitude of goods (both private and public, material and non-material). This assumption seems so obvious that we feel some embarrassment at stating it, but the obvious also requires elucidation. The fact that men are 'acquisitive,' or in search of goods, leads to a great deal of their political activity as well as to an explanation of it. Economists, of course, have long made this postulate their basic assumption and explanation of economic behavior, and psychologists have employed some variations in their analysis of drives, wants and needs. Political theorists such as Machiavelli, Hobbes, Locke, for example, also thought in similar terms. The significance of this assertion of motivation is that many people turn to political affairs as a means of achieving at least some of the diverse goods they desire (both private and public, but particularly the latter). Demand for goods and services on the part of governments as well as individuals is a major datum for political analysis. Which goods are demanded, by whom, how and with what success are basic questions, as one might have gathered from previous discussions of resource allocation and distribution. What becomes of special interest to the political scientist is understanding situations where the quest for such goods leads to cooperative or antagonistic and competitive behavior.

Each person would prefer more to fewer or less of such goods. Again, we have adapted an essentially economic assumption about preferences and behavior. We think it applies to almost all behavior, not just to behavior in the marketplace. Humans generally want to increase satisfactions rather than to limit or restrict them, whether the desired goods are satisfying in a quantitative or qualitative manner. A citizen who puts great emphasis on America's military strength wants more defense hardware and not less; a citizen who travels a great deal generally prefers more to fewer miles of better rather than inferior highways. The citizen who values education generally puts it in terms of more and better education. The worker would prefer more to fewer wages; the employer, more rather than less monetary rewards for himself. Similarly the liberal espouses more rather than less freedom; the conservative, more rather than less order; the administrator, greater not less efficiency; the elective official, more not fewer votes. Have we made our point?

There is a limit to the satisfactions afforded by any one good. There are qualifications to the above assertion; specifically, people can become satiated with any single good. In economic terms, the law of diminishing marginal utility sets to work placing a limit on the amount of any particular good a citizen might wish to consume or use. In terms of public goods, there is some point at which alternative claims and uses become equally competitive. Or, in the colloquial sense, 'there can be too much of a good thing.' In the above examples we might note that those who want to see more and better transportation do not want all of the public budget devoted to highway expenditures. There would be little point in having the entire country paved and, besides, we would miss alternative pleasures thus foreclosed.

The law of diminishing marginal utility says little more than this: The extra utility or benefit which one derives from the consumption or use of each additional unit decreases as it is consumed. At some point the added consumption will no longer add to total utility; indeed it may become dis-utility. Each candy bar eaten may add to one's pleasure until ten have been eaten and one becomes sick. We think the logic also applies in the case of such public goods as highways, welfare, defense, police protection, etc. Citizens would become 'satiated' with them and would prefer to employ resources for other purposes and acquire other sources of satisfaction. The importance of this relates to such things as the types and quantities of public goods preferred. Different citizens have different satiation points for different goods. This fact is of extraordinary significance in the political life of a society as we shall see in Chapters 10 and 12. The problem for political systems is to arrange choices given these limitations and differences. How this is done will be the subject of the remaining chapters in Part 1. The normative problem of what constitutes optimal collective choices and processes will be discussed in Part 2.

For the moment consider Figure 1-3 which illustrates our axioms about the preferences for more rather than less and the idea of diminishing marginal utility. We have included the total utility and marginal utility curves for two citizens with regard to some public good. Note how each derives different amounts of total as well as marginal utility from the use of that good. A little later in the book (Chapters 10 and 12) we hope to demonstrate how these elementary observations, if properly understood, can facilitate political trades or bargains.

Figure 1-3
Total and Marginal Utilities of a Public Good

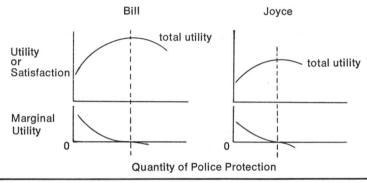

Quantity of Police Protection

In Figure 1-3 are illustrated some hypothetical satisfactions derived from police protection for two citizens—Bill and Joyce. The uppermost curve depicts the total utility derived by each from increasing amounts of protection, while the lower, downward sloping line shows the additional or marginal satisfactions derived from each additional amount of protection. Joyce apparently is satiated rather quickly. Bill's point of diminishing returns appears to set in at a somewhat greater amount of police protection. The point at which total utility no longer increases is the same as the point at which marginal utility equals zero and crosses the base line. These two points are joined in the figures by a vertical dotted line. Any further police protection fails to add to the satisfaction of our two citizens. The significance of these facts will become more apparent in subsequent chapters as we attempt to explain the preferences and behavior of citizens and how they might improve their shares of whatever they want in the way of public goods.

Persons place different valuations on goods. We do not all wish to have possession or command of identical sets of either private or public goods, nor of identical ratios or combinations thereof. This is fortunate not only because it introduces greater variety into life, but also because it enables men to have a division of labor in society and make exchanges with one another. If all wanted identical goods in identical quantities and the goods were scarce, as most would surely be, we would have nothing but competition and conflict; indeed, conflict of the most serious nature. The fact that men tend to place different valuations on goods enables them quite often to make peaceful, mutually profitable exchanges and to be more

effective in their efforts in producing and acquiring goods. As Durkheim
put the matter:

> In the same city, different occupations can co-exist without being
> obliged mutually to destroy one another, for they pursue different ob-
> jects. The soldier seeks military glory, the priest moral authority, the
> statesman power, the businessman riches, the scholar scientific renown.
> Each of them can attain his end without preventing the others from
> attaining theirs. . . . The oculist does not struggle with the psychia-
> trist, nor the shoemaker with the hatter, nor the mason with the cabi-
> net maker, nor the physician with the chemist, etc. . . . The closer
> functions come to one another, however, the more points of contact
> they have; the more, consequently are they exposed to conflict. . . . As
> for those who have exactly the same function they can forge ahead
> only to the detriment of others.[2]

Political systems afford different men the opportunity of competing for the
same objects such as public offices, but they also enable men to seek different public goods by forming alliances and engaging in other cooperative
endeavors such as trades or exchanges through which they can acquire
more of the goods they desire.

Once more we can make use of a convenient and simple diagram to
illustrate our axiom. In Figure 1-4 we have drawn what economists call
'indifference curves' showing a series of combinations of two public goods
(police and fire protection in dollar terms) preferred by two citizens. Each
point along a single curve represents a combination of protections of equal

---

Figure 1-4

Preferences Among Public Goods

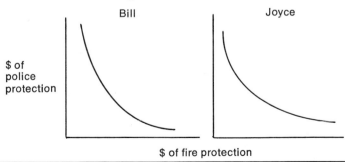

[2] Emile Durkheim, *The Division of Labor in Society* (Glencoe, Ill.: The Free Press, 1933),
p. 267.

worth to the citizen—thus the term indifference curve. The citizen will regard any of these combinations as equally rewarding. The higher the curve or the further it is from the point of origin the more preferred are those combinations illustrating our axiom about men preferring more to fewer goods.

The slopes of the curves tell us the rates at which Bill and Joyce are willing to substitute or exchange police and fire protection. The steeper sections of the curves indicate a willingness to give up larger amounts of police protection for smaller increments of fire protection, while, conversely, the flatter areas of the curves indicate less willingness to surrender police protection unless in exchange for much larger amounts of fire protection. The reason for this change in willingness is simple: As one gains more of a good he places less value on it while he places more value on that which he has but little of. Thus, he is willing to give up more of that which he has in abundance to gain possession of the scarcer good. As you can readily see, the indifference curves say much the same as our earlier utility curves but they say it in ways which are more useful for some purposes. These purposes will become clarified in later chapters.

All choices and behavior entail costs in the use of resources. Resources are those goods put to use in the attainment of other preferred goods. The most obvious kind of resource is money with its great versatility as a medium of exchange. It can 'stand for,' or purchase, a great variety of things one wants for the good life. Too bad its value also depends upon a limitation of supply! There are other important resources which are valued because of their usefulness and limited supply. Energy, for example, whether in human effort, horsepower, or kilowatts, must be spent in the effort to achieve goods. One's time, attention, activity can also be conceived as being spent on one thing, rather than another. In this sense, even if nothing else were used, one's time spent on making choices for himself about what he likes and wants to do is an expenditure of resource. The limitation of time, money, effort, attention and so forth implies a further aspect of cost in that its expenditure upon one thing forecloses its use for another. Given the multitude of preferred goods and the tendency to desire more or better combinations of things, this becomes an important kind of cost consideration. If a citizen decides to ring doorbells for his preferred candidate he will not only spend a good deal of his time, energy and costs of transport, but he will have to give up alternative pursuits for those resources, which might have been watching TV, reading a book or playing poker.

Choices are constrained by subjective values and perceptions of the desired goods. Because men make decisions or choices and seem to have some control over themselves and their resources, we are, as political scientists, interested in accounting for the choices that are made. While we wish to simplify things at the start, we want to be realistic too. Social sciences have often been accused of a deterministic view of man's behavior, seeing it as subject to great forces, or directed and influenced by people and institutions beyond the individual's control. We do not wish to foreclose this possibility—sometimes, someplaces. But on closer examination, these forces and influences must be explained in terms of the receptivity or vulnerability of the human being to them. Let us again start with the individual and consider first the mediating processes by which the person comes to recognize and respond to the external world. We refer to the subjective elements in the human personality: perceptions, attitudes, norms, values, beliefs and expectations. Goods must first be identified and defined somehow for the person (perception) and some valuation process must take place on the basis of his attitudes, values and norms before preferences can be determined. Even further, a person must make some estimate of feasibility before he invests too much in the matter: How likely is he to win satisfaction by his investment of resources (expectations)? How important is the object of preference compared to competing ones (values and beliefs)? How easily may it be attained in terms of permissible behavior (norms) and the obstacles and perceived limits on one's resources in the outside world? All these may be considered as values and possibilities to be subjectively assessed when deciding what one wants and the situation in which one wants it.

Of course there are many means by which these subjective factors are influenced for each individual: by his learning experiences of all sorts and of course by the nature of the external environment which sends such stimuli to him. We may identify important processes in society which tend to guide and even control these experiences and stimuli to some extent through major institutions and practices. More about these later. Fortunately, individuals bring with them differences in genetic makeup, and tend to deviate somewhat as they encounter special experiences or react in their own way, therefore developing their own unique styles or combinations. For some purposes we can by-pass uniqueness and individual differences and note generally that such and such behavioral pattern is associated with certain demographic characteristics or other factors. But the connecting link between the behavior and other characteristics must be socio-psychological in nature. How people acquire these subjective orientations; how these influence behavior; what patterns there are; and what consequences these all hold in the working of political systems are very important questions to answer.

In societies both resources and choices are affected by the preferences and behavior of others. This postulate begins with the reverse aspect of the above. If people react and make choices with regard to their external environment, then that environment is affecting them in important ways. What it makes available to be chosen, how it teaches what should be preferred and in what manner, and what it presents as the possibilities for doing so—all can be viewed as influences on the reacting person. More important, there is a situation of *interdependence* involved. No perception without stimuli, no learning of orientations without experience and precept, no attainment of goods whether material or non-material without their being available. As Aristotle has said, "Man is a social animal," and that word *social* makes all the difference. Even the most ardent Zen practitioner must first learn about it and then be left alone, or allowed the auspices to pursue his quest. The choices and behavior of each person take place in the context of others doing so as well. As we consider this, we shall be thankful for the variety of preferences and their marginal utilities as postulated earlier and for at least some of the guidance and learning that puts bounds on each person's claims to the goods in life. Otherwise we might have what the philosopher Hobbes described as life in the "state of nature": "solitary, poor, nasty, brutish and short!"

The future is uncertain. Whether the world would be a better place if most things were more certain is debatable; in any case, the fact of the matter is that it is an uncertain place in many respects. The uncertainty that exists is not so erratic that daily predictions cannot be made with a fairly high level of confidence; rather, as the time span which we wish to predict and control is lengthened the uncertainty generally becomes greater. This seems to hold for social and political matters even more than elsewhere. While we can treat many future events in terms of the probabilities with which they might occur, we cannot eliminate uncertainty. We can try, however, to reduce it. The role of uncertainty in politics is particularly important in explaining the behavior of individual voters, leaders and especially nation-states in their international dealings. Since these persons and entities cannot foresee the future actions of others with much certitude, it is necessary for them to include the uncertainty element in their calculations and decisions. They can do so by assessing the degree of *risk* involved in what they might choose to do, i.e., the estimated probabilities of things going wrong rather than right. Things will not always go as anticipated; mistakes will be made in domestic and foreign policies, in individual voting choices, in the administration of programs such as public works. And great inefficiencies are apt to occur in the vast undertakings of large-scale political systems such as those of the U.S.A., the U.S.S.R. and China. A theory of politics which does not consider the role of uncertainty and risk cannot explain very much. We need to know how men cope with these problems and how these, in turn, affect their perceptions and behavior.

The resources of society are scarce and have alternative uses. How nice life would be if scarcity did not occur. Then one could conceive of a society without politics, at least as we know it, and without Hobbes' state of nature either. How nice if we had a limitless government treasury, unbounded time for attending to our private desires and public pleasures and endless assurance that we could have what we asked for, whether it be money, blondes, cars, brains, pot or quiet and beauty. Alas, some have more than others, but few persons even come near having all that they want in life. And two earlier postulates sharpen enormously the consequences of overall scarcity. One is the previous axiom that men prefer more to less or fewer of most things they like. With most men preferring more, most of the time, we can expect that conflicting demands will be made upon the short supply of resources. Not all men will acquire all that their aspirations dictate. The result is apparent: The competition will disappoint many concerning their shares of the scarce values. Further, the fact that demand is greater than supply leads to higher values placed on resources. Then the other postulate concerning interdependence presents another sort of problem. One cannot just hit his fellowman over the head to get what he wants if that man in some way is needed to provide the very object of desire. One cannot get a car unless there are those contributing to its production, nor a blonde unless available and consenting, nor lots of money in the public treasury unless there are those who have contributed to it. This raises tantalizing questions and possibilities as to the ways one gets others to contribute to one's own preferred goals and what one has to give or to do for that to happen. Perhaps the goals of some are complementary to those of others, and exchanges can take place or agreements to join in common pursuits. Maybe an equilibrium or balance could be reached between the amounts of resources suppliers are willing to provide and the quantities users are willing to take at the given values, i.e., exchange rates. But often goals don't coincide or complement so easily. Maybe agreements about goals and resources will be 'forced,' by agreement upon prior rules for decision or by some tougher measures and tactics. How this may take place is dealt with in Chapters 9 through 11.

The second part of this postulate is also interesting and commands our respect: namely, scarce resources have alternative uses. The land, labor, capital, organizational skills that are found in a society may be employed for different purposes both private and public. In the short-run we may assume that the quantities of these resources—as stated above—are limited. This being the case plus the fact that men prefer different goods creates a situation in which decisions must be made on the proposed use of the resources. Shall we use our limited supplies of manpower to build hospitals or to fight a war? Shall we use our capital to build a road in West Virginia or a dam in California? Shall we use the scarce organizational skills of some citizens to run the Marine Corps or General Motors? These are all allocation problems concerning the use of resources. If a resource can be used in only one endeavor we have a different problem, but since most resources can be employed for an almost infinite variety of social purposes and private wants, decisions must be made about their employment. Scarcity and alternative uses are as crucial postulates in political life as they are in the marketplace, and we shall be concerned with them in Chapter 2.

The resources of power are limited and have alternative uses. In order to acquire the use of public goods citizens must first be able to influence which goods are to be produced and how they are to be distributed among the users. If this influence is to be exercised one must have various resources that enable him to affect the decisions and behavior of others who participate in the making of authoritative decisions. The formal right to participate is important but may not be sufficient by itself; but if one has some money, status, formal powers, a strategic role in society, personal charisma, or skills in political bargaining, he can do much more toward altering public policies and actions. That is, he can influence the choices and behavior of other participants or decision-makers by using these resources in ways affecting them, as rewards, punishments, controls, exchanges and the like. Recent studies of community power structures and decision-making, especially, have strongly emphasized the role of resources in accounting for political decisions. Much of political man's activities are concerned with improving his resource investment as well as its employment in daily political life. Questions we will want to consider in subsequent chapters revolve about this resource base and the most effective way in which to employ it. Who gets how much of the public benefits and who pays how much of the costs are both vitally affected by the societal distribution of power resources through which these decisions are influenced.

The fact that power resources are limited and have alternative uses implies that choices must be made about their use. If resources were unlimited no such decisional dilemma would be faced; one could do anything he wanted with them. Since resources are limited and can be employed for different purposes, goals, or policies, the individual citizen and leader must decide how, where, when and how much of each resource to employ. Again, the element of cost, i.e., using a resource in one line of endeavor usually, although not invariably, means that it cannot be equally and effectively employed elsewhere. To be sure, not all resources can be used for the same ends in different sets of circumstances. Money typically is less effective within a monastery; what is charisma in India may not be in America; what constitutes status in one community may not in another. So the effective employment of one's own resource base is crucial. Knowing one's resources as well as those of potential allies and opponents is essential to effective action as we shall claim in Chapter 12.

Society is organized in ways that enable and regulate the making of interdependent collective choices. We may start with the individual as a unit, and indeed will always return to him in evaluating the costs and satisfactions of what happens to him politically, but we must also consider the collective or social unit. Given many wants, limited resources, interdependence and mutual influences, how do these all work together without pulling society apart? Fortunately we do not have to deduce society logically, because it is there, in constant operation, but we have tried to suggest logically why it is convenient to have an on-going system. Setting up agreements to exchange resources, to engage in competition and to communicate wants and needs all of the time in order to make out all right is pretty difficult. We have an economy and a great variety of marketplaces; we have families which get us started out; and we are continually guided about what to do in the home, play group, at school, church, on the job and through the media. Life is structured for us concerning most of the things that are highly valued in society, saving us the exhaustion and at least some of the helplessness and error of individual effort. So, too, is this the case regarding political effort, and the organization and processes by which this is done are the major concern of this book. We see this especially in Chapter 8 on the political division of labor and role allocation, and in all our earlier chapters on the problems and outcomes of political allocations, distributions, regulations and collective choice. Thus we have started with the individual but have brought him into the context of the political situation. What he wants depends on others, what he gets and gives will affect others and be affected by them, and there are many possibilities of how these will come about. We first begin the analytics by examining these possibilities. Then later we assess the values involved and propose strategies, offering political 'payoffs,' we hope, for those special individuals who have had the added experience of reading this book.

A Summary Checklist of Generalizations

Teachers have frequently noted the difficulties students encounter in attempting to summarize what they have read. All too often they get lost in details, illustrations, particulars as they boldly and indiscriminately underline each sentence. We think it important to know what an author has to say, to be able to summarize his views accurately, fully, and clearly. We also think it useful to read critically but reading critically entails knowing what an author wishes to say and, in fact, does say.

In this chapter certain points have been made that should enable the student to read more profitably the remainder of the book, as well as to shape his own perspectives on politics and political study.

1. Certain basic problems are confronted in all political systems.
    a) These problems may be discovered by reading the words of political scientists or by studying extensively social interaction and trying logically to simplify its basic postulates.
    b) The basic problems can be viewed as decisional problems or outcomes involving the mobilization and allocation of scarce resources; distribution of benefits and costs; rules and controls; division of labor and recruitment of decision-makers; and adapting to and coping with uncertainty through time.
2. Societies employ sets of political processes which handle social and

public aspects of these problems of individual preferences and interdependence.

   a) Every polity displays regularities which make certain forms of calculation possible.

   b) *Each polity is, in some respects, like*

      all other polities, in the choices and processes it must employ;

      some other polities, in the nature of its resources, scarcities and competing values;

      no other polity, in its own solutions and their particular consequences.

3. It is useful in studying political systems and individual behavior to take certain things for granted. A list of such postulates was presented on page 15, and discussed on pages 15-25.

Problems and Applications

Exercises, questions or comments directed toward using the concepts and generalizations discussed will conclude each chapter of this text. The purpose is to give the reader some practice in political analysis and problem-solving as he goes along. Hopefully this is a more effective learning device than memorization and subsequent forgetting. Some will be simple analytic exercises, some will be interpretive questions, and others could be turned into more extensive projects. Often there is no single solution to these exercises, though there may be a best one. The most profitable way to pursue the possibilities is with other readers, in classroom or study discussion. In some cases the exercise is open-ended and can be structured further by the instructor or student's own preferences and the resources available.

This first chapter was intended as a general introduction and survey, so these exercises will be aimed primarily at interpretive discussion.

1. The daily newspaper furnishes an unending source of the variety of issues and problems of politics. We find them useful as illustrations of our approach from actual situations, in the United States and abroad. Can you identify the types of issues involved in the headlines preceding this chapter, in terms of our outline of political problems? What are the kinds of problems involved in the current major issues dealt with in your local or school newspaper?

2. Pages 27-31 present different newspaper lists of governmental agenda and activity. They are good indicators of the varying dimensions of formal governmental activity and suggest how the basic problems confront the official decision-maker. We have identified basic problems confronting Congress and the President at a given time. Can you do likewise for the other agenda?

THE DAY IN SACRAMENTO
By Associated Press

THE GOVERNOR

Defended his governmental economy drive and criticized top state higher education officials for temporarily barring admission to the state university and colleges in reaction to that drive.

Appointed William Symons Jr. of Inyo County and Prof. Frederick Morrissey of Berkeley to the State Public Utilities Commission.

Again said a tax boost this year is inevitable.

Proposed his anti-crime program, aimed mainly at cracking down on smut and giving more control over crime to local authorities.

THE ASSEMBLY
Bills Introduced

Genocide — Seeks to end harassment of Jews and Negroes, makes it illegal to advocate genocide, sets forth penalties for action ridiculing a class of people when near a group of them; AB 141, McMillan (D-Los Angeles).

Recall—Provides uniform recall provisions for officers of certain governmental bodies; AB 148, Porter (D-Compton).

Water—Increases pay of Water Commission chairman from $2,000 to $2,500, increases commission staff, loosens ties between commission and Water Resources Department; AB 150, Porter.

Insurance—Tightens state control of life insurance training; AB 151, Knox (D-Richmond).

Unification — Eliminates requirement that school district unification elections be held every two years in nonunified districts, and that high school district boundaries guide unifications; requires instead that surveys be made every two years that might lead to unification; AB 146, Burke (R-Huntington Beach).

License—Permits state to suspend or revoke collection agency license if licensee fails to pay a judgment against it; AB 145, Burton (D-San Francisco).

Drunk — Revokes new state law requiring chemical sobriety tests for suspected drunken drivers or loss of license for six months; AB 144, Burton.

Report—Makes it a misdemeanor to knowingly and falsely report emergency, makes it a felony if such report results in death or serious injury; AB 140, Knox.

Election—Eases rule making it almost impossible for minor party to get on primary election ballot, spells out procedure for selection of Presidential electors by minor party; AB 137, Z'berg (D-Sacramento).

Aid — Restores $5 cut made in state benefits to certain old or disabled persons when Medicare took effect in 1965; AB 136, Elliott (D-Los Angeles).

Fair — Prohibits use of state name to promote or advertise world's fair without specific approval; AB 135, Biddle (R-Riverside).

Tax—Allows state tax exemption for personal effects and household furnishings above $100; AB 134, Thomas (D-San Pedro).

Court—Boosts from 2 to 3 number of judges in El Cajon Municipal Court; AB 133, Wilson (R-San Diego).

Judges — Increases retirement benefits for certain judges who took office in 1959; AB 132, Bee (D-Hayward).

Moving — Provides that condemnors shall pay up to $200 for persons whose residences are condemned and who must move up to $3,000 for business moves; AB 143, Burton.

Beach—Makes permanent the temporary law that the state pays one half the cost of local participation required by federal law authorizing beach erosion control projects; AB 142, Porter.

THE SENATE
Bills Introduced

Governments — Requires legislature to say specifically when it is preempting a lawmaking field from local governments and says it isn't legislative intent to preempt any field; SB 66, Sherman (R-Berkeley).

Crimes — Allows arrested persons to have their records kept secret if they were not convicted of a crime; SB 71, Carrell (D-San Fernando).

Secrets—Makes it a crime to take from a company any item involving a trade secret and says theft of an idea alone is not a crime; SB 69, Lagomarsino (R-Ojai).

Tax — Exempts personal effects and household items in excess of $100 value from personal property taxation; SB 68, Petris (D-Oakland).

Legislators—Removes requirement that a court delay a case being argued by a legislator who is also a laywer while he attends legislative sessions or committee meetings; SB 70, Sherman.

Credentials—Exempts all teachers with master's degrees from junior college credential requirements; SB 65, Alquist (D-San Jose).

Administrators—Exempts junior college administrators from state credential requirements; SB 64, Alquist.

Board — Makes State Board of Education elective for four-year instead of eight-year staggered terms and leaves state superintendent of instruction an elective office; SB 63, Whetmore (R-La Habra).

Loitering—Declares state has not preempted field of criminal legislation on loitering; SB 67, Sherman.

Los Angeles Times, Jan. 18, 1967.

MAJOR BILLS IN CONGRESS

Saturday, Sept. 16, 1967

ABBREVIATIONS: C—In Committee; R—Reported; F—On Floor; P—Passed; D—Defeated.

Bill	House	Senate	Classification
Revises the Social Security System, increases benefits by 12.5 per cent, and authorizes $3.2 billion for 1968 (HR 12080)	P	C	Distribution (benefits) · Allocation (resources)
Authorizes $2.8-billion to aid foreign countries (S 1872, in conference)	P	P	Allocation · Allocation
Authorizes $75-million in fiscal 1968, and $300-million the following year, to assist state and local governments in reducing crime and strengthening law-enforcement facilities (HR 5037, S 917)	P	C	Control · Division of labor
Prohibits racial discrimination in Federal and state jury selections and in housing and employment practices, and outlaws threats or injury to persons seeking or urging others to seek enjoyment of various social benefits (HR 2516, S 1026)	P	C	Distribution (rights, status) · Control
Revises Congressional committee procedures, extends and strengthens the lobby registration law, provides for minority staffing on committees; and calls for Congressmen to have a month-long vacation every August (HR 2594, S 355)	C	P	Rules and regulations · Division of labor
Prohibits the use and manufacture of wiretapping and eavesdropping devices except in matters related to national security (HR 5386, S 928)	C	C	Distribution (benefits) · Control and rules
Establishes greater Federal control over the traffic in and importation and sale of firearms (HR 5384, S 1)	C	C	Control
Expands the authority to assist air pollution research, and establishes regional air quality commissions, pollution standards for industry, and inspection programs for anti-pollution devices on automobiles (HR 4279, S 780)	C	P	Adaptation · Division of labor · Rules and regulations
Authorizes $3.4-billion in fiscal year 1969 for aid to elementary education (HR 7819, S 1125)	P	C	Distribution (benefits) · Rules and regulations
Revises the copyright law, extending the duration of current protection and bringing under copyright protection certain electronic and performing arts (HR 2512, S 597)	P	C	Distribution (benefits) · Distribution (benefits)
Provides Federal subsidies to pay for specific campaign expenses of Presidential and Congressional candidates (HR 4890)	C	C	Allocation (resources)

28

Rules and regulations
Distribution (benefits, symbolic)
Mobilization of resources
Allocation (resources)
Distribution (benefits)
Allocation (resources)
Distribution (benefits)
Rules and regulations
Division of labor
Control

C P

P R

C C

P C

Extends existing election laws to cover all primaries and conventions, limits the amount any person can contribute to a candidate, removes restrictions on political spending and calls for full disclosure of contributions and expenditures (S 1880) C

Establishes a corporation to help finance educational television and radio programs, and extends for five years the Educational Facilities Act of 1962 (HR 6736, S 1160) .... P

Authorizes $2.25-billion for the antipoverty program in fiscal year 1968 (HR 8311, S 1545) (ordered reported) .... R

Amends and extends the Higher Education Act of 1965 and other college aid programs (HR 6232, S 1126) C

Requires that by the 1972 elections no state have a population variance of more than 10 per cent between its largest and smallest Congressional districts (HR 2508, in conference) .... P

Prohibits travel or use of interstate commerce facilities with intent to incite a riot or other violent civil disturbance (HR 421) .... P

PRESIDENT'S ACTION ON MAJOR BILLS

Jan. 10, 1967, to Sept. 16, 1967

ABBREVIATIONS: A—Awaiting Action; S—Signed; V—Vetoed.

Allocation (resources)
Division of labor
Rules and regulations
Distribution (burdens)

S

S

Appropriates $12.2-billion to finance military operations by the United States in Vietnam (PL 90-18) .... S

Extends the military draft for four years and limits Presidential authority in effecting proposed draft changes (PL 90-40) .... S

The New York Times, September 18, 1967, page 28.

SUMMARY OF ACTIONS
BY PALO ALTO COUNCIL

The Palo Alto City Council Monday night:

—Voted 8-4 to build a heavily landscaped electrical substation behind the Eichler Swim and Tennis Club, 3539 Louis Road.

—Approved by an 11-1 vote — Councilman William P. Rus dissenting—a subdivision ordinance amendment that would require large (over 400 units) subdividers to dedicate land for elementary school sites. City Attorney Robert Michalski warned that the amendment might be unconstitutional on grounds that it would be confiscatory and discriminatory, but noted that no court tests have been made.

—Approved parking time limits for the block surrounding the new Palo Alto Office Center: 24 minutes along University Avenue; two hours along Cowper Street and Lytton Avenue; and no parking along the southerly side of Tasso Street.

—Passed, 7-5, an "after the fact" resolution endorsing establishment of a Santa Clara County Planning Policy Committee of the Inter-City Council. The planning advisory group was created last month by the ICC, composed of representatives of the 16 cities and Santa Clara County.

—Delayed consideration of widening studies on West Bayshore Frontage Road for further review by the council's planning and procedures committee, which recommended the studies to ease peak hour industrial employe traffic tieups.

—Declared a philosophy favoring protection of upstream creek channels against erosion caused by increased runoff that would accompany development of the foothills. The council voted to initiate a pilot study on headwater storage basins — seeking the cooperation of Los Altos and Los Altos Hills — under the auspices of the Black Mountain Soil Conservation District.

—Defeated on a 6-6 vote a proposal to reiterate the council's two previous positions regarding the Santa Clara County Expressway program, phase II: That Palo Alto wants a one-year delay on the $114 million phase II program to allow completion of a county public transportation study, or—if delay is refused by county supervisors— to seek complete exclusion from the program, due to go to voters in May.

—Defeated on a 7-5 vote a proposal to instruct the city delegate to the Association of Bay Area Governments (ABAG) to vote against a "regional home rule" government plan this Friday unless a city proposed amendment regarding election of representatives to the group's executive board be adopted.

— Tabled a proposed $4,000 traffic engineering study for the Embarcadero Road-El Camino Real intersection to await the impact of traffic pattern changes caused by reconstruction of Palo Alto High School. Councilman Philip Flint objected to the exclusion of Churchill Avenue from the study by an earlier council action, noting a strong relationship between the two cross-street traffic patterns.

— Unanimously approved a design contract for a $115,000 pedestrian overcrossing at Bayshore Freeway and Oregon Avenue.

—Voted a unanimous resolution of appreciation "for excellent and loyal service" to former Assistant City Manager Cecil S. Riley, who left for a similar post in Oakland last week.

Palo Alto Times, Dec. 14, 1966, p. 39.

THE PROCEEDINGS
IN WASHINGTON

YESTERDAY

(June 6, 1967)

THE PRESIDENT

Had breakfast with Democratic Congressional leaders; lunched with Secretary of State Rusk, Defense Secretary McNamara, and special assistants Rostow and Christian; announced the appointment of Capt. James A. Lovell Jr. as his special consultant on physical fitness.

THE SENATE

Debated the Middle East situation; passed and sent to the House a joint resolution creating a 7-man national commission on product safety to protect consumers from dangerous household products.

The Labor and Public Welfare Committee cleared the Administration's railroad strike bill.

Financing committee heard

several Senators support tax allowances on political contributions, rather than direct treasury subsidies to finance political campaigns.

THE HOUSE

Discussed the apparent Israeli victories in the Middle East; moved towards passage of agriculture appropriations bill.

Judiciary Committee approved a bill to fine flag burners up to $1,000 and imprison them up to one year.

Commerce Committee heard statement by Secretary McNamara that a nationwide railroad strike would be intolerable in the light of the Vietnam war and the situation in the Middle East.

DEPARTMENTS & AGENCIES

State Department announced that United States will break diplomatic relations with Egypt as a "reciprocal" action following the official word that Cairo is withdrawing recognition of the American Government.

Defense Department announced that approximately 20 military transport aircraft were being sent from Europe to Libya to evacuate military dependents.

F.P.C. said that the power shortage that spread over parts of four states Monday started with a failure of a power line of the Philadelphia Electric Company.

SCHEDULED FOR TODAY

(June 7, 1967)

President Johnson has no appointments.

Senate meets at 10 A.M. House meets at noon.

General Walt, former Marine commander in Vietnam, holds news conference, noon.

The New York Times, June 7, 1967, p. 11.

3. Using the newspaper further, try to analyze an extended account of a local issue. Try to analyze in a meaningful way the sequences and inter-relationships of the basic problems involved, as revealed in this article from *The New York Times* of May 29, 1967.

SUBURBIA RESISTS GROWTH PRESSURE

By Ralph Blumenthal

Important battles over zoning are being fought in New York's suburbs. The outcome will determine the physical environment of the communities and, to a large extent, their quality of life.

It will determine whether residents will be able to live in seclusion by preventing the construction of apartment houses near their homes, whether others will be able to lighten their tax load by inviting industries into their towns, whether people and businesses seeking the advantages of the suburbs will be allowed to go there, or be forced to hunt space elsewhere.

Arithmetic delineates the nature of the conflict: There are now eight million people in the 17 suburban counties. Within two decades, if the population trend continues, there will be five million more.

"Right now," warned Sy J. Shulman, Westchester's planning commissioner, in a recent speech, "the suburbs are in a lull before the storm."

The problems of where to put those people and how to pay for their schools, roads, policemen, firemen, sewage disposal and other necessities of modern living have aroused not only the suburbs, but also the federal and state governments, civil rights groups and business interests.

The way each of the 500 zoning boards in the metropolitan area handles its job is crucial. The boards promulgate the ordinances that control the number, types and use of buildings in any given area. Their decisions cannot help but reach beyond their own enclaves, affecting surrounding communities, New York, Newark and the other cities in the region.

A study by The New York Times of the boards' actions shows that in many instances the suburbanites, distressed by what could prove an explosive population growth, are increasing the minimum size of plots on which structures may be built, thus making it increasingly difficult for newcomers to settle in the suburbs.

The following representative cases demonstrate the scope of the problem:

¶In Norwalk, Conn., a civil rights group has gone to court to try to prevent a tightening of the zoning code, charging that it will set up an economic barrier that will keep Negroes from moving to Norwalk.

¶In Orangetown, in Rockland County, residents are trying to keep out apartment houses, which they say mean more children and higher school costs. But they are trying to attract industries, which pay taxes.

¶The town of Harrison, in Westchester County has rezoned a section of Purchase to allow Pepsico, Inc., to convert a 112-acre polo club into its world headquarters so that it can collect more taxes. Residents of Purchase, with an eye to protecting their estates, have threatened to form an independent village to keep Pepsico out.

Numerous government agencies are trying to bring more order out of the present confusion, contending that something must give to accommodate the increase in the suburban population, which will result from city migration and from internal growth.

President Takes Action

Among moves contemplated or under way are the following:

¶In January, President Johnson warned that policies that stunt growth are "the springboards from which many ills of urban life flow" and appointed a 16-member commission under the chairmanship of former Senator Paul H. Douglas of Illinois to look into zoning policies, as well as other development issues.

¶In Connecticut, the General Assembly has debated the zoning issues, sometimes bitterly, and is expected to appoint a legislative committee to study the problems.

¶In New York, the Legislature passed a bill this year requiring localities to submit zoning changes to county planning boards, where they exist, if the land involved is within 500 feet of a state or county road. The county agency can reject changes, but the local board can then override the county agency by a vote of a majority plus one. A joint legislative committee is now preparing a report that may call for more sweeping changes in the local zoning power.

A New Jersey situation shows how one community's plan can hurt another. After apartment builders were barred or severely restricted by certain communities, some concentrated on an area where they were welcomed — West Orange.

In West Orange, one garden apartment development was built right up against the town line of Short Hills, where residents wanted no part of the development.

"How would you like it?" demanded one Short Hills woman, standing on the lawn in front of her $50,000 contemporary ranch home and glaring at the development across the street. "This entire monstrosity wasn't even on record when we moved in two years ago."

Such situations are possible because each incorporated municipality in the area—and there are 500 of them — can adopt any zoning ordinances it wants. This authority was delegated by Legislatures to give the individual communities "home rule" over what may be built, where it may be built, and how it may be used.

Appeals against rulings by the zoning boards may be taken to the courts. But the courts, with a few notable exceptions, have been reluctant to interfere with what has generally been regarded as a legislative matter. So the boards, in most cases, wield near absolute power.

Although members of zoning boards are appointed rather than elected, in general their decisions reflect what the electorate thinks, inasmuch as they are appointed by elected officials. And the elected officials are very sensitive to zoning issues.

The population growth combined with a statistic from Westchester County shows why the federal and state governments are worried. In 1955 Westchester County could house a population of 3 million residents under zoning regulations then in effect. Today, because residents began requiring newcomers to settle on larger and larger plots of land, the population capacity has shrunk to 1.8-million. (Westchester has about 870,000 residents now.)

Rezoning One's Neighbor

In 1950, according to a survey by the Regional Plan Association, the average zoned vacant housing lot in the five-county region of Fairfield, Bergen, Middlesex, Passaic and Westchester was 9,176 square feet. In 1960, the average size, because of local upzoning, had grown to 19,334 square feet. (An acre is 43,560 square feet.)

One of the principal questions that officials are beginning to face now is whether a community can continue to decide policies that may profoundly affect a neighboring community as well.

"In Greenwich," said William H. Hernstadt, a local property owner who has been crusading for years against zoning laws that have prevented him from selling his land for commercial development, "no one can get elected unless he swears on the Bible, under the tree at midnight, and with a blood oath to uphold zoning."

Along with Greenwich, Scarsdale shows what a community can do to remain an island of quiet homes in a sea of business, apartment and industrial development if it follows stiff zoning requirements over a long period.

There is no industry in Scarsdale and there are almost no poor people.

A light industrial plant paying high taxes could significantly ease the tax burden of Scarsdale residents. But they prefer to shoulder the tax load and keep things as they are.

Where there is no zoning or where requirements are loose, as on Central Park Avenue, just outside Scarsdale, or on Sunrise Highway in Suffolk County, the area has become a neon panorama of gas stations, eating places and stores and offices.

What many communities in the suburbs are seeking—

and what virtually none has found—is the exact mixture of zoning control to protect homes and green space and yet foster development that brings in tax revenues.

Lenient zoning that encouraged indiscriminate apartment development in Parsippany-Troy Hills, N.J., helped that town double in population from 25,000 to 50,000 between 1960 and 1967. Now town officials have declared a moratorium on further apartment construction.

In the last seven years, the town had to increase its police force from about 20 men to 52 and the building department from one man to five as well as other increases in town services, all of which meant a greater cost to the taxpayer.

However, zoning critics contend that growth need not raise taxes too much if a community attracts the proper industry — the most lucrative source of municipal revenues since it requires relatively

small municipal expenditures for services.

Besides, say the critics, such as Salem Shapiro, a private planning consultant from Stamford who is advising the national association for the Advancement of Colored People in its antizoning suit in Norwalk, government in the form of zoning power has no business limiting development to protect the interests of certain residents.

"The issue," he said, "is whether you can use the powers of government for this amoral purpose."

A supporter of strict zoning, Everett Smith Jr. of Greenwich's opulent Round Hill section, denies that zoning is aimed at setting up racial barriers.

"It has nothing to do with racial or religious factors. It's just economics," he said. "It's like going into Tiffany and demanding a ring for $12.50. Tiffany doesn't have rings for $12.50. Well, Greenwich is like Tiffany."

The New York Times, May 29, 1967, p. 1, 13.

4. Through the centuries political philosophers have emphasized different aspects of politics, relevant to their concerns and the issues of the day. Using the following definitions and descriptions identify the writer's major concerns and conception of politics.

a) "By the study of politics is here meant the study of influence and the influential." Harold D. Lasswell, "Politics: Who Gets What, When, How," in *The Political Writings of Harold D. Lasswell*, Glencoe, Ill.: The Free Press, 1951, p. 443.

b) "The state is the organization of the public effected through officials for the protection of the interests shared by its members." John Dewey, *The Public and its Problems*, Chicago: Allan Swallow Incorporated, n.d., p. 33.

c) "The activities of political interest groups imply controversy and conflict, the essence of politics." David Truman, *The Govern-mental Process,* New York: Alfred A. Knopf, Inc., 1959, pp. 502-03.

d) "And so with government of any kind: no ruler, in so far as he is acting as ruler, will study or enjoin what is for his own interest. All that he says and does will be said and done with a view to what is good and proper for the subject for whom he practices his art." Plato, *Republic,* New York: Oxford University Press, 1945, Book I, Chap. 3, p. 24, F. M. Cornford, ed.

e) "When several villages are united in a single complete community, large enough to be nearly or quite self-sufficing, the state comes into existence, originating in the bare needs of life, and continuing in existence for the sake of a good life." . . . "Hence it is evident that the state is a creation of nature, and that man is by nature a polit-ical animal. . . . But justice is the bond of men in states, for the administration of justice, which is the determination of what is just, is the principle of order in political society." Aristotle, *Poli-tics,* Book I, Chap. 2, in *Introduction to Aristotle,* Richard Mc-Keon, ed., New York: The Modern Library, Random House, Inc., 1947, pp. 555-557. (© Oxford University Press)

f) "All wise princes should . . . consider not only present but also future discords and diligently guard against them; for being fore-seen they can easily be remedied, but if one waits till they are at hand, the medicine is no longer in time, as the malady has become incurable; it happening with this as with those hectic fevers, as doctors say, which at their beginning are easy to cure but difficult to recognize, but in course of time when they have not at first been recognized and treated, become easy to recognize and difficult to cure. Thus it happens in matters of State; for knowing afar off (which it is given to a prudent man to do) the evils that are brew-ing, they are easily cured." Niccolo Machiavelli, *The Prince and the Discourses,* 3, New York: The Modern Library, Random House, Inc., 1950, pp. 10-11. (© Oxford University Press)

g) "A sagacious legislator of a republic, therefore, whose object is to promote the public good, and not his private interests, and who pre-fers his country to his own successors, should concentrate all author-ity in himself; and a wise mind will never censure any one for having employed any extraordinary means for the purpose of establishing a kingdom or constituting a republic." . . . "The law-giver should, however, be sufficiently wise and virtuous not to leave this authority which he has assumed either to his heirs or to any one else; for mankind, being more prone to evil than to good, his successor might employ for evil purposes the power which he had used only for good ends." Machiavelli, *Discourses, op. cit.,* IX, pp. 138-139.

h) "A *Common-wealth* is said to be *instituted,* when a *multitude* of men do agree, and *covenant, everyone, with every one,* that to whatsoever *man,* or *assembly of men,* shall be given by the major part, the *right* to present the person of them all, . . . every one, . . . shall *authorize* all the actions and judgments, of that man, or assembly of men, in the same manner, as if they were his own, to the end, to live peaceably amongst themselves, and be protected against other men." Hobbes, *Leviathan,* II, 18, Oxford, England: Basil Blackwell Publisher, n.d., p. 113.

Bibliographical Notes

This opening chapter has formed an outline for the remainder of the text. As such, it has merely noted but not elaborated upon the major themes. Outlines or conceptual frameworks are, as the jargon has it, a dime a dozen; they will always be that for they are easy to put together. In any case, our framework was derived from a variety of sources. First let us recommend most highly a great classic in the modern vein, which has treated all these problems with great insight and analytic skill for his time. We are speaking of Alexis de Tocqueville's *Democracy in America,* New York: Vintage Books, Alfred A. Knopf, Inc., 1945 (Vol. I, generally on resources and division of labor; Vol. II, the first book of which contains information on symbolism that is politically relevant; the second book, on motivation and goals; the third book, on distributive questions, material and symbolic; and the fourth book, on change and stabilization). The breadth and imagination of his interpretation is fortunately becoming widely admired by modern social scientists.

In political science resource mobilization has only recently been emphasized as a basic problem of politics, most frequently in the studies or comparisons of developing nations. See Gabriel Almond and G. Bingham Powell, Jr., *Comparative Politics; A Developmental Approach,* Boston: Little, Brown and Company, 1966, particularly Chapters 8 and 10. Also, A. F. K. Organski, *The Stages of Political Development,* New York: Alfred A. Knopf, Inc., 1965, treats some mobilization questions in "Stage Two," as does David Apter, *The Politics of Modernization,* Chicago: The University of Chicago Press, 1965, in Chapters 10 and 11. A most interesting special kind of resource mobilization is treated by national security analysts and some of their studies may be illuminating for their systematic approach to the problem, e.g., Klaus Knorr, *The War Potential of Nations,* Princeton, N.J.: Princeton University Press, 1956, or Harold and Margaret Sprout, eds., *Foundations of National Power,* 2nd ed., New York: D. Van Nostrand,

and Company, 1951, Chapter 4 (note the formula for national power on page 111). For a broadly historical and comparative account of national mobilization and resource management try S. N. Eisenstadt's *The Political Systems of Empires,* New York: The Free Press of Glencoe, 1963.

The entire problem of resource allocation for different uses is a major topic of economics textbooks; we suggest you look over any one of the numerous ones now on the market. Being an important concern of theirs, economists have long proposed rules and general criteria for dividing resources between public and private uses. Even the master of the "laissez faire" economy, Adam Smith, in *The Wealth of Nations,* New York: The Modern Library, Random House, Inc., 1937, found some major tasks for which society's resources should be channeled through government. John Kenneth Galbraith brings the debate to bear on modern issues and he often 'turns on' his economist critics by his facile phrases and far-ranging critiques. See his book, *The Affluent Society,* Boston: Houghton Mifflin Company, 1958 and, for rejoinders, Edmund S. Phelps, ed., *Private Wants and Public Needs,* New York: W. W. Norton and Company, 1962. Planners are continually confronted with the allocative question, and none more so than those prescribing methods and standards for a socialist or communist system. Note the broad-gauged and systematic treatment of Oskar Lange and Fred M. Taylor, *On the Economic Theory of Socialism,* Minneapolis: University of Minneapolis Press, 1938. A partial counterpart in our own system is found in the recent 'revolution' in methods of treating defense budgets, for example, in Charles J. Hitch and Roland N. McKean, *The Economics of Defense in the Nuclear Age,* Cambridge: Harvard University Press, 1960.

The distribution of benefits and costs has been alluded to in the familiar title of Harold Lasswell's "Politics: Who Gets What, When, How," in *The Political Writings of Harold D. Lasswell,* Glencoe, Ill.: The Free Press, 1951. Even more recently, the non-material aspects of the question have been emphasized by Murray Edelman in *The Symbolic Uses of Politics,* Urbana: University of Illinois Press, 1964. The whole range of distributive issues is cited by Gabriel Almond as an important category for comparing nations, in his essay, "A Developmental Approach to Political Systems," *World Politics,* XVII, No. 2, January, 1965, pp. 183-214. This piece might be especially useful for the person with considerable background in the social sciences, as it too treats political problems on a broad societal basis, citing major works, and bringing a somewhat different perspective to most of the subjects we surveyed here. Looking back, we cannot help but cite the great and revolutionary theorist of the (mal)-distribution of costs and benefits, Karl Marx. He not only sought to document empirically the condition of the poor and oppressed, but to present a 'scientific' theory of why that comes about in *Das Kapital,* i.e., *Capital,* New York: The Modern Library, Random House, Inc., n.d. Later theorists such as Gaetano Mosca in *The Ruling Class,* New York: McGraw-Hill Book Company, Inc., 1939, or Robert Dahl, *Modern Political Analysis,* Englewood Cliffs, N.J.: Prentice-Hall, Inc., 1963, Chapters 3-5, have dealt with the distributive question in less caustic fashion. In the American context, the question of 'who gets what' can generate a good deal of heat, and there is a lively tradition of the political exposé. A classic case is Charles Beard's *An Economic Interpretation of the Constitution of the United States,* New York: The Macmillan Company, 1913, and for more recent versions see the mounting literature on the 'military-industrial complex,' both in popular and scholarly form. Modern economists have been able to treat distributive problems in far more analytic (and somewhat less emotive) form, with regard to material costs. Two very helpful recent sources are James Buchanan, *The Public Finances,* Homewood, Ill.: Richard D. Irwin, Inc., 1960, and Bernard T. Herber's *Modern Public Finance,* Homewood, Ill.: Richard D. Irwin, Inc., 1967. Richard Musgrave's *The Theory of Public Finance,* New York: McGraw-Hill Book Company, Inc., 1959, is a modern classic, a major contribution to both economics and political science (although the latter discipline has yet to accord that recognition). Parts 1 and 2 contain the relevant political theory.

Political division of labor has long been a staple topic of political science. Perhaps the greatest treatments are still Plato's *Republic,* F. M. Cornford, ed., New York: Oxford University Press, 1945, and Aristotle's *Politics, op. cit.* They were equally concerned with descriptions and prescriptions regarding the best ways to organize a state. Their classifications may be questionable, but few have improved upon them. We also suggest that you read or review Locke's *Second Treatise of Government,* New York: The Macmillan Company, 1956, Rousseau's *Social Contract,* New York: E. P. Dutton and Company, 1950, and Hobbes' *Leviathan,* Oxford, England: Basil Blackwell Publisher, n.d., for alternative analyses and prescriptions regarding the ways in which political systems have been formed and ought to be structured. View their prescriptions as calculations of actual consequences stemming from various premises about man and his goals in society. Note how they propose to organize the political system to bring about preferred behavior and goals. A very succinct classic which beautifully employs this mode of reasoning is Madison's essay #10 in the *Federalist Papers,* New York: The New American Library, 1961, pp. 77-84.

The problem of control or regulation has been considered by all sorts of philosophers and social scientists. Machiavelli considers the ways in which leaders can and do control their people in *The Prince, op. cit.* Lasswell and Kaplan in *Power and Society,* New Haven: Yale University Press, 1950, provide a broader perspective on control and regulation. Roberto Michels in his brilliant *Political Parties,* Glencoe, Ill.: The Free Press, 1949, dealt in detail with leadership control and why there are leaders and the led. Economists consider control in a different way; they devote much energy to comparisons of governmental and nongovernmental controls of economic forces. Perhaps the best introduction to such efforts may be found in Robert A. Dahl and Charles E. Lindblom, *Politics, Economics, and Welfare,* New York: Harper and Brothers, 1953, especially Part IV. The psychological aspect of political control is brilliantly suggested in Czeslau Milosz' *The Captive Mind,* New York: Alfred A. Knopf, Inc., 1953. While there are many modern studies of manipulation by propaganda and 'brainwashing' which emphasize sinister uses, the observation of psychological controls was treated as more natural and pervasive in the earlier classics, as in Walter Bagehot's *Physics and Politics,* Boston: Beacon Press, Inc., 1956, and Graham Wallas' *Human Nature in Politics,* Magnolia, Mass.: Peter Smith, n.d. Charles Merriam, in *Political Power,* New York: McGraw-Hill Book Company, Inc., 1934, suggests a psychological theory of power emphasizing its attractions ("credenda" and "miranda") to the subjects of a regime. And, of course, we could not neglect the crucial role of law in the fabric of political controls. A most profound work which covers many aspects of the meaning and workings of the law and is quite relevant to the social science perspective is Julius Stone's *The Province and Function of Law,* Sydney, Australia: Associated General Publications Pty., Ltd., 1946. For the American experience, James W. Hurst's *The Growth of American Law,* Boston: Little, Brown and Company, 1950, treats the operation and uses of legal rules with relevance to the political and social system.

Adaptation and stabilization as political problems are another staple of political science. The classic approaches are again those of Plato and Aristotle, for both were primarily concerned with the instability of regimes. Their proposals with regard to divisions of labor were designed to attain some degree of adaptability in the case of Aristotle and complete stabilization of political life in the instance of Plato. We also recommend an analysis of the *Federalist Papers, op. cit.,* for the federal union of the proposed Constitution of the United States was seen by Hamilton, Madison and Jay as a flexible and sturdy means of meeting the problems and dangers from within and without the country. Modern literature abounds in analyses of the problems of adaptation and stabilization, from questions of international crises and conflict, to such internal issues and dilemmas as those regarding population pressures, health and disease, urban ills and rural stagnation, development and economic growth. More and more frequently these matters are dealt with in the systematic context of the basic problems we have surveyed in this chapter. As some outstanding examples, we would recommend Karl W. Deutsch, *The Nerves of Government,* New York: The Free Press, 1966; Rupert Emerson's *From Empire to Nation,* Cambridge, Mass.: Harvard University Press, 1960; Myron Weiner's *The Politics of Scarcity,* Chicago: University of Chicago Press, 1962; Charles Wolf, *Foreign Aid; Theory and Practice in Southern Asia,* Princeton, N.J.: Princeton

University Press, 1960; Martin Meyerson and Edward C. Banfield, *Politics, Planning and the Public Interest,* Glencoe, Ill.: The Free Press, 1955; Robert C. Wood, *Suburbia, Its People and Their Politics,* Boston: Houghton Mifflin Company, 1959; Kenneth B. Clark, *Dark Ghetto: Dilemmas of Social Power,* New York: Harper and Brothers, 1965.

Subsequent bibliographical notes will be less extensive and more specific with regard to the subjects of each chapter. But first, with this broad overview, we hope you will acquaint yourself with some old and honored classics, and some very good modern contributions. Each can serve as inspiration in its own way in the continuing quest for political enlightenment.

Tax Limit — Yes Or No?

Levy Limitation Proposal Would Affe

U.S., State Income Payments Total

Los Angeles Times, Jan. 1, 1967, Los Angeles, California

The Oregonian, Oct. 9, 1968, Portland, Oregon

Hidden Costs of Vietnam

Year Of Austerity' In Portla

scalation Are Showing

The Oregonian, Nov. 8, 1967, Portland, Oregon

BONN — Chancellor
urt Georg Kiesinger's
rave budgeteers ope
967 with deepest anxie
to how they are going
idge the gap that yawn
vesomely between wha
nn will spend and wha
will earn.
Los Angeles Times, Jan. 1, 1967,
Los Angeles, California

The New York Times, June 16, 1967, New York, New York

Spain Set to Float

BUDGET CUTS BAR

$80-Million Issue

RESERVE CALL-UI
COSTLY TO ISRA

ART TRIPS ABROAD

Tax on Commuters
Yielding Only 50%
Of City Prediction
The New York Times, Aug. 5, 1967,
New York, New York

Stores Close and Servi
Lag as Men Enter Force
The New York Times,
May 28, 1967,
New York, New York

State Department Calls Off
Third of Troupes' Tours
The New York Times, Dec. 27, 1967,
New York, New York

Defense Budget
To Top $73 Billi
During Fiscal 196

chool Budget Pinch

JOHNSON SAYS U.S.

any Cities Cut Back
ducational Programs
s Voters Balk at Costs

CAN PAY FOR WAR
AND ANTIRIOT AID

nd Issues, Tax Increases
Rejected; Kindergarten,
Bus Service Are Affected

Says Nation Is Rich Enough
for Both—Names Top Aide
to His Riots Inquiry
The New York Times, Aug. 5, 1967,
New York, New York

resident to Seek Additio

$9.4 Billion for Milita
Spending for Fiscal 19

sting State, Federal Aid
The Wall Street Journal, April 13, 1967,
New York, New York

Road Projects Face Del
The Wall Street Journal, Jan. 18, 1967, New York, New York

Chapter 2

Mobilization and Allocation
of Resources

If Chapter 1 made any sense we can assume that every society has some
kind of political system which produces public goods and services for the
satisfaction of at least some citizens. If this is so, we are confronted with a
variety of rather interesting questions concerning decisions about *which
goods are produced, in what quantities, how* and *who makes the decisions.*
We are interested in the public allocation of resources through public
policies to various public activities on the part of governments and groups
of the society. How much of the total income and wealth of the nation is
devoted to public goods and services? Which goods and services are thus
produced? In what ratios or proportions? How are they produced—by public
or private persons? We are asking what are usually viewed as economic
questions but these questions are resolved by political rather than economic
systems. Consumers and producers do not decide how much of our national
income will be spent on defense but citizens and politicians do. So we must
analyze *political decision-making* or, as some say, *'collective decision-
making.'* As we will discover in Chapter 10, a variety of political or collective
decision-making processes are used in different societies. Ethiopia, the
United States and China, for example, do not employ the same procedures,
rules and criteria. Nevertheless there are enough similarities among some
nations to allow us to characterize them as having essentially the same type
of problems and decision processes. But more on that later.

41

The main problems of this chapter are (1) the mobilization of resources by governments and (2) the allocation of those resources to particular objectives or programs of action. We begin with the second problem because that is the issue which appears more prominent in the minds of citizen and leader alike. The subject of how resources are acquired and in what quantities will follow. However determined or in what order decisions are made, it is clear that the mobilization and allocation of resources are among the most crucial and divisive issues in all systems which permit issues to be debated. In some societies mobilization of resources presents greater problems because the means of acquiring them are not as highly developed. Most under-developed nations confront this difficulty at present. Advanced industrial societies are more concerned with the problem of allocation than with mobilization; where resources are more plentiful, demands for their alternative uses are far more numerous and insistent than is the case in the less advanced nations. Still, no nation has achieved a utopia of endless resources and costless means for their acquisition and use.

Resource Allocation

If there were plentiful resources enabling everyone to have all the things they want, we would not have to write this section. But resources are limited and not everyone can have everything he wishes; some allocative decisions must be made. As individuals must allocate their personal resources so must groups and societies. How much is spent on defense, on social welfare, on agricultural subsidies, on highways, on urban renewal, on education, on care for the aged, on police and fire protection? Decisions on these plus a myriad of other problems and goals are made continuously in every system. Perhaps we can learn a bit about why these are collective choices, and how they come to be so.

Public/Private Goods Ratios

As we observed in the first chapter, it is logically possible for a society to produce almost all public goods or all private goods or any combination thereof. The decisions that are made in a system (many decision-makers may make the choice) will result in some ratio of public and private goods. How much of the national income is spent as a result of private decisions and how much by public officials or bodies? We can illustrate this with simple graphs (Figure 2-1). The graphs depict not only the total 'product' of a nation but also the respective supplies of public and private goods available to their people. The total supplies of goods and services or national income could be explained by economic theory. But the ratio of public and private goods and the total supply of public goods cannot be accounted for by economic theory alone; we must employ a 'political-economic' theory. That we shall try to do.

Figure 2-1
Choice Between Public and Private Goods

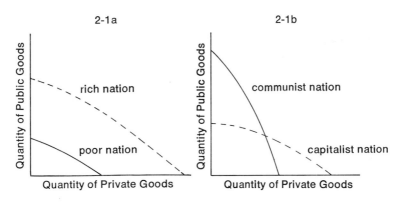

In Figure 2-1 the choice between public and private goods is illustrated in terms of a set of curves depicting the situations of a poor and a rich nation (2-1a) and a communist and a capitalist nation (2-1b). The curves are constructed by noting a point on the vertical axis which would indicate the quantity of public goods if all resources were devoted to those uses and a similar point on the horizontal axis which measures the quantity of private goods that could be produced if all resources were allocated to that end. The actual curvature of the connecting line should suggest that various combinations can be produced and that a decision to produce more of one type of good necessarily restricts the amount of resources available for the other type good. The two curves of Figure 2-1a are hypothetical descriptions of the state of affairs in both a poor and a rich nation. Obviously, the latter can produce more of both public and private goods. The curves of Figure 2-1b, on the other hand, refer to the choices of communist and capitalist nations, regardless of their resource base. We could assume—although it is unrealistic—that the two hypothetical nations had equal supplies of resources. Still, each might produce quite different combinations of goods. The communist nation typically engages in the public production of more public goods while the capitalist nation tends to produce proportionately more private goods using private productive processes.

No nation devotes all its resources to one type of good nor do they rely exclusively upon either public or private production and distributive processes; varying combinations of both are typically employed. Not only can a wealthy nation spend more on all goods but the richer nations tend to devote proportionately greater resources to public goods than do the poorer nations. Some evidence on this matter is available and arrayed in Table 2-1. Note that the table contains but twenty-eight of some 120 nation-states and that they are all non-communist nations. There appears to be a positive relationship between the wealth of a nation (as measured by its per capita income) and the amount or percentage of the gross national product devoted to public uses, but the relationship is not perfect, i.e., the nation with the highest per capita income (U.S.) does not spend the highest percentage of

Table 2-1

Per Capita GNP and Expenditure of Government as a Percentage of the GNP

Nation	Govt. Expenditure/GNP (1959)	Per Capita GNP (1957)
West Germany	30.1%	$ 927
Austria	28.8	670
France	28.7	943
Sweden	27.9	1380
Italy	26.9	516
United Kingdom	25.6	1189
Norway	25.2	1130
Netherlands	24.4	836
Finland	24.3	794
Belgium	24.2	1196
United States	23.8	2577
Canada	22.8	1947
New Zealand	21.9	1310
Denmark	21.3	1057
Ireland	20.9	550
Greece	20.3	340
Congo (Leopoldville)	20.2	92
Brazil	18.9	293
Pakistan	18.0	70
Burma	17.0	57
Portugal	16.4	224
Barbados	15.8	200
Spain	15.3	293
Australia	14.7	1316
South Africa	14.6	395
Japan	13.9	306
Jamaica	10.8	316
India	8.3	73

Source: Bruce M. Russett, *et al.*, *World Handbook of Political and Social Indicators* (New Haven: Yale University Press, 1964), pp. 58, 155-57.

its GNP for public goods, nor does the nation with the lowest per capita income (Burma) spend the lowest percentage for public purposes. There does seem to be a strong tendency on the part of richer nations to spend more through the public sector, however, and a lesser tendency for the poorer nations to do so.

No matter how wealthy a nation, none can have all the private and public goods all its citizens and officials might ideally prefer. The production possibility curves in Figure 2-1 show the maximum combinations that are possible at any given time. This means of course that choices must be made between the production of public and private goods since all the necessary resources for both kinds are typically unavailable. Some sacrifices are required. The cost of acquiring more private goods is the public goods not produced; the cost of acquiring more public goods is the private ones that are sacrificed. The accompanying newspaper item illustrates more dramatically what this entails than any words on the part of the authors. Waging a war imposes sacrifices of both private and public goods and services. It also may have a variety of other economic consequences such as higher

---

Uniforms, Bombs and Bullets

WAR COSTS SQUEEZE HOME FOLKS

By Sally Ryan

NEW YORK (AP) — Heavy spending for the war in Vietnam is squeezing civilians and industry at home.

The Defense Department has poured billions of dollars into the nation's economy to buy uniforms, food, bombs and bullets.

To meet the needs of the fighting men in Vietnam, some manufacturers have had to cut back on production for civilians.

Shortages of men's clothing have been reported by some department stores.

Factories note shortages of copper, electronic and chemical products, machine tools, small motors, forgings and castings, computers and aircraft engines.

Defense industries had unfilled orders totaling $24.6 billion in November. By May they had jumped to $27.3 billion.

The shortages extend to transportation of many kinds, and to labor and credit.

The final tally on defense expenditures for the year ended June 30 is expected to be over $55 billion, $800 million more than predicted as recently as January. This year it may top $60 billion.

The Vietnam spending on top of the domestic boom has touched off inflationary pressures.

The most noticeable pinch comes from the military's expanding manpower needs, subtracting men from the work force when they are needed in industry to meet the demands of increased military production.

Then the mills at home are pressed to clothe and feed them.

The problem is particularly acute in clothing and textiles.

In fiscal 1965, the Defense Department spent $317.2 million on clothing and textiles. In the year ended June 30, it spent $1.149 billion, and the current year the defense supply agency in Philadelphia estimates it will run another $800 million.

"It will cut into civilian supplies, but not any more than it has to date," an agency spokesman said.

The Defense Department is having trouble getting bids on many military orders as a result. Of 330 firms asked to bid on making waterproof clothing bags, four submitted bids. Of the 86 asked for cotton denim cloth, one bid. Of 261 asked to make fliers' nylon twill jackets, three submitted proposals.

The Boeing Company and Douglas Aircraft postponed delivery of some commercial jetliners, awaiting engines from United Aircraft Corporation, which is giving first priority to military production.

The military also has first priority on trucks. Civilian deliveries are running behind schedule.

Heavy military shipments to the West Coast contributed to an acute boxcar shortage this spring.

A fleet of tugs and barges sent to the harbors and beaches of Vietnam has left the West Coast with a tight supply for domestic commerce. The supply of qualified personnel is critically short.

Machine tool makers are operating under priority-rated orders, making equipment for helicopters, shrap-

nel, bombs.

Producers of copper and aluminum are subject to priority orders, too.

In steel, there are priority orders for steel pilings, plate and corrugated sheet.

There are indications that housing construction is falling because some mortgage lenders have stopped making new loans.

The Associated Press, July 28, 1966.

interest rates, tighter loan markets, shortages of labor, inflationary tendencies and reallocation of certain resources because of military priorities. All these economic consequences stem from decisions of government to prosecute a war and would be reflected in the changing shape of the production possibility curves.

Much of the political process in all nations concerns precisely the problems we have just described: how much of the nation's wealth and income will be used by government and decided upon by political processes? We might also note that the question must consider the moving of the production curve outward, that is, the expansion of the resources and productive capacity of the nation. When this is the case, debates frequently take place over how desired goals can best be realized. Typically, during the twentieth century the more conservative American citizens have believed that the curve can best be moved outward by limiting or decentralizing governmental activities so as to facilitate the private businessman and his production of private goods. This requires that the proportion of the national income allocated to public goods be minimized. Liberals, however, have contended and fought for expanding the public sector, i.e., the production and/or distribution of goods by the government. In earlier centuries conservatives were among those who wanted powerful central authorities, while liberals wanted weak central governments and more powerful local governments to make allocative decisions.

Choices Among Public Goods

The resource allocation problem of society is not restricted, however, to choices between public and private goods; that is only the beginning for there are still choices among public goods. Normally these two aspects or choices are made more or less simultaneously in the minds of advocates. The overall size of expenditures is not generally the first and exclusive order of business which must be completed before internal allocations are made. Decision-makers would find it difficult to make such a sweeping choice without considering the goals involved, so they tend to deal with these choices segmentally, or by assuming certain 'givens' as to resources available. Again, we can resort to a simple diagram of the possibilities. Consider Figure 2-2 in which the choice concerns the ratios of two hypothetical public goods—social welfare and defense.

Figure 2-2
The Allocation of Public Goods

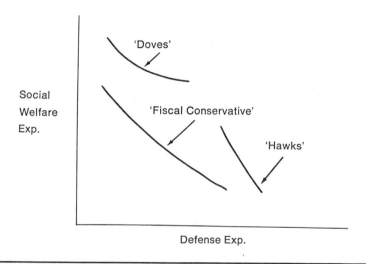

Men may fight bitterly over the allocation of resources to such goals as welfare and defense. Some men ('hawks') want to give the military more funds while others ('doves') want to cut them drastically and shift monies to domestic welfare. Others ('fiscal conservatives') would cut both, to keep total government expenditure down. Hardly an item in a nation's budget goes unnoticed, but the very size and number of expenditures are so great now that few officials in any government can master the entire set. Consequently, most politicians, interest groups and citizens pay most attention to those items in which they have a direct personal concern, i.e., in improving their shares and preferences or preventing other groups from doing better. Few of us want to pay the costs of improving another person's position in society. And we generally want to elicit more resources to improve our own situation. The great allocative problem then consists of deciding which goals to pursue and how to pay for them.

We do not wish to suggest that individuals or groups, insofar as they have a role to play in making these choices, decide on the basis of strict and

dispassionate economic rationality, for they seldom do. Many of these decisions are made without reference to a budget; instead they are often fought
out as great ideological or symbolic issues concerning human rights and
duties (cf. Chapter 4). Few white citizens know how much money is spent to
improve the status of the Negro in America but all know that an intense
struggle is taking place over their respective statuses; precisely what it
costs is an unknown to the average citizen. Yet he is involved in such battles;
goals are established and resources allocated. The leaders of interest groups
may more often have a fairly precise idea of the allocative problem, the
choices to be made and the costs to be paid. And they are the ones who make
most of the direct decisions within their organizations and attempt to influence public policy.

Other variations in the choice of public goods might be usefully introduced at this juncture. Politicians and citizens are confronted not only with
choices over alternative goods such as defense and social welfare but also
with alternative projects within the same type of benefits. A clarification
may be had in the form of an example: Congressmen compete over funds
for building post offices, atomic installations, military establishments, dams,
etc., for their respective districts. If an atomic installation is to be constructed next year, there must be some means of deciding where it is to be
located. Normally, more than one area in the country is available and useful. Or, suppose a new dam is to be built. Is it to be constructed in Oregon or
in Tennessee? This is an allocative decision. It must be resolved through
political processes. How politicians might be aided in making optimal
choices is an important problem; such matters will be considered in Chapter 13. To what extent their choices can be improved is an open question
but in the meanwhile politicians must make allocative choices and do so
within a more or less given framework of rules, institutions and political
cultures operative within their respective nations or communities.

It should be mentioned at this point (more extensive analysis in
Chapters 12 and 13) that all choices between public and private goods
are not inherently contradictory. In other words, spending money on one
project need not necessarily mean the sacrifice of another project. In fact,
expenditure on one may promote or complement others. A good example
is governmental spending on public works during depressions. Additional expenditures by governments may actually increase the incomes of
private citizens, who may in turn spend their added incomes on more private goods. Carry-overs or 'spill-overs' of benefits work in both directions
when social and private goals are compatible or complementary. But, at any
given time and with *given* resources, the choices are more frequently of the
either/or types. We hasten to remind readers that nations do not have to
surrender to given times or to given resources. They can increase their
resource base or the efficiency with which it is employed and, of course, time
changes things whether one wants it to or not. Conservatives are generally

impressed with the givens or constraints while radicals and liberals seem impressed with unused opportunities to change. How do you view the situation?

The discussion has focused upon certain necessary crucial allocative choices that individuals, whether voters or politicians, and governments make as a part of their everyday political lives. But we have said little about what actual choices have been made by governments. On what do governments spend their money? How are their resources allocated among the multitude of possibilities? Fortunately, we have some figures on precisely such allocative choices (though only by expenditures as a measure of resource allocation). A summary of this data is provided in Table 2-2.

Several things should be noted in reading the table: (1) breakdowns are in terms of very general categories so details about each class of expenditure are absent; (2) the range of public goods is in most cases not too different for all these European governments regardless of their political processes and income levels. This suggests an earlier point of ours that some governments are faced with similar problems, constraints, and therefore, choices; and (3) the spread among expenditures for most classes of goods is not very significant, i.e., the range from the highest to the lowest expenditures is not pronounced. Since countries like Spain and Great Britain have different cultures as well as political systems, one might expect their budget choices on economic allocation to be a reflection of such differences. Apparently, the universality of some social problems and public goals for these western systems prevents this from happening.

Time Preferences

Another essentially allocative decision involved in the choices of governments and citizens concerns a time preference. Public goods may satisfy *present consumption* or *expected future wants*. The former is easy to understand; we generally prefer the present enjoyment of goods to uncertain future satisfactions. Provision for future needs may be thought of as an 'investment' that is expected to pay off at an assumed rate for some unspecified time period. For example, road repair is intended to satisfy present needs, while building a super-highway in an area that has yet to be developed may be thought of as fulfilling or providing for an expected future need. Our government is, today, attempting to reach the moon; there is little present payoff in such an endeavor but there may be a future value, as military and space officials contend.

What makes this distinction and decision so important is the fact that most of us most of the time place a far greater emphasis or value on immediate satisfactions. Reaching public investment decisions for the future is seldom easy or popular because the satisfactions are not directly enjoyed and may never be, since estimates may go wrong and opportunities may be lost

Table 2-2

Percentage Distribution of Government Expenditures (Excluding Expenditures for Defense and Social Security) by Function, Selected Countries, 1956

Country	Total	Education and Culture	Justice and Police	General Adminis- tration	Transport and Communi- cations	Subsi- dies	Hous- ing	Public Debt Manage- ment	Other
All levels of government									
France	100.0	21.2	6.7	11.5	19.4	11.3	12.3	7.3	10.3
United Kingdom	100.0	22.6	4.6	9.5	16.0	10.8	12.4	24.1	—
Germany	100.0	25.8	10.2	14.1	14.5	2.4	15.5	8.8	8.7
Norway	100.0	20.3	3.4	10.4	20.8	23.3	4.7	6.4	10.7
Switzerland	100.0	23.4	8.2	16.2	14.9	12.1	11.9	13.3	—
Central government only									
Austria	100.0	19.9	9.8	26.9	27.5	10.0	1.5	4.4	—
Belgium	100.0	19.1	3.6	9.0	12.3	7.9	2.8	21.5	23.8
Finland	100.0	28.1	4.2	13.9	24.6	25.8	—	3.4	—
Luxembourg	100.0	14.6	4.2	16.7	25.0	16.7	2.1	14.6	6.1
Netherlands	100.0	16.1	6.1	9.2	13.4	14.4	5.6	13.4	21.8
Sweden	100.0	35.0	6.8	12.0	19.9	13.5	—	10.8	2.0

Source: J. Frederic Dewhurst, *et. al.*, *Europe's Needs and Resources* (New York: Twentieth Century Fund, 1961), p. 420.

forever. *Uncertainty* then plays a great role in private and public decisions about the future. Because delayed consumption, or worse, an uncertain promise will bring sacrifices, we usually demand some form of compensation. In the private economy savers demand interest payments; indeed they also demand them from the government for any loans they may make for future public projects. But most delayed consumption on the part of taxpayers is forced by the government whether citizens wish to sacrifice or not. The great investment projects of the U.S.S.R., for example, were financed by edict of a government whose people had no direct voice in the decision to promote future development at the expense of present enjoyment. Again we can present the choice—whoever makes it—in the form of a curve. Figure 2-3 depicts what we mean.

Figure 2-3

Time Preferences for Public Goods and Services

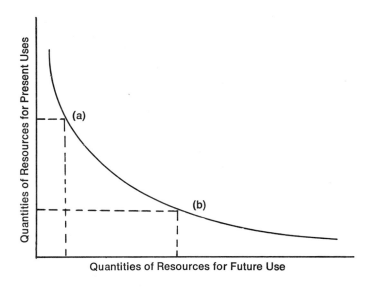

Quantities of Resources for Future Use

The curve in Figure 2-3 illustrates a set of time preferences on the part of a person or a government, i.e., the combination of preferred uses of resources. Each point on the curve indicates the respective quantities of resources that a person or government might like to see devoted to both present and future uses. Thus (a) indicates a government which prefers to spend most of its resources for present consumption or uses, while (b) indicates a government which prefers fewer quantities used in the present and more devoted to the production of future uses. The shape or slope of the curve indicates the rate at which a person or government is prepared to sub- stitute resources for either present or future use. The steeper portions of the curve denote a greater willingness to surrender resources from present con- sumption for future use, while the flatter sections of the curves indicate a greater unwillingness to give up present consumption. We are most willing to invest in the future when we have ample or plentiful resources for the present; we are least willing to surrender present consumption when we are confronted with scarcities. We *must* live for today and not tomorrow. Many governments have considered it necessary to force their peoples to save and invest as a nation if economic development is to take place. Russia and China are good examples. Since we cannot, given scarcities, use all capital goods to satisfy present needs or vice versa we have a dilemma; to allocate a resource to one time period rather than another requires us to make real sacrifices. Generally, the more allocated to the present, the less is available for the future; the more capital made available for future uses, the less available to satisfy today's demands.

Politics is inevitably bound up with questions of this type although they may occur less frequently than our other two types of allocative deci- sion conflicts. Nevertheless, political debates over research and devel- opment budgets, space explorations, future military needs, educational facilities, the location of housing developments, urban renewal, and many others entail choices between the present and the future. The newly- developing nations are peculiarly involved in these dilemmas since their rulers want some immediate satisfactions for their needy subjects but also know that the nation will never become better off until it has acquired capital development projects promising higher future incomes and inde- pendence in world politics. The example of the U.S.S.R. is always upper- most in their minds, for that once backward nation became at least the second most powerful nation within forty years, largely because Lenin and Stalin opted for future development and sacrificed the current needs of two generations. Those who now live better in the Soviet Union do so partly because those rulers forced their parents to sacrifice and 'save' for the future. They did this by inspiration and command, controls and fear, rewards and penalties, and even by the taking of countless lives. But they succeeded. It would appear that the eighty or so underdeveloped nations are for the most part future-oriented, but their leaders generally do not wish to employ the mass intimidation of a Stalin. Cases in point are India and The Peoples Republic of China, both of whom are attempting with quite different polit- ical systems to develop for the future: China is striving for a more central- ized command system while India is relying on a decentralized, competitive bargaining system. Which will succeed better? At what costs?

The situation in the newly-developing nations is rather different in a number of ways from that of wealthy nations. In most new nations present consumption takes a much greater proportion of the gross national product than it does in industrialized nations because the new nation's GNP is so much smaller that investment is extremely difficult to encourage and maintain. In less developed countries, for example, 73-75 per cent of the GNP is devoted to current private consumption while in the United States it is less than 66 per cent.[1] Still, the latter can provide a vastly higher standard of living because its GNP is so much greater than that of developing countries. Most of the less-developed nations consume more than 68 per cent of their national product in daily private consumption. The governments of these nations find themselves in the unhappy position of wanting to achieve conflicting goals with extremely limited resources. On the one hand, their stability and popularity are partially dependent upon fulfilling current needs and wants, while on the other hand they realize that their resource base can be expanded only by considerable sacrifice and discipline. To rely upon outside sources is viewed as political dependence and control, a fate many would prefer to avoid, given the former colonial status of most of these countries. The simple little curve of Figure 2-3 illustrates a source of profound policy dilemma.

Mobilization of Public Resources

The allocative problem is described only in part by assessing the pattern of resource. The supply of resources is also a major problem. Governments require the well-known factors of production, just as do economic enterprises and private organizations, namely land, labor, capital and the appropriate productive technology. This is not surprising. In an earlier day some great empires used massive quantities of resources, especially land and labor, in such public enterprises as extensive agricultural irrigation, military conquest and the construction of public buildings and monuments.[2] Consider the scale of governmental operations required to build the pyramids of Egypt or the Great Wall of China, and the kinds of skills needed. The growth of the modern nation-state has been identified with developments in the techniques of public and military administration and with newer forms of public endeavor, such as organized exploration and scientific discovery, or planned economic development and the operation of many sorts of enter-

---

[1] Simon Kuznets, *Modern Economic Growth: Rate, Structure and Spread* (New Haven: Yale University Press, 1966), p. 426.

[2] Some interesting research has been done on the mobilization activities of ancient empires. Cf. Karl A. Wittfogel, *Oriental Despotism* (New Haven: Yale University Press, 1957); S. N. Eisenstadt, *The Political Systems of Empires* (New York: The Free Press of Glencoe, 1963). The latter volume has an unusually complete bibliography of historical materials.

prises. The nature of the demand for public resources has changed accordingly, and the governments have shown a variety of capabilities for resource acquisition, some of them rather unique. Consider the current extent to which governments do own and manage actual capital assets, land and manpower.

The U.S.A. can serve as a somewhat surprising example of public ownership because it is still regarded as the home of private enterprise with an ideology stressing private initiative, profit and property. The federal government, alone, owns and controls the use of more than 765 million acres of land, or approximately 34 per cent of the total land area of the nation.[3] Ironically, the federal government has come to own more than 44 per cent of the land in the conservative state of Arizona and 98 per cent of Alaska.[4] Much of the property is held in the form of forest preserves, parks, military installations, highways, grazing and pasture land, and sites of government buildings and installations. The value of all this land cannot be accurately estimated because market prices have not been determined. The United States Government assesses the value of these buildings and land at more than $69 billion and this is probably a low estimate of the current market value.[5] And, of course, many capital assets of government have a symbolic worth which cannot be estimated. Nevertheless, periodic efforts are made to place some comparable dollar values on the assets of governments. One such effort, now dated but still instructive about trends, is that of Solomon Fabricant, illustrated in Table 2-3. Even when price adjustments are included to deflate the estimates, the increase in governmental property holdings and values is considerable. The value rose from $8.4 billion in 1902 to $50.9 billion in 1946 (in terms of 1929 prices).

The government has also increased its use of the nation's manpower. Public employment is now a major industry. In 1962, all levels of government in this country employed more than 12 million persons, roughly one-sixth of the entire labor force.[6] While short-term fluctuations in public employment are experienced, the trend has been ever upward. From 1929 to 1962 governmental employment increased at twice the rate of the labor force increase. We need not detail the composition of the increase except to say that military personnel have shown the greatest increases, as well as the most fluctuation, during the past three decades. The reasons for this should be apparent. What is less apparent is the substantial gain in state and local employment. The percentage of the labor force employed at these levels has increased from a total of 5 per cent in 1929 to 9.2 per cent in

---

[3] U.S. Bureau of the Census, *Statistical Abstract of the United States, 1967*, 87th ed. (Washington, D.C., 1967), p. 201.
[4] *Ibid.*
[5] *Ibid.*, p. 202.
[6] Frederick C. Mosher and Orville F. Poland, *The Costs of American Governments: Facts, Trends, Myths* (New York: Dodd, Mead and Company, 1966), p. 134.

Table 2-3

Government-Owned Nonmilitary Assets, 1902-1946 (billions of dollars)

	1902	1912	1922	1929	1939	1946	1922	1929	1939	1946
			Excl. Roads and Streets				Incl. Roads and Streets			
Book values										
Incl. defense corporations	3.8	7.3	15.4	21.1	30.9	51.4	20.5	31.9	47.8	68.8
Excl. defense corporations	3.8	7.3	13.0	21.0	30.7	36.1	18.1	31.8	47.6	53.6
*1929 prices**										
Incl. defense corporations	8.4	14.3	18.9	23.3	33.8	50.9				
Excl. defense corporations	8.4	14.3	15.9	23.2	33.6	35.8				

* Conversion of book values to 1929 prices changes the 1929 book values because the assets of 1929 are valued on the books at the prices prevailing in the years when the assets were acquired.

Source: Solomon Fabricant, *The Trend of Government Activity in the United States Since 1900*, p. 15, copyright © 1952 by the National Bureau of Economic Research, New York, New York.

55

1962.[7] Most of the increase is found in the educational activities of these governments. In short, the public employment of manpower has been one of the most rapidly growing areas of employment since 1929.

Other modern nation-states have displayed similar developments during the twentieth century. All apparently have confronted similar demands for increased services and faced similar developmental problems as their societies increased in population, density and complexity of activities.

The Means of Mobilization

Governments, as we have mentioned, are organizations with some rather unique characteristics and capacities for resource mobilization. In the first place, governments, if they are well established, possess the ultimate authority or right to exercise control over the citizenry, a right which no other social organization can legally claim. This august authority, in fact, means the legal power to compel the citizen to contribute resources, including even his property or his own labor, as in the case of compulsory military service. If such edicts are resisted, governments can still, by force of superior power, compel men to behave and contribute against their will, and we all know of examples—prisons and concentration camps.

Interestingly, in spite of the enormous influence of patriotism, no state in history has ever depended solely upon voluntary contributions. Men may love their country and die for it in wartime, but rarely do they contribute money to it on a voluntary basis. Resources for continuing government operations are usually acquired by taxation, borrowing in the open market, operating enterprises, resorting sometimes to confiscation or to imperialistic ventures and the exploitation of other peoples, or by trying to enlist fervent support for national projects through propaganda and political organization. These means have been employed by all governments. But each of these means also depends upon the technological and administrative capabilities of the government in question. While the modernized nation-state may have little difficulty mobilizing sufficient resources under normal conditions, such is not the case in many newly-developing nations. They are often seriously lacking in the basic resources, including administrative techniques and skilled personnel, sufficient to realize their ambitious public goals.

Taxation

Taxation is regarded today as the most common way of acquiring resources; in the United States it provides about 75 per cent of all public

---

[7] *Ibid.*, p. 139.

revenues and consumes about 25 per cent of the GNP. The taxation system of a nation is dependent on the nature and distribution of wealth and income, the state of tax administration or technology and the political doctrines which assist in justifying what can be taxed, how and when.

Patterns of taxation have varied greatly throughout history and still do vary among nations. Amounts levied and collected differ as greatly as the political means by which they are decided. The patterns of incidence—who pays how much of the total tax bill—and the impact relative to income also vary greatly among nations. These matters will be developed in detail in Chapter 5.

Borrowing and Debt

Few governments consistently mobilize sufficient resources by taxation. Even in the exigencies of wartime it is generally considered inexpedient to raise all revenues by taxation. The reasons are both political and economic. While taxes can bring in the largest sums by far, totals are not completely predictable, nor do governments always trim their sails when such sums fall short. The differences can be made up in other ways which have greater short-run flexibility. One way is by selling bonds, that is, borrowing from those who can afford and are willing to purchase government securities. The government must, like all borrowers, eventually repay the loans and compensate the lenders with attractive interest payments. While debts may be repudiated, and often have been, most governments, especially democratic ones, feel a strong obligation to maintain the trust of their own citizens and especially those at home or abroad who have the means for such investments. While many Americans worry about the astronomical sums of their public debt as conveyed in per capita or aggregate amounts, the debt is a tribute in a sense to the trust and willingness of investors. In any case, it should be compared with other kinds of lending and indebtedness. More recently, state and local indebtedness has increased while the relative federal debt has decreased; and total private debts have increased substantially during the last thirty years.[8]

In Chapter 5 public borrowing will be assessed in more detail and on a cross-national basis.

Governmental Enterprises and Market Operations

As we have seen, governments perform many services and supply a multitude of public goods which are financed from public treasuries. While many public goods are distributed without direct cost to users, an increasing number are also sold. Many public goods are indivisible and cannot be

---

[8] *Ibid.,* pp. 99-101.

sold to individual consumers, but as governments produce goods comparable to those of private economy, fees can be attached and payment
can be required. In this country, about 15 per cent of the total revenues are
acquired through sales, fees and other charges.[9] Postal receipts, tolls, school
lunch charges, parking fees, public utility charges, public housing rentals,
fees for use of various facilities such as airports, liquor sales, recreational
charges, are typical examples of services and goods for which governments
charge users. In nations with considerable nationalization of industries one
can expect that such charges are a more common feature of public activity
and contribute a larger portion of the total revenues. As citizens who are
taxed resist further compulsory payments, we may expect that the resort
to user charges will increase.

The fact that governments can charge for services and goods means,
of course, that they are in business and operating in the market.[10] Government enterprises are becoming more significant elements of even capitalist
systems and they seem destined to be used even more so in the future. Just
why nations adopt or pursue more market activities both as buyers and
sellers is a question which will be taken up below.

Mobilization of Support

We save for the end the best and most valued resource which governments always seek—and indeed create, if they can. It is the resource of citizen support in all its forms and dimensions. All the material supplies and
monetary funds available may count for little without a social and political
environment which facilitates their use for public purposes. Support is the
political resource par excellence, yet often the least understood by the critical onlooker. Much of governmental activity and effort to muster such support is especially viewed with suspicion by the democratically oriented
American. Only as we look at other systems do we begin to understand
clearly that no government—repeat, *no* government—has long survived
without engaging the resources of popular support, in some or most forms.
At a minimum, this requires commitment and energy on the part of major
participants in governing systems, from top decision-makers to officials and
workers in the public service. Even more so, in modern industrialized and
participatory systems, this must include the dedication and contributions of
a greater number of active citizenry and, hopefully, from the standpoint of
the governors, the acquiescent attachments of the potentially active or the
passive 'giver' of other resources.

Some writers have referred to this important source of governmental

9 *Ibid.,* p. 71.
10 See Lloyd D. Musolf, *Government and the Economy* (Chicago: Scott, Foresman and
Company, 1965), Chaps. 5-6, for a succinct treatment of the government's role as a buyer
and seller.

efficacy in terms suggesting a circular process: that governments and leaders by their own efforts mobilize such support and focus it upon the desired ends. This certainly appears to be an important task of leadership in new nations, revolutionary regimes, and countries trying to modernize and develop from traditional economic and political forms. Thus Karl Deutsch has described an important and pervasive aspect of political development as the "social mobilization" process and has characterized its basic dimension as "the general propensity or availability of persons for recommitment." The recommitment of human concerns and energies can include occupational and residential mobility, changes of human relationships in jobs, communities, associations and therefore changes of roles, identifications and expectations.[11] Thus we can conceive of a resource reservoir of people made available for new loyalties and tasks, once they are 'stirred up,' shaken free of older ties and motivated to seek new opportunities. Of course these opportunities may be offered by other than governmental leaders—one thinks of earlier industrializing processes in western systems where entrepreneurs mobilized resources for private productive purposes. But for a variety of reasons—including the state of technology, the magnitude of ambitions to modernize, and the nature of resistances—political leadership in these changing systems takes on a very large part of the effort to mobilize the efforts and skills of the peoples, as well as their political loyalties. One scholar, David Apter, has used the term "mobilization systems" to emphasize the political features of systems where there is a very intense, centrally directed modernizing or industrializing effort. He notes the important role of an explicitly formulated and propagated ideology (or a 'political religion'); the need for a strong hierarchy of command; a party of solidarity; and special roles for youth, the military, and the civil service.[12] However, the author sees this as an 'extreme' type of political answer to demands for change in a system, contrasting it to other forms which he calls "neomercantilist" and "reconciliation" types of systems.

Given the subject Apter is analyzing, these are quite useful distinctions; but we would note that *all* political systems mobilize human resources, though their methods, objects and levels of effectiveness may vary considerably. At one extreme, perhaps, we can conceive of only a minimal level of acquiescence and loyalty being thus mobilized among the populace. But even in highly decentralized countries it is far more likely that a whole array of legal encouragements, symbolic exhortations and public examples will remind the people that public pride and duty are just as deserving of effort as individual endeavor. We shall have more to say about this in discussing the division of labor, for what are called 'political socialization' processes

---

[11] Karl W. Deutsch, "Social Mobilization and Political Development," *American Political Science Review*, 55 (Sept., 1961), pp. 493-514.

[12] David E. Apter, *The Politics of Modernization* (Chicago: The University of Chicago Press, 1965), Chaps. 6, 7, 10.

are typically the very diffuse means by which citizens and political activists are called into participation and service.

Why Do Governments Grow? Expansion of the Public Sector

Newspapers, many Republican leaders, 'Jeffersonian Democrats,' most conservatives and even the New Left periodically lament that 'creeping socialism,' or state bureaucratization of life, has become fact in even this most 'capitalistic' of countries. The lament is based on historical fact: from what we know most societies have been administering increasing proportions of their resources through governmental and political processes. We see evidence of this from the increasing proportions of the national income that are taken by taxation, increasing public expenditures, and by the increasing use made of governmental enterprises. Governments own vast quantities of property; they employ vast numbers of citizens; they control many productive enterprises and they engage in many other economic activities. Lest the reader be unaware, consider some figures on the matter.

The more than ninety thousand governmental units of the United States during 1965 took in a total of more than $202 billion from a gross national product of about $681 billion.[13] Some $165 billion was derived from taxation, meaning each of us paid an average per capita sum of about $860 during that year. With these dollars our governments employed nearly 10.5 million persons from a population of about 195 million people. This works out to an average of about 5 per cent of the total population working for government. Their total income amounted to $4.8 billion. These employees and Americans generally worked the resources of the richest nation and government in the world.

With this resource base our governments engage in an almost endless list of activities. Research and development programs were sponsored and executed by government to the tune of $14 billion during 1965. More than $29 billion of insurance business was conducted by the many governments during 1964. In one of the more traditional activities of government—highway construction—our governments built or contracted for 3.6 million miles of roads at a cost of about $5.5 billion. Other construction during 1964 was contracted for by public sources to the extent of almost a third of the total building done in the nation; the governmental proportion amounted to $20 billion in a total of public and private construction of $66 billion. These highly selective figures on resource mobilization provide but the barest set of indicators of the enormous scope of resource management by American governments. Few other governments manage so

---

[13] Tax Foundation, Inc., *Facts and Figures on Government Finance*, 14th Biennial Edition, 1967 (New York, 1967), pp. 17, 32.

huge a resource base, although some governments (the U.S.S.R. in particular) manage much larger proportions of the societal factors of production.

Furthermore, as we look abroad we find that public ownership is no longer an unusual thing, nor practised solely by socialist governments. The countries listed in Table 2-4 are all non-communist regimes, and the greatest amount of public ownership does not always coincide with the countries typically labeled as more 'socialistic.' By now we must have confirmed the suspicions of the conservatives and stimulated some leftists, so we must turn to inquire into the causes of this remarkable state of affairs. In short, why has resource mobilization and allocation come to be so much of a political problem?

Demand for Public Goods

A most direct and somewhat simple explanation for the growth of governmental activities is that people want increasingly more things from their governments, and their governments are more than willing to oblige. This disarmingly simple generality is quite commonly heard from the critic who despairs of the insatiable greed of people to 'sup at the public trough' and of the conniving politicians who thus can bribe the citizenry into maintaining them in power. The trouble is, the circularity or mutuality of causes is almost too simple to apply to the real political world. How long could such a system of mutual benefit exist without confronting the question of who pays the costs?

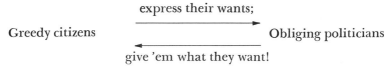

Somebody must be forced to pay for the 'goodies' thus generated, and at what point does the greedy citizen become a rebellious taxpayer? We will examine this question in greater detail in Chapter 5, but let us move on to more sophisticated versions of this basic generalization which have been advanced by some rather respectable scholars and worriers about the public sector.

One such sophisticated approach would be to show *under what political conditions* demands for public goods might prevail over resistance to the costs and might succeed in persuading politicians to respond favorably. In other words, one could spell out the special circumstances which might cause citizenry and politician to cooperate in this manner. This essentially was the nature of the reflection that Alexis de Tocqueville gave to the subject in his classic study, *Democracy in America,* based on his observations of this country in the 1830s.[14] De Tocqueville begins with a comparative gener-

---

[14] Alexis de Tocqueville, *Democracy in America,* trans. Phillips Bradley (New York: Vintage Books, Alfred A. Knopf, Inc., 1945), I, Chap. 13.

Table 2-4

Per Cent of Government Control of Industries in Which Government Ownership or Participation Is Substantial, Selected Countries, about 1955

Industry and Country	Per Cent	Industry and Country	Per Cent	Industry and Country	Per Cent
Coal mining		Natural gas		Electrical equipment	
Austria	94	France	Substantial	Austria	42
France	98	Italy	94 (methane gas)	Italy	30
Germany	26	Other minerals		Transport equipment	
Italy	100	France	Potash monopoly in Alsace	Denmark	13
Netherlands	60	Italy	Effective government control of mercury	Finland	33
Sweden	44 (peat)	Forest resources*		France	20–33
U. K.	100	Iron and steel		Italy	40
Crude oil		Austria	95	Norway	More than 15
Austria	100	Finland	56	Sweden	10
France	Substantial	Germany	5	Automobiles	
Germany	16	Italy	80 (pig iron)	France	33
Italy	20		50 (steel)	Germany	About 40 but state ownership not permanent
Iron ore		Norway	66	Italy	10
Austria	100	Sweden	Minor	Chemicals	
Germany	35	U. K.	10–15	Austria	13
Italy	76	General machinery		Denmark	Minor
All metal ores		Austria	20	Finland	28
Austria	Almost complete	Denmark	2	France	8
Finland	96	Finland	16	Sweden	Minor
Sweden	69	France	16		
Norway	Substantial state participation in private companies	Italy	13		
		Norway	Minor		

Source: Dewhurst et al., op. cit., p. 439.

alization about the encouragements used by different regimes to produce wealth. He observes that despotic systems take more wealth from
the citizenry and tend to restrict production. Contrariwise, a political
condition of freedom encourages the production of more goods than it de-
stroys or takes away, so that a free country's resources rise at a greater rate
than taxation. Then de Tocqueville considers the political opportunities of
the citizenry in terms of what they already have in the way of wealth. He
sees society divided into three *relative* strata: the wealthy, the middle classes,
and those without property or the workers. Like Aristotle in antiquity, he
sees the middle classes as the most economical in the policies they would support because they are not rich enough to bear the cost of public spending lightly. He views the wealthier classes as more likely to be generous
in financial administration because they would view their contribution in
taxes as relatively less burdensome. But the lower classes would most certainly be extravagant in their support of spending programs from which
they would gain more than they would lose, given their relative inability to
contribute to the public coffers. Then de Tocqueville examines the political
condition, finding that the kind of 'pure' universal suffrage practiced in the
United States would give the poor a far greater chance to express their
preferences, being the majority (as he saw it in the 1830s).

> In democracies, where the rulers are poor and in want, they can
> be courted only by such means as will improve their well-being, and
> these improvements cannot take place without money. When a people
> begin to reflect on their situation, they discover a multitude of wants
> that they had not before been conscious of, and to satisfy these exigen-
> cies recourse must be had to the coffers of the state.[15]

Perhaps we can diagram de Tocqueville's reasoning as follows, noting the
conditions he would attach to the earlier, rather simplistic model we
presented.

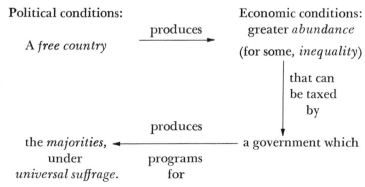

---

[15] *Ibid.*, p. 224.

Note also how much more easily such reasoning from certain conditions is susceptible to comparative testing. De Tocqueville made a brave effort, given the inadequate information available in his time. He tried to compare the relative prosperity of France and the United States and then compare their governmental expenditures. But he was defeated even in trying to dig up comparable budget figures for a composite of all levels of government in the two systems, let alone in finding some broad measure of relative prosperity. After making the try, with a very long footnote containing interesting comparisons, he came to a familiar conclusion:

> Hence we must conclude that it is no less difficult to compare the social expenditure than it is to estimate the relative wealth of France and America. I will even add that it would be dangerous to attempt this comparison; for when statistics are not based upon computations that are strictly accurate, they mislead instead of guiding aright. The mind is easily imposed upon by the affectation of exactitude which marks even the misstatements of statistics; and it adopts with confidence the errors which are appareled in the forms of mathematical truth.

Yet, in the spirit of persistent inquiry, he continues the quest as best he can:

> We abandon, therefore, the numerical investigation, with the hope of meeting with data of another kind. In the absence of positive documents, we may form an opinion as to the proportion that the taxation of a people bears to its real wealth, by observing whether its external appearance is flourishing; whether, after having paid the dues of the state, the poor man retains the means of subsistence, and the rich the means of enjoyment; and whether both classes seem contented with their position, seeking, however, to ameliorate it by perpetual exertions, so that industry is never in want of capital, nor capital unemployed by industry.[16]

This seemed worthy of quoting at length, for de Tocqueville admirably exemplifies here the best in empirical scholarship: Know what you are looking for, and why; try your level best to get the most relevant and accurate data to test the case; but if you cannot, reflect on the best possible substitutes, and make your evaluations as carefully as you can.

Another quite sophisticated form of reasoning about public resources and expenditure also tends to emphasize the element of public demand as a determinative factor. We are speaking of the economists in public finance, who have based their analysis on comparisons with demand-making in the

---

[16] *Ibid.*, p. 232.

marketplace. What, they have asked, is similar in the public sector to the processes of the market, and how can the 'production of public goods' be explained in comparable terms? Their reasoning typically starts with the assumption that individuals have an array of preferences, most of which can be satisfied in the private economy by goods and services which are produced, priced and distributed there. But there are other kinds of goods for which people have preferences which are not so easily sold or distributed through the market system because they cannot be easily priced and sold in separate units, e.g., highways, sanitation services, national defense. Then there are other goods which will not be produced by the ordinary enterprise, e.g., space exploration, and other such high risk or high cost projects as dams and irrigation systems, atomic energy development or operation of extensive canals and bridges. To be made accessible, these kinds of goods must be publicly produced and generally made available to all. In this way, economists come to a definition of *public goods* in terms of the peculiar nature of the product as compared to the kinds of goods generated through the market system. A pure public good is thus indivisible in the sense that its use and enjoyment by one citizen does not preclude its use by others.

But the economist is not only interested in discerning and describing public goods, their kinds and amounts. They wish to explain *why* and *when* they will be so undertaken, and when they will not. It is here that some of the major analysts have developed rather elaborate theories starting from the basic premise of 'consumer' or public demands which must be met by governments rather than private enterprise. For example, Richard A. Musgrave, in his very important work, *The Theory of Public Finance*,[17] begins in this fashion in his first chapter, "A Multiple Theory of the Public Household." To understand the nature of public wants, he starts with the ideal conditions in the private market and notes those "market imperfections" which will call for public policies in order to meet the ideal standard of the optimal allocation of resources. Then he considers the case of "social wants," where consumer sovereignty is still presumed to prevail but what is desired are the kinds of public goods described above. The problem becomes, how do people express their preferences for these goods, if the regular market channels are not available? With the perspective of a U.S. citizen, Musgrave very easily draws the analogy of the vote as a means of expressing preferences in democratic political systems. If such preferences were expressed through the political process, he says, ". . . the problem is to determine the kind of voting process or group decision that offers the best approximation to the solution . . . that would be chosen if true preferences were known."[18] Of course, Musgrave develops this reasoning, starting from

---

[17] Richard A. Musgrave, *The Theory of Public Finance* (New York: McGraw-Hill Book Company, Inc., 1959).
[18] *Ibid.*, p. 11.

quite simplified premises, in order to use the very effective tools of economic analysis to the greatest extent possible. Assuming the existence of public wants similar to private wants is one such highly useful simplification. But even this needs further clarification, for perhaps these public goods are not so easily discerned or designated as is a very particular and specifically visible item purchased in some market. To this possibility which would undermine an economic approach considerably, Musgrave replies:

> Let us look upon our preference for the individualistic over the organic view as a matter of value judgment and be content to show that our formulation makes empirical sense. I see no reason why individuals should not be able to evaluate the benefits they derive from the satisfaction of social wants, along with the benefits they derive from the satisfaction of private wants.[19]

Note that this is still a logical assertion and not an empirical test of whether and where this is the case. Yet, Musgrave goes still further with another logical kind of want, in this case different from the expression of what the 'sovereign consumer' would have. Suppose that, still aiming at ideal allocations by market criteria, some wants "are considered so meritorious that their satisfaction is provided for through the public budget, over and above what is provided for through the market and paid for by private buyers."[20] These the author calls 'merit wants.' If these are imposed, as against actual consumer preferences, in policy programs, they must be explained in some other fashion. Musgrave makes references to 'matters of learning and leadership' for explaining how these wants come about.[21] Yet he does not treat them as a major impediment to the economic analysis of public goods, because they are also decided upon in political processes and, to that extent at least, are comparable to the resolution of issues about priority of social wants over private preferences.

Now all this sounds very abstract, and indeed it is. The pure economic 'explanation' of the demand for public goods is performed in terms of general 'utility' criteria, possible kinds of preference orderings, and derived indifference curves. It doesn't sound like de Tocqueville at all, but in seeking general solutions to the abstract formulation of the problem, the economist may help considerably to provide better measurement tools which will aid in testing more precisely the kind of theorizing which de Tocqueville had found so frustrating. Yet in common applications such assumptions can easily be confused with empirical explanations. No sensible economist believes

---

[19] *Ibid.*
[20] *Ibid.*, p. 13.
[21] *Ibid.*, p. 14.

that governments could or would act in the same way that ideal markets would respond to consumer demand. But he will tend to make the consumer-sovereignty and free market exchange model a first approximation for what happens in the public sector. And therefore, in summary fashion, he may use the language of 'public demand for public goods' as shorthand form for what are known to be quite intricate decision processes in the political system. In this fashion, for example, one economist explained the growth of government to members of the Joint Economic Committee of the U.S. Congress, using these terms:

> . . . We now have different standards of 'necessity,' and as a nation we have higher consumption aspirations than we had in the past. The same facts, not surprisingly, also hold with respect to our public spending. Just as we have come to demand more and better quality products from the private sector of the economy, we have come to demand more and better quality 'products' from government—the public sector. We want more and better quality schools, roads, hospitals, and recreational facilities, more adequate provision for the aged, unemployed, infirm, and needy children, increased attention to our natural resources, more provision for public safety, etc. As a consequence of this growth in public demand, virtually every government function has been expanded since 1900.[22]

We might diagram this simplified economic theory of the formation of public goods as follows:

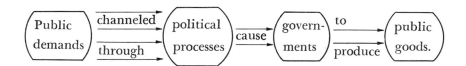

Public Goods as Increasing Necessities in Complex Societies

Man's capacity to produce goods and services, at least in the western world, has grown enormously during the past two centuries. So has his capacity for participating in highly organized modern life. Increasingly large and complex enterprises, growing cities, ever more vast organizations and bureaucracies, greater networks of communication and transportation—all

---

[22] Arnold M. Soloway, "The Growth of Government Over the Past 50 Years: An Analytical Review," in *Federal Expenditure Policy for Economic Growth and Stability*, U.S. Congress, 1st Sess., Joint Economic Committee, November 5, 1957, pp. 19-59.

seem to be undeniable trends as societies continue to modernize. In several
ways this growing complexity and interdependence can be viewed as requiring an ever greater governmental role in society. The methods by
which governments discern and meet these necessities may vary considerably,
depending upon the form of government and the nature of its leadership. It
may or may not come through an expression of public demands. It could instead come from the politically 'insulated' decisions of dictators, or planning commissions, or cabinets and ministries. Indeed, before theories of
individual choice and market behavior became so elaborate, some notable
earlier studies of public finance treated this expanding relative share of
government as an inevitable 'law,' tied directly to the growing economy and
technology. Such apparently was the perspective of H. C. Adams, writing in
this country in 1898.[23] It was even more clearly expounded as a law by the
German scholar, Adolph Wagner, who undertook to explain the increasing
public expenditure of a variety of governments on the Continent and in
North America, which the studies of his time, in the late nineteenth
century, clearly revealed. In his own words:

> The "law of increasing expansion of public, and particularly
> state, activities" becomes for the fiscal economy the law of the increas-
> ing expansion of fiscal requirements. Both the State's requirements
> grow and, often even more so, those of local authorities, when adminis-
> tration is decentralized and local government well organized. Recently
> there has been a marked increase in Germany in the fiscal require-
> ments of municipalities, especially urban ones. That law is the result
> of empirical observation in progressive countries, at least in our West-
> ern European civilization; its explanation, justification and cause is
> the pressure for social progress and the resulting changes in the rela-
> tive spheres of private and public economy, especially compulsory
> public economy.[24]

Wagner's reasoning proceeds in terms of broader societal conditions and
their changing impact on the role of the state. 'Social progress' refers to economic and technological developments which have important compounded
effects in modern society, leading to more state intervention. For one thing,
as social and economic life became more atomized and the divisions of la-

----

[23] H. C. Adams, *The Science of Finance* (New York: Henry Holt and Company, 1898),
Chap. 2, cited in Alan T. Peacock and Jack Wiseman, *The Growth of Public Expenditure
in the United Kingdom* (National Bureau of Economic Research, Princeton University
Press, 1961), p. 17.
[24] Adolph Wagner, "Three Extracts on Public Finance," in *Classics in the Theory of
Public Finance,* Richard A. Musgrave and Alan T. Peacock, eds. (New York: St. Martin's
Press, Inc., 1964), p. 8.

bor increased, the sources of societal conflict would proliferate. Concomitantly, developing organizational capacities would lead inevitably to more centralized administration and would enhance the ability of the state to conduct larger enterprises more efficiently. With these dominant trends in mind, Wagner reviews the major functions of governments and indicates how each will expand. First, governments must maintain law and order, and their enforcement activities will have to increase to meet the tensions and disorders of modern life. Second, as governments improve their capacity to produce, there will be more occasions where private enterprise would not or could not assume extensive operations as efficiently or with as great a stability of commitment. Here Wagner viewed the device of the public corporation as increasingly useful, especially for developing such 'newer' resources as steam power, or for replacing private monopolies. Finally, governments provide economic and social services, such as postal, education, banking; and again capacity and effectiveness would favor an increasing public share. In each sphere, therefore, there is increasing necessity for public control and activity to meet the problems of social progress.[25] The diagram that follows is an attempt to summarize his reasoning:

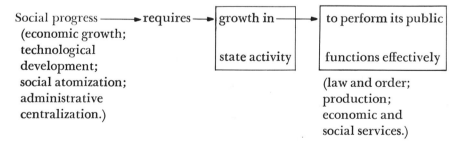

Social progress ——→ requires —→ growth in —— → to perform its public
(economic growth;   state activity   functions effectively
technological
development;   (law and order;
social atomization;   production;
administrative   economic and
centralization.)   social services.)

Economies of Scale and Complementarities

Several of the processes or forces that Wagner suggests have been phrased in more modern economic terms by present-day analysts. For example, centralization may be explained in economic terms by calling attention to *economies of scale*, in broadening the scope of enterprise and management. If governments have the requisite scope and capacity, they may then enable a more effective use of resources, although decisions to that effect may not at all be automatic. Whether as 'demands' or 'command decision,' such rational criteria must somehow be built into the political system as well. Another sort of economic explanation is related to the private proliferation of goods, along with increasing interdependence. The availability

—————————
[25] The above summary of Wagner's views was aided considerably by the discussion of Alan T. Peacock and Jack Wiseman, *The Growth of Public Expenditure in the United Kingdom* (Princeton: Princeton University Press, 1961), pp. 16-19.

or use of one good may require a *complementary* good or service to be produced. For example, the millions of cars and trucks and motorcycles that are produced by private corporations and owned by private citizens require extensive road systems if they are to be of any use. Given the many needs that motor vehicles fulfill, one can readily understand why billions of dollars must be spent on creating and maintaining highway systems. In principle, these highways could be produced by private entrepreneurs for a profit. Most people—even capitalists—are not likely, however, to believe that we would have an efficient highway system if private persons administered it. High investment requirements and a doubtful profit situation are not conducive to making a private enterprise of highways. As more cars are produced for profit, more public highways are also demanded. The same is true of air transportation; private companies and their passengers demand more and better airports, traffic management, regulation of the system and safety. These needs are most easily provided for by governments. They are complementary to private activities. And so it goes for many other complementary public facilities that are demanded by private users. Can you name some others? Think of public programs and services which directly serve privately induced needs.

Compensatory Action, Subsidies and Competing Goods

We might continue to speak in economic terms of compensatory public programs which meet economic needs when and where the private economy has failed. Each citizen is, for example, frequently confronted with costs he must bear which are caused but not borne by those responsible for them. Such costs are labelled external costs by economists. As might be expected the citizen may turn to government for aid in reducing such burdens. The term compensatory has been popularized in designating certain monetary and fiscal policy measures in Keynesian economic doctrine when they are used to balance or make up failings in the private economy. The term can be applied to poverty programs as well as military expenditures when viewed as a means of stimulating the economy. Subsidies may also have similar effects but are usually viewed as a means of assisting private producer groups who cannot survive or flourish if left to the choices of the private market. In addition to subsidies and compensatory programs, we can observe an array of goods offered by government which compete with goods produced and distributed in the market by private entrepreneurs. One can borrow books from a public library instead of buying them, use public parks instead of private lawns, buy public power instead of a private utility's services, ride in public transportation instead of one's own car or boat. These programs are usefully viewed by the economic analyst in terms of needs served, and they may very well then help to explain why the need was met through public means. Typically, though, the precise decision to turn to the public sector is not so automatic. One usually finds economists adding further criteria for such decisions: the economies of scale, as above; or the lack of private alternatives, as where the special properties of public goods come into play. Or further, they may build in the assumption of public demands but leave it to others, primarily political scientists, to explain when and how this comes about.

Political Responses to Private Ills

Most empirical investigations of increasing governmental activities indicate that the rate of growth in public programs tends to be uneven. There are periods of rapid growth and proliferation, and then relatively stable periods when the public sector proceeds only in proportion to growth in population or output per capita, or may even retrench as compared to the private share (see Chart 2-1). In the United States, for example, there were two periods of great peacetime expansion in federal agencies in this century, one, the decade of the 1910s, and the other during the post-depression New Deal period of the 1930s. This has inspired many political analysts to reflect upon the political processes which result in rapid public change, as compared to periods of relative quiescence. The political theories of significant policy change tend to emphasize the role of activists, whether few or many, in broadening the public sphere, and to emphasize the political ideas and events which relate directly to these changes.

Of course there is no inherent reason why policy changes should all be positive and not negative. Like the business cycle, could not the production of public goods rise and fall as well—especially in electoral systems where different administrations come into office? Most political analysts have assumed no inexorable direction to political events, and have seen alternation as quite likely in some kinds of policies. Perhaps we may dissect the different elements of policy change in order to see more clearly what is attributed to political events. First, these analysts seldom concern themselves with growth in the public sector due to ongoing programs about which there is little controversy. That is, they would tend to take for granted, in this country, such expanding services as the postal system, the increasing burdens of the decennial census, the mounting literature put out by the Government Printing Office. Where the commitment is firm, the operation an established one, and the services tied to other growing sectors in the system, growth becomes a foregone conclusion. Its explanation is neither profound, nor politically of much interest. What is of greater interest are the additions of new programs or significant alterations in ongoing ones. What causes rapid acceleration of services, outstripping population growth rates? What brings new programs to government, new functions or matters to be managed? These have most intrigued political analysts, and we might note some major thoughts along these lines.

Chart 2-1

Federal Expenditures, Annually, 1794-1952

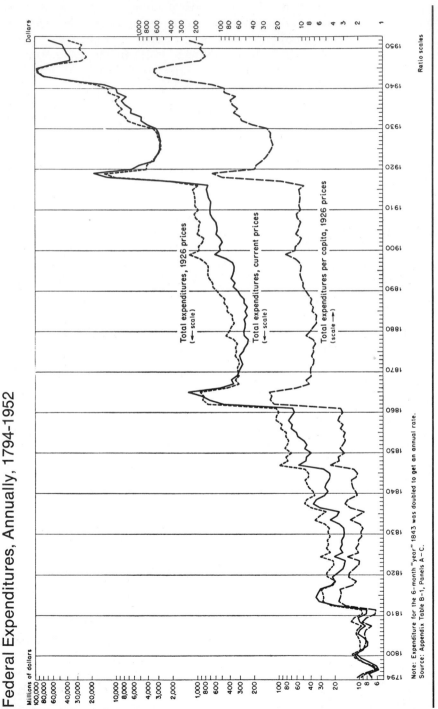

Note: Expenditure for the 6-month "year" 1843 was doubled to get an annual rate.
Source: Appendix Table B-1, Panels A – C.

72

Source: M. Slade Kendrick, *A Century and a Half of Federal Expenditures*, p. 4, copyright © 1955 by the National Bureau of Economic Research, New York, New York.

Political reasoning, unlike economic, may start with the assumption that political institutions, as with other major 'establishments' in society, may more typically be resistant to change. The status quo, or the 'power structure,' may not necessarily be as responsive to new demands as the marketplace would tend to be. If changes tend to come in clusters, or irregularly, would it not be more politically savvy to look for the factors which finally overcame the resistant thresholds? In this sense, the political analyst more often looks for movements, crusades, or intense pressures put on government to change—and most likely to expand—its services. The classic cases have been the farmer movements of this country such as the Populist stirrings of the late nineteenth century, or the various combinations of farmer organizations and big city progressives in the early years of this century. Many note that most farm programs were in response to such farmer pressures, when these became so widespread and intense that responsive change was certainly less costly than continuing to do nothing. Now farmer discontent can also be attributed to economic factors, for it is typically noted that the farmer in this country at least, gets most agitated when the prices for his crops fall. Yet his demand had to be organized and expressed politically, and the programs to help him were not assumed directly, in the sense that individual market demands would be met.

In electoral systems there is available a relatively broad channel through which the membership of organized movements *may* express their preference for change. This is a possibility only, until one knows more about the conditions under which elections are held, and how much the demand for certain changes can be identified with electoral choice. In this country and in Britain, at least, the scholar can find good evidence that elections upon occasion have resulted not only in party or electoral turnover but also have resulted in policy changes and expansion of programs. We can draw several tentative hypotheses about policy changes, and especially expansion of government, from the lessons of history, and then leave it to future chapters to explore the strategies of change in a more detailed manner.

Hypotheses About Overall Policy Change

1. *In some political systems, policy changes will stem from new combinations of majorities which are identified with intensely felt demands.*

The Jeffersonian revolution in this country appears to be only the first of several such 'new majorities,' although it is not easy to test this, given the problems of evidence for earlier times. Certainly in recent times one has witnessed the policy changes due to notable coalition shifts. As one scholar has noted:

In 1932 the country, in the midst of a great depression, used a demoralized and disorganized Democratic party to produce the greatest reversal of public policy in American history. This happened not because the Democratic party was an ideal vehicle for this task but because it was the only instrument available.[26]

This most obvious case has been followed by another most unusual recombination in 1964, when southern states deserted the Democratic Party in large number, to be replaced evidently by many moderate-thinking persons who normally vote Republican. The resultant expansion in Great Society programs was only surpassed by the increasing military effort in Vietnam. Without going into all the 'intervening variables,' we will rest with the assertion that the newly composed majority for that year was followed by one of the most remarkable increases in overall federal expenditure witnessed since the years of World War II and the Korean war mobilizations. We might finally note another way in which new majorities may come about, using the peculiar case of the Civil War years. The seceding southern states lost much of their representation in the federal Congress, so that the newly formed national Republican Party found itself in an extraordinarily dominant position. The 'radical' legislation that resulted was often belligerently directed at the South, but there were also added general programs such as a new Department of Agriculture, a Bureau of Education, and the first internal revenue tax.

2. *Governmental expansion results from successful efforts of groups seeking restitution of private losses.*

We will add a further political premise to what may be labelled compensatory public goods produced by governments. If there are burdensome private problems, it is not always simple or easy to turn to the government for redress, as the economic logic of externalities would suggest. We have noted there must be organized effort or broad channels made available and, most of all, an intensity of effort and sense of the relevance of public remedies. All this in sufficient amount may lead to added or changed programs. Therefore we must note not only the presence of felt needs but the activation and political efficacy of the demands as well. Thus, we not only note that protective tariffs perform economic functions but look also to the political occasions when they are instituted and to those activated elements which have successfully expanded or changed them. Social security and public insurance programs have been instituted by many governments at different times, and one should investigate the occasions when they are successfully advocated. In the astute formulation of E. E. Schattschneider, policy change comes about when the issues are so defined as to broaden the 'scope of conflict' to include the aggrieved and the 'have nots' as new partici-

---

[26] E. E. Schattschneider, *The Semi-sovereign People* (New York: Holt, Rinehart and Winston, Inc., 1960), p. 86.

pants in electoral choice. John Kenneth Galbraith also emphasizes such a conflict premise in his famous theory of countervailing power, whereby the weaker economic groups facing strong opponents in the marketplace would turn to government for support in winning economic redress.[27] He cites the success of farmers' organizations and of labor unions in achieving protective legislation.

In conclusion, one can view many new expenditures and services as restitution for groups feeling so embattled or deprived as to turn actively to government.

3. *In pluralist or competitive situations governments may be expected to produce policies which gain rather than lose electoral support.*

We may attribute some 'cost-benefit' analysis to political leaders, always remembering that the essential unit of value is not currency so much as a more ephemeral but earnestly-sought thing we call support. Politicians must win elections. Given the uncertain world of competitive type systems, one may expect leaders or governments to attempt to please or placate the more demanding groups by public policies meeting their preferences. As we shall see later, explanations of the 'pork barrel' and 'logrolling' tend to emphasize the relatively costless gains of combining benefits for as many people as possible, given available resources. Here policy must be analyzed in terms of what is to be given, with what resources and how these policies will affect voting at the next election. But what about dictatorial systems? Do they escape such encouragements to government expansion? We have to consider particular cases. We see in revolutionary regimes—and especially the communist ones—great expansions of the government role over the pre-revolutionary regimes.

Also, one notes that redistributive schemes (land, income, rights or statuses) are often the rallying cry of revolutionaries and often pursued by the new rulers. But subsequent repression of resistance, forced drafts of resources and general impositions of cost require more explanation: either in terms of force, terror, inspired patriotism or promises for the future. Some have proposed a 'law of diminishing dictatorship'; namely, the longer the regime in power, the fewer the realized promises, the more the disillusionment of supporters, the more likely the rulers will have to concede more present gains to the many. If this is so, we could expand our generalization to these systems, too—in the long run, that is.

4. *Governments will revise regulations and controls more often than domestic distributive expenditure and service programs.*

While this point rests on discussions in future chapters, we would like to include it here in view of its relevance to public resources. Taking away

---

[27] John Kenneth Galbraith, *American Capitalism: The Concept of Countervailing Power* (Boston: Houghton Mifflin Company, 1952), Chaps. 1-4.

expected benefits is a very risky course of policy change. It is difficult to find examples where a government has done so, when any considerable number of people were involved. Instead, social welfare benefits tend to be extended, even under more 'conservative' administrations, such as Eisenhower and Churchill's; veterans' benefits are extended as a matter of right to younger generations of war veterans; and all forms of assistance generally proceed upward. Yet there are alternations in policy programs and we think they will more often take place in nonexpenditure areas. Anti-trust suits have fluctuated considerably since the first legislation of 1890. Tariff rates, interest rates and margin requirements for securities also have frequently been raised and lowered. There would appear to be several reasons for such patterns, as contrasted to that of steady or rapid growth. For one thing, there is the effect of a party alternation in electoral systems—or even of some 'proto-electoral' coups and successions. New regimes may seek relief for the aggrieved who have not been bearing the costs of regulation. The Anti-Federalists reversed the pattern of alien and sedition prosecutions, and later heirs of Jefferson lowered tariff rates when they came into office. Anti-trust prosecutions have tended to increase with Democratic administrations and decrease with the Republicans in office. One should also very likely expect alternations such as 'get tough,' or 'go slow' policies where there are high costs in sustaining crack-downs, and a good deal of adaptive evasion by target groups. This seems often to be the case with regard to campaigns against vice or rackets in American cities. At any rate, the point is not to view growing government as the only—or inevitable—form of change involving public resources. There is just as much a logical case for governments to ease up on costly or unrewarding efforts by seeking less costly alternatives as there is to expect Wagner's 'law' of increasing expenditures to be operative. The hypothesis must be tested, of course, by more than just the pattern of expenditure. Perhaps that is why we find less attention paid to this possibility.

5. *In ordinary times official or dominant ideologies will serve to limit government expansion.*

Students of government policy have frequently noted that periods of relative stability in expenditures and programs are typically accompanied by dominant beliefs that existing program levels are 'right' or 'proper,' and should *not* be precipitously exceeded. There are, in other words, constraining ideologies which serve in ordinary times to keep public spending and services down, or at least to impose limits on rates or amounts of increase. In the United States, for example, ideologies of laissez-faire, states' rights and local autonomy had this effect during much of the prior century and earlier decades of this one. Presidential vetoes and Supreme Court decisions often struck down venturesome new policies, such as a series of presidential vetoes on congressional internal improvements legislation prior to the Civil War, or the series of state and national laws for welfare, economic protection and benefits struck down as unconstitutional by the Supreme Court in the first two decades of the twentieth century. Demands can be denied, therefore, if the deniers believe they are doing so on behalf of 'right principles.' A most pervasive case of this sort has been the prevailing norm of 'budget-balancing' versus 'fiscal irresponsibility,' which has guided executive and legislative policy-making since the very early years of the Republic. And such ideologies gain in plausibility where public costs are more visible than the benefits. One study of federal fiscal policy since 1789 has indicated how frequently Presidents and their Treasury secretaries labored under such explicit premises of fiscal constraint.[28] More recent Keynesian doctrines of compensatory spending to stimulate a faltering economy are thus quite revolutionary, insofar as they have transformed official precepts of appropriate expenditure.

6. *Wars and severe crises generate major governmental expansion, with an aftermath of significantly enlarged public activity.*

A crisis removes normal constraints on behavior, as the value placed on survival knows few bounds. In cases of a severe threat to the polity or society, governments are turned to as the most resourceful and forceful instrument of defense and restoration. The expansion of public resources can be quite remarkable in terms of what was considered possible prior to the emergency. Governments are seen as justified in taking more from the private sectors of activity; and people are typically called upon to make sacrifices and work harder, which further expands the resource base at public disposal. The larger or longer the war, the greater the mobilization demands in terms of money, material and manpower. Even with considerable war damage nations-in-arms reveal a great capacity to expand productivity by tapping hitherto unused supplies of labor, resources and service, and by invention and improvement of technology. Since war is a collective effort, government controls are also expanded: to mobilize resources more effectively, to draft manpower, to curtail private diversion of goods and to ration or manage the disbursement of what is left; to guide production, regulate behavior and to carry out protective defenses more effectively. The elaboration of control marks a great change not only in the level or magnitude of government activity but also in its nature and impact. What is ordinarily considered by the citizenry as repressive or costly may be supported as necessary and patriotic. Governments are allowed broader means and confront fewer obstacles and resistances. Again, under emergency situations, such expansion is a dramatic transformation.

There is considerable evidence that what is thus done is not likely to be completely undone—or dismantled—after the period of crisis. The aftermath of modern wars in Britain and the United States has seen a far greater

---

[28] Lewis H. Kimmel, *Federal Budget and Fiscal Policy, 1789-1958* (Washington, D.C.: The Brookings Institution, 1959).

relative role of the central government than normal growth rates would have achieved, given the pre-war trends. That is, wartime brings a disproportionate increase in government activities, even after the subsidence of the emergency effort. These considerations have led two analysts of the British case to generalize about the 'concentration' and 'displacement' effects of 'social upheaval' upon levels of government activity. They comment about these as follows:

> . . . Changes in social and political ideas and institutions, as such, may condition the evolution of the functions of government, and may also affect the nature and significance for public expenditures of such social upheavals as wars. Conversely, the displacement effect may be the origin of lasting changes in ideas and institutions; periods of war are, for example, a fruitful source both of new ideas about society and of new administrative procedures.
>
> . . . During periods of social upheaval such as wars the political opposition to change is weakened, and the pressures for concentration can break through. At the same time, an event such as war has different impacts at the central and subordinate levels of government. The central authority assumes responsibility for the prosecution of the war, and it is consequently at the central level that new tax revenues (which are the basis for the later permanent growth of the public sector) are concentrated. This must imply a relatively faster growth in central functions, in the absence of a deliberate decision to hand over new responsibilities for expenditures to local governments after the disturbance is over. Further, the needs of war become more important than such issues as local autonomy, and abrogations of local independence are tolerated that would have been unacceptable at other times. Once the change has been made, it is easier to make it permanent, and such a step may indeed become unavoidable. Finally, the periods of disturbance may (though they need not) be characterized by a social cohesion that reinforces among other things, the demand for uniform standards of public services. The result of this will of course depend upon the country concerned and upon its state of economic development; it must always encourage a concentration of responsibilities at higher levels, but whether the concentration will be at the center or at some intermediate level must depend upon particular conditions.[29]

Other occasions of crisis, such as a great depression and its aftermath—and, we suspect, great natural disasters as well—would also fit this pattern.

---

[29] Peacock and Wiseman, *op cit.*, pp. 28, 30.

Case Studies

Some of the more general and abstract formulations of the past pages may be made more concrete and meaningful with a few case studies of resource mobilization and allocation in specific countries. The cases we have selected are meant to illustrate various facets of mobilization and allocation; for example, one deals with citizen attitudes toward governmental fiscal policy (expenditures and taxes), while another presents hard data on federal allocative choices in the United States. Still another case study considers the obstacles to resource development and mobilization in four fairly representative underdeveloped countries.

Case Study #1   Citizen Attitudes on Fiscal Policy in the U.S.A. (1960-61)

Our overall discussion has concerned abstract problems from the more general perspective of the system, and our tabular presentations have dealt with overall government resources and allocations. Such presentations necessarily leave out the individual citizen and his views of these same choices. This 'oversight' is not as great a problem in non-democratic polities as in democracies where individual preferences are solicited to a much wider extent. In the democracies there is more explicit concern with the perceptions and information levels of citizens on mobilization and allocative problems. As will be the case in so much of our discussion we must use data collected on American citizens, because there is less available as yet on other countries. Oddly enough, American survey researchers seem to have tapped attitudes on practically everything but allocative policies. We have been able, however, to locate two very good systematic studies of public attitudes on fiscal matters and we have summarized their main findings to illustrate the possibilities of attitude surveys on such substantive issues.

In a nation-wide survey, The Survey Research Center at the University of Michigan undertook an investigation of attitudes toward governmental spending and taxation as a part of a more inclusive study of political and economic attitudes. Eva Mueller, an economist at the Center, analyzed the results and came to a number of interesting and important conclusions. We have organized her study in the form of a number of propositions or generalizations based on the evidence or explanations of her study. We suggest that you consult the article, itself, for her supporting analysis.[30] The more relevant generalizations are as follows:

1. Judging fiscal policies (governmental spending and taxation) in terms of national or long-term general benefit seems . . . to be a task beyond the grasp of most people.

---

[30] Eva Mueller, "Public Attitudes Toward Fiscal Programs," *Quarterly Journal of Economics,* LXXVII (May, 1963), pp. 210-35.

      a) There is a lack of congruence in thinking about fiscal programs.

      b) Most do believe that the federal government has great capabil-
ities for influencing the level of economic activity and for bringing about the proper functioning of the economy.

2. Attitudes toward individual programs differ sharply.

      a) A large majority have favorable attitudes toward a number of
major government expenditure programs.

      b) While the desire for extended government services is pro-
nounced in *all* income groups there are distinct differences in
the kinds of services which are desired.

      —All income groups strongly support more aid for older people
and aid to education.

      —Lower-income groups prefer aid to the needy, aid for the
unemployed, hospital and medical care, public works more
than higher-income groups.

      —Aid to small business and highway construction receive wid-
est support in the upper-income groups.

3. The majority of Americans do not formulate ideas as to how the
level of taxation, much less the system of taxation, might be altered.

      a) There is not much general information on the relative fairness
of income, sales and property taxes.

      b) There is no evidence that the existing federal debt causes
great concern or uneasiness.

      c) There is widespread acceptance of current tax levels.

      d) Support for programs goes down when added taxes are made a
condition.

Miss Mueller goes on to say that self-interest is only a partial explanation of attitudes toward fiscal programs since she discovered that the upper-
income groups were as much for added governmental expenditures as lower-
income groups. This finding has been supported in a study by Wilson and
Banfield,[31] who claim that many higher income voters support added governmental expenditures in referenda which are of no direct manifest value
to them. The authors term this tendency 'public regardingness,' the opposite of self-interest. However, one may question their findings because the
particular public goods voted upon tend to be more useful to higher income
groups, contrary to the authors' contention. Such public projects as court-
houses, government office buildings, parks, roads and bridges are probably
more useful to, or used more by, middle and upper income classes than the
very lowest income receivers. In any case, Banfield and Wilson do not attempt to check the frequency of use of various public goods among the

---

[31] James Q. Wilson and Edward Banfield, "Public Regardingness as a Value Premise in
Voting Behavior," *American Political Science Review*, LVIII (December, 1964), pp. 876-87.

citizenry, so we do not really know whose interests or values are being better served by each type of good and expenditure. Whatever is the case, the authors have shown that non-homeowners tend to vote in overwhelming numbers for projects which are financed by taxes on property holders, while middle income property owners tend to be less enthusiastic for public expenditures which will be financed out of property taxes. A rough sort of rationality seems to prevail among these two economic groups. What seems less rational, in a narrow sense, is the support which the high income earners provide for public projects. Banfield and Wilson believe that these citizens are 'rational,' i.e., concerned about the costs they pay, but that they have a civic end in mind rather than a narrow personal income or status goal. Such citizens are felt to take pride in the public sector, at least in cities and towns. We are inclined to believe this is also the case, but to make a special virtue of the practice seems unwarranted, until the flow of the relevant civic benefits are better understood. In a sense the city, its appearance and services, are always of more value to the better-off than to the disadvantaged. Note who drive their out-of-town guests about showing off the community—not the poor!

These two studies are harbingers of more attitudinal and voting analyses of citizens on substantive policy issues. You would be wise to consult them at first hand.

Case Study #2   Federal Allocative Choices in the US.A. (1966-67)

In our first case study we reviewed two studies dealing with citizen attitudes and voting behavior with respect to fiscal or allocative matters. As we all know, such inquiries have limited value in predicting or explaining the actual allocative choices made by an entire political system. The budget which a nation finally enacts may or may not be in accord with public opinion—if there is an informed attitude at all. We are not likely to know since no attempts have ever been made to determine national opinion on the size and composition of an entire national budget of billions of dollars. In the final analysis all we have to go on are the end results—the budget itself.

Our case study deals with the actual 1966 and the proposed 1967 budget. Table 2-5 lists the allocations according to 'function,' i.e., the kind of government activity and the total amount of such expenditures. A number of features in these outlays require comment. First, the largest single activity of the federal government was providing national defense and waging war. Over one-half of the total budget was devoted to these tasks in 1966 and 1967 while all other activities consumed less than half of the available money. Parenthetically, we may recall that many conservatives in Congress waged an economy drive to reduce certain non-defense expenditures even more than the budget indicates. Those wishing to reduce the budget were not all in agreement on how much to cut from which programs; typically, congressmen wanted to cut parts affecting other areas than their own states

Table 2-5

Administrative Budget Expenditures, 1966 and 1967 (Fiscal years. In billions)

Function	1966 actual	1967 estimate
Administrative budget expenditures:		
National defense	$57.7	$70.2
Excluding special Vietnam	(51.9)	(50.8)
International affairs and finance	4.2	4.6
Excluding special Vietnam	(3.9)	(4.1)
Space research and technology	5.9	5.6
Agriculture and agricultural resources	3.3	3.0
Natural resources	3.1	3.2
Commerce and transportation	3.0	3.5
Housing and community development	.3	.9
Health, labor and welfare	7.6	10.4
Education	2.8	3.3
Veterans' benefits and services	5.0	6.4
Interest	12.1	13.5
General government	2.5	2.7
Allowances:		
Civilian and military pay increase		
Possible shortfall in asset sales		
Contingencies		.1
Interfund transactions (deduct)	.6	.8
Total, administrative budget expenditures	107.0	126.7

Source: *The Budget of the United States Government, 1968* (Washington, D.C.: U.S. Government Printing Office, 1967), p. 18.

and districts. Secondly, note that interest payments on the national debt rank as the second most important expenditure. The significance of this fact is two-fold: (1) the magnitude of the gross debt is very large (over $321.5 billion, or about 55 per cent of the national income[32]) and (2) interest payments are made to those who can afford to lend the government money, meaning the higher income receivers. Among these creditors are the federal reserve banks, commercial banks, insurance companies and other corporations. Even some federal agencies hold a portion of the government's debt. Lest you worry about the burden of the debt, recall that private debt is at least twice as large as the public debt and that the growth in our national income far exceeds the growth rate of the debt itself.

Other notable features of the budgetary allocations include an increasing proportion going into 'health, labor and welfare.' The table does

---

[32] U.S. Bureau of the Census, *Statistical Abstract of the United States: 1966*, p. 388.

not show long term changes but they have occurred. Veterans' benefits and services are also substantial items (5 per cent) and are on the increase because of the frequency of war and growing numbers of veterans entitled by law to some form of compensation. You may note that one category, 'general government,' was allocated 2.3 per cent of the budget; that means it really did not require much money for the other miscellaneous management activities of the government itself, even though this includes the costs of Congress, the federal court system, the FBI and the Internal Revenue Service as well! Those economizers who feel that government is terribly inefficient and that great sums could be saved by more 'businesslike' procedures are apt to be somewhat disappointed for there is so little room to save here. If the entire sum were subtracted from the budget it would not affect very many citizens' pocketbooks very much. If one wishes to effect savings one had better concentrate upon defense expenditures. Any other area is apt to provide but marginal savings.

We should also emphasize that budgetary allocations in the United States are seriously constrained from year to year. In other words, a new administration cannot wipe the slate clean and begin an entirely new budget either in the aggregate or in terms of its internal composition. Far too many projects are firmly established by custom, law and opinion to be eliminated or seriously adjusted. No President can decide not to pay the interest on the debt, nor to suspend veterans' benefits. No President could realistically reduce the defense budget by a half or a third. It is simply a political impossibility. Such a man would be impeached if he even tried. And among the impeachers would be many well-known economizers. All that a government can realistically expect is to adjust most established expenditures by rather small percentages, and most of them in an upward direction. It has been easier to increase expenditures than to reduce them. Furthermore, some expenditures are easier to manipulate than others. We have already indicated that the 'sacred cows' include interest payments, veterans' benefits, and national defense; to these three we may add subsidies, particularly those to the shipping industry, agriculture and the airlines.

A careful perusal of the national budget is a necessity in political analysis for it summarizes the great allocative decisions we have discussed in earlier pages. Budgets are not particularly inspiring documents nor are they easily understood, but they are political documents and a resultant of the political processes of a nation. As such they offer suggestive hints about the distribution of political resources, the values of a nation, its problems and resources. We believe that political scientists ought to spend more time analyzing these reports.

Case Study #3   Resource Allocation in Peru, Ecuador, Colombia and Nicaragua (1953-1960)

Resource allocation in the underdeveloped lands is a particularly interesting and important if depressing problem, not only for those directly involved but for Americans who wish to see them develop into effective nation-states, able to provide their people with a decent standard of living. Their problems often appear insurmountable and perhaps for that reason many rely on government to devise and conduct development plans. Of course, reliance on government investment and direction of economic development varies considerably among these countries as do specific plans and allocations of resources by their governments.

We have chosen four Latin American countries as cases in point: Ecuador, Colombia, Peru and Nicaragua.[33] None of these countries is very democratic or socialistic in its goals and economic practices, but all show quite different patterns of resource allocation regarding monies devoted to social and economic development, general governmental and military expenditures. Peru, one of the less democratic Latin American nations, has allocated the smallest amounts of its national budgets to social and economic development (public works, education, health, agriculture, labor, etc.) and the most to military objectives. Peru's defense expenditures have averaged about 25 per cent of the budget for the period 1945-1960. On the other hand, Ecuador devoted anywhere from 61 to 76 per cent of its public budgets to social and economic development from 1950 to 1960. Colombia and Nicaragua allocated resources to social and economic development at a rate somewhere between the amounts assigned by Ecuador and Peru. Figure 2-4 depicts all these proportions for the four countries during the 1953 to 1960 period. We may note in Figure 2-4 that the four countries are devoting increasing percentages of their budgets to development but at different rates. Furthermore, Colombia and Nicaragua have proceeded in a rather erratic fashion, with Colombia showing much greater annual variations. ·We do not know the reasons for these varying annual changes. Perhaps you might inquire more deeply into the problem than we have been able to do. These four nations, unlike the much more democratic Costa Rica, for example, have seen fit to spend much more on military hardware and control.[34] Costa Rica has seldom spent more than 4 per cent of its budget on the military as contrasted with one-fifth to one-quarter of the budgets in the cases of Peru, Colombia, Nicaragua and Ecuador. In nations with average per capita national incomes of less than $409, as in the case of Colombia, and only $205 in the instance of Peru, contributing to the military budget inevitably imposes a severe sacrifice on the people. How much more rapidly social and economic development might take place with significant reductions in military spending is difficult to say. But optimal resource allocation during the early stages of development can produce considerable marginal gains.

---

[33] Our discussion is based on Charles W. Anderson, *Politics and Economic Change in Latin America* (Princeton, N.J.: D. Van Nostrand Company, Inc., 1967), Chap. 11.
[34] *Ibid.*, p. 331.

Small increases in investment can, in other words, result in far greater additions to the national income.

Figure 2-4

Proportion of Public Budget Devoted to Social and Economic Development—1953–1960

(Peru, Ecuador, Colombia, and Nicaragua)

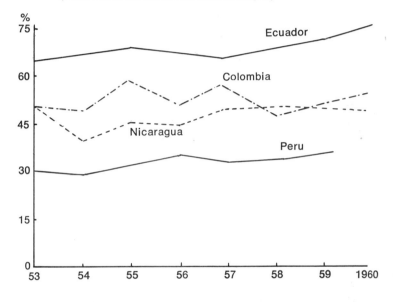

Source: Based on Charles W. Anderson, *Politics and Economic Change in Latin America* (Princeton: D. Van Nostrand Co.. Inc., 1967), pp. 330-31.

The rather skewed resource allocations of many Latin American countries are undoubtedly products of widespread military rule over the decades. While established elites—and even military elites—may pursue enlightened allocative policies, the probabilities that they will do so appear less promising than in the case of more democratic civilian leadership. There are signs of change, though, as development becomes a more prized goal in all societies—regardless of political system. Even military regimes require economic development, if for no other reason than to provide an industrial base for more effective armies. However that may be, Latin American nations appear to be increasingly restless, and one consequence may be a reallocation of societal resources to more productive uses.

Generalizations to Explore About
Resource Mobilization and Allocation

We have ranged over a good deal of data and explanations concerning public resource mobilization and allocation as general features of political systems. We suggest many possibilities in summary form below; these are the kinds of claims we and others have made which call for much further consideration by the interested person than we have been able to give in this chapter. None of these statements is an absolute certainty. The reader should consider them critically and if possible discuss them with others. What objections or conditions should be made? What cases or examples cause you to support or reject these generalizations? How could they be tested empirically? Do they appear obvious, logically contradictory, or perhaps even circular in meaning? Many of these we do not quite agree with either, but they have been presented by others, or offered by ourselves, as an initial venture in testing the generality of what we think we know about the resources at the disposal of governments.

Resource Mobilization

1. Governments tend to take resources where there are fewer costs or resistances.
2. Governments will tap the most lucrative and promising kind of resources for a given system, subject to the constraints of extremely powerful groups.
3. Benefits will be exchanged for revenues more frequently in democratic and industrial societies than in non-democratic and non-industrial nations.
4. Means of governmental resource mobilization will change with the technological state of management and control.
5. The governments of industrialized nations prefer automatic and indirect revenue extraction to those methods requiring direct administrative impositions.
6. Conflicts among citizens over methods of raising revenue are likely to be more numerous than conflicts over the aggregate size of the budget.
7. Desirable expenditure goals outweigh cost considerations in deciding the size and rate of growth of the budget.
8. Governmental expansion or contraction takes place with the advent of new political coalitions.
9. As real income increases, the demand for all goods (public and private) increases.
10. Wagner's Law: The public sector will increase in size and importance with the increase of social complexity.
11. 'Displacement Effects': Wars and similar emergencies generate increases in the level of public expenditures which are only partially reversible.

12. Among voters, party identification has only a weak relationship to fiscal policy attitudes.
13. Voters tend to judge particular taxes from the point of view of immediate personal benefit.

Allocations Among Public Goods and Services

1. Among nations the allocation of resources to military consumption varies far more than does the size of the civilian share.
2. Governments seldom know for certain the specific revenue sum they will have to allocate among various uses.
3. While the desire for extended governmental services is pronounced in all income groups, there are distinct differences in the kinds of services which are desired.
4. Social security programs are most preferred among lower income groups, while public works projects receive wider support among middle and upper income groups.
5. Those public goods which are complementary to private goods are more likely to be produced by governments than those which are competitive.
6. Goods produced under conditions of decreasing marginal costs are more apt to be produced by governments.
7. Programs involving regulations and costs will fluctuate more widely than those involving benefits and services.
8. In democracies governments will choose those allocations which are most intensely preferred by most citizens.
9. Public expenditures conferring present benefits are preferred by most citizens to programs of public investment or deferred consumption.
10. People seldom judge tax and expenditure policies in terms of long-term or general benefit.
11. When conditions are stable official agencies tend to seek short run incremental gains.

   We repeat that these propositions are not asserted as truths both because the empirical foundations for them are at present too limited and because some of them are quite likely subject to logical disproof in part or in their entirety. We offer them because they have been asserted, often as a part of the conventional ambiguous wisdom, by someone. They must all be further refined and rigorously tested. It is our hope that the task will appeal to many more political scientists in the future than it has in the past.

Problems and Applications

1. If one wished to measure the extent to which compulsion is used in different political systems to mobilize resources, how might he proceed? What are some good indicators of compulsion? Is it possible to measure compulsion?

2. Suppose you are an official adviser to an underdeveloped nation and are requested to provide policy recommendations on breaking out of the vicious cycle of limited governmental resources. What would you suggest? Why?

3. If a democratic nation is extremely poor in resources, which *public* goods and services are most likely to be produced? And, which will be sacrificed? Why?

4. If a nation is experiencing an increase in production of the following private good, which public goods are most likely to experience an increased demand? Why?

Private Goods	*Public Goods & Services*
automobiles	?
hallucinatory drugs	?
aircraft	?
private pleasure boats	?
ocean freighters	?

5. Can you think of any reasons why state and local spending has been rising at a faster rate than federal *non-defense* spending during the past forty years?

6. Table 2-6, on page 89, from Russett, Alker, Deutsch and Lasswell, *World Handbook of Political and Social Indicators*, New Haven: Yale University Press, 1964, p. 63, shows the relative shares of all governmental spending for selected countries, as related to GNP. What sorts of plausible hypotheses would be relevant, as explanations of differences? How would you explain the below-average ranking of the United States?

7. Chart 2-2 on page 90 estimates the long-term trend in U.S. federal expenditures proportional to GNP since the Constitutional period, based on current economic reporting and earlier approximations. What relevant factors can be related to the different periods of stability and growth? Does incremental growth appear to be the dominant trend?

8. Contrast the above chart, for relevant periods, with Chart 2-3, on page 91, from Peacock and Wiseman, *The Growth of Public Expenditure in the United Kingdom*, National Bureau of Economic Research: Princeton: Princeton University Press, 1961, p. 57. What political factors would one want to check against the periods of rise, decline and stability of expenditures? What economic and social factors?

9. If you wished to cut back the federal budget by 25 per cent, which items would you reduce or eliminate? Why? Assess the political feasibility of your proposals.

Table 2-6

Expenditure of General Government, Social Security, and Public Enterprises as a Percentage of GNP[1]

No. of Cases	28
Mean	32.2
Median	33.7
Modal Decile	VI
Range	39.3
Standard Deviation	10.2
Percentage of World Population	41

% of Table Population	Case Deciles	Rank	Country	Expenditure/ GNP	Range Deciles
	I	1	Sweden	52.9	I
		2	United Kingdom	45.3	II
	II	3	Austria[2]	43.8	III
		4	New Zealand	43.2	
		5	Japan	42.3	
	III	6	Netherlands	41.2	
		7	France	40.1	IV
		8	Italy	39.9	
	IV	9	West Germany[2]	38.8	
25.6					
		10	Canada	37.4	
		11	Finland	36.9	V
	V	12	Norway	36.5	
		13	South Africa	35.6	
	VI	14	Burma	34.3	
		15	Belgium	33.0	VI
		16	Congo (Leopoldville)	32.9	
	VII	17	Ireland	32.5	
		18	Australia	30.5	
		19	Denmark	29.9	
	VIII	20	United States	27.9	VII
		21	Greece	26.2	
		22	Portugal	22.8	VIII
49.5					
	IX	23	Brazil	18.9	IX
		24	Pakistan	18.0	
64.8					
		25	India	17.7	
	X	26	Barbados	15.8	X
		27	Spain	15.2	
		28	Jamaica	13.6	

[1] Years are 1959 except Denmark, India, Ireland, and New Zealand (1958), and Spain (1957).

[2] Not all public enterprises included.

Chart 2-2

Federal Expenditures as a Percentage of National Product (1799-1951)

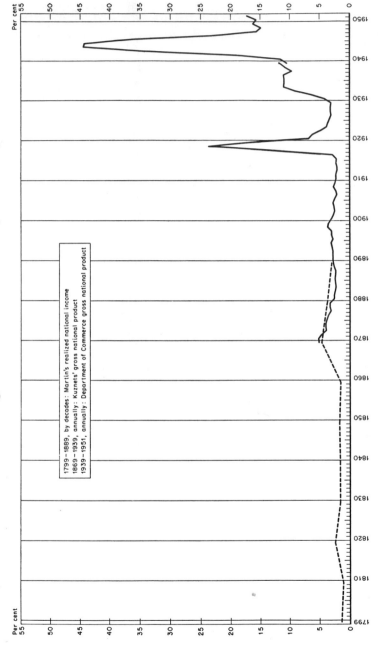

1799–1889, by decades: Martin's realized national income
1869–1939, annually: Kuznets' gross national product
1939–1951, annually: Department of Commerce gross national product

Source: M. Slade Kendrick, *A Century and a Half of Federal Expenditures*, p. 9, copyright © 1955 by the National Bureau of Economic Research, New York, New York.

Chart 2-3

War Related and Defense Expenditure

Total Government Expenditure and Its War-Related and Defense
Components, in Relation to Gross National Product, per Head of
Population, at 1900 Prices, 1890–1955

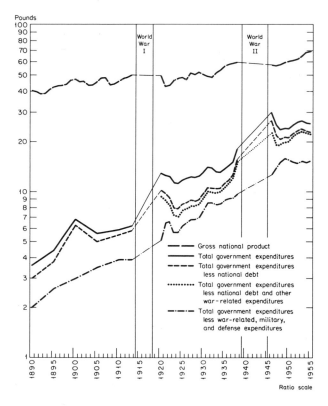

10. The production possibility curves in Figure 2-5, on page 92, contain a number of points (a, b, c, d). Please identify what each means and how they might be related to the supply of resources and the efficiency with which they are employed by the government.

11. On page 92 is a newspaper account of one man's explanation for the growing demands for public services. Please comment on Mr. Smith's remarks.

Figure 2-5

Production Probability Curves

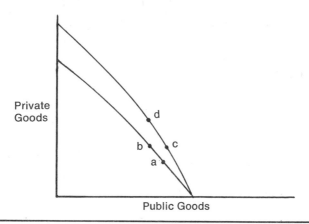

STATE FINANCE DIRECTOR HITS
PRESSURE FOR MORE SERVICE

SAN FRANCISCO (AP) — State Finance Director Gordon P. Smith blames individual citizens for a 13,800 per cent jump in federal expenses and a 7,700 per cent hike in state costs the past half century.

Smith, in an address Friday to the Commonwealth Club, contrasted the percentages with the statement that "our national population has increased only 100 per cent during the last 50 years."

Adding that local governmental costs soared 2,000 per cent in that time, Smith declared "the principal cause of the astronomical rise in domestic government costs has been a gradual erosion of private will, personal initiative and self-reliance on the part of too many Americans."

He termed the situation a paternalism in which local governments also lean on the state governments and the states lean on the federal government.

"It is obvious that far too many of us look to our government to serve our needs, rather than looking to ourselves," he said. "As a result, a large measure of our personal freedom has been sacrificed, and it has cost us dearly."

EXPANDED ROLE

He asserted that although the bulk of federal budgeting involves national defense, "its domestic programs have gone far beyond that ever envisioned by the creators of this nation."

California's budget, he said, has jumped from $1.7 billion of 10 years ago to more than $5 billion today. It has been more than a 200 per cent boost in the budget compared to a 48 per cent population increase in that decade, he said.

Smith stated that California, whose governmental costs rate 11th highest in the world "and we don't even have a foreign policy," faces five basic fiscal problems:

—Paying off the debt left by the past Democratic administration.

—Reducing budgets.

—Adopting a tax program.

—Revamping Medi-Cal and other major programs.

—Providing property tax relief.

Palo Alto Times, Saturday, July 8, 1967.

Bibliographical Notes

Whereas our readings note at the end of Chapter 1 grappled with a condition of affluence, i.e., almost too many titles to select among, this chapter faces a poverty condition, at least with respect to political science. Political scientists have not studied resource allocation very often; consequently it becomes necessary to consult economic studies. We advise this course with some hesitation because the language of economics is highly specialized and formidable to the beginner. In any event, you might at least sample a few such studies to gain the feel. We suggest the following items.

On the general matter of resource allocation the best we can do is suggest textbooks in public finance. Many of them are dull and much within them is irrelevant to a political scientist, but they seem to be improving in both regards. Our favorites are James M. Buchanan's *The Public Finances*, Homewood, Ill.: Richard D. Irwin, Inc., 1960, and Bernard P. Herber's *Modern Public Finance*, Homewood, Ill.: Richard D. Irwin, Inc., 1967. At a far higher level of difficulty is the modern classic, Richard A. Musgrave's *The Theory of Public Finance*, New York: McGraw-Hill Book Company, 1959. Parts 1 and 2 are basic contributions to both economics and political science. Francis Bator's *The Question of Public Spending*, New York: Harper and Brothers, 1960, is the most readable discussion on the allocation of resources in the United States during recent years. For an historical account of the same consult Solomon Fabricant, *The Trend of Government Activity in the United States since 1900*, New York: National Bureau of Economic Research, Inc., 1952. A useful compilation and analysis of costs may be found in Frederick Mosher and Orville Poland's *The Costs of American Governments: Facts, Trends, Myths*, New York: Dodd, Mead and Company, 1966.

Political scientists are only now beginning to do research on the allocation of resources, but we predict that before you have finished college the volume of publications on resource mobilization, allocation and costs by political scientists will be considerable. Each issue of the professional journals finds increasing concern for these matters as a part of a more general concern over explaining public policies, i.e., why nations or governments pursue the policies they do, or allocate resources in the manner they have chosen. One example of this interest may be seen in Thomas Dye, *Politics, Economics, and the Public: Policy Outcomes in the American States*, Chicago: Rand McNally and Company, 1966. The interested student will find most of the recent relevant literature cited in that book.

Students interested in governmental expenditures and revenues should consult *The National Tax Journal,* a quarterly dealing with various aspects of taxation in the United States. While many of the contributions are somewhat esoteric, a fair number are understandable to the layman. Those readers who have an interest in local and state governments might well like to look at two recent compilations of materials and analyses published by the Joint Economic Committee of the Congress of the United States. The volumes are entitled *State and Local Public Facility Needs and Financing*, 89th Cong., 2d sess.; Washington, D.C.: Government Printing Office, 1966, with Volume 1 on needs and Volume 2 on financing. Publication date was December of 1966. Somewhat similar but much briefer accounts have been issued by the Tax Foundation, Inc., also in 1966, entitled *Handbook of State and Local Finance*, Research Publication No. 7, new series, New York, and *Fiscal Outlook for State and Local Government to 1975*, Research Publication No. 6, new series, New York. None of these several volumes makes good bedside reading, but they are valuable and required reading for those interested in these problems.

If one wishes to consider resource mobilization and allocation within specific areas of policy we suggest James R. Schlesinger on *The Political Economy of National Security*, New York: Frederick A. Praeger, 1960, Jerry Miner on *Social and Economic Factors in Public Education*, Syracuse: Syracuse University Press, 1963, Otto Eckstein on *Water Resource Development*, Cambridge: Harvard University Press, 1965, and Wilbur R. Thompson's *A Preface to Urban Economics*, Washington, D.C.: Resources for the Future, Inc., 1965, distributed by Johns Hopkins Press in Baltimore. A highly readable, although dated account of the history of taxation in the United States is Sidney Ratner's *Taxation and Democracy*, New York: John Wiley and Sons, Inc., 1967. Here we may learn how various taxation systems came into being and why.

Some interesting statistical studies of changing governmental resource levels have been done during recent years. Among the more able and better known studies is Morris A. Copeland's *Trends in Governmental Financing*, (National Bureau of Economic Research) Princeton: Princeton University Press, 1961, an attempt to trace fiscal developments in the United States up to 1960. A more theoretical book on somewhat the same matters is *The Growth of Public Expenditure in the United Kingdom*, (National Bureau of Economic Research) Princeton: Princeton University Press, 1961, by Alan T. Peacock and Jack Wiseman. Their critique of Wagner's Law and suggested substitute theory of the growth of public expenditures has been influential in economics. We have made use of it in this book and this chapter. Another study, *The Growth of Public Employment in Great Britain*, (National Bureau of Economic Research) Princeton: Princeton University Press, 1957, by Moses Abramovitz and Vera Eliasberg, considers one aspect of the mobilization process as the title indicates. It is a useful complement to the Peacock and Wiseman volume as well as relevant to students of public policy or Great Britain. We would like to see more of these types of analyses for more countries. At present, the most general and comparative book on the problems of this chapter as well as the next two is E. S. Kirschen, ed., *Economic Policy in our Time*, Amsterdam: North Holland Publishing Company; Chicago: Rand McNally and Company, 1964, 3 volumes. Volume 1 deals with general theory and attempts to summarize the specialized country studies of economic policy found in the other two volumes. Accordingly, all three deal with policy-making, economic objectives, and governmental instruments for their achievement. Part 2 on "The Decision Making Process" is a refreshing addition to political science, at least as we conceive it. We strongly recommend these three volumes, but with a special emphasis on Volume 1, because of the authors' attempt to treat policy in a comparative framework so that one can witness the variations and common denominators of policy and policy-making among the western democracies.

Two rather special items in our personal library and in the preparation of this textbook are *Europe's Needs and Resources,* New York: Twentieth Century Fund, 1961, and *America's Needs and Resources: A New Survey,* New York: Twentieth Century Fund, 1955. These hefty studies, each over 1,000 pages, were written under the editorship of the late J. Frederic Dewhurst and his associates at the Twentieth Century Fund Foundation. They have been a most important source of data for us in both our writing and our classroom teaching. We are heavily indebted to the authors and pleased to express our gratitude in this context.

Ruler of Swat Installs Benefits of Welfare State
The New York Times, July 20, 1967, New York, New York

Negroes' Dilemma

Home inspection ruling
favors householders
Palo Alto Times, June 5, 1967, Palo Alto, California

Middle Clas

Rent subsidy
plan supported
Palo Alto Times, Jan. 13, 1967, Palo Alto, California

Reaps Benefi
Eugene Register-Guard, Jan. 7, 1968, Eugene, Oregon

Jersey Central Files Bankruptcy P
As Bid for More State Subsidies Fa
The Wall Street Journal, March 23, 1967, New York, New York

$2-MILLION GIVEN
TO CANADA'S ARTS;
Federal Council Grants Go
to Performing Troupes
The New York Times,
Aug. 13, 1967, New York, New York

Students in Church Schools Get
$60-Million a Year in Public Aid
The New York Times, Nov. 4, 1967, New York, New York

SUBSIDY DECLI
FOR AIR CARR
Off $7.3-Million in the
Year 1967, C.A.B. Re

The over-all subsidy
...ers declined approxi
...-million in the fisca
1967, and a further dec
$6.4-million is expected
current year, the Civil
...tics Board reported y

In its revised annual
of "Subsidy for United
Air-Carriers," the agency
cast that subsidy paymen
the fiscal year 1968 would
$59.2-million compared
last year's $65.7-million. I
fiscal year 1966, payment
...led $73-million.
The New York Times,
Dec. 14, 1967,
New York, New York

Republicans
Plan Fight
On Benefits

RURAL AREAS LOSE
AS ECONOMY GAINS
But Fewer Regions Require
Federal Aid, U.S. Says
The New York Times, June 3, 1967, New York, New York

Vietnam & Veterans
War Builds Pressure
To Lift Benefits for All
Former Servicemen
The Wall Street Journal, Jan. 18, 1967,
New York, New York

WASHINGTON (AP) — Sen-
ate Republicans vow ... floor
...ight against a proposed record
...oost in Social Security benefits
...hey contend has a financing
...eature pc..ged to help Demo-
...rats in the 1968 elections.
Eugene Register-Guard,
Nov. 10, 1967,
Eugene, Oregon

Tax Relief Seen for Industry
Involved in Pollution Curbs
Eugene Register-Guard, Oct. 6, 1967, Eugene, Oregon

Northrop Unit Recei
$6.1 Million Army O
The Wall Street Journal, Dec. 8, 1966,
New York, New York

Chapter 3

The Distribution of Goods
and Welfare

The discussions of Chapters 1 and 2 directed attention to political systems and governments as producers and distributors of valued products or benefits intended to serve both private and public needs and wants. While we may be accustomed to viewing economic systems in this light many citizens find it difficult to consider political systems in an analogous way. Still, governments do provide many goods and services which we would find extremely difficult to provide for ourselves or through private enterprise. Many of these goods, which we have termed public goods, are of such a nature that they could not be produced and marketed (or as efficiently) by private firms; however, many goods now provided by governments were once and still are in some nations supplied by private persons. We shall have need, therefore, of fairly precise definitions of the product or output of the polity if we are to understand distributive problems. What a polity has produced or how its resources are allocated has an important bearing on who gets how much of the output.

Types of Public Goods and Their Consumption

A complete inventory of the goods and services distributed by governments is beyond our needs; suffice it to say that such an inventory would probably run into several volumes if all nations were surveyed. If we were to study such a list and classify that great variety, we might well devise a classification not unlike one used by economists. Typically, the economist arranges goods into two basic types: (1) pure private goods, and (2) pure public goods. The purely private goods are defined so as to include only those which can be individually exchanged generally through a market, at a price, to a specific consumer. In other words, exclusive possession and consumption of the goods is possible. Thus, if one purchases an automobile he may legally claim control over its use and employ the courts to enforce his claims of ownership.

On the other hand, a citizen cannot claim exclusive individual consumption or possession of such governmentally distributed services as national defense, parks, police protection and highways. Such services and facilities are equally available to many and cannot be readily sold in a free market. Because exclusive possession cannot be maintained, economists have often spoken of pure *public goods* as being 'indivisible.' In fact, most public goods are not of the pure type but can be and are divided or distributed among the populace, usually in unequal portions. These are often referred to as *mixed* or *quasi-public goods.* Some members of society derive more police protection than others; some citizens benefit more from national defense expenditures than others; some citizens use the parks more than others; some members acquire more advantages from a stable monetary system than do others, etc. In the present chapter we will inquire into the distributive problem as it relates to public goods whether in pure or mixed forms; make some estimates of actual distributive outcomes; and, hopefully, provide some useful explanations of these outcomes or payoffs.

We will also consider in some detail an area of governmental activity in which distributive payoffs are quite visible and countable. We refer to actual payments by governments of income to citizens; such payments are called *transfer payments* because they are, in effect, transfers of income from some citizens (taxpayers) to other citizens (recipients). Whereas the production of public goods and services consumes or uses up scarce resources, transfer payments do not; government simply transfers income or purchasing power from one person to another. While measurement of the distribution of true or pure public goods almost defies solution, transfer payments are easily identified in terms of their destination or recipients, and easily measured because they are made in monetary terms. Public records are kept for most of these types of payments and while they may not always be readily accessible, as in the case of welfare recipients in some societies, it is far easier to quantify transfer payments than it is general public goods and services.

While the most conspicuous products of the government are its public goods and transfer payments, one of its most important activities has to do with the creation and distribution of *opportunities* for its citizens.

Most governmental actions and policies either directly or indirectly, whether intentionally or not, serve to distribute advantages which affect different persons' welfare and status in personal or private spheres. For example, governments often allow professions the power to establish their own rules of admission, thereby enabling those who already practice to decide who else may practice. Or, the zoning decisions which local governments usually make determine how one may use his property and thus how profitable a use he can make of it. Governments grant monopoly powers to utility concerns and allot contracts among business firms. And they protect certain spheres of behavior in the name of rights and freedoms. In these and countless other ways, governments affect the welfare of their citizens; in so doing they alter the distributive patterns of the economy and society through control over the opportunity structure of a society.

Estimating Exchange Relationships and Relative Benefits

Many transfer payments are easily measured and specifically identified by recipient when the government pays directly: relief payments, unemployment compensation, crop parity payments, aid to dependent children, business subsidies. Many mixed goods and services are almost as easily identified as to their relative value for the recipients: school lunches, water and power supplies, medicare benefits, postal services and so forth. We can also identify the direct contributions made to government by various individuals and enterprises when they are in the form of cash payments. But *who paid how much for which goods received* cannot be directly ascertained in the public sector, as it is in the private. We can conceptualize the problem in the form of a diagram, as in Figure 3-1. Citizens A, B and C in our hypothetical polity are all engaged in a somewhat indirect and ambiguous set of exchanges mediated by a government and a political system. The exchanges are ambiguous to the extent that the amounts paid in and collected by individuals are not easily measured, and they are also ambiguous to the extent that citizens cannot determine who pays whom. The exchanges are indirect because the government is the intermediary which makes the crucial decisions with regard to both parties. Clarifying the relationship between these transactions is not easy, but the effort to shed some light on the question continues.

As we have observed, transfers are indirect; in short, taxpayers and beneficiaries do not make direct exchanges as buyers and sellers do in marketplaces. Instead, the political system through its officials collects monies, makes decisions about how those funds are to be used and redistributes the income or benefits. No taxpayer knows exactly to whom his payments go, nor does any recipient know from whence his benefits come.

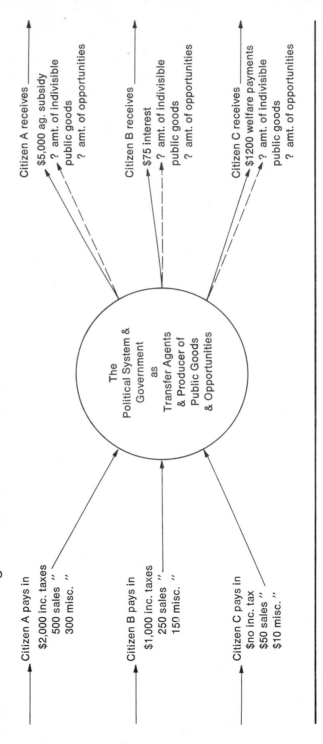

Figure 3-1

Possible Exchange Relationships
Between and Among Citizens and the Government

Citizen A receives

$5,000 ag. subsidy
? amt. of indivisible
    public goods
? amt. of opportunities

Citizen B receives

$75 interest
? amt. of indivisible
    public goods
? amt. of opportunities

Citizen C receives

$1200 welfare payments
? amt. of indivisible
    public goods
? amt. of opportunities

The
Political System &
Government
as
Transfer Agents
& Producer of
Public Goods
& Opportunities

Citizen A pays in

$2,000 inc. taxes
   500 sales "
   300 misc. "

Citizen B pays in

$1,000 inc. taxes
   250 sales "
   150 misc. "

Citizen C pays in

$no inc. tax
  $50 sales "
  $10 misc. "

In some respects it is probably a good thing that we do not know whom we are 'supporting' or who 'supports' us, for if we did some rather difficult situations might arise. Yet, social science investigations have enabled us, as the following studies illustrate, to identify the broad flows of transfer payments. We do know a great deal about which income groups, among others, pay which taxes and how much. We do know which groups tend to benefit from certain governmental expenditures, policies and practices. Our case studies are designed to illustrate these facts.

Some Case Studies of Relative Benefits

Case Study #1   Total Tax Burdens and Benefits as a Per Cent of Total Income in the U.S.A. (1961)

The Tax Foundation, Inc., of New York City has estimated how much tax various income groups pay the government and how much they receive in the way of public goods and transfer payments.[1] To do so they had to make rather broad judgments about such matters as allocating the 'worth' of rather expensive pure public goods like national defense and transportation, according to the relative proportions of families in the various income levels. Further assumptions had to be made about the unknown extent of tax collections and distributions, as estimates of the actual incidence of costs and contributions. The graphic result of their effort is shown in the following Chart (3-1), where they depict the aggregate exchange ratios of different income classes of citizens with their governments in terms of relative benefits and burdens. While the idea and effort is exemplary, there could be a great deal of disagreement about how the conclusions are presented. The study suggests a strong imbalance of these exchanges by calculating cost and benefit levels in terms of percentages of the income base, which means the very long white bar at the low income level reflects a value of benefits actually less than the much shorter white bar at the other end of the income levels (i.e., about 112% × $2,000 as compared to about 17% × $15,000). Thus one's judgments about equities might change were the standard of comparison put in different terms. We should also offer a note of caution about the demarcation of income levels. The way a range of values, such as incomes, is defined and divided can change the resulting bar graphs considerably. In this case, especially, the two end categories of incomes pose problems of interpretation, in terms of what they represent. 'Over $15,000' can comprehend an enormous income range which is averaged on the bar graph into one burden-benefit ratio. Many

---

[1] *Tax Burdens and Benefits of Government Expenditures by Income Class, 1961 and 1965* (New York: Tax Foundation, Inc., 1967).

Chart 3-1

Total Tax Burden and Expenditure
Benefits as a Per Cent of Total Income
by Income Class (All Families—1961)

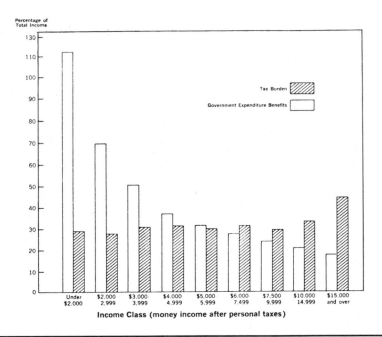

Source: *Tax Burdens and Benefits of Government Expenditures by Income Class, 1961 and 1965* (New York: Tax Foundation, Inc., 1967), p. 13.

such fine points are discussed in the study, its notes and appendices. We call attention to them here because the major use of estimating such exchanges of burdens and benefits is an evaluation of who enjoys the relative advantages in the system. This study shows one interesting possibility.

Now note a contrasting method of tracing the incidence of certain tax payments, by income level. Joseph Pechman in his book *Federal Tax Policy*[2] reports on actual payments made, as reported in a selected sample of individual income tax returns. A reduction in tax payments is, of course, a direct means of increasing one's personal income or net worth. Chart 3-2 shows the actual effective rates for paying income tax when the exemptions and deductions made by these individuals are traced along a continuous

---

[2] Joseph Pechman, *Federal Tax Policy* (Washington, D.C.: The Brookings Institution, 1966).

Chart 3-2

Influence of Various Provisions on Effective
Rates of Federal Individual Income Tax, 1964 Act[a]

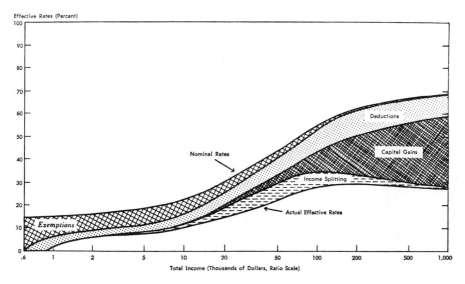

Effective Rates (Percent)

Total Income (Thousands of Dollars, Ratio Scale)

[a] Based on 1962 incomes, with rates applicable beginning Jan. 1, 1965.

Source: Joseph A. Pechman, *Federal Tax Policy* (Washington, D.C.: The Brookings Institution, 1966), p. 66.

range of respective incomes. This chart very graphically shows the relative benefit of different tax provisions in reducing the nominal rates of the tax laws. We see the importance of exemptions up to about the $10,000 income range; and the very greatly enlarged benefit of capital gains provisions for incomes over $75,000 actually causes relative effective rates of payment to decline! Thus, what is considered in its formal provisions to be the most equitable tax in terms of 'ability to pay' becomes less so when actual payments are assessed. It pays therefore to qualify or check indirect and aggregate estimates of cost and benefit balances wherever there are means to do so.

Case Study #2   Federal Grants to State and Local Governments Compared to Contributions, U.S.A. (1962)

Another means of comparison that is quite meaningful in federal systems is the relative exchange relationship of the local unit with the central government. What the local citizenry contributes to the federal government in taxes could be compared to what they receive 'collectively' in federal expenditures. One study, again by the Tax Foundation, worked out an even more difficult comparison.[3] It took just the federal grants-in-aid to the states, a form of transfer payment between governments, and estimated, by states, the proportionate tax contribution to all these grant programs combined. Thus relative redistributions can be assessed, as illustrated in Table 3-1. One could say that living in Alaska, Vermont, Louisiana

Table 3-1

Federal Grants to State and Local Governments and Estimated Burden of Grants, U.S. (1962)

States	Amount contributed to federal grant programs	Amount received in federal grants	Amount paid for every dollar of aid received
Delaware	$ 24.5 (millions)	$ 10.9 (millions)	$ 2.12
New Jersey	210.5	99.8	1.80
Connecticut	108.2	54.0	1.64
New York	655.6	406.7	1.52
Wyoming	7.8	10.9	.45
Louisiana	56.8	163.6	.44
Vermont	8.3	11.6	.35
Alaska	5.9	30.7	.19

Source: *Allocating the Federal Tax Burden by State* (New York: Tax Foundation, Inc., 1964), p. 30.

or Wyoming is more profitable for the citizen than living in Delaware, when considered in these terms. However, we should know how much of federal grants to the states will be applied to general public goods at the local level (such as airports and roads), and how much of such sums flows to particular groups and strata in the form of transfer payments (public welfare, for example) or quasi-public goods and services (such as education). In political analysis therefore we want to answer a variety of such questions as: Which groups pay out more than others? Why do some receive more than others? What reasons are there for the unequal flows to and from different states or areas? How do such inequalities square with general principles of equity and fairness? And what do they say about the effective output of the political system?

---

[3] *Allocating the Federal Tax Burden by State* (New York: Tax Foundation, Inc., 1964).

Varieties of Distributive Goods

As noted in discussing resource mobilization, the valued goods in a system may change over time, and so too will the capacity of governments to satisfy various citizen claims on the public sector. Governments can give away what they have; they can use resources to generate the goods and services conferred; and they can create or maintain valued perquisites which are passed on from one recipient to another, or shared by particular individuals and groups. The variety of such distributive possibilities should be kept in mind, especially where most concern tends to focus on just the more obvious cases. We shall try to illustrate some of this variety, from the obvious to the more obscure, and note in the process the kinds of appropriate information—available or desired—and the kinds of questions to be answered.

Case Study #3   Distribution of Subsidies: U.S.A.

In this country the subsidy is a frequent political issue, and opinions about its desirability abound. Since it frequently takes the form of cash payments, this is a quite visible distribution for any recipient or group. Recently the Joint Economic Committee of Congress has received information on the relative distribution of subsidies for major economic sectors, and Table 3-2 shows some figures for the latest year they were made avail-

---

Table 3-2

Net Expenditures on Subsidies and Subsidy-Like Programs of the Federal Government, 1964 (In millions of dollars)

Agriculture	$5,168
Business	1,251
Labor	457
Homeowners & Tenants	−51

Source: Joint Economic Committee, *Subsidy and Subsidy-Effect Programs of the U.S. Government*, 80th Congress, 1st Sess., 1965 (Washington, D.C.: U.S. Government Printing Office, 1965), p. 22.

able.[4] It shows in summary fashion quite clearly the great disparities in the net flows to the different sectors. The agricultural sector, consisting of less

---

[4] Joint Economic Committee, *Subsidy and Subsidy-Effect Programs of the U.S. Government*, 80th Congress, 1st Sess., 1965 (Washington, D.C.: U.S. Government Printing Office, 1965).

than 10 per cent of the population, received almost five times as much as the other three groups combined! Of course there is some overlap in the designation of the recipient groups—home ownership runs across the other three. But as a measure of the relative public aid being 'given freely' to assist each economic endeavor or situation, it tells a story in its own.

Note in the case of homeowners and tenants the federal subsidizing agencies received more than they granted; while their loan programs are direct aids, unlike farm commodity loans, they do tend to make a 'profit' for the government! These particular distributions need to be explained. Think of the possibilities for explaining why each group got what it did in 1964. Try again after you have completed the reading of Part 1 of the book, or after reading the entire volume.

Some advance speculations may not, however, be inappropriate. Certainly they will assist an appreciation of the remaining case studies and the difficulties social scientists face in explaining some of the more obvious 'facts of life,' which nevertheless stand in sharp contrast to conventional values and wisdom. Various theories or considerations have been advanced to account for this generosity to the farm sector, especially. Among them have been the following:

1. Farmers have a greater need for the governmental assistance.

2. Farmers are more virtuous people.

3. The structure of the political system is such as to increase the bargaining power of the farmers.

4. Farmers are highly-skilled politicians.

5. Farmers are lucky.

6. Society needs farmers and farm produce.

7. Farmers are well organized and led.

The above possibilities can, in principle, be tested in such ways that the data of Table 3-2 may be explained. One could construct some imaginary tests and anticipate what findings would account for the fact of farmer superiority in acquiring subsidies and, alternatively, the respective 'failures' of business, labor and householders to do as well at the 'public trough.'

Case Study #4   Federal Distribution of Public Lands in the U.S.A.

Evaluating distributions of goods in nonmonetary forms will often pose great problems of estimation, and lose much of the comparability that makes money exchanges so useful to study. Sometimes there are other units for weighing benefits and assessing the patterns of distribution. The case of public lands in the United States shows some of the possibilities and also points up the problem of shifting values in the nature of policy goods.

There are remarkably complete records about federal land distributions since the beginning of this government as a result of the sales and legal records kept by federal land office agents. These provide data for long-term comparisons, at least with regard to the parties directly receiving the lands. As a result, there are some very good studies of U.S. land policies, from which we can get an idea of shifting patterns of distribution. In the earliest period the land was distributed as a highly individualized benefit: granted as a free bounty to veterans or sold to individuals at very cheap prices, in small parcels, limited in size by law. The Homestead Act of 1862 made free land a matter of right for any settler, who would presumably develop and farm the land. As Figure 3-2 shows, this transfer of lands was primarily concentrated in the Middle West, where unsettled fertile acres

Figure 3-2

Distribution of Federal Lands in Homesteads

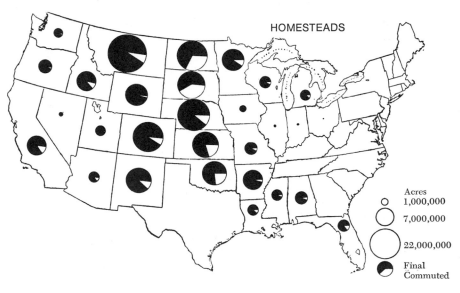

Reprinted with the permission of the copyright owners, the Regents of the University of Wisconsin, from Benjamin Horace Hibbard, *A History of Public Land Policies* (Madison: The University of Wisconsin Press, 1965), p. 410.

were fairly accessible. But the land had other uses too, as a means for speculation, or for exploiting its other economic assets and resources—i.e., its forest products and minerals and its wildlife, or its use for transport, rights of way and commercial sites. In spite of legal precautions, there was a great deal of 'slippage' from original recipients to speculators and various enterprises. The final incidence of benefits in this sense requires far more investigation; thus Chart 3-3 indicates only the first stage of 'dividing the pie.'

Chart 3-3

Disposition of Public Domain
Total Acreage: 1,399,000,000

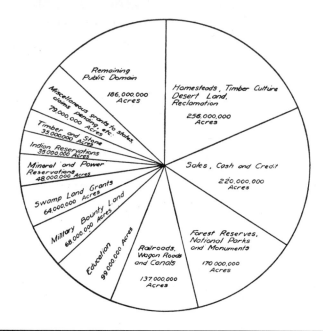

Also, the federal government gave land directly to encourage some types of endeavor, such as local public education or the construction of roads, canals and railroads. Though this land was a direct transfer in these cases, the ultimate purposes envisaged have the character of public goods whose benefits would be general in their distribution.

Where the land was less desirable, the government had more difficulty finding takers, without increasing the amounts and often providing other rewards and incentives for developing lands which were arid, rocky or swampy. This suggests something of an exchange, rather than an outright transfer. The shift in the nature of the good distributed is even more obvious in the present federal management of lands, where grazing, lumber or mining rights can be leased by private enterprise, or where recreational privileges can be enjoyed for a fee. But as with game reserves and wilderness areas, the 'good' remains under governmental control, managed or conserved, presumably, for future generations of users. How can we compare the relative values and beneficiaries of land uses here? Conservationists would see these long-run values as public goods. We would have a hard time estimating an ultimate price for these, comparable to the earlier type of direct transfers of land. This may also be the case with many other types of goods generated by governments. One thinks of the various informational and research services—weather forecasting, crop research, nuclear and space explorations—which have immediate and quite measurable benefits to specific individuals and enterprises. Yet the fund of skills and knowledge remains a public good for all potentially to enjoy. This also reminds us that we frequently make calculations differently for the short run and the long run. Calculations of relative advantage are most typically applied to the short run, for the more immediately affected groups and persons.

Case Study #5   Speculations About Distributions of Rights and Statuses

It would be very misleading to leave the distributive question as primarily a matter of who gets what economic values. In fact, there is increasing concern these days with the role of government as a distributor of rights and statuses. But systematic study of these patterns is often more difficult, because the 'letter of the law' often obscures actual practices; or legally intended statuses are subverted by private economic and social practice. At the risk of placing more credit or blame on government than it deserves, we may note some kinds of such non-material goods which people hope to gain, and often do, from their governments.

We tend to take for granted the basic status of citizenship, yet the criteria by which it is conferred and withheld are crucial distributive questions. Where citizenship is taken for granted as a general rule, the 'cost' side is more typically noted; that is, when and where this basic status is denied or withdrawn. Some of the more positive prerequisites of citizenship, the 'rights' of voting, fair trial, free speech, are also most in evidence when their denial or abuse is contested. But anyone concerned with the general enjoyment of such goods should also study more carefully the ongoing patterns of distribution and practice. Thus the United States Civil Rights Commission found it had to observe and report on the actual exercise of the vote by American Negroes, especially in the South, to determine where and when progress was achieved.[5] Sometimes the formal procedures and machinery make general rights and privileges relatively inaccessible to many: holding elections during the workweek, requiring presence at a specified polling place, requiring residency, limiting the time the polls are open and so on. We think many of these things further handicap certain

---

[5] U.S. Commission on Civil Rights, *Report, Book 1, Voting; Book 2, Education* (Washington, D.C.: U.S. Government Printing Office, 1961).

groups in the enjoyment of these goods, which then flow to the privileged remainder. In another area, the incidence of criminal penalties can also tell us about relative privilege, and such devices as public defenders and legal services for the poor are recent attempts in this country toward balancing some of the scales of justice.

Also, note those special statuses conferred by the political system, where not only economic benefits are involved, but also a variety of services and 'honorific' blessings. Veterans are most bountifully honored in return for their service and sacrifice; and the many symbolic honors paid war heroes must certainly be considered as well. Political systems might well be compared as to status distributions, by such items as their statuary and honor rolls, ceremonies and legends. But wherever possible, actual enjoyment of privileges should also be assessed; one thinks of the sad lot of many poor and hungry American Indians whose status rests solely on the legends and noble depictions of their ancestors!

We only suggest here some possibilities about patterns of status, rights and privileges as distributed in a political system. It certainly deserves more systematic study, and indeed there are beginning to be some interesting attempts at comparing these patterns in different countries. The most persistent efforts are being made under United Nations auspices, although frequently the reports on rights and statuses in separate countries are extremely hard to compare, even where there is concrete behavioral evidence.[6] There is some promise that the attitude survey will provide this comparability, by interviewing samples of citizens directly about their expectations and satisfactions from the public sector, should the design and administering of questions be appropriate and sensitive. A notable venture in this direction is the study of five countries by Gabriel A. Almond and Sidney Verba, *The Civic Culture*,[7] which seeks to relate political attitudes of citizens to patterns of participation. Tables 3-3 and 3-4 show this, and reveal interesting variations among these selected formal democracies. What judgments would you draw from the variations? What further information might be helpful about patterns of distribution of such 'satisfactions' *within* each country?[8]

---

[6] See David H. Bayley, *Public Liberties in the New States* (Chicago: Rand McNally and Company, 1964), for a cogent summary and commentary upon the state of affairs in the new nations as well as for a convenient bibliography of United Nations reports on human rights.

[7] Gabriel A. Almond and Sidney Verba, *The Civic Culture: Political Attitudes and Democracy in Five Nations* (Princeton: Princeton University Press, 1963). Another useful survey of attitudes involving interviews with nearly 20,000 persons from thirteen different nations is Hadley Cantril's *The Pattern of Human Concerns* (New Brunswick, N.J.: Rutgers University Press, 1965).

[8] Cantril, *op. cit.*, should prove useful in providing data for questions on the distribution of 'satisfactions' as well as 'dissatisfactions.'

Table 3-3

Expectation of Treatment by Government Bureaucracy and Police, by Nation* (in per cent)

Per Cent who say	U.S. Bureauc.	Pol.	U.K. Bureauc.	Pol.	Germany Bureauc.	Pol.	Italy Bureauc.	Pol.	Mexico Bureauc.	Pol.
They expect equal treatment	83	85	83	89	65	72	53	56	42	32
They don't expect equal treatment	9	8	7	6	9	5	13	10	50	57
Depends	4	5	6	4	19	15	17	15	5	5
Other	—	—	—	—	—	—	6	6	—	—
Don't know	4	2	2	0	7	8	11	13	3	5
Total per cent	100	100	98	99	100	100	100	100	100	99
Total number	970	970	963	963	955	955	995	995	1,007	1,007

* Actual texts of the questions: "Suppose there were some question that you had to take to a government office—for example, a tax question or housing regulation. Do you think you would be given equal treatment—I mean, would you be treated as well as anyone else?" "If you had some trouble with the police—a traffic violation maybe, or being accused of a minor offense—do you think you would be given equal treatment? That is, would you be treated as well as anyone else?"

Source: Gabriel A. Almond and Sidney Verba, *The Civic Culture: Political Attitudes and Democracy in Five Nations* (Princeton: Princeton University Press, 1963), p. 108. Reprinted by permission of Princeton University Press.

Table 3-4

Amount of Consideration Expected for Point of View from Bureaucracy and Police, by Nation* (in per cent)

Per Cent who expect	U.S. Bureauc.	U.S. Pol.	U.K. Bureauc.	U.K. Pol.	Germany Bureauc.	Germany Pol.	Italy Bureauc.	Italy Pol.	Mexico Bureauc.	Mexico Pol.
Serious consideration for point of view	48	56	59	74	53	59	35	35	14	12
A little attention	31	22	22	13	18	11	15	13	48	46
To be ignored	6	11	5	5	5	4	11	12	27	29
Depends	11	9	10	6	15	13	21	20	6	7
Other	0	–	–	–	1	2	6	6	–	1
Don't know	4	2	2	1	8	11	12	14	3	4
Total per cent	100	100	98	99	100	100	100	100	98	99
Total number	970	970	963	963	955	955	995	995	1,007	1,007

* Actual texts of the questions: "If you explained your point of view to the officials, what effect do you think it would have? Would they give your point of view serious consideration, would they pay only a little attention, or would they ignore what you had to say?" "If you explained your point of view to the police, what effect do you think it would have? Would they . . . [same choices as before]?"

Source: *Ibid.*, p. 109.

Case Study #6   Distribution of High-Ranking Positions in Liberia (1960-1961)

There is another type of good which is produced quite directly by the political system: positions of honor and employment in government and political organizations. The high-ranking positions, and those well paid, are especially important to consider as distributive goods. After all, charges of nepotism and patronage are political issues just for that reason. Of course, rewarding relatives or those faithful to one's cause brings advantages to the patron too, whether simply the paying off of old obligations or assuring continued loyalty and support. And the position conferred is often a favor that can be taken away; the disloyal can often be dismissed and the job-holder who becomes a liability may be disposed of. In such cases it is a kind of conditional good that is distributed, at the pleasure of the benefactor, so to speak.

The case of Liberia may be a rather amusing example of the extent to which family ties may be exploited politically, although we hesitate to say how it might be viewed by the average Liberian. As Figure 3-3 indicates, marrying into the Tubman family is a rather rational act for any Liberian with political ambitions for high office. This is undoubtedly an extreme case among countries today, but European monarchies flourished on this principle in the past, and anthropologists report many small or tribal systems where family ties are the basis of public rewards. More generally, family ties are a powerful claim wherever prestige, power and income are distributed; and that means everywhere in the world. In our own system it is not uncommon for legislators to employ their wives, local party organizations to be maintained by one or a few old families and elective office to pass from father to son, or brother to brother! And in an earlier period, when this country was much smaller and the national leaders tended to be a more intimate group, family ties could be more systematically effective than they usually are today. Note the numbers of top administrative office-holders that had family relationships in this country's first seven administrations, as shown in Chart 3-4. The chart depicts the family relationships of twenty-one members of Jackson's administration who had relatives serving in previous administrations and the particular Presidents they served. Given Jackson's image as a representative of the 'common man' it is somewhat remarkable to find him depending so heavily upon elites from previous administrations.

Most modern nations have managed to place some limitations on the use of this public resource for such direct favors to kin. The sheer numbers of positions, the skills required, the 'bad image' which nepotism has incurred, the need to cement broader loyalties and to reward broader ranks of people—all of these discourage the practice. Instead, concern is general-

Figure 3-3

Family and Politics in the Republic of Liberia, 1960-61

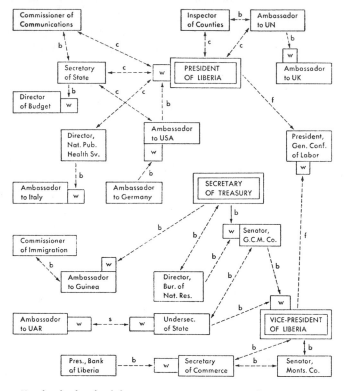

Key: b = brother; f = father; c = cousin; s = sister; w = wife.

ized to the question of what kinds of groups tend to be thus favored in
modern systems. There is much evidence that elite strata tend to monopolize
favored positions over time, and that even in modern society, such elites
tend to be perpetuated to some degree through family, educational and
social positions. There are many studies of Great Britain in which the elite
backgrounds or affiliations of office holders are identified, and the role of
the school system is especially noted. Table 3-5 shows an interesting comparison over a considerable period of the class status of those chosen for
British Cabinet positions. The aristocracy, while of declining relative
strength in British governments, is still favored considerably by two parties,

Chart 3-4

Family Relationships in the
First Seven American Administrations*

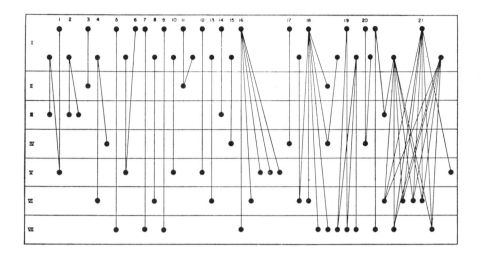

* Showing family relationships between members of Jackson's elite and members of previous elites. I: Jackson; II: John Quincy Adams; III: Monroe; IV: Madison; V: Jefferson; VI: John Adams; VII: Washington. Persons who were appointed more than once have been placed in the administration in which they first served.

Source: Sidney Aronson, *Status and Kinship in the Higher Civil Service* (Cambridge: Harvard University Press, 1964), p. 155.

especially when compared to its much smaller proportion of the general populace. And the working class got a proportionately better role in the earlier part of this century than later, when the middle class share gained somewhat. These shifts in patterns revealed here relate only to the topmost political positions. Other studies have examined the systematic bias of employment in the civil service jobs as well, but most certainly popular deference and attention flows to these top positions.

It is typically assumed that such special benefits distributed politically along class lines reflect a 'cultural lag' from which the new world was able to escape. But the study of earlier high appointments in America shows very strongly the domination of political posts by the top social class.[9] Table 3-6 gives the distribution of top appointive offices for the administrations

---

[9] Sidney Aronson, *Status and Kinship in the Higher Civil Service* (Cambridge: Harvard University Press, 1964).

Table 3-5
Class Structure of Cabinets, 1868-1955, According to Party*

	1868–86		1886–1916		1916–35		1935–55		1868–1955		
	Cons.	Lib.	Cons.	Lib.	Cons.	Lab.	Cons.	Lab.	Cons.	Lib.	Lab.
Aristocracy	13	15	26	23	19	3	20	1	60	32	4
Middle Class	8	14	21	28	33	12	40	14	86	54	25
Working Class	—	—	—	2	1	19	2	19	3	3	36
Total	21	29	47	53	53	34	62	34	149	89	65

* This breakdown concentrates on the two major governmental parties. It leaves out one Labour Cabinet minister for the period 1886-1916 and all Liberal ministers since 1916. Owing to the fact that nine ministers sat in Cabinets of two different parties the total for the three parties adds up to 303 and not 294.

From *The British Political Elite* by W. L. Guttsman, Basic Books, Inc., Publishers, New York, 1963, p. 79.

of Adams, Jefferson and Jackson; it may surprise the reader to see that Jefferson was as 'democratic' as Jackson, who has had the reputation of first turning the spoils of office over to the lower classes! The difference between the Federalist and the Jefferson and Jackson administrations was only a matter of degree. Later studies indicate there may be some of the same kind of changes in the United States as in Britain.[10] Top posts come to be shared more with the middle class, but in the absence of a labor party here, the chances for direct choices from the working class are mighty slim, until the worker has first 'pulled himself up by the bootstraps'!

Table 3-6
Social Class Positions of Elite Members

	Adams (N = 96)		Jefferson (N = 100)		Jackson (N = 127)	
	Num-ber	Per cent	Num-ber	Per cent	Num-ber	Per cent
I (Upper class)	83	86	74	74	95	75
II (Middle class)	4	4	7	7	9	7
III (Working class)	1	1	2	2	5	4
Unknown	8	9	17	17	18	14
Positions filled by men in financial difficulties at time of appointment	5	5	10	10	7	6

Source: Sidney Aronson, *Status and Kinship in the Higher Civil Service* (Cambridge: Harvard University Press, 1964), p. 99. [Class designations added.]

More typically in the modern scene occupational, ethnic and even religious statuses are the subjects of controversies as to fairness in political appointments. The political leader must 'balance the ticket' to honor such group identifications, and formal official ceremonies take into account such groupings. While many expect the lowly born to prove their competence before receiving top honors, few contest the far greater original advantages for those already in the top strata, for receiving political honors and offices.

---

[10] For a contemporary report see the detailed statistical survey of the social and personal characteristics of civilian and military leaders in the United States by W. Lloyd Warner, *et al.*, *The American Federal Executive* (New Haven: Yale University Press, 1963). Donald R. Matthews' *The Social Background of Political Decision-Makers* (Garden City: Doubleday and Company, Inc., 1954) is a brief but cogent survey of leadership backgrounds with materials on U.S. national officials and those of some other nations, in some cases for considerable periods of time.

Welfare Spending and Redistribution

At least from the days of the Elizabethan Poor Laws in England, the care of the destitute and disabled has been a major public issue. The dominant belief, during the budding days of capitalism, was that poverty signified laziness or at least a fall from grace and that the dole should not be a reward for doing nothing. This resulted in the public provision of some minimal sustenance, publicly supported almshouses, workhouses and disciplinarian orphanages to instill the virtues of thrift and hard labor. On into our own colonial and frontier days, there was constant vigilance to see that poverty and dependence were not rewarded by excessive public 'benefits.' In the case of public bounties and pensions for veterans and hospital benefits for merchant seamen, the expenditure was viewed as a reward for service. Similarly, farmers got their share of benefits, with an aura of virtuous right attached to it. In this sense, these transfer payments were aids to specific groups, who had some special reason for deserving them, according to the grantors.

There were, to be sure, resurgent dissenting philosophies and movements, claiming man's right to equal treatment and goods and viewing poverty as accidental or deliberate misery inflicted in the process of industrialization. Novelists such as Dickens, crusading social workers such as Jane Addams, members of elites taking charity seriously and articulate social theorists, all played a role in helping to shift the climate of opinion. But more directly, the actual experiences of increasing industrialization have altered the meaning of welfare programs. The recurrent downturns of the business cycle, the increasingly visible plight of factory labor, the organization and agitations of workers and the unemployed created very direct political demands for public solutions on the part of broader groups of active citizenry. One also notes that these citizens could increasingly resort to the ballot box to express their discontents, encouraging the tone of officialdom to change from disdain to sympathetic concern. In any case, social benefit expenditures have been extended to a broader target group, with the explicit purpose of providing basic income security. Not that the controversiality of the 'welfare state' has subsided—at least not in this country—but one can now examine the flow of social security and welfare expenditures in terms of the assumption that it is intended to minimize hardship among more broadly defined strata of the citizenry.

There are several kinds of governmental benefits to meet the newer aims, not all of them in the category of transfer payment. In this country, there are several kinds of public insurance programs carried on, such as the social security system financed by mandatory payroll taxes, with the receipts earmarked for trust funds, from which payments are made (Old Age, Survivors and Disability Insurance). There are joint financial arrangements, with employers contributing as well as employees (unemployment insurance), and other federal inducements to state or local governments to conduct their own public insurance programs (as with workmen's compensation). Such compulsory forms of protection can achieve wide coverage and can serve to channel a large flow of income payments through the public sector. It is indeed a service, forced on all alike, or at least on those directly reached by the benefit provisions. In the United States, Congress initially excluded the self-employed, who tended as a group to be the most strongly opposed ideologically. Some categories of service work continue to elude the system (much part-time domestic help, for example), and some have been kept out as political concessions to intensely opposed groups.

There are other services and goods made available to the needy which are more difficult to estimate in terms of the relative degree of ultimate benefit. Hot school lunches, the disposal of agricultural surpluses through food coupon plans and free mailing for the blind, for example, can be fairly easily accounted for as to amounts but difficult to compare in relative value to other kinds of aid. At this point we shall again have to stay with cases involving direct money transfers, as most of the studies have been done by economists on that kind of data.

There are several kinds of questions worth exploring about such benefit programs. One consideration is the relative scope or importance of such transfers, as compared to all other forms of income flows or to all other kinds of public programs. Another significant question is the degree to which it reaches the relevant population groups: those incapable of earning a sufficient income, and in various categories of dependency and disability. Another central question of program effectiveness is the degree to which these programs do provide a sufficient cushion for the economically disadvantaged, i.e., enough compensation to achieve the basic living standard anticipated. Further, and of much interest to economists and those concerned about poverty, do these programs effectively redistribute income so as to lessen significantly the degree of inequality generated by the private marketplace? Actually, a full answer to this and the other questions ought to consider the structure and effects of taxation as well. We shall consider this in the next chapter on the paying of costs, and in our more theoretical treatment of the problem of inequality. At this point we shall mainly deal with the benefit side of the equation, because these programs are more positively and directly related to governmental efforts for the provision of welfare.

Case Study #7   Some International Comparisons of Social Security Expenditures

Nations do not all devote equivalent amounts of public monies to any given program or activity, and social security is no exception. In fact, the range of variation in total amounts, percentages of the GNP, and allocations among various types of programs is considerable, as Table 3-7

Table 3-7

Social Security Expenditures, by Type of Program,
as Per Cent of National Income, Selected Countries, 1957

Geographical region and country	Social Insurance and assimilated schemes	Family allowances	Public employers	Public health services	Public assistance and assimilated schemes	Benefits for war victims	Total[d]
Western Europe							
Austria	11.1	1.6	3.1	—c	1.0	1.2	17.6
Belgium	8.1	2.5	3.2	0.4	1.2	1.0	16.3
Denmark[a]	6.0	0.6	1.1	2.4	1.6	0.1	12.0
Finland	3.6	2.3	1.3	2.2	1.7	0.8	12.0
France	8.5	5.1	3.5	—	0.9	1.3	18.9
West Germany	13.7	0.3	3.3	0.1	1.6	2.3	20.8
Ireland[a]	5.5	1.2	1.3	2.8	0.6	—	11.5
Italy	7.3	3.2	2.8	0.2	0.4	1.7	15.2
The Netherlands	7.7	1.8	2.0	—	0.8	0.1	12.3
Norway[a]	5.3	0.6	1.7	1.4	1.0	0.1	10.1
Portugal	1.6	1.0	1.5	0.4	2.0	—	6.5
Sweden	6.5	1.1	0.7	2.7	1.6	—c	12.9
Switzerland	4.8	—c	1.1	1.5	1.4	—	8.7
United Kingdom[a]	4.7	0.7	0.7	4.3	1.6	0.6	12.1
Eastern Europe							
Poland[b]	2.6	2.3	0.2	2.4	—	0.1	7.7
Yugoslavia	6.3	3.0	—	0.6	0.1	0.6	10.3

North America							
Canada[a]	3.4	1.7	0.3	1.7	0.8	0.8	8.7
United States[a]	3.0	—	0.6	0.5	0.9	1.1	6.0
Central and South America							
Chile	3.0	3.0	3.4	0.4	—	—	9.7
Guatemala[a]	1.1	—	0.3	1.7	—	—	3.1
Australasia							
Australia[a]	5.8	—	0.5	1.2	0.2	1.4	9.1
New Zealand[a]	8.9	—	0.8	2.2	0.1	1.0	13.0
Asia							
Ceylon[a]	—[c]	—	1.3	2.1	0.8	—	4.2
China (Taiwan)	0.2	—	—[c]	0.3	0.3	—	0.8
India	—[c]	—	0.5	0.5	—	—[c]	1.0
Japan[a]	2.8	—	1.8	0.6	0.8	—	5.8
Africa and Middle East							
Israel[a]	4.4	—	—	2.2	0.6	0.3	7.7
Tunisia	0.4	1.6	2.0	1.7	—	—	5.7
Turkey	0.4	—	0.7	0.2	—[c]	—	1.3
Union of South Africa[a]	1.4	0.1	0.6	1.8	—[c]	0.5	4.5

[a] Data relate to the fiscal year 1956-57.

[b] Administrative expenses are not included.

[c] Less than 0.05.

[d] Individual percentages may not add to totals because 1) of rounding errors, 2) administrative expenses that are not allocated to a particular program (or group of programs) are included in the total in some cases, and 3) transfers between programs are not included as a separate item.

Source: Margaret S. Gordon, *The Economics of Welfare Policies* (New York: Columbia University Press, 1963), pp. 18-19.

clearly indicates for a fairly recent point in time. This survey of some thirty nations depicts a range in total expenditures from 1 per cent of the national income in the case of India to more than 20 per cent in the case of West Germany. The median percentage is 8.7 per cent found in Canada and Switzerland. The United States spent 6 per cent of its overall income on social security. Apparently the major program in most of these nations is social insurance, particularly for retirement and old age. Perhaps the popularity of such programs stems from the fact that all people expect to grow old and retire from active work, whereas the other programs benefit much smaller proportions of the population.

An interesting set of questions arise in connection with Table 3-7 concerning reasons for the distributions. We may casually observe that both democratic and non-democratic nations sometimes spend corresponding proportions of their national income: the United States, Poland, Portugal and Israel, all devote similar amounts to social security. And, we may also note that the nations which are thought to have the highest standards of living tend to spend more on social security than do the poorer or less developed nations. Why should that be the case? In looking over the figures, would you propose cultural, economic or other social and political factors as most related to the variations? How, where or in which cases?

Case Study #8   Income Redistribution in Denmark

We know that the Danish government, like all other nations, engages in the collection of taxes and the distribution of various benefits. Fortunately we can learn much more from the results of a fairly sophisticated research project conducted in Denmark by three Danish economists on governmental redistribution of income.[11] Their research is highly complex, but its meaning is relatively simple. Among the conclusions the authors came to were these: (1) Just under one-third of the total income redistributed was accomplished by using progressive taxes while the larger remaining amount was redistributed as a result of social benefits, particularly old age pensions. (2) Industrial wage employees tended to pay for their own benefits and in effect also paid for a large part of the income of non-industrial persons, including farmers. (3) Employees and the self-employed paid a great part of the income of retired persons. In a sense the younger members of Danish society support the older, but everyone grows older so eventually the younger, more productive citizens will in turn be supported in old age. Finally, the investigators concluded that if one studied the entire set of redistributive measures one would find a less than coherent

---

[11] K. Lemberg, N. Ussing, and F. Zeuthen, "Redistribution of Income in Denmark," in Alan T. Peacock, ed., *Income Redistribution and Social Policy* (London: Jonathan Cape, 1954), pp. 55-89.

system, with various programs serving contradictory ends. Economists, however, tend to value consistent economic ends more than consistent political ends which may be attained by inconsistent economic policies!

Case Study #9   Transfer Payments in France

France, like the other democracies, has seen an increasing percentage of its national income and governmental budgets go into transfer payments or redistribution. One study claims that in 1938 the amount of all transfer payments was 51.7 per cent of the government budget and rose to 55.5 per cent in 1955.[12] The author, Wallace C. Peterson, seems to feel that the trend will continue. We do not know. The major increases have been in transfer payments to individuals, primarily as a result of social security and other welfare programs. The net amount going to businesses has not changed much, amounting to about 11.2 per cent in 1955. Social Security payments on the other hand increased from 15.8 per cent in 1938 to 30.2 per cent in 1955. As a consequence the proportions spent on governmental consumption of goods and services for the performance of the broader tasks of government declined during that seventeen year period.

In addition to analyzing the redistributive activities and outcomes of government on the payment side of the ledger, Peterson also studied the distribution of taxes since one's net financial position vis-à-vis the government necessarily includes what one must pay as well as receive. Interestingly, Peterson contended that the distribution of taxes, at least those he studied (income, social security), strongly points to the conclusion that the farmers, and non-active people (retired, injured, etc.) pay less than their proportions of the income of the nation would indicate as their share, while the self-employed and wage earners pay more than their respective share.

In conclusion, Peterson observed that the basic income structure of France was one of inequality, modified only slightly by the sum-total of redistribution going on via transfer payments and taxation. And the overall redistribution across the social classes remained minimal. Most redistribution seems to be taking place *within* each social class as evidenced by the fact that farmers and 'non-actives' do better while workers pay more.

If the situation is as Peterson suggests, conservatives need not be as apprehensive about the future as they appear, while liberals and radicals might worry all the more, since the redistributive activities conducted by governments do not appear to result in significant changes in the income structure of society. The alterations have not been dramatic in France nor any other country that has been studied. Of course, most studies do not go far enough back in history to enable analyses of long-term change. Some day investigators may find some way to do this.

---

[12] Wallace C. Peterson, *The Welfare State in France* (Lincoln: University of Nebraska Press, 1960), p. 41.

Case Study #10   Redistribution in the United States

The United States must be the most thoroughly studied nation in the world with respect to income distribution; this is also probably true for most questions one might ask about a society. In any case, there are continuing efforts in the United States to study the effects of governmental activities on income redistribution.

One such study, by Stauffacher, found that a considerable amount of redistribution had been brought about by the federal government during the New Deal era.[13] For example, Stauffacher claims that government transfer payments accounted for about 27 per cent of the income of those receiving less than $780 per year. One may think this is a small sum but during the depression of the 1930s it was enough for many to survive on. The lower third of families paid about 5 per cent of the taxes and received some 26.8 per cent of direct money flows from the government. The upper third (then earning over $1450) paid around 83 per cent of the federal taxes and received 60 per cent of the income payments of the government. Those who had annual incomes of over $4000 (2.4 per cent of the population) paid about 50 per cent of the taxes but received only 22 per cent of the income payments.

More recent studies of income distribution in the U.S. generally argue that the income patterns before and after taxes and government expenditures *are* different and tend to work in the direction of greater equality of incomes. The most widely known study holds that changes in income shares since the 1930s have been striking. Simon Kuznets, the Harvard economist, has claimed that his "exhaustive" studies showed the share of income held by the upper income groups (particularly the upper 5 per cent) to have declined some 28 per cent from 1939 to 1946.[14] He further contends that the decline has been fairly consistent since as far back as 1919. Unfortunately, Kuznets did not attempt to determine the distribution of pure public goods as benefits. What that might have done to his final conclusions we cannot know, for the problem of definition and measurement would be immense.

In still other studies Alfred H. Conrad and John H. Alder each attempted, independently, to study the market distribution of income and redistributive consequences of American governmental policies for different years (Adler for 1938-39 and 1946-47; Conrad for 1950).[15] Both appear

---

[13] Charles Stauffacher, "The Effects of Governmental Expenditures and Tax Withdrawals Upon Income Distribution, 1930-1939," in *Public Policy, II* (Cambridge: Harvard University Press, 1941), pp. 232-62.

[14] Simon Kuznets, *Shares of Upper Income Groups in Income and Savings* (New York: National Bureau of Economic Research, Inc., 1953), pp. xxxv-xxxix.

[15] Alfred H. Conrad, "Redistribution Through Government Budgets in United States, 1950," in Alan T. Peacock, ed., *Income Redistribution and Social Policy* (London: Jonathan Cape, 1954), pp. 178-267. John H. Adler, "The Fiscal System, The Distribution of Income, and Public Welfare," in Kenyon E. Poole, ed., *Fiscal Policies and The American Economy* (New York: Prentice-Hall, Inc., 1951), pp. 359-409.

to be in rough agreement that government, through its taxation practices, patterns of resource allocation and redistributive activities, has partially succeeded in income redistribution. The lowest income groups on the average have improved their shares while the upper classes have not, except during the 1938-39 period when all but those who made over $7500 increased their shares after both taxes and benefits had been calculated. During the 1946-47 period the lower income groups profited from their relationships with the government while the upper groups typically suffered 'losses.' We doubt, however, that any higher income families would therefore want to exchange positions with lower income people!

Directions of Redistribution

While there are many advocates of greater equality in the distribution of income and welfare, they should not inherently assume that all changes proceed in that direction alone. Changes might also be made in the direction of greater inequality or simply remain the same, i.e., no redistribution. Or as we have seen in some of the studies, redistribution may take place horizontally within the same income group. What evidence has been garnered shows that divergent tendencies may be observed in different countries and through different time periods. Some economists, for example, have maintained that labor's share of the national income in United States has not changed in fifty years, while others have shown that some redistribution has taken place between the upper and lower classes but not within the middle class. Still others have claimed, as did Peterson in regard to France, that most redistribution took place from workers to the aged. The famous theorists Pareto and Lorenz argued that redistribution was, in the long run, impossible; inequality was a natural fact of social life. Governments could not and should not attempt to contravene nature. We shall discuss such differing views on inequality after the following chapter on costs and burdens.

Political Redistribution of Income: How Much? From Whom? To Whom?

Our case studies have illustrated a number of benefits distributed by governments in terms of outcomes, for particular countries and times. They have provided some hints on the degree of redistribution. The more interesting question about political aspects remain, however. Can we generalize further about the extent to which different types of polities have attempted to redistribute income? What are the political aspects of income redistribution?

We must begin by saying that controversy still prevails on all these problems because not only is redistribution difficult to measure, but little systematic political study has been made of the problem. Nevertheless, we cannot simply suspend judgment but must use whatever information is available and make what inference we can. The cases we have noted, plus a few others, all seem to indicate that:

1. Both democratic and non-democratic governments have in fact attempted deliberately to redistribute income;

2. They have succeeded to some small degree but much less than the full goals visualized by their advocates;

3. The directions of redistribution have not always been in the direction of greater equality.

A few remarks about each of these propositions is in order.

Governmental Efforts to Redistribute Income

All governments affect the creation and distribution of income in some manner or other, to some degree, and in some direction, whether through inadvertent or deliberate policy. The mere fact that governments tax and thereby reduce personal incomes as well as spend those same taxes on public programs necessarily means that redistribution of incomes will most likely occur. The additional fact that governments select certain means of financing rather than others; that they tax at some rates rather than others; that they provide particular exemptions and not others necessarily means that they take different amounts from each citizen's income. These considerations, along with choices on the allocation of resources and spending programs, can change the prior distribution of income by the marketplace.

We have observed, especially during the past two decades, a protracted and important effort on the part of many governments to substitute the polity for the economy, to increase as well as shift more income to the lower-income groups. Socialist and communist systems have made this an explicit policy. The western democracies, including the United States, have also made some efforts in this direction with varying degrees of success. While evidence is hard to come by, especially for the new nations and communist systems, it would seem that the latter have tried harder to achieve equality. As far as we can determine, nations such as the Soviet Union have increased their standards of living and perhaps affected a redistribution, but they have not eliminated some serious inequalities. Differential wages and salaries tend to be paid among occupations as they are in market economies. The more highly educated, skilled and motivated persons draw greater incomes and acquire more status and influence than do the less well-educated or skilled persons. The supply and demand for talent is not made irrelevant by the substitution of planned economies for market systems. Whether complete equality of incomes can be attained and whether it is desirable will remain major questions for some time to come.

Extent of Redistribution

For all the study devoted to this problem by economists precious little in the way of definitive results have been attained. The reason is fairly obvious: imputing incidences of income, taxes and governmental expenditures is not an exact science. In addition, we know very little about the historical changes that may be involved, especially the political ingredients of success or failure in attempting redistributive policies. Our case studies all strongly suggest that relatively little has been achieved, thus far, by way of political redistributions, among the democracies. This is not to say that more could not be accomplished; it could be, but no one should expect radical changes in societies which already enjoy broadly based high standards of living and in which the expectation of moving up the ladder of relative personal success appears reasonable to many citizens.

The major roadblock to greater redistributions of income and welfare, more generally however, remains political in nature. Those who enjoy greater incomes have greater political power or resources with which to protect their positions than do those who have lower incomes. The latter groups cannot as easily mobilize to advance their interests. Why this is the case we must defer to Part 2 where we deal with various political processes.

Who Gets What?

We are back to one of our original questions—who gets what? Or, more explicitly: Who gets what from whom? Politically, this is most often the crux of the question. The political system imposes compulsory extractions, and bestows its benefits by rules outside the usual economic processes. But to what extent it succeeds in intervening successfully is also a political question.

First, we are inclined to believe that the greatest inequalities of income are found in the less developed nations with low per capita incomes. There is good evidence for this part of the claim. There is some, but not as much, evidence for the further claim that most of these same low income nations with great inequalities are non-democratic or at least less democratic than the higher income nations. Since there are many more of the less developed and less democratic nations, we expect that whatever redistribution goes on via government in these systems is in the direction of furthering the interests of the wealthier families. In short, most governments have served to protect and improve the fortunes of the rich. Their taxation systems tend to be regressive while their expenditure policies tend to advance the upper income groups at the expense of the lower classes. Not all poor nations ignore the poor citizens; those which have had communist revolutions or coups by 'modernizing' elements tend to take more of the resources of the upper classes—often initially through outright confiscation —and redistribute them to the poor in the course of undertaking rapid economic and social mobilization. Such nations have included East Germany, the East European nations, Cuba, China, North Vietnam, North Korea, Egypt, Ghana and perhaps others now undergoing leadership changes. Right-wing or traditional non-democratic nations are still more numerous and they are the ones in which the least amount of redistribution in the direction of greater equality has occurred. This is not to say that some such redistribution may not come about either as a result of governmental ignorance or even as deliberate policies of redressing some wrongs and ensuring the stability of the rulers' positions. A great many nations in Africa, Latin America and to a lesser extent in Asia may be said to be nations without explicit commitment toward greater equalities.[16]

Western democracies, on the other hand, are nations with some commitment to redistribution and some knowledge of ways to achieve it. As we have seen from our case studies the most likely course of redistribution—to the extent that it occurs—is from the upper to the lower classes, while the middle class pays its own way in taxes and receives about what it contributes toward the operations of the polity. With most social insurance systems there is some horizontal redistribution within income classes, especially among lower income brackets. Explicit policies toward income security tend to reach primarily those only temporarily or conditionally denied incomes: the retired and aged, those paid off from jobs or injured while working. Relief and welfare programs have also been typically justified as temporary aids and are not intended to shift the structure of income flows in the entire economy. Students inclined to worry about the alleged drift to the welfare state ought to study the details of welfare programs with care; most such programs do relatively little to redistribute income.

Problems and Applications

1. Develop an explanation or theory to account for the distribution of subsidies found in Table 3-2. You might proceed by consulting the various considerations suggested on page 106. Which make the most and the least sense? How can one proceed to test these theories?

---

[16] See Charles W. Anderson, Fred R. von der Mehden, and Crawford Young, *Issues of Political Development* (Englewood Cliffs, N.J.: Prentice-Hall, Inc., 1967), Chaps. 9-11.

2. Rank the following public benefits in terms of ease in measuring who receives how much of them. Explain or defend your ranking.

National defense   Public education
Police protection   Veterans' benefits
Agricultural subsidies   Urban renewal
Highway construction   Weather reports

3. Most, if not all, studies in income redistribution make it amply clear that governments cannot, or have not, been able to produce marked redistributions in the short-run. If this is so, how can we best account for the fact?

4. Evaluate these two statements:

"Voters are much more cost conscious (tax aware) than they are benefit-oriented, because costs are more visible and measureable than are the benefits of public expenditures."

"Voters will approve of additional public expenditures where there is no clear-cut accounting of the distribution of costs."

5. Rank order the most likely preferences for the listed public goods by each of the following groups. Defend your preference rankings for each group and specify the relevant conditions. (1) Lower income receivers; (2) middle income; (3) upper income; (4) Negroes.

Airport improvement   Highway beautification
A new civic auditorium   Urban renewal
Increased aid to dependent children   Conservation
Lower tuition at state university   Public parks
Community action programs   Medicare

6. Different levels of government, i.e., local, state or provincial and national, tend to produce and distribute different goods and services; in short, they have a division of labor. What types of goods and services do they tend to specialize in and why?

7. Try predicting how voters might respond if their various governments sent them an annual statement indicating their personal or family shares in the public benefits. Do you think it would: Alter their views of government? Change their voting habits? Irritate or please them? Make them more patriotic? Cause them to support or oppose higher public budgets?

Bibliographical Notes

Social scientists have been investigating the distribution of income, power and social status for a long time, but the element which has received the least attention has been the role of public goods and services. We have already learned of some reasons for this situation; they need not be repeated here. The fact that increasingly more of our total income is controlled by governmental expenditures and taxation will, however, encourage social scientists to pay much greater attention to the distribution of public goods. They will have to assess more carefully how and for whom these benefits flow.

The best work on public goods and the redistribution of income by governments is found in the writings of a number of persons we have already cited in previous chapters. Thus, we call to mind the most advanced treatment to date, by Richard Musgrave, *The Theory of Public Finance*, New York: McGraw-Hill Book Company, Inc., 1959, especially Chapters 4-6; and the pioneering work of James M. Buchanan in *Public Finance in Democratic Process*, Chapel Hill: The University of North Carolina Press, 1967. A still more recent volume on *Public Spending*, New York: McGraw-Hill Book Company, Inc., 1968, by a distinguished political economist, Roland N. McKean, deserves your attention not only for its direct relevance to these concerns, but for its simple, clear approach. We recommend Chapters 2 and 4, at this point. Perhaps the best short treatment of governmental redistribution of income to be found in a textbook is that of Donald S. Watson, in *Economic Policy: Business and Government*, Boston: Houghton Mifflin Company, 1960, Chapter 23. Chapters 24 and 25 are on specific aspects of redistribution, namely social welfare and farm policies.

Measurement of benefits stemming from public goods is extremely difficult, but efforts are being made to identify and measure incidence. One such collection of efforts may be found in *Measuring Benefits of Government Investments*, Washington, D.C.: The Brookings Institution, 1965, edited by Robert Dorfman. This reports on efforts by several economists to measure values for various governmental programs involving research, outdoor recreation, civil aviation expenditures, urban renewal programs, etc. Greater success seems to have been obtained in identifying generalized benefits than in the determination of who gets how much of these same benefits.

Two recent studies on Latin America not only contribute to our knowledge of Mexico and Latin America generally but also shed some light on the question of benefit distributions. James W. Wilkie in *The Mexican Revolution*, Berkeley: University of California Press, 1967, attempts to relate federal expenditures and social change since 1910. In doing so he provides information on the allocation of resources but less directly on distribution since he makes no effort to establish which groups benefit from which expenditures. Yet the nature of the expenditures does give strong hints concerning the *intended* beneficiaries. A less detailed but more extensive coverage of governmental spending is presented by Charles W. Anderson in *Politics and Economic Change in Latin America*, Princeton, N.J.: D. Van Nostrand Company, Inc., 1967. Part 2 comes closest to our interests and should be consulted along with Wilkie's work as examples of a type of investigation which is likely to include nations in other parts of the world.

The above citations all pertain to economic benefits that can to some extent be measured in money terms. Other benefits are conferred that cannot so easily be translated into dollars and cents, yet they are as important and, in some instances, far more crucial for some groups, particularly those suffering social and political disadvantages as well. We have in mind the less tangible benefits of social status and esteem, political rights and efficacy, as well as education, housing, and employment. But there are many ways to document and assess such conditions, and a fine example is *The Report of the National Advisory Commission on Civil Disorders,* New York: Bantam Books, Inc., 1968 (also available from the U.S. Government Printing office). Very effective documentation can be found on the plight of Negroes in the United States with respect to the conditions of life for this racial minority: from inadequate housing and medical care; denial of education and employment, divorce, family instability and crime; police harassment without effective protection; and many other miseries that most whites need not worry about. Whatever the goods or benefits derived from living in this country, Negroes acquire far less than their just shares. You might want to compare this report with the classic investigation by Gunnar Myrdal, *An American Dilemma,* New York: Harper and Row, 1962, written during the late 1930s and first published in 1944. The focus and intention of the two reports are different, but the stories they have to tell about racial discrimination are remarkably alike though more than twenty years separate their publication. A very thorough study of the relative benefit of education for Negro and white youngsters, compared under varying conditions, is reported in *Equality of Educational Opportunity, Summary Report,* U.S. Department of Health, Education and Welfare, Office of Education; U.S. Government Printing Office, 1966, better known as "The Coleman Report," named for the very able sociologist who directed the project, James S. Coleman. This is an exemplary effort at measuring the value of a public service through controlled comparisons of its effects on different groups under varying circumstances; similar efforts could be done for many other public activities including employment services; hospital, health and rehabilitation programs; job training programs; even area redevelopment and urban renewal; or such amenities as recreational facilities and library services. And such studies can assess a greater variety of relative advantages and disadvantages flowing from governmental programs, for many other kinds of groups—by ethnic, age, income, or residential divisions, for example.

There is a continuing body of literature which laments the current 'maldistribution' of goods and benefits in this country, as it relates to the public sector. We have noted Galbraith's well-known castigation, *The Affluent Society*, Boston: Houghton Mifflin Company, 1958, in our first bibliographical note. Even more perceptive about the victims of inequality in this country is Michael Harrington's *The Other America*, Baltimore: Penguin Books, 1963, where graphic depiction of those most slighted is related to a political thesis about their 'invisibility' and lack of political influence. The impact of this book can be found in many of the recent action programs set up publicly or privately to do more for—and by—these groups. There have been many works critical of U.S. military and space policies for gravely increasing inequalities, as well as furthering less desirable public ends. Seymour Melman's *Our Depleted Society*, New York: Dell Publishing Company, 1965, takes this approach, and uses a variety of data relative to inequalities in this country and among nations.

The best general summary of elite studies is Suzanne Keller's *Beyond the Ruling Class*, New York: Random House, Inc., 1963, which surveys theory in the light of empirical findings. Chapters 7, 8, 9 and the Appendices indicate what evidence there is about patterns of advantage, rewards and opportunities for what Keller defines as "strategic elites," including several political types. Joseph A. Schlesinger's *Ambition and Politics: Political Careers in the United States*, Chicago: Rand McNally and Company, 1966, looks at the subject in terms of the structure of available political opportunities. Chapter 10 presents the conclusions by systematic propositions. Political patronage, once the subject of so many journalistic exposés, certainly deserves more systematic study in spite of its apparent relative decline. Theodore Lowi indicates what can be done, in terms of the patronage available to a New York City mayor, in his book *At the Pleasure of the Mayor*, New York: The Free Press, 1964, by showing patterns of preferences in appointments over time. An imaginative treatment of the less legitimate forms of dispensing favors, and the social and private valuations involved, is found in Arnold A. Rogow and Harold D. Lasswell, *Power, Corruption, and Rectitude*, Englewood Cliffs, N.J.: Prentice-Hall, Inc., 1963.

Los Angeles Times, Jan. 18, 1967, Los Angeles, California

eagan Outlines
-Step Crime War

Asks Local Ordinances to Control
Sex and Public Decency Offenses

Furious Hindus riot
over cow slaughte

Palo Alto Times, Nov. 7, 1966, Palo Alto, California

Tennessee House OK's
'monkey law' repealer

The New York Times,
Nov. 29, 1966,
New York, New York

The New York Times, July 31, 1966,
New York, New York

GEORGE V STATUE

NDALS DESECRATE
DACHAU MEMORIAL

TROUBLES INDIAN

Nationalists Ask to Replace
Royalty With Gandhi

San Francisco Examiner & Chronicle, April 13, 1967,
San Francisco, California

Legal Artificial Insemination
Of Humans Voted in Oklahoma

The New York Times, May 5, 1967, New York, New York

TEACHER OPPO
THE TERM 'NE

Urges Federation to
for Use of 'Afro-Amer

The New York Times,
Dec. 10, 1966,
New York, New York

ONN. Nov. 29. The Munich
e disclosed today that a
ish memorial at the site of
former Dachau concentra-
camp was desecrated by
dals some time this week.

he monument was smeared
swastikas and painted
s saying. "Juden raus aus
schland" (Jews get out of
nany).

e vandals painted anti-
rican slogans saying. ("Am
ome."

San Francisco Examiner & Chronicle, April 2, 1967, San Francisco, California

Bitter Fight on
Film in School

South Carolina Pleads
For State Sword Retur

The Oregonian, April 3, 1968, Portland, Oregon

ARK BACKS LAW
N FLAG BURNING

The New York Times,
May 11, 1967,
New York

The Woodside Town Council,
reaching to its ordinances for
finition of family, ordered
town staff Monday night
"clear up" within two
what council members
"hippie pad" at 95 Med-
way Road.

Hippie is the current term
for persons living outside accepted social restraints.

Palo Alto Times, April 12, 1967,
Palo Alto, California

Nation's War Dea
To Be Remember

San Francisco Examiner & Chronicle, May 28, 1967,

UNDAY CLOSING
T STAKE IN UTAH

Anxiety in Belgrade

Linguistic Quarrel Stirring
Of a Widened Serbo-Croat Rivalry

The New York Times, March 25, 1967, New York, New York

The New York Times,
Dec. 20, 1966,
New York, New York

Commons Approves
Bill on Homosexuals

INDIANS DISPUT
TATE ON WAM

roquois League Den
Return of Ancient B
Locked in Museu

ernor Will Decide on Bill
hat Mormons Backed

The New York Times, March 11, 1967,
New York, New York

The New York Times,
March 25, 1967,
New York, New York

Chapter 4

Symbolic Public Goods: Identifications, Status and Morality

One of the great cliches has it that 'man does not live by bread alone.' In political life there are not only the material allocative and distributive problems and choices discussed in Chapters 2 and 3, but also problems involving the distribution of loyalties, identifications, social status, and morality. These particular 'goods' can be created or produced and distributed by governments just as income, opportunities and power are created and allocated. As some citizens acquire more income and other public goods so, too, do some citizens acquire greater status, and have their morals more honored than those of other citizens. Although these symbolic goods are not consumed and transferred in the form of material objects, they are at least as crucial to most men and are far more important to many, as we shall see. In the event that any reader doubts us, let him prove that he would prefer less to more status; that he would rather see another's morals more honored than his own; that he would wish political honors to be bestowed on a group he dislikes. We suspect most readers will share our view that symbolic goods are valuable and most men have intense preferences about them. In any event, we shall proceed on the assumption that people covet both symbolic and material goods and that governments have an enormous impact on their creation and distribution.

Political systems and governments produce symbolic goods to fulfill a great variety of needs or wants. In so doing they, in a sense, earn a profit if citizens accept what is offered for 'sale'; but if governments fail to meet strongly felt symbolic 'demands' they must (1) redistribute existing goods; (2) create new symbolic goods which will fill the needs; or (3) attempt to reshape citizen wants and preferences. In fact, all governments work on both the supply and the demand for their goods and services just as do private organizations. Politicians, like businessmen, constantly advertise or display their products, their policies and promises. And citizens, if presented with opportunities, will manifest their preferences. Democracies, of course, institutionalize various practices in certain ways to enable such expression.

Citizens 'consume' symbolic goods, not in a literal sense but in the sense of deriving satisfactions from them just as they derive satisfaction from material public goods. Each citizen may prefer different combinations of symbolic goods and, in fact, he does. But unlike the marketplace, the polity is more restricted in its efforts to satisfy all demands. All men cannot have all they want in the exact proportions they prefer. Politicians typically attempt to satisfy as many as possible, but they cannot fulfill all such wants. Symbolic goods, as we shall see, pose some peculiar problems of distribution quite unlike those of material goods.

In this chapter we consider the gratifications citizens derive from *national identifications* or patriotism and the political issues these arouse when men are unable to agree about these important matters. In the second section we deal with issues of *social status* as affected by governmental and political processes, while in the third section we consider some *moral goods* over which men may struggle.

The Nation and Patriotic Identifications

A walk through most small towns and particularly through state and national capital cities is an instructive experience in understanding one very basic element of social and political life. On such an imaginary walk, one is apt to encounter much of the physical symbolic apparatus of the polity and government. The city hall, courthouse, post office, police station and fire department; the flag, seals of office, war memorials, historical monuments; uniformed police, meter maids, or military personnel; historic paintings and other reminders of traditions are commonly encountered on any such tour. In capitals one finds even greater proliferation of such political and patriotic displays to remind the visitor of his honored heritage of leaders and events. While we take many of these symbols for granted there are occasions in the histories of all nations when this is not so—when such identifications are questioned, authoritative symbols attacked, and men challenge one another's citizenship or patriotism. But more often in the stable regimes this vast and intricate symbolism simply reinforces loyalties and provides political aesthetics or gratifications for citizens. Neither the great totalitarian states nor the newly-emerging nations take these symbols of cohesion and loyalty for granted; vast and expensive efforts are made at indoctrination and control in the former, while the latter struggle for new identifications and loyalties where traditional ties have prevailed among a people without a sense of national citizenship. The state, thus, attempts to manage both the supply and demand for these goods.

The point in all these observances and symbols is to represent the society or the national heritage and unity by stressing symbols that have affective meaning for most men in a society. Each generation attempts to pass on that heritage to its successors. And each generation expects its members to respect the symbols. What might happen to a person who trampled the American flag at the busiest corner in your home city or town? Disrespect to the flag is usually regarded as a crime. Disrespect for other political symbols may not always be criminal but it is certainly not encouraged and usually is strongly frowned upon through the use of informal sanctions. The political system is a prime user of symbols and, as such, produces as well as distributes them. Revolutionary movements usually develop their own special symbols to replace those of the status quo. Indeed, as one commentator noted, symbols are often all a new revolutionary movement has! Nazi Germany, the U.S.S.R., Red China have all created impressive new sets of physical symbols and symbolic behavior: a new vocabulary of politics, a new set of uniforms, a new set of slogans, a new style of behavior for its leaders and followers, mass demonstrations, new symbolic ideals. Each has created a new ideology or verbal symbols that have meanings for the true believers as well as for the enemy who fears them. Each treats these symbols and beliefs as tools of politics to be consciously manipulated for great social goals. Each honors a new flag and makes great heroes of their founders or heads of state.

The democracies of the West also have their political cultures and symbols. We have suggested as much with the illustrations used at the beginning of the chapter. Just as a fascist culture may differ from a communist culture, so may the culture of democracies. British political culture is quite different from the American and Canadian. In the former, status, the monarchical tradition, pageantry and deference contrast with the much greater egalitarianism, informality and openness of the American. Canada, on the other hand, has a somewhat different mixture. The general point is that all nations have political cultures made up of precious beliefs, values, norms and affective symbols (both material and verbal). One becomes a citizen when he has internalized or accepted these elements of the culture to such an extent that he as a person is identified with them. Thus an American is easily distinguishable among other peoples because he carries a particular and even somewhat unique political culture with him wherever he might travel.

Nations devote substantial portions of their resources to the inculcation and maintenance of political cultures. The amounts themselves are, of course, subject to allocative decisions since these resources can also be employed for other purposes. Consider for a moment the vast expenditures of time, energy and money that go into the educational systems of most societies. A large part of these educational funds is, in turn, used for creating 'good' citizens imbued with appropriate ideals, beliefs, norms of behavior; in short, shaping their demand for symbolic goods. Or, consider the vast amount of land, labor and capital that has gone into the physical symbols of a nation-state and its polity: expensive public buildings and incredible numbers of art work dedicated to political themes. Every local government and national government allocates substantial funds to celebrate annual political rites or ceremonies. The inaugurals of national leaders are elaborate and expensive; so are their funerals. Consider the highly valuable amounts of real estate that are maintained in the form of tombs, memorials and monuments honoring the forefathers and military heroes of the nation. Among the most valuable real estate in such historic locales as Boston, for example, are those which contain the remains of American heroes and founders. Increasingly we find that the architecture of public buildings is among the most impressive in the country. So the symbolic apparatus of integration, identification and loyalty are vast, intricate, moving, powerful and costly.

Because they are all these things, political symbols are not only a basis for cohesion in society and for personal satisfaction but also a potential source of cleavage, for one man's satisfactions may not be another's. A nation cannot have two flags of equal worth. Some of the most compelling and intense crises, some of the most profound issues in every society revolve about the symbolic order. As we suggested above, respect and affection for the symbols is a most sensitive matter for both the patriot and the deviant. That is why cases of treason or disloyalty are so crucial and emotion-laden. Socrates in ancient Athens, Joan of Arc in early France, Burr in America, Trotsky in Russia, the Hiss case in recent United States history, are names and events of great import, not only for their times but all times in the histories of the respective nations. All groups have definitions of loyalty and disloyalty; these definitions have served to make bitter enemies at times and to draw countless others into emotional fervor and dedication. Loyalty to the nation-state is the prime loyalty for many men today. And, even in those areas where loyalty is still focused on the family or locality, we see it breaking down and newer, larger, more encompassing loyalties to nations being created. Nationalism is the name usually reserved for these identifications, as contrasted with the localism or parochialism of more particular ties.

Men do not ordinarily bargain about their loyalties, for loyalty is basically a non-instrumental and highly diffused identification. Few men calculate their loyalties for nation-states in the manner they may calculate their interests in the allocation of resources and the distribution of material

benefits. Indeed, most of us would be very distrustful of a person who calculates loyalties at any level, whether to friends or his nation. One characteristic of these commitments is that they are formed very early and tend
to remain highly stable throughout life. The feelings about allocation and
distribution may be strong, but they are hardly a match for the fervor, the
depth of association, the intensity of a commitment to a nation-state. Men
will, in fact, die for their nation's honor and survival, but they will bargain
over their taxes and material benefits. Few will die for any other organization or group. And, these same men can inflict terrible injury upon those
whom they suspect of being less loyal than themselves. Witch hunts, 'red-
baiting,' accusations, physical harm have all been known to occur in most
modern nation-states which are presumed to be highly rational societies.
In prisons, we are told, even hardened criminals ostracize the political
prisoner accused of treason, sabotage or espionage.

Whereas in more normal times the rationality of the skilled bargainer
prevails, during the great loyalty issues the emotionality of the superpatriot
prevails. Men no longer demand more or less but either/or. Because the
'stakes' are high, the intensity of the struggle and the demands are also high.
Resolution of the issue becomes extraordinarily difficult and unstable as
contrasted to allocative issues. Whereas compromise and logrolling are
thought to be reasonably honorable solutions to most allocative and distributive problems, they are considered dishonorable for those intensely
concerned with loyalty issues. One must not compromise with the 'devil' or
his loyalty is surrendered. Witness the treatment which twenty-one American 'turncoats' of the Korean war received from this country as they returned to confess their errors. Perhaps never again will they be treated as
ordinary citizens, either by their government or fellow citizens. So the give
and take of ordinary politics is absent from the great symbolic issues of
loyalty to the nation.

Symbolic issues of loyalties can occur in less intense or violent form,
such as questions of competing loyalties, for example, between two levels of
government or between overlapping forms of political community. The
degree of conflict involved probably depends on the manner in which the
issue is presented, and how much of a threat is seen to deep-seated attachments. In federal systems such as the United States there are continuing
questions of whether the federal, state or local government should have the
major role in various programs, which provoke debate over relative attachments as well as matters of competence, resources, etc. The framing of the
Constitution itself had this symbolic dimension, as did the question of
support for the United Nations organization have for numbers of concerned
citizens. Issues of dividing authority, or of ironing out relative spheres, are
more likely to be debated than fought over, to the degree they do not call
for complete replacements of one loyalty by another, or require absolutely
exclusive commitments.

In all these cases, the symbolic aspects are important not for their own sake, but as references to more important and meaningful relationships between the citizen, his government and the general political order. Loyalties are not established by a government's producing flags, nor are ceremonies alone sufficient to evoke lasting attachments. But these symbols may evoke pride, deference, honor, as standing for generalized attributes of the regime and the government's performance. What the government does, and how it does it, may affect these sentiments over the long run or after many instances but seldom as the result of one act or program. Scholars have tried to define the less tangible meanings of these symbolic public goods in many ways. The quest is as old as political thought itself, but we shall cite just a few modern attempts at definition and methods of analysis.

Certainly the term *authority* suggests one generalized attribute of the regime to which the citizenry is oriented. Max Weber linked this attribute to citizen sentiments and behavior by the concept of legitimacy, the acceptance of power by followers or subjects as being right, i.e., justified by their sense of political values.[1] He was especially concerned with how this legitimacy was engendered by the kind of performance in leadership roles in the political system. He viewed charismatic leadership as generating profound political loyalties, a 'do or die' devotion based on beliefs in the magic or 'grace' of the leader. Such leadership can serve to re-establish or create political bonds in times of instability or change, yet suffers the problems of long-run erosion. On the other hand Weber viewed political authority based on traditional or on legal-rational authority as more stabilized and less personalized. The latter he considered basic to modern forms of bureaucratic performance, enabling a conditional sort of loyalty based on instrumental ends. Weber, therefore, links his concern with the mode of authority generated by the political system, to the perceptions, roles and performances of followers. Somewhat similar is Seymour M. Lipset's view that the legitimacy of the political system is related to its effectiveness as perceived by its subjects—getting the job done in conformance with their expectations.[2] Again, it is a generalized attribute of governmental performance as assessed by the citizenry.

While this form of public opinion is viewed as having important consequences for the ongoing operation of the polity, it is important to note that it is related to the reactions and beliefs of citizens, not just their material well-being or advantages. It therefore also suggests attitudinal forms of measurement or some sort of inference about the subjective beliefs of citizens.

---

[1] Max Weber, *The Theory of Social and Economic Organization*. Trans. A. M. Henderson and T. Parsons. Edited with introduction by Parsons. (New York: Oxford University Press, 1947), Part III.

[2] Seymour Martin Lipset, *Political Man* (Garden City: Doubleday and Company, Inc., 1960), Chap. 3.

Subjective beliefs and values are most emphasized by those scholars who have viewed the symbolic aspects of the political order as important for contributing to the citizen's *sense of identity,* especially in new nations and with transitional societies. Psychological analysis has been employed by Lucien Pye,[3] for example, to assess the amount of trust and rational conduct among civil servants, concluding that modernizing nation-states must resolve the conflicts in identity of its leaders before the stability and effectiveness of the system can be assured. Daniel Lerner[4] and Leonard Doob[5] have similarly explored the problems of developing nations through the socio-psychological expectations of their subjects. Perhaps the most profound exploration in depth of the sense of political identity was done by Robert J. Lifton[6] concerning the effects of 'brainwashing' in China. Following the psychoanalytic theories of identity, especially as developed by Erik Erikson,[7] Lifton concludes that the political aspects of identity are deeply embedded in the human psyche and that their deliberate and systematic transformation by the Communists created profound disturbances in the victims. This extreme case serves to underscore the relevance of psychological measures for understanding the nature of political loyalty and its relationship to authority and legitimacy in the political system.

But we can also observe many other behavioral indications of the central importance of political loyalty in a variety of political settings. Governments do expend much effort to encourage or delimit loyalties. In the police state or military dictatorship a great deal of governmental effort is directly related to containing disloyalty. Countless subjects have lost their lives as enemies of the regime, or have been imprisoned as political prisoners for behavior judged disloyal. In times of tension, even jokes ridiculing the authorities can put a subject in prison, and writers, publicists or articulate intellectuals are very frequently subject to suspicion, censorship, trial, imprisonment or banishment for their expression of dissenting ideas. Many an unhappy chapter has been written in the lives of every nation involving such episodes. Even the United States has legally documented this fearfulness, with the Alien and Sedition laws by the embattled Federalists and, in this century, with many state and federal anti-subversive

---

[3] Lucian W. Pye, *Politics, Personality, and Nation-Building* (New Haven: Yale University Press, 1962).

[4] Daniel Lerner, *The Passing of Traditional Society* (Glencoe, Ill.: The Free Press, 1958).

[5] Leonard W. Doob, *Communication in Africa* (New Haven: Yale University Press, 1961); *Becoming More Civilized* (New Haven: Yale University Press, 1960); and, *Patriotism and Nationalism* (New Haven: Yale University Press, 1964).

[6] Robert J. Lifton, *Thought Reform and the Psychology of Totalism* (New York: W. W. Norton and Company, Inc., 1961).

[7] Erik H. Erikson, *Childhood and Society* (New York: W. W. Norton and Company, Inc., 1950).

laws aimed at advocacy of alien ideologies and seditious utterances. Totalitarian regimes have had far more devastating purge trials; most recently we have witnessed Communist China's great 'cultural revolution' apparently aimed both at dislodging 'reactionary' officials and redefining patriotic beliefs for the younger generation. Thus, official political doctrines as enunciated by leaders, as well as legislation, court cases and public records, serve as important sources for assessing such general symbolic goods in the form of definitions, proscriptions and exhortations.

And we can also measure some of the quantitative or performance dimensions of public programs as symbolic dimensions of public goods, where they are regarded by citizens as reflecting general attributes of the nation and regime. The publicity, display and parading of weaponry has come to symbolize the power of one's own nation versus those abroad; a source of pride in the militant or nationalist regime, especially. Many developing countries today want to display their progress in industrialization by great dams and hydroelectric works, factories, farm machinery and the like, as the Soviet Union did in its early years, because these are the major efforts and concerns of their governments. All programs and activities in this sense have their symbolic aspects, i.e., effects upon the citizen, but our concern here should be with the actual consequences of symbols and not merely our own speculation about various personal meanings of political events.

Status Issues

Not all symbolic issues are concerned with such generalized matters as loyalty, nor are all allocative and distributive issues matters of material benefits and pure rationality. Symbolism is intertwined in all these processes but in somewhat different ways. We cannot fully understand what takes place in resource allocation and distribution processes and outcomes without taking account of the symbolic aspects and symbols. And so we will attempt to unravel these connections. It will not be easy so we beg your patience and indulgence.

As we have seen, the issues of allocation involve competing uses of social resources, while issues of distribution involve division of the benefits and costs that are created. There are non-material aspects to such distributive issues. Men seek social status or high regard as well as income and they concern themselves in different ways over correct behavior and beliefs. For example, this finds expression in movements for equality and rights of various sorts, most recently with the Negro civil rights movement and demands of the past decade in the United States. While the Negro certainly wants a greater share of the nation's material benefits in the form of jobs, education, better housing, security, etc., he is also concerned with these distributive benefits as they symbolize his recognition, regard or status as a full-fledged citizen in the society. The most eloquent Negro plea is for full citizenship, for respect, for manhood. This plea is a highly emotional one because it is so fundamental. It is only partially conveyed by getting a somewhat better job, a slightly higher salary or even being able to command high incomes as do some sports heroes and stars. Rather the claim is full and free recognition as an equal human being, commanding the same treatment white men accord one another. The slights of everyday life can be even more burdensome than the poverty. Probably the demand for recognition is so frustrating, too, because it cannot be readily accomplished by passing laws. Civil rights laws alter the formal status of the Negro as a citizen, enabling him to vote and to sit in a restaurant, but they cannot easily alter the feelings of the white man who administers election laws or the white bigot who runs a restaurant. The white man can offend the Negro through such subtle means that the Negro may wish he never entered the restaurant. Daily courtesies and attitudes cannot be readily legislated in any system.

When men struggle to maintain or achieve status, and evoke moral judgments, they do more than struggle over more or less income and material goods. Many of the most intense and long drawn-out political battles are over these status and morality matters. They occur not only over racial relationships, as in this country, Britain, or South Africa today; but among language groups, as in Belgium, Canada and India; and generally among a variety of cultural sub-groups, including ethnic, religious, nationality and sectional cultures. The Civil War in the United States certainly had its allocative and distributive aspects as many historians have noted, but the intense feelings about that war can only be accounted for by viewing the struggle as one deeply involved with rights, obligations and statuses.

A man's esteem and standing in the world is a precious thing; when it is demeaned he is likely to do battle. As a political issue it can be intensely divisive in terms of hostility, resistance, conflict. The general norms of fair play, reciprocity, give and take, are not so likely to prevail. The sense of solidarity of the offended group may be turned against the legitimacy of the system itself, or against the integrity of incumbent authorities.

Social status is a distributive good because it entails the ranking of men into higher and lower categories. Some individuals and groups are accorded greater deference than are others. We know this from personal experience; we not only evaluate others but are in turn thus evaluated by others. Political systems participate in this ranking by according greater or less recognition upon its members and by differential treatment as noted previously. Officials reflect different status values in both formal and informal ways; citizens receive differential accord in a variety of roles and group memberships. In the United States, for example, it has been typical for the white Anglo-Saxon Protestant to reap more such rewards and accord than others. And the higher the formal position, the more difficult its attainment by those possessing the less honored social attributes. In Britain the upper-class has been honored far beyond all other classes. A degree from Cambridge or Oxford counts for much more and is found more frequently among top officials than a degree from a provincial university. In the Soviet Union, officials like to advertise their worker or peasant backgrounds, but different leaders have tended again to reward some regions and subgroups more highly than others, in appointment policies and various other attentions.

As times change, new groups do tend to receive greater recognition from governments. In Massachusetts, for example, the Anglo-Saxon patricians have been succeeded in significant numbers by Irish and Italian politicians. In this country we have elected a Catholic President, installed a Negro cabinet member and Supreme Court Justice, and members of other racial and ethnic groups have attained many other offices. So too have there been changes in Britain and other countries. But there have also been racial and religious pogroms, exclusion and persecution of a variety of subgroups. We cannot posit any necessary law of progress here.

Again, we may note that status and esteem may be best assessed subjectively, by psychological and attitudinal measures. The attitude survey is especially useful for exploring distributive patterns, if the instruments and methods are sufficiently sensitive and objective. But one should also look for other empirical measures, in laws and official actions; in the activities and situations of citizens. We have especially noted the patterns in attaining political office. There are many other such indicators which can be gleaned from the public records of political systems and from systematic observation and accounts of events.

Morality Issues

A morality issue or good is characterized by a judgment of the rightness or wrongness of a person's behavior or beliefs and values. Everyone makes moral judgments of others' activities because such judgments are inescapable. In the United States, for example, one hears some people exalt work, saving, property, 'minding one's own business' and condemn laziness, lack of discipline, loose sexual mores, and slothful or indolent behavior. Usually it is the more substantial strata who make these moralistic judgments about 'lower class' elements who have yet to be fully assimilated. One finds this sort of phenomena in most nations; it is not unique to the United States.

Morality is a substantial part of symbolic goods, processes and issues. Politics are often seen not so much as matters of adjustment and compromise as matters of right and wrong, of moral and immoral distinctions. Very nearly any aspect of life can be so regarded at some time by someone. Typical issues involve sexual behavior, crime, alcohol and drugs, dress, religion, language and aesthetics. Not infrequently these form a syndrome of related issues and values; nor should this be unexpected. If one has strong views about one issue, he is expected to have strong views about the others. As a result, these views often reinforce one another to produce very deeply felt values and beliefs. Those who take the 'wrong' views are thought to be worthy of contempt and punishment. They must be eradicated from society, severely controlled or closely watched; if they are not, they will bring society to ruin.

The opponent is not viewed as a competitor but as the devil incarnate, or the enemy of decent people. Those leaders who take on the devil in combat are highly honored for their fearless conduct and often feel a profound sense of self-righteousness. Those who, like the police, control deviants, are viewed as heroes. Symbolic gestures of contempt, control and indignation are highly prized for they show recognition of evil and, symbolically at least, attack it. The indignant person, at times, seems more concerned with expression of his anger and fears than he does with instrumental and rational control of the persons and things he loathes. But that is not completely irrational because the symbolic actions may indeed end in highly successful repressive controls. The temperance movement in the United States did succeed in enactment of an amendment to the Constitution; its repeal has not removed all the social strictures against liquor consumption, nor all the legal restrictions either.

Often we find political scientists believing that the only sources of status and moralistic politics are the more fundamentalist groups of the Right. Actually, few groups have managed to avoid being fanatics on status and moral issues. Each of us has both his instrumental as well as emotive and symbolic concerns and issues. No citizen can avoid—nor do we believe should even attempt to avoid—expressive action. To list a few of the symbolic-expressive issues and movements in history should suggest the wide range of groups involved at one time or another. Socialist parties have been highly moralistic and indignant movements—at least until they come into power and contend with so many instrumental issues and problems. Populist groups of the latter nineteenth century in the United States are another case in point, viewing as they did the vested interests as immoral exploiters. The Nazis had their own brand of moral fanaticism, and many dictatorships in traditional systems have decreed strict moral rules. A great many professors have viewed the world through highly moralistic lenses in which the good and bad played their historic roles out to some conclusion, not unlike western movies. Practically all religious groups have identified moral issues in politics, and politicians frequently invoke some crusading fervor against the moral dangers of their times.

The range of moral issues is about as inclusive as life itself. All choices in political systems can, no doubt, be viewed or translated into moral questions although some areas appear to lend themselves to this translation more easily and frequently than others. Try identifying some of the times and partisans of the following issues, in this country alone:

crime   liquor consumption
communism   religious education
Catholicism   school prayers
anti-semitism   civil liberties (speech, press,
corruption   assembly, arrest, etc.)
religious symbols   immigration and immigrants
fluoridation   blue laws
housing restrictions   miscegenation
    and zoning   sexual conduct
education principles   national flag
languages   nudism
racial integration   personalities of leaders
obscenity   civics textbooks

What about some hypotheses and empirical tests? Are moral issues most likely to occur in societies which have strongly repressive cultures, i.e., values and beliefs which stress disciplined behavior and negative sanctions to control wrongdoing? Is behavior viewed more tolerantly in less repressive societies and sanctioning accordingly minimized? Do societies with powerful religious traditions tend to be more moralistic than the less religious, or do the more protestant types of religions tend to be more restrictive than non-protestant faiths? Have morality or issues thereof been a more prominent feature of western Protestant countries than most other nations? Are 'live and let live,' 'give and take,' 'to each his own,' more popular aphorisms in some kinds of societies rather than others? Is it the case that some western nations have endured democracy less as a commitment to certain moral rules than to the free play of allocative and distributive issues without such punitive consequences? Or do all systems require some strong moral strictures? Again, we suggest both attitudinal and behavioral measurement, but frankly acknowledge a great problem in such measures for effective comparison. Until critically assessed, however, theories about moralism in politics must be handled with care, and not simply as a cover for one's own biases.

Resolution of Symbolic Issues

When the resolution of differences is defined in terms of quantitative benefits or costs it is possible to compromise by either redistributing existing supplies or creating more for all, but when a good or issue is specified in terms of 'right or wrong,' resolution is not so easily attained through addition or division. How can citizens whose beliefs about 'right' are at issue compromise their respective convictions? How can citizens divided over an obscenity issue devise an acceptable solution? How can a race who believes itself naturally superior to another devise a set of relationships that is acceptable to the 'inferior' group? Issues such as these try the souls of politicians caught in their midst. Compromise solutions require extraordinary imagination on the part of leaders and usually some diminution of intensity or commitment on the part of the involved citizenry. Imagination and diminution of passion are not always forthcoming, and acts of force and violence often mark these issues, across all nations. Seldom are there passionate conflicts over purely material allocative and distributive issues, for few men find it meaningful to risk their lives over a matter of subsidies, the income tax, or highway construction. But men have battled and died throughout history over religion, national honor, personal status, civil rights, moral behavior.

The extraordinary power of these symbolic issues is thus demonstrated by the greater incidence of violence in their resolution than is the case with purely material distributive problems. It is also illustrated when groups which have common or complementary economic or material interests are unable to coalesce because symbolic differences prevail. Poor whites and blacks in the United States probably could materially benefit by a political coalition, but no such direct coalition has been established. Hindus and Muslims in India have taken countless lives over religious beliefs when they might have cooperated to improve their meager existence. Obviously they have not done this because religion is regarded as far more important than their standard of living. In 1966 the world heard of a riot by more than 100,000 Hindus protesting the slaughter of India's sacred cows. The army had to use force to quell the demonstrations. Numerous race riots in the United States have been set off by some perceived insult or injury on the part of a white police officer toward Negroes. An international diplomatic incident was caused in India a few years ago when the family of the American ambassador named its cat after a religious figure. Diplomats have shown their hostility toward other nations by walking out of conferences and national ceremonial events. The elaborate social courtesies of international diplomacy are taken most seriously by all nations. When they are breached, serious consequences may follow. A careful reading of the newspapers each day will produce numerous incidents of national and racial slights, apologies, retributions, etc. While such symbolic behavior may have been more significant during the era of aristocratic monarchies we would be foolhardy to demean them today. The democracies and the newer communist societies have no doubt reduced and altered the forms of etiquette, but etiquette continues to provide both ludicrous and important issues and events.

Case Studies in Political Symbolism

A few case studies are offered in the interests of concreteness for those who would like to see efforts to apply major propositions to actual events.

These case studies have been selected to illustrate our points in a number of different contexts: religious symbols in a medium size northwestern city of the United States; traditional political symbolism in an industrialized democracy; revolutionary symbolism in the context of a stable totalitarian state; and the evolving symbolism of a newly-developing state. We hope in time there will be more effective means of systematic assessment of the symbolic dimension across issues and societies.

Case Study #1   The Cross Issue in Eugene, Oregon

This case concerns the display of the Christian cross, public property and an issue of religion and state. Sometime in 1964 a University of Oregon fraternity and a group of local businessmen arranged to have a 90-foot lighted concrete cross constructed and erected on a bluff in a city park overlooking the city of Eugene, Oregon. The cross was erected without the previous legal permission of the city council, although the council retroactively approved the project. The cross—given its height and bright lighting—was visible at night for many miles around the city. Its presence immediately provoked an intense and widespread interest since some opponents claimed it was offensive to non-Christians and was placed on public property, a clear violation, in their opinion, of the American tradition and law concerning the separation of church and state. A subsidiary criticism related to the cross being placed on city property without formal permission of the city government. Others fiercely upheld their right to view and be comforted by a symbol which meant so much to them.

Various interest groups formed both in defense of and against the cross, public meetings were held, and countless letters to the local newspaper were published establishing the pros and cons of the issue. Subsequently, the dissidents made a legal issue of the matter and in the summer of 1966 it began its way through the court system for adjudication.

This brief account of the incident suffices to illustrate one way in which a highly symbolic issue can arise and be handled. Religious issues are typically very emotional because they involve a person's deepest beliefs, commitments, and relationships to the ultimates of human life and its meanings. Those who wrote letters to the editor defending the cross on public lands did so with the most profound convictions. They could not easily appreciate how a religious symbol such as a cross in a Christian nation could possibly be controversial. For anyone to derogate the cross or question the legal proprieties of its location was incomprehensible. Such critics must be atheists, communists or both. On the other hand, the dissidents tended to be somewhat snobbish in their worldliness and contempt for the 'little old ladies in tennis shoes,' for fundamentalists and believers in religious over secular law. Neither group was very willing to listen genuinely to the other.

The city council voted its support of the cross with but one dissenting vote. They also, as practical politicians, attempted to find compromise solutions, but the nature of the issue, as we have said, makes compromise difficult. One such compromise was to light the cross only on religious holidays rather than every night of the week as was the original intention of the sponsors. The fact that the cross was less visible made it less offensive to those who disapproved of its presence, while the retaining of the cross, itself, at least partially satisfied defenders of the faith. Then, too, costs of electricity were paid for by private persons and not the city government. Various defenders pointed out that an old wooden cross of much less grandeur had occupied a similar position for years and no one complained. Apparently size and lighting created a problem of visibility and intensified symbolic responses.

Logically, the critics should be against any cross—no matter how small —on the property. But they were not. One wonders whether a further reduction of the conspicuousness of the cross would have been an effective solution to the problem. Practical solutions may be provided for symbolic issues, but they require finesse. Separation of church and state has, of course, been a great compromise of a symbolic issue for many nations for hundreds of years, so symbolic issues do have solutions and sometimes very mundane ones. The bussing of Negro and white students in order to establish different racial relationships is another example of an indirect quantitative 'solution' to a highly emotive symbolic issue. The specific ratios and distances involved are the variables politicians and citizens can and do alter in order to achieve mutually acceptable decisions. But often resolutions of contentious symbolic issues are difficult because a people cannot easily have a little more or a little less of the valued symbol; a little more or less of religion is usually not feasible among believers and non-believers.

While the cross issue was, and remains, primarily a moral rather than distributive or status problem, aspects of the latter were involved. Casual impression suggests that many of those who supported the cross on public property were lower-income religious people, and elderly retired persons, while those who opposed tended to be middle- and upper middle-class, essentially non-religious persons, of considerable education. Like all issues this one had its intermingling of other types of issues and unstable coalitions of unlike people with but partially shared interests and values. There were also some very high income, high status and educated persons allied with fundamentalists, those with lower incomes, and anti-communists, in supporting the cross. As so often happens, such coalitions infrequently meet face to face; if they did, maintenance of the alliance might prove difficult.

Religious issues will continue to play an important part in the political processes of the United States. How often they become intensely divisive remains to be seen.

Case Study #2   Traditional Symbolism in an Industrialized Nation

We now consider a situation quite different from the previous case study; we wish to describe the highly integrative symbolism of monarchy (a traditional or feudal element) in an industrialized and democratic nation—Britain. The case is interesting because of the seemingly disparate elements, and yet the success of such symbolism in making Britain a most cohesive nation is beyond doubt.

The British monarchy is ancient and highly institutionalized. Its attendant ceremonial pageantry is a focal point of the nation and its traditions, and likely to be so for a long time even though the monarch has little effective political power. The monarchy is a symbol in itself, a symbol of the nation and empire or Commonwealth, as it is now termed. The maintenance of monarchy is a treasured element of the conservative notion of social life and so fortifies the loyalty of conservative citizens, which includes most in the upper-classes, significant portions of the middle-classes and a smaller percentage of 'Tory workers.' All those who appreciate national traditions, unity, duty, social deference among the classes, are reassured by the monarchy. The behavior of the monarch is therefore of the greatest importance in maintaining respect. Consequently, one finds that monarchs and their families are closely circumscribed in their manners and behavior in order not to offend anyone. The Queen devotes much of her daily schedule to participation in symbolic integrative activities including charity work, dedications, the honoring of various hallowed institutions and those activities that are regarded as legitimate and require support. The British monarchs have not engaged in direct policy-making or politics for a long time since that would make them controversial and thereby reduce their widespread appeal as unity symbols among citizens who are otherwise divided sharply over issues. A factor in its success is the magnificent pageantry that accompanies the monarch's doings, the great visibility and drama of unusual dress, ceremony and courtesy. The coronation is above all else a ceremonial occasion in which all of Britain may partake in the national life. The very rarity of these coronations makes them the more valuable and moving. The mystery of power, the majesty of authority, the beauty of the occasion, all make the coronation memorable and meaningful to those whose daily lives may well be rather drab existences.[8]

We do not wish to speculate too much about the psychological meanings of monarchy, but it would seem unrealistic to claim that such institutions are meaningless for ordinary men. We have little doubt that the monarchy in Britain fails to 'send' some people and is even actively ridiculed and rejected by others, but such responses have not managed to

---

[8] An excellent exchange of views on the role and significance of the monarchy in Britain may be read in Edward Shils and Michael Young, "The Meaning of the Coronation," *Sociological Review*, 1 (1953), pp. 63-81; and Norman Birnbaum, "Monarchs and Sociologists: A Reply to Professor Shils and Mr. Young," *ibid.*, Vol. 3 (July, 1955), pp. 5-23.

secure a sufficiently powerful appeal to lead to the abolition of the monarchy. In other lands they have.

We should note in closing that Britain has evolved a sharp differentiation of function in politics: that of the Prime Minister performing the daily grind of politics while the symbolic functions are carried out by the Crown. In the United States, on the other hand, one finds the President performing both roles, with interesting consequences, since activities that lead to successful performances in one role may be the complete antithesis of what is required for effectiveness in the other. But we allow you to puzzle your way through the intricacies of instrumental and symbolic roles and behavior.

Case Study #3   Symbolism in a Stable Communist Society

When the Soviet Union came into being, many of the respectable elements of the West were appalled by the norms of the new system and well they might, for the Soviets deliberately reversed basic tenets of Victorian morality and manners. The highly controlled, moralistic beliefs and behavior of the upper middle-class stood in sharp contrast to the 'vulgar' behavior of the equalitarian communist leaders, whom we suspect took their own moral satisfaction in offending the proprieties of the hated bourgeoisie. This was accomplished by crude language, common clothes, elimination of upper-class etiquette, and contempt for the sanctified bourgeois institutions of family, property and business; not to mention Soviet ruthlessness in their suppression of native middle- and upper-classes, as one might expect in such a revolution.

In place of the symbolism of the feudal Czar and westernized upper-classes, the new leaders elevated the symbols of communism: a flag stressing human struggle and solidarity (the red color; the sickle and clenched fist); leaders wearing simple clothes, the strident slogans of revolution and redistribution, of bread and work. Ironically, to most people the word 'communism' was itself offensive with its conflict connotations in a world that believed in 'peaceful' individual competitiveness and inequality. As the Soviet Union became more secure and stable in the world, its symbolism began to be altered. Conventional military symbols became more prominent as did signs of inequality among citizens. So, too, the behavior of Soviet diplomats became impeccable, in the best western traditions. Emphasis upon Russian history rather than the Soviet Union once more became acceptable. Soviet citizens now stress merit and uncommon skills rather than common sacrifice to build the new nation. The leaders in recent years have become less fearsome than Stalin. Indeed, they are almost models of dull respectability. The fire and energy of the first generation of revolutionaries are obviously gone, much to the chagrin of the Chinese communist leaders who want more aggressive policies, actions and symbols.

The Soviet Union is routinizing its symbolic life as have most other stable nation-states. The early aura of an embattled nation seems to have died down considerably during the last decade or so. Newer revolutionary nations make the Soviet Union look stodgy. Perhaps Americans are, therefore, less concerned about the Russians because they see other more menacing enemies still under the influence of revolutionary symbolism.

Some of these broad generalizations might be more concretely illustrated by reference to the verbal symbols contained in the constitutions of the United States and the Soviet Union. Contrast the Preamble of the American Constitution with that of selected articles in "Chapter I" of the Soviet document.

Preamble to the U.S. Constitution

WE THE PEOPLE of the United States, in Order to form a more perfect Union, establish Justice, insure domestic Tranquility, provide for the common defence, promote the general Welfare, and secure the Blessings of Liberty to ourselves, and our Posterity, do ordain and establish this Constitution for the United States of America.

Chapter I. The Social Structure—Constitution of the U.S.S.R.

ARTICLE 1. The Union of Soviet Socialist Republics is a socialist state of workers and peasants.

ARTICLE 2. The political foundation of the U.S.S.R. is the Soviets of Working People's Deputies, which grew and became strong as a result of the overthrow of the power of the landlords and capitalists and the conquest of the dictatorship of the proletariat.

ARTICLE 3. All power in the U.S.S.R. belongs to the working people of town and country as represented by the Soviets of Working People's Deputies.

ARTICLE 12. Work in the U.S.S.R. is a duty and a matter of honor for every able-bodied citizen, in accordance with the principle: "He who does not work, neither shall he eat."

The principle applied in the U.S.S.R. is that of socialism: "From each according to his ability, to each according to his work."

If our constitution were stated in Soviet terms we might find some amusing translations. For example, Article I might read "The United States of America is a capitalist state of managers and stock-holders." You might try your hand at substituting American phrases for the crucial Soviet terms.

Case Study #4   Political Symbolism in the Newly-Developing Nations

Many commentators on the newly-developing areas have noted a certain impatience and sense of inferiority on the part of their leadership as they incessantly compare themselves with the western world. A defensiveness appears in many forms; for example, such countries as Indonesia, Ghana, Brazil and Egypt have all engaged in great and expensive construction projects including vast universities, airports, airlines and industrial works that go well beyond rational economic requirements. Such modernized investments are of little utility where complementary investments have not been provided for in a systematic way. One result has been that the investments are frequently underemployed. They appear to foreign observers as monuments to folly. That they are created is more explainable in terms of symbolic achievement. Vast construction projects are a sign of modernization, a visible symbol that the new state can command the techniques or assets of modernity.

Still another interesting symbolic aspect of these societies is the continuing presence of highly expressive emotive and often traditional symbols representing older ways of life and of authority in particular. Western-educated leaders frequently wear traditional and elaborate dress, especially on ceremonial occasions, and often revert to other older customs also. Traditional dress and habit, of course, honor the past and the elders, while attempts at modernization represent the new and the aspirations that will one day supplant the older tribal or traditional way of life. Still, the ancient beliefs and traditions will continue to play their roles and sometimes in very amusing situations as the following newspaper item from the *Eugene Register-Guard* (Aug. 6, 1963) relates:

> Nigeria's 221-pound labor minister with responsibility for sports engaged the services of a rain doctor Tuesday to ensure there will be no downpour Saturday night when Dick Tiger defends his world middleweight boxing title against Gene Fullmer.
>
> Minister Joseph Modups Johnson will drive around the town with a local medicine man to "persuade people he is on our side," he told newsmen.
>
> This is Nigeria's rainy season and when it rains in Nigeria it really rains.
>
> "People aren't buying tickets because they think the fight will be washed out," the minister said. "Of course I don't believe in rain doctors myself but there are still a lot of Nigerians who do."
>
> Johnson said it was customary for Nigerians to engage a rain doctor on the eve of a wedding to make certain there was good weather for a ceremony.
>
> "I did it myself," he recalled. "It still rained but at least guests could not blame me."

Traditional societies then embrace the symbolism of past, present and future but in quite different ratios. Some still emphasize the past (usually the more conservative) while others (usually the revolutionary regimes) emphasize the present and future. Thus, left-wing dictatorships in China and Cuba wage immense and costly campaigns to build for the future. The entire society is mobilized to work at an intensified rate in an effort to catch up to the western nations. Leaders constantly promote gigantic collective goals and add their exhortations for the costly mobilization of resources. The labor, idealism, enthusiasms and skills of youth are especially important here, and leaders are anxious to tap these valuable resources. Personal involvement in highly emotional collective enterprise is the goal. Nations need not be left-wing dictatorships to promote these activities but they tend to be so at present. In an earlier day, Nazi Germany attempted such mobilization; today, we find Israel encouraging its youth to sacrifice, work on the collective farms, and become imbued with nationalism and service to the nation rather than personal success. One finds similar sorts of endeavor for idealistic youth in the western systems—the Peace Corps and civil rights movements, for example, but seldom so pervasive or so manipulable in these established political systems.

Political symbolism in the newly-developing areas is fascinating because it is intended to be so expressive and all-pervading in social life. Western European symbolism tends to be far more lofty, more traditional and deferential than emotive and expressive. In transitional systems aspiring leaders and citizens alike expect and permit a degree of expressiveness that most western leaders do not. The flamboyance, affectivity and demonstrativeness allowed among some Latin or African leaders, for example, tends to be embarrassing to Englishmen and Americans. When President Johnson embraced the President of Mexico he pleased Mexicans but probably made Americans uneasy. The five-hour 'harangues' of a Sukarno or Castro would be intolerable in the United States where being 'businesslike'—meaning rational, unemotional, instrumental, controlled and 'to the point'—are highly valued forms of behavior. Historically, democracy was established in a 'legal-rational' kind of normative and symbolic environment; it will be interesting to watch the development of democracy in highly expressive societies.

Individual Behavior and Symbolic Issues

Our generalizations and case studies on symbolism in the polity and symbolic issues aid us in understanding political cultures. But it does not complete the description or explanation. We have need for more systematic data on individual perceptions and behavior in connection with symbolic objects. As is usual, we are forced to rely mostly upon studies of a few countries where extensive opinion surveys have been carried out. The findings may be representative of people elsewhere, but we cannot be sure until further cross-national study is done.

Several propositions might be more carefully investigated. The *first* is do the voters make clear-cut distinctions along the lines that we have, i.e., consciously contrast material and symbolic issues, or are they part and parcel of the same phenomenon for the average voter? *Second,* to the degree they are distinguishable, have the material, self-interest issues involving policies on resource allocation and the distribution of benefits in the past appeared to exercise greater influence over the outcomes, than symbolic issues? *Third,* do voters have a high level of accurate information about the nature of very many issues, or do they tend to entertain a few very general considerations but are unable to articulate them clearly? *Fourth,* it has been found that large percentages (half or more) of the voters are unable to determine the positions of political parties on basic issues of the campaigns, so are they able to decide which party is closest to their own preferences in public policy in any precise way, or do they have more or less coherent belief systems about which party is more favorable on the general issues of public policy and governmental performances? *Fifth,* do voters assign greater importance to symbolic issues when material issues diminish in salience? *Sixth,* do voters seem to differ more sharply over the symbolic issues and much less so on economic or material issues?

The findings may even reveal that symbolic issues do not create highly intense sentiments; rather, in terms of voting, the surveys may tend to elicit differences among citizens as party members, where overall integrative symbols are not as salient. This is well illustrated by a rather ingenious set of graphs designed by a British political scientist to measure the extent of partisan cleavage among British citizens. Figure 4-1 depicts the cleavages over a range of twenty-two issues of which twelve are labeled as 'humanitarian-liberal' and 'foreign affairs' or roughly symbolic in our terms; the remaining issues (13-22 on the graphs) are economic or material issues. Issue number 1, for example, was capital punishment; number 2 was corporal punishment; number 10 dealt with opinions on South Africa. Number 13 concerned the level of taxation; while the issue which created the greatest cleavage was number 22 on whether the government or the trade unions were responsible for the increase in the cost of living. It is quite clear that economic issues were the source of greatest differences during the years of these issues (1959-61).

Of course, symbolic issues may be said to have dominated during certain periods, e.g., the McCarthy era (1950-54) in America with its emphasis on communism and subversion. Any symbolic issue may be extraordinarily contentious; the Dreyfus Affair in France before World War I was one dramatic case. During one period of American history slavery was an enormously important symbolic issue, dividing the nation for several decades until a civil war produced a resolution. And today civil rights and the race problems, or 'law and order,' are again the predominant concern of most American citizens. Some scholars believe that symbolic issues are most

Figure 4-1

Conflict and Consensus on Issues in Great Britain (1959-61)

Proportion of electors of the two main parties favouring a right-wing (or pro-government) answer on individual issues

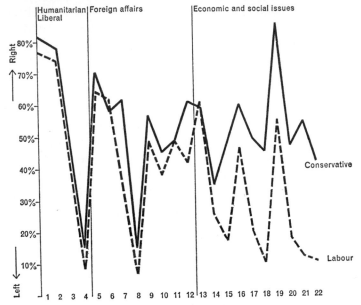

Percentage variation from the average proportion of electors favouring a right-wing (or pro-government) answer

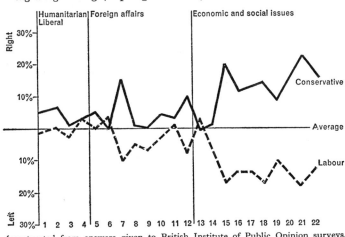

(constructed from answers given to British Institute of Public Opinion surveys, 1959–61)

Source: Jean Blondel, *Voters, Parties, and Leaders: the Social Fabric of British Politics* (Baltimore: Penguin Books, Inc., 1963), p. 78.

likely to appear during times of affluence; their evidence is not always formidable or convincing. Since symbolic issues of status, morality and patriotism are rarely found in pure and isolated form, it is exceedingly difficult to measure their independent frequency and impact. Until precise distinctions are systematically applied, we cannot identify the conditions of symbolic issues.

Symbolic Issues and Rationality

A reading of Chapters 3 and 5 will probably leave most readers with a rather distinct impression that people and nations are quite rational political beings, in the sense of knowing what they want and how to get it. Such a reading would be erroneous as well as superficial, but we concede that the tenor of the present chapter would suggest the opposite case. An equally superficial reading of this chapter would probably suggest to many readers that we believe voters are quite irrational when symbolic issues come to the fore. Perhaps we should clarify the matter of different types of issues, processes and the possibilities of rational behavior in dealing with them.

We emphatically do *not* believe that men are purely rational or purely irrational; nor do we believe that men are rational about some political problems (such as allocation, distribution and regulation) and irrational about still others, such as loyalty, status and moral concerns. The events and problems of political life do not sort themselves out into such neat non-overlapping categories. No one is purely rational and few are purely irrational under all conditions. No issue is solely symbolic or instrumental. We attain some degree of rationality depending upon a whole host of conditions, many of which we cannot as individuals control. Some of these conditions of rationality are fairly well known to social scientists. Advice is given in Chapters 12 and 13 on becoming more rational in a political order, but for the present we limit ourselves to generalizations concerning types of issues and the possibilities of greater or less clarity about the kinds of public goods over which citizens and leaders may contend. We are indebted to Lane and Sears' very useful summary; they in turn are indebted to a generation of social psychologists, survey analysts and experimental psychologists, who have worked on similar programs involving cognition and perception. Lane and Sears set forth conditions which we believe are useful for reflecting upon the possibilities of rational action on the kinds of issues we have discussed throughout these last four chapters.[9]

1. The more vague the referents of the issue, the greater the tendency toward irrationality.

---

9 Robert E. Lane and David O. Sears, *Public Opinion* (Englewood Cliffs, N.J.: Prentice-Hall, Inc., 1964), Chap. 7.

2. The more remote and difficult the consequences are to assess, the greater the room for irrationality.

3. The more abstract the terms of the issue, the greater the tendency toward irrationality.

4. Issues dealing with matters commonly repressed invite irrationality.

5. Socially 'unpopular' views are more likely to stimulate irrationality in others.

6. Issues that pertain to people, as distinct from more purely instrumental matters, will encourage irrationality.

Most, if not all, of these conditions should be reasonably self-evident; however, a few words about them may help. Concerning 1: A vague issue is one which permits people to entertain almost any sort of view of how it relates to reality where there is little explicit information on what the relevant facts may be. One cannot then disprove a person's views. Number 2 should be familiar enough; one finds it difficult to assess alternative policies when the consequences of each choice are so distant and indirect. A policy is expected to have certain consequences, but what are they? The average citizen views many of the policies of his government as distant and indirect in their impacts upon him. Again he can entertain less than pure rational conceptions. Proposition 3 suggests that most citizens cannot reason well outside of the concrete problem areas. Political issues of all types, but more often the symbolic ones, offer many purely abstract formulations for the citizen. In such cases the citizen is more likely to take the position which is personally satisfying on other grounds. Less rational needs and identifications may come to the fore here. Number 4 is an interesting constraint on rationality if one views morality issues as emotively charged with deep feelings of sin and guilt. When the issues concern behavior considered to be socially or morally unacceptable, fears and anxieties may be expressed with intolerant or repressive reactions. Sex and violence are such subjects of taboos; the result is a good deal of irrationality about how to control these tendencies and what we think about people who do not share our apprehensions. Socially unpopular positions also draw irrational responses from citizens, as witness the treatment frequently accorded the political heretic whether in the United States, the Soviet Union, China, or elsewhere. Lane and Sears seem to think that both conditions 4 and 5 are based upon the unconscious elements of our personalities. A hatred of communism, for example, may be based upon a hatred of authority which, in turn, is based upon a hatred of one's father. The consequences of communism are therefore not rationally apprehended by such a person. The last condition (6) says that we tend toward greater irrationality when we confront personalized symbols, including various ethnic, religious and racial groups, than we do in dealing with straightforward instrumental issues or problems that do not involve our direct identifications and stereotypes. Feelings of trust and distrust tend to crowd out the direct consideration of positions and proposals. Polls have shown that many American voters during the 1950s felt a certain distaste for Richard Nixon but could not state its basis. Nor could those who felt deeply grieved by the death of President Kennedy any more easily define the loss. If rationality means the objective assessment of a situation, these then are the irrational aspects of politics.

We are inclined to think that being rational even about allocative and distributive problems is exceedingly costly, but that if objectivity and controlled emotions are to be achieved by the individual, he is more likely to do so on these problems than he is on those which tend to evoke more purely symbolic issues. We shall see that regulatory issues fall somewhere in between. But there is no point in being dogmatic about these distinctions. Some men can be quite as irrational (hopefully not so many now) about balancing the national budget. Others treat the gold reserve of the nation as a great symbol of something or other. Some citizens no doubt believe strongly that a sales tax or income tax is evil; economic issues in our society have often been susceptible to the same irrationality. A few citizens are irrationally fearful that taking more than 25 per cent of the national income for public goods is unthinkable; as we learned in Chapter 2 many nations in fact do, and live very well. We can only conclude that such irrationality can prevail in any area of policy-making. But we also believe that more favorable conditions are encouraged in certain choice situations than others. The more an issue involves expression, taste or basic beliefs and identifications, the more likely it is to provoke non-rational responses.

The fact that this may happen does not mean such issues must be repressed in order to promote rational political behavior. To the contrary, we believe that a fine appreciation of the difficulties involved in achieving some degree of objectivity will aid us in extending the realm of compassionate and intelligent discussion. Self-insight and perspective can be encouraged even when feelings run high; where the nature of intensities and reactions are understood there is greater likelihood of intelligent response. But repression as a means of control only invites the irrational reaction.

While the realm of intelligent analysis ought to be expanded we do not propose to eliminate (even if possible) the affective and expressive symbolism accompanying issues and their resolution. The deepest meanings of politics tap these dimensions, and we generalize them in terms of such ideas as equality, freedom, justice and right. Life would be barren were these concerns absent and the relevance of politics would be reduced to the trivial. Political motivation and aspiration have to do with the symbolic aspects, and differences as to their content and meaning will always be at the heart of political involvement.

Problems and Applications

1. Suppose you were considering a research project on the national flags of the world. What might you ask about them? Why? Can you think of any indicators, indices, measures, that might be employed in your analyses?

2. How can we account for the fact that many citizens will settle for symbolic reassurances concerning political issues rather than actively demand effective resolution of them?

3. Compare the symbolism of the courts and legal processes with those of either a city council, a state legislature, or the Congress. Explain both similarities and variations.

4. If you were asked to prepare a set of campaign speeches for either a Republican or Democratic candidate for the presidency what sort of verbal and other types of symbols would you incorporate into his addresses and behavior? Why?

5. How do you interpret the meaning of the symbols the new revolutionaries have adopted, such as army fatigues, bandoliers, berets, beards, slogans, etc.?

6. Compare the verbal symbols of the American and U.S.S.R. national constitutions. What are the significant differences in language and objects of veneration? What reasons are there for these differences?

7. If you were a Democratic President in favor of a guaranteed annual income for the poor, how would you reassure the conservatives that this was a good idea or policy?

8. Why do the leaders of many nations wear uniforms? You might want to determine which national leaders do and what types they wear before answering the question.

9. Analyze the symbolism of "The Star-Spangled Banner" or some other national anthem.

10. If you like historical studies and library work, try your hand at analyzing the rather intense issue in Canada, especially during the early 1960s, over the design and adoption of a new national flag. How do you suppose Americans would react if proposals were made to adopt a new flag? Why?

11. Discuss the following news item from the *San Francisco Examiner* of Dec. 26, 1966 (p. 35) as a symbolic issue.

COURT BRIEF DEFENDS 'CUSSING OUT' OF COP

Washington—(UPI)—When a policeman grabs you by the back of the belt, it just may be "socially necessary" to yell about it in a string of four-letter oaths.

That's the view expressed by the American Civil Liberties Union in a brief filed with the U.S. Court of Appeals.

The brief contends citizens have the right to make their remarks in as colorful or flagrant a manner as they choose.

It was filed in behalf of a man arrested for disorderly conduct who expressed himself freely and was charged with a second count of disorderly conduct.

The brief notes colorful expletives release aggressiveness "which might otherwise explode in physical violence."

12. In what sense are the following newspaper headlines symbolic issues, and why?

"Palo Alto GOP Group to Honor New Citizens"

"President Salutes Teachers"

"War Victim Denied 'Funeral Support' "

"Spain's Jewry Now May Teach Hebrew"

"Indians Disputing State on Wampum"

"U.S. Upgrades Ties with Bulgarians and Hungarians: Diplomatic Relations Raised from Rank of Legations to Ambassadorial"

"Civil Rights Movement Spurs Interest in Role of Negroes in History"

"Anti-Bigotry Bill Voted in Albany"

Bibliographical Notes

Our problem in these notes stems from plenty rather than scarcity, for interest in symbols and symbolism is widespread among the social sciences. We may begin, however, with a reminder to consult the footnotes for they contain some excellent discussions of various aspects of political symbolism.

As general introductions to the problems considered in the present chapter we suggest Charles E. Merriam, *Political Power*, New York: McGraw-Hill Book Company, Inc., 1934 (now available in a paperback edition, New York: Collier Books, 1964), with special attention being paid to Chapter 4, on "The Credenda and Miranda of Power." With regard to loyalty or national identifications, see Harold D. Lasswell's "World Politics and Personal Insecurity" in *A Study of Power*, Glencoe, Ill.: The Free Press, 1950. In Part 2 on "Symbols" he analyzes not only loyalties, but the demand for other symbolic reassurances including security, equality and supremacy. Older, yet highly insightful analyses, were provided by Walter Bagehot in *Physics and Politics*, New York: Alfred A. Knopf, Inc., 1953, and *The*

English Constitution, New York: Oxford University Press, 1933, where a distinction is made between the "dignified" and the "efficient" roles played by the monarch and prime minister in Britain. These two classics were originally published in London in 1872 and 1867, respectively. Graham Wallas, another distinguished Briton, dealt with symbols in *Human Nature in Politics,* Boston: Houghton Mifflin Company, 1909 (reprinted by Peter Smith, Magnolia, Mass.), but unlike our conception, viewed them as essentially irrational elements in political behavior. Thurman Arnold, a well-known trust-buster of the New Deal days, also viewed symbols as important, and basically non-rational, if not irrational, because they serve to conceal the actions of the powerful and prevent others from being rational in political life. Arnold's book is aptly entitled *Symbols of Government,* New Haven: Yale University Press, 1935.

More recently, two American political scientists have reconsidered the roles of symbolic goods, in theoretical as well as empirical terms. Murray Edelman has written about *The Symbolic Uses of Politics,* New Haven: Yale University Press, 1964, and in particular has emphasized their use as a means of appeasing citizens who demand some policy. Thus, he points out how laws are passed (symbolic) but not strictly enforced, and how preambles to legislation can be used to symbolize concern and 'hoodwink' people into a symbolic reassurance that all will be well once the law is on the books. A former colleague of his, Joseph Gusfield, took the temperance movement as a focal point for his inquiries into moral issues and symbolic politics. In a brief but cogent and well-reasoned volume Gusfield analyzed the movement which ended up in restricting the production and distribution of liquor in this country. *Symbolic Crusade,* Urbana: University of Illinois Press, 1963, is the title of the study. We think you will enjoy reading it even if it suggests that your grandparents may have been more status-conscious in adopting the Prohibition amendment to the Constitution than just concerned with the evils of intoxicating beverages. Nevertheless, we find his sympathy with the plight of declining or threatened status groups in society a more realistic means of understanding some of the fervor of such issues.

Peter Odegard dealt with the same movement but from a quite different perspective; we suggest you consult this old minor classic—*Pressure Politics: The Story of the Anti-Saloon League,* New York: Columbia University Press, 1928. Whereas Gusfield concentrates upon the symbolic meaning of prohibition, Odegard focused on the political strategies and organizational efforts made by the Prohibitionists. They were rather shrewd politicians and utilized the symbolic aspects of their issue very effectively.

Leaders may, as the above citation suggests, use symbols in a highly rational manner, whether by deliberate manipulation or unconscious insight. A variety of studies illustrate this proposition. Walter Lippmann's *Public Opinion,* New York: The Macmillan Company, 1927 (reissued by

The Free Press, 1965), is a classic statement on mental stereotyping and its impact on politics. Frederick L. Schuman's *The Nazi Dictatorship,* 2nd ed., revised, New York: Alfred A. Knopf, Inc., 1936, in Chapters 8-10, has some compelling descriptions of Nazi techniques in converting and mobilizing the masses. In the case of our own country, Vernon Van Dyke has written about the use of our national "race" with the Soviet Union in order to gain support for the United States' space program. The book is *Pride and Power,* Urbana: University of Illinois Press, 1964, a most suggestive title.

Since one of our case studies was on the developing nation-states, we suggest you look over two chapters in *Old Societies and New States,* New York: The Free Press of Glencoe, 1963, edited by Clifford Geertz. Read Geertz's own chapter, "The Integrative Revolution," and David E. Apter's "Political Religion in the New States." One has the feeling after reading such essays that it is easier to note the peculiar symbols of another people than to recognize one's own and their functions. In any case, such studies should enable us to gain greater insight into the contrasting uniqueness of the American political culture. If these two sources are not enough to convince you about the significance of symbolization we suggest that you skim through Lucian W. Pye and Sidney Verba, eds., *Political Culture and Political Development,* Princeton, N.J.: Princeton University Press, 1965. Not only do the editors provide a useful introduction and set of conclusions about comparative cultures, but there are interesting chapters on such countries as Japan, England, Germany, Turkey, India, Ethiopia, Italy, Mexico, Egypt and the Soviet Union, written by authorities on those nations. Not much of this material is cast in terms of this text, but the connections should not be too difficult to establish or at least perceive. Of all the studies of symbolization in the newly-developing states we are inclined to believe that the best one is Herbert Feith's "Indonesia's Political Symbols and Their Wielders," an article found in *World Politics,* XVI (October, 1963), pp. 79-97. The conflict between economic rationality and very real psychological needs is made apparent, as the (then) ruling group under Sukarno opted for the latter course of action in the allocation of resources. As we now know, a reallocation might have saved Sukarno. Symbols can also cost money.

A great deal of the research on symbols is characterized more by its literary quality than by systematic measurement and controlled investigation. Some efforts have, however, been made to reduce the amount of pure speculation as to the meaning of symbols. For the most part this work has been done on verbal symbols, in other words, on language. One such endeavor is "content analysis" and it is characterized by its concern for quantification of language patterns. Content analysis has been applied to such obvious matters as political speeches, propaganda, campaign platforms, Presidential inaugural speeches, communist writings, newspaper columns and editorials, television programs and other forms of communication. The basic idea is to be as exact as possible about who says what to whom and in what way. What the "recipients" of such messages or symbols may believe is also of considerable interest, but this aspect has been explored mostly by psychologists and psychoanalysts. Rorschach tests and thematic apperception tests, for example, have been frequently employed as means of finding out how people interpret the symbols they are confronted with and how these relate to basic concerns. In a political context we suggest reading Robert Lane's *Political Ideology*, New York: The Free Press of Glencoe, 1962, based on an extensive set of interviews with fourteen working-class males from New Haven, Connecticut. For explanations of content analysis you can do no better than consulting the following volumes: Harold D. Lasswell, *et al.*, *The Comparative Study of Symbols*, Stanford: Stanford University Press, 1952; Ithiel de Sola Pool, *Symbols of Democracy*, Stanford: Stanford University Press, 1952; Harold D. Lasswell, *et al.*, *Language of Politics*, New York: George W. Stewart, 1949; and Ithiel de Sola Pool, ed., *Trends in Content Analysis*, Urbana: University of Illinois Press, 1959. These books may not be especially exciting to read, but they are highly instructive on the methods and possibilities of content analysis. Most "political culture" studies could be considerably improved were they to apply such systematic methods. Perhaps the very best model for such research would be David McClelland's *The Achieving Society*, Princeton, N.J.: D. Van Nostrand Company, Inc., 1961, a remarkable comparative study using attitude surveys as well as content analysis and combining these with a variety of other "harder" data on economic and social activity.

Eugene Register-Guard, Nov. 14, 1967,
Eugene, Oregon

ons Hear Woes

The New York Times, Aug. 15, 1967,
New York, New York

The New York Times,
July 6, 1967,
New York, New York

Canada

Annexations
Said Costly

NEWARK RIOT LOSS
PUT AT $10,251,200

COAST HOTELS GET
NEW ASSESSMENTS

Hikes Old
Age Tax

ERAGE TAXES UP
$25 PER PERSON

City Survey Finds 20% Was
in Looted Liquor Stock

Property Re-evaluaion Aids
Hilton, Hurts 2 Others

San Francisco Examiner
& Chronicle,
Dec. 26, 1966,
San Francisco, California

ort Gives Data for State
nd Local Collections
The New York Times,
Aug. 19, 1967,
New York, New York

Property tax relief doubtful
as state fiscal demands mount

Palo Alto Times, June 7, 1967, Palo Alto, California

The New York Times,
June 10, 1967,
New York, New York

The New York Times,
July 27, 1967,
New York, New York

anchers' Threats To Withhold
unds Add Fire To Tax Revolt

NEVADA TO IMPOSE
A MAJOR TAX RISE

Aid on Taxes Is Ba
For Divorced Fa

The Oregonian, Nov. 28, 1967, Portland, Oregon

Sales Levy Set at 3 Cents
—Gamblers Affected, Too

WASHINGTON, July
AP)—The Senate Fi
mmittee approved a H
ssed bill designed to
etter tax break to div
hers on expenses of
.n.

FFLUENT FOUND
TO ACCEPT TAXES

Israel Increases Her Taxes and Will Float Loans

The New York Times, June 5, 1967, New York, New York

udy Says They Don't Cut
Output to Avoid Levies

The New York Times, Nov. 21, 1966,
New York, New York

Canada Tax Study Urges Reforms to Shift
Bigger Load to Firms, High-Income Grou

The Wall Street Journal, Feb. 27, 1967, New York, New York

The Wall Street Journal, Feb. 24, 1967, New York, New York
WASHINGTON —The Treasury's tax-policy
chief sharply criticized a variety of corporate
income-tax rules and practices, including the
advantages a corporation can gain by having
a large number of subsidiaries.

enior citizens — anyone who
hed his 65th birthday
. 31, 1966 — receive seve
ortant advantages on th
nal income tax return
Palo Alto Times, Jan. 13, 1967,
Palo Alto, California

$120-MILLION SPENT
ON 1966 ELECTION

$20-MILLION L
IN CIGARETTE

Income Levies Barred in 2 States

Record for Midterm Ballo
Comes to $2 per Voter
The New York Times, Aug. 19, 1967,
New York, New York

The Wall Street Journal, Nov. 10, 1966,
New York, New York

Smuggling Biggest F
Goodman Tells Co
The New York Times,
Dec. 20, 1966,
New York, New York

ew Dutch Premier Plans
$200-Million Tax Increase
The New York Times, Nov. 29, 1966,
New York, New York

Chapter 5

The Distribution of Costs

In Chapter 2 we dealt with some general problems of resource mobilization and allocation, indicating kinds of choices which would also affect the distribution of benefits and costs. In Chapters 3 and 4 we explored the benefits produced by political systems and concluded, among other things, that distributive inequalities are a major fact of political life. In this chapter we will pursue much the same theme, but through an investigation of the distribution of burdens among the people. Mobilizing and allocating resources to societal goals necessarily entails costs; resources are consumed or used up. The question, then, is: whose resources? Who pays how much of the costs of the maintenance of a political system?

This chapter is concerned with a variety of burdens. Some are *mandatory costs* such as taxes, while others are *participation costs* in the form of money, individual effort and time. And, still others are the indirect and often unintended burdens or 'external' costs experienced by citizens as a result of the decisions or activities of others over whom they have little control. For the sake of convenience, we label these various costs as *external burdens,* and we shall consider them in the order below, with first some thoughts on why these are assessed as costs.

1. formal collective burdens
    a. money costs (fees, taxation)
    b. real costs (land, labor, effort, time)

2. costs of political participation

3. external or indirect costs

Means of Assessment

Acquiring the needed resources can be accomplished, as we have seen, in a variety of ways, including taxation, user-fees, license charges, income from governmental operations and enterprises, eminent domain, lotteries, labor drafts, concentration camps, borrowing, and conquest or exploitation of other nations. Note that we have not included voluntary contributions as a major source. While there are times when citizens may volunteer their services to government, as in wartime, for fire fighting, and other such crises, very few citizens would voluntarily send money to the government on a regular basis, or give a lifetime of uncompensated service to it. One reason nation-states do not get individuals to make regular voluntary contributions is that many of the public goods generated are then freely available to all, including those who would not pay. The generalized products of government do not therefore command automatic prices paid by all those who benefit. One can see the definite temptation for all to want to be freeloaders, but then who would be the producers of such things as law and order, public safety, and so forth? Instead, governments institute compulsory payments and requirements of services and support which quite directly place the burdens of maintaining government on the citizenry. It is unusual to find a nation-state in the world which can muster widespread voluntary support, especially from outside its jurisdiction, as in the case of Israel. During the first three days of the Arab-Israel War of 1967, American citizens contributed some $22 million to the Israeli cause. British citizens offered nearly $17 million, and many citizens of both nations volunteered their services for the emergency.[1] One has to consider here the unusual circumstances and the special ties that Israel has. Occasionally, we read of some lonely soul who bequeaths the United Nations an entire estate, but the very rarity of such gestures makes it newsworthy and causes the more commonsensical person to shake his head in wonderment. In spite of their obvious love and loyalty, most citizens in most countries consider it highly legitimate to reduce their shares of the collective burdens. Compulsion is, therefore, absolutely fundamental to the assessment and distribution of burdens if the society is to enjoy collective goods in the long run. This is particularly the case when some people oppose some ends for which public monies are spent. All of us oppose at least some of the activities of our governments. Some, like folk singer Joan Baez, refuse to pay a portion of their income taxes for supporting the Vietnam war, while others object strenuously to redistributing income to the poor or subsidizing the farmer. Accordingly, some of the most bitterly fought issues involve

---

[1] "Mideast War Brings Unprecedented Jewish Contributions of Funds," *The Wall Street Journal* (June 10, 1967), p. 2.

who will suffer the burdens of supporting the public sector. Complicating the matter is the fact that the resources we contribute to government go, for the most part, into a general fund from whence particular projects are financed. We seldom know precisely what our monies will be spent on in the polity. Only a few programs have special earmarked funds which can be employed only for specified purposes. In contrast, all monies are earmarked in the marketplace, and the buyer pays the costs directly for the enjoyment of his own preferences.

Formal Collective Burdens: Taxation

Commonplace examples of money burdens are relatively easy to list, but their market and political significance is neither simple nor apparent. While we know a great deal about the market repercussions of taxes, we know very little about the political consequences of revenue decisions on the part of governments. We cannot pretend to offer a systematic summary of the economic reactions of people nor need we do so, but it is useful to remind ourselves of the wide range of economic responses because they may, and frequently do, lead to further consequences. Public officials must be concerned with both the economic desirability of altering taxes and their political acceptability.[2] A particular tax program may be highly useful because of its market consequences, but totally unacceptable among certain voter groups. In Table 5-1 we have arranged some typical taxes and their incidence among taxpayers along with some predictions about likely voter attitudes and behavior.

The rough estimates of Table 5-1 simply illustrate the distributive consequences of various common taxes and the likely direction of popular attitudes toward the imposition of each type of burden. While few citizens can escape taxation in the modern state many escape particular taxes either by passing them on to others to pay, or by legal exclusion or exemption. If one does not own property one does not pay property taxes, except those amounts that property holders may be able to pass on in the form of higher rentals. To be sure, many citizens are not fully aware of tax incidences, but there seems to be a rough understanding of who pays most of each general type of tax. Approval appears to rest upon the size of one's income and whether the particular tax reduces that income by notable amounts. Only under dire circumstances are most people generous in approval of greater taxes upon their income and assets. Thus, income taxes tend to be

---

[2] See pages 407-08 for a most interesting account of President Johnson's political considerations in forming his tax policies of 1967.

Table 5-1

Taxes, Tax Incidences, and Political Responses

Tax	Incidence	Probable Political Responses
Progressive Income Tax	According to Ability to Pay	Lower Income Group approval Higher Income Group disapproval
Property Tax	Property Holders and/or Renters	Property Holders disapproval Renters disapproval only where the tax costs are recognized
Sales Tax on Necessities	All who consume necessities, but falls heaviest on lower income groups	Higher Income Receivers approval Lower Income Recipients disapproval Businessmen-collectors disapproval
Excise Tax on Liquor	Consumers of liquor and perhaps the vendors	Moralists approval Users disapproval Sellers disapproval

adopted and increased during popular wars when the need for revenue is particularly pressing. Political man is highly sensitive to taxation and its distribution even though his information levels are minimal.

While taxes are needed by governments to finance their activities and while taxpayers are conscious of the income effects of taxes, both groups are similarly aware of other non-financial uses of taxation. For example, most nations have enacted some tax programs which are designed not to increase the coffers of the government but to control various types of behavior in the community. Heavy taxes on cigarettes, liquor, drugs and firearms are intended not only to produce revenue (which they do in great quantities) but also to control the production and use of these commodities. An intense moralist wants to reduce the consumption of liquor; one way is to make the price prohibitive by a heavy tax. Sulfurous matches were taxed out of production by the United States Government when it was discovered that they were poisonous. We suspect that consumption of alcohol might increase considerably if all taxes were removed from its price. Conversely, the manipulation of tax policies can encourage certain activities, chiefly by reducing rates or increasing exemptions. The oil industry in this country is induced to further explorations of new properties by the simple policy of granting them a tax reduction of 27½ per cent for doing so. Many industrialists have profited from federal tax policies which grant tax reductions for further investment.

One might note that even so otherworldly a group as the churches are not oblivious to the role of taxes as controls and as reductions from their incomes. Many churches have supported the use of taxes to control undesirable behavior, including smoking, drinking and gambling. At the same time, they have lobbied rather successfully in resisting taxation of church properties and religious activities. Churches have been notably successful in all these endeavors in most western democracies, including the United States. In fact, the practice of exempting churches from taxation rolls was started as far back as the fourth century under Emperor Constantine as part of his plan to encourage the spread of Christianity. Edward Fiske, of *The New York Times*, has estimated the value of church tax exempt property in the United States to be about $80 billion.[3] Such a lucrative source of revenue during great scarcities of public revenue is apt to draw the attention of legislators. Most churches may, however, be counted upon to resist taxation.

This discussion raises one of the less recognized questions in political science, namely, the range of types of monetary burdens imposed by different nations. The different methods for levying monetary costs are crucial issues in all nations, yet little comparative political study has been done on

---

[3] "Religion: To Tax or Not to Tax," *The New York Times* (May 28, 1967), p. E-7.

them. We know that different nations have quite different arrangements in this regard. Richard A. Musgrave, a distinguished student of public finance, has found that Latin American nations do not rely on the income tax to the same extent as do the United States and Western European democracies.[4] Latin Americans have come, instead, to depend upon indirect taxes and customs duties, with property taxes falling somewhere between. Taxes on business corporations are also minimized. One obvious conclusion is that the lower-income groups in these countries shoulder a disproportionate share of the burdens.

In the United States chief reliance is placed on the graduated personal income tax, which contributes more than a third of all tax revenues at all levels of government. More than half of the federal government revenues come from this tax, while at state and local levels sales and property taxes supply the major source of resources. Whereas the United States places a heavy dependence on direct taxation (personal and corporate income, property) most Western European democracies and the underdeveloped countries are characterized by a marked preference for indirect taxes, i.e., taxes which are initially levied on one citizen or group but eventually passed on to others to pay. Such taxes include the sales tax, various excises, custom duties and 'turnover' taxes at various stages of the productive and distributive processes. Perhaps 45 per cent of the tax revenue in Europe comes from indirect taxes.[5] Table 5-2 contains data for 16 nations on the matter of direct and indirect tax choices.

As Table 5-2 clearly shows, variations in the tax mix are very great, ranging from a total of 87.7 per cent direct taxes in the United States to a low of 17.7 per cent in the instance of Nigeria. While these figures are quite dated they are not likely to be radically different today in most of these systems. If this is so, how should one account for the considerable variation in tax policies, not only among nations at different stages of economic development but among industrialized nations with similar political systems? The democracies at the head of the table have fairly different combinations of taxes. Yet all these systems in which there is widespread participation in politics tend to have more direct taxes than those with less. Why might this be so?

Distribution of the tax burden depends on the rates imposed as well as the type of tax .The most conspicuous tax in this instance is that on personal income. We can illustrate the considerable variations that existed around the late 1950s for three countries: United Kingdom, Denmark and the United States. Table 5-3 depicts the approximate personal income

---

[4] "Estimating the Distribution of the Tax Burden," in *Problems of Tax Administration in Latin America* (Baltimore: The Johns Hopkins Press, 1965), pp. 31-75.

[5] J. Frederic Dewhurst, *et al.*, *Europe's Needs and Resources* (New York: Twentieth Century Fund, 1961), p. 431.

Table 5-2

Per Capita Income, Direct Taxes as a Percentage of Total Tax Revenue (1948-55)

Country	Average Per Capita Inc.	Direct Taxes as % of Total Tax Rev.
United States	$1,730	87.7%
Canada	1,200	54.0
Sweden	1,040	48.5
New Zealand	960	68.5
Belgium	810	41.5
United Kingdom	740	49.8
France	650	49.1
Netherlands	500	47.1
Chile	370	31.1
Brazil	240	31.5
Costa Rica	230	19.6
Colombia	220	25.7
Mexico	190	22.9
Egypt	130	20.3
Ceylon	120	25.0
Nigeria	80	17.7

From *Poor Lands, Rich Lands, The Widening Gap*, by L. J. Zimmerman. © Copyright 1965 by Random House, Inc. Reprinted by permission.

tax for a married but childless couple in each income group for the three nations. Note that the tax was lower at all levels for the American than for his counterparts. Note, too, that the increase in rates was highest in Britain but that the rates on the lowest income levels are much higher in Denmark than in the United States and Britain. Some interesting political questions are presented by the data of Table 5-3, problems which are by no means easily resolved. For example, how can we account for the considerable variations among these nations in terms of both the absolute amounts of the tax and the rates at which each income level is taxed? Or, we might ask this question: why are the upper income groups willing to pay such high taxes, if they have so much political influence? Perhaps, they are neither willing nor as influential as some believe. Your answers may be as good as those of most political scientists for we are only now beginning to pose questions about the determinants of public policy. Tax policies are an important and interesting place to begin. Elements of a theory or explanation will be forthcoming in subsequent chapters.

Tables 5-2 and 5-3 point up a most difficult research problem—that of producing valid and reliable comparable data for several nations, even for such a quantifiable matter as taxes. Variations in monetary systems, tax

Table 5-3

Approximate Personal Income Tax at Various Income Levels, for a Married Couple Without Children: U.K., Denmark and the U.S., Late 1950s

Income Level	United Kingdom, 1957-1958	Denmark, 1955-1956	United States, 1958
$ 725	—	$ 44	—
1,100	$ 22	90	—
1,400	78	140	$ 10
2,000	225	300	122
2,800	472	625	266
4,300	935	1,200	512
5,600	1,400	2,000	788
7,000	1,975	3,100	1,022
11,200	4,000	5,400	1,940
14,000	6,380	7,600	2,568
28,000	15,620	17,275	7,574
140,000	118,560	121,000	82,524

Source: J. Frederic Dewhurst, *et. al.*, *Europe's Needs and Resources* (New York: Twentieth Century Fund, 1961), p. 435.

legislation, actual incidence and effective rates, all serve to make comparative tax burden studies extremely difficult to conduct. A highly rational person who wished to calculate all his potential tax burdens for a variety of countries before selecting one for his residence would be hard put to locate the relevant information. In most cases, however, the costs of acquiring and interpreting sufficient evidence would probably outweigh the benefits. Yet it is common for cities, states and nations to enact some visible tax inducements for persons and businesses who are potential residents and entrepreneurs. There are some kinds of obvious disparities that the concerned and well-informed group can take advantage of. One case is that of film makers and performers who consider taxes as well as other production costs in choosing to work abroad. Many newly-developing nations, American states and municipalities compete for business and investors by offering tax reductions and even tax moratoriums.

We know there are tremendous variations in tax systems, but we do not know nor can we easily calculate actual total tax incidences, on a personal basis, especially because of hidden taxes and particularly those which can be shifted to others. At best, estimates can be made according to income class. We think we are also justified in claiming that the tax burden is subject to great national variations, that it is unequal within nations, and that in far too many lands it is highly regressive. Such facts, if they can be discerned, could testify to the weak political positions of the many, the legal facility of some, and the illegal ingenuity of those who would escape paying their shares of maintaining order and other public benefits. Those who have the resources of power can acquire more of the benefits as well as reduced shares of the burdens. This is not to say that the wealthy do not pay more; they do. But, they may be able to avoid proportional sacrifices. In some nations they succeed with ease; in others only with considerable effort. And, in a few, such as Great Britain, they have lost out to national need and the growing political power of the lower income groups. At the end of this chapter are listed a number of generalizations pertaining to governmental tax preference and policies. They should be of some value in accounting for the kinds of observations we have just made.

Burdens of Participation

Every reader must know from personal experience in club, fraternal, social service and other voluntary organizations, that collective projects are burdensome; someone must make decisions and others carry out the work. All this activity is usually regarded as onerous, as something to be avoided whenever possible. The same is true, if not more so, of national political systems with their more generalized and impersonal collective goals and enterprises. In a later chapter we study the political 'division of labor' in order to gain some insight into the variety of ways in which political work may be allocated among the citizenry. In this section we treat of somewhat the same problems but with a greater emphasis on the 'cost' side.

Some forms of burdens are the costs paid by those who engage in active participation, i.e., in influencing decisions. These costs typically take the form of sacrificed time, energy and other resources which might be used to good advantage in other pursuits.

The most obvious and least admirable costs are those borne by citizens who must endure forced labor, military drafts and enslavement by governments which can command services with little or no compensation. A less brutal type includes the more sophisticated and subtle 'arm-twisting' employed by political leaders to induce valued citizens to perform political tasks. Then, there are the 'poor souls' who have to participate, whether by command of leaders or compatriots, or of conscience. The sense of compulsion can be equally as forceful, when citizens feel unable to shirk such bothersome or onerous duties as enduring patriotic rituals—even seven to twelve hour marathon addresses by leaders in some dictatorships! Voting or other required expressions of support may be quite compulsory and ritualistic—not just in communist nations; and there are those who do not enjoy marching in parades, saluting flags and standing for anthems.

We must also think of the voluntarily paid costs of citizens who participate in politics, especially the activists at higher levels who run for public office, contribute money, campaign, or lobby for policies. These people pay heavy personal costs in pursuit of their choices. Most policy-making public officials come to be overburdened with work; they seldom know an eight hour day and they seldom enjoy family privacy. Top leadership roles impose particularly strenuous demands on their incumbents as there seems to be no controllable boundary or limit of time and effort that can be devoted to the problems they confront. It is difficult indeed to imagine a calculation of the marginal utility of the next hour of rest when the 'responsibility' of the leader is an expectation that he can and must cope with all problems and come up with perfect solutions under baffling conditions. Equally burdensome are the conflicting demands made on them by constituents who need worry only about their own preferences. The leader is usually expected to be all things to all men. When he is not, he must endure criticism—often unwarranted—and protect himself as best he can. Because leaders are powerful and have high social status they are particularly susceptible targets for the disgruntled. Not infrequently they are targets for assassins—or for rocks, eggs and spittle! And, as some Presidents have been wont to claim, they are lonely at the summit. The awful responsibilities of decision are theirs, especially during wartime and crises when millions of lives or fortunes may be at stake. But, even in more tranquil times the burdens of choice are immense. The personal and social costs of poor decisions are great and, for the sensitive, they are difficult to bear with any joy. Failures of leadership can sometimes be disguised or rationalized, or blamed on others, but not always. And all too often a leader may be blamed for policies and actions over which he had but the most limited control. In short, while leadership has its rewards (there does not seem to be a shortage of aspirants), it also has its burdens even if they may be voluntarily assumed.

At lesser levels, politically active persons and groups may also pay heavily for whatever rewards they may achieve. Those who perform the mundane tasks in political organization must pay real costs in the form of sacrificed time that might have been enjoyed in some other pursuit, and must use resources that might also have been employed elsewhere, perhaps for still greater gains. The size of the differential, between what is and what might have been, can also be considered a cost of political activity. Much of the work done, in political parties, campaigns, movements and associations, goes unpaid. Answering phones, licking stamps, ringing door-bells, requesting financial support, arranging and running meetings, debating with opponents, are frequently tiresome jobs. They must be, for there is never enough manpower around party headquarters!

The rewards of politics may be substantial, but the costs of participation are heavy and for the lower ranks especially heavy because there are so few substitutes or aids in the endeavor—they cannot so easily contribute money to buy services, nor bring in other resources as well—i.e., prestige, skills, etc. Also at the lower levels there may be less immediate compensation, either of a material or symbolic nature. One must be sustained in the drudgery by the sense of larger events of which one is but a part. And further, political affairs are divisive, and its practitioners are often denigrated. One may enjoy the camaraderie and loyalties of political service, but it also makes one a target for abuse and contempt. In some nations political action is frowned upon and the politician is accorded a status appropriate to such estimations or evaluations. In any case, the politician normally holds an ambivalent status, meaning he is the object of both affection or admiration and hostility. President Franklin Roosevelt was simultaneously both the most beloved and hated man of his times in the United States.

One special kind of cost endured by those who participate in politics is the cost of uncertainty, i.e., acquiring and using information to overcome that uncertainty. In order to be more successful, political leaders require vast amounts of diverse information about their constituents, alternative solutions to public problems, strategies and tactics of their opponents, rules of the game, and all sorts of expectations and constraints. The average citizen who wants to know what he is voting on also requires information. A government or bureaucracy has even more need for a greater variety of more precise information than an individual voter or politician. Devising workable and acceptable policies, resolving differences, and explaining the positions of an agency or even the government itself, has led to millions of dollars and manhours being spent in every major nation. It has also led to covert and forceful methods of acquiring information, such as espionage, criminal investigations, wiretapping and other means of surveillance on both external enemies and fellow citizens. How much is actually devoted to the quest for politically relevant information is probably impossible to estimate.

The distribution of participatory costs can only be guessed at in terms of some broad categories of 'payers.' We are inclined to believe that among the democracies such costs are most broadly paid by the middle- and upper middle-classes. Of course the highest echelons of top leadership pay heavily here, but they are a very small number relative to general strata of the population. The middle-class predominates in the political affairs of such nations as our own. The less educated, the poor and the most disadvantaged in the society tend not to participate, except spasmodically, so they do not bear as much of these kinds of costs. They do shoulder another type which we discuss in the next section of this chapter. The costs of participation fall on those who engage in it; thus the label, participatory costs. However, there is one form of participatory cost borne by the under-privileged: that is the cost of reform. Whenever great reform movements, including the revolutionary, occur we may expect that those who man the guns, march in the demonstrations, riot and rebel will pay heavily for their attempt to participate in order to change things. In the racial rioting of the 1960s in the United States, it has been the Negroes who have marched and suffered injury and death at the hands of police and others. Seldom is the white man killed or his white residential districts bombed and burned. As in all wars, the direct costs of violence or rebellion fall most heavily on those who wage it to overcome their inefficacy and oppression.

Indirect or External Burdens

The costs we have discussed are all best thought of as direct burdens which the citizen has either voluntarily undertaken or had to assume, as in the instance of political participation, or costs which he, as a citizen, is required to pay to sustain the efforts of the system which he supports, as with taxation. These latter type costs are generally endured because they pay for public goods created by the polity. The costs we are about to analyze do not have either of these characteristics; instead, they are burdens which are felt by citizens who have had little if any say in their imposition. Then, too, these costs are generally not thought to be deliberately or legitimately assessed against people but simply result from the actions of others in the pursuit of their preferences and interests. In other words, as some groups are active and participate in decisions, others—outside the interaction— often experience deprivations and injury of some sort. Some political scientists would say such persons are 'outside' or excluded from the system. Since they cannot participate, they cannot defend their interests; they cannot improve or defend their positions and as a result, suffer losses.

What are some of these indirect or external costs? And, who pays them in various systems? As we observed that the middle- and upper middle-classes tend to pay many of the more normal participatory costs, we may now observe that external costs are generally paid by those strata who do not participate in the political system. A major reason for inability to participate is the lack of political resources which, in turn, stems from poverty, disadvantages, disability, or repression. Such groups are helpless in the face of rules that penalize or discourage them and of superior resources among other groups; they suffer from a cultural deprivation which discourages effective participation. In more extreme cases, as in autocratic systems, vast numbers of citizens are deliberately kept down or excluded from effective participation. In the Union of South Africa and in the American South, black men experience such oppression; in revolutionary communist systems bourgeois elements have been repressed by government; in other lands various other minorities experience similar treatment. Both governments and private persons, or both, can be the source of these oppressive costs.

Some of the forms of indirect costs are not so obvious as outright oppression. For example, we consider cynicism, apathy, alienation, frustration,
despair, hopelessness and fear as typical manifestations of the burdens some
men endure in all systems. Note that these particular costs are not expressed
in terms of a necessary monetary assessment by a government to support its
activities but are subjective experiences felt by people as they attempt to
relate themselves to the political order. The fact that they are subjective
does not prevent the social scientist from detecting and explaining them.
Nor is he prevented from measuring them, for it is possible to observe
whether few or many citizens experience them, and it is possible to observe
the relative intensity of feeling. Many social scientists have measured the
extent and intensity of these costs for a number of societies. Of course, a
number of governments would prohibit such inquiries among their populace. The bibliography gives some titles of studies in nations which have
permitted questioning of its citizens.

We should note that the costs we are discussing are not all products of
political systems, alone. Each of us, for example, is frustrated for many
reasons which have nothing to do with our citizenship roles; we may experience personal problems in our family, school, occupation, church, union
and other private activities. As governments increase their activities and
power we must expect that they will become the source of more of these
costs. In fact, the uniqueness of twentieth century totalitarianism has produced a magnitude of such costs unknown in previous history. Until such
time as the number of democracies increases we may expect little diminution of oppression and fear. And, until such time as the democracies, themselves, extend genuine participation to those who have not had that right,
we may expect cynicism, apathy, alienation, despair and frustration to continue. We may also assume that political systems, regardless of type, will
continue to control their members in the pursuit of what are regarded as
highly legitimate ends; accordingly those who are controlled in the interests
of others are likely to experience injury, deprivation, loss of opportunities,
loss of individual liberties, and perhaps, reductions in their income and
status. And since punishment or penalties are important elements of control, we may expect that some citizens will continue to endure heavy
burdens for not following the rules and for engaging in punishable conduct.
Whether such rules are fair and just exercises of power or not, they inflict
burdens.

As men normally attempt to reduce their respective shares of the collective money costs of a system, so some of them will attempt to reduce their
shares of the psychological burdens. In fact, a major cause of political action
is the desire to reduce these costs. No better example can be cited than the
continuing efforts of American Negroes to decrease their share of these
unfortunate burdens. And, the efforts of men throughout history to overcome the oppression and fear they feel has led to countless revolts, civil

wars, rebellions, assassinations, even under hopeless odds for success. Recent insurgency movements, the tragic rebellion of the Hungarians against the Soviet-backed communist leadership of the 1950s and the recent Czech situation serve to remind us of the courage of men to be the master of their own destiny. As Michels advanced a 'law of oligarchy,' perhaps we can advance a conflicting 'law of democracy,' a tendency to want freedom. Michels, himself, ended his justly famous book, *Political Parties,* with these words, reflecting both pessimism and faith in these counteractive tendencies, even in democracies:

> The democratic currents of history resemble successive waves. They break ever on the same shoal. They are ever renewed. This enduring spectacle is simultaneously encouraging and depressing. When democracies have gained, a certain stage of development, they undergo a gradual transformation, adopting the aristocratic spirit, and also in many cases the aristocratic forms, against which at the outset they struggled so fiercely. Now new accusers arise to denounce the traitors; after an era of glorious combats and of inglorious power, they end by fusing with the old dominant class; whereupon once more they are in their turn attacked by fresh opponents who appeal to the name of democracy. It is probable that this cruel game will continue without end.[6]

Case Studies

The distribution of burdens, which occurs in many forms, as we have seen, does not come about in one grand sweep. For the most part, governments do not make 'once and for all' decisions on such matters but tend to decide in a more *ad hoc,* unsystematic way through unrelated and accumulated lesser decisions. As these decisions are made and become institutionalized in their application they become more difficult to unravel or revise in any fundamental sense. To be sure, revisions of taxation schedules and practices are a frequent occurrence but most typically of an incremental nature. There are even strategic reasons why, short of revolutionary change, governors would prefer not to make an issue of what everyone should pay, all at once. It is like the proverbial hornet's nest, which if prodded would result in all being stirred up with the most potent buzzing the loudest. We shall consider the strategies of reform later, but wish here to emphasize one frequent consequence of such incremental decisions made over a period of time. However they occur and for whatever reasons burdens are imposed,

---

[6] Roberto Michels, *Political Parties: A Sociological Study of the Oligarchical Tendencies of Modern Democracy* (New York: The Free Press, 1962), p. 371.

their additive effect is quite likely to be highly unequal in impacts on the citizenry when judged as a whole. Some of the inequalities can be neatly illustrated with a series of short case studies. We begin with the United States.

Case Study #1   Total Tax Burdens in the United States (1961-1966)

During the fiscal year of 1965 the many governments of the United States received approximately $203 billion from citizens whose gross national income was in the neighborhood of $681 billion. The total dollar intake from taxation alone was just over $145 billion. In terms of the average per capita tax load this would amount to about $860 per person if all were giving equally to the maintenance and operations of our governments. Contrast this situation with that of 1902 when the average annual per capita tax amounted to $18.[7] Of course, earnings were also considerably less than now. But we all know that per capita figures are not very meaningful; not all citizens are taxpayers, either because they do not directly earn taxable incomes, or they do not themselves pay for things on which there are taxes, fees or some form of monetary returns to government. Many persons, therefore, did not pay as much as $860 and some others, including the authors, paid considerably more than that amount in income tax alone.

Economists encounter a great deal of trouble estimating the incidence of tax systems, but they have not given up the effort. Because of this difficulty they often differ in their respective estimates. Still, there is considerable agreement about the major findings. One such study, conducted by the Tax Foundation, Inc., of New York City for the year 1961,[8] has concluded that the total tax burden of federal, state and local taxes is approximately proportional up to a family annual income level of $10,000. This range includes about 91 per cent of the families. The meaning of such an estimate is that most such units pay roughly the same proportions of their respective incomes. According to the details of the report, those receiving under $2,000 pay about 27.3 per cent of their income in the form of taxes while those who earn just under $10,000 pay about 28.7 per cent of their income to various governments. Those receiving from $10,000 to $15,000 pay a calculated 30.9 per cent of their annual earnings and those with incomes of over $15,000, an average of 44.1 per cent. Actually, those who earn between $3,000 and $4,000 pay relatively higher proportions of their income than do those with incomes of just under $10,000. And note that some 29.4 per cent of all families earned less than $4,000 in 1961.

These figures do not convey the fundamental notion that these roughly

---

[7] These figures are taken from *Facts and Figures on Government Finance, 14th Biennial Edition/1967* (New York: Tax Foundation, Inc., 1967), pp. 21, 23, 32.

[8] *Tax Burdens and Benefits of Government Expenditures by Income Class, 1961 and 1965* (New York: Tax Foundation, Inc., 1967), pp. 13-15.

equal proportions of income paid out in taxes fall with unequal force on income recipients. It is much more costly for a person earning a small salary to pay 25 per cent of his income than it is for a person with an income of $25,000. The latter, after taxes, still has nearly $19,000 with which to live while the man who gives up one-fourth of $4,000 ends up with but $3,000, a difference of nearly $16,000 in income after taxes. The Tax Foundation study did not include an analysis of the tax structure and its incidence among those who earn over $15,000, probably because they numbered only 9 per cent of the total population. No doubt some of them paid in more than 50 per cent of their incomes (primarily income tax), but as one comes to the very large income earners, one finds greater opportunities and resources for limiting one's tax liabilities. Lawyers and accountants can often easily reduce the amount of taxable income each fiscal year. Tax laws are filled with 'loopholes' and exemptions designed to favor certain groups. These are not necessarily sly nor illegal practices; they are institutionalized means of reducing taxes for those who have the resources to make use of them. Thus, each income level tends, according to this and other studies, to pay different types of taxes, in different amounts, and to different governments. We need not detail these complex findings further, except to observe that intense struggles over tax alternatives are understandable when each tax imposes different burdens on the citizenry. If you wish to shift your burden, you will have to pay the costs of complex calculations and be careful about the types of taxes you support, as well as the strategies of the politicians who advocate them!

Investigations into the incidence of taxation typically, if not exclusively, concentrate on income groups or levels without indicating which social groups receive varying levels of income. One need not, however, be a genius or extremely well informed to form some estimation of the earning power of major social groupings. For example, those who make higher incomes in the United States tend far more than proportionately to be white, to have higher social status, to possess one or more college degrees, to be Protestant or Jewish, and to reside in the larger urban areas. Those who live on the smallest incomes tend more to be lower-class whites, Negroes, Mexican-Americans or Indians; to be the aged, poorly-educated, and from rural areas or big-city slums; to hold unskilled jobs or be unemployed. Middle-income ranges contain those great numbers who are white, have reasonably skilled jobs, have at least a high school education, live in suburbs or residential neighborhoods, and are seen as enjoying the 'typical American way of life.' These various groups and income levels not only share differently in the distribution of burdens, but share unequally in the benefits conferred by the polity and government.

Case Study #2   Taxation in Latin America

Detailed estimates of tax distributions in less developed lands are seldom available and often questionable because the economic data on which the estimates are prepared are highly deficient. Governments in these nations are not as yet well equipped to gather social and economic statistics. However, estimates are made. One such attempt has been conducted by Richard Musgrave for ten Latin American countries: Argentina, Bolivia, Brazil, Chile, Colombia, Ecuador, Paraguay, Peru, Uruguay, and Venezuela for the year 1958.[9] Needless to say, the results may now be somewhat dated, but the overall conclusions are not apt to be seriously wrong for so short a period.

Musgrave contends that the incidence of the overall tax structure is regressive in the lower income groups and that the effective tax rate in several countries is highly erratic, frequently being subject to personal bargains with government officials. The overall burden of taxation is much lower than in more developed western industrialized nations with democratic politics. For example, the lower income groups seldom paid more than 14 per cent of their income in the form of taxes while in several countries the average rate for all income levels was under 10 per cent. Only in Venezuela was the average as high as 35 per cent for the upper income groups and the overall average just under 27 per cent. Once more we remind the reader that the income levels of the Latin American nations are far below those of the United States. A lower tax rate is meaningless in itself; one must consider the sacrifice made in terms of relative capacities to pay as well. And, finally, citizens seldom compare their personal situation with that of people in distant lands; rather they compare themselves with their fellow citizens. On these grounds, the lower income groups in Latin America can legitimately complain about the strongly regressive character of their tax burdens.

Case Study #3   Taxation in the Soviet Union

Economists know a great deal about formal Soviet tax policies and practices and the general incidence of burdens, but it is more difficult to discern the actual distribution of taxes and burdens in Soviet life. Franklyn D. Holzman, for example, has written extensively on Soviet methods of taxation, uses of taxes, the history of tax practices, and analyzed various trends in the aggregate burden.[10] But, he found it impossible to get direct data on the distributive question.

Those who study Soviet fiscal policies face the difficulty of acquiring reliable information, plus the difficulty of comparing even reliable data with western cases, because the cultural definitions of burdens are not comparable. Holzman tried two different ways of calculating burden levels for

---

[9] "Estimating the Distribution of the Tax Burden," in *Problems of Tax Administration in Latin America* (Baltimore: The Johns Hopkins Press, 1965), pp. 31-75.

[10] *Soviet Taxation: The Fiscal and Monetary Problems of a Planned Economy* (Cambridge: Harvard University Press, 1955), especially Chapter 10 on "The 'Burden' of Money Taxation."

the Russian people using different estimation techniques, and both suggest a very high rate of taxation. The size of that average burden is unbelievable unless one takes into account the fact that the citizen is afforded many services for his ruble of taxes which the American citizen acquires through private enterprise. Holzman's estimate for the period around 1949 was an average per capita rate of more than 50 per cent of the personal income and at times almost two-thirds of that income was returned to the state as taxes.[11] While the taxe rate is unusually high, one should take into account also the abnormal post-war period of reconstrucion with its shortages of consumer goods, and the additional possibility that Russian citizens, unlike Americans, may not perceive these tax levels as so burdensome, in spite of the fact that Americans have much higher incomes. We may tentatively infer these things but adequate evidence is not directly available. In any event, later policy changes under Stalin's successors have reduced the rate of the income tax and eliminated enforced bond purchases which served to reduce the citizen's disposable income.

Who pays how much of the Russian burden remains to be explored. We know that income differentials are found there as in the United States, but whether the wealthy pay more taxes and how much more is still most difficult to ascertain.

Case Study #4   Incidence of the Draft in the United States (circa 1967)

Taxation is bound to raise questions of equity, but hardly as profound as those raised about compulsory military service, especially in times of armed conflict. Those who are called may have their lives taken, incur disabilities, and have their lives interrupted in a variety of inconvenient ways. Thus, when not all serve, who shall serve? Drafts do not fall equally upon all. Most obviously, women are not included in most systems, nor the elderly and very young. Some men may not have to serve, and of all those who do, only some will be directly engaged in combat and perhaps suffer injuries or death. While fate or luck are not political factors, the basic choices are matters of public policy and may indeed become intense political issues. The incidence of such serious burdens must be attributed to many decisions and human factors; and in the United States this includes various phases from the basic legislative and administrative rulings, to the decisions and informal criteria of local draft boards, as they then come to affect the available supply of manpower.

During the Vietnam war, the military draft in the United States has been borne unequally by various groups in several ways. First, of course, it excluded women, and was aimed primarily at young, unmarried men in the age bracket 19 to 25. Of these young men, the pattern of formal exemp-

---

[11] *Ibid.*, pp. 254-56.

tions has tended to exclude undergraduates until graduation, graduate students in some professions, ministers, reservists, and occupational categories deemed critical. In effect the pattern of choice has come to fall very heavily on certain groups: those with the least education, the unemployed, those with unskilled jobs; and these tend much more than proportionately to be Negroes, Mexican-Americans, Puerto Ricans in this country and members of similarly less fortunate minority groups. In short, more native-born whites who come from middle- and upper-class families and can afford good educations can remain home to enjoy the opportunities and fruits of civilian life during these crucial years.

The case of Negroes is especially interesting in view of their many problems in civilian society. While the non-white population of the nation is about 11 per cent (mostly Negro), the percentage of Negroes drafted during 1966-67 was about 16 per cent. Some 17 per cent of the sergeants in the Army are Negro and the Negro soldier tends more often to end up in the fighting units rather than rear echelons. The proportion of Negroes in elite fighting units, such as the paratroops and marines, is also higher than equality would require. This being the case, the casualties suffered by Negroes are well out of proportion. At the same time, Negroes still find it exceedingly difficult to become commissioned officers, although they do better in the Army than the Navy with the greater weight of its traditions.[12]

What makes this experience and case study so fascinating (and abhorrent to many) is the fact that badly disadvantaged groups in civilian life find themselves doing the fighting for the advantaged. Even more ironic is the well-known tendency of blacks to re-enlist at a much greater rate than the whites. Miserable as an enlisted man's life may be in war, it would seem that it has more to offer than a return to civilian status in the ghettos or poor rural areas. How else can one explain this fact? Civilian life holds few realistic promises while military service offers comparatively more rewards, although at some risk. Young men, however, are not always very risk conscious. In any event, life in a ghetto or in a community maintaining white supremacy can also be rather risky.

Some Highly Tentative Generalizations

Highly reliable comparative information about the distributions of national burdens is hard to find and perhaps even more difficult to relate to political processes and systems. Nevertheless, we have managed to find some highly interesting propositions about the burden of taxation. Most of

---

[12] The information for the above paragraph was derived from *The New York Times* articles dated January 3, 1966, p. 6; March 5, 1967, pp. 82-83; March 7, p. 33. See also the issue of April 29, 1968, pp. 1, 16.

these propositions are scattered about in the literature of public finance. Unhappily, they are not always very well stated and more often than not are written as after-thoughts. In any case, we have extracted some of these generalizations, not because they have been proven true, but for their subject-matter and relevance to the content of this chapter. Each proposition is followed by a brief resumé of plausible reasons why it may be at least partially correct and why it should, therefore, be subject to further investigation and testing.

    1. *Democratic systems (i.e., those with higher degrees of citizen participation, competition and bargaining) tend to depend on direct taxation to a greater extent than the non- or less democratic systems.*

We have already encountered sufficient evidence of this tendency in Table 5-2 to justify the observation. It has also been noted by a variety of economists in the course of their work in underdeveloped nations. Direct taxes tend to be more progressive and less susceptible to being shifted than indirect taxes. This being the case, democratic nations might understandably pursue such direct revenue sources because many more lower income groups find it to their advantage and have an opportunity to participate in expressing their interests and preferences. On the other hand, it is also evident that among the western democracies one does not find quite as strong a positive relationship between voting participation and dependence on direct taxation. This suggests that if the political process is important in shaping the choice over taxation instruments it must pertain to some other element of politics than just voting, for the United States has the highest percentage of direct taxes and a lower voting turnout than most European nations. We suspect that there are some intervening variables, including some non-political ones, which might aid in explaining the observed facts. In any case, democratic polities on the whole do rely more on direct taxes than do the non-democratic or less democratic.

    2. *The more democratic-type systems place a greater reliance on the progressive personal income tax than do the non- or less democratic systems.*

Perhaps the most obvious explanation of this generalization is self-interest on the part of the vest majority of income recipients. The less affluent generally prefer taxes based on ability-to-pay over other forms. Given the opportunity to choose, they and their leaders will more than likely vote to approve progressive income taxes, whereas the elites and higher income groups in less democratic nations will understandably act to prevent any such distribution of burdens; given their superior political power they can succeed in shifting the burdens to the middle and lower income categories. But we would have to investigate further the alternative explanation that the more democratic (or older?) the systems, the more the cultural norms of equality and fairness are accepted by the higher income strata as well. What evidence or tests can you think of? Anyway, as a nation becomes more democratic, one should expect to find a more equalitarian tax structure in terms of incidence of relative burdens. One can note that progressive income taxes were not enacted in these western systems until the electorate had grown considerably in size and influence. But then in the United States the national income tax was first resorted to in wartime, when more people can be more easily called upon to contribute their share. This question calls for further exploration in terms of the timing and strategies of such changes. More about that in later chapters.

3. *Most governments tend to prefer inflation to taxation as a means of financing their activities.*

Testing this generalization might be a bit difficult because one must decide whether he is interested in actual governmental policies or the attitudes and preferences of politicians. Still, history offers an interesting collection of cases in which governments have allowed, or used, inflationary devices as a means of coping with heavy demands from various segments of their populations and with the outside pressures from the international sphere. Inflation is an attractive short-run policy solution to many problems, especially if it can be controlled and allowed to occur slowly without undue severity on those whom it tends to hurt. Debtors and those interested in low credit costs tend to favor inflation for it makes more funds available and payment of their debts easier, while their creditors would lose more and therefore tend to oppose inflationary tendencies. Fixed income recipients also suffer and accordingly would tend to mount hues and cries against visibly inflationary policies. Bankers, and 'little old ladies' with relatively fixed and small incomes would find themselves in alliance on this issue.

Whether inflationary or deflationary policies are pursued could depend to a considerable extent on the balance of power among the populace. Deflation can harm some segments of the population greatly, as the deflationary policies of the Johnson Administration apparently did during 1966-67 with respect to the construction industry. Interest rates and down payments were allowed to rise, with the consequence that construction companies, their employees, the lumber and construction industry's suppliers, and ultimately the prospective consumers of these goods, all felt the 'pinch.' Western democracies have generally tended to pursue mildly inflationary policies ever since World War II, or at least that is the consequence of what has, and has not been done. While some citizens have been hurt, more seem to have benefited by the controlled inflationary efforts of their governments. But it is, of course, difficult to trace all the effects of such economic phenomena. How long such policies should be pursued is an unresolved question among economists and others.

4. *Most governments prefer increasing the rates of established taxes to imposing new taxes.*

Governments, as we have seen, tend to prefer the route of least resistence. Such behavior is hardly unexpected since most men would rather reduce their costs than maintain or increase them. And governments consist of men. Most governors tend to be persons of intelligence and perception as well as experience. They may learn that active citizens prefer known to unknown costs and that, in general, change is regarded with hesitancy. Politicians, given their dependence on voters, may be inclined to over-estimate resistance, if anything, so that they will be most cautious about imposing new burdens, particularly if they are major ones. Increasing tax rates, or their base, and imposing new forms, are all unpleasant and un-welcome alternatives; the politician would therefore probably select the least evil given the opportunity. So will the citizen, except under unusual circumstances, such as a popular war. If something must be done, it would therefore tend to be in the direction of increasing tax rates or the bases of assessment, rather than inventing new burdens for the ubiquitous and sad little taxpayer we see portrayed in typical political cartoons.

5. *Individual citizens tend to be more cost than benefit conscious with respect to public policies.*

We advance this generalization with some reluctance because it has not been adequately tested, if tested at all, by political scientists. We are also cognizant of the fact that ordinary individuals are aware of or feel both the returns and the costs in most of their daily behavior and attempt to achieve favorable balances. But political life, especially at the level of entire nation-states, is not identical with daily social and economic activities; the fact that it is not introduces some important consequences for behavior and choice, as well as suggesting an explanation.

A number of economists have argued that nations and governments should present citizens with electoral choices in which they can simultane-ously decide on their preferred benefits and costs; few systems enable this opportunity. We suspect that if citizens were allowed the choice they would cut both the size of the overall budgets and allocations for particular pro-grams by varying amounts. Most elections on financial matters simply pre-sent the benefit or the cost side without reference to the other. Such situa-tions are, of course, most unlike a market where a buyer learns about the alleged values and costs at the same time. Perhaps, this is why conservative thinkers tend to support reforms which force the citizen to confront costs of public programs, while more liberal writers tend to favor the reverse. The latter are sensitive to the values of public programs while the conservative views the burdens in sharper perspective.

There is some evidence on perceptions of taxation among American taxpayers. Most of it suggests that the ordinary taxpayer is not very well informed even about the amounts he pays. For example, one inquiry[13] shows

---

[13] Norbert L. Emrick, "A Pilot Study of Income Tax Consciousness," *National Tax Journal*, XVI (June, 1963), pp. 169-73, and "A Further Study of Income Tax Consciousness," *National Tax Journal*, XVII (Sept., 1964), pp. 319-21.

that about 55 per cent were able to estimate their income tax liability within plus or minus limits of 10 per cent while more than one-fourth erred by more than 20 per cent. And, the investigator found that there was some slight tendency to underestimate the liability. One reason may be the withholding practice by the employer where the taxpayer does not have to calculate his own tax and pay it in person each month or year. Another student found that those who believe the income tax to be fair were also far more accurate in their estimations of tax burdens.[14] Awareness of indirect taxes is even less accurate than of the direct tax on income. But the least awareness of fiscal matters pertains to the benefit side. Thus what little evidence there is of such matters supports the assertion. Most citizens cannot identify very many of the public goods they consume or use each day. One of the authors of this book has queried his classes on this matter on many occasions and found abysmal ignorance about the range and types of benefits created and distributed by their governments!

Even where benefits are perceived they are difficult for the citizen to evaluate since they have no opportunity to price them in a market. How much are the sidewalks worth to you? How much value can you attach to national defense? to police protection? to fire protection? to the parks you may visit? Assigning a value or worth to these vital activities of the government is very nearly impossible; as a result most of us do not make the effort. In spite of considerable ignorance about taxes many more citizens are aware of them and could produce a figure roughly indicating their share of such common ones as income taxes, property taxes, licenses and the sales tax. For these reasons we believe the typical taxpayer to be more conscious of his burdens than of his benefits.

   6. *The outer limits of the tax burden are unknown.*

   A considerable amount of public debate in the democracies has been over the most appropriate methods of taxation and the outer limits of individual and national burdens. Some contend that when the government extracts over 25 per cent of the national income in the form of taxation, dire consequences will flow for the operation of a market economy and that citizen support for the government will wane. A few such prophets in this country have even attempted to enact constitutional guarantees along these lines as well as to declare the progressive income tax unconstitutional. The good citizens of Nebraska voted out both the sales and income taxes in 1967. The importance of these matters is at least partially attested to by the slogan of the American revolution, 'No taxation without representation.'

   These attempts to protect the pocketbooks of citizens, whether effec-

---

[14] J. V. Wagstaff, "Tax Consciousness Under Withholding," Ph.D. dissertation at the University of Virginia and reported by James M. Buchanan, *Public Finance in Democratic Process* (Chapel Hill: University of North Carolina Press, 1967), p. 185.

tive politically or as symbolic gestures, are related to the notion that some ceiling or maximum level of taxation must be enacted in order to avoid terrible consequences. Reasons are advanced about the reduced motivation to work, dangers in the political administration of resources, the inflationary possibilities of huge public budgets, and the simple immorality of taxation—all in support of the thesis to limit taxation. Unhappily, there is little evidence to suggest the precise limits. The proportion of the national product taken over in taxes varies considerably from one nation to another. Some of the most stable democracies take over a third of the national income for taxation. And some of the least stable democracies consume less than a third of the national product.[15] And under wartime conditions few question the enormous amounts extracted by governmental authority. In short, the amount of taxation, whether thought of in terms of individual payments or the aggregate amount, that a nation can tolerate and still function effectively is unknown. There may not be a set figure or ceiling, in general, although different nations at different times may show more or less tolerance. We suggest extreme caution in entertaining any generalization which claims that the limits of human endurance are about to be reached.

Explanations

We have explored, in a tentative manner, some of the aspects of distributing burdens in a political system. Among these aspects were governmental choices and behavior, individual perceptions and information, and actual distributive outcomes. We cannot rest assured that the data of this chapter or that of Chapters 2 and 3 will remain valid for very long. But, in any case, we have yet to account for these distributive outcomes regarding benefits and burdens. Why do some groups acquire more benefits and others less? Why do some people shoulder more of the burdens than others? Why is inequality so pervasive in both areas?

The answers to these questions are, we believe, quite similar, as is also the case with the allocation of resources. The elements of such explanations can be briefly summarized with reference to the *participants and processes* of policy-making which have differential consequences for allocation and distribution; the larger *cultural context of values and moral claims* respecting appropriate ends or goals; and the *distribution of political resources* among competing actors in the nation. All of these elements are more or less stable, i.e., factors which tend to persist. The cultural context is probably most enduring, the political processes (stemming from basic political

---

[15] See Table 2-1.

institutions) perhaps somewhat less so, and the kinds of participants and their resources most likely to vary over time. Thus, existing distributions of burdens, as is the case with existing distributions of benefits and the allocation of resources, need not be what they have always been. They can, have been, and are being altered. A revolution, for example, may alter these choices in a most radical way. Partial reforms may also generate new distributions, although at a much slower rate. How one may affect these patterns is explored in Part 2, Chapter 12. Criteria for how burdens *ought* to be shared are explored in Chapter 13.

The full working out of this theory or explanation will take several chapters; in fact, the remainder of the book. But, before going further we ask the reader to consider the more basic and general question of the value and meaning of inequality. After all, it is one of the most burning issues of our—and other—times. So we should like to reflect for a moment on the problem as it has been developed by various thinkers. In short, we want—while distributive questions are now foremost in your minds—to present the major explanations and justifications of inequality.

A Discourse on Distributive Inequalities

We have deliberately headed this final portion of the chapter with the term 'Discourse' because there is no single widely-accepted theory accounting for variations in rights, privileges, benefits, costs and burdens. Our apologies to the great French philosopher Rousseau, who tackled this problem in an inimitable way with a somewhat similarly entitled, though more extensive essay. Because these distributions are so crucial we are intensely concerned with finding explanations and justifications. Those who receive more from society and the polity are apt to prefer explanations which justify their greater shares while those who receive less or pay more apparently prefer a rationalization of their 'failure' and a claim for a better share. Typically the explanations of the well-off have been based upon some notion of 'just dessert,' either in terms of natural superiority or achievement through self-discipline and hard work. The aristocracy in Europe has generally emphasized its 'natural' superiority, while in the United States the well-off tend to claim their privilege is due to their hard work and skills.

Another aspect in attempting an explanation has been to view inequalities as either the products of nature or of 'artificial' institutions. Some theorists have asserted that inequality is a kind of natural law and that nothing can be done about it by man's efforts whether individual or collective; there will always be the less able, less talented, less deserving, or so the argument goes. Man, it is said, cannot legislate equality of treatment and rewards. Those who are appalled by inequalities usually contend that differentials of rewards are the product of human institutions and decisions; as such they can be altered for the better. One need not reform man; rather reform the institutions which engender and protect the privileged. Perhaps a third school of thought exists which attempts to combine the two positions, i.e., argues that inequality is a fact, but that disparities can be considerably reduced and ought to be. Let us consider some of these theories or explanations in greater detail.

Natural Inequality

One finds the theory of natural inequality being propounded throughout history. In the early Greek city-states some five centuries before Christ, a great philosopher—Plato—stated the case with a kind of poetic clarity that has never been equalled.[16] For Plato, inequality was a fact of life and not an unpleasant one at that. Because he observed profound differences among men he felt it necessary to recognize and take account of such facts in constructing an ideal state or passing judgment on existing states. Plato believed that there were four types of men based on variations in their natural abilities:

> Philosopher Kings (the fewest)—rarest talent
> Guardians (second fewest)—second rarest talent
> Artisans (most numerous)—third rarest talent
> Slaves (a sub-stratum)—least rare abilities

In Plato's view each of these groups performed a specific function in the life of a city-state; meeting these functions is a requirement of maintaining such an organization or system. Individuals are required to fulfill the various roles on the basis of their natural abilities as developed by education. Thus the most courageous are cast in the roles of guardians (both government decision-makers and soldiers); those who are manually skilled, not as intelligent and courageous do the 'dirty' work of the state, i.e., all the mundane economic tasks; while the last group consisting of non-citizens simply service the entire state as lowly servants or slaves.

We note that Plato's system of stratification or inequality was based upon natural variations as modified by education or training and experience. Plato was generous enough to allow men to compete for advancement, but the culture obviously stressed the inequalities rather than the basic equality of men. Because of this unique combination of natural inequality and highly institutionalized competition for roles, Plato's theory has proven attractive to many intellectuals who see their own skills as recognized and accorded a higher status in such a society.

---

[16] *The Republic* is a basic work for political scientists.

Another great theorist who emphasized natural differences is more of our time—the Italian mathematical economist and sociologist, Vilfredo Pareto. In a four-volume work entitled *Mind and Society*,[17] Pareto elaborated his sociological theory of man and society, contending that among other things society was and always will consist of but two classes, the rulers and the ruled, with the former again divided into two sub-classes—the "lions" and the "foxes." These two types of rulers have alternated with one another in the history of every society—what Pareto labeled the "circulation of the elite." There could be no such thing as democracy or rule by the people, only changes of rulers. The reason this is so is natural, i.e., men are unequally endowed with intelligence, courage, skills, etc. Pareto, unlike Plato, did not stress the complementary nature of differences and how they could and should be harmonized into a social system; rather he seemed to see these differences as the effect of conflict producing winners and losers. Life is continual conflict.

Two other theories ought also to be mentioned in this connection—Mosca and Michels—both of whom agreed with Pareto that democracy was largely a sham, though in quite different ways. In Mosca's terms:

> Among the constant facts and tendencies that are to be found in all political organisms, one is so obvious that it is apparent to the most casual eye. In all societies—from societies that are very meagerly developed and have barely attained the dawnings of civilization, down to the most advanced and powerful societies—two classes of people appear—a class that rules and a class that is ruled. . . .[18]

In Michels' words, the basic fact of political life is "the iron law of oligarchy," namely that "who says organization says oligarchy."[19] Michels' theory is a more modernized explanation than those of Pareto and Mosca because it is based on a recognition of both natural and artificial differences. Perhaps one should not say artificial, for Michels believed that organizations fill certain needs, such as a need for leadership, that are simply facts of life, to be described neither as natural nor artificial, but as necessities. Michels argued with great cogency that individual members of organizations have emotional needs of identification with leaders, that the leaders have control over many greater resources than the followers and that their motivations to be or remain leaders are powerful. And, finally, organizations, especially if they are 'combat' organizations such as political parties, business firms and interest groups, have need of strong leadership

---

[17] *Mind and Society* (New York: McGraw-Hill Book Company, Inc., 1935), p. 193.

[18] Gaetano Mosca, *The Ruling Class* (New York: McGraw-Hill Book Company, Inc., 1939), p. 50.

[19] Roberto Michels, *Political Parties* is now available in many paperback editions.

in order to survive. Michels, it should be pointed out, did not welcome these 'facts'; rather he desired democracy but despaired of its ever being fully possible. Pareto and Plato preferred inequality and belabored those who worked for greater equality.

The theory that inequality, political or otherwise, stems from natural inequalities in abilities is, of course, an attractive one to the better-off; but the theory has some logical inconsistencies that disturb the more or less objective student. For example, we know from the studies of scientists that most characteristics of human beings as they relate to performances or abilities to do various things—such as pass IQ tests, run the one-hundred-yard dash, lift weights, do problems in arithmetic—are distributed in the form of a bell-shaped curve or the curve of normal distribution (Figure 5-1). We note that the curve is more or less symmetrical, meaning that if we take a sufficiently large number of people, the largest number of them will have average ability and the number of persons with greater or lesser ability is about the same on either side of the median. We might expect that the distribution of, say, economic skills or political skills and therefore of income and political power, would reflect this same normal curve of distribution. But, as we have seen, this does not seem to be the case. The more typical distribution of the good things of life is skewed or asymmetrical indicating, once more, that the few receive more per capita than do the many. There are many people with less than average (mean) benefits and many fewer people with more than average (mean) benefits.

Figure 5-1

Typical Distributions of Abilities and Benefits

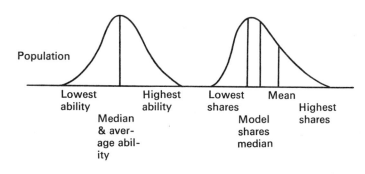

Population			
Lowest ability	Highest ability	Lowest shares	Mean
	Median & average ability		Model shares median	Highest shares

---

If abilities are distributed in a normally-expected way we might tend to feel that the benefits ought to reflect this fact. Should this occur benefits would also be normally distributed. But this is not the case and never has been. Moreover, although the range of abilities may be fairly great we suspect that the range of rewards or benefits is still greater. A person may have an IQ of 60 and receive $4,000 a year while a corporation executive may have an IQ of 120, or twice as high, but receive an income of $500,000 a year, or 125 times as much. The logic of the abilities argument if restricted to IQs would have the executive earning $8,000. Such extraordinary differences leave us with the somewhat uneasy feeling that something is unfair and, in any event, requires some other type of explanation than the ones offered by Plato, Pareto and their followers.

Artificial Inequality

Here we wish to present those explanations which focus on or explain why inequality prevails in terms of certain men's decisions or choices and not as natural imperatives about which we can do little. Whereas the former group of theorists tended to welcome inequalities, this group bemoans the fact that men treat one another so unequally. We must stress the fact that this group agrees that inequality is pervasive, but accounts for the facts with quite different factors.

Among the theorists we have in mind are Karl Marx, John Dewey, C. Wright Mills and a host of other thinkers who have all stressed democracy and equality as ideals. These theorists believe that the similarities among men far outweigh their differences and as such should be emphasized rather than the distinctions. The problem for this theory is to account for the fact that so many inequalities prevail; how could this have come about when man is created morally equal?

The explanation generally has it that some men have been able to secure advantages in a society and once having them not only wish to retain them but have the necessary resources to do so. Advantage then begets and reinforces advantage; disadvantage reinforces disadvantage. Those who can inherit great sums of money, acquire superior education, public office, etc., can dominate others and do. The allocation of these resources of power, privilege, status, property is accomplished by processes which do not admit of much equality, and so we all begin life with varying probabilities of achieving the better things of life. Those who have the advantages are not apt to allow them to go by default; attempting to wrest their privilege away is heartbreaking. Because this explanation of disparity is marked by hope for change, its adherents are always on the verge of disillusionment because they believe such artificial inequalities can be reduced, but the resources of the enemy are so great that progress is slow and painful. Some of these theorists believe that inequality, though bad, will persist in the real world. However, they are few in number. The more numerous social theorists contend that inequality is not entirely inevitable and so long as it exists, produces evil consequences. The good society would be one in which something much more near full equality would prevail.

Institutions, laws and such, will need to be reformed in order to achieve this state; and man will need to be re-educated to behave less in conflict and competition, and more in brotherly love and mutual assistance.

Much of what we know about distributive inequalities is due to the critics of inequality; the defenders have been rather reluctant to advertise the facts. Inequalities in income were best measured by a conservative— Lorenz—but the research has been done mostly by unconventional economists; inequalities in economic power have been discussed mostly by Marxists, Socialists, American 'institutionalist' economists; and status differentials have been minutely researched by angry sociologists who are disturbed by these same differentials. The documentation is impressive. Inequalities in political power, such as in representation, have also been thoroughly researched and condemned by concerned political scientists. As expected, these same highly committed and imaginative social scientists have also made suggestions ranging from minor to thoroughgoing changes in order to reduce or eliminate alleged inequities. Various of these suggestions have been pursued in different societies and with varying degrees of success. If a person is appalled by inequalities perhaps he can think of some means for reform. How can we measure their effectiveness?

The New Synthesis

As the social sciences have developed during the twentieth century and more particularly during the last few decades, new and more sophisticated theories have been constructed and elaborated to explain inequalities in wealth, status, power and income. The origins of these theories have been found in different branches of the social sciences: status differentiation has been explained most frequently in sociology, power differentials in political science, and income variations in economics. Each of these explanations takes on quite different appearances in accordance with the methods of the particular science; thus, the distribution of income in economic theory can be and is stated in highly mathematical terms while social status and power have been done in statistical fashion and using ordinary English. In spite of great variations in methods of analysis and presentation all these theories have some common features. First, inequality is regarded as a fact. Second, measurements of the degree of inequality are stated in much more precise terms (quantitatively) than was the case with earlier theories. Third, and this may be the most crucial feature, the explanation of prevailing inequalities is done in terms of individual choices and artificial constraints on men. Nature does not enter the picture very much. Change in the patterns of inequality are less easily observed, but further change is normally predicted. Sometimes it is argued, especially in economics, that the rate of change is normally slow but change is certainly conceivable, unlike the theories of Plato, Pareto and even Michels. Generally, too, the explanation of variations in status, power, and income are related to the choices that men make within whatever range of choice is possible. For example, in the case of power, we find Robert A. Dahl[20] claiming that inequality is best explained by these factors:

1. Variations in the initial distribution of power resources (income, status, skills in using resources, education)

2. Variations in the confidence or estimate that men have of success

3. Variations in alternative opportunities

4. Variations in value placed on political action.

Dahl and others attempt to explain why some men are more political than others in the above terms and why some men realize their ends or acquire more favorable decisions. None of this explanation rests on the immutable laws of nature or God; they are not fore-ordained outcomes. A considerable amount of the responsibility for one's power potential and actual power is seen as the individual's in this analysis. The same is true in economic theory: what one gets from the income distribution of a market-economy is seen as dependent on the contribution one makes as evaluated by others in their demand for those services. The same explanation has been employed to explain status differentials as a measure of the rewards that society pays for contributions to society. High-status people are presumed to have earned their status because others place a high value on a contribution that is in relatively short supply. Few men can realistically hope to be President; and, since such service is in great demand, the President receives great deference and power. He also receives a high income. The same can be said of Mickey Mantle and Willie Mays.

The constraints or initial givens that confront us in determining our share of distributive gains are related primarily to variations in the resources available to us and in the alternative opportunities. Those who are fortunate enough to have selected the right parents have an enormous advantage in terms of both resources and opportunities. Each person, in a democracy, can affect both of these factors to some extent; and a few persons through dint of hard work, motivation and luck can overcome serious handicaps and acquire great influence in the polity. We often make heroes or devils of such persons. Generally, the improvements one can make in his resource base are sharply limited; generally, the extension of alternative opportunities is also limited. Within broad limitations the individual could make significant gains if he values political action enough to put forth the necessary effort.

---

[20] *Who Governs?* (New Haven: Yale University Press, 1961), p. 274. See also the same author's *Modern Political Analysis* (Englewood Cliffs, N.J.: Prentice-Hall, Inc., 1963), Chaps. 3, 5 and 6.

The new synthesis explaining inequalities is somewhat complacent in that it claims that one finds a variety of political resources in democracies so that a citizen who is a bit shy on one resource may be well off in regard to some other. A diagram might show the possibilities. In Table 5-4 we have a hypothetical list of citizens in the U.S. with a ranking of their power position in terms of their respective resources. In order to suggest the possibilities of quantification and comparison we have inserted hypothetical scores or ranks for each person with respect to each resource. Finally, a total score has been included to illustrate the total power potential of each person. In actual research all the relevant terms (resources and ratings) would have to be carefully defined and stated so that numerical testing is feasible. Our purposes are served by a more casual assignment of ratings. Sketchy as this is, we doubt many readers would question our estimates.

Table 5-4

An Inventory of Political Resources (1967)

Citizens	Income	Status	Role	Infor-mation	Skill	Moti-vation	Total Score
Mitchells	med.	med.	low	high	med.	low	poor 4th
President Johnson	very high	very high	very high	very high	very high	very high	1st
Sec. of Def. McNamara	high	high	high	high	high	high	2nd
Senator Morse	high	high	high	high	high	very high	3rd

You can see where the authors stand in company with Johnson, Mc-Namara and Morse at mid-1968. We have some resources, but they are no match in deciding public policy with these three gentlemen. Our income (joint) puts us higher than the majority of incomes, but it is far below those of at least two others in the table. Our status as professors is also far below the others, but again above many occupations. Our roles are mostly private whereas the others hold elective or appointive offices of great formal power and authority. We possess a good deal of information about politics, especially, but it is that of political scientists and not of practitioners in office. Thus it is less relevant and immediately useful in policy-making. The same can be said of our skills; they are the ordinary skills of political scientists and teachers, not politicians and administrators. Again we rank moderately high in the social structure of the nation but rather low in terms of power potentials to decide upon policies at the national or any other level.

Some further observations must be made in order to complete the analysis. First, the above table ranks only *potential* power not actual power in that the table does not show whether the actors employ their resources, or their relative effectiveness and efficiency if they do. You are safe in concluding that we do not use our political resources as often; if we could bank them and draw interest we might show a hefty balance after some years. But we cannot. Resources that are not used tend, like iron, to rust; they certainly produce little or nothing. Then, too, the table implies that we evaluate all resources equally. This would be a serious mistake in practice. Each resource is not equal under all conditions. Income is not the equal of learning, virtue or piety in a monastery. If we were to be precise in assessing the worth of each resource we would have to include different weightings. For example, we could say that it is possible to 'earn' or be assigned ten points as a maximum for income; eight points maximum for status; six points maximum for role; and so on to a total of, say, four points for some other resource. The consequence would be that a person might score very low on several resources but very high on an important one and therefore be deemed potentially powerful, or another might have significant amounts of several low-scoring resources and still end up with medium or low power potential.

Another qualification must also be entered: the same resources may not be equally useful in every area of policy-making. High medical skills may make one a power in the AMA and even on the national level with respect to medical policies, but such skill and information are usually not deemed useful resources when issues of foreign policy or agriculture arise. In order to determine where one stands one must relate his resources to a range of issues or policy problems. You can experiment a bit on this dimension in Table 5-5. Try rating yourself or your family.

What this discussion adds up to is this: inequalities are a fact of life in every political system and society. In some they are 'cumulative disparities,' i.e., each compounds the others, while in other systems, especially the highly decentralized (bargaining systems), one finds more 'non-cumulative' or 'dispersed inequalities.' Everyone is unequal—more or less—but in different walks of life. Perhaps relatively few persons are permanently disabled in politics. There are elites, but they are not always composed of the same persons. The situation is quite different in stable, hierarchical systems (monarchies, dictatorships, etc.). There the inequalities are still more pronounced and the chances of significant change slighter. Inequalities tend to be more cumulative and reinforcing.

The new synthesis or modern theory of inequality is 'tough-minded' in that it recognizes the existence of elites and inequalities, but it tends to be cautiously optimistic about the possibilities of change and possibly more sanguine about change than was the case with earlier critics of in-

equality. Even the language of the new theory is less emotive and con-
demnatory; perhaps for this reason it irritates those whose belief in equality
is deep and passionate.

Table 5-5

Resources and Issues: A Personal Inventory Sheet

Resource Scores	Issues				
	Civil Rights	Labor/ Management	Vietnam War	School Bond	Local Property Tax
Income					
Status					
Role					
Information					
Skill					
Motivation					

Problems and Applications

1. How could we best account for the following facts concerning the distribution of taxes among Americans during 1961.

Income Level	Total Tax Bill as % of Incomes, 1961
Under $2,000	27.3%
2,000-2,999	26.3
3,000-3,999	29.4
4,000-4,999	29.1
5,000-5,999	29.4
6,000-7,499	28.6
7,500-9,999	28.7
10,000-14,999	30.9
15,000 and over	44.1

Source: *Tax Burdens and Benefits of Government Expenditures by Income Class, 1961
and 1965* (New York: Tax Foundation, Inc., 1967), p. 19.

2. Assume you are President of the United States and wish to consider the political feasibility of altering the national tax structure. Which of the two following alternative tax reforms are most and least likely to win public support under each of the accompanying conditions?

Alternative Tax Reforms	*Conditions*
a. National sales tax at 3 per cent	Limited War
	Inflation
b. Across-the-board income tax increase of 3 per cent	Stable price level
	Republican Party victory in the last mid-term Congressional elections
	Democratic control of Congress (55 per cent majority in both Houses)

3. The following are figures on the relative tax revenue shares of the United States federal, state and local governments. What have been the most striking changes in the long run? What appears to be the more recent direction in relative shares—and how would you project it up to the year 2000? What major explanations would you offer for the trends?

	1913	*1950*	*1960*	*1965*
Federal	30.2	68.8	68.0	64.6
State	11.6	15.5	15.9	17.9
Local	58.3	15.6	15.9	17.5

Data from U.S. Bureau of the Census, *Pocket Data Book, USA 1967*, and Bernard P. Herber, *Modern Public Finance* (Homewood, Ill.: Richard D. Irwin, Inc., 1967), p. 124.

4. In the fall of 1967, Governor McCall of Oregon, a Republican, proposed a new tax program which would include (1) a 3 per cent sales tax on all retail purchases in order to provide property tax relief; (2) a small increase in corporation income taxes; (3) a rebate of some $12 per year to each family to partially offset the incidence of the sales tax. Analyze this proposal in political terms. Try to hypothesize why the Governor would advance these particular reforms and how they might have been received by Oregonians, generally, and especially the legislature and electorate, if asked in a referendum to vote directly on the issue. What kinds of information about the state would you most like to know, in order to assess the situation?

5. What possible justification is there for the following observations? Give supporting arguments for your case:
"Voters are more interested in receiving additional benefits than they are in having tax reductions." (Beginning student in Political Science)
"But the President, noting that 'you'll never get pickets asking for higher taxes,' has expressed doubt that he can ignite a public clamor for the

proposed 10 per cent surcharge on individual and corporate income taxes." (News item, October, 1967)

"But then, as a New York taxi driver said to me the other day with a straight face: 'Who am I to tell the Government what to do with my money?' " (Letter to the editor, *The New York Times*, October, 1967)

6. What could be the reasons why the federal government has never prosecuted a former great heavyweight boxing champion for failure to pay several millions of dollars in back income tax?

7. Why have the many attempts to reduce or eliminate the 27½ per cent tax exemption for oil depletion allowances failed thus far (1967)?

8. Under what conditions would the recipients of welfare expenditures and services most likely protest a relative shift in resources from their program to war expenditures? To education? To space exploration? Why?

9. What kinds of issues of the distributive or allocative sort would most likely activate politically the following groups? Why?

Farmers	Suburbanites
Migrant farm workers	Alienated non-voters
Elderly persons on pensions	Small property owners
College students	College faculty

Bibliographical Notes

In addition to the footnote citations dealing with rather specific problems we should like to suggest a number of more general sources about burdens in the modern state. Once more Bernard P. Herber's *Modern Public Finance*, Homewood, Ill.: Richard D. Irwin, Inc., 1967, is a most readable and useful volume. Part 3 on "Financing the Public Sector" is the most relevant for the problems of this chapter. A more advanced but less comprehensive volume is that of James M. Buchanan, *Public Finance in Democratic Process*, Chapel Hill: The University of North Carolina Press, 1967. Also of considerable use, especially in understanding American practices of decision-making with respect to taxation decisions, is a chapter by Charles E. Lindblom entitled "Decision-Making in Taxation and Expenditures" in *Public Finance: Needs, Sources, and Utilization*, Princeton: Princeton University Press, 1961, pp. 295-329. A quite different kind of book which not only has influenced this particular chapter but the entire text is Anthony Downs' *An Economic Theory of Democracy*, New York: Harper and Row, 1957. While its abstractness may repel some, most of it is actually fairly easy reading. Downs attempts, among other things, to deduce why democratic governments would enact the types of revenue or taxation policies they do, given some assumed calculations and choices of leaders and voters concerning relevant elections. One of the first comparative empirical studies of American state economic policies is that of Thomas Dye, *Politics, Economics, and the Public,* Chicago: Rand McNally and Company, 1966. In this study, Chapter 7 is devoted to an analysis of the tax and revenue policies of the fifty states. Of particular importance are pages 188-191, 193-200. Dye challenges a number of commonly held beliefs about which states employ which tax policies. We strongly suggest that you consult this volume if for no other reason than the prospect that many more like it will follow. Two books which we have found enlightening on federal taxes include Joseph A. Pechman's *Federal Tax Policy,* Washington, D.C.: The Brookings Institution, 1966, and Robin Barlow, *et al., Economic Behavior of the Affluent,* Washington, D.C.: The Brookings Institution, 1966. The former is a major, non-technical discussion of the general features of our federal taxation system. It also contains many useful appendices of historical statistical data on taxation. The latter book is a detailed empirical analysis of just what the title says, but among the more relevant chapters is Chapter 11, "Tax Consciousness," which will probably upset some preconceived notions on the responses of the affluent to taxation. Since many readers may come from relatively affluent families, we know you will be curious. Similar surveys on citizen attitudes toward taxation may be found scattered throughout two books by the psychologist-economist, George Katona: *Psychological Analysis of Economic Behavior,* New York: McGraw-Hill Book Company, Inc., 1951, and *The Powerful Consumer,* New York: McGraw-Hill Book Company, Inc., 1960. Curiously, the voting surveys by American political scientists have almost totally ignored attitudes toward revenue and expenditure policies, yet they are, as we have seen, among the most crucial policies made by all governments.

Another curious lacuna in political science are studies of the political process by which taxation decisions are made. Fortunately, this oversight is beginning to receive attention. One portent is the recent investigation by Thomas J. Anton, *The Politics of State Expenditure in Illinois,* Urbana: University of Illinois Press, 1966. In spite of the title, there is a good deal on taxation. The book is written by an angry scholar who disapproves of the way these policies are made. There is one notable pioneering venture in our discipline, concerning the politics of avoiding costs and cumulating benefits on tariff legislation during the 'business era' of the late 1920s: *Politics, Pressures and The Tariff,* New York: Prentice-Hall, Inc., 1935, by E. E. Schattschneider. With a good empirical sense and fine discernment, this analyst contrasted the formal, legitimized rules of tariff-making with the actually operative 'rules of the game' by which legislators and businessmen settled the question. The cost-consciousness of the active business interests and the non-representation of other roles leads Schattschneider to recommend a set of counteractive strategies. Using the techniques of modern polling and communications analysis, Raymond Bauer, Ithiel de Sola Pool and Lewis Dexter in *American Business and Public Policy*, New York: Atherton Press, 1964, bring the methods and issues of tariff policy up to date, assessing particularly what has happened to the business 'interests' now that foreign trade concerns are so closely related to tariffs. In Chapter 9, especially pages 148-49, there are interesting conclusions about the 'American business ethic' on the question of imposing costs, indicating why political action on the subject may not directly reflect ideologies and personal preferences.

Taxation and the allocation of costs in the newly developing nations has been less subject to scrutiny than it has in the United States and western Europe. The United Nations, however, issued a comprehensive investigation in 1955 entitled *Taxes and Fiscal Policy in Under-Developed Countries*, Technical Assistance Administration; Geneva, July, 1951; New York, 1954. A most detailed and useful case study of a particular country is *Public Finance in a Developing Country: El Salvador*, Cambridge: Harvard University Press, 1951, by H. C. Wallich and J. H. Adler.

Participatory costs have been dealt with at both theoretical and empirical levels. The former mode of analysis has been thoroughly and brilliantly handled by James Buchanan and Gordon Tullock in *The Calculus of Consent*, Ann Arbor: The University of Michigan Press, 1962. They consider "decision-making costs" in Chapter 8. Anthony Downs also discusses "the costs of information" in his *An Economic Theory of Democracy*, *op. cit.*, particularly in Chapters 5 and 11-14. These two books are musts on the list for 'participatory costs.' To these theoretical examinations one must add Edward C. Banfield, *Political Influence*, New York: The Free Press of Glencoe, 1961, Chapters 8-11, and Robert A. Dahl's *Who Governs?* New Haven: Yale University Press, 1961 (Chapters 24-26), for more theory and a wealth of detailed facts about the costs of participation in Chicago and New Haven, Connecticut. Another useful empirical analysis is that of James Wilson, *The Amateur Democrat*, Chicago: University of Chicago Press, 1962, a study of political clubs, their operations and memberships, in a number of American cities.

The question of indirect costs has become a very timely issue these days, with so many movements actively claiming redress on the part of the many—right and left. Perhaps the most popularly received treatment was Michael Harrington's *The Other America*, New York: The Macmillan Company, 1962, which vividly describes the plight of the "invisible poor" who are not only unable to be active and effective in politics, but are not even "seen" by the mainstream of Americans and thus are ignored by these people pursuing their own daily concerns. One can say that at least a temporary effect of Mr. Harrington's book was to gain for some of these groups more visibility on the part of at least some political activists. Murray Levin's small book on *The Alienated Voter*, New York: Holt, Rinehart and

Winston, Inc., 1960, explores the painful dimensions of alienated attitudes, with the help of a practicing psychiatrist, and his interviews enabled him to distinguish which groups of the citizenry feel which costs the most. In a follow-up work, *The Compleat Politician*, Indianapolis: Bobbs-Merrill Company, Inc., 1962, the author then proposes strategies for both the alienated and the politicians of Boston, where both studies took place. An interesting comparative study of alienated voting is Hadley Cantril's *The Politics of Despair*, New York: Basic Books, Inc., 1958, in which he explores the kinds of choices of those voting communist in France and Italy. The timing of his study enabled him to assess the impact of the Hungarian revolution, and the interviews quoted are fascinating.

The paying of costs is a central point in E. E. Schattschneider's *The Semi-Sovereign People*, New York: Holt, Rinehart and Winston, Inc., 1960, for he views political participation as contingent on whether issues concern those matters on which people can directly assess their own losses and gains. This is a most incisive modern treatment of a political context in which the decisions effecting costs are made by some and endured by others.

On the more official level, one of the most illuminating inquiries into the extent of non-participation in voting and the possibility of progress is found in the 1961 United States Commission's Civil Rights Report, *Voting*, Book 1, Washington, D.C.: U.S. Government Printing Office. Because it had to concern itself with the plight of the American Negro in the South, the Commission explores concrete evidence of official actions which can serve to inflict costs on others in the outcomes of policy-making. A broader attempt at comparing such costs in different societies and political systems is hard to find. Some good hints, though ambiguous, can be read in Almond and Verba's *The Civic Culture*, Princeton: Princeton University Press, 1963, a comparative analysis of citizen attitudes in five nations: United States, Mexico, Great Britain, Germany and Italy. Most relevant are Chapters 3 and 4 on political cognition and feelings toward government and politics. You will find some interesting variations.

Evasion of Tax on Foreign Stocks

Seen Continuing Despite New Rule

The Wall Street Journal, July 18, 1967, New York, New York

The New York Times,
July 18, 1967,
New York, New York

India Weighs
To Sterilize Fat
Of Three or M

SELF-REGULATION
URGED FOR FUNDS

States Find Law

WN PUTS TEETH

N DOG-LEASH LAW

Dealers Are Told to Fight
Any 'Oppressive' Curbs
The New York Times, Oct. 23, 1967,
New York, New York

The New York Times, Jan. 3, 1968,
New York, New York

Don't Stop Strike

Eugene Register-Guard, June 12, 1968, Eugene, Oregon

Britain to Continue Strong Control of Ri

In Prices and Incomes Through June 196

The Wall Street Journal, March 26, 1967, New York, New York

New State Rules May Prove

ostly, AOI Delegates Told

Eugene Register-Guard, Oct. 6, 1967, Eugene, Oregon

The Wall Street Journal, May 19, 1967,
New York, New York

New Incinerator L

In New York Spar

Suit as Owners Bu

abor Law Violators

ith Government Wor

aid to Be Under Study

CREDIT PRESSURE

REMAINS STEADY

Real Estate Board Will
City Enforcement of
Governing Apartment

FL-CIO Says Johnson Ask
Justice Agency to Investigate
If Orders Should Be Halted
The Wall Street Journal, May 9, 1967, New York, New York

Indicators Show No Change
in Federal Reserve Aims
The New York Times, June 7, 1968,
New York, New York

DETROIT SETS UP
'LISTENING POSTS'

System Is Designed to Alert
Officials to Racial Unrest
The New York Times, July 10, 1967,
New York, New York

Chapter 6

Regulation and Problems of Control

Citizens may or may not be aware of the various allocative and distributive aspects of the polity, but they are usually very conscious of the regulatory activities of governments. Many tend to discuss public issues as though governmental activity were confined to regulation or control. Or at least that's what often bothers them most. The idea that government is interfering with one's freedom or the right to do as one pleases usually inspires of intense opposition to new public proposals in any system. Almost every public activity has its regulatory aspects, aimed at controlling or directing behavior to some degree. Even symbolic aspects of the public order have their rules of respect and maintenance, such as the required courtesies for the flag and national anthem and rules on their appropriate use. Distributive or allocative programs require rules to govern their application, such as criteria for selection or denial of recipients, permissable procedures of application, of notice, of appeal, and the like. Almost all governmental activity by its nature is 'regularized,' that is, performed in accordance with designated rules.

The Problem of Regulation

Thus governments not only command, produce and distribute resources in the political system, but they also exercise control over the behavior of the members of the system. Or to turn the generalization around: Another product of the political order is the regulation of the behavior of its members. Of course, we shall admit of variations, degrees and conditions. Public control is hardly all-embracing or single-purpose, at least in most situations and regimes, and public efforts at control often fall short of their intended ends. But to most people this is the essential quality of the political system and the central concern of politics: namely, the exercise of power over people. Perhaps some definitions are in order concerning a matter potentially so all-embracing.

We shall treat as regulation that aspect of government performance intended to affect the behavior of others. There are a variety of terms that reflect forms of regulation: command, control, influence, manipulation, persuasion, suggestion. And the means of regulation may be as varied: from formal laws and rules, to informal guidelines or suggestions; from negative threats or costs to positive inducements or rewards; from indirect suggestion or contrivance to very direct compulsion exercised on the person.[1] Further, regulations may be the direct aim of governmental effort, or be intended as instrumental for achieving other ends. In other words, the object may be 'law and order' for its own sake, or just part of programs providing services and benefits or imposing taxation and such. As we shall see, control choices are complicated by the fact that governments strive to achieve multiple goals involving a great variety of allocations, distributions of benefits and burdens, as well as symbolic goods. What serves one end may work against or less well for others.

Granted the impossibility of a society without rules of conduct, and the high probability of conflicts and contradictions accompanying them, the problem becomes more realistically one of degrees and kinds of regulation in terms of priorities of purposes. The effort or effects of control must be related to these goals and not simply considered in terms of some generalized antipathy. A control seldom implies restriction and nothing else; a control over one person's behavior may be a necessary means to promote or insure some other person's liberty. In this sense regulation can be a sort of 'zero-sum game' where the liberty and goals of one citizen are often achieved at the expense of another. This kind of conflict relationship invites resistance or resentment and entails many problems of enforcement and effectiveness. Such a conflict situation, where one gains *only* if another gives up something, probably explains much of the bitterness attached to

---

[1] Three useful general treatments of politics which stress control are George E. G. Catlin, *A Study of the Principles of Politics* (London: George Allen & Unwin, Ltd., 1930); Charles E. Merriam, *Political Power* (New York: McGraw-Hill Book Company, Inc., 1934); Harold D. Lasswell, *Politics: Who Gets What, When, How* (New York: McGraw-Hill Book Company, Inc., 1936).

regulatory issues. This need not be present in distributive and allocative problems, where the issue may be posed in terms of mutual if unequal gains. But more about that in Part 2. At this point we should take a look at some typical public controls and see how they actually work.

Tools of Control

Governors, administrators, dictators and even political philosophers have shown ingenious capacity for devising controls over men. Actual physical compulsion is the most obvious form, as with traditional use of military or police forces and prison systems, for example. The techniques of rendering or threatening physical violence can be quite sophisticated in the modern age. So too are medical and psychological means of compulsion.[2] Less sinister but often equally compelling are economic and material arrangements leaving very little choice to subjects, such as providing income or job opportunities where alternatives are limited. But most states do not rely on such complete command or control of behavior. Most rules and regulations are aimed at guiding or limiting choice, prohibiting or favoring some behavior, and providing some kinds of *positive inducements* or *negative sanctions* to that end. The positive or negative implements are supplied from whatever resources the government commands, whether physical force, economic and material goods, or symbolic goods.

It should be noted that the typical political system has a legitimate if not effective monopoly on coercion in most societies. So notable has been this feature of political life that many political scientists have considered it *the* distinguishing property of government. Whether this is exclusively so hardly seems worth debate; the chief point is that governments are very powerful and that they can employ a whole gamut of devices for realizing their goals. Even in the most constitutional of societies one finds innumerable and varied controls being used on the citizenry. We would be remiss in our scholarship, however, if we did not note that most other 'lesser' groups in society also exercise a great many of the above mentioned controls over their membership and others as well.

The heterogeneity of controls can be simplified somewhat by a few simple classificatory statements. Generally speaking, controls may be categorized according to some important dimensions or properties affecting their usage. For example, controls may be usefully conceived as operating

---

[2] For a frightening but fascinating analysis of 'brainwashing' in modern times see Robert Jay Lifton, *Thought Reform and the Psychology of Totalism*, New York: W. W. Norton and Company, Inc., 1961, referred to in the bibliography of Chapter 4 on symbolic public goods.

either *directly* or *indirectly* upon the object of regulation. In the former case the subject is given the rule or directive, along with some implicit or explicit encouragement to comply. In the latter instance, the government's efforts are aimed at affecting a situation or environment within which the citizen behaves. The government attempts to affect certain assumed crucial elements in the situation in such a way that the citizen will respond in certain predictable ways. In other words, he need not be told directly to do this or that; instead, he more or less voluntarily responds to stimuli or signs that the government has provided.

Indirect controls to some extent conceal the controllers. The citizen may believe that he is freely directing his own behavior in response to an impersonal situation. Direct controls, however, are aimed as the terms suggest, directly at the citizen by the government. No intermediaries are involved; he is simply told to do something or refrain from a specific action. Most governmental control probably is of this direct type because it requires less sophistication of technique. Examples of direct controls include the requirement of taxes on income, property or transactions; traffic laws and policing; military drafts and service; and the rules of criminal and civil law generally. Indirect controls are found most frequently in the area of economic policy; such methods as general fiscal, monetary and market regulations, while posing direct requirements for some, are aimed indirectly at a great many economic choices in the marketplace. In communist societies such as the U.S.S.R. and its allies much greater use is made of direct controls and planned economic decisions governing the major uses of resources.

A second characteristic of control concerns the *sanctions* that accompany their use. Controls without sanctions are not controls unless they are successful in obtaining the desired conduct. Accordingly, the nature of the sanction is most important in determining the effectiveness and cost of particular controls. Needless to say we cannot be completely confident about the effectiveness of sanctions for it is often very difficult to measure effectiveness. Sociologists usually type sanctions as either *negative* or *positive* inducements. Another set of labels might be penalties and rewards. If one does what the controller wants he may be rewarded; if not, he may be penalized. But going further, a reward that is missed or denied can be considered a penalty or cost, too. Or the satisfaction of avoiding a penalty may provide a 'reward' if only through a sense of relief. Law abidingness may in itself become a positive source of satisfaction, as many socialization studies indicate.

Another characteristic requires brief mention: Controls can be either *formal* or *informal*, i.e., the former are stated in legal or explicit terms, whereas the latter are more diffused, casual, or left unstated. The latter may be more effective than the former for certain reasons and circumstances, but the point here is the form of the control, not its effectiveness. Most governmental control efforts are to some degree formalized into laws for reasons of clarity, visibility and consistency, but most such efforts have to rely on a great variety of informal controls as well. We will consider the formal aspects at greater length because they are so characteristic of governments.

Perhaps it will help to illustrate in concrete ways the kinds of control choices that can be made. Figures 6-1 through 6-4 are graphic illustrations from a very noteworthy contribution of an economist and a political scientist. Some fifteen years ago they attempted to explore the dimensions and problems of public controls in a manner which has been most valuable for our discussion. You can, no doubt, especially if you have studied economics or public policies, designate other possibilities.

Let us consider a common type of situation in an industrial society. The value of money is decreasing and governmental leaders wish to heed the clamor of some to halt inflation. This may be done in a variety of ways, both formal and informal, directly and indirectly, using both positive and negative inducements.[3] Of course, various combinations may be considered with varying degrees of expected success. A typical governmental control designed to slow down inflation is illustrated in Figure 6-5. Let us assume a government is interested in reducing the amount or rate of consumer spending. One way of achieving this is to prevent consumers from acquiring and spending more income. This may be partially accomplished by tightening loans made by banks. Compliant behavior on the part of the consumer in this case comes from reducing his potential supply of money. It would be exceedingly difficult, except during wartime, for a government to apply direct controls with negative sanctions that would halt inflation and not incur the wrath of voters. Many governments therefore follow policies and use controls which will indirectly do the job. Home buyers, for example, may tend to blame the economy or private sector as the source of their frustrations rather than the government. Besides, administering indirect controls is generally less costly since fewer administrators are required and fewer regulations must be enforced.

Thus one way of partially preventing or controlling inflation is to make the borrowing of money difficult; in other words, to control the supply of money by controlling its price—the interest rate. This could also be accomplished by a variety of other means including certain debt policies, increased taxes and reduced governmental borrowing. Whichever ones are used the government begins the process of control either by altering its own operations or attempting to influence other economic agents or organiza-

---

[3] Citizens who are concerned but confused by inflationary problems should consult some introductory economic text concerning 'macro-economics' or national income determination for discussions of the basic problems. One of the most readable is Robert L. Heilbroner, *The Economic Problem* (Englewood Cliffs, N.J.: Prentice-Hall, Inc., 1968), Part 2.

Figure 6-1

A Continuum Showing Some of the Choices Available Between Compulsion and Information by Government Action, as Illustrated by Techniques for the Settlement of Industrial Disputes

Compulsion ← → Information

Above the line:

- Highly organized "voluntary" back-to-work movement supported by local govt., police, businessmen, etc.
- President's back-to-work appeal
- Fact-finding boards with power to recommend settlement
- Fact-finding boards without power to recommend settlement
- "Cooling-off" requirements
- Mediation
- Conciliation
- Informal advice from and consultation with government officials

Below the line:

- Compulsory arbitration
- Injunction
- Militia
- Voluntary arbitration
- Compulsory arbitration where no effective means of enforcing the award is at hand

Above the line: techniques commonly considered as those of " education," "persuasion," and "appeals to reason."
Below the line: techniques commonly considered as those of " power," "coercion," and "orders."

Source: Diagrams 2, 3, 4, 5 (pp. 12, 14, 15, 17) in *Politics, Economics, and Welfare* by Robert A. Dahl and Charles E. Lindblom. Copyright 1953 by Harper & Row, Publishers, Incorporated. Reprinted by permission of Harper & Row, Publishers.

Figure 6-2

A Continuum Showing Some of the Choices Available Between Direct and Indirect Controls, as Illustrated in Techniques to Control the Level of Employment and Spending

Direct Control ← → **Indirect Control**

Nationalization permitting directives on investment / Variations in public expenditures	Licensing of private investment	Anti-trust	Variations in grants-in-aid to state and local govts.	Regulation of terms of credit in private transactions, as in installment buying	Appeals to business on price policy or to unions on wage policies	Bond sales to consumers	Taxes and subsidies / Manipulation of interest rate and central bank policy / Secondary effect of public expenditures

Source: *Ibid.*

Figure 6-3

A Continuum Showing Some of the Choices Available Between Voluntary and Compulsory Organizations

		Contract-ing members of Agric. Adj. Admin.	NRA code groups					The nation-state
							Social security systems	
						An American state		
			Land-use planning districts	Tax districts	Municipality			
		Guilds and syndicates				Guilds and syndicates		
Advisory councils	Civil service							
		Professional and busi-ness organi-zations	Union with maintenance-of-member-ship rule	Closed-shop union	Class and status groups			
Small private clubs	Political parties			Business firm where annuity is lost on separation	Business groups with delegated govt. power: e.g., news-print users in Great Britain			
	Pressure groups	Unions						

Above the line: organizations commonly thought of as governmental.
Below the line: organizations commonly thought of as private.

Voluntary

Source: *Ibid.*

Figure 6-4

A Continuum Showing Some of the Choices Available Among Kinds of Public Agencies According to the Degree to Which the Agency's Operations are Prescribed by a Hierarchical Superior

Above the line: British governmental agencies.
Below the line: U.S. governmental agencies.
Placement of British and American agencies is not comparable.

Above the line (British governmental agencies):

BBC — Coal Board — Local govt. — Bank of England — Organization and Management Division, Treasury — Courts — Cabinet Secretariat — Ministry of Pensions / Stationery Office

Below the line (U.S. governmental agencies):

Autonomous agencies: e.g., trustees of the New Haven commons — Semi-autonomous agencies such as the Port of New York Authority — Atomic Energy Commission — Supreme Court — TVA — Securities and Exchange Commission — Regulatory commissions — Reclamation Bureau — Interstate Commerce Commission — Budget Bureau — General Acctg. Office — Unemployment compensation — Veterans' Administration

Source: Ibid.

Figure 6-5

A Typical Governmental Control Over the Economy

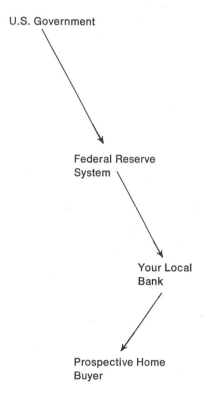

U.S. Government

Federal Reserve
System

Your Local
Bank

Prospective Home
Buyer

DIRECT

INDIRECT

Through one or more of its agencies
(Congress, President, Federal Reserve
Board, Treasury, etc.) poses requirements for the Federal Reserve System
(direct controls on reserve sizes, redis-
count rates) to be imposed on the
semi-public Federal Reserve Banks in
order to control the supply of money.

The Federal Reserve Banks respond
by following the order and thereby
money becomes easier to loan or
harder to loan.

The local bank finds itself in a
position of being required either to
increase or decrease its reserves and
must adjust its interest rates to
borrowers.

The borrower should respond to
the local bank interest rates
and down payment requirements
by engaging in the form of
behavior expected and predicted
by the governmental officials.

tions. For example, a government can influence the behavior of banks,
thereby affecting the behavior of individuals whenever they consider borrowing additional sums. The government does not apply a direct negative
sanction in the sense of writing a letter saying one cannot borrow from the
bank; rather it institutes direct or indirect controls through the Federal
Reserve which loans money to your bank. By raising interest rates or restricting the amount of money available, the Federal Reserve can make
money 'tight,' and the local bank, if it wants to make a profit, has little
alternative but to raise the interest rate on money its customers may borrow.
Or, if the local bank increases the down payment requirement for loans on
houses, e.g., the prospective buyer may not be able to borrow funds. If

enough people are affected by these policies, the supply of money or velocity of money transactions will decrease and inflation will presumably be stemmed.

A more detailed list of controls would include all those which are most commonly used to regulate the economic system: the national budget with its plans for revenue and expenditures; regulations of specific practices such as monopoly and trade; subsidies and loans or guarantees of loans; tax and insurance requirements; charters and licenses; publicity and investigations; operational requirements and privileges, as with public utilities; operation of public or mixed enterprises; mediation and arbitration of industrial disputes—all are examples of the extensive array of control instruments employed by governments to achieve public goals.

We might note that one of the reasons we choose to emphasize and illustrate economic controls is because knowledge of them is far more complete than it is in most other areas. Economists have been most diligent in cataloging and assessing the utility of these controls, and even in proposing new forms. The reader might try systematizing the instruments of control used in such other areas as family life, crime, social welfare, international relationships, or some other sphere of activity familiar to him. How, for example, do public authorities and university officials regulate student behavior?

Objects of Control

Unhappily, we find it hard to name an area, object, or person that has not been subjected to control by some political system at some time. So, it seems best and most economical simply to say that persons and groups are the ultimate objects of governmental controls, most typically in terms of their activities, relationships, positions and perquisites. Thus, we find governments controlling the economy as to work conditions, the supply and quality of commodities, wages, rents, profits, land, labor, markets, capital and means of corporate organization and finance, to name but a few. There is control of political behavior with regard to parties, interest groups, basic rules and rights, campaigning and elections. So, too, for religion (believer's rights, church and ministerial privileges and practices); sexual behavior (definitions of sexual morality; rights and relationships of sexes); and other social behavior (moving, traveling; family and marriage relationships, duties, and rights; education; race and other group relationships), including the aesthetic and expressive realm as well. Every government in the world today exercises some kind of control over each of these areas of daily life. The controls are more or less extensive; more or less formal or direct; more or less positive or negative; more or less legitimized; more or less effective. The quantity of controls is incredible in each area. If you doubt this consult a law library for relevant code books for just the most formalized. The more complex the society, the greater the number of controls and, probably, the greater the number of indirect and subtle forms of operation.

We may rest somewhat reassured that even with the extraordinary numbers of controls in a modern nation-state, we will not be immediately and continuously affected by all. Most citizens are oblivious most of the time to most regulations. Controls are not directed at every citizen but at certain categories of actions and relationships. When we enter one of these relationships or categories of action we are then subject to the controls of that area. As long as one remains unmarried, for example, he need not worry too much, if at all, about the laws of marriage and family. Actually, he can go about his life as though he were a free man. But whatever one does, there will be some degree of control affecting it. No one can escape entirely from the political system and government, even if he should wish to ignore it.

Because economic systems seem capable of endless expansion and differentiation of forms and techniques, there are probably more laws on the statute books of industrialized nations governing economic affairs than any other single area. And the reasoning about regulations tends to be more explicit; the subject of more specific theory and formal study. Economists differ about which controls to employ under given conditions, but it is clear that such controls are used pervasively by the governments of the world. No comprehensive inventory of regulations and areas or objects of control has been made but there have been occasional efforts to suggest which elements of an economy are most susceptible to control. Robert E. Lane, for example, has concluded that industries in the following categories are most likely to be influenced by governmental controls:

1. The industry is a natural monopoly (transportation, utilities).

2. The industry deals with matters critical to the defense of a nation (atomic energy, shipping, aircraft production).

3. The industry receives a substantial share of its patronage from the government (road building, munitions).

4. The industry is particularly subject to foreign competition (copper, wool, meat, shipping).

5. The industry depends upon natural resources under governmental control (lumber, hydro-electric and all extractive industries).

6. The industry is 'sick,' i.e., cannot achieve conditions of competition in which a substantial portion of the industry operates profitably (dry cleaning, coal mining).

7. The industry is composed of some large efficient firms considered

threatening by many small independent firms (drugs and grocery stores).[4]

Economists have formulated sophisticated reasons, or rationales, for control of the above industries, but these reasons need not concern us now; in Chapter 13 we will advance some of them as guides for policy-making. For those who detest governmental supervision yet plan on careers in the private sector, the word must be loud and clear—stay out of the above industries. On the other hand one must consider whether the private regulations of other enterprises cannot be equally as restrictive.

Some Problems in Regulation

Many citizens believe that governments are all-powerful and can achieve any goal they desire; nothing could be further from the truth. Governments continually fail to achieve objectives, even those pursued most efficiently. Leaders who would control confront a series of problems, obstacles, conditions. This is especially so in complex, decentralized societies. Decision-makers, confronted with various sets of givens and much uncertainty, are required to make interdependent decisions over which each one has but a limited amount of control. The choice of an optimal control or means of achieving goals will be dealt with at length and in detail in Chapter 13. For the moment we want simply to create some awareness of the difficulties involved in planning and controlling by government.

Decision-makers are normally in a position of choosing among alternative goals and alternative means. Frequently these are the focus of political contention and conflict. When the scholar views policy-making in retrospect he is sometimes inclined to believe that the decision-maker had no alternatives; that there was one proposal, one best way designated, or too many limitations to approach the problem in more than one way. Decision-makers on the other hand generally perceive themselves as having to make choices, often in the midst of the tug and pull of different advocates and positions. If the latter is correct then the decision-maker must make a whole series of interlocking decisions about goals and means. What are they?

Decision-makers must decide whether to aim toward a single goal or multiple goals. If the choice is the latter, some relationship or rank order must be assigned, i.e., the order of priority or importance, and especially whether the various ends are in conflict, are complementary, or are independent of one another. The significance of this is all-important for the

---

[4] *Political Life: Why People Get Involved in Politics* (Glencoe, Ill.: The Free Press, 1959), pp. 325-326.

selection of means and resources to achieve them. The means and resources chosen can as easily mitigate or intensify conflicts, can bring about complementary ends or maintain independence of objectives. So a very crucial part of attaining goals has to do with the assessment of ways to achieve them and their consequences.

For example, the maintenance of 'law and order' in a community may pose a whole series of questions to be answered:

1. Should the authorities devote more effort to public education about traffic safety and crime prevention or emphasize expanded activities of traffic and foot patrolmen?

2. Will added police activity intensify certain citizen dissatisfactions which may lead to greater evasions or resistance?

3. Would traffic accidents and violations be better deterred by more stoplights, traffic direction or the presence of visible patrol cars?

4. What order of priority should be given to the prevention and/or control of different types of crime?

5. Will all groups of citizens get equal police protection?

6. Should the major effort be aimed at overcoming present inefficiencies or extending the kind or scope of police programs?

7. Are there informal means of encouraging compliance to reduce the costs (money, time, compulsion) of investigations and court trial?

We could go on elaborating more refined questions but these seven are typical and illustrate major problems confronted by the administrator and politician in making choices. Achieving goals is a problem in the relationship of means and ends.

When a policy-maker begins to study a problem, select goals and devise means he knows—especially if he is experienced—that not all alternative means are equally effective. He also knows that he is often poorly informed about the comparative effectiveness of all the alternatives. He also wishes to estimate the comparative costs of the alternatives, since they normally vary, and he generally must make such estimates with only partial information.

In some control areas a policymaker will need to know whether the proposed control is automatic or must be enacted anew and adjusted by separate decisions as each new circumstance arises. By automatic we mean the control is set in motion and operates in response to changes of an objective indicator. For example, income tax rates can be tied in with certain economic indicators of employment, production, or volume of business investment so that as the latter indices go up or down the tax rates automatically go up or down. Or, traffic lights can be geared to volume of traffic or time of day. Probably only a very small percentage of the controls used by governments are automatic.

Some instruments of control are employed continuously to achieve goals through time while others are a sort of 'one shot' operation. Subsidizing an industry or agriculture has been a continuous and somewhat automatic operation for many years in the United States. On the other hand a control may be employed once or for the short-run and in diminishing amounts as the goal is achieved. Thus, small business loans are made with the expectation that the enterprise will make its own way after the initial help. Or disaster relief focuses all its efforts on the initial recovery period. That is, overcome the immediate problem, period.

We have already discussed the problem of direct and indirect controls so we need not dwell further on it. Positive and negative sanctions may be illustrated from the area of farm programs. If the problem is overproduction, resulting in low prices for the farmer, the government may choose between methods tackling causes, or the consequence itself. Crop restriction may be positively induced by offering 'conservation' payments on the land retired from cultivation. Or the effects may be met by a (positive) compensation for the income which would be denied by an oversupplied market (parity prices). One particular means chosen in federal farm programs has been a loan to the farmer in return for which the farmer gives the government the surplus amount of his produce which is then stored indefinitely or used in some other program. The loan thus turns out to be a benefit payment, but compliance is achieved, and in a positive manner, with the dignified symbolism of a loan rather than a dole! However, another device using negative sanctions is to have the farmer vote on the question of market quotas and, if the referendum passes, crop restrictions go into effect with penalties for violators. Note how the voting serves first to legitimize this more direct and negative form of regulation.

Still another problem to be faced by decision-makers involves the probabilities of unintended consequences flowing from the choice of instruments. It is relatively rare for an instrument of control to have but one known consequence or set of consequences. This fact implies the possibility of unwanted or at any rate unanticipated consequences which may be either good or bad, or both. As we learn more about controls we may be better prepared to anticipate more of the consequences. Figure 6-6 shows what we mean in the case of a progressive income tax.

Of course, once a particular control comes into being and is used we learn more about its functioning and consequences. When the progressive income tax was initiated, there were many predictions about its consequences; some have been proven correct and others in error. We are still learning about the operation of personal income taxes, and indeed about all taxes and other types of controls. For example, we are only now beginning to

Figure 6-6

Consequences of a Progressive Income Tax

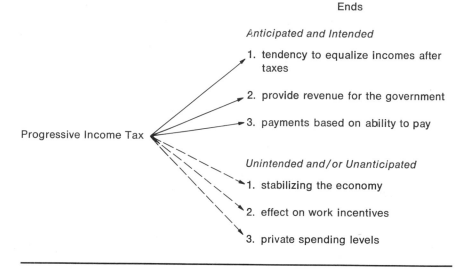

Ends

Anticipated and Intended

1. tendency to equalize incomes after taxes

2. provide revenue for the government

3. payments based on ability to pay

Progressive Income Tax

Unintended and/or Unanticipated

1. stabilizing the economy

2. effect on work incentives

3. private spending levels

learn about regulations that are more or less successful in achieving racial integration. We still know very little about which economic programs would further resolve the problems of agriculture. We have, however, made great progress in the diagnosis and control of the business cycle and, to some degree, of the overall levels of employment, thanks largely to the methods derived from the ideas of Keynesian economists.

Finally, we want to know about consistency among controls and goals. Above all we wish to minimize conflicting consequences that follow from a set of policies. When more than one control must be used, as is generally the case in complex systems, the possibilities of mutually contradictory consequences increase. A good example is found in American agriculture: Government research and conservation services on the one hand encourage increasing production and productivity, while several of the programs mentioned previously induce the farmer to restrict his production. While land-grant college extension services teach means of expanding production, the Department of Agriculture administers a series of restrictive controls on farmers' production, or handles unwanted surpluses. In the long-run this may not be inconsistent if the number of farmers is reduced but individual and total productivity is increased. Many contend, however, that there is an inherent inconsistency in retaining, by subsidies, more farmers than the economy needs. The general point is that governments typically do not wish to negate something they have set out to do, nor to incur consequences that are unwanted whether consistent or not with the major goal(s). Occasionally, unintended 'beneficial' consequences are produced; we should welcome such luck but not count on its regularity. Robert K. Merton, the distinguished Columbia University sociologist, once popularized the term 'serendipity' as a label for accidental benefits[5]; subsequently a folk music group adopted the name for reasons we know not. In any event, welcome serendipity—that most scarce, beneficial, unintended effect of public efforts. It is better, however, to plan good consequences than to depend upon Dame Fortune.

Various of these considerations may be more fully illustrated with some case studies and diagrams.

Case Studies

Case Study #1   The Achievement of Equal Education

Recent years have witnessed a great struggle on the part of the Negro population in the United States to improve their situation. There has been some success in achieving legislation designed to improve their incomes, status and political rights. One such piece of legislation, the Elementary-Secondary Education Act of 1965, allocates federal funds to local school boards for educational purposes and designates various criteria that local school districts must meet in order to qualify for funds. This, too, is a regulation aimed at equalizing educational opportunity. It can be assessed according to the dimensions we have just discussed. Try your hand at characterizing the types of controls employed and make some predictions about their relative success. Title I of the Act, given below, and Figure 6-7 ought to help you get started; to complete the job will require much further research and perhaps even a term paper!

As signed into law, PL 89-10, the Elementary and Secondary Education Act of 1965:

Extended for two years, through June 30, 1968, Title I of PL 81-874, which provided federal aid for school operations and maintenance in school districts "impacted" by the presence of federal installations.

Further amended PL 81-874 by adding a new Title II which:

Declared it the policy of the United States to provide financial

---

[5] The general problem is ably discussed by Robert K. Merton in "The Unanticipated Consequences of Purposive Social Action," *The American Sociological Review*, 1 (Dec., 1936), pp. 894-904. The concept 'serendipity' was initially used by Merton in *Social Theory and Social Structure* (Glencoe, Ill.: The Free Press, 1957), pp. 103-108.

assistance to local educational agencies serving areas with concentrations of children from low-income families.

Authorized the U.S. Commissioner of Education to distribute funds to state educational agencies which would in turn distribute them as basic grants to eligible local educational agencies for fiscal years 1966-68 and as special incentive grants to local educational agencies for fiscal years 1967-68.

Directed the Commissioner to reserve up to 2 per cent of the funds appropriated for basic grants under this title for allotment among Puerto Rico, Guam, American Samoa, the Virgin Islands and the Trust Territory of the Pacific Islands.

Stipulated that where the Commissioner determined satisfactory data to be available (to make the following computation), the maximum basic grant to a local educational agency in fiscal 1966 would equal 50 per cent of the average per-pupil expenditure in each state multiplied by the number of 5 to 17 year-old children in the school district from families with an annual income below $2,000, or with a higher income resulting from aid to dependent children relief payments. Where information was not available by school district, the maximum basic grant would be determined by county (computed in the same manner), with funds allocated among local agencies in the county in accordance with criteria prescribed by the Commissioner.

Provided that for fiscal 1967-68, Congress later would establish the percentage of the average per-pupil expenditure and the annual family income level to be used in determining the allocation of funds.

Limited basic grants for fiscal 1966 to a maximum of 30 per cent of a local educational agency's budget for that year.

Stipulated that to be eligible for a basic grant, a local educational agency had to be located in a school district in which the number of school-age (5-17) children of families with incomes under the specified low-income figure ($2,000 or relief payments during the first year) totaled at least 100 or were at least equal in number to 3 per cent of all of the school-age children in the district, whichever was less; in no case, however, could an agency receive a grant if it had less than 10 such children. Where information was not available on a school district basis, an agency would be eligible if there were 100 children from low-income families in the county in which the agency was located. In special cases, eligibility would be determined in accordance with regulations prescribed by the Commissioner.

Provided that each local educational agency eligible to receive basic grants in fiscal 1967 could receive a special incentive grant not to exceed an amount equal to the total number of children in average daily attendance at public schools during fiscal 1965 multiplied by the amount by which the average per pupil expenditure for fiscal 1965 exceeded 105 per cent of such expenditure for fiscal 1964. For fiscal 1968, the expenditure factor was changed to 110 per cent of such expenditure for fiscal 1964. Federal funds could not be included when calculating average per pupil expenditures.

Stipulated that to receive a basic or special incentive grant, a local educational agency had to submit an application which had been approved by the appropriate state educational agency upon the state agency's determination that the application met certain criteria provided in the bill.

Included as criteria for an acceptable application: (1) that the local agency take into account the number of educationally deprived children in area private schools and make provision for services such as dual enrollment, educational radio and television and mobile educational services in which such children could participate; (2) that property derived from funds provided under the title would be retained by a public agency; (3) that local agencies would annually evaluate and report to state agencies on programs under the title; (4) that projects be coordinated with local community action programs under the 1964 Economic Opportunity Act (PL 88-452).

Required any state desiring to participate in the program to submit through its state educational agency to the Commissioner of Education an application providing assurance that (1) payments under Title I would be used only for programs and projects approved by the state agency and that the agency would comply with the provisions of the title; (2) proper fiscal control and fund accounting procedures would be adopted; and (3) the state agency would make periodic reports evaluating the effectiveness of payments under the title and such other reports as were necessary to enable the Commissioner to perform his duties.

Directed the Commissioner, upon finding that there had been a failure to comply substantially with any assurance and after reasonable notice and opportunity for hearing to the state educational agency, to withhold further payments under Title I, or notify the state agency not to make further payments to local agencies affected by the failure.

Stipulated that the Commissioner could disapprove an application only after reasonable notice and opportunity for a hearing to the state educational agency.

Authorized the Commissioner to reimburse a state for costs of administering Title I, but the payment could not exceed an amount equal to 1 per cent of the total amount of basic grants paid to the state in a year for distribution to local educational agencies.

Prohibited payments to any local educational agency for which the state agency found the combined fiscal effort, as determined by regulations established by the Commissioner of Education, of the local agency and the state to be less than that in fiscal 1964.

Provided for judicial review of the Commissioner's actions, with respect to approval of state applications or the withholding of funds, in the United States court of appeals for the circuit in which the state is located.

Directed the President, within 90 days after enactment of the bill, to appoint a 12-member National Advisory Council on the Education of Disadvantaged Children to review the operation of Title I. Directed the Council to report its findings and recommendations to the President by March 31 of each year following enactment of the bill.

Figure 6-7

Equalizing Educational Opportunities

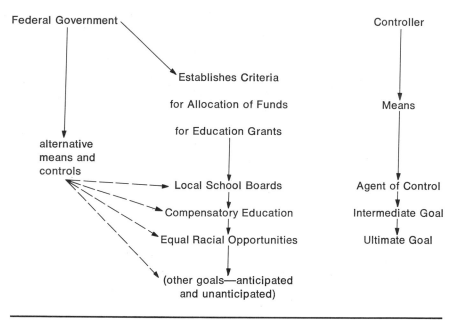

In Figure 6-7 we have attempted to depict some aspects of the means-ends relationships involved in governmental policy to achieve greater equality of educational opportunities, especially for black citizens. The solid lines or arrows illustrate the direction of the main controls and relationships among controllers while the dotted lines suggest some unspecified alternative means and controls for achieving the same ends. Note that the chief agent of control is the local school board which is offered an option with respect to complying with the federal criteria. Compliance means receiving needed funds, while the cost of non-compliance means the denial of funds. The board's choices are severely constrained by the opportunity costs set by the government's criteria. Note also that while reduction of racial inequalities is listed as a generalized ultimate goal, no mention is made of it in that portion of the Act which we have quoted. Instead the problem is treated as one of improving the lot of deprived children from low-income families. Yet much of the impetus for the legislation was prompted primarily by black protests of the 1960s.

Two other facets of regulation could be suggested by Figure 6-7. First, more democratic governments perhaps prefer using controls which depend upon voluntary compliance, or at least the pretence of voluntary cooperation; and, second, most goals can be achieved by multiple means. The latter possibility is conveyed by the dotted lines in Figure 6-7. Federal officials could, in principle, work for the achievement of racial integration by dealing directly with school boards, by various adult occupational training programs, by inducing business to assist in training and hiring Negroes, by persuasive speeches on the part of the President and other leading officials.

A very considerable part of the daily work of politicians and administrators is concerned with devising complementary means to achieve fairly widely accepted goals. Fortunately, public officials in democracies turn to citizens for suggestions on how best to cope with their common problems. While all these activities may be neatly diagrammed for textbooks they seldom occur in such simplified and orderly ways in daily political life. A reading of the newspapers ought to cure one of any such delusion.

Case Study #2   Equalizing Economic Opportunities in Agriculture

Let us consider a much more complex situation diagrammatically. Our previous case could have been made more intricate and therefore more realistic but we wanted to start on a 'simpler' scheme. Figure 6-8 is arranged somewhat differently and in greater detail and scope to illustrate what generally faces a politician or administrator and, of course, a society when an attempt is made to solve a farm problem.

Note the complexity of 'superior ends,' 'objectives of specific programs,' the 'major means' and 'program measures' as well as the interdependence of each element. Those who devised all these intricate measures can, no doubt, inform us on the difficult political problems they encountered in achieving each element of the total program, of the compromises and promises, conditions and restrictions they had to make in order to approach any of their ends. Now that these various programs have been enacted the administrator can, no doubt, tell us, as can the affected farmers, about the administrative difficulties and the partial successes and failures. Each program and each means involves complex relationships among many people,

Figure 6-8

Equalizing Economic Opportunities in Agriculture

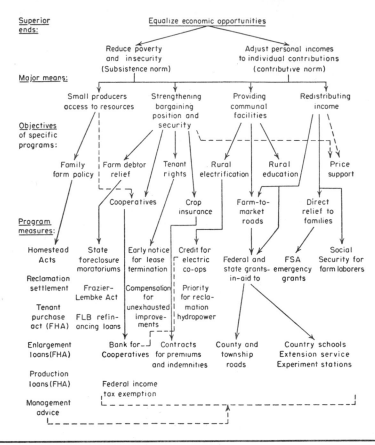

Source: Ranier Schickele, *Agricultural Policy* (Lincoln: University of Nebraska Press, 1954), p. 323.

none of whom probably behave precisely as the authors of the policies might prefer. In Chapter 13 we will discuss criteria for evaluating the success of such government programs.

Case Study #3   Policies for the Redistribution of Income

Most, if not all, western democratic-type systems have pursued policies which are in part designed to redistribute income from the richer to the poorer. How successful these policies have been is still questionable, but economists seem generally agreed that some redistribution has occurred during the past forty years in the United States and Great Britain. Whether successful or not, our concern is with the nature of the regulations governing the means and their variety. As we have pointed out there is usually more than one path to any given objective. The redistribution of income is a case in point. Generally speaking, redistribution can be accomplished by taking from the rich, or by improving the earning capacities and incomes of the poor, or by varying combinations of both. Most systems with high levels of political competition and bargaining employ such combinations. Table 6-1 is intended to show some possibilities among the instruments of control.

Table 6-1

Policies for the Redistribution of Income

Alternative Means (Policies and Controls)	Intended and Unintended Objectives
Affecting High Income Persons	
1. progressive income tax	
2. corporation income tax	
3. inheritance taxes	
4. luxury taxes	
	Income Redistribution?
	Economic Stabilization?
Affecting Low Income Persons	Increased Productivity?
	Increased Consumption?
1. old age assistance	Effect on Investment?
2. social security	Inflation?
3. unemployment insurance	
4. assistance to blind, disabled, destitute	
5. minimum wage	
6. subsidized public housing	
7. public medical services	
8. surplus food programs	
9. family allowances	

Various other features of Table 6-1 should be noted: Even though control situations have arisen in which the number of alternatives is highly restricted, politicians more often discover that their imaginations are the major obstacle. In Table 6-1 we have listed four alternative policies designed to affect directly higher-income receivers and nine policies which affect lower-income persons. Any or all may be applied, depending upon their political acceptability and economic feasibility. Actually, then, the intended objective of redistributing income may be realized through a number of complementary policies or instruments of control. But whether there are also contradictory policy programs and regulations has not been explored here. A lenient capital gains tax, or other significant tax exemptions would appear to be kinds of rules with conflicting consequences, as Chart 3-2 indicates in our case study of total tax burdens and benefits in Chapter 3 (Case Study #1).

Case Study #4   Some Comparative National Variations

In this case we illustrate some of the common and unique controls and policies employed by different governments, during the recent past, as they confronted a similar situation. The common problem was inflation during 1955-58. Briefly, the inflation of that period was mild but of a fairly long duration and it was experienced in varying degrees by at least eight nations in Europe and the United States. Table 6-2 is a summary table of the policy efforts undertaken by each of the eight nations to control the situation.

Table 6-2

Summary of Policy Measures Taken by Eight Nations to Control Inflation, 1955-58

BELGIUM	FRANCE
Public finance	
Reduced budget deficit (increased indirect taxes by 11%).	Reduced expenditures.
Delayed government investment and reduced local authorities investments to give work to unemployed.	Increased direct taxes on corporate enterprises incomes and indirect turnover tax.
Subsidies to flour and rayon industries.	Exempted certain items from indirect taxes.
Taxes on enterprises incomes: excess profit tax of 5.5%; did not extend accelerated amortization.	Suppressed customs duties on many consumer goods.
Reduced indirect tax on some foods, flax, fabrics, tobacco and pharmaceutical products.	
Reduced indirect import tax and customs duties on some foods and all meats.	
Money and credit	
Raised bank rate (2.75 to 4.5%).	Increased bank rate (and penalty rate applied above rediscount ceilings).
Restricted rediscounting for some exports.	Reduced rediscount ceiling and raised floor on public notes.
Control of hire-purchase transactions.	Selective credit policy attempted by persuasion.
Restricted credit to investment and construction through control of financial institutions.	Limited extension of medium term credit (control of financial institutions).
	Controlled hire-purchase transactions.

	Borrowing from enterprises and households.

Direct controls

Loosened control of private imports of food.	Used State import trading to import consumer goods.
Imported Danish butter (State trading).	Price control: lowered some prices (gas); general freeze on industrial prices.
Control of private exports, mainly food.	
Price control: set maximum prices and profit margins on domestic and imported goods; expanded price control list; extended time required to declare a price rise; agreement with coal mines on coal prices; warnings against price rises.	

Exchange rate

	Disguised devaluation of 20%.

GERMANY	ITALY

Public finance

Budget surplus on current account.	Decreased budget deficit.
Selective lowering of customs duties on some manufactured and agricultural goods.	Slowed down rate of government investment.
General customs duties reduction by 20 to 25%.	Reimbursement and reduction of indirect taxes on textiles and some agricultural products.
Dropped all tax exemptions for exports.	Suspended customs duties on some raw materials.

Money and credit

Raised bank rate (3 to 5.5%); later reduced to 3.5%.	Raised interest rates on discounts and advances.
Raised reserve ratios in general and on foreign held bank accounts.	Directives to reduce the demand for credit.
Selectively adjusted rediscount terms.	Treasury notes allowed only as legal reserves of banks.
Abolition of special discount privileges for export financing.	Established funds to insure export credits.
General reduction of rediscount ceiling.	Increased rate on deposits.
Restrictive open market operations.	Increased rate on 9-year bonds.
Persuasion to limit hire purchase transactions.	

Direct controls

Liberalized control of private imports (OEEC,* dollar).	Liberalized OEEC imports and imports of raw materials.
Exchange control: removal of all restrictions on foreign travel.	Price control: relaxed public utility prices and decreased raw material prices.
	Relaxed rent control.

---

* Organization for European Economic Cooperation

Table 6-2 (continued)

NETHERLANDS	NORWAY

Public finance

Decreased expenditures.	Increased Central Government budget sur-
Decreased sugar subsidy.	plus.
Transfers to households: accelerated (war	Increased some food subsidies.
damage).	Introduced sugar subsidy (later abolished).
Increased tax on enterprises incomes, plus	Introduced special investment indirect tax
accelerated tax collection and suspended	of 10% affecting non residential con-
fiscal investment allowance.	struction and motor vehicles.
Increased some indirect taxes.	Taxes on enterprises incomes: enacted
Decreased social security contributions	new depreciation allowances; reduced
(unemployment).	reserve fund tax.
Raised social security contributions (0.9%	Reintroduced customs duty on machinery
decrease in wages).	(from June 1954).

Money and credit

Borrowing from enterprises (5-year	Government borrowing from enterprises
Treasury certificates to bind bank liq-	and households.
uidities).	Raised bank rate (2.5 to 3.5%).
Bank rate raised three times.	Introduced reserve ratios.
Reserve ratios: agreements by banks to	Quantitative stop on state bank loans.
keep cash reserves at Central Bank.	Directives to restrict lending for investment
Restrictive control of hire-purchase	goods, non essential consumer goods
transactions.	and mortgages.
	Stricter control of private companies bor-
	rowing by new issues.

Direct controls

Liberalised control of private imports from	Control of private imports: liberalised 'reg-
OEEC.	ulated' import licensing and quotas; ex-
Control of private oil exports.	tended free-lists of imported OEEC prod-
Reimposed price control on some con-	ucts.
sumer goods, public utilities etc.; But	Controlled main agricultural prices.
increased a few prices.	Control of investment: building licenses
Control of investment: decrease of invest-	generally reduced; quotas for industrial
ment in public enterprises.	and school buildings later increased.

UNITED KINGDOM	UNITED STATES

Public finance

Pruned investment programmes.	Tightened expenditures.
Increased tax on distributed enterprises	
profits (22.5 to 27.5%).	
Increase of indirect taxes.	

Money and credit

Raised bank rate several times, once to 7%.	Raised bank rate (1.5 to 3.5%).
Directives to banks to reduce advances.	Open market operations.
Reintroduced control of hire-purchase	Increased savings bond interest rate
transactions.	Continued public debt lengthening pro-
	gramme.

Control of private enterprises borrowing: Capital Issues Committee expected to examine applications more stringently.

Control of financial institutions: raised stock market margin requirements; tightened terms on government guaranteed mortgages; but later eased them.

Direct controls

Price control: persuasion by the Council on Prices, Productivity and Incomes; nationalised industries encouraged to peg their prices.

Source: E. S. Kirschen, *et. al., Economic Policy in Our Time* (Amsterdam: North-Holland Publishing Company, 1964; distributed in U.S.A. by Rand McNally & Company, Chicago), Vol. I, pp. 320-323.

While some of the actions taken may be unfamiliar or obscure to many readers, Table 6-2 does convey a sense of the great variety of economic controls as well as illustrate some common policy choices for dealing with inflation. As political scientists, we are primarily interested in comparing different forms of control, regardless of their relative economic effectiveness. In order to suggest the range of our concern we list a set of hypotheses which illustrate the type of questions and answers a political scientist might produce in response to Table 6-2. Some of the relevant data that might be considered are shown in Table 6-3. On the basis of these crude facts, which of the following hypotheses are best supported by Table 6-3? The table ranks nations from first to last in terms of four different variables which may have something to do with influencing policy choices.

Tentative Hypotheses:

1. The greater the electoral "sensitivity" (column 4, Table 6-3), the more likely the government is to resort to indirect controls.

2. The more socialist the country, the less need to resort to indirect monetary manipulations.

3. The more centralized the government, the greater the array of methods used to combat inflation.

4. The more prosperous or industrialized the country, the greater the variety of means to combat inflation.

Conceivably the factors listed in Table 6-3 are of little relevance; perhaps other variables, including political cultures, class stratification, and power structures, etc., are more influential in determining the governmental fiscal and monetary policy choices. Or, inflation may be viewed as a somewhat different phenomenon in each country thereby prompting somewhat different combinations of policies for dealing with it. In any event, we want you to

Table 6-3
Selected Political and Economic Rankings of Eight Western Nations

Economic productivity per capita	Socialist or public ownership	Centralization of government	Electoral "sensitivity" of government
1. United States	1. France	1. France	1. United Kingdom
2. Belgium	2. Italy	2. United Kingdom	2. United States
3. United Kingdom	3. United Kingdom	3. Netherlands	3. West Germany
4. Norway	4. Norway	4. Belgium	4. Belgium
5. France	5. West Germany	5. Italy	5. Norway
6. West Germany	6. Netherlands	6. Norway	6. Netherlands
7. Netherlands	7. Belgium	7. West Germany	7. Italy
8. Italy	8. United States	8. United States	8. France

Note: These rankings vary in reliability, in terms of data used, and kinds of criteria applied. From left to right, the first is most reliable and is based on GNP/per capita figures from Bruce M. Russett *et al., World Handbook of Political and Social Indicators* (New Haven: Yale University Press, 1964), Table 14, p. 155. Somewhat less reliable is the second ranking, derived from various evidence out of J. Frederic Dewhurst *et al., Europe's Needs & Resources* (New York: Twentieth Century Fund, 1961), Chapter 13, pp. 436-442. The third is a composite ranking based on expenditures, revenues, employment and relative authority, as derived from Russett *et al., op. cit.,* Tables 13, 14, 17, 20, 21; and from the Kirschen volume (cited in Table 6-2), pp. 31-34. The fourth is a less reliable, judgmental ranking, based on a compound evaluation of directness of voter choice of the government, frequency of elections and alternation of governments, and degrees of changes or shifts in governing coalitions. A 'panel of experts' of our colleagues appeared to agree most at the extreme ends of the dimension.

think about control policies as important products of political systems which should be explained. Table 6-3 is merely offered to stimulate the imagination about possible determinants of such policies.

Limitations on Governmental Control

Such novels as Orwell's *1984* and Huxley's *Brave New World*, and many popular newspaper accounts clearly imply that there are no limitations on the capacities of modern governments to control their citizens. Put in the extreme, such writings imply that *everyone* could be *completely* controlled in *every aspect* of his life *all of the time*. But a moment's serious reflection should make one skeptical of such omnicompetence. True, governments are often powerful, but many are not and none can exercise a total monopoly of power. The reasons for this statement will be made clear in a moment.

First, we should like to insist that many governments are not powerful at all. They cannot, especially in the newly-developing states, perform even the most basic and required functions of government found in more stable systems. The provision of a monetary system that is reasonably stable, law and order that are respected, the capacity to raise their own revenues and to provide commonplace services, not to speak of all the benefits that more developed systems offer, are either not performed or they are performed without much efficiency. The fact that so many riots, rebellions and civil wars occur is direct evidence on the point. Failure to provide order and other public services and goods can only mean that governments lack the full capacity to obtain designated ends; they cannot control all of the circumstances involved. Government or governing cannot be equated with complete control. As much as our imaginations conceive the possibility, we have not yet seen such a 'total command' situation prevail over time in any known political system. Modern totalitarian regimes strive mightily toward this end, proceed with means well beyond traditional forms of governing power, and yet there remain persistent resistances, evasions, and spheres of private choice, however small. Perhaps we may contend that no dictatorial regime can forever impose itself on men. As Roberto Michels[6] maintained that an 'iron law of oligarchy' constrained democracies, so we maintain that an 'iron law of democracy' limits the role of dictatorships, to some extent at least.

The evidence showing limitations on capacities to control may be plentiful and apparent but the reasons for this state of affairs are not. Let us spell out a few of the more plausible.

---

[6] *Political Parties: A Sociological Study of the Oligarchical Tendencies of Modern Democracy* (Glencoe, Ill.: The Free Press, 1949).

We may proceed by examining the capacities or capabilites of govern-ments (governors) to control and the capacities of the governed to resist or remain indifferent. Rulers who wish to control all behavior all of the time are apt to be surprised at the magnitude of the problems and limitations. American presidents in recent years have remarked on the very serious limi-tation which they feel in trying to realize promises and programs.[7] But dic-tators in nations without such an institutionalized set of restraints also learn that they cannot do whatever they want, whenever they wish. One reason for this state of affairs stems from the fact that dictators are human beings sub-ject to human foibles and physical constraints. They, too, must sleep and eat; they, too, have limited information and imagination; they, too, are con-fronted by historical traditions that cannot be wiped out; they, too, are con-fronted by real social problems that cannot be abolished by fiat. A dictator in an underdeveloped nation may want to see his country industrialized and perhaps eventually democratized. He cannot enact the prerequisites for these developments if they do not exist. He may encourage and even accel-erate some of them, but one lifetime is generally insufficient to industrialize and democratize a people even where the procedures are understood.

Dictators are not supermen who never make mistakes in policy, and even those who may be exceptional leaders are dependent upon others for information and administration of programs. The best information about a problem may not be good enough; and if it were, and the program were well-designed, the administrators who run it may administer badly or in-efficiently. Good intentions are not enough. Mistakes are made and controls prove ineffectual; the program fails; the goals are not achieved. Indeed, this is a frequent event in most underdeveloped nations and even in China and the U.S.S.R. where power is very highly concentrated. One hardly needs to add examples in the United States, France or Great Britain where economic, domestic and foreign troubles plague both rulers and their expert advisers. Societies are far too complex to be easily controlled. No dictator can rest assured that his assistants will be sufficiently capable and not make errors, either in providing advice or carrying out orders. No executive can shoulder the entire decision-making burden; he must delegate authority and in so doing lose some degree of control. Even a Stalin must have been impressed by the number of 'givens' in life. Any member of a 'power elite' today must think wistfully of the security of prerevolutionary monarchs.

Let us shift for a while to the position of the ordinary citizen. He is

---

[7] Limitations on presidential power is a major theme in Richard E. Neustadt, *Presidential Power: The Politics of Leadership* (New York: John Wiley and Sons, Inc., 1960). Another study in which obstacles to effective leadership decision-making are emphasized in both the United States and Russia is Zbigniew Brzezinski and Samuel P. Huntington, *Political Power: USA/USSR* (New York: The Viking Press, 1963); see especially their case studies in Part 2.

the object of the control and in part the instrument. His position may well be extraordinarily weak by comparison with most governmental officials. But there is also enormous potential power which citizens in the aggregate may have, whether organized or not. Rulers no doubt would prefer all citizens to behave in perfect conformity with the scheme they have designed, but usually they do not. Some actively rebel; others perform at less than optimal rates; and most are probably quite indifferent to many of the plans and pleas of the government. And, in most states, under certain conditions, one or more of these responses seems possible. Rulers who wish to industrialize, for example, cannot expect to work their people twenty-four hours a day; nor can they expect that all will perform at the most inspired levels. If workers make errors one cannot simply kill them and solve the labor problem! If a society is preliterate it cannot be made literate overnight. And, governments surely cannot attain all these ends simultaneously. There will be many grievances and objections to various collective endeavors, and seldom for purely 'ideological' reasons. The communist world has most recently learned this lesson in many areas. Suppression of all dissension is nearly impossible and quite undesirable. The Soviets, for example, have learned to encourage certain criticism of governmental industries in order to achieve greater efficiency. The Polish, Czech and Yugoslav communist leaders are forced to listen, and even bow, to some forms of dissent. In communist China the energies of youth were turned against certain leadership figures and 'restive' elements, then the students threatened to become unmanageable in turn.

Neither should one underestimate the ingenuity of man to avoid work or the paying of costs; to do so is to miss another important limitation on the capacity to control. Governments must enlist the support and resources of their citizenry to achieve collective goals. Regulations are a means to this end but are seldom enjoyed for their own sake. People often avoid or minimize compliance with the commands of others—unless there are more direct or immediate rewards or costs forthcoming. Governments must therefore use additional resources—and rules—simply to mobilize these vital resources, while vicious circles of resentment and resistance may threaten to increase both the controls and the resistance. Evasion (legitimate or not) of income taxes, avoidance of military service, ignorance of various regulations, covert or 'underground' practices, 'padding' a payroll or stretching out work on a government job are but a few of the practices found in all countries to minimize one's contribution to the working of the system. It is difficult for the controller to regulate and minimize such practices. In the Soviet Union we find the government actually ignoring black markets and certain kinds of profit-making, and pursuing various non-socialist practices of management in order to achieve their production goals. We find the Polish regime coexisting with an avowedly non-communist Church. We find the U.S. government reluctant to prosecute some forms of draft evasion or tackle some areas of tax delinquency to the full letter of the law. The costs of doing so would outweigh the gains involved. Governments most often have to face a set of conditions or givens; power to command compliance may be well beyond their reach. In summary we may list all these limitations as follows:

SOME REASONS FOR LESS THAN COMPLETE GOVERNMENT CONTROL

Government

High costs of control effort
Lack of effective techniques
Lack of sufficient information
Complex interrelationships
Contradictory program requirements
Insufficient rewards and/or penalties
Lack of resources

Citizenry

Indifference to governmental goals
Lack of immediate incentives
Substitute means to proscribed ends
Conflicting social or personal goals
Ease of evasion
Social support for deviance
Resistance to burdens or costs

Conditions of Success

We are about to suggest that control processes are more successful under certain conditions. Put another way, one finds effective control when these conditions pertain and less successful control when the conditions do not prevail to the extent necessary for complete achievement of the goals. Actually we are not as confident about this as we should be; reliable information is not extensive. But various cases and some logic should help our case if empirical evidence is wanting. In any event, those who govern cannot await all the evidence; they must act. We must learn continually from their experience and efforts. One further qualification: each of the conditions we enumerate may be found in greater or lesser degree and not often as either/or states. Our contention is that the more of these conditions and the more of each condition, the greater the likelihood of success. And, of course, administrators and politicians may assist in the creation as well as exploitation of the conditions.

Condition #1   Consistency of Goals and Controls with Citizen Values and Norms

Citizens are forced to do some things they would rather not do and are required to refrain from doing still other things they would like to do. Granted that this is the case, we still maintain that control is most successful when it is consonant with or 'takes advantage' of citizen values and norms. When this is the case people will accept the control more readily and make its enforcement easier, less costly and more effective. If a control is not consistent, there will be a rise in costs of administration and a reduction of efficiency. Recent American experience with altering racial relationships through public regulations ought to make these claims understandable. Public efforts (various federal policies) have tended to work best in areas where anti-Negro sentiment is less intense or widespread and works least well in areas such as the South where views are very deeply embedded in the white culture and attitudes. However, we also witness trouble in labor unions where job interests clash directly, e.g., in apprenticeship systems. Our earlier example of Prohibition comes to mind as another instance in which a control was inconsistent with the norms and preferences of most of the adult American public. As a consequence violations were many and control efforts were very expensive and only partially successful. When men believe in the goals for which controls exist and the actual controls are consistent with that goal, then men are more likely to assist in honoring the objective through self-policing. Thus, one sees higher degrees of compliance and volunteered services during wartime; and most traffic laws concerning order, direction, etc., are automatically observed by drivers. But those who are alienated from the major values and goals of the official directives may feel no compulsion to honor a government's efforts at control; why should they?

Consistency of goals and values can actually occur in more than one way. They may be *shared* by controllers and controlled alike, as with the shared concern that the country survive a war. Or they may be *complementary* or reciprocated values, where the citizen gets what he wants while granting the controller what he wants. Thus the citizen may observe a stoplight for reasons of personal safety, while the city is more interested in having a more orderly and expeditious traffic flow. Here one might also add a sub-condition of relevance. The citizen observes or complies with those rules which are perceived as relevant to the achievement of his own goals and values. Without such salience, there would be no perception that the government's rules had something to do with the citizen's goals and values.

Condition #2   Consistency with the Values and Norms of the Controllers

Just as citizens obey laws they do not like, so law enforcement officials and administrators enforce laws they may not personally like. But again the effectiveness and efficiency of such enforcement is likely to increase if the controllers are in sympathy or at least not actively opposed to the laws.

A good example may once more be found in the southern states where many law enforcement officials, especially local police, are adamant against the civil rights laws. Since the police have the support of the white citizens, they can 'enforce' federal laws with minimal effort, while enforcing local statutes—more consistent with their own values—with a vengeance. If stringency against some groups is socially sanctioned, officers will act aggressively—as they frequently do—against deviant groups. In business regulation, scholars have noted a tendency for regulatory commissions to 'come to terms' with the interests they regulate. Their survival is insured by their sympathy for the goals and problems of the enterprises, while their regulatory fervor subsides as they experience the costs of resistive pressures and attacks.

Alternatively, we may observe that administrators who crusade for their programs are apt to work harder at making them successes; during the Great Depression one found many administrators who were also reformers and zealots for the New Deal. As a consequence they labored hard and long with boundless enthusiasm. Apparently administrators do the same after successful revolutions in most new nations. Their acceptance of new values is a source of great inspiration and dedication. The U.S.S.R., China and Cuba, for example, have had such periods of collective dedication and zeal. As the revolutionary fervor or independence ages and becomes routinized, zeal drops and conventional bureaucrats administer controls in more routine ways. Professionalism breeds a new form of behavior. Technical skill or experience, rather than dedication to social values, tends to be honored among administrators. Perhaps the concept of *reference group* is helpful here. An administrator will conform most to the norms and values of salient reference groups, but different times or situations will determine the rankings of reference groups and whether these identifications will aid the efforts to control, or run counter to them.

In sum, if administrators believe in the regulatory 'mission,' they are generally more likely to do a good job.

Condition #3   Tolerable Costs of Change

Controls that are designed to alter established ways of living may be expected to be costly and resisted by those made comfortable by the established patterns. The able administrator and politician will anticipate such responses and attempt to lay the groundwork carefully so as to allow citizens more time to adjust and do so gracefully. Controls that are sprung on people suddenly and without warning may succeed if the power to enforce them is sufficient, but such application of power is often too costly from the governmental perspective. So it is generally the better part of wisdom to develop and publicize the control and its purposes. The rationalization or defense of the control should be more successful when done in terms that are consistent with the culture. The same control may be defended in quite different terms in different societies. What a German will accept as a legitimate reason for a control may be less acceptable to, say, the French or English.

Controls which are expected to have been publicly discussed and rationalized are likely to prove more successful, given the above conditions, than those which have not had this preparation. One qualification comes to mind, however; in the absence of those conditions, surprise may be necessary for effective control. For example, government price control and rationing would be self-defeating if a government announced well in advance that it was seriously considering rationing a particular commodity. One hardly need be an economist to recognize that such an announcement will send consumers of that item scurrying to the market to hoard before rationing takes effect. Under these circumstances governments must be somewhat secretive or defeat their own purposes. Here the conflict of goals and the entailed costs dictates further considerations.

Condition #4   Adequate Sanctions: Penalties and Rewards

Policies and laws that are adopted without adequate sanctions or rewards are less likely to succeed if they succeed at all. Those who are to be controlled do not alter their behavior simply because a policy has been announced. One form of reward, of course, is the type mentioned in condition #1, the perception of compatibilities of goals and values. Formal provision for rewards and sanctions must make up for the absence of any such shared public and private values. If penalties or rewards are inadequate policy goals are less likely to be achieved. If the rewards are considered inappropriate, compliance may not be forthcoming. An award of money, for example, is not typically an appropriate one within a church; it is a most appropriate reward in an economic system. In other words, rewards and penalties must be salient and legitimated, and be sufficiently available or applicable to alter behavior. If a government wishes to pursue a policy of encouraging investment by private businessmen in plant and equipment it must offer monetary rewards or inducements and not just generalized verbal thanks from the President. Only a shared sense of urgency would allow the symbolic award to be sufficiently satisfying. Likewise, the quantity of the inducement must be sufficient to make the businessman believe it a profitable act to invest his cash. A typical way of doing this, incidentally, is to allow businesses tax reductions for such actions as investments. In some instances the rewards may be more than enough to change the behavior; many economists and legislators believe that a 27.5 per cent depletion allowance for the oil companies is a bit too much. In other words they believe these companies would continue to explore for oil even if they got a smaller reduction. What allowance is minimally necessary is really a pragmatic question, requiring evidence or experimentation.

Occasionally one encounters some rather strange and even bizarre cases involving rewards on the part of governments. Germany, under Hitler, offered rewards (monetary and prestige) to increase the population —and even provided institutions to promote 'patriotic mating.' Some South American governments turn over tax collection to private persons and groups for a percentage cut. The inducement to do a zealous job of collecting is, of course, a greater profit. In the United States, the Internal Revenue Service has offered a percentage of recovered taxes to citizens who inform on those who cheat the government. Interestingly, the Internal Revenue Service does not publicize this reward system, and those who inform are usually less interested in the cash reward than in taking revenge on someone they detest, such as an ex-husband or business partner. Perhaps this latter case is one of inappropriate or unnecessary rewards. An angry mate or cheated partner is rewarded simply by seeing the other person caught and penalized. Apparently, there are few informers; we think this is so because informing is regarded as an immoral act and informers would fear exposure in turn. There is another area in which informing is used rather extensively by government officials in all nations, including our own, and for which rewards are offered. Police employ informers all the time. In specific cases they may bargain with a criminal to inform for a reduction in his sentence or penalty, or for protection. Apparently the concessions are sufficient to induce informing.

There are also comforting instances of reward-induced compliance with government regulations. While people are inclined to believe that most regulations are punitive, one can point to more positive ones where direct inducements have applied. For example, it is a common practice among local governments to award taxpayers who pay their property taxes on time with a small percentage reduction. It is common for military forces to award valor with medals. Federal grants in aid are more likely nowadays to be offered with a variety of criteria or prerequisites to be met by recipient states, agencies or groups. And defense contracts have frequently been used to induce nondiscrimination in employment practices.

Condition #5   Acceptance of the Controllers

Where regulations are negative, controllers may come to share the typical status of the control itself. In fact, the controller may become the convenient object of hostility. This being the case, a prime condition for a successful control is to have the controller be at least minimally acceptable to those who are being controlled. Of course, we do not mean this in a literal sense—that every policeman and administrator be acceptable to every single citizen over whom he may have some control; that is impossible and unnecessary. But it does seem that governments gain by having controllers with whom the citizenry can identify or respect. The latter may be achieved by the appearance of neutrality and 'objectivity,' by expertise, or by symbols of authority. A uniform is one visible symbol of training or special service—the robe of a justice; the forester's green uniform; the policeman's outfit and badge; even the postman's blue serge. Identification, on the other hand, calls for familiarity or some positive sympathy with the regulators. Wise governments have administrators who speak the local language, whose origins may have been in the relevant area, or who may now live there. A persistent demand in the United States has been for local control, a demand for local officials who understand the local people and problems. Blacks want black policemen; Puerto Ricans want their own kind; so do white men. Other societies have experienced the same phenomenon. The British 'bobby' has traditionally been considered a rather lovable law enforcer. He tends to be 'of the people' he regulates. The recent organization of black youth in 'cooling-off' squads to prevent riots in the United States is another effort in this direction.

Gauging the Effects of Regulation

It is not a simple matter to determine what a well-regulated political system is, or what it should be. Advocates of law and order do not always make clear whether they view lawfulness as a product of individual moral constraints, more effective social norms and institutions, or rigorous law enforcement by governments. If the latter is stressed some would seriously raise the question of whether greater use of legal sanctions and controls does not amount to an admission of failure. That is, repressive regimes may *look* more orderly, but at the very high cost of using force and fear to command obedience. Most would prefer systems where greater reliance is placed on positive inducements, or complementary goals and values, and indirect or informal guides to behavior rather than direct and formal sanctions. But the former are by definition ubiquitous and less visible, and it would be an enormous task to measure the relative amounts or impacts of such indirect encouragements to lawful behavior.

A more common way to evaluate degrees of law and order is by noting the relative incidence of crime and violence. In the United States much concern has been voiced over growing crime and delinquency, and the question of law and order in these terms has become a major political issue. Rioting and demonstrations are seen as the culmination of the trend of increasing murders, rapes, muggings, property thefts and the like. The country is seen as 'going to the dogs.' Given this degree of attention, indeed alarm, let us consider some problems of measurement and evaluation before closing the chapter. A case study may point up some of the dilemmas of jumping to drastic conclusions too easily.

Case Study #5   Reporting Crime Statistics in the United States

While most people will assert that statistics *can* lie, there seems to be no public questioning of the increasing crime rates as reported by the FBI in the United States. One scholar, Albert C. Biderman, has not only rigorously challenged such a simple conclusion, but has also offered reasons why it is believed so strongly. In a chapter of the book, *Social Indicators*, Biderman shows that statistics can serve as symbolic authority for what people want to believe, not as evidence to be assessed critically.[8] His own analysis of the FBI, *Uniform Crime Reports*, so widely publicized by the popular press, leads him to the following conclusions:

1. The errors and biasing factors affecting the Crime Index largely operate to show spurious increases, rather than decreases, in the rate.

2. The Crime Index does not provide a sound basis for determining whether criminal behavior is increasing or decreasing in the United States.

3. The Crime Index is highly sensitive to social developments that are almost universally regarded as improvements in the society. Thus, it is altogether possible that year-to-year increases in crime rates may be more indicative of social progress than of social decay.[9]

The variety of reasons for misleading conclusions about the reported crime rates brings home the point about the ambiguities in the meaning of law and order. Biderman notes that people tend to identify the reported Crime Index with what is actually the smallest portion reported: murders, rapes and other violent acts. Actually the rate of murders, the author noted, slowly dropped over the years, and even forcible rape, relative to population, remained constant. And each was negligible relative to other types of reported crimes, affecting the overall rate by little more than 1 per cent up or down. Another category, aggravated assault and battery, tended to be so loosely defined that police reported largely non-violent acts if there were any possibility that the acts might have become violent. Yet many forms of illegal acts of force were not reported at all. Organized crime, covert intimidation, extortions, abortions, and such go largely unreported. One cannot, therefore, prove increases or decreases of all violent acts without time-trend information.

But the most ironic aspect of today's crime statistics is the great degree to which they are based on reports of stolen goods. Biderman notes that it is more than coincidental that the large increase in this kind of crime parallels two spiraling economic trends: The production of portable goods in the economy generally and growing inflation. The former makes more things available for theft, especially the ubiquitous automobile, and the latter

---

[8] Albert C. Biderman, "Social Indicators and Goals," in Raymond A. Bauer, ed. *Social Indicators* (Cambridge: Massachusetts Institute of Technology, 1966), pp. 68-153.
[9] *Ibid.*, p. 115.

makes more goods qualify for reporting in the Crime Index, whose criterion for indexing is a value of $50 or more. From 1953 to 1963 the average of all stolen goods reported to the police rose from $43 to $82, sufficient to create an exponential increase in those indexed crimes which would have been categorized as petty larcenies were prices not inflated. Another way in which industrial prosperity contributes to this increasing rate of crime is through the great growth of insurance practices whereby more thefts must be legally reported (including a number of probably fraudulent claims); and through the greater demand for police efficiency and the rewards (in salaries and funds) based on such expanded reports. To balance this 'property-laden' crime growth, the critic notes, are the great number of recovered goods of larger value, especially of stolen automobiles, where registration and license procedures enable more likely recovery. Ninety-one per cent of the cars stolen in 1963 were recovered the same year. This, too, is a product of modernity, but the alarmed citizen is not given this statistic to balance his fears. Thus, Biderman concludes that not only are "growing crime rates" a highly misleading claim, but indeed these widely publicized statistics reflect quite the opposite, namely: "(1) more widespread and intense identification with the norms of the national society, (2) greater integration and effectiveness of the economic and social systems, and (3) more effective operation of the formal agencies of control, such as the police and courts."[10]

Attitudes Toward Regulation

Another method of assessing the effectiveness and impact of controls is to look directly at the responses of the regulated. In the area of crime this is not easy, given the covert nature of such violations of law. But in the areas where legitimate activities and enterprises are regulated, this may be done in a variety of ways. For example, trends in anti-trust enforcement activity (such as numbers of cases and their disposal) can be compared to the trends in business mergers and combinations. Or the attitudes and responses of the businessmen who are the targets of such rules can be examined directly, much as public symbols can be evaluated in terms of their direct effects on people's attitudes.

Case Study #6   The Regulation of Businessmen (U.S.A.)

One such study—on the regulation of businessmen—contains a rather thorough attempt to get at the perceptions of businessmen toward regulations sometime after World War II.[11] Twenty-five New England business-

---

[10] *Ibid.*, pp. 115-116.

[11] Robert E. Lane, *The Regulation of Businessmen* (New Haven: Yale University Press, 1954).

men were interviewed at length about their views on some of the more outstanding regulatory acts in the United States (such as the Sherman Anti-Trust Act and Federal Trade Commission Act). These businessmen responded as one might expect: They tended to be critical about most aspects of regulation but especially about what Lane, the author, termed "deprivations of freedom and power," "deprivation of certainty and security," "deprivation of money," "deprivation of equity vis-à-vis other groups."[12] About 50 per cent of the criticisms dealt with these themes. The second most important set of criticisms pertained to what the businessmen felt were detrimental actions to "the public good." Confusion, failure to achieve purposes, unanticipated public damages, and detriments to prosperity were common statements. About 35 per cent of the criticisms were based on these themes. Defective administration, meaning inefficient personnel and red tape, were commonly raised complaints. Confusion and "wrongheadedness" was the major single complaint and observation (18.2%). One can draw the obvious conclusions about the difficulties of regulation in such an antagonistic climate.

Case Study #7   Cross-National Comparison of Attitudes (1959-60)

In a cross-national study (based on national samples of citizens in five different nations: U.S.A., U.K., Italy, Germany, Mexico) Almond and Verba report many interesting views of government control, bureaucrats, and the citizen's relationships to them.[13] We can only sample this rich and rewarding study by Almond and Verba; we hope readers will look into it further regarding these as well as other problems of politics.

One might begin with a brief summary and table from the Almond-Verba discussion of feelings that citizens have about their general freedom. The authors were interested in finding out the degree to which people felt free to discuss politics and with whom. Their findings may be somewhat surprising to some readers. Table 6-4 shows the distribution of responses.

The authors have also informed us that there are substantial variations among the five nations with respect to the amount of 'consideration' and 'expectation of treatment' that citizens feel they will receive from governmental bureaucrats and police (see Table 3-3 in Chapter 3). Generally, Americans and Englishmen more often feel they will get serious attention and equal treatment, while Germans and Italians expect much less, and Mexicans least of all. The police and the bureaucrats appear to be viewed in quite similar terms. The authors did not attempt to determine the attitudes of specific groups such as businessmen or racial or ethnic minorities within

---

[12] *Ibid.*, pp. 16-35.

[13] Gabriel Almond and Sidney Verba, *The Civic Culture* (Princeton: Princeton University Press, 1963), Chap. 4.

Table 6-4

Political Discussion and Feelings of Freedom or Restriction in Such Discussion, by Nation (in %)

Per Cent Who	U.S.	U.K.	Germany	Italy	Mexico
Discuss politics and feel they can talk to anyone or most people	54	50	32	21	18
Discuss politics and feel they must avoid it with many or almost all people	22	20	28	11	20
Never discuss politics	24	29	39	66	61
	100%	99	99	98	99

Source: Gabriel Almond and Sidney Verba, *The Civic Culture: Political Attitudes and Democracy in Five Nations* (Princeton: Princeton University Press, 1963), p. 120. Reprinted by permission of Princeton University Press.

each nation. Recent analyses in this country strongly suggest that black citizens, for example, do not trust the police and have little faith that they will be treated on a par with whites. We suspect that the Arabs in Israel may have a similar lack of faith in Jewish administrators; that Flemish citizens distrust French-speaking Belgian officials; that Hindu and Muslim citizens and administrators in India have a mutual antagonism; that French-Canadians have little affection for some English-Canadian bureaucrats and police. Hardly a country is without its own minorities who are at odds with the majority and who resent the controls as determined and administered by officials from that majority.

Thus there can be significant differences in feelings about control both within and among nations. What these feelings mean regarding the effects of control efforts is not a simple one to decipher. For example, one study finds that some Soviet citizens have a great fear of the secret police, even though most Soviet people approve of the control exercised over the economy by the state and tend to believe that a state ought to own the basic resources, produce and distribute most goods and services—and even further, that such a state ought to be powerful but benevolent toward the individual person.[14] Such attitudes are in sharp contrast to those encountered in the United States, for example, where governmental control is more expressly disliked, where socialism is a bad word, where private property and

---

[14] Raymond A. Bauer and Alex Inkeles, *The Soviet Citizen* (Cambridge: Harvard University Press, 1959), Chap. 11.

its associated rights are highly regarded. A control that is readily and widely acceptable in Russia may not stand a chance of being applied in this country. So there are varying levels of acceptability of types of controls, of degrees of control and of controllers among the nations of the world which do not necessarily vary in proportion to the numbers or scope or incidence of rules and regulations. The few studies we have managed to find illustrate some of the interesting problems which certainly need further exploration in order to understand what control consists of and the role of controllers and the controlled.

Problems and Applications

1. Rank the following types of controls in terms of the likelihood of their acceptance by American farmers, i.e., which controls are most likely to be acceptable, least acceptable, and matters of indifference. You will probably have to do some research on the controls. Justify your ranking!

parity prices

acreage controls (direct)

subsidies to control production

tax adjustments for compliance with crop controls

marketing agreements with the government

quality controls administered by governmental agents

2. A lumber dealer who is a friend of the authors claims that his prices could be reduced if he did not have to spend so "damn-much" time filling out governmental forms concerning his inventories, taxes, employee deductions, etc. If possible, arrange collective or individual class interviews of some small businessmen to determine just how much time they put into such activities, as well as to learn the nature of their objections and the depth of their feelings. If this is not possible, try some organized observation of zoning or other local regulatory procedures, using descriptive analysis or check-lists of the participants' positions and the intensity of their responses.

3. If someone claims that people in the Soviet Union are more controlled than Americans, how might one proceed to measure the extent of that control over ordinary citizens? What are some of the indicators of regulation? How can you measure the intensity of control, i.e., the imperativeness of a rule? How can you decide how much of a person's life is controlled by government? Is it possible to make cross-national comparisons of these measures that are meaningful? You might consult Almond and Verba's *The Civic Culture*, Boston: Little, Brown and Company, 1965 (paperback), particularly Chapters 4 and 8; Robert Lane's *Political Ideology*, New York: The Free Press, 1962; or Webb, Campbell,

Schwartz and Sechrest, *Unobtrusive Measures,* Chicago: Rand McNally and Company, 1966, for suggestive ideas on determining or inferring the opinions of citizens regarding controls and controllers.

4. Prepare an analysis, with a model showing influences (using arrows), of why the Prohibition Amendment (18th) to the United States Constitution was so difficult to enforce. Are there any general lessons that can be learned from that experience which should be of value in determining what can be controlled and how? Defend your answer!

5. Many students of administration have contended that it is easier to control behavior than feelings and beliefs. What are your views on the matter? Illustrate your position with analyses of situations involving public regulation of race relations, religion, business conduct, sexual behavior, family life, curricula of universities, traffic control.

6. Suppose you have been retained by the government to measure the *effectiveness* of police in controlling crime and protecting 'law and order.' How might you proceed? Divide your proposed study into various categories of police work: For example, traffic, homicides, petty larceny, robberies and whatever other standard classification of crimes you can locate. Be prepared to find variations of effectiveness in each area. Can you explain why such variations are apt to occur?

7. Try your hand at constructing a utopia in which there are no regulations, no regulators and no regulated citizens. How would the needed tasks for survival and the good life be provided? If you cannot devise a solution, look at one of the famous political utopias proposed, and see how a utopian handles the problem of regulation.

8. How might we best explain the fact that different democracies devote varying amounts of their national budgets to police activities. For example, in 1966 various European countries spent the following percentages of their national budgets on police work:

Germany 10.2%	Netherlands 6.1%
Austria 9.8%	Finland 4.2%
Switzerland 8.2%	Belgium 3.2%

9. Rank-order the following areas of activity in terms of (a) effectiveness of control by formal governmental regulation; (b) cost of enforcement. Indicate how you might proceed to make such determinations.

miscegenation	communist propaganda
obscenity	student dress
false and misleading advertising	firearms control
air pollution	billboards
divorce	cigarette smoking

Table 6-5
Crime-Complaint Data for 10 Cities

	Murder and Non Negligent Manslaughter	Forcible Rape	Robbery	Aggravated Assault	Burglary	Larceny $50 & Over	Motor Vehicle Theft	Total Crime Index
New York City	5.9	16.3	195.5	221.5	1,074.0	978.8	414.3	2,900.3
Chicago	10.3	26.2	358.2	252.8	628.9	374.1	660.4	2,306.1
Los Angeles	6.5	39.7	224.2	293.8	1,647.2	986.7	679.5	3,877.8
Philadelphia	6.5	20.2	88.9	148.6	423.4	171.6	268.9	1,128.0
Detroit	9.2	32.9	366.3	157.7	1,248.1	468.0	559.8	2,841.9
Baltimore	14.3	26.1	263.3	335.1	778.5	669.2	614.4	2,700.9
Houston	16.7	15.4	178.3	218.8	1,375.5	441.7	465.2	2,711.5
Cleveland	11.0	11.3	199.2	95.4	520.7	97.8	540.0	1,475.3
Washington D.C.	14.3	13.9	325.6	314.0	979.0	467.1	595.3	2,709.2
St. Louis	9.9	31.6	230.3	220.1	1,232.8	262.1	540.3	2,527.1
Average rate of cities 2–10	11.0	24.1	248.3	226.3	981.6	437.6	547.1	2,475.3

Source: *The New York Times*, February 21, 1967. The figures refer to the number of crime complaints received for each 100,000 of population in the ten largest cities in this country. The total Crime Index is the sum of the major crimes during the first nine months of 1966. Thus, Los Angeles is first in the total number of complaints.

10. Explore, in detail, problems of regulation by government for any one of the specified areas in problem nine.

11. Which segments of the population in this country do you feel are most regulated? What sorts of controls are exercised? Why do you believe these segments are most regulated?

12. Table 6-5 was issued by the New York City police department and published February 21, 1967 by *The New York Times*. It shows the distributions of crime complaints made by citizens for the major cities listed, and provides an overall Crime Index from such data. What kinds of explanations might apply to the variations among different kinds of crime complaints? Which kinds of complaints are most likely to underrepresent the actual incidence of such crimes? Which *might* be overrepresented? What explanations could be offered for the kinds of variations among the cities? Would the circumstances of how the complaints are reported affect the figures in some way?

Bibliographical Notes

The literature on regulation and control is both plentiful and of high quality, partly, we suspect, because these functions of government are so ubiquitous and significant. A great many basic treatments of politics are based on the notion that the chief characteristic of political systems and governments is their exercise of control. As a consequence much attention has been paid the various aspects of control discussed in this chapter.

Two books we suggest are of considerable historical interest in this regard, Karl Wittfogel's *Oriental Despotism*, New Haven: Yale University Press, 1957, and S. N. Eisenstadt, *The Political Systems of Empires*, New York: The Free Press, 1963. Both deal with ancient polities and their methods of control over resources and human beings. Both suggest that totalitarian methods are not just twentieth century phenomena. Another useful volume, consisting of an analysis of control in modern totalitarian systems, is that of Carl J. Friedrich and Zbigniew K. Brzezinski, *Totalitarian Dictatorship and Autocracy*, New York: Fredrick A. Praeger, Publisher, 1956. Their conception of such systems is based solely on the extent of control. Recent events in the communist countries suggest that they overestimated the thoroughness and efficiency of communist governmental control. Riots, coups, near revolutions and recent economic reforms all indicate that greater decentralization may take place and that more individual choice could be a possibility. On the Soviet Union itself, we strongly recommend Merle Fainsod, *How Russia is Ruled*, Cambridge: Harvard University Press, 1963, and in particular, Part 3 on the "Instruments of Rule." A case study of considerable interest is that by Sidney Ploss, *Conflict and*

Decision-Making in Soviet Russia: A Case Study of Agricultural Policy, 1953-1963, Princeton: Princeton University Press, 1965. This book is about many things besides control but the attempts at handling the vast agricultural transformation of the Soviet Union are, in fact, efforts to control a basic industry.

As with Fainsod's effort to analyze the Soviet Union, we find Herman Finer's *Mussolini's Italy,* New York: Grosset and Dunlap, Inc., 1965, a fine piece of scholarship on a non-communist one-party state. Parts 4 and 5 deal with the institutions of control and the "manufacture of obedience." A much more diffused but still useful compendium of control in preliterate societies is a recent volume edited by Ronald Cohen and John Middleton, *Comparative Political Systems: Studies in the Politics of Pre-Industrial Societies,* New York: The Natural History Press, 1967. Because primitive governments are not as formalized and social control is more diffused throughout the social structure, we commend this volume to your attention for the sharp contrasts it affords with the control activities of both modern dictatorships and democracies. We learn much about ourselves by studying people who run their affairs in quite different ways.

Of course, we must also look directly at our own systems. In the case of the United States, students have a great wealth of studies concerning regulation of various activities in the nation. In particular abundance are the works on business regulation. For example, a good general volume, although very long and detailed, is Harold Koontz and Richard W. Gable, *Public Control of Economic Enterprise,* New York: McGraw-Hill Book Company, Inc., 1956. Another highly useful, although more theoretical treatment of regulations, may be found in Robert A. Dahl and Charles E. Lindblom, *Politics, Economics and Welfare,* New York: Harper and Brothers, 1953. Chapters 8 and 9 deal with bureaucracy as the best known case in regulation, but all of the book is really about various types of control including the price system, bargaining and 'polyarchy.'

Among the several excellent case studies is Robert Lane's *The Regulation of Businessmen,* New Haven: Yale University Press, 1954, a somewhat unique treatment of regulation because he studied the perspectives of the regulated, i.e., the businessmen. From these analyses Lane attempted to formulate the conditions which contributed to successful control. We have made use of the book in this chapter. A minor classic is Victor A. Thompson's *The Regulatory Process in OPA Rationing,* New York: Columbia University Press, 1950. The perspective in this case is that of administrators who attempted to formulate and administer controls over prices during World War II. We consider it one of the better books we read as graduate students. Another favorite, quite different from any noted in this bibliography, is Alexander Leighton's *The Governing of Men,* Princeton: Princeton University Press, 1945, a study of an American 'relocation' camp for

Japanese during World War II, by a participant who was one of the administrators. It is a highly reflective, sensitive analysis of control in a strange, and we hope not to be repeated, experience.

Regulating Business by Independent Commission, Princeton: Princeton University Press, 1955, by Marver H. Bernstein is a thoughtful analysis of a typical American means of coping with business regulation. For those who like more specific detail we suggest consulting Edwin A. Bock, *Government Regulation of Business: A Casebook,* Englewood Cliffs, N.J.: Prentice-Hall, Inc., 1962, a collection of several highly readable case studies of federal regulatory actions.

One of the more unique empirical investigations on law and compliance in political science is that of Richard M. Johnson, *The Dynamics of Compliance,* Evanston, Ill.: Northwestern University Press, 1967, a study of the effects and reception of a particular Supreme Court decision in a single rural school district in central Illinois. The decision dealt with the religion-in-school issue which the Court has faced in some recent cases. Not only is the study unique in the sense of investigating the consequences of a specific court decision, but also in the sense that the author attempted to discover conditions under which a decision will or will not affect behavior. Among other conditions, Johnson concludes that the Court secures greater compliance when citizens are convinced that it has made its decision with calm deliberation, and has employed esoteric rules of law. We strongly suggest that you read this interesting and valuable book.

A recent reader compiled by Samuel Krislov and Lloyd D. Musolf, entitled *The Politics of Regulation,* Boston: Houghton Mifflin Company, 1964, is of considerable use because it contains articles on a whole host of regulatory issues, none of which may be said to have permanent solutions.

Issues of regulation and control may be universal but they have their unique applications in specific nations and types of political systems. We have suggested as much by noting some general volumes on historical systems and a number of scholarly inquiries into American problems. Perhaps among the most fascinating analyses of control are those which pertain to attempts by socialist and communist states to plan entire economies, i.e., make basic choices on what to produce, how to price goods, distribute income, plan investments, and how to coordinate through government what the private market does in free enterprise systems. Oskar Lange and Fred M. Taylor (the former a chief planner in Poland until his recent death) wrote what many regard as a classic entitled *On the Economic Theory of Socialism,* New York: McGraw-Hill Book Company, Inc., 1938. This work explains how a socialist economy can be operated by adopting some of the decision-rules or criteria of pricing found in private economies. This book is not descriptive, but rather prescriptive, and its proposals have been partially adopted by some communist societies. Another cogent treatment, also by a chief planner, this time in the Netherlands, is Jan Tinbergen's *Central Planning*, New Haven: Yale University Press, 1964, a volume which describes both what takes place in centralized planning in socialist-inclined states such as the Netherlands and what ought to govern in such societies. The book is considerably easier reading for the non-economist than is the Lange-Taylor volume. A much more difficult one than either of these two is Benjamin N. Ward, *The Socialist Economy*, New York: Random House, Inc., 1967, in which the author attempts to analyse the operations and the consequences of three different versions or types of socialist economy. Not all communist or socialist economies function in the same way, we might add, nor do all so-called capitalist systems. Perhaps the two best and most readable analyses of the Soviet Economy are Abram Bergson's *The Economics of Soviet Planning*, New Haven: Yale University Press, 1964, and Alec Nove, *The Soviet Economy*, New York: Frederick A. Praeger, Publisher, 1961. The former is a distinguished American student of Russian economics while the latter is an equally distinguished English economist. Both point out similar dilemmas and problems in running a planned economy but both are highly objective evaluators of the gains and costs in such systems. They are important readings for anyone interested in how the U.S.S.R. handles its control problems concerning economic behavior.

The books cited thus far have been written mostly by political scientists and economists, as may be expected, but other social scientists—particularly sociologists—have also been intensely interested in understanding control as a general phenomenon in society. In fact, without the sociologist's perspective we would have difficulty classifying governmental controls, for they have provided a more general framework within which to place them. For a general treatment read Harry M. Johnson, *Sociology: A Systematic Introduction*, New York: Harcourt, Brace and World, Inc., 1960, especially Chapter 20 which deals with social controls. Similar sorts of chapters may be found in most introductory sociology textbooks. We should observe that most sociological treatments of control deal with non-governmental controls and therefore with the less formal, less legal, less visible, but no less important regulatory activities. Informal norms are a special province of the sociologist and are often written about in the context of roles or norms of behavior. Governmental regulations are simply viewed as a particular class of control.

An important theoretical consideration, although difficult reading, is that of Talcott Parsons, *The Social System*, Glencoe, Ill.: The Free Press, 1952. He views control as one of the twin basic processes for maintaining the social system, the other being socialization. Controls are those activities which are used to handle situations in which the individual cannot or will not be a self-policeman. Socialization presumably 'internalizes' the approved motivations and behavior for most men, most of the time, so that they will do the 'right' thing. Governments, however, cannot rely upon voluntary behavior alone.

In later chapters we will reconsider the problems of regulation and control from a 'normative' or policy perspective, i.e., offer advice on the best types of controls in a more or less democratic polity. At that time we shall continue these bibliographical notes with a number of others that are primarily concerned with the question of how best to regulate whatever should be regulated.

Greeks to write
new constitution
Palo Alto Times, May 31, 1967, Palo Alto, California

Javits Asks Long-Range P
In Slums to Avert Rising U
The New York Times, May 23, 1967, New York, New York

Strife Keeps Yemen
In Political Turmoil
The Oregonian, Aug. 7, 1966, Portland, Oregon

Colombians impatie
with slow reform
Palo Alto Times, May 17, 1967, Palo Alto, California

Albany Opposes Change in Legislative Str
The New York Times, April 2, 1967, New York, New York

Marcos Optimistic on Solving
Social Ills Plaguing Philippines
The New York Times, March 14, 1967, New York, New York

Junta Chief Scores Tribalism in Sierra
The New York Times, March 30, 1967, New York, New York

Nigeria braces
for civil war
Palo Alto Times, May 29, 1967, Palo Alto, California

Detroit Race Riot
Of 1943 Started
In a Traffic Tie-Up
The New York Times, July 24, 1967,
New York, New York

Viets Pon
Land Refo
The Oregonian,
June 21, 1968,
Portland, Oregon

BOTH SIDES RIGID
ON FUND REFORM
The New York Times, July 31, 1967,
New York, New York

Czechoslovak Reform Traced to Economic Lags
Intellectuals' Ferment and
Student Protests Also 'Center of World Rev
Listed as Factors
The New York Times, Nov. 7, 1967, New York, New York
The New York Times,
May 30, 1968,
New York, New York

Chapter 7

Uncertainty and Change: Problems of Adaptability and Stability

In 1900 there were fifty-five nations; today there are at least 120. In 1900, monarchies constituted about 22 per cent of all political systems; in 1968, they constitute but 8 per cent of the present total. In 1900, communist and fascist nations were unknown; today we find at least fifteen communist states and a smaller number of essentially fascist systems. Empires have shrunk drastically in size and number; at least sixty-five new states have come into being since 1900 and most of them, since 1945; new forms of politics have been established; two great world wars have been fought in the twentieth century and countless deaths have resulted. Civil wars, riots, rebellions have been commonplace; indeed, over 1200 revolts occurred during the years 1946-59. Individual nations have undergone great institutional changes during the past century. France, for example, has had five republics, a monarchy and a dictatorship. Germany has experienced a monarchy, a weak democracy, a Nazi dictatorship and now, hopefully, a stronger democracy—all in the past fifty years. Within a period of three months during 1966, seven governments were toppled by military coups in Africa. Nine coups have taken place between 1962-1967 in nineteen Latin American countries and more than eighty since 1930.

Catalogues of facts are, in themselves, meaningless but they do dramatize certain trends and themes of great import to citizen, politician and political scientist alike; namely, that the world is changing rapidly although not everywhere at the same rates, nor in the same directions, nor in the same ways. Great upheavals occur in some lands while the status quo prevails elsewhere and, occasionally, both exist in the same land. Why should there be such great variations and why should the political world have changed so much in the last sixty years? Where are we headed? These are the basic questions posed in this chapter. We warn that the answers are not singular; many theories on change contend in the marketplace of ideas. Perhaps the many facets of change will become better related and clarified as we proceed. Perhaps.

What Is to Be Explained?

Studies of social and political change sometimes leave one with an impression that their authors are not sure what they want to analyze and explain. The inevitable result is a bewildering profusion of ad hoc indicators and facts that appear to confirm the notion of constant alteration. We prefer to reduce this vast confusion to a few critical dimensions: (1) changes in the *performance* of political systems, (2) changes in the basic *institutional structure* of the system itself and (3) changes in *control of governments*. Political science has been most concerned with the second and third types of change. Since we have not devised measures of governmental performance equal to our measurements of national income or productivity, political scientists have had less to say about it in any general, comparative sense. We believe that some measures of political system performance or output are possible and suggest that change be studied in the context of performance as well as basic institutional structures.

Political scientists are not likely, however, to rest content with analyses of institutional and performance changes; most would also like to study change in terms of persons or groups occupying major governing roles which constitute the polity. In particular, we want to focus on changes of top leaders because they are so crucial an element in the process of initiating and carrying out both performance and institutional changes. Our concern with this aspect of political change is enhanced by the wealth of data about leadership changes; leaders are usually the most visible aspects of governments. Political scientists have been most assiduous in their studies of leaders and leadership, whether in the form of party groups, military dictators, old fashioned nobility, or other types of modern elites. We should be remiss if we did not make use of this rich source of materials.

Some Changes in System Performances

Earlier chapters identified various performances of the political system, particularly the production and distribution of various public goods and services. We believe it is possible to measure variations in output of these goods and services through time and to explain these variations. For some purposes this means simply counting the kinds of governmental activity or the amounts of money spent on them. We want to count them just as an economist wishes to count actual physical output of goods, stock market activity or consumer behavior. So, too, would we wish to know the miles of improved highways constructed each year; the number of crimes solved; the number and kinds of new recreational services provided; the efficiency of the fire department and post office in meeting demands; the defense capabilities of nations and so forth. For other purposes we may prefer or need estimates of the worth of these goods and services, calculated, perhaps, by adding up their costs in terms of dollars and cents. Such governmental accounting affords us one rather easy and clear method for measuring changes in performance through time, as well as enabling comparative studies of many nations and types of political system, providing the records are at all comparable. For example, we know that industrialized nations have far greater outputs of public goods and services than do the newly-developing nations. But it would be useful to know the differences more precisely, and the trends, whether toward greater or less international inequality.

It would appear that most nations allocate a far greater proportion of their resources today through political processes than they did a century ago; it would also appear that most nations currently produce and distribute far more *public* goods and services than was the case in earlier years. We suspect, too, that governments produce and administer far more controls and regulations than ever before. There is evidence that governments also produce a much greater variety of public goods and services; in other words, governments have expanded the scope, quality and nature of what they do. Since there is no convenient worldwide survey of changes in public products, performances, or the relative role they play in social systems, we must depend upon illustrations to make our points.

At the turn of the century United States governments (all levels) administered about 10 per cent of the gross national product; at present they handle between 25 and 33 per cent of the GNP.[1] If one were to measure the total resources consumed by the United States government we would note an increase of a little more than 350 per cent from 1900 to 1950, and if we added military expenditures, as we must, the increase would have been more than 500 per cent. These figures gain in meaning when we take account of the fact that national income only doubled during that period. The rise in the governmental share of the nation's resources was more than twice the rise in the nation's total product. There was also a six-fold

---

[1] The above figures are taken from Solomon Fabricant, *The Trend of Government in the United States Since 1900* (New York: National Bureau of Economic Research, Inc., 1952), p. 25.

rise in governmental employment and a similar increase in capital assets held by the government.

Another interesting measure of change in the government's role within a society is the proportion of government employment. We may assume that changes in the numbers of bureaucrats, soldiers, police, etc., are indicators of the varying importance attached to what governments are empowered to do: resource allocation, the distribution of benefits and costs, the production of rules, regulations, symbols and statuses. Presumably the greater the proportions of these governmental agents the greater their significance in social life. For example, studies of Great Britain have shown that total government employment has risen from 3.6 per cent of the working population (1891) to 24.3 per cent of all workers in 1950.[2] In Britain there were 2.57 government servants per 100 citizens in 1901 while fifty years later the figure had increased to 6.53, presumably serving the needs and desires of British citizens. A major reason for the increase stems from the fact that Britain has many more nationalized industries today than does the United States. In communist countries the proportions working directly for government are of course vastly greater than in either the United States or United Kingdom.

Overall performances of political systems have changed greatly as they have absorbed greater proportions of the national resources and individual incomes. We have seen some fairly accurate and reliable measures of such changes. But they do not tell the whole story. The interested citizen and political scientist is also concerned with the changing *composition* of the governmental product. Are public allocations of resources different from the past? Data on these problems are wanting; we have but fragments, from here and there, and for limited periods of time.

Generally it seems that governments have been increasing both the amounts spent on traditional functions of government and creating new goods and services, as well as regulations. Entirely new programs have been invented and conducted by governments in industrial systems, including most welfare activities, transfers of incomes, and the direct production and distribution of goods and services by governmentally-owned or controlled enterprises. Social security, unemployment insurance, child welfare, scientific research in all program areas, including nuclear energy and space explorations, are relatively new governmental endeavors. Provision of public education, recreation, health services and controls are quite recent innovations on the part of most governments.

We should point out, however, that expenditures do not vary uniformly among governments and that quite different variations may be

---

[2] The figures are taken from Moses Abramowitz and Vera Eliasberg, *The Growth of Public Employment in Great Britain* (New York: National Bureau of Economic Research, Inc., 1957), pp. 25, 107.

found on the part of any single government. For example, national expenditures for traditional programs in the United States displayed moderate growth through the late nineteenth century. But in this century two world wars stimulated enormous expenditure increases—to nearly half of this nation's GNP in World War II. Other periods of rapidly increased spending are found during the New Deal when emergency relief and social security programs were developed, and during the 1950s and 1960s, when expenditures first for Cold War armaments and then for Great Society welfare programs were added.[3] Past and present defense, education and transportation, for example, now take the bulk of the public dollar in this country. Their respective importance, however, differs considerably in other nations. For example, defense expenditures varied from 25.7 per cent of Jordan's GNP to .02 per cent of Jamaica's national product in one comparison of eighty-two nations circa 1960.[4] Certainly similar variations could be found in other public programs of industrialized and democratic nations. But the kinds of changes and their reasons need far more systematic observation than we have found thus far.

Control activities on the part of governments are more difficult to measure through time but indicators may be found which provide rough approximations. For example, the proportions of police in governmental employment have changed greatly during the last seventy-five years in Great Britain. In 1891, the police constituted about 25 per cent of local government officials; in 1950, they constituted only 5 per cent of the local officialdom. On the other hand, the proportions of police to the total population has shown a slight increase since 1851 when there was but one policeman for every 1,215 persons, while today Britain has a policeman for every 703 persons.[5] Other regulators (better known as bureaucrats) have increased greatly in all western nations. Like the police, such bureaucrats can hardly be described as just controllers since they also perform vital services. But in performing a service for some citizens they necessarily control those who must abide by the rules. We can regard the enormous increase in numbers of government employees as a partial indicator of both increasing services and regulations, since the latter are seldom self-enforcing. Our impression is that the increase in numbers of governmental employees in the newly-developing nations is even more remarkable than has been the case in western history—remarkable because the rate of increase is probably higher.

One of the more persistent surprises of political life is that a leader

---

[3] M. Slade Kendrick, *A Century and a Half of Federal Expenditures* (New York: National Bureau of Economic Research, Inc., 1955), Occasional Paper #48 (revised), pp. 14-15.

[4] Bruce M. Russett *et al.*, *World Handbook of Political and Social Indicators* (New Haven: Yale University Press, 1964), pp. 79-80.

[5] Abramowitz and Eliasberg, *op. cit.*, p. 72.

may promise one set of policies and soon thereafter pursue a totally opposing set. This may be because of uncertainty in political situations, a matter we dwell upon in detail in subsequent chapters. Or it may have to do with the constant problem leadership faces in maintaining political support. In any event, policy changes are a prime fact in all societies, whether leaders or institutions change or not. While historians and others have written countless volumes on domestic and foreign policy alterations, relatively little of this detail and data has been systematized into useful generalizations. Our observations tend, therefore, to be impressions and should not be accepted as gospel truth without further inquiry.

We wish we knew more about the rates and directions and conditions of policy changes. For example, which types of polities are most and least adaptable in recognizing the need for changes of policy? Under which conditions will citizens accept change most readily? How long has it taken for changes in various policy areas, including foreign and domestic concerns? How do policy changes come about in various societies?

Foreign Policy Changes

Studies of policy-making, particularly the historical or case study type, tend to show that few nations pursue the same public policies for long periods of time without alteration. New policies in foreign affairs, new policies covering domestic matters are the subject of debate everywhere. As America has evolved from a newly-developing nation-state to its present preeminence it has pursued foreign policies with radically different objectives and means, including expansionist "manifest destiny," protected isolation, collective security, armed international policeman. Britain has alternated from balance-of-power policies to those of imperial command, and more recently to those of a lesser power in a bi-polar world. France, Germany and the U.S.S.R. have all changed policies in equally dramatic ways and never more so than when they turn their resources to war.

There is nothing which so pervasively changes the policy priorities and activities of governments as the outbreak of war—and no one would deny the magnitude of all its other consequences as well. Probably the most ambitious study of the patterns of war-making by nations was that directed by Quincy Wright, conducted, ironically, just prior to World War II and reported in a massive compendium entitled *A Study of War* (recently republished with an updated postscript on recent war policies).[6] The accompanying tables (7-1, 7-2) reflect only slightly the many extensive attempts of the author and his associates to document comparative dimensions and trends in the military policies of nations. Note variations in the incidence of wars as reported for the nine half-century periods listed in Table 7-1.

---

[6] Quincy Wright, *A Study of War*, 2nd ed. (Chicago: University of Chicago Press, 1965).

Table 7-1

Summary of Participation in Wars in Modern Civilization by Important States, by Fifty-Year Periods, 1480-1941

State	1480–1550	1550–1600	1600–1650	1650–1700	1700–1750	1750–1800	1800–1850	1850–1900	1900–1941	Total
England (Great Britain)	6	6	7	10	8	7	14	13	7	78
France	10	10	6	8	4	4	11	12	6	71
Netherlands	1	1	2	8	5	2	2	0	2	23
Spain	12	7	11	6	7	5	6	7	3	64
Empire (Austria)	13	4	3	8	7	5	6	3	3	52
Prussia (Germany)	0	1	1	3	4	4	2	3	5	23
Savoy (Italy)	0	0	4	1	5	2	1	5	7	25
Denmark	2	1	3	5	1	3	3	1	1	20
Sweden	2	6	4	4	5	3	2	0	0	26
Poland	3	4	7	5	3	2	1	1	4	30
Russia (U.S.S.R.)	2	6	7	8	7	10	10	4	7	61
Turkey	6	5	5	4	3	5	5	5	5	43
United States	0	0	0	0	0	2	4	2	5	13
Japan	0	0	0	0	0	0	0	2	7	9
China	0	0	0	1	0	0	0	4	6	11
World	32	31	34	30	18	20	41	48	24	278

Source: Quincy Wright, *A Study of War*, 2nd ed. (Chicago: The University of Chicago Press, 1965), p. 650.

Table 7-2

Summary of Certain Characteristics of Wars of Modern Civilization, by Fifty-Year Periods, 1480-1941

Characteristic	1480–1550	1550–1600	1600–1650	1650–1700	1700–1750	1750–1800	1800–1850	1850–1900	1900–1941	Total
No. of wars fought:										
Mainly in Europe	28	31	31	26	18	13	15	14	11	187
Mainly outside Europe	4	0	3	4	0	7	26	34	13	91
Total	32	31	34	30	18	20	41	48	24	278
Average duration of wars:										
Fought mainly in Europe	3.5	4.9	8.2	4.9	4.9	3.6	3.7	1.1	3.7	
Fought mainly outside Europe	1.0	0	1.0	7.2	0	3.0	4.1	2.8	3.6	
All wars	3.8	4.9	7.6	5.2	4.9	3.4	4.2	2.7	3.6	
Types of war participated in by European states:										
Balance of power	18	12	13	14	13	10	8	12	11	111
Civil	4	14	14	8	5	5	8	9	3	70
Defensive	6	5	4	4	0	0	0	0	0	19
Imperial	4	0	3	4	0	5	11	13	4	44
Total	32	31	34	30	18	20	27	34	18	244

Types of war participated in by non-European states:

									Total
Balance of power	0	0	0	0	2	0	10	16	8	36
Civil	0	0	0	0	0	1	4	4	3	12
Defense	6	5	4	4	0	0	2	0	0	21
Imperial	4	0	3	4	0	5	11	13	4	44
Total	10	5	7	8	2	6	27	33	15	113

Types of war participated in by all states:

									Total
Balance of power	18	12	13	14	13	10	17	23	15	135
Civil	4	14	14	8	5	5	11	12	5	78
Defensive	6	5	4	4	0	0	2	0	0	21
Imperial	4	0	3	4	0	5	11	13	4	44
Total	32	31	34	30	18	20	41	48	24	278

Source: Adapted from Wright, *ibid.*, p. 651.

Why the rise and fall of apparent aggressiveness for each state? Do the fluctuations match the rise of certain empires, the flowering of nationhood, or
perhaps the times of relatively superior economic power? Are there some
countries which appear consistently more aggressive through most of these
periods? If so, would you be inclined to attribute it to cultural peculiarities,
persistent economic problems, or perhaps continuing geographic vulnerability to other states? Check your theories systematically against the figures in terms of what you think are the significant variables, and score the
degree of confirmation, if any.

Note in Table 7-2 the characterization of types of wars in these same
time periods. Do these provide better clues as to the typical kinds of conflict
situations confronted by states during these centuries? What kind of war
tends to engage the greatest number of states? Can you think of reasons
why? This is richly suggestive of explanations about policy change from a
broader perspective than simply considering the kind of political leadership or the institutional relationships within one nation-state. External
demands and threats also provoke policy responses, and Quincy Wright
explores these in terms of the problems of arms races, of imperial expansion
and the competitiveness of contiguous nations over several types of goods or
resources. In the text added more recently, Wright reaffirms some of the
more important 'causes' of wars in the light of experience: (a) reaction to
perceived threats; (b) national enthusiasm for ideals; (c) frustration over
unsatisfactory conditions attributed to a foreign scapegoat; (d) belief in
the utility of threats of war or war itself as an instrument of independence,
policy, prestige, or power; and (e) conviction that military self-help is necessary to vindicate justice, law, and rights if peaceful negotiation proves
ineffective.

War is not the only means of conducting international relations. But
what is of greater significance, here, are changes in foreign policies, whether
peaceful or not, which entail considerable domestic consequences. Unhappily we cannot provide neat lists or tables of foreign policy responses for all
the nations of the world, but we can suggest some generalizations which
pertain to such changes as well as indicate the nature of foreign policy-
making. Foreign policy-making is hardly unique although it does have elements which are somewhat special as contrasted to domestic governing.
Perhaps the most important of these elements is the fact that nations react
more as independent entities than as units in a common political system.
There is no widely accepted single government of the world; there are only
partial and temporary agreements among various nations to act in certain
ways. Hopefully these agreements will lead to further accords and eventual
world-wide rules which achieve more general compliance.

Foreign policy is subject to change and even to sudden alteration and
reversal partly because of the nature of the international scene as just described. Nations and their leaders find themselves involved in conflicts

under conditions of great uncertainty. Accordingly, flexibility is highly valued. So, too, is the acquisition of information to overcome that uncertainty. Under these conditions it is very difficult to formulate specific principles and decision rules which enable successful adaptability to all circumstances. Policies do not reflect single goals, nor are they highly articulated or widely understood. Instead, policies are frequently ambiguous and often denied if challenged. What one typically finds is a bewildering confusion of statements, actions, non-actions, presumed intentions and incidents. The entire maze defies complete understanding. With all this uncertainty and conflict, both potential and real, no wonder policy-makers tend to be suspicious and refuse to commit themselves for fear premature judgments may become embarrassing at some later date. One gains the impression that foreign policy-makers tend to react rather than plan and that they seldom react to different emergencies in the same way. Thus the search for consistency and continuity in the external responses of nations can be quite frustrating. Adaptability is most likely to mean reacting in such a way that things do not get completely out of control.

Domestic Policy Changes

Whether foreign or domestic policies show greater stability or change is still open to question. It probably depends on the stage of a nation's development. We have the impression, however, that domestic policy-making in the modern nation state is a constantly evolving process which embraces more kinds of concerns, yet it may be easier to understand than foreign policy efforts. We suspect, too, that domestic policy-making is performed under somewhat less uncertainty than is typically the case in international politics. As a result, policy change and innovation can be somewhat more deliberate, i.e., rationally adaptable. We do not wish to push these points too far for many countries do not have highly institutionalized polities in which information processing, policy planning, and thus policy change, can be controlled. As we shall suggest below, modern states and those pursuing modernization, whether democratic or not, do attempt to control their circumstances and intelligently plan for the future and aspire to improve the lot of their people. We believe, also, that knowledge about domestic problems and their resolution is more complete than knowledge about international politics. Certainly the possibilities of controlled change are greater where uncertainty can be reduced.

In domestic policies we find many kinds of innovative policy-making. During our own time one quite innovative policy effort with far-reaching consequences has been the adoption of Keynesian precepts about how to stabilize economic conditions and maintain prosperity. As mentioned in the last chapter, the governmental effort depends upon an understanding of many direct and indirect economic relationships. Note what appears to be a maze of great complexity in Figure 7-1. At the right-hand side you will see the major desired end-effects or goals the government is supposed to aim for: growth, price stability, and high levels of production and employment.

Each of the intersections in the diagram is a link in the vast and intricate interrelationships that constitute a modern economy; each of these points or links is one which government can affect more or less directly, more or less effectively in its efforts to control the workings of the entire system. Conservatives tend to prefer minimizing the number of governmental actions or prefer to affect certain linkages instead of others, while liberals seem to prefer controlling more links and often those which conservatives want to see unhindered. Each school of thought tends to view some links and policies as more efficacious than others; for example, conservatives like to manipulate investment decisions by entrepreneurs while liberals tend to prefer manipulation of consumption choices.

Very seldom have non-economic policy programs been integrated conceptually in such a complex system of interdependent relationships. But we expect more such innovative ventures, in such areas as environmental health, metropolitan renewal, distressed areas and even informational procedures for governmentally conducted research. Can you conceive of some of the dimensions and ramifications of policy efforts in each such case? Think of a model or a system of interrelated elements affecting the problem which the government should (ideally) be seeking to control. Such broad-gauged, coordinated policies may indeed come in the wake of distress analogous to the Great Depression which ushered in the Keynesian approach. In Part 2 we shall approach such problems in terms of strategies for political effectiveness and guidelines for public policies.

The adoption of the Keynesian approach to guiding and controlling the economy is an especially good illustration of domestic policy change of the deliberative sort. For one thing, the analysis and policy prescriptions of Keynesians were stoutly resisted by many as dangerous doctrine. Yet the appeal and adoption of these new policies was chiefly in response to a major domestic crisis—depression. The adoption took more than twenty-five years of effort on the part of many people, including economists, politicians and even businessmen. The advocates of Keynesian ideas had to learn politics and even adjust, refine and revise some of the original tenets of Keynes. Much of the change was in the direction of according to government greater power; while this was widely evident, the intricate nature of Keynesian solutions was not widely understood. The policies could not be easily popularized by slogans or appealing symbols, as in the case of many programs conferring direct benefits. In short, the history of the adoption of Keynesian economic analysis and policies vividly illustrate a modern effort at policy change.

Figure 7-1
An Economic Model for Policy Choices

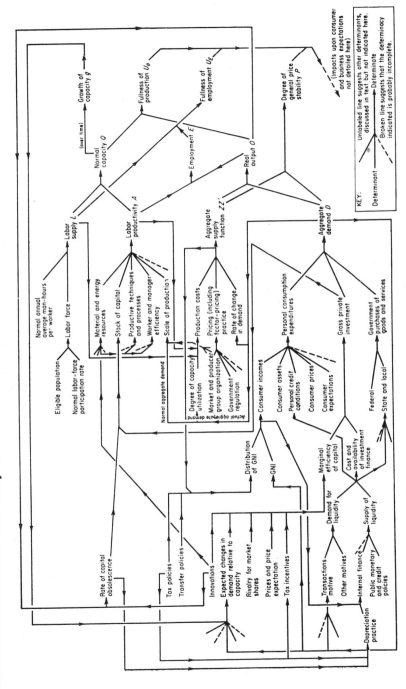

Source: John P. Lewis, *Business Conditions Analysis* (New York: McGraw-Hill Book Company, Inc., 1959), p. 274.

Of course there are many ways in which governmental programs are introduced or significantly changed, and some of these we dealt with at length in Chapter 2 on the mobilization and allocation of public resources. The growth of population and increasing interdependence can to some degree create a political demand sufficiently effective to introduce new or expanded programs and services by governments. We especially noted the innovative effect of new political coalitions at the national level in this country, whether brought about by political movements, by the crucial issues of 'critical elections,' or by conflict and distress as was the case with the Civil War Republicans or the New Deal Democrats. Other nations may have their own peculiar 'thresholds' to be overcome politically, and only far more systematic research will reveal the broader patterns of domestic policy innovation in different kinds of systems. We must also note the other side of the coin, namely, the many resistances or constraints on great policy innovation. One cannot take for granted one form of change without also trying to explain the obverse, i.e. successful denial, delay, or avoidance of policy demands and problems.

Old Questions and New Information

In the absence of systematic study it seems most appropriate to outline what crucial kinds of information should be developed by the new student of political change. Modern scholars are increasingly turning their attention to these subjects, and there are many auspices and funds now available to encourage systematic comparative research along these lines. Thus we urge the student to look for this kind of data in the most recent literature, documentary sources and reports of comparative research. First, the kinds of data to look for and then some guideline questions which should be answered in order to achieve the kind of understanding of change we are urging here:

1. Measurements of governmental products, i.e., the supply of public goods and services. We will want to know the determinants of that supply through time. For example, how does the supply of natural resources affect the amounts and kinds of public goods? Does the structure of political systems affect what governments do? Which types of polities are most effective in generating public goods?

2. Measurements of changes in policies. Which policy areas (for example: foreign; trade; labor, business regulation; taxation; subsidies; law enforcement; labor conditions; agriculture; manufacture; etc.) are most stable? Which most subject to fluctuation? Which areas show rapid growth? Decline? When and where does substantial innovation occur?

3. Are there regular stages through which policies are initiated, processed and adopted? If so, how are they best designated? How long a period of time does each stage 'require'? Are these stages different in different systems? Or are there similarities across systems? What institutions or participants are identified with each stage?

4. Why do policies change through time, or remain more or less constant? Are the explanations to be found in type of political system? Incidence of social problems? The power structure of the nation? The stage of the economy?

5. When policy changes, especially dramatic ones, are made, how are they justified to the decision-makers and citizens? Are there different approaches in the degree to which the policy change involves regulations and controls, distributive benefits and costs or symbolic status goods?

6. Which political systems are most responsive to changing conditions? Of what sort?

7. When do political systems of different types adopt similar policies? There is some evidence that social security policies, as we noted in Chapter 4, are quite similar regardless of the type of polity. Could this be the case for other policies? Is this imitation? Or similarity of needs and demands?

8. How aware are people of the policies of their governments, and who do they believe is responsible for them? Do they know about changes in policies? How (i.e. through general publicity and mass media, specialized channels, etc.)? Evidence may be found in some voting studies to the effect that relatively few citizens have accurate information on many of these matters. Why? Who would tend most to have relatively complete information about important kinds of policy changes?

9. What are some of the special ingredients of innovations in policy-making (i.e., technological 'breakthroughs,' commission studies, agitation and publicity, coalitions of interest groups or elites, etc.)?

In Chapters 9 and 10, we advance some ideas relevant to these questions. We wish it were possible to list and discuss a number of sound general propositions about policy changes and system performances but the present state of inquiry does not enable us to do this with any confidence. At best, one finds plausible but largely implicit generalizations made about policy changes, and many tantalizing insights. In some cases these generalizations are explicit but typically based on a few case studies or the perspectives of a particular observer. Most comparative research still tends to be descriptive of events without more extensive empirical tests. However, one can glean a variety of views and propositions from a careful reading of research efforts designed for other purposes. The following list of ad hoc generalizations constitutes an effort on our part to state and illustrate what remains rather implicit and unsystematic in the general literature of political science on policy changes.[7]

1. Elected leaders prefer flexibility to stability while bureaucrats tend to prefer assurances of regularity in policy making.

2. Foreign policy is not really 'made' but more often managed on an ad hoc basis by dealing with events as they come.

3. Even in their most imaginative actions most governments will react to situations rather than try to control them.

4. Contingency policies cannot detail or anticipate all the relevant details of social and political behavior; and the details may be the most important considerations at the moment of confrontation.

5. Most policies are the product of immediate opportunity and chance, while the others are the 'inevitable' consequences of many partial past choices enacted without knowledge of future consequences.

6. Most established policy programs show a regular growth pattern in the context of increasing population and economic and social development.

7. Crises are of extreme importance in creating opportunities for policy innovation, although severe stress frequently leads to very costly control solutions.

8. New policy proposals are usually initiated by groups reacting to intensified burdens and frustrations.

---

[7] Variations on the above propositions can be found in a variety of studies. Our statements have been influenced by the following sources: Raymond A. Bauer, Ithiel de Sola Pool and Lewis Anthony Dexter, *American Business and Public Policy* (New York: Atherton Press, 1964); Pendleton Herring, *The Politics of Democracy* (New York: W. W. Norton and Company, Inc., 1940); Albert O. Hirschman, *Journeys Toward Progress* (New York: The Twentieth Century Fund, 1963); David Braybrooke and Charles E. Lindblom, *A Strategy of Decision* (New York: The Free Press of Glencoe, 1963); Wallace S. Sayre and Herbert Kaufman, *Governing New York City* (New York: W. W. Norton and Company, Inc., 1960); E. E. Schattschneider, *The Semi-Sovereign People* (New York: Holt, Rinehart and Winston, Inc., 1960).

9. Policy innovations are usually slow and piecemeal, but subject to periodic bursts of imagination and implementation.

10. Policy planning and policy choices are rarely well coordinated across different subject areas.

These few propositions about policy changes amply illustrate the still impressionistic character of thinking about policy change. The chief utility of such statements appears to be in calling to our attention important matters and some highly plausible observations about those phenomena. It would be presumptuous of us to advance these and other similar generalizations as well-substantiated and well-known propositions of political analysis. We feel the quest is just beginning and we look forward to tests or validation during the coming years. A most useful immediate task in which students as well as professors can participate is that of systematizing the propositions currently found scattered throughout political studies about policy change.

Changes in Institutional Structures

We turn now to a more familiar area but one which is deceptively easy to discuss: changes in the basic structure of the political system. We are all familiar with extreme changes such as the Weimar Republic's rapidly turning into a totalitarian Nazi regime; a monarchy in Italy changing into a Fascist dictatorship; an ancient monarchy in Japan being converted into a parliamentary system; a monarchy in Russia changing into a communist dictatorship; and in our own time countless colonial societies becoming independent and forming various types of polities, sometimes of rather brief duration. But what has, in fact, changed? Usually political scientists mean the power structures or relationships between the leaders and led are altered in more or less significant ways. This may mean either that actual participation has been changed or that the rules or roles by which such relationships are 'structured' have been altered. If rulers had been selected by hereditary principles (monarchies) and are subsequently selected through competitive elections we have had a major structural change. These are the types of concern one finds among political scientists.

To speak of change in structure generally requires that we be able at least provisionally to classify political systems so that we can say that one type has become or is in the process of becoming another type. All manner of typologies or classifications have been suggested since the time of Plato and Aristotle; in fact, Aristotle himself used a set of some twenty-eight or twenty-nine types and subtypes.[8] They were constructed from a total of six

---

[8] Some of the problems involved in classification of political systems are exemplified in the following contemporary attempts to establish some order in the study of nation-states:

basic or major types. We will not review these types but note simply that studying changes of structure typically will begin with some rough classification of structures, if for no other reason than economy of expression. It is simpler to say that a dictatorship succeeded a monarchy than to list and elaborate all the details of the changes. If a typology is a good one its author has presumably supplied us with some crucial definitions of dictatorship and monarchy so that we know what he is describing. Therefore our first step should be to identify those aspects of political structures or institutions which are considered to be of critical importance in identifying this basic type of change.

Political scientists, as well as most other people, have tended to use the word 'institution' to designate any ruling body, or ongoing organization of government, in a very concrete way. They tend to visualize the actual body of men, and even the building in which it resides, as the embodiment of the institution. Actually, sociologists have contributed a much more relevant definition of institutions by reminding us of their very important non-physical attributes. What is important about institutions are not the persons but rather their specific roles; and what is important about their roles are not the informal practices, but the more basic formalized relationships and rules of performance. Thus political institutions consist of spheres of authority and duty which have rather explicit doctrines justifying them. They tend to have explicit norms specifying the appropriate ways of doing things, i.e., rules about duties, procedures and relationships. The term 'institutionalization' suggests these attributes when they are developed in any sector of human activity: in family life, the economy, religious sphere, or in the polity. The explicit doctrine and rules serve to regularize the practices, and to maintain their legitimacy at least to the degree that they are taught, practiced and thus accepted, honored and shared.

Let us return to political institutions and how these basic forms may change. Most political typologies since Plato and Aristotle have identified changes in the *composition of political authority.* They talked about rule by one, the few or the many or, in other words, dictatorship, oligarchy and democracy. They also identified *the values the rulers served,* Plato choosing a simplified dichotomy of selfish or unselfish, and Aristotle adding some thoughts on the notion of compromise or the 'golden mean.' There are many more complex combinations; as we noted above, Aristotle went to consider-

---

Gabriel Almond and G. Bingham Powell, *Comparative Politics: A Developmental Approach* (Boston: Little, Brown and Company, 1966), Chaps. 9-10; Robert A. Dahl, *Modern Political Analysis* (Englewood Cliffs, N.J.: Prentice-Hall Inc., 1963), Chap. 4; Fred R. von der Mehden, *Politics of the Developing Nations* (Englewood Cliffs, N.J.: Prentice-Hall Inc., 1964), Part 4; Charles W. Anderson, Fred R. von der Mehden, and Crawford Young, *Issues of Political Development* (Englewood Cliffs, N.J.: Prentice-Hall, Inc., 1967); and, G. Lowell Field, *Comparative Political Development* (Ithaca, N.Y.: Cornell University Press, 1967).

able lengths in making such distinctions. Today many of the elaborations have to do with the organization of *specialized governing tasks* and with *procedural rules*. Governments may be typed as to whether they use electoral systems, parliamentary procedures for lawmaking, or divisions of governing responsibilities among several independent formal bodies, such as the separation of powers with their checks and balances as it operates in the United States. The emergence of *political parties* as a means of competing for, capturing or maintaining control of government has given rise to further classifications, usually in terms of whether there is a dominance of one or competition among two or more parties for the top governmental positions. Other scholars prefer to center on the question of whether there is competition among different *elites* for the command of governmental power or, instead, dominance, collusion or perhaps outright conflict relationships among them.

These only touch upon possible structural comparisons in today's world of complex and differentiated institutions, although the above have been dealt with most frequently. But we should also add another dimension of concern to many, namely changes in *the legitimating norms and values* of the governing system. Today we often hear these referred to in terms of the 'isms': communism, capitalism, fascism, socialism and whatever else is considered a major competing political ideology. The honored German scholar Max Weber tried a different approach to this question, distinguishing different ways of legitimating political power.[9] As we have mentioned earlier, in Chapter 4, he designated the basic alternatives as traditional, legal-rational, and charismatic. The first legitimizes the relation of ruler and ruled in ascriptive and time-honored ways (e.g., royalist or conservative values); the second does so in the mode of contract, or exchanges of promises (as with constitutions and bureaucratic relationships); and the third describes the kind of heroic or gifted leadership which in unsettled times commands a following through devotion and belief in the personal powers of the leader.

There is nothing which is necessarily magical or lasting about these typologies, for the political institutions of this world can conceivably evolve in many unique or unforeseeable ways in the future. It is sometimes hard to make the new forms fit some of these older categories, and scholars strive mightily to invent more appropriate types and terms, such as 'transitional' systems (modernizing or at least leaving the traditional norms and structures); 'mobilization' systems (high integration and change through party solidarity, hierarchy and ideology); 'fused,' 'prismatic' and 'diffracted' societies (designating the degree of differentiation of all social structures,

---

[9] See, Max Weber, *The Theory of Social and Economic Organization*, trans. and ed. by A. M. Henderson and Talcott Parsons (New York: The Free Press, 1946).

including the political); or 'totalitarian' systems (suggesting a very pervasive scope and penetrating techniques of political control). Chart 7-1 summarizes some of these types to illustrate the diversity of concepts. One could always continue the list for different political units and purposes: strong mayor/council-manager/weak mayor; or judicial review; checks and balances; due process of law; and so forth. Many of these attributes would go together for different systems; for example, you can select many categories from the chart which are characteristic for the United States. Some may only apply to a limited set of countries and have no exact parallels in others and, of course, every category may have quite special meanings depending upon the use and the user.

Chart 7-1
Commonly Used Typologies

Political Structures	Processes		Norms and Values
Monarchy	Autocracy	Hereditary	Theocratic
Republic	Oligarchy	Electoral	Royalist
Dictatorship	Democracy	Revolutionary	Constitutional
Totalitarian			
	One party	Representative	Traditional
Tribal	Two party	Communal	Legal-rational
National	Multi-party	Bureaucratic	Charismatic
Imperial			
	Executive	Modernizing	Nationalist
Federal	Legislative	Transitional	Communist
Unitary	Judicial	Mobilization	Capitalist
Pluralist			Fascist
Monolithic			
Fused			
Prismatic			
Diffracted			

Theories of how institutions change in political systems approach the problem in different ways. One is to posit the likely changes from one such type to another, as did Plato and Marx (illustrated in Figures 7-3, 7-4). Another is to analyze degrees of vulnerability to change, without specifying a necessary direction or form, as we shall discuss further under the general subject of stability. Most common among modern scholars is the effort to explain institutional changes in terms of broader or more basic factors at work in the environment of the political system, in the economy or society at large. Contemporary theories of modernization or revolution often start from economic situations, or events which cause social distress and psychological dissatisfactions which are then brought to bear on the political system. We shall try our hand at incorporating these approaches too. At any rate the task begins with good definitions of which political institutions have changed and how—the dependent variable to be explained. Whatever the typologies, the important next step is to identify the nature and degree of change to be explained. Good definitions ease the problem of effective comparative description and measurement—a task still found difficult by most of today's scholars. While we have not emphasized institutions as such in our approach thus far, but rather the performance or tasks of governments, this provides an appropriate place to remind the student of the kinds of institutional changes one must account for today.

In the great sweep of history scholars have emphasized the marked progression from small, communal political systems to those having wider scope and more impersonal or formal kinds of organization. The establishment of large empires was certainly a major step in the use of formal law or bureaucratic command to integrate more people and territory under one rule, however loose it may have been in ancient times. The development of the western nation-state as a unit was accompanied by newer legal norms of sovereignty and contract and increasing differentiation of formal institutions and relationships in the polity. New concepts of roles, rights and duties; methods of command, decision and adjudication; and greater distinctions between religious and civil or public and personal values marked the literature and rhetoric of those centuries. As we come into this century the complexity of political forms and roles is managed, or at least met, by increasingly sophisticated technologies. Today we witness an incredible number of new nations breaking the bonds of empires and tribal systems, striving to catch up with the modern giants. By the early 1960s more nation-states had been created than in any century before (about seventy more than had been created in all previous centuries); these include fewer monarchies (about fifteen) but more dictatorships (fluctuating greatly from about twenty to thirty); more constitutional regimes (somewhat over fifty); and some totalitarian regimes (sixteen) new to the twentieth century but now evolving into less terroristic forms than the earlier Nazi and Stalinist types. We have seen the elaboration of democratic forms: forty-one governments broadly representative, eight somewhat more oligarchic, and about forty-three having but some appearance of representative structures or procedures, according to one recent count. About forty-three had some party competition, and nine more had one party which actually dominated—as compared to thirty-four non-democracies where there was a one-party monopoly and five systems which have no parties at all.[10] There were about forty-two presidential regimes, often ruled by one party. There were about fifteen parliamentary regimes and approximately twenty-five systems com-

---

[10] Figures derived from Arthur S. Banks and Robert B. Textor, *A Cross-Polity Survey* (Cambridge: The Massachusetts Institute of Technology, 1963), Chap. 3.

bining parliaments with some royalist or monarchical roles. This enumeration could continue, in terms of bureaucracies, legal procedures, elites and the like. The basic institutional trends should be apparent, but the numbers will continue to change, and we simply caution that you update these figures. What will the future hold? More bureaucratization and related technological capacities, to be sure. New forms of integration and decentralization are becoming possible, and many predict more supranational organizations will assume significant political tasks.[11] Whether there will prove to be more or less competition of parties and elites, different uses or substitutes for elections, more revolutionary and fewer constitutional regimes, are points hotly argued today. We invite you to check up on more recent trends and indicators.

Leadership Changes

Since we cannot be certain that performance and institutional changes are either equivalents of or correlated with changes in the leadership of political systems, we must investigate this dimension of political systems as an independent matter. To be sure, one can provide plausible connections among these elements but few have done so on a systematic basis. In any event we want to look into the matter of changes in leaders and consider possible relationships to institutional rules and system performance. What kinds of changes are possible and when do they occur along with performance or institutional variation, or when do they not?

For many, the crucial problem of leadership change is the question of political stability. One view relates instability to the rapidity of changes in top leaders, while another would emphasize stability as the institutionalized means of assuring periodic and regular renewal of elites. Again, a most useful way to begin an inquiry is simply to note all such changes, and then compare the incidence and kinds of change across nations. One such study was based on the relative turnover of chief executives which each of eighty-seven nations experienced during the period 1945-1961.[12] Admittedly this is a fairly brief span of time over which to measure changes, but since data are available, it is of historical interest to compare those countries for that period. Note the relative ranking of countries by the stability index used. The higher the score or index in Table 7-3, presumably the greater the stability or lower the rate of changes in executive leadership, according to one definition noted above. But note the obvious: both non-democratic and democratic nations have a wide range of scores.

---

[11] Bruce M. Russett, *Trends in World Politics* (New York: The Macmillan Company, 1965).

[12] Bruce M. Russett *et al.*, *World Handbook of Political and Social Indicators* (New Haven: Yale University Press, 1964), pp. 103-104.

Table 7-3

Executive Stability:
Number of Years Independent/
Number of Chief Executives, 1945-1961

No. of cases: 87	Percentage of World Population: 70
Mean: 4.38	Median: 3.00 Range: 16.46

Nations	Per cent of Table Population (cumulative)	Stability Index
Ethiopia, Liberia, Portugal, Spain, Taiwan, Yugoslavia		17.00
India, West Germany	24.8 (through India)	14.00; 12.00
Albania, Poland, Sweden, Switzerland, Yemen		8.50
South Vietnam, East Germany		7.00; 6.00
Afghanistan, Australia, Canada, Saudi Arabia		5.67
Ghana		5.00
Austria, Czechoslovakia, Luxembourg, Mexico, New Zealand, Nicaragua, Norway, South Africa, U.S.S.R., United States	56.6	4.25
Malaya		4.00
Argentina, Bulgaria, Cuba, Honduras, Netherlands, Romania, United Kingdom		3.40
South Korea		3.25
Guinea, Morocco, Philippines, Tunisia		3.00
Chile, Ireland; Burma, Ceylon, Israel	74.6	2.83; 2.80
Colombia, Costa Rica, Denmark, Paraguay, Peru, Turkey, Uruguay		2.43
Libya; Guatemala, Iceland, Venezuela		2.20; 2.13
Sudan; Ecuador, El Salvador		2.00; 1.89
Pakistan; Bolivia		1.75; 1.70
Belgium, Brazil, Haiti, Italy		1.55
Finland, Nepal, Panama, Thailand		1.42
Indonesia; Hungary, Japan		1.33; 1.31
Egypt, Greece, Iran		1.21
Jordan; Iraq, Lebanon: Laos		.84; .81; .78
France		.68
Cambodia, Syria		.54

Source: Adapted from Bruce M. Russett and Hayward R. Alker, Karl W. Deutsch, Harold D. Lasswell, *World Handbook of Political and Social Indicators* (New Haven: Yale University Press, 1964), pp. 103-104.

There are a good number of dictatorships at the top of the list, but also at least three democracies among the top four ranked scores; there are several traditional regimes, some developing countries, some communist regimes;

some very new and some very old states. The bottom of the list shows a somewhat similar mixture of types. It is, in any case, extremely difficult to relate high executive turnover with one set of political institutions alone. Perhaps most ironic is to find the U.S. and the U.S.S.R.—the two opposing leaders of the bi-polarized international system of that time—appearing together somewhat above the midpoint of the entire range. For those who prefer stability in executive office, it may be of some comfort to note that most of the established democracies are found in the middle ranks rather than at the extremes, although with plenty of company from other types of systems, too.

But, of course, what is more relevant for democracies is party alternation and not just turnover of persons occupying executive office. The meaning of personnel changes is very intricately tied to the institutional context; in dictatorships a change in the person of the dictator is most meaningful if it goes farther than a mere 'palace coup' which typically is a shift within the same elite or strata; in competitive democracies it is party turnover and not just the man in office; even in communist systems the scholar tries to see if the composition of the new elite has shifted, or if the turnover in top leaders ushers in new programs. Thus turnover in top personnel can indicate any degree of change, from a mere transfer within a strata or group to a more pervasive alternation. Personnel changes provide a more useful means of assessing change when compared with performance and institutional dimensions. When all three change together, the political transformation is profound indeed, whether instituted by peaceful convention, violent revolution or, say, a negotiated treaty of peace. Sometimes political institutions are changed, but with a continuity of leadership that may belie the scope of change, and then performance checks become important. We can think of instances where a political leader 'went to the people' with a demand for more power, as DeGaulle has done more than once in France; or where the leader has devised a new constitution incorporating some representation, as in Spain; and yet the question of performance changes is an open one in those cases. New forms may not lead to new policies or even to significant new roles, and continuity in leadership may provide the first clue. In any case, alternation of top leaders is typically the most visible kind of political change, and it is a challenge to the student of politics to discern the relevance or meaning attached to it. Let us explore, as an example, the question of changes in party control of the government.

Strangely enough, political scientists have not compiled comparative tables or charts which conveniently summarize party control over time for the democracies. It is really very difficult to state any generalizations about the longevity or stability of control by individual parties or coalitions. Casual impression has it that party control or coalition control of national governments tends to be fairly stable, i.e., a particular party or coalition of parties will maintain itself in power for more than one term. Thus, the

Republican Party controlled the Presidency of the United States for fifty-six of seventy-two years during the period of 1860-1933. Only Presidents Cleveland and Wilson interrupted this long period of Republican domination. And since 1933, the Democrats have controlled the Presidency except for eight years of Republican rule under President Eisenhower. In Great Britain, the Labour Party has held control of Parliament and the Cabinet on only four occasions since the inception of the Labour Party and only two of these incumbencies have been of any duration (1946-50 and 1964-   ). The Liberal Party in Canada dominated national politics from 1935 to the late 1950s when the conservatives under Diefenbaker temporarily gained ascendancy. The Labour Party in New Zealand has likewise held majorities or control of the Parliament and Cabinet for most of the period since 1935. In Norway, coalitions of leftist parties controlled sixteen of the twenty-four governments between 1882 and 1963. These few examples should suffice to suggest that alternations in party control of government among the western democracies takes place infrequently and that once a party is able to gain national office it is in a good position to maintain that power for more than one term. It is relatively rare for parties to alternate constantly with each election. Various studies of party control in American state offices strongly confirm this generalization.[13] Very few states are genuinely competitive in the sense of having each political party in a strong position to oust the other at every election. Many more states are characterized by having a single party dominating the scene for extended periods of time. Think of the one-party Southern and New England states which have had one party in power for long periods since the Civil War. Traditionally the Republicans have had difficulty winning a Southern election while the Democratic candidates have had little chance until recently to win public offices in New England and some Midwestern and plains states.

A number of theories have been advanced to explain this persistent pattern of party control. These explanations have included a number of possible variables, sometimes contradictory, including human inclinations to stay with the familiar, voter satisfactions with government performance, or human indifference and low turnouts; electoral and other institutional arrangements which favor the incumbents; or superior resources available to the party which controls governmental distributions of benefits. Some-

---

[13] Austin Ranney and Willmoore Kendall, *Democracy and the American Party System* (New York: Harcourt, Brace and Company, 1956), Chap. 7; Joseph A. Schlesinger, "A Two-Dimensional Scheme for Classifying the States According to Degree of Inter-Party Competition," *American Political Science Review*, XLIX (December, 1955), pp. 1120-1128; Robert T. Golembiewski, "A Taxonomic Approach to State Political Party Strength," *Western Political Quarterly*, XI (September, 1958), pp. 494-513; David G. Pfeiffer, "The Measurement of Inter-Party Competition and System Stability," *American Political Science Review*, LXI (June, 1967), pp. 457-467.

thing can be said in defense of each of these explanations, especially if it is used in connection with others.

While the causes of party continuity are interesting, many citizens and scholars are more interested in the policy or performance consequences of whatever degree of party change there is in a nation. Unfortunately, few firm, dependable generalizations can be made about policy alternations; we believe that party changes, especially those which are ushered in with huge majorities, do alter policies. But such occasions are rare. One scholar, the late V. O. Key, Jr., asserted, with some evidence, that there were only two such major or "critical" elections in the United States since the late nineteenth century (1898 and 1928), i.e., elections in which new electoral alignments and new elements of the population made their force felt in the choice of Presidents, Congressmen and Senators.[14] The social reforms of the New Deal were a product, Key believed, of the critical 1928 elections, and the more remarkable reforms of the Labour Party in Great Britain after World War II may be similarly explained. But many more elections appear to be reinforcing, or reinstating, in the sense that they simply continue the broad policy outlines that are currently operative in society. Changes as a result of such elections may be termed marginal. The chief concern is with, say, the size of an appropriation for a major social program, not with whether such a program should be adopted or repealed. As we have noted, and will expand upon in Chapters 9 and 10, critical elections, startling party changes and dramatic policy reversals or reforms generally come about as a response to deep crises and shifting power relationships in a society. Since neither of these occurrences is an everyday matter, swift and profound party and policy shifts have been rarities rather than commonplaces. But history, of course, need not always repeat itself and there may be good reasons for contrary developments in the future.

The task of identifying the scope of leadership change in dictatorial systems deals more frequently with institutional or class affiliations of the new and old leaders since the gauge of voter support which exists in competitive electoral systems is lacking. Kremlinologists have probably carried this kind of scholarship to its ultimate refinement. In the earlier years of the Soviet regime, such scholars could compare the class backgrounds of the new revolutionary leaders with those of the previous aristocratic regime. Later, they preferred to trace recruitment of Soviet leadership from various bureaucratic and party positions. Now, they tend to emphasize the institutional sectors, the geographic regions and the occupational strata since these factors may provide either the power base for top leadership or the resources

---

[14] V. O. Key, Jr., "A Theory of Critical Elections," *Journal of Politics*, XVIII (February, 1955), pp. 3-19.

for opposition, or the typical ladders of recruitment to the top ranks. As noted by one student of Soviet political succession, Myron Rush, personal rivalries and interests will arouse many factions during a Soviet succession crisis, but the resources for success must reach beyond the top level of leadership. "A faction's strength is reflected in its representation in the regime's top organs, but the substance of that strength is the faction's influence in institutions and social groups."[15] Rush noted four chief sources of Soviet political power:

1. The institutions of dictatorship: the Party machinery, the state bureaucracy, the system of productive enterprises, the army and the political police—with some subsidiary organizations such as legislative bodies, trade unions, 'intellectuals' and youth groups.
2. Territorial bases of power: some part of the above who are leaders in a large city or Union-republic.
3. Professional groups: those with strong institutional identifications, such as the economic technicians.
4. Personal influence: where the prestige, personal associations or popular following may cut across institutional and professional lines.[16]

More complete documentation of any alternation in relative weights of these power sources will be more revealing as more such successions of top Soviet leaders occur. It will be especially valuable to compare these to other communist or dictatorial systems, to see if there are any common leadership trends in these now highly institutionalized political regimes.

The western scholar has been most interested in communist leadership changes as a test of the stability of these regimes. Succession periods are frequently discussed as crises, based on an assumed (or projected) legitimacy problem in such revolutionary regimes. For some these crises are seen as offering a chance for repressed peoples or groups to rise up against the regime; others view revolutionary leaders as charismatic and thus unable to transfer the right to rule; and still others depict such totalitarian systems as inherently arbitrary, where succession must be fought out among those who have garnered most of the means of control or force. Each of these hypotheses needs more confirmation by objective evidence before being related to turnover in top leadership. Have there been signs of popular revolts or resistance during successions? What are the indicators of loss of

---

[15] Myron Rush, *Political Succession in the USSR* (New York: Columbia University Press, 1965), p. 84.

[16] *Ibid.*, pp. 84-85.

legitimacy, from Lenin to Stalin, Beria-Malenkov-Khrushchev, and Brezhnev-Kosygin? There have been purges and banishments, to be sure, and forceful efforts at control, but their incidence and pattern suggest they are more related to the consolidation of powers for existing leaders than to the actual succession struggle. We urge the student, therefore, to ascertain first the actual patterns of change, and then test as carefully as possible the explanations offered. As we study these systems over a greater length of time, we see that the institutional context is more likely to stabilize succession, as Rush points out, than to crumble with successive transitions at the top.

By contrast, consider a form of leadership succession which typically occurs in more forceful and seemingly arbitrary fashion and with greater frequency in many systems. We are referring to coups d'etat, the forceful change of rulers by a group, most typically military, which has conspired behind the scenes. Secrecy, surprise and force are the key elements, and to many this is the ultimate in political instability. The incidence of such coups enables extensive comparison and examination. One scholar noted that of the fifteen nation-states created between 1945 and 1955, nine had suffered military coups; of thirteen states created between 1918 and 1944, six experienced military revolt and dictatorship. And of those forty-six states in existence for more than a century, "no less than twenty-six of these have suffered from some form or other of military intervention in their politics, usually of a violent kind."[17]

These coups represent a case where high instability of political leadership does not necessarily entail any significant pattern of change in either institutions or policies. Even though violent, they do not constitute a revolution, for no major restructuring of institutions typically is entailed. And they are seldom based on any planned policy changes; rather, they are directed to the seizure or transfer of power itself. As S. E. Finer notes in his most extensive comparative survey, these coups tend to occur in those states with a colonial or dynastic heritage which remain as oligarchies, or in those autocracies without ideological legitimation.[18] The persistence of the old institutional forms, with the old elites commanding power, is the typical context. But, as Finer notes, there are crucial divisions among the elite: personal or regional identifications or rivalries among different elements of the old elite, whether religious, political or economic. The tempting solution is to use force to settle differences, to restore order or the 'right' rule, and the military most often possesses the key command of armed force. It is disciplined, skilled, and has the cohesion to carry out a conspiracy with dispatch and secrecy. They have a sense of mission that can easily be identi-

---

[17] S. E. Finer, *The Man on Horseback: The Role of the Military in Politics* (New York: Frederick A. Praeger, Inc.; London: Pall Mall Press, Ltd., 1962), p. 2.

[18] *Ibid.*, pp. 3-4.

fied with saving the nation by intervening to restore the right rulers, practices, or to take command of the situation for the sake of order.

The pattern appears to continue and spread: in Latin America and the Middle East, and now increasingly in Africa and the newer Asian nations. The Latin Americans, who are old hands at violent overthrow, distinguish kinds of coups in terms of whether the blow is aimed simply at removing the head of state, or at replacing many governmental positions, or at establishing an outright military dictatorship, or is merely intended as a brief intervention.[19] Chart 7-2 indicates a useful diagram of the modes, levels and results of such cases of military intervention. It would be most useful if some enterprising scholar would supply the relative frequencies of each possible relationship in the diagram, so that we could discern more precisely the directions in current trends.

Note further the implications for instability in these situations. While these are not revolutionary transformations of institutions, violence or force is used and the change is unexpected, i.e., lacks the regularity or predictability of institutionalized processes. They are beyond the reach of popular participation, just as are royalist or communist successions, but the nature of the intervention deprives them of any of the typical means of legitimation. In this sense institutional instability is involved, and creates the situation for the coup as the beginning of the flow chart suggests. This form of instability can be related to another aspect of public performance, that of maintaining law and order. Military rule in these situations may be justified in terms of establishing order, but performance tends to bely the promise. The resort to force to capture government is only symptomatic of the general incidence of political violence in the system. Table 7-4 (pp. 288-89) indicates the high incidence of violence in such countries given to coups. And the frequency of occurrence of coups in the same country strongly suggests that they do not solve the problem of disorder any more than they change substantially the basic structure of the system. In these cases the sources of instability persist, and change in top personnel, even though violent, is only symptomatic of a more basic condition.

The Problem of Adaptation: Challenge and Response

The emphasis upon stability seems to many to be inherently conservative. It focuses upon order, continuity, regularity and strongly suggests that the known ways are to be preferred to the unknown. But the political prob-

---

19 *Ibid.*, Chaps. 10-11. See also Irving L. Horowitz, "The Military Elites," in Seymour M. Lipset and Aldo Solari, eds., *Elites in Latin America* (New York: Oxford University Press, 1967), pp. 150-153.

Chart 7-2
Some Variations in Coups d'Etat

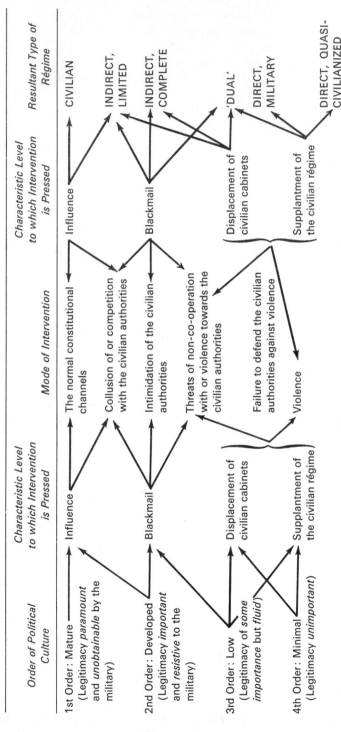

Order of Political Culture	Characteristic Level to which Intervention is Pressed	Mode of Intervention	Characteristic Level to which Intervention is Pressed	Resultant Type of Régime
1st Order: Mature (Legitimacy *paramount* and *unobtainable* by the military)	Influence	The normal constitutional channels	Influence	CIVILIAN
2nd Order: Developed (Legitimacy *important* and *resistive* to the military)	Blackmail	Collusion of or competition with the civilian authorities	Blackmail	INDIRECT, LIMITED / INDIRECT, COMPLETE
3rd Order: Low (Legitimacy of *some importance but fluid*)	Displacement of civilian cabinets	Intimidation of the civilian authorities	Displacement of civilian cabinets	'DUAL'
4th Order: Minimal (Legitimacy *unimportant*)	Supplantment of the civilian régime	Threats of non-co-operation with or violence towards the civilian authorities	Supplantment of the civilian régime	DIRECT, MILITARY / DIRECT, QUASI-CIVILIANIZED
		Failure to defend the civilian authorities against violence		
		Violence		

Source: S. E. Finer, *The Man on Horseback: The Role of the Military in Politics* (London: Pall Mall Press, 1962), p. 168.

lem of change has another very important aspect, too. If the world is constantly changing it may not be certainty but flexibility that is the most important problem for the polity. New policies and maybe even new methods and forms may more appropriately meet the challenges of changing conditions, of continuing conflicts and new threats. Those who are concerned with the political problem of adaptation see the political enterprise as one of problem-solving, of creative solutions, of continuing innovation. They would prefer to view political power as an instrument for changing the existing approaches, a means of intervening in an ongoing system and redirecting its energies and purposes. Here change is honored as a most important product of the political system, the most direct and effective mechanism in society for providing solutions, resolving differences and dissatisfactions, achieving goals in new contexts, and guaranteeing appropriate performance.

Planned, Orderly Change

Perhaps the most idealistic approach to political adaptation centers upon the rational and deliberative capacity of governments and rulers, and the peaceful force of enlightenment in guiding men to cooperative, collective endeavor. There are points of historical confirmation, too. Some great political events of our own nation were instances of planned and deliberated change of rather basic institutions, such as the creation of new forms of government (both democratic and theocratic) by America's early settlers, and the even more extensive abandonment of the Articles of Confederation and the enactment of the Constitution. On a lesser level, city councils, state legislatures, Congress, the courts and many administrative agencies deliberately originate change or carry it out each day. There may be discussion and dissension, but it is peacefully resolved, and at least those who win feel that the solutions more often than not were for the better. And many who engage in these processes for any length of time tend to become proud of the methods and procedures, to admire the ingenuity of their solutions, compromises and means of reaching agreement on an issue. In most responsible decision bodies there are strong influences toward agreement, courteous cooperation, a climate of enlightenment and propriety. One must consider non-democratic cases also. We might also point out that very great changes have been ushered in within our century through the planned programs of the communist governments. Some came to power through violence and revolution, but once established they proceed to sponsor extensive deliberate change to alter the entire institutional framework of society. Coordinated planning and direction are conceived as essential in the communist state, and thus knowledge and skill in producing public goods is accorded a high place. We would not wish to dismiss the disturbing implications of the more forceful methods, but it would be quite unrealistic to see such governments as solely a network of harsh dictators

Table 7-4

Incidence of Internal Wars in Latin America—1946-1960*

	Warfare	Turmoil	Rioting	Terrorism-Small Scale	Terrorism-Large Scale	Mutiny-Military	Coups-Military	Administrative Coups	Quasi-Private Coups	Military Plots	Totals
Argentina	1	1	10	16	1	5	1	8	1	13	57
Bolivia	1		23	2		5	3	3		16	53
Brazil			27	4	1	2	2	7	1	5	49
Br. Guiana			3								3
Br. Honduras			1								1
Chile			8	1				6		6	21
Colombia	1	1	30	8			2		5	5	52
Costa Rica	3		5	8						3	19
Cuba	1		26	48	2	2	1	7		13	100
Dominican R.			1		1			2		2	6
Ecuador			14	2		6	4	2		13	41
El Salvador			2				2			5	9
Fr. Guiana			1								1
Guatemala			12	10	7	2	1	5		8	45
Haiti			12	13	3		4	3		5	40
Honduras			5	2		1	2			1	11
Mexico			22	5						1	28
Nicaragua	1		2	7	1	1	1	1		2	16

Country									
Panama		17	2	1		3	2	4	29
Paraguay	2	6		1	3	7	1	9	29
Peru		11	2		5	2	2	1	23
Uruguay								1	1
Venezuela		15	2		5	4	2	8	36

* Materials drawn from *Internal War: The Problem of Anticipation* (Appendix 1), a report submitted to the Research Group in Psychology and the Social Sciences by Harry Eckstein (Smithsonian Institution, January 15, 1962).

Original Source: *The New York Times Index.*

Source: Irving L. Horowitz, "The Military Elites," in Seymour Martin Lipset and Aldo Solari, eds., *Elites in Latin America* (New York: Oxford University Press, 1967), p. 151.

and policemen. The planner and the methodical bureaucrat have also performed increasingly significant roles in order to make such systems work.

It is interesting to note that at present the governments of the U.S.S.R.
and Czechoslovakia, and perhaps other communist regimes, too, are consciously experimenting with the adoption of western capitalist-type markets
and price systems. This is a most profound change, from their ideological
perspective, but it points out a major dilemma of planned problem-solving.
Early classical economists, and many of their descendants who defend free
enterprise or capitalism in the West today, have extolled the superior
'rationality' of the market system. In their ideal conception, pricing and
exchange in the marketplace can more efficiently allocate scarce resources
and coordinate a myriad of individual or decentralized decisions so that
wealth is produced with no force or command involved. This was coordination by what Adam Smith labelled the 'invisible hand' of the marketplace,
which satisfied both the self-interested individual (or firm) and realized the
public good at the same time. Adam Smith scoffed at the thought that any
one person could presume to know what the public interest was in any
determinate sense—the crucial article of faith for the planner, socialist or
otherwise. We must caution here that both views tend to be ideal conceptions. Just as the Soviets now try to decentralize and use market mechanisms, so do the free enterprisers justify or live with far more governmental
interference and direction than their free market ideal should tolerate.
Again, we must examine the particular adaptive processes as they take
place in different political contexts, and see what contrasts and trends the
evidence offers.

Responsive Capacity

In part the differences found in the two systems may represent contrasts in emphasis upon *what* problems are considered to be the most important for adaptive responses through political means. In the more democratic
systems there is a lot more concern with the ability of governments to meet
the demands of its members. The political arena is viewed as a place where
citizens bring their own problems and grievances, their desires and aspirations. The government's job is then viewed as dealing with these demands
by helping, conciliating, adjusting or arbitrating. The 'rational' solution
here may have to be compromise, halfway measures or even delay, depending upon the nature of the demands. This is a recurrent problem in democratic theory: whether to appease the very intense feelings of some, follow
simple majority rule criteria, or grant some appeasement or satisfaction to
as many as possible. "The greatest happiness of the greatest number" (as the
utilitarian philosopher Jeremy Bentham put it) is not an easy formula to
follow in actual problem-solving situations. Just try applying it to some
major issue of demand-making in this country. We are sure that at some
point, if you have any empathy for the differences in values and claims of

all contending parties, you would find relief in resorting to an imposed solution in terms of what *you* feel is just. Economists, who have evolved rather esoteric theories of demand-making, refer to this as the problem of interpersonal comparisons of utility in collective choice.

There are many other real-life difficulties in assessing political adaptation as a responsive capacity of governments for meeting citizen demands. We have to ask whether all citizens or groups are equally active and efficacious about expressing what they want, or gaining equal access in a highly diffused and complex political system. One test of the adaptive capacity of governments here would be a check on the number and kinds of participatory opportunities available to members for expressing themselves about matters of concern to them. The question goes beyond legal right or availability of such channels, to whether they are actually used and with what effects. Electoral turnout should be related to responses in leadership, policy performance and even institutional change, to the numbers of complaints about the ability of officials to resolve the source of trouble, etc. But what about the wants of the more quiescent or less visible elements of the citizenry? Is it the responsibility of governments to divine what these wants 'really' are? How do governments know? May this turn out to be rational planning in another guise; that is, defining what is good *for* people by one's own vision or expertise?

Of course political adaptation should be weighed against the scarcities of public resources, the degrees of conflict or competition of competing claims, the efficacy of governmental authority and the ease or facility of controls, the sensitivity to symbolic and status solutions, and so forth. Those who emphasize demands prefer to simplify the task by checking levels of satisfaction and dissatisfaction during the life of an issue. The opinion pollsters often phrase it in terms of "do you feel the President is doing a good job?" or "how do you feel about . . . . . ?", and public responses may be analyzed for trends. The course of such change in feelings about issues could easily be illustrated with a series of graphs showing various stages of conflict leading to a final acceptance of demands for change by the status quo supporters. Figure 7-2 shows what happens in the typical case. Notice that the changes stem from the 'Left' in these graphs; the 'Right' is usually thought to support the status quo, but changes can of course originate anywhere in society. Hitler was actively supported by the Right but he initiated all sorts of dramatic changes when he gained power. In the democracies, change has historically been the rallying cry of the parties of the Left. These graphs vividly illustrate the possible slowness, or speed, of resultant opinion change under different circumstances.

Even the most orderly change may be subjectively upsetting to some segments of society; witness the resistance and hysterical responses of many whites to recent black demands. The integration of classrooms has upset many parents and students, the guarantee of free choice of residence

Figure 7-2

A Natural History of Political Change

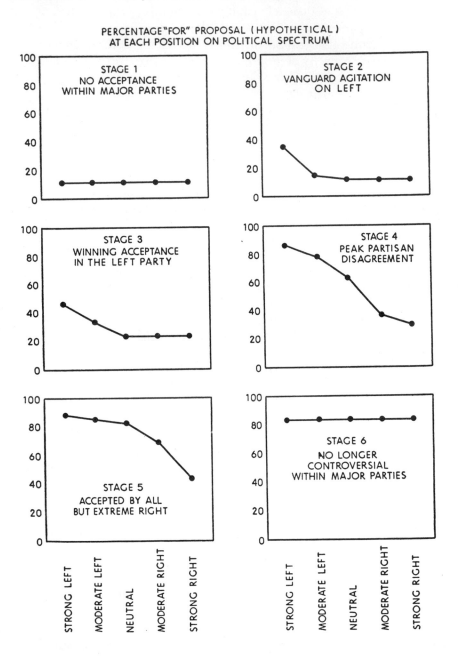

PERCENTAGE "FOR" PROPOSAL (HYPOTHETICAL) AT EACH POSITION ON POLITICAL SPECTRUM

STAGE 1
NO ACCEPTANCE
WITHIN MAJOR PARTIES

STAGE 2
VANGUARD AGITATION
ON LEFT

STAGE 3
WINNING ACCEPTANCE
IN THE LEFT PARTY

STAGE 4
PEAK PARTISAN
DISAGREEMENT

STAGE 5
ACCEPTED BY ALL
BUT EXTREME RIGHT

STAGE 6
NO LONGER
CONTROVERSIAL
WITHIN MAJOR PARTIES

STRONG LEFT — MODERATE LEFT — NEUTRAL — MODERATE RIGHT — STRONG RIGHT

Source: Bernard Berelson *et al., Voting* (Chicago: University of Chicago Press, 1954), p. 208.

has aroused white fears and antagonisms, and we find intense opposition expressed both by covert intimidation and overt demonstration. The uncertainties of change mean that the precise benefits and costs are seldom scientifically ascertainable, and when they are, some citizens may not be convinced or they may still object on other than rational grounds (e.g., being forced, injured pride, nostalgia for the old, etc.). Eric Hoffer, the profound and literate longshoreman, said there is an 'ordeal of change.'[20] Who knows how it will all work out? The comforts of routine are widely appreciated. And of course, citizens may experience many less visible effects of intended change, which create further reactions and demands. In terms of systems theory, there is a continuous cycle of 'feedbacks' both visible and non-visible, material or otherwise, direct or indirect, from government action to the new phase of citizen demands. We may not always be able to follow the complex linkages, so focussing on citizen demands and satisfactions appears a simpler alternative. And to many democratic theorists, such as Bentham, John Dewey, and Gabriel Almond and Sidney Verba more recently, this citizen-government relationship is the crucial one in public life, where government responsiveness and respect for citizen's desires can develop a high order of civic culture.

Modernization

The case of newly-developing states is a fascinating contrast in the present context because most of these nations are led by men who, educated for the most part in western universities, share the western scientific and liberal values. They have learned to place a very high value on secular progress, including democratization and industrialization, and are both ambitious and impatient about modernizing their own countries. Anxious to lead their countrymen out of ancient practices they often attempt to institute broad-scale social and economic changes which would indeed be unsettling to the older citizens, to many of the established institutions and their elites, and even to those elements abroad whose interests or concerns are affected. The leaders see their political task as moving or converting the citizenry to accept these ends and to dedicate their efforts and resources to them.

This rather all embracing political effort has been characterized by the term 'mobilization system.'[21] Centralized political leadership plays a crucial role in arousing new citizen loyalties for devotion to new tasks, and they do so with all available resources: by the authority of charisma, ideology or precept, through the cadres of a militant and obedient party organi-

---

[20] Eric Hoffer, *The Ordeal of Change* (New York: Harper and Row, Publishers, 1952).

[21] David E. Apter, *The Politics of Modernization* (Chicago: The University of Chicago Press, 1965), especially Chap. 10.

zation and, if lucky, by the dedication and skills of the military and other public servants. Thus the uncertainties of change are to be appeased by the newly inspired faith—what some have called the political religion—and the securities of old institutions are to be replaced by the encouragements and satisfactions of the new forms of political integration and identity. The political conditions for change are thus created first, and the efficacy of this mobilization should break old bonds, in theory at least. But the leaders must know the content of the task to which all this must be devoted. *What* is to be done?

The hope has been that rational social and economic planning can direct these forces of change. Many of these nations pursue explicit socialist goals and even employ planners to assist in the formulation of national policies for achieving these goals of modernization, often within stipulated periods, such as the famous five-year plans of the U.S.S.R. and India. As might be expected, the advisers and the experts sometimes differ with one another not only about appropriate goals but over the most effective ways of achieving these goals. For example, some economists advocate 'balanced' growth while others favor 'unbalanced' and incremental change.[22] The former approach claims that all the plans for change must be consistent, i.e., if a government plans on importing or building so many automobiles it must plan on constructing an appropriate number of miles of highways, have a sufficient number of spare parts, mechanics and gasoline stations in the appropriate places. This all seems reasonable, but the unbalanced growth theorists claim that change never took place this way in history and, furthermore, there are unforeseen advantages to inconsistencies. Such inconsistencies act as inducements to correct the errors. If there are too many cars built it may stimulate gasoline dealers and highway builders to renew their efforts.

As there are different economic planners so there are different social and political planners who deal with problems of population, health, education, political institutions, administration, etc. In each of these areas, as we have noted, great changes are expected and stupendous efforts are required to achieve them, sometimes against the will of many members of the society. The experts have learned that reform in one area is usually contingent upon reforms of a certain kind in other areas. Economic growth cannot be easily attained without educated people who are disciplined in the ways of industry and who value material goods. A population that grows too rapidly may outrun resources for sustaining healthy people. A non-

---

[22] The balanced growth theory is perhaps best exemplified in Ragnar Nurske, *Problems of Capital Formation in Underdeveloped Countries* (New York: Oxford University Press, 1953), while the unbalanced growth approach is chiefly associated with the name of Albert O. Hirschman, *The Strategy of Economic Development* (New Haven: Yale University Press, 1958).

literate people may not be able to contribute quite as much to the political life of the nation as they could if educational attainments were higher. A people accustomed to traditional authority cannot readily adapt themselves to democratic processes which require some skepticism and a willingness to criticize in public and to take an interest in political affairs.

All these obstacles are dealt with at greater length in Chapter 14 but for the moment the focus is on the capacity of newly-developing nations to meet their problems of adaptation in a world they did not create and which their leaders and the young would like to see significantly altered. The fact that the western world and the Soviet Union have faced these problems in the past has encouraged the new states to emulate them and to hire western consultants to help speed modernization. Many newly-developing nations began in revolution and violence, but most seem determined to meet the problems of their own aspirations by the deliberate application of intelligence and information to their situations. Adaptation of the givens confronting them, and planned redirection, has become one of the major political tasks of the mid-twentieth century.

Intelligence in Problem-Solving

We should especially emphasize a very important aspect of orderly, institutionalized change, whatever the form. If there are public problems to be solved, adaptation will be dependent upon the degree of knowledge and understanding of them and the perception of possibilities about what can be done. The caliber of relevant information about different aspects of the problems, whether stemming from citizen demands or from centrally formed conceptions of needs and goals, is crucial. Information has become a most highly valued political resource, to the point that public leaders today are seldom without their press secretaries, and an ever-increasing part of the public bureaucracies today are engaged in gathering, creating and managing information, rather than in simply running enterprises, extending services, or commanding obedience. Intelligence takes different forms in terms of its contributions to the adaptive task. There is *strategic intelligence,* which deals with political factors such as military involvement, foreign policy, or even campaign and developmental strategies. *Diagnostic information,* which trained experts are expected to provide, concerns the economy, health and safety, agriculture, poverty and race problems, or urban congestion. The expert is supposed to tell the decision-maker what is happening and why—what are the causes, trends and the like. And we might label as *creative intelligence* that most crucial form in which information is selected and combined or proposed in new ways as solutions and procedures for defining and meeting the problem. In the political realm such problem-solving must combine both diagnostic and strategic considerations, a point often overlooked by experts and reformers. The creative aspect of politics and policy-making is often unrecognized or denied, as if the solutions and policies would always be those of the familiar past. Many seek to relate new policy forms with 'technological breakthroughs' but ignore the political strategies which accompany actual policy changes. To comprehend what is possible requires a knowledge of both available techniques or capacities *and* possible means of bringing them about in the political system, whether domestic, foreign or both.

Today we see a tremendous specialization and institutionalization of such information, often referred to in business and government as 'research and development.' Most, if not all, governments actively support research and development of new ways of doing things in practically all human concerns. Billions of dollars are devoted to the improvement of productivity, military technology, transportation, medicine and even, nowadays, to how men behave in society. In the United States the precedents go back to the public training and support of engineers, geographical exploration, public health and agricultural research. More recently a far greater share has been spent on military research than on peaceful pursuits; a higher public value has been placed on how to defend ourselves than on getting along with others, in health and well-being. There has been an increasing amount of public resources devoted to solving the problems and aiding the planning of developing nations abroad, both by the major industrial nations and through international organizations. How successful this effort will be is another matter. The western or modernized world places an almost unscientific faith in the scientific method for ameliorating the condition of man.

Violent Political Action

We have finally to consider that aspect of change with which many readers have become very concerned—the occurrence of violence in bringing about political change. While we dealt earlier with the use of force in the coup d'etat, we are now interested in the broader ways that violence serves as an instrument of political change: revolutions, riots, insurrectionary movements, brutality and terror, to name some other forms. These occurrences are far more disruptive, more coercive, perhaps more rapid and more costly than the ordered or institutionalized forms of promoting change we have just discussed. Such incidents are fearful and exciting, the stuff of the daily newspapers. They have been the concern of great political philosophers such as Plato, Aristotle, Marx and Sorel; they are found in the modern doctrines of Mao and Guevara, and in those of some domestic militant groups; they are treated as well by modern military and social science theorists.

Our prior discussion indicated an interest in great changes involving entire societies and political systems but little was said about how changes occur other than through relatively peaceful, institutionalized processes. Many of the great political changes the world has experienced have proceeded, however, under the most violent of conditions: the American, French, Russian and Chinese revolutions are good and well-known illustrations. Certain civil wars, such as the American and Spanish, are also apropos. Peaceful political and social processes did not work; since no agreement on them appeared possible, revolution, civil war and rioting came to determine the outcome.

National wars and domestic violence in the forms of civil wars and rebellions are probably the most notable types of violent political action but they are not the only ones. Violence assumes many other forms, including police brutality, concentration camps, secret police activities, street demonstrations, assassinations, lynching, and vigilante activities. No nation escapes any of these occurrences but they do differ remarkably in the incidence of total violence and in the choice of techniques or forms. The United States could very well lead among western democracies for the number of assassinations of leading officials; we have lost more Presidents during the last 100 years than any of these nations. Four of some thirty-six Presidents have now fallen to the assassin's gun. During the last eight (1960-68) years we have lost a President, a Senator, and at least a half dozen important civil rights leaders. Vigilante justice in the Old West is cited by historians as part of the tradition of using forceful means to solve political problems in America; so, too, the frequent lynchings which went unpunished in the South. And so-called riot control has taken its toll of persons, especially Negroes, during the late 1950s and 1960s. These recent events may remind us of the significant role played by violence in all walks of American life for most of its history. We need not, however, be masochistic, because the record of political violence in history for other countries is even more depressing. Several millions of Europeans, especially Jews, were systematically murdered by Germans during the Nazi regime. Perhaps fourteen millions of people were deliberately murdered and brutalized by Stalin's orders in the Soviet Union. Estimates run into the hundreds of thousands of Indonesians slaughtered during the repression of the communist coup in 1965-66.

Since violent behavior can be identified in some fairly obvious ways one may say country A is subject to more violence than country B, and B more than C, that is, ranked according to some measure of the frequency or extent of such occurrences. Recent years have seen an increasing concern for such measurements, beyond the raw counts of events as portrayed in Table 7-4 on the incidence of internal disturbances. One such method of ranking which suggests relative amounts of violence has been presented by Russett and associates, and involves counting all deaths due to domestic group violence and scoring the nations in proportion to their population size. We show the result in Table 7-5, where we have selected a number of nations to depict the range of variations as well as to indicate those places where domestic violence has been most prevalent during the immediate past. The figures are now dated (the time period was 1950-1962) and we are sure that more recent events would add considerably to the scores of some nations.

Table 7-5

Deaths from Domestic Violence
Per One Million Population, 1950-1962

Nation	Deaths Per One Million Pop.
Cuba[1]	2,900
Hungary	1,335
Indonesia[1]	860
Bolivia	663
Iraq[1]	344
Colombia	316
Philippines	292
Argentina	217
Burma[1]	152
Honduras, Venezuela	111
Paraguay	60
Guatemala	57
South Korea	49
Brazil, Portugal	1.0
Belgium, Turkey	.9
Czechoslovakia, U.S.S.R.	.7
France, Uruguay	.3
Italy, Saudi Arabia, Spain	.2
Japan	.1
West Germany	.02
United States	.01
Australia, Canada, Denmark, Finland, Ireland, Liberia, Netherlands, New Zealand, Norway, Romania, Sweden, Switzerland, Taiwan, United Kingdom, Yugoslavia	.0

[1] Based on rough approximation. Precise data unavailable.

Source: Bruce M. Russett *et al., World Handbook of Political and Social Indicators* (New Haven: Yale University Press, 1964), p. 99. Selected from Case Deciles I, II, VII, VIII, IX and X.

This partial listing of deaths resulting from domestic political violence should give pause to any reader who thinks the world is becoming more peaceful in its pursuit of political changes. The sociologist, Pitrim Sorokin, once estimated the amount of violence the world has known since the time of the Greek city-states; his considered judgment, based on large quantities of statistical data, was that the twentieth century is by far the bloodiest in history. And his studies were conducted before World War II! Since World War II the world has experienced at least twelve limited wars, forty political assassinations, seventy-four rebellions for national independence, and more than 162 revolutions, riots and rebellions, including those which took place during recent years in the United States.[23] Who can deny that violent political action is a pervasive feature of international and domestic politics?

Further recitations of the history of political violence are not really necessary to make our point: violence is a major means of expressing political preferences and achieving them. As such it must be treated as *normal* and frequently as a rational choice. Revolutionists, assassins, police, armies and other agents of violence may be perfectly rational and deliberate about the employment of violent means. Indeed, we train our police, National Guard and military to be calm, deliberate and rational when selecting violent strategies and tactics. Such well-known revolutionists as Lenin, Mao, Guevara and others have developed highly sophisticated theories and strategies of revolution and warfare. We insist that violent politics is not necessarily an irrational form of behavior, if by rational we mean deliberate and purposive. And, we may add, violence frequently pays off whereas other means either do not or at a lower rate of return. War was considered the only way to stop Hitler. No society has been able to eliminate the need for police and enforcement procedures; civil rights in the United States have been advanced by the threats of violence and the destruction of private property on the part of the blacks; and most parents find that at some time or other they must apply the rod or force to get the recalcitrant child to do what he is told. While we prefer seeing violence minimized there seems little point in denying that it fills the pages of history, that it is now very much present, and that many manifestations of violence are rational.

Why nations should vary so much in terms of their resort to political violence is still an open question among scholars. We cannot pretend that political science has a settled answer although there are a number of plausible theories emanating from psychology, sociology and political science. Some aspects of these explanations are now considered in the broader context of general theories of political change. We begin with three classical versions: (1) Plato's theory of the causes and sequences of change; (2) Marx's theory of social change and its political implications; (3) some cyclical theories; and, finally, (4) an attempt on our part to synthesize a number of more modern social science conceptions.

---

[23] "Is Insurrection Brewing in the US? An Expert's Appraisal," *U.S. News and World Report* (Dec. 25, 1967), p. 33.

Further treatments of violence are offered in different contexts in Chapter 10 which deals with conflict as a major policy-making process and in Chapter 12 which is concerned with establishing strategic guidelines for the politically active.

Some General Explanations of Political Change

As we have said in previous chapters, explanations or theories of political behavior and systems are numerous and sometimes conflicting. Once more we have an opportunity, or perhaps for some readers the dismal anticipation, of considering still more conflicting theories. But that is primarily the fault of man and not just social scientists. Because change is so multi-faceted we are apt to see theories concentrate on different questions or aspects and therefore present different explanations. Actually many of these theories may be more complementary than conflicting for precisely this reason. We sample only some of the better-known general theories and once more we begin with the incisive work of Plato, whose theory of change is remarkably systematic for so poetic a thinker. It is also still germane and not just an archaic curiosity for pedants.

Plato's Theory of Continuous Degeneration

Plato was an unhappy aristocrat and tended to see the events of his day as a retrogression from some alleged higher moral order of life. He saw political systems as changing from one type into another in a somewhat stabilized fashion, i.e., a predictable sequence of events. The variables or factors with which Plato dealt were (1) moral worth, (2) types of polities, (3) time. We show these factors and Plato's prediction of the path of change diagrammatically in Figure 7-3.

The predicted course of events goes through a familiar pattern of continuous 'degeneration' and ultimate 'redemption' when the 'savior' in the form of a philosopher-king sets things on their proper paths. The philosopher-king will accomplish this by reading Plato and following his public policies. Once the utopia (Republic) is instituted, political life will be stable, productive and enriching. All of Plato's prescriptions were designed to arrest the downward chain of events and replace them with a complementary division of labor where everyone would be content to have a proper role, performing appropriate tasks and behaving in specified, regularized ways. Plato was a fine writer but not always a very good empirical analyst, for his theory about the inevitable sequence of changes has not been borne out. But his explanations of the origins of change in various systems are still of considerable interest. In brief, Plato argued that the source of change was generally to be found in the ruling classes; more specifically, he

Figure 7-3

Plato's Model of Change, Oversimplified

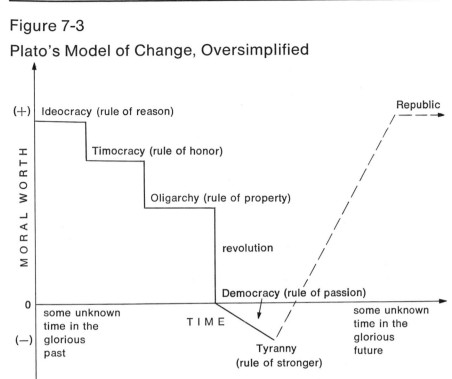

believed that dissension resulting from selfishness was the prime cause of
change. As selfishly competing leaders sought to better themselves, they
looked for allies and often found them among other classes; the allies were
incited to participate in politics, creating still more widespread and intense
conflict. So there were coups, rebellions and civil wars. Plato did not like
such change because he identified each step with a lowered moral worth or
'injustice.' How selfishness originated in the first place is not adequately
explained. But 'first causes' seldom are. It was his intention to diagnose
the moral ills of society so that he could prescribe a permanent cure for the
disease. He proposed a cure for selfishness that need not be developed here,
as we are emphasizing his conception of the source of change. But we cannot resist mentioning that his solution involved an ingenius combination
of the use of a legitimizing myth, censorship and education of the sort we
refer to today as political socialization.

Plato sketched a predicted path of political change but not a table of
timing and probabilities which we believe would be needed for a theory
of such broad political transformations. But a deterministic theory does not

allow for probabilities and Plato did not see fit to provide a timetable for future reference.

The Marxian Explanation

We come now to a man who also was not a political analyst in any strict or narrow sense. Marx was a general social theorist who focused upon a particular set of factors causing major political change and, like Plato, was concerned with setting society right. He developed a theory of social change that has profound theoretical implications and very great current political relevance. So we will want to see how he went about explaining political change.

First, we should emphasize that he had certain preferences about change, as did Plato. But unlike Plato, he preferred change since his ideals were to be attained from it. He did not see things getting worse in the same way Plato did; things would get worse until the day of the revolution when a new society could be brought about free of the old evils. But unlike Plato, Marx spent more time on the causes and process than on the cure.

Marx saw history as a process of gradually increasing conflicts among men, conflicts of a class-type based on the ownership and control of the means of economic production. A few men controlled these means and most others worked for them. The former exploited the latter because they had the opportunities and were induced by social values and norms that permitted exploitation and indeed made it inevitable or necessary regardless of personal values. As the means of production changed, the nature of the classes changed. By the time of nineteenth century capitalism, two distinct classes had emerged: the bourgeois and proletariat. These two classes would ultimately do battle in a great revolution as the situation of the worker and the unemployed become intolerable. Guided by a communist vanguard the workers would emerge victorious; and they would establish a 'dictatorship of the proletariat' until such time as classes, exploitation, government, power, inequality and alienation would all disappear. Government was simply an agent of the bourgeoisie and had, therefore, to be destroyed. The actual forms or structures of political systems were regarded as of relatively little consequence; all acted as oppressors of the peasants and workers. The general historical process of change can be represented as in Figure 7-4.

Marx, like Plato, saw change as highly conflictive, determinate in the sense of proceeding through certain stages, predetermined in its result, and utopian in its final stage. Marx's heroes were different people as was the content of their values, but they were unselfish in the sense of being devoted to a true ideology. Both Marx and Plato planned for an ideal state in which men would find fulfillment. In Marx's vision this would be

Figure 7-4

Marx's Model of Change, Oversimplified

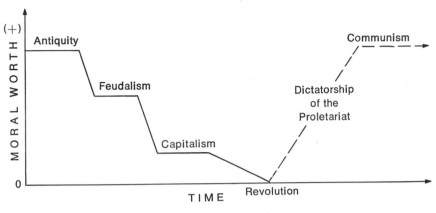

a communist society guided by the formula 'from each according to his ability, to each according to his need.' With this rule for settling allocative and distributive conflicts, Marx foresaw a society which did not need the compulsion of government, thus the state would 'wither away.'

While there are certain formal similarities in these two theories we must not confuse their substantive analyses. Plato viewed the original source of change as the effects of selfishness within a small governing elite, while Marx detected the impetus to social and political change as stemming from productive technology as it affected economic relationships. Marx was more attuned to the impersonal economic dimensions of modern life while Plato was more sensitive to interpersonal relationships among rulers. Historically we might say that Plato provided a useful theory for his time but not for Marx's time when industrialization was a major facet of changing conditions. Plato's theorizing also was more concerned with political life than was Marx's work, even though the political implications of the latter are now more apparent. Accordingly, Marx exercises a much greater influence over contemporary social science and political ideas.

Since Marx did not attempt to detail the political systems or political characteristics of his social systems, it is somewhat difficult to extend his general theory of social change to politics. As with Plato, Marx's 'inevitabilities' did not come with definite timetables. Marx really provided us with a general theory of socio-economic systems and not of political systems. This difference is particularly notable for Marx says little about how his future utopia would work as a classless society; nor does he even spell out the properties of that intermediate stage after the revolution which he called 'the dictatorship of the proletariat.' Scholars have debated endlessly on what the communist political systems might be or become. Thus far those labelled as such have been either dictatorships or totalitarian systems. And each such system has shown different degrees of transformation from their former states. And there are many signs throughout the communist world of further evolution; what the future will bring we do not know. But we must note that Marx developed a most remarkable political weapon for bringing about change: an ideology for communist movements. He did so in both emotional and analytical or theoretical terms. He was not the self-conscious strategist that Adolf Hitler was in *Mein Kampf*, that Machiavelli was in *The Prince*, or that Mao and Ché were on guerrilla warfare. But *The Communist Manifesto* is full of the spirit which would inspire his followers for decades to come. Note the universality of its concluding slogan: "Workers of the world unite!"

Cyclical Theorists: Pareto, Mosca and Michels

The theories of Plato and Marx stressed a view of change which held that a succession of events took place which never repeated themselves. Once each phase was completed another took its place until the utopia was attained. Each saw a different number of stages and each found quite different occurrences within those stages or phases. Various other theorists have wondered, however, whether human life does not repeat itself and in a sense 'get nowhere.' Change takes place, but the course of events forms cycles. Vilfredo Pareto was one such theorist; to a lesser degree, his countryman, Gaetano Mosca, was another, as was Roberto Michels.[24] These early twentieth century thinkers believed that mankind consisted of two classes: the rulers and the ruled. The rulers were subject to change but it was an alternation of types of rulers rather than a succession of types of political systems. Pareto was to label this phenomenon the "circulation of elites." All that is ever discovered in reading history, he said, is a succession or alternation of elite groups. Pareto called the different leadership types "lions" and "foxes," terms used to suggest their typical modes of behavior in governing and acquiring power.

In our terms, Pareto might have maintained that the allocation of resources, distribution of benefits, controls and symbols of power changed

---

[24] Vilfredo Pareto, *The Mind and Society,* trans. and ed. by Arthur Livingston (New York: Harcourt, Brace and World, Inc., 1935); Gaetano Mosca, *The Ruling Class,* trans. Hannah D. Kahn, ed. and revised by Arthur Livingston (New York: McGraw-Hill Book Company, Inc., 1939); Roberto Michels, *Political Parties,* trans. by Eden and Cedar Paul (Glencoe: The Free Press, 1949). For an interesting interpretation of these analysts see James Burnham, *The Machiavellians: Defenders of Freedom* (New York: The John Day Company, Inc., 1943).

but little. Perhaps the symbols (he termed legitimating ideologies as "derivations") and controls employed varied most while the distributive aspects varied the least. The rulers would continue to receive more benefits because they exercised control of power. Furthermore, he believed that cycles resulted because humans were inherently unequal; some people had political skills and others did not. Genetic differences could not be altered with the speed of environmental factors, if at all, so the outcome of necessity had to be a set of rulers and the ruled. Michels, whose theories were more complex, admitted non-genetic factors into his theories—stressing primarily the idea that organizations, especially competitive ones, require leadership in order to survive. And once leaders are required it is difficult to displace them because of their functions and superior resources.

Pareto, Mosca and Michels, unlike Plato and Marx, were men of varying degrees of pessimism. The latter two believed that after all the trials and tribulations were over (and they could be surmounted), a utopia would emerge. Not so the cyclical theorists. All that man could anticipate was more of the same, and this is not a very enticing prospect unless one is a misanthrope. This may be one reason why cyclical theories have not had much appeal to contemporary social scientists.

These three great bodies of thought do not exhaust the theoretical possibilities although they illustrate some major strands of thought about the conditions of stability and change. Most, if not all, the social sciences are currently very much engaged in constructing new, and hopefully better-grounded, theories which can be tested against reality with some semblance of control. Grand theories about the rise and decline of whole civilizations, such as those of Sorokin, Toynbee and others, continue to be produced, but this generation of social scientists is more modest in its aims and more rigorous in its methods. We cannot summarize all the relevant literature but we can point out some of the factors which contemporary theorists stress. In the following sections conditions are described which make for greater political stability as well as those which encourage instability.

A Contemporary Synthesis:
Some Conditions Favoring Stability

Phrases like 'we live in an era of transition,' of 'great changes,' are certainly true but they do not inform very much. Change is often confused with any activity which goes on all of the time. But we may also observe great continuities and even stabilized rates of change. Many facets of the political life of nations are quite predictable on a day-to-day, month-to-month and year-to-year basis. If this were not so, governing would be more difficult than it is and the study of politics would be impossible. We do not suppose that most of you are particularly worried about what American political life will be tomorrow or the next day. People in some areas of the world no doubt would like to see more and swifter changes since their present existences are so miserable and unrewarding. But change brings uncertainty, great costs to some, and usually occurs at an intolerably slow rate. Some societies have remained basically continuous for thousands of years. Why is this so for political systems? Are there factors which work to maintain the status quo and lessen change in its scope, rates, successes? We believe so.

Satisfactory Exchanges

A great deal of what men do and do not do can be explained quite simply in terms of the satisfactions they derive from existing ways of doing things. Politics seem to pose no unusual problems in this regard. In Chapter 1 we wrote that political systems—even the worst ones—produce valued goods and services for their members and do satisfy many wants or preferences of the citizenry. To the extent that there is gratification one can expect the government to be respected and supported, and its continuing existence guaranteed. Political systems must, of course, face a kind of demand curve for their goods and services just as private firms must in the market. As indicated in the first chapter, the demand for public goods and services may be affected by the actions of the polity. If a society has few resources it may survive only if the demand for public goods and services is sufficiently low. On the other hand a rich nation may be faced with a very heavy demand for services and goods and, not being able to meet them, would engender dissatisfactions. The United States, for example, has enormous capacity for producing both public and private benefits but the demands for both are also extremely high; we are a consumption-oriented society. Perhaps people in some of the newly-developing nations are more satisfied than we are even though the level of production is disproportionately lower. Increasing demand and scarce supplies would lead to problems, but so would surplus supplies and restricted demand. Where supplies and demands can be equated, stability is encouraged. In other words where the citizens acquire all they want from the leaders and the latter attain all the support they want from followers or citizens, one finds a reasonably satisfied society and a more stabilized political system. Neither party has a strong reason for challenging the existing framework of institutions or rules. But where the citizens or the leaders are dissatisfied in terms of not having their expectations met, one may find trouble sooner or later. We are assuming that men generally prefer having more rather than fewer goods and services, other things being equal, and that they prefer superior to inferior quality. Dissatisfied aspirations, then, are a major cause of frustration and disruptive behavior; unsatisfied hopes may lead to demands for greater adaptation, innovation and, therefore, change.

We have indicated in a previous chapter why some systems may be more productive than others; we have yet to explain the demand curve for public goods and services. Why do some people expect much' and others so little? The demands that citizens make for public goods and services are to a considerable extent a product of received expectations or learned responses from previous generations. What we want from life and the political system is largely learned; we are not born with hereditary demand curves etched in our heads and hearts, or with purely derived self-interests. We are taught or socialized into wanting certain goods and services and in certain preferred combinations.[25] As we grow older we learn more from personal experience and less from others, but we continue to learn; we acquire preferences for some things rather than others, and these are reflected in our demands on the polity. In many societies—particularly the more traditional and autocratic—citizens are socialized to be quiescent, deferential and to mind their own business while the leaders run society. In others, such as the United States, most citizens are taught to believe they have rights and that the political system is but a means for protecting these rights and fulfilling their expectations and demands for a better life. Gradually, however, the citizenry of the newly-developing nations are acquiring notions about politics more akin to the pragmatic ones of the West. The mass media and more frequent communication and exchanges across societies will serve to stimulate this process.

Our general point has been that satisfactions aid in the preservation or maintenance of a system; dissatisfactions, however, do not mean automatic changes and revolutions. People who are dissatisfied frequently do not have the necessary resources or the opportunities to implement their hostility and grievances. But more of that later. Let us look at some comparative data about relative levels of general satisfaction with society and political systems. These data from opinion surveys conducted in recent years were referred to earlier. In *The Civic Culture*, Gabriel Almond and Sidney Verba described the "political cultures" or beliefs and values of representative samples of citizens in the United States, United Kingdom, Germany (West), Italy and Mexico. They used a standardized questionnaire in order to get comparable answers. Among the questions put to the respondents was this one: "Speaking generally, what are the things about this country that you are most proud of?" Table 7-6 displays the results. Notice the unusually large number of favorable responses toward the polity on the part of Americans compared to the responses of Germans and Ital-

---

[25] The literature on political socialization is now quite extensive. We suggest Herbert H. Hyman, *Political Socialization* (Glencoe: The Free Press, 1959); Fred I. Greenstein, *Children and Politics* (New Haven: Yale University Press, 1965); and, Leonard W. Doob, *Patriotism and Nationalism* (New Haven: Yale University Press, 1964). The latter volume is less about childhood socialization and more about the psychological aspects of adult patriotism.

ians. Note also the variation among the different aspects. Which do you think are the most relevant for political stability, as we have discussed it here? The case of Mexico is also interesting in this regard but we will leave it to the reader to figure out why, or he may consult the book.

Table 7-6

Aspects of Nation in Which
Respondents Report Pride, by Nation (in per cent)

Per cent who say they are proud of	U.S.	U.K.	Germany	Italy	Mexico
Govt. political institutions	85	46	7	3	30
Social legislation	13	18	6	1	2
Position in international affairs	5	11	5	2	3
Economic system	23	10	33	3	24
Characteristics of people	7	18	36	11	15
Spiritual values & religion	3	1	3	6	8
Contributions to art	1	6	11	16	9
Contributions to science	3	7	12	3	1
Physical attributes of country	5	10	17	25	22
Nothing or don't know	4	10	15	27	16
Other	9	11	3	21	14
Total % of responses*	158	148	148	118	144
Total % of respondents	100	100	100	100	100
Total number of cases	970	963	955	995	1,007

* Percentages exceed one hundred because of multiple responses.

Source: Gabriel Almond and Sidney Verba, *The Civic Culture: Political Attitudes and Democracy in Five Nations* (Princeton: Princeton University Press, 1963), p. 102. Reprinted by permission of Princeton University Press.

Presumably a nation in which pride is expressed for its institutions is one in which greater rather than less stability will be found. Conversely, the less pride, the greater the instability. These are rather broad inferences, to be sure. You might compare the data of Table 7-6 with those of Table 7-3 or 7-5 to determine whether there is any positive relationship between satisfactions (pride of institutions) and certain facets of system stability. Also try explaining whatever you discover.

Hadley Cantril in *The Pattern of Human Concerns* attempted to determine what the people of some fourteen different countries felt about their situations, their hopes and fears, their general concerns during the late 1950s. Among the many things he learned was one of considerable interest in explaining the maintenance of political systems. People in these countries (listed in Tables 7-7 and 7-8) seemed to be much more concerned

Table 7-7

Personal Hopes by Country

Country	Economic	Family	Health	Values & character	Job/work	Social	International	Political	Maintain Status quo	Total
						Personal hopes				
Brazil	68%	28%	34%	14%	8%	1%	1%	—%	1%	155%
Cuba	73	52	47	30	14	4	3	15	1	239
Dominican Republic	95	39	17	15	25	2	—	9	—	202
Egypt	70	53	24	39	42	9	2	4	—	243
India	70	39	4	14	22	8	—	—	2	159
Israel	80	76	47	29	35	10	12	2	4	295
Kibbutzim	41	74	24	59	51	63	23	3	6	344
Nigeria	90	76	45	42	19	14	—	—	—	286
Panama	90	53	43	26	26	3	—	1	1	243
Philippines	60	52	6	9	11	5	—	—	—	143
United States	65	47	48	20	10	5	10	2	11	218
West Germany	85	27	46	11	10	3	15	1	4	202
Yugoslavia	83	60	41	18	20	4	8	—	2	236

Source: Hadley Cantril, *The Pattern of Human Concerns* (New Brunswick, N.J.: Rutgers University Press, 1965), p. 169.

Table 7-8
Personal Fears by Country

Country	Economic	Health	Family	Interna-tional	Values & character	Job/work	Social	No fears	Political	Total
Brazil	30%	42%	17%	3%	7%	2%	2%	4%	1%	108%
Cuba	47	42	24	5	23	4	3	9	15	172
Dominican Republic	82	29	25	1	4	10	1	—	9	161
Egypt	46	42	30	4	23	20	2	11	4	182
India	51	23	19	—	5	6	2	8	—	114
Israel	55	58	44	27	10	10	4	6	2	216
Kibbutzim	33	52	48	48	45	20	51	2	4	303
Nigeria	65	64	27	1	17	2	14	8	5	203
Panama	57	64	37	3	7	6	1	1	2	178
Philippines	38	25	30	23	2	7	1	3	1	130
United States	46	56	25	24	3	5	3	12	5	179
West Germany	51	51	14	50	3	2	2	2	8	183
Yugoslavia	33	60	26	27	5	2	2	3	—	158

Source: *Ibid.*, p. 170.

over personal problems than great political matters or issues. The percentage who indicated some kind of concern over politics were extremely limited in all cases. The average amount of concern shown over directly political matters was only 4 per cent. The highest percentage of political fears was reported in Cuba, the Dominican Republic and West Germany, each of which had recently experienced political turmoil and crisis. All other types of personal fears and hopes seem much stronger and more widespread.

Nations and their political systems may not of course provide many satisfactions for very many citizens and still survive rather successfully. Why? The answer, if there is one, seems to lie in the fact that many people are unaware of the political relevance of their 'problems' and what might be done about them. Many are too depressed or unaware to have aspirations and make higher and more frequent effective demands upon the political sector. Their passivity, a product of centuries of fatalism, means they must endure incredible poverty and wretchedness without thought of turning to political leadership and aid from government. Mere survival and acquiescence to authority are the primary responses to life. No government or political system is threatened under such circumstances. What discontent there is cannot be focused on means of solving problems politically without some information or reason to expect gains from that approach. Cantril tells us that such people cannot assign themselves or their nation any sort of ranking in terms of the satisfactions enjoyed. They have no basis for comparison. So we see that a person may be either satisfied with his system in a conscious positive sense or may be simply passive and unaware; in both cases the result is to aid in the maintenance of the system. In the one instance it is because of a conscious positive evaluation of the system as worth preserving while in the other it is preserved because no one thinks to evaluate its adaptive performance and challenge authorities for failures.

Positive Loyalties and Sacrifice

Political life, however, consists of more, than a balance-sheet of satisfactory exchanges between citizen and government. There are conditions in which citizens are induced to give to their country far more than what they will receive. The notion of a calculus of interest falls far short of explaining many forms of political action whereby citizens passionately support their governments at great cost or discomfort, and quite often with no apparent promise of long-run gain for themselves except as they may believe in glory or comfort in the hereafter. Instead of the usual expectations and demands, their political identifications, or what we call patriotism, may be uppermost. Men sacrifice their properties and lives for the defense of their nations. They sometimes spy and inform for their countries at great risk; some people will work long and hard when they feel their nation is imperiled and they care to preserve it.

Apparently the survival of the nation appears more important than the continuance of other social groups for a great many humans. What seems so remarkable is that relatively few citizens, at least among western democracies, actively disavow their nationalities and nations. Is it not meaningful that many people refer to their countries as the mother or fatherland? Patriotism is seldom taken lightly and especially when the source or focus of one's political identity is threatened. Under certain crisis conditions, therefore, stability is reinforced. In any case, positive loyalty, affection for one's political institutions, have caused many to see their duty as serving the state and its leaders.

Of course, leaders who have an investment in stability are not unaware of the degree to which this can preserve and enhance their own tenures. A crisis or sense of external threat can divert people from their more immediate dissatisfactions and political discontents. These fierce loyalties can be turned against enemies of the regime, or any group threatening to change the existing order. There is a point at which this too becomes highly unstable or conducive to change, as we note in the tragic history of some nations. A nation under crisis conditions may transform itself to the eventual regret of those who really cherished the old ways. The degree to which patriotism actually serves stability must always be assessed.

Limited Opportunities and Resources

We all know from personal experience that we may be highly dissatisfied with something but powerless to do much about it. Such is the case with most men in all nations. Those who are most dissatisfied are generally the ones who have the fewest opportunities or resources to affect a favorable change. Every effective political system is distinguished by the fact that it has a monopoly of force or something approaching one that can to some degree prevent dissidents from spreading their dissatisfactions and creating social changes and convulsions. Formal and informal controls, fear, reprisals can be employed, and are, by those who wish to maintain a particular system and its patterns of distribution against those who want something else. Concentration camps, work camps, prisons, death chambers and firing squads are constant features of the maintenance of all too many political systems. Can one blame an ordinary citizen in such a land for wanting to keep quiet and mind his own business? He knows all too well what is in store for him should he attempt to express his discontent in public or even in private. Armies and police are employed to keep men in line; they need only make periodic examples of a few to frighten most potential dissidents. Few opportunities may be allowed for people to make their demands or expectations known to the rulers, and even fewer resources would be permitted to make them known even against the will of the rulers.

It must be a truism that one cannot implement one's goals without resources. The state typically has a preponderant command of the symbols and means of terror, violence and suppression in autocratic and totalitarian nations. One cannot successfully fight armies and police with sticks and stones for very long. And few wish to be so suicidally heroic where even the symbol of the deed will perish. There are no statues of the brave revolutionists in Hungary or Posnan, Poland.

Some Conditions Favoring Change

The absence or relative absence of the above-noted factors making for stability will of course aid in stimulating change. Where satisfactions are not being provided in adequate amounts one may expect to find potentials for change; where expected contributions and satisfactions are poorly defined by the society one may find a potential for change. But absence of certain factors is not enough to insure that change will in fact take place. Certain other factors must be present for both orderly legitimate change and minor or revolutionary upheavals in entire political systems and society. Let us first consider legitimate types of change which are usually narrower in scope and affect lesser processes and outcomes.

Legitimate, Orderly Processes

A price of survival in a changing environment is to change oneself. Political systems in reasonably stable societies generally provide for some degree of adaptability. All western democracies, for example, have some (written or unwritten) provisions for changing the formal structures of government. Article V of the United States Constitution stipulates how the Constitution itself may legitimately be altered. Quite basic institutional changes can be and have been made in accordance with these procedures. Formal specifications about how policy decisions will be made and how the decision-makers will be selected also allow for considerable flexibility and change. All western democracies have witnessed some changes in the effective power structure (decision-makers) during the past 100 or more years. The western constitutions do not say which classes, persons or parties are to hold power; they simply state some of the procedures for distributing formal political power. Likewise, all western nations have witnessed some great policy changes, as we have indicated in earlier pages. Few constitutions attempt to dictate policies which successive generations must pursue; they state only the ground rules by which policy contenders must or should abide in their collective decision-making. And as stated above, the rules may themselves be altered with changing circumstances.

What permits a society to allow and even encourage change? We think there are a number of factors that enable people to view change (orderly, controlled) with favor and even excitement. The first is the perception of the citizens: man may be socialized to believe in the advantages of change. Some forms of change may be viewed as almost automatic progress. Western peoples in particular have been so taught throughout at least the past two centuries. The great historical movements of discovery, science, nation-building, capitalism, democracy and socialism have all encouraged and honored change. The most conservative of western citizens are apt to believe in a great deal more change than would be conceivable to a member of a highly traditional society. Most of us like to believe that life will be better for our children and grandchildren. Most of us also like to believe that it is now better than it was in, say, the nineteenth century. So we do not always fear change. This being the case, we are prepared to entertain reform as a reasonable alternative.

Our faith in change is not without good reason: change has in fact provided for increasing satisfactions. Nothing is so self-confirmed as success. Fact has reinforced many of our expectations and aspirations. If this did not happen we would be more reluctant to change. We might add that change is also as highly regarded in other than the western world; apparently most Russians, for example, believe they are far better off today than a decade ago, and certainly better off than fifty years ago. The leaders of newly independent nations also strive to make this claim, and we even see many traditional leaders caught in new styles of making promises for the future.

A faith in change is, of course, insufficient to guarantee that change will take place. Still other factors must be present. Again we must emphasize the availability of resources and opportunities for those who promote change. The history of reformers without resources is legion. Successful reformers are those who have had strategic access to the necessary resources for winning their case. He who wishes to alter the basic rules or the policies of a nation must mobilize sufficient *leadership, money, support, appropriate symbols, and relevant information and pursue successful strategies* to prevail over opponents.[26] Reform or change may be valued but specific changes must be won over opposition. As we noted earlier, some segments of the population value change less strongly while others profit from the existing structures and decisions or policies.

In nations which permit the resources of power to be somewhat dispersed some change is possible and normally occurs. Yet resources must not be so dispersed as to be incapable of mobilization in complex systems—a

---

[26] Failures to mobilize effectively are ably discussed in James H. Meisel, *Counterrevolution: How Revolutions Die* (New York: Atherton Press, 1966).

kind of political paralysis which many in pluralist systems fear. Change may take place in more centralized systems as well, but then it is a problem of whether the rules permit it or the rulers will accept it. In traditional systems resources are concentrated and leaders have not wanted institutional change. But in newly independent and communist systems, in particular, we often find that dictators are promoting change faster and perhaps in different directions than their citizenry might want if they had a choice. These leaders value modernization highly and often have ambitions to compete in the international scene. Past centuries have seen similar types of leaders: Peter the Great, Ataturk of Turkey, Bismarck are some rulers who tried to modernize their societies often against great resistance on the part of powerful nobles and suspicious peasants. Yet favorable conditions of change are by no means always present, and many peoples still have not changed very much. The twentieth century has probably seen more important social and political changes than any previous century. It is to be expected: change is more highly valued and the resources for change are more plentiful.

Conditions and Stages of Revolutionary Activity

We deal now with a very different 'kettle of fish,' the conditions and stages of revolutionary activity. Note that we speak of activity, not revolutions; the latter are less frequently encountered and are a special variation of the former. By revolutions we refer to forceful transformations of the political system, especially its institutions and personnel. A nation may experience revolutionary efforts and not undergo a full-scale revolution. So we write primarily of the conditions for the activity and not of its success or outcomes.

Revolutionary changes are generally not welcomed as a standard element of everyday living, so conditions which encourage and cause such changes are apt to be rather different from those which support orderly, institutionalized changes. Most people want changes but not revolutions where the means are so costly and the results so uncertain. In this sense most people would reject Jefferson's idea that a revolution every twenty years is a good thing, unless he meant by that the peaceful discussion and renewal of political forms. The conditions that spawn the hatreds and violence of revolutionary activity are not collectively and rationally decided; they occur as the result of many processes in the existing regime; events that trigger open conflict are not necessarily meant to produce revolutions. Some modern theorists see the major cause of revolutionary change as related to changes in the realization of popular aspirations or needs. The absolute levels of aspirations and need satisfaction appear to be less important than what happens to them through time. More specifically, it has been contended by James C. Davies that the most favorable condition for revolutionary activity is one in which a long-term increase in actual need satisfaction is suddenly reversed, terminated or, we may add, the rate of increase begins to show a decline.[27] Aspirations and expectations of the good life continue to increase while the sense of need satisfaction levels off or actually decreases. A convenient means of depicting this set of relationships is found in Figure 7-5. Such divergences logically may occur at any level of economic development. Evidence regarding the level of development which is most favorable for revolutions is still too fragmentary to make a confident choice.

We agree with Davies that men who have been accustomed to receiving increasing satisfactions and who suddenly find their expectations thwarted are more likely to consider revolutionary appeals and activities worthwhile. Still, they may not act on this possibility and they certainly may not be successful if they do. Since time lags and uncertainties are generally experienced in most human activity, profound dissatisfactions engendered by the growing gap between expectations and reality among some people is only a preparatory stage for genuine revolutions. If the attitudinal response is to become a successful revolution, a great many other phases must be passed through successfully. Various social scientists have tried their hands at reconstructing the stages of revolutions; we will try more of the same. Chart 7-3 is a brief schematic presentation. The stages noted are not distinct time processes that can be rigidly applied to the events of the day. But, in general, we may observe both the interactions and the progression of stages, and of levels of conflict. Then, too, we are less willing to believe that history is an inevitable sequence of events in the sense that once a given stage has been initiated, governmental reactions will be automatic and greater conflict must automatically follow. Some stages may result in a resolution of issues, or the conditions causing them may change. For example, it is generally believed by historians that the British aristocracy was able to prevent or reduce revolutionary activity because it responded to new demands at an early stage and managed to satisfy significant new aspirations so that revolution became a less plausible alternative means of change. And certain of these stages may also be prolonged or aborted as they work themselves out.

One of the problems of studying revolutions has been their paucity, but since the twentieth century is the century of revolutions, political scientists may find enough data to allow more empirical generalizations to be made instead of case studies. If this is so we may eventually have more rigorous comparative tests of the conditions, sequences and time-spans of revolutionary activity.

---

[27] James C. Davies, "Toward a Theory of Revolution," *American Sociological Review*, 27 (February, 1962), pp. 5-19.

Figure 7-5
Need Satisfaction and Revolution

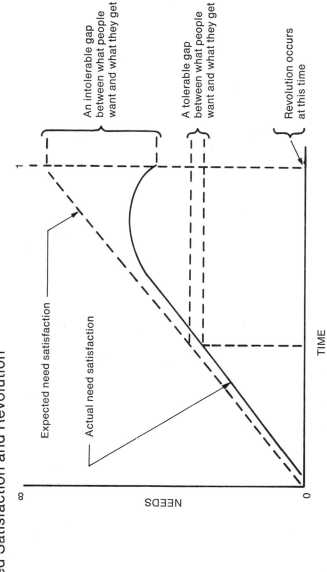

Source: James C. Davies, "Toward a Theory of Revolution," *American Sociological Review*, 27 (February, 1962), p. 6.

Chart 7-3
Stages of Revolutionary Effort

Stages	Revolutionary Activity	Ruling Elite Reactions
I	Dissatisfaction (expectations/reality gap)	
II	Public symptoms of disturbance	Rejection of policy and/or policy changes
III	Organizational activity (overt and covert)	Symbolic or negative reactions
IV	Overt demonstrations	Repression by authorities
V	Open warfare	Retrenchment and defections
VI	Capture of government	Capitulation
VII	Removal of old regime	Trials, exile, death
VIII	Revolutionary regime begins	

The Problem of Popular Support

We think of revolutions as vast, violent upheavals which strain the deeper bonds of the system. In the process citizen loyalties must be transferred or eliminated. New institutional relationships are established, sometimes extending the popular base and/or involving new forms of participation for new groups or strata. We think of revolutions as not being ultimately successful without capturing broad support among major segments of the citizenry.

This is in great contrast with the coup, where the use of force is selective and very rapid, an excising at the top which need not shake the political order very deeply. But even more significant as a testimony to the great distance of ruler and ruled in coup situations is the fact that so forceful and illegitimate a blow to a government does not evoke widespread popular revulsion and resistance to the interlopers. Many have noted that in the long run the perpetrators of coups must struggle with the problem of legitimacy—and, as often as not, lose out to other coups. They generally fail to build any new system of popular support, and the internal disorder, violence, repression and elite rivalries tend to erode their hold on power.

Thus one can say that of the two violent forms of change the revolution is an event which ultimately has adaptive consequences in creating a new order, whether the observer approves the form and manner or not. Indeed, perhaps the true test of a revolution is the degree to which it has crystallized some degree of broader popular support in the new regime. We may not wish to believe it, but that was the case with the Russian Revolution, as well as the French, American, Mexican, and Egyptian revolutions.

We have some reason to doubt that this was equally true in some of the Eastern European communist takeovers, which began more like the palace coups of old. But lest we be skeptical about the legitimizing powers of revolution, think of the many ways it is honored by all such regimes. Symbols of revolution deal at great length with the sacrifice of the people, their courage and persistence, and also with the heroism and wisdom of the revolutionary leader. Much of the glory of the revolution is its creation of new bonds between ruler and ruled which are far stronger than any which may have existed in the old order.

Revolutions in this extensive, popular sense are relatively late occurrences in history. Marx identified them with the structure of the industrial order, and believed that capitalist economic conditions would intensify the alienation and misery necessary to bring them about. Today's revolutionary theorists have had to reconsider Marx's tenets to make them applicable to the peasant societies of traditional systems. The first stage of creating a revolutionary condition in such a context is to develop an awareness of the promise of revolution for the peasant who is not so much alienated from as tied to the old ways. Should this stage be achieved, popular support of the opposition movement must next be developed in the form of acquiescence to its operations and active shelter of its fighting forces. By the final stages there must be positive, active loyalties on the part of significant numbers of the citizenry. Thus the stages of revolution and guerrilla warfare have to do with the degree to which the popular base allows open insurgency and eventual seizure of power. The stages of this guerrilla form of revolutionary movement are outlined rather simply in Chart 7-4. Note here the two different reactive effects (government and people) of guerrilla strategies. Consider the possible situations on either side which may abort such revolutionary attempts. Note also that efforts to convert many people in traditional systems may take much more time, and that the relatively small numbers of initial revolutionaries may have a very long way to go. This wearing away of the old is suggested by Mao's term, "protracted conflict."

Distributions of Support and Changes in the System

Most men do not act as fanatic loyalists or revolutionists most of the time nor are political systems completely successful in fulfilling all expectations and aspirations.[28] And most men do not demand but one form of governmental response to maintain their loyalties. The balance of satisfactions on the part of most citizens is favorable, if very marginal, in many societies.

---

[28] One of the more thorough theoretical discussions of support is contained in David Easton, *A Systems Analysis of Political Life* (New York: John Wiley and Sons, Inc., 1965), Parts 3 and 4.

Chart 7-4

Stages of Guerrilla Warfare

Stage	Guerrilla Strategy	Popular Reactions	Government Reactions
I	Terrorism	Awareness	Fear and reprisals
II	Diffused, limited military engagements	Permissiveness	Military search and destroy missions
III	Larger scale attacks by highly organized forces	Volunteered support	Efforts to crush rebels without harm to the people
IV	Control of land areas and people		Tacit surrender of control
V	Conventional warfare	Political identification	Strategic retreat to strongholds
VI	General offensives	Massive support	Major defeats
VII	Takeover of government		Capitulation

We may learn much about tendencies to change by conceiving these satisfactions as distributed among people in different degrees of strength in support or opposition to the regime. For example, in the western democracies satisfactions may be so distributed that most people display a favorable balance, although a small proportion may be negative and some even highly so. And there would also be a few for whom vigilant patriotism is their most intense pleasure. We know that Marx depicted an intensely opposed communist vanguard, a negative "army of the unemployed," a growing number of negatively class conscious workers, a smaller group of relatively contented bourgeoisie, and a highly satisfied capitalist elite. Thus both a widespread and increasing polarization could be observed. In countries ripe for guerrilla warfare one usually finds a very small group with intensely negative feelings toward the regime who are thus motivated to start the guerrilla movement, a very large group of indifferent peasants, and a relatively small number of positive supporters of the regime; even the military and bureaucracy may be largely indifferent or satisfied as long as their kind shares power.

We have great difficulty documenting such distributions of intensities and relative support. We are not simply loyal or disloyal but more or less so regarding a great many political objects and activities of government. Many scholars have distinguished the different objects of such feelings. One person may be a fanatic about the great ideals of the society, less impressed by the institutions, highly devoted to a specific leader, negative toward some policies and highly favorable toward still others. Another person may adhere to a precisely opposite combination. We would maintain there is no inevitable order of stability in the feelings likely to be accorded one or another of these objects. The question of salience and intensity is related more to the situation of the person and what he regards as politically crucial to his future. And the question of how many others feel the same way is also a matter of empirical inquiry, as we have suggested here.

If enough members of a society feel exceptionally strong about a political matter, whether values, institutions, laws, policies or leaders, they are likely to take action if other conditions permit. Systems in which one finds an entire population sharply and intensely divided is one in which peaceful change is unlikely. Even in systems with a 'passionate minority,' as opposed to a moderate majority, trouble is apt to occur. Settlement of issues and the maintenance of satisfactions are made increasingly difficult and uncertain. Probably the most stable and peaceful situation is one in which most citizens feel moderately for or against most policies and laws. Being less than highly intense allows a person to remain loyal by not having his loyalty tested with each new development, issue or problem. Daily or recurring conflicts of high intensity are too demanding on both the individual and the system.

But let us be emphatic about one point: we do not know the maximum amounts of conflict that either the citizen or a polity can tolerate and still maintain effective government. Apparently, a great deal of conflict can be sustained and the support of the citizenry still remains. If decisions can be made and are of such a nature that solutions do not necessarily alienate large segments of the population, loyalties will be preserved and perhaps even strengthened. Whatever the critical points may be, systems do break down as our recitation of facts about change in the beginning pages of this chapter suggest; on such occasions the minds and souls of men are tried and brother may fight brother. In the final analysis what seems so unbelievable is that so few outright civil wars have occurred. We hope that our analysis has stimulated thought about why this is so.

Problems and Applications

1. Rank the following policy changes in terms of their acceptability to you and to some designated group. Explain your ranking.
   a) an across-the-board income tax increase of 10 per cent
   b) school bussing to achieve racial balance in a city of 500,000 people
   c) a decrease in U.S. military aid to developing nations by 25 per cent

    d) a 10 per cent increase in subsidies to farmers

    e) a constitutional amendment to increase the terms of congressmen to four years, coinciding with presidential terms

    f) a constitutional amendment providing for a national presidential primary

2. Analyze the following possibilities of basic institutional change.

    a) democracy ⟶ monarchy

    b) monarchy ⟶ democracy

    c) dictatorship ⟶ democracy

    d) democracy ⟶ dictatorship

    e) monarchy ⟶ dictatorship

3. Many political observers have contended that status quo forces have a superior position in society compared to those urging change, yet we note a great amount of political change in this chapter. How can we resolve this apparent contradiction or paradox?

4. What kinds of problems and considerations must leaders in a democracy confront whenever they attempt to introduce change (any kind) which dictators can ignore? Are there any similar considerations for both sets of leaders?

5. Some political theorists maintain that violence is a necessary cost which must be paid in order to achieve any changes which are significant. Comment.

6. Devise some measures for plotting changes over the long run, say, 100 years, with respect to one of the following phenomena:

    a) electoral participation in the United States

    b) the growth of bureaucracy

    c) expenditures on welfare, military, highways, education

    d) numbers of different types of polities

· 7. In a society such as the American, change is viewed as an almost automatic good. How can a person who wishes to slow down, or at least question the benefits of change rationally, defend his position in terms that will be acceptable or persuasive to those who favor continual change?

8. Make some predictions about possible future changes concerning one or more of the following items. You might wish to date your predictions in such terms as the next decade, next quarter of a century, next 100 years. Provide a rationale for these prognostications.

    a) the number of democracies in the world

    b) racial relationships in the United States

    c) frequency of revolution

    d) number of world wars; two-nation wars

    e) various alliances: U.S.A.-U.S.S.R.; U.S.S.R.-China; China-U.S.A.; France-Yugoslavia; Cuba-Mexico, for example

9. It is often said that youth are radical and the aged are conservative. How could we proceed to test such a claim?

10. Some theorists are continually amazed at the number of revolutions, coups, assassinations and civil wars while others are continually amazed at the dearth of them. How can we account for these opposing perspectives?

11. The following table (7-9) was prepared in the course of an investigation by Ivo K. and Rosalind L. Feierabend, "Aggressive Behaviors within Polities, 1948-1962: A Cross-National Study," in *The Journal of Conflict Resolution*, X (September, 1966), pp. 249-271. They examined the relationship between social frustration and political stability. They scored what they selected as political conflict behaviors for each country, giving each event a score along the stability dimension so that a general election would be put in the 0 category, resignation of a cabinet official in the 1 position, peaceful demonstrations in 2, a significant assassination in 3, mass arrests in 4, coup d'etat into 5, and civil war at 6. These various kinds of events were combined in scores for each nation, placing them therefore in similar fashion along the stability line. New Zealand scored the lowest and Hungary the highest among the 84 countries thus rated for that time period, meaning that the latter had far more serious occurrences than did New Zealand and 82 other countries during 1948-1962.

    What do you think of these rankings? Are there any surprises? Why? Given the relative position of the United States, how would you describe its stability? Do you find any difficulties identifying stability with such a rating of intensities of conflict? Can you add other indices or dimensions of stability? Relate this kind of ranking to our discussion of change in terms of institutions, performances and personnel. Do you see it as a good predictive approach?

12. Figure 7-6 on page 326 affords you an opportunity to draw some curves relating intensities of support and opposition to a political system with their distributions among the population. On the basis of what has been presented in this chapter, or your own views, construct a hypothetical set of curves representing (1) a relatively stable western democracy, (2) a situation such as that found in Cuba just prior to its revolution, and (3) the condition of any other particular country that interests you.

Table 7-9

Political Stability among Nations, 1955–61

Country	Score
France	499
U. of S. Af.	495
Haiti	478
Poland	465
Spain	463
Dom. Rep.	463
Iran	459
Ceylon	454
Japan	453
Thailand	451
Mexico	451
Ghana	451
Jordan	448
Sudan	445
Morocco	443
Egypt	438
Pakistan	437
Italy	433
Belgium	432
Paraguay	431
USSR	430
Nicaragua	430
Chile	427
Burma	427
Yugoslavia	422

Country	Score
Tunisia	328
Gr. Britain	325
Portugal	323
Uruguay	318
Israel	317

Country	Score
India	599
Argentina	599
Korea	596
Venezuela	584

0	1	2	3	4	5	6
N. Zealand 000	Norway 104	W. Germany 217	Canada 317	Panama 422	Turkey 583	Indonesia 699
	Netherlands 104	Czech. 212	U. S. 316	Ecuador 422	Lebanon 581	Cuba 699
	Cambodia 104	Finland 211	Taiwan 314	China 422	Iraq 579	Colombia 681
	Sweden 103	Romania 206	Libya 309	El Salvador 421	Bolivia 556	Laos 652
	Saudi Arabia 103	Ireland 202	Austria 309	Liberia 415	Syria 554	Hungary 652
	Iceland 103	Costa Rica 202	E. Germany 307	Malaya 413	Peru 552	
	Philippines 101		Ethiopia 307	Albania 412	Guatemala 546	
	Luxembourg 101		Denmark 306	Greece 409	Brazil 541	
			Australia 306	Bulgaria 407	Honduras 535	
			Switzerland 303	Afghanistan 404	Cyprus 526	

Stability ——————————————————————— Instability

Source: Ivo K. and Rosalind L. Feierbend, "Aggressive Behaviors within Polities, 1948-1962: A Cross-National Study," *The Journal of Conflict Resolution*, X (September, 1966), p. 253.

Figure 7-6

Cumulative Distributions of Citizen Support

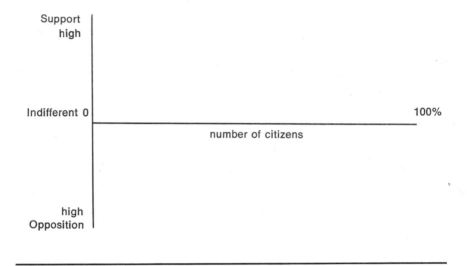

Bibliographical Notes

Social scientists ritualistically lament the state of knowledge about social change, but it remains a fact that more research and writing is done on change than any other single subject. In fact, not to write on change is to place oneself on the defensive.

The vast supply of materials makes it difficult to know where to begin. This being the case, we will cite only some very well-known and accessible works and ideas. Perhaps the most convenient introduction to the entire field of change is Wilbert E. Moore's *Social Change*, Englewood Cliffs, N.J.: Prentice-Hall, Inc., 1963, a brief but thorough typing of social change from the perspective of a leading sociologist. Alterations through time take place in different ways in different societies and sub-systems. Change in a polity is quite different from change in an economic system, but no one has the time to study all forms of change, least of all the harried student, so henceforth we will concentrate on political change.

The most dramatic change is, of course, a revolution; accordingly, scholars have devoted a great deal of their attention to it: the causes, courses and strategies, forms and consequences. As noted, the first philosophers to speculate in a disciplined way about revolutions were Plato and Aristotle. We need not review their work again, but suffice it to say that some scholars still maintain that Aristotle's treatment of the problem in Book V of the *Politics* is the best and most concise consideration to date.

Many other political philosophers have since attempted to fathom the meanings of revolutions, and we have especially noted the major work of Karl Marx; we invite you to explore the extent of his writings beyond his well known polemic, *The Communist Manifesto*, first published in 1848. Marx's writings are available in many editions, as are the more practical applications of V. I. Lenin. *What is to be Done?* New York: International Publishers, 1929, is the best brief treatment by Lenin of how the transition to the true communist state may come about. Whereas many liberal nineteenth century thinkers believed in some sort of inevitable progress toward democracy and personal freedom, we have noted some pessimistic doubters. Vilfredo Pareto's cyclical theory of political history is set forth in a four volume work entitled *Mind and Society*, ed. by Arthur Livingston, New York: Harcourt, Brace and Company, 1935, which the student may find interesting to examine but very difficult reading. Similar responses to the liberal views were put forth by Roberto Michels in *Political Parties*, Glencoe, Ill.: The Free Press, 1949, first published in 1915, and by Gaetano Mosca in *The Ruling Class*, ed. by Arthur Livingston, New York: McGraw-Hill Book Company, 1939. Mosca's theories were first advanced in the 1880-90s.

While such men may remain skeptical about revolution there is no shortage of violent political upheavals. In fact, the twentieth century now treats them as commonplace, so plentiful are they that several research institutes have been set up to study the subject, conferences have been convened, and hundreds of articles and books published during the past two decades on these dramatic occurrences. From all this work have come some notable studies, including Crane Brinton's *Anatomy of Revolution*, Englewood Cliffs, N.J.: Prentice-Hall, Inc., 1938, a modern classic in which both the causes and stages of revolution are derived from three case studies in revolution. Another well-known analysis is that of Hannah Arendt, *On Revolution*, New York: Viking Press, Inc., 1963, a passionate account of the meanings of revolution. Readers who prefer aphorisms should enjoy the remarkable Eric Hoffer's insights into change entitled *The Ordeal of Change*, New York: Harper and Brothers, Publishers, 1964. For budding social scientists who prefer more technical terms we suggest Chalmers Johnson's *Revolutionary Change*, Boston: Little, Brown and Company, 1966, a book which covers most phases of revolutionary activity. One product of a conference is *Internal War, Problems and Approaches*, New York: The Free Press, 1964, edited by Harry Eckstein. A number of distinguished American social scientists contributed their ideas and research to this volume. Another conference product—this time of more philosophically-minded scholars—is a volume edited by Carl J. Friedrich, *Revolution*, New York: Atherton Press, 1966.

Of course, revolution is but one type of political change. Contemporary scholars are interested in all types and particularly the attempts of newly-emerging nation-states to modernize. Revolutions may be a phase in that development; in any case, countless writings are available for the curious, all with the word 'development' in their titles. A beautifully written earlier work is that of Rupert Emerson, *From Empire to Nation,* Cambridge: Harvard University Press, 1960. A sensitive and well-written account of change in the Middle East and North Africa is Manfred Halpern's *The Politics of Social Change,* Princeton: Princeton University Press, 1963. The well-known book of Daniel Lerner, *The Passing of Traditional Society,* Glencoe, Ill.: The Free Press, 1958, deals with the Near East and uses survey data on attitudes. The findings of the study point out many of the difficulties of instituting change. Similarly, Albert O. Hirschman, an economist, deals with problems of mobilization in *Journeys Toward Progress,* New York: Twentieth Century Fund, 1963. Historians quite naturally have also speculated about change. Among the best recent summaries is C. E. Black's *The Dynamics of Modernization,* New York: Harper and Row, Publishers, 1966, which synthesizes much modern theory about the difficulties of modernization. Black is able, as an historian, to place these events into a much broader time span than do most social scientists. A similar attempt, with a more controversial theory attached, is A. F. K. Organski's *The Stages of Political Development,* New York: Alfred A. Knopf, Inc., 1965. In this volume, Organski attempts, as the title suggests, to elaborate "stages" through which development occurs, an attempt which has also been made by such theorists as Sorokin, Toynbee, Walt W. Rostow and others. Some scholars question the purpose of classifying stages, especially when the evidence concerning their periodicity and inevitability is so scant.

For a recent brief attempt to describe development at a level appropriate to undergraduates we nominate Lucian W. Pye, *Aspects of Political Development,* Boston: Little, Brown and Company, 1966. Pye is especially attuned to the psychological dimensions of change at the individual level. At the societal level and written from a very different value orientation is Irving Louis Horowitz's *Three Worlds of Development,* New York: Oxford University Press, 1966. David Apter's *The Politics of Modernization,* Chicago: University of Chicago Press, 1965, deals with mobilization systems and alternatives, in a somewhat abstract sociological approach. Apter has no single neat theory of change, but he does have many good observations.

The extensive literature on electoral, personnel and policy change will be dealt with elsewhere in this text, but we shall mention a few very relevant or readable works, mainly about the American situation. Samuel Lubell gave a rather lucid account of electoral change with his theory of "ins" and "outs," found in *The Future of American Politics,* New York:

Harper and Brothers, 1951, 1962. While somewhat dated, the book is still helpful in thinking about electoral parties as coalitions. John K. Galbraith ventured a provocative thesis about American policy change in his book, *American Capitalism: the Concept of Countervailing Power*, Boston: Houghton Mifflin Company, 1952. It is quite useful to consider his approach to policy change with that of E. E. Schattschneider in *The Semi-Sovereign People*, New York: Holt, Rinehart and Winston, Inc., 1960, where electoral and interest group approaches are contrasted.

Bibliographical notes on change can go on endlessly unless one simply calls a halt. We will, but not without citing two excellent if quite different books: one is Homer Barnett's near classic, *Innovation*, New York: McGraw Hill Book Company, 1953, in which the author attempts to explain the basis of cultural change. He deals in particular with the incentives to change and acceptance or rejection of changes. Read it! Another fine volume is Barrington Moore's *Social Origins of Dictatorship and Democracy*, Boston: Beacon Press, Inc., 1966, an analysis of how these systems have come into being in the modern world, with rich historical material. In the final chapter of this text we will have occasion again to refer to Moore.

President's Role
To Be Examine
Eugene Register-Guard, Nov. 19, 1968, Eugene, Oregon

Commerce chief
recruiting aides
Palo Alto Times, July 11, 1967,
Palo Alto, California

Eugene Register-Guard, Jan. 7, 1968, Eugene, Oregon
They've Reached T

Politician Tabbed as 'Pr
Christian Science Monitor, April 10, 1957, Boston, Massachusetts

Decentralized Government Called Decisive Issue
The New York Times, May 21, 1967, New York, New York

HE LONG WAY UP
Time, Nov. 15, 1968,
New York, New York

Be Delegate If Packaging the Char
You Want Start

% OF SENATORS
RE MILLIONAIRES
In Politics
Iron River Reporter, July 26, 1956,
Iron River, Michigan

Makers of New Constitution D
Putting All Their Eggs in One
The New York Times, Sept. 22, 1967, New York, New York

rvey Indicates as Many as
30 May Surpass Mark
The New York Times, March 5, 1968,
New York, New York

The G.O.P.'s Big Gain
Time, Nov. 15, 1968, New York, New York

Massive Gerrymande
Mapped in California
By 38 Congressmen

* * *

Jersey Senate Judiciary Group
Expanded to Shift Power Base
The New York Times, Dec. 11, 1967, New York, New York

GOP, Democratic Lawmak

The Sagging Power Structure
The Wall Street Journal, July 27, 1967, New York, New York

'Boss Rule'
The Oregonian,
July 12, 1968,
Portland, Oregon

Quietly Carve New Distri
Designed for Mutual Bene
The Wall Street Journal, Nov. 9, 1967, New York, New Yo

Chapter 8

Political Division of Labor
and Role Allocation

Consider the following facts and the problems they entail: the United States has a population of approximately 200 million, of whom about 115 million are 21 years of age and older. In our constantly evolving political and governmental systems, we have created a complex structure consisting of some 530,000 elective public offices; about 10.5 million civilian governmental positions; nearly three million persons in the armed forces; more than 15,000 interest groups; two major and a host of minor political parties; a national, state, and local set of governments which total more than 90,000, and a tripartite separation of powers at each level with many more independent commissions and agencies as well.

A basic problem is obvious: *Who is to do what* in this huge and complex system? No one person can handle all the responsibilities nor can all 115 million adults participate equally in all the jobs that must be done. Recognition of this elementary need for political specialization led the founding fathers to propose a formal division of labor which would allow different individual citizens to perform different tasks or services in a variety of different offices and roles. The problem, then, is to decide which persons will perform which services with what resources, and this in turn requires many decisions on the division of labor since many alternative forms are available. In short, *how shall the political system be organized to perform its various tasks, and how shall individuals be allocated, assigned, or recruited* to the various political roles, offices and work?

We will have relatively little to say here about how different political systems or structures came into being, but we will have much more to say about how various societies recruit and allocate persons to perform political roles once these divisions of labor are established. In short, we have the same problem in political science as the economists have in describing economic divisions of labor, or the sociologist in depicting the performance of the great variety of social roles. The explanations may not be the same but the general problem is analogous.

More specifically, we need to know which divisions of labor are used; which processes are employed for allocating persons to positions; and how citizens are motivated and prepared to perform different tasks and roles. These are all interesting and crucial questions for leaders especially, as well as for political scientists and other specialists on the matter. We will consider them, therefore, as major problems of politics.

Specification of Political Roles

Societies seldom if ever create an entire political division of labor with a single conscious act; rather the divisions tend to evolve through time and countless choices, experiences and resolutions of problems. Societies which are stabilized and institutionalized have full-fledged political divisions of labor, a great part of which will be highly formalized, i.e., explicit, visible and generally recognized or accepted as such. Many nations are still developing political divisions of labor and, until such time as they are stabilized, it will be difficult to describe them very accurately. Whatever the stage of development, political divisions of labor consist of various citizens performing the inevitable complementary tasks of political life.

A polity may be partially defined as those sets of roles which are concerned with the making and implementing of public choices which we discussed in earlier chapters. A role, in turn, may be thought of as a position or task which is specified in terms of a set of responsibilities or duties to perform, norms or rules for doing the work, resources for accomplishing the task, and a set of rewards or compulsory inducements for the incumbent or person who performs the role.[1] Citizens typically perform a great variety of such political roles, many of which may seem quite private or informal to

[1] A vast literature on roles has been produced by sociologists during the past twenty years. Almost any introductory sociology textbook can serve as a useful supplement to our discussion. For those who wish more advanced analyses we suggest Bruce J. Biddle and Edwin J. Thomas, eds., *Role Theory: Concepts and Research* (New York: John Wiley and Sons, Inc., 1966). A less technical but much more philosophical and reflective volume is that of Dorothy Emmet, *Rules, Roles and Relations* (New York: St. Martin's Press, 1966).

them. Thus, one may be a politician, a consumer of public goods, a voter, and a spectator of political events all more or less simultaneously. A person behaves somewhat differently in each of these roles because he is faced with different problems and operates within different contexts of rules, cultural, expectations and resources. Some people, of course, become highly specialized in political activity and tend to stress such roles above the others; they become professional politicians or administrators, while others perform only occasionally and remain essentially amateurs. Figures 8-1 and 8-2 illustrate some ways to contrast the broad mixture of social roles all of us

Figure 8-1

Some Possible Adult Roles in the U.S.A.

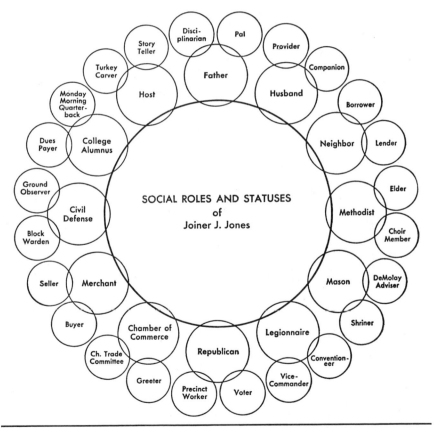

Source: Figure 46 (p. 316) in *Sociology*, Rev. Ed., by George A. Lundberg, Clarence C. Schrag and Otto N. Larsen. Copyright 1958 by Harper & Row, Publishers, Incorporated. Reprinted by permission of Harper & Row, Publishers.

Figure 8-2

Some Roles of a State Legislator

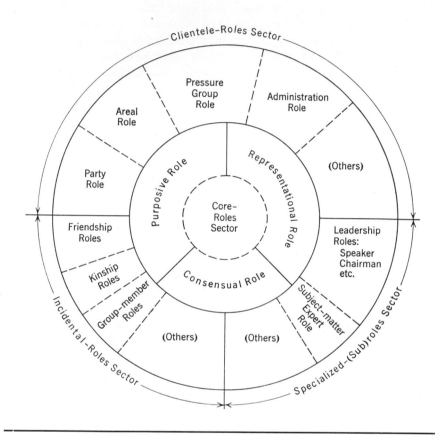

Source: John C. Wahlke, Heinz Eulau, William Buchanan, and LeRoy C. Ferguson, *The Legislative System* (New York: John Wiley and Sons, Inc., 1962), p. 14.

perform with a highly specialized set of roles, such as those pertaining to a professional political office.

An adequate description of such role combinations or even of a particular role in a polity requires a substantial amount of work, much of which may not be particularly useful for all research purposes. Nevertheless, some aspects may be highly useful in explaining and predicting certain political behavior. When we know a citizen's rights, responsibilities, resources, etc., we have fairly good predictors of a great deal of his behavior and influence in the political system. Note we said 'fairly good' and not perfect predictors. But even the most complete description of the formal divisions of labor or role structure will not enable certain predictions of actual behavior. Citizens may not exercise their rights or responsibilities; officials may exceed their formal powers or fail in their duties. No constitution can possibly convey a sense of how a President, for example, actually behaves on a daily basis. Still, it would not be possible to account for either the behavior of a leader or an ordinary citizen without some knowledge of the formal roles he is expected to perform. All qualified voters may not vote but all who vote must have been qualified. So it is imperative to have some notion of the formal division of labor or role structure of a political system to begin to understand the behavior of individuals and practical daily political processes. It is also imperative if we are to understand how collective decisions are made and public goods are produced and distributed.

We have included a 'job sheet' or role description form to illustrate some of the more pertinent considerations about political roles and services (Figure 8-3). The left-hand column lists a random selection of political offices while the top row lists various important though partial aspects of the roles. Complete descriptions of each set of roles are likely to entail a great amount of detail because the description cannot be reduced to single words. The powers of a particular governmental office such as a Prime Minister are not readily summarized in a few neat, clear-cut statements. Most political roles are combinations of both ambiguous and fuzzy expectations concerning actions to be performed, including some mandatory actions, some prohibited actions and some actions that are optional or discretionary. Yet there are broad areas of agreement about many of these roles if they are visible, formalized, and familiar to the persons describing them. Literally thousands of volumes have been written on these aspects of political roles in various nations. Yet political roles and tasks are always being redefined and altered, with new insights and perspectives emerging. A President's role in the United States today is very different in terms of its powers and responsibilities from what it was in 1800. The same is true of most other political roles throughout the world. Consider the position of the typical monarch in 1800 with that of today.

A full set of job descriptions should convey an image of the political system as an enormous, complex division of labor guided by a vast network of norms or sets of prescriptions, proscriptions and options. Each member has his behavior and services 'structured' or guided by the norms which define his role(s). These guides may be more or less explicit, more or less formal, more or less precise, more or less imperative. The more of each of these characteristics, the more completely specified is the role. As we have stated earlier, in highly institutionalized and stable systems one finds the overall division of labor and many more individual political roles to be highly explicit, formalized, precise and imperative. In the transitional or modernizing

Figure 8-3

Role Description Form

Role	Must Do	Must Not Do	May Do	Formal Powers	Informal Resources	Term of Office	Social Status	Mode of Selection
U.S. President								
British Prime Minister								
French Mayor								
Chief of Primitive Tribe								
Swedish Voter								
Spanish Dictator								
Chairman People's Republic China								
U.S. Senator								
Japanese Emperor								
Secretary-General, UN								

nations the new roles are usually less explicit, less formal, less precise, less imperative. As a result citizens do not have confident guides; what may and may not be legitimately done has yet to be determined. Under such conditions force or command may be the deciding factor, or even caprice and impulse. We can clarify these considerations rather simply with a chart such as that in Figure 8-4 where the role structures of three kinds of nations are scaled in terms of more or less of each particular attribute. In principle, political scientists can estimate these properties and locate roles or entire political systems as 'profiles' on the chart.[2] In fact, it is very difficult to devise more accurate measures than these somewhat subjective relative rankings. Nevertheless, the conceptualization should be useful.

Some brief definitions or explanations of the various role attributes referred to in Figure 8-4 may clarify some of the contrasts which social scientists have observed. You may wish to check these definitions against our judgments of the profiles. Would you agree or disagree?

Interchangeability indicates the degree of ease with which roles can be transferred from one person to another, or with which the same person can assume many different institutional roles. If a role has elaborate training or recruitment requirements it will typically have low interchangeability. In polities some examples of high interchangeability would be ones in which a general often serves as president, say, or where a citizen can also be a legislator in a town meeting. *Imperativeness* relates to the degree of requiredness or expected conformity to specific behaviors identified with the role. If there were high imperativeness, non-performance would inevitably result in serious sanctions, whether informal or formal. Can you imagine the President of the United States not going to the Inaugural ceremony, the general in the field refusing to take command, or an ordinary citizen of Britain failing to show courtesy and deference to the monarch? The more imperative a norm, the more predictable is the behavior of the role incumbent. When highly imperative norms are violated, we are typically shocked or concerned; there must be strong reasons for breaking imperative roles. For example, why would devout members of a religious order leave their traditional roles and join a guerrilla movement? When would a head of state voluntarily surrender the sovereignty of his nation? When does a dedicated citizen of one country spy for an enemy power? Can you think of facilitating circumstances?

Visibility pertains to how observable the role and its performance are, and thus how well it is known to most members of the system. In a small primitive band, all roles typically have very high visibility; many persons

---

[2] Figure 8-4 and the accompanying discussion were at least partially influenced by Gabriel Almond, "Comparative Political Systems," *Journal of Politics*, 18 (August, 1956), pp. 391-409, and Gabriel Almond and G. Bingham Powell, *Comparative Politics: A Developmental Approach* (Boston: Little, Brown and Company, 1966), especially Chaps. 9-10.

Figure 8-4
Some Basic Attributes of Roles and Systems

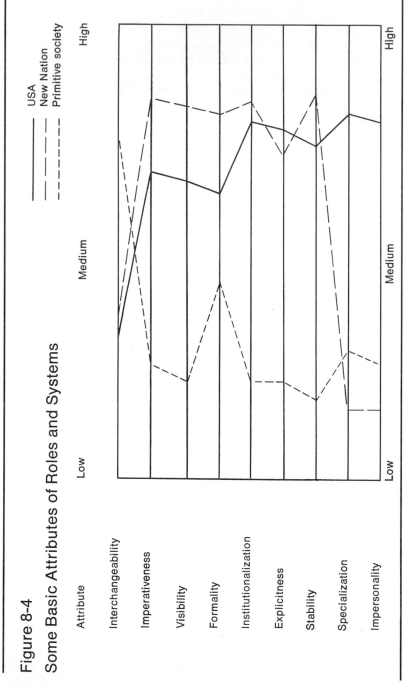

feel this is equally true of small-town America. The United States has more role visibility in politics, with its constant mass media attention, than does a traditional royal system such as those in nineteenth century or earlier Europe. And of course, most dictatorships and totalitarian type systems have very low visibility of effective decision-making roles, however much the mass media plays up the ceremonial roles of their leadership. *Formality* of roles refers to very explicit and very impersonal norms of observance, usually commanding deference or 'social distance.' Roles with high formality typically involve rituals of courtesy or ceremony which cast an aura of dignity over proceedings. The coronation ceremony in Great Britain abounds in this attribute; the convening of the U.S. Supreme Court would provide some of that flavor; but so, too, the traditional academic processions and some aspects of committee or council meetings in campus or local affairs. Bureaucracy and the military are the sectors of modern political life most noted for their highly formalistic behaviors, on the job, at least. *Institutionalization* has been discussed in the previous chapter and, as applied to roles themselves, it refers to their acceptability as the appropriate or basically *right or authorized* ways of doing things. Most public officials have highly institutionalized roles in modernized or complex political systems, as do the leaders of highly stable primitive tribes. When the values accorded the role are considered central or crucial to the society, then one is likely to observe this feature, unless the political roles are undergoing great change and the new forms are not yet widely accepted. Thus charismatic leadership, in the beginning, is non-institutionalized, but leadership becomes institutionalized as it evolves a more stabilized and accepted set of expectations.

Explicitness is a matter of the degree of clarity in the role specifications. The detailed elaboration of specific rituals as, say, in the traditional Roman Catholic Church is one form of this attribute. But so, too, the extremely delicate or complex tasks of many modern professions, such as surgery and medical practice generally. The political profession in the United States is still rather low along this scale, at least so far as running for office is concerned, but most believe it is becoming more explicit in its rules and precepts as the study of political strategies progresses, and the techniques of polling, public relations and the like become more elaborate. The practice of the law, of course, is highly explicit, as are most bureaucratic duties and the skills generally which go into the management of organizations and their resources. *Stability* has to do with the enduring nature of the role, either in terms of its being viewed as necessary to the society or highly rewarding to the person performing in it. The former case is nearly akin to institutionalization, but the latter suggests that many roles may persist because the occupants like them so well. Or if there are *any* beneficiaries from the performance of the role at all, this may be sufficient to ensure its prolonged existence. In this sense the American political boss possessed a rather stable role with benefits for many—and much personal enjoyment—even though it was not institutionalized in the eyes of the broader membership of society. While bosses had to work behind the more formal, institutionalized leadership, the manipulation of patronage and personal rewards for their following brought them many returns, and we see the role persisting in many situations even today. Popular distaste does not automatically banish political roles. Apparently there are many stable roles or relationships involving non-legitimate activities (such as the underworld) which few scholars have yet explored at any length from the political perspective. There apparently is a whole criminal argot conveying much about what such role occupants do and why; after all, it is important for them to know.

Specialization refers to the degree to which roles and their tasks are discernibly different. Some scholars refer to this as role differentiation and think of it as an important feature of advanced social systems. It is tied to social and technological complexity and such features as bureaucratization and professionalization. We might also note that the greater the specialization, the less likelihood of interchangeability of roles. As some critics put it, in our 'credential society' there are many specialized professional and bureaucratic positions which can be attained only after meeting rigid educational and skill criteria. Yet housewives can still be voters and husbands and fathers can also be politicians. In other words, one can still combine many sorts of differentiated roles. Indeed, there is one school of elite theory which claims that there is a great deal of role interchange across official positions at the very top where key decisions are made. In fact, the British have honored (i.e., institutionalized) non-specialization of top decision-makers by their tradition of the gentlemanly 'amateur' who is given a broad humanist-type education at their prestige schools.

Impersonality of roles refers to the degree to which their performance is not identified with the specific person involved. Some roles, such as those of movie stars, are liable to vary enormously in the relevant norms and expectations, depending upon the kind of 'personality' or image projected by the particular star. To some degree top politicians in this country share that same attribute; they are considered celebrities and convey unique attributes to their following. Sometimes there is an element of charisma, such as many were inclined to attribute to those in office bearing the Kennedy name during the mid- and late 1960s. Some sociologists would label this an *ascriptive* status attribute, inherited rather than achieved. Consider alternatively the impersonality of most traffic officers, judges, voter registrars, and similar officials. In new nations there is likely to be very little impersonality attached to most new roles because the roles are occupied by well known figures of the prior revolutionary or independence movement. But in these situations the personal propensities of the leaders may create precedents for future incumbents, contributing to greater impersonality as they become the accepted form. Historians feel that George Washington contributed much toward such an impersonal 'style' and performance for the Presidency in its earliest years, but there have been succeeding Presidents who left the stamp of their personality upon the norms of presidential performance as well. How one would measure the lasting effects of these is harder to tell, except as we can trace the innovations to subsequent formal role prescriptions, with the ultimate influence found in new norms which become imperative. You might say it is a case of one man's proclivity becoming another man's role imperative.

The usefulness of these dimensions will vary in terms of what the scholar or student wishes to do with them. As we have noted, they may help explain regularities and continuity in the performance of roles. Roles are the basic units in the political divison of labor, thus organizing the ways of meeting the problems we have been treating: mobilization of resources, allocations to collective goals, distributions of burdens and benefits, the creation and distribution of symbolic goods and statuses, application of controls, stabilization and adaptation. Hence many of our generalizations about how these are done may depend on the nature of the particular role attributes. The many types of systems or divisions of labor can thus be compared along many lines, involving those attributes: interchangeability, imperativeness, visibility, formality, institutionalization, explicitness, stability, specialization and impersonality.

We are inclined to believe that each political division of labor has a particular set of more or less consistent policy-making processes. Nations which may be located on the right side of Figure 8-4 will have one combination of processes while another, located differently, will develop a different combination. Likewise—and this is most important in the context of this chapter—such systems develop particular combinations of recruitment rules and processes. Similarly, individual political behavior found in each society is vitally affected by the role structure of the polity, since the role structure defines the permissible, mandatory and prohibited forms of political activity and interaction. So much for the attributes of individual roles within which men act politically; let us look briefly at the possible combinations of role structures and how they may serve political systems in different ways.

Role Structures and Political Interaction

We hope we have persuaded you that the concept of roles can be quite useful for understanding how the behavior of individuals is organized for certain tasks and relationships in the social system. Since it provides a very important link between the individual and the larger structures and processes, we do not have to talk about politics either at the level of pure personalities, with their unique characteristics, or at the very impersonal and abstract level of formal structures and procedures, as if people didn't count at all. Let us recount here some of the ways in which the characteristics of roles can be related to specific types of political structures, and how they may also vary in the ways they induce and affect behavior.

Start simply by noting that roles relate persons to one another. The relationship consists essentially of mutual expectations or understandings. And larger sets of role relationships will make up the 'structure' of an area of political activity. We can conceptualize, and even diagram, the nature of these sets of relationships and how they specify the behavior of persons toward one another. Note the several diagrams in Figure 8-5. The most typical convention in political and organizational charts is to depict *power* or *authority* relationships. But there are several other kinds of relationships which can be designated in these ways, many of them equally as important to understand. We might want instead to depict communications networks, status relationships, friendship ties, or any other way human beings relate to each other. However, in political systems power and authority relationships are very important, so we begin by considering these.

Most typically we think of power and authority relationships as hierarchical, from 'top' positions of command to those at the bottom who must obey. The formal organization chart displays this, and typically the lines depict the formal chain of command, from superior to subordinate positions. Thus you may have identified models I, II, or V in Figure 8-5 as symbolizing the rudiments of command in an organization, although very simplified. In formal organizations there is also the conventional assumption that it is the duty of those in subordinate positions to report upward along the same lines which also designate responsibility to one's superior. In this sense the relationship entails a constriction on formal interaction as well. For example, in model V of Figure 8-5, those in the positions at the bottom, C, D and E; should thus report only to their direct superior, B, who in turn deals with the top position, A, as the single line indicates. The administrative norms of command and obedience will formally specify these channels and constraints, and in principle, at least, any inferior who makes a habit of circumventing his boss (B) over job problems would be disciplined. Combining these command and communication precepts we can make some distinctions about the different authority structures reflected in those three figures. Model II suggests a rather autocratic arrangement where inferiors deal *only* with their superior and, assuming the strict conventions, he has both a monopoly of command *and* of the information each reports to him. In contrast, Model I shows a line between B and C, and could thus symbolize their duty to communicate or share information, on a formally equal basis, while also interacting with their superior in the conventional manner. Here the superior's command would not be the only kind of communication formally relevant to their job performance.

If we are considering an hierarchical organization, the horizontal line between 'equals' in the organization may be considered a consultative sort

Figure 8-5

Some Typical Role Structures

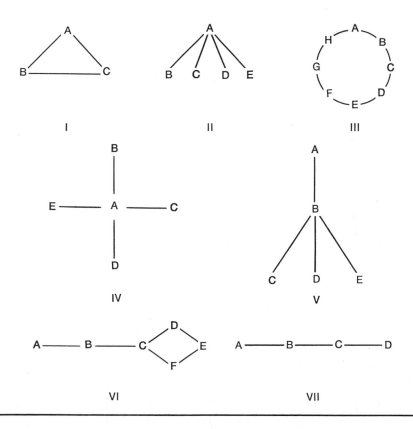

of relationship, involving shared information without the suggestion of command. Frequently crucial decision-makers will not only have a command relationship with subordinates, but also a consultative or staff relation where information is supposed to be autonomously given, that is, unbiased by a position of subordination. This is sometimes suggested by a lateral line directly to the superior, and often a dotted line is used to convey the consultative nature of the staff position, rather than command over operations. Thus in Figure 8-6, the organization chart of the Department of State, the Arms Control and Disarmament Agency is designated as an advisory body to the Secretary. The lateral line to the Agency for International Development and the Peace Corps suggests that these agencies maintain a degree of operating autonomy from the other units in the department, but the solid lines to the Secretary indicate a reporting relation over operational matters.

There is no magic in these diagrams, but they aid in conceptualizing

Figure 8-6
Organizational Chart of the Department of State

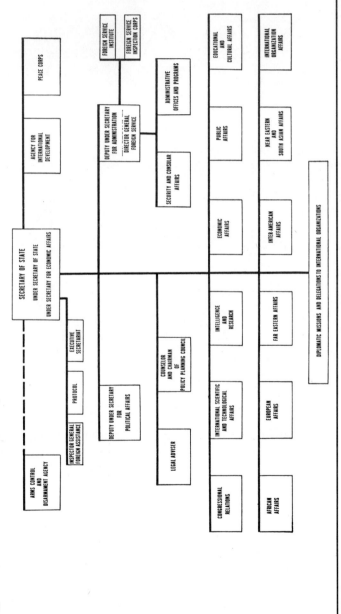

Source: Office of the Federal Register, *United States Government Organization Manual*, 1966-67 (Washington, D.C.: Government Printing Office, 1966), p. 609.

different aspects of role relationships in formal organizations. We might note some further distinctions. There is much attention given in western legal precepts to delegation of authority, whereby operating discretion is granted a subordinate, but with some form of checking or review by the grantor. Model V could suggest this, with A being the delegator and B the actual director of operations. In business organizations, A might be the Board of Directors and B the manager of the firm. In the United States Army, A could be the civilian superior, the Secretary of the Army, and B the top military commander, identified as the Chief of Staff. If you look in the *United States Government Organization Manual* at the charts for the military departments you will note that the proliferation of staff about the offices of the Secretaries, and at the military command level, are not mixed with direct chain of command to the operating forces. For the military especially, the distinction between staff and command lines are quite crucial. The information function is extremely important, but it is a special type of relationship.

Another form of delegation is the electoral relationship. In democracies the belief in popular sovereignty is institutionalized in periodic election of the top governmental officials. In some ingenious diagrams of political relationships, Alfred De Grazia (Figure 8-7) has chosen to designate this by the dotted line. In the United States the electorate chooses officials who are formally independent with regard to each other, however much they may have to work together in the business of governing. Note that the 'weak mayor' and 'strong mayor' systems in Figure 8-7 both designate an autonomous council, although in the latter, both positions can generate ordinances. The Council-Manager form is more nearly like the business-type delegation of authority, with the council as 'board of directors.' The former example of complete autonomy between elective bodies also applies to our national government with its separation of powers between President and Congress. This contrasts strongly with the British scheme of integrated powers, i.e., interchangeable roles for top leadership.

But for all the concern with hierarchy in political affairs, there are many significant relationships of equality as well. Less attention has been paid to the formal relationships of equality as far as organizational precepts are concerned, except that those who like hierarchies tend to view them as inefficient. Actually there are many political forms embodying positions of equal standing, where duties and responsibilities are shared equally in the formal sense. We may call these *collegial* bodies, where no member has command over another, and all can communicate with each other, and indeed are supposed to. The legislature is a typical case, as is a city council and any other elected committee. Each member gains his authority from an electorate, and sits in the body as a formal equal to all other members. Their rights typically involve the exercise of a vote in the major decisions of the body, the command of relevant information for casting a vote and the right to be heard in turn. Within the body there can be a delegation of tasks or

Figure 8-7

Major Structures of Local Government in America

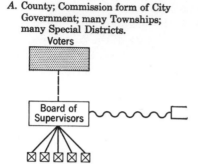

A. County; Commission form of City Government; many Townships; many Special Districts.

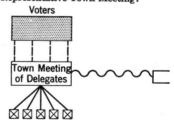

B. "Weak–Mayor" form.

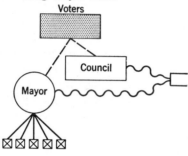

C. "Strong–Mayor" form.

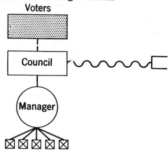

D. Council–Manager form.

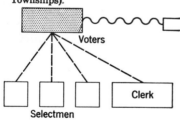

E. Town–Meeting form (and many Townships).

F. Representative Town Meeting.

Key to Drawings
- – – – – Signifies Election
- —— Signifies Appointment and Control
- ☒ Department Head
- ∿⊏ Ordinance or Legislative Power

Note:
Voters are often organized in districts to elect supervisors, councilmen, commissioners, or delegates. At other times, all voters cast ballots for the whole number of officers (election–at–large)

Source: Alfred De Grazia, *The American Way of Government,* National, State and Local Edition (New York: John Wiley and Sons, Inc., 1957), p. 857.

election of leadership for certain functions, and each member may have command of a staff aiding him in performing his duty. But the principle of collegial equality is essential, especially on the matter of talking and voting. In Figure 8-5 this relationship might be represented by Model III. If one also wanted to indicate an emphasis upon open communications among all members, they might draw additional lines between H and F, H and E, A and F, A and E, A and D, B and E, and B and D as well. This would result in a rather complex grid, especially if the members in the body were increased, so perhaps the circular interconnections will suffice. The idea of complete communication of information between all members is in sharp contrast to the division of responsibility in the formal command systems. One therefore expects the processes of choice to be more 'political' in the sense of more argument and persuasion, i.e., reciprocal interaction. More about that very shortly.

Let us consider some other possible role relationships, forgetting about command or equality for the moment, and think about communication links. In the sense of personal interaction, the top command position of a formal organization can be quite invisible or inaccessible to subordinates at the bottom of the pyramid. Every intermediate superior increases this distance, and the fellow at the bottom could conceivably know only his immediate superior, or know higher-ups only in the very formal sense of seeing them, but without communicating, aside from the courtesies due formal superiors. In some organizations this distance is used to preserve the invisibility of superiors, where their identity might endanger operations. Espionage organizations frequently rely on communication links that maintain maximal invisibility; should any member be caught and forced to tell he could name but a few out of the whole operation. Many underground organizations operate on this principle, and insurgent or subversive units are inclined to do so, too, so far as they fear betrayal or discovery. The Communist Party's classic cell block structure involved another consideration, too. Each cell was a unit of equal comrades who worked together, maintaining the militancy and fervor expected of revolutionary groups. But each cell would have contact restricted to a few crucial links with a superior so that they would know little or nothing about the rest of the cells and leadership positions. The relevant diagram might look something like Model VI in Figure 8-5. Distance and invisibility served to protect the overall party organization, while maintaining a strict command principle for militant operations; and yet the advantages of collegiality and cooperation could presumably thrive at the bottom. There can conceivably be no end to the ingenious combinations of such roles, given the tasks to be done and the desired mode of operations.

Reflect on each of the models in Figure 8-5 again. This time consider possible communication patterns and how each position might be affected in terms of *distance,* possible *visibility,* and the *ability to share information.* Note that without any hierarchical assumptions, Model I comes to represent a situation of complete equality in terms of direct inter-action with the two others and equal communication paths. It connotes the immediacy of a small group and the complete visibility and ability to exchange information. It might be an informal group where the communi-cation is spontaneous, or a committee which shares all tasks. But Model II shows a structure of unequal communication, even if no command assump-tions were made. In this situation A monopolizes information from the others. If such a situation emerges even on an informal basis, A's strategic position in communications would give him advantages. Depending on the task or purpose of the group, he might take all the winnings, or emerge as leader, or become the 'fall guy' should one of the other members 'squeal' to the police. At least as formally symbolized, we cannot be sure the other members know one another, and the division of labor here would indicate they do not depend on one another. Actually, Model IV may symbolize this more appropriately when we are considering communication rather than command relationships. Position A is here specified as crucial for whatever E, D, C, and B learn about or from each other. How would you feel, as C, in this model as compared to C in Model I—a little 'left out'? Actually, ana-lysts of interaction patterns note that those out at the end of communi-cations chains, so to speak, or limited with regard to whom they may ex-change information, tend to lose the rewards of having immediate exchanges with the others. If the information is highly valued, A would get by far the most rewards from the situation in IV, while C should prefer the situation in I. And by this criterion, think of how A and D would feel in the case of Model VII, with two intermediary links, and even greater distance, in this sense, from those farther along the communication line. When we think in terms of such rewards, we can feel sorry for a boss who is confined to talk-ing only with his lieutenant in command. This notion of distance, when combined also with the status dimension (where one has the exclusive status of being at the top) gives great meaning to the saying that the 'leader is lonely.'

The analyst of group processes, especially those involving decision-making and the performance of tasks, should be quite sensitive to other aspects of role relationships, too. We have dealt here with the formal and prescriptive sort because most governing bodies are guided by rules of law and formal principles of organization; these are so frequently the starting point in learning the basic principles of procedure. We have also noted com-munications relationships, and suggested some other elements which may be related, namely those of social distance or status, and what we might call social and information rewards. The status dimension figures very strongly in some political situations, where prestige figures or other enjoyers of status (celebrities, hero figures, etc.) may create their own lines of attention and deference quite different from the formal conventions. Some notable administrative subordinates have used their individual status to gain some degree of autonomy from their superiors (J. Edgar Hoover, Admiral Hyman Rickover, for example). Sometimes we note strong loyalties or affective ties which cross formal organizational lines. Thus party or regional affiliations have often created rather cohesive factions within legislatures, and loyalty to a President from one's own party may cause the legislator to act differently from his colleague who does not feel this constraint. Cross-cutting loyalties may become complex, but the analyst cannot dismiss them if they affect the outcomes of decision or performance significantly. In brief, then, roles tend to structure behavior through imposing norms and constraining opportunities for interaction. Role analysis and communications study enable us to make better predictions of political interaction. Indeed, men create roles and norms in order to control or at least influence behavior; and others attempt to reform them because they prefer other forms of behavior and/or political outcomes.

Recruitment and Allocation of Services

Having pictured the political system as an intricate assemblage of positions or roles and institutions which assist in defining appropriate political behavior, we are left with the problem of describing how individuals are recruited and assigned to perform services in various roles. As individual citizens we are anxious to know and predict how we will fare and what we must do in whatever system we may live; likewise political scientists are interested in knowing how political tasks will be allocated and personalities and political roles 'matched.' This is logically similar to the problem individuals and economic systems confront in allocating the factors of production: who will labor? who will save? who will invest? who will rent? who will manage firms? Generally, we may say that some six ways have been used in political systems to assign, recruit, or allocate men to political roles and offices:

1. random selection
2. prescriptive criteria
3. competition
4. conflict
5. command
6. bargaining

Random selection has been used in the form of lotteries, as in some ancient Greek city-states, and is now used in selecting panels for jury duty in the United States and occasionally in drafting men for military service. The Greek city-states used the lottery to fill governmental offices on the assumption that most offices were essentially simple and all citizens could do the work. Such random procedures emphasize the principle of equal availability, either as a device for sharing costs equitably or, perhaps, for sharing the good life if one believed, as did the Greeks, that public service was ennobling. Of course not all in Greek society were citizens, and thus eligibility for this service was preserved for a somewhat select group of peers. Note also the connotations of fairness of the jury trial requirement in the United States, where judgment by one's peers is considered in principle, at least, to be safer than a decision by a higher authority when a major offense is in question. But the legal counsels are given quite a bit of discretion within that requirement to sift out potentially biassed jurors, so that the presumed randomness is hedged quite a bit. As we have mentioned earlier the impact of the military draft in the United States has been less than fully random. Built into the law are quite a few prescriptive criteria for exemption. Many contend that a pure lottery system would be much fairer when not all serve. Of course another equalizing principle could be prescribing that everyone serve, as in universal military training which some advocated for this country just after World War II. Today some would prefer a universal service approach, with varieties of peaceful service as alternatives to the military. Can you see some problems, in principle or practice? Can you think of any other solutions to the fairness principle? Where else might you like to see random selection procedures apply?

Prescriptive criteria are best illustrated by hereditary rules for selection of leaders, as with European royalty. As long as the criteria are fulfilled (i.e., the blood line lasts, etc.) this kind of procedure has the merit of automatic selection, which should save all concerned some anxiety or uncertainty, and should rule out any competition or conflict, ideally at least. It is very crucial in these types of selection processes that the rules be explicit and unambiguous or there may be much interpretation and argumentation over how they apply. Even hereditary principles may fall into difficulty here, as the history of European royalty has well attested, with ultimate resolution often depending upon the force of arms. Prescriptive criteria are usually related to basic legitimizing values. In a way, these values will usually justify an essential inequality of selection. But legitimizing values do change over time and, consequently, the particular selection criteria. We see that the hereditary principle is fast fading with the passing of traditional systems. During the age of feudalism, and in some surviving primitive societies, it applied to almost all positions: for religious, political, family and economic life, as well as for political leadership. The laws of inheritance still have political implications, as when the millionaire's sons gain prominence so easily—at least in non-communist systems. But no longer is heredity regarded as appropriate for political office in most systems. Even the English House of Lords is viewed as an anachronism, and its powers have been carefully trimmed.

Today the most prevalent prescriptive criteria have to do with modern concepts of skill or competence, and are most likely to prevail for bureaucratic positions. The typical mode of eligibility is some certification of competence, usually the professional's license, the appropriate degree or requisite education, or sometimes by examination or some demonstration of skill. Sometimes competition is also involved, as we shall note below, but only among those selected few who qualify. In an era of expanding technology, the selective mode determines who serves for increasing numbers of public service positions. It dominates what one might call the middle and upper-middle level of public employment, where skilled services are most relevant—military officers, engineers, technicians and scientists, public health personnel, social workers, naturalists and foresters, agronomists, communications experts, economists, accountants and even social scientists. The vastly expanding professions and skilled trades in society become a very important source for the personnel who make the public sector run. And it makes the formal education system of the society a very crucial channel for mobilizing and training this talent; some see this influence as already problematic. Whoever is out of the educational system is thus denied access.

We must also note that experience and seniority are prescriptive criteria which have been widely applied in public institutions as well as private. The seniority principle in Congress is widely attacked, for many see it as bringing senile incompetents to positions of committee leadership where crucial decision-making powers are lodged. It favors those who have safe seats, whether due to a highly stable constituency (such as rural areas and especially in the South), or to a party machine (as in the urban East and Midwest), or to an ethnic affiliation for a concentrated minority (as with urban ghettoes). The principle itself may not be opposed so much as those it tends to favor. White Southerners may not support it if more Negro legislators become committee chairmen, while their own 'old men' pass from the scene. Interestingly, the critics of seniority tend to ignore its application in the military services, in unions and in the civil service—and, yes, even in the education profession! Now and then it becomes an issue concerning Supreme Court tenure, for the retirement age of 70 is permissive, not mandatory. But again, it is brought up as an issue mainly in terms of perceived ideologies and loyalties of the justices. And it is very often tied to the political battles of the 'ins' and 'outs.'

When one is defending the principle of seniority it is customary to point out the virtues of experience. Thus 'insiders' will tend to honor it more than 'outsiders'; those who like the institutionalization of leadership roles will favor it against those who prefer 'fresh blood' or merit criteria. Traditionalists will defend it, especially if they believe there is no formalized training which can effectively equip the incumbent for his role and the kinds of decisions he must make. For example, many feel the Supreme Court is not just another court, but is highly 'political' and needs a different form of wisdom from that dished out in most law schools or practiced on the bench. Indeed, most political practitioners in top offices tend to have that feeling about their jobs, that political experience is its own best teacher—and some even carry this to a very self-congratulatory mystique. However, in modern political systems the final judge of worth tends ultimately to be performance and outcomes, although institutional lapses and lags are a very common phenomena.

We must note that what we call 'prescriptive' is very similar to what sociologists have labelled as 'ascriptive.' But they usually contrast *ascription,* such as inherited statuses or personal attributes, with *achievement,* or the notion of winning awards and positions by merit or impersonal standards. We include both, for politically each of these forms of selection has an automatic form of operation and thus reduces ambiguity and/or conflict by the operation of the rule.

Institutionalized competition is one of the more interesting inventions of man, especially as it applies to the selection of political leaders. The political party is indeed a very recent phenomenon, which developed in western systems where elections had become institutionalized. Political competition in any large society requires extensive organization, if it is at all to approximate the democratic ideal of popular choice of leadership. And, as we will note in Chapter 14, the conditions which maintain competition are rather fragile, and the competitive process is often more a facade than reality. Nevertheless it is a vital institution in this country at least, and recent evidence indicates that more, not fewer, electoral districts are becoming competitive. The crucial value in competition for public office is that it enables a form of popular choice. Without competition, the electoral system becomes simply a means of expressing support, as it is in most communist systems, and as many fear it may become in the democracies, where one dominant party or ruling group is persistently returned to power. The great economic theorist, Joseph A. Schumpeter, is often credited with emphasizing electoral competition as the prime characteristic of democracy. Robert Dahl has, in turn, based his definition of 'polyarchy' on this conception.[3] Polyarchy presupposes, in Dahl's thought at least, a sufficiently pluralistic society so that alternative bases of support can be maintained, yet a society not so polarized as to degenerate into a conflict of classes, regions or sectors.

But elections may not be the only form of institutionalized competition. In general, any contest for a position which has designated rules for winning should be included in the type. Examination systems can thus be competitive, and the civil service uses them extensively. Here the principle of merit rather than popular choice is the legitimating norm. We will have

---

[3] Joseph A. Schumpeter, *Capitalism, Socialism and Democracy* (New York: Harper and Brothers, 1942), Chap. 22; Robert A. Dahl, *A Preface to Democratic Theory* (Chicago: The University of Chicago Press, 1956), Chap. 3.

more to say about some of the rigors and costs of competition in the pages ahead, but will note here that many have viewed competitive elections as a potentially unstabilizing element in the political system and yet others have viewed them as a great stabilizing device. The former note all the strains and intensities of fierce competition and fear that the outcome will not be accepted, that a disappointed party may turn to other means, or that people generally will tend to lose their tolerence toward oppositions. Others point to the legitimizing value of popular choice in systems with political diversity. They note, as Max Weber once suggested, that elections afford a candidate the opportunity to capture some aura of charisma in the excitement of the contest, although analysts have had difficulty 'proving' this one way or the other. We revert to our earlier discussion of stability, and emphasize again that there are other attributes of system performance which must also be considered in deciding whether any designated process is unstabilizing or not. But if instability is identified with uncertainty, there is no doubt that a truly competitive election or selection process must build in doubt as to who may win. If that raises more fears than hopes, then we should worry for the system.

Conflict is still another means of allocating positions. We think of pure conflict processes wherever the losing side also loses its standing in the system; where the victor takes all and banishes or attempts to eliminate the opposition. Thus the period of nation-building in Europe brought a great deal of conflict as to which royal contender would rule the new nation or jurisdiction. Conflict was also carried on covertly, as many written histories tell us, in countless court intrigues which degenerated into stealth and violent measures unknown but to the few. It pays to remember those times when we view with dismay the many forms of conflict over office and jurisdictions in new nations and revolutionary regimes today. Of course the scale of potential slaughter or purging of contenders seems much more ominous today and one cannot dismiss that lightly. But the elimination of conflict is not easy for any new system, and repression of it may be the worst policy.

Between institutionalized competition and outright conflict are many degrees and variations. A most interesting study of the political selection processes in Latin America by Charles Anderson suggests that even the more violent or forceful aspects of contending for office in many of those countries have their somewhat stabilizing rules and understandings. Excepting the very few 'real' revolutionary situations, he sees most such selection processes as abiding by the rule that "new power contenders may be added to the system, but old ones may not be eliminated."[4] The way for

---

[4] Charles W. Anderson, *Politics and Economic Change in Latin America* (Princeton, N.J.: D. Van Nostrand Company, Inc., 1967), p. 104.

'outside' groups to be accepted as participants in determining who governs, is for them to demonstrate a "power capability." The military can do this most easily, and often bloodlessly, by symbolic display of power, as in marching the troops through a capital, a show of forces and weaponry at strategic places, and so forth. The unions have their classic weapon in the general strike which can threaten the urbanized sectors. And students, as we increasingly learn, can be quite adept at the mass demonstration—an old art, apparently, in the Latin systems. Each such forceful technique can be viewed therefore as a 'threat' which gains access to the selection process for the successful wielders. Their success is thus achieved with less than outright force, i.e., just by threatening, and still less by chaotic violence, depending upon the degree to which the 'rules of the game' are implicitly understood by those involved. Anderson claims the process thus turns into "one of manipulation and negotiation among power contenders with reciprocally recognized power capabilities."[5] We might label this form *regulated conflict*.

In addition to these four methods, one also finds *command* procedures being used to select and recruit people for political roles. By command we mean rules which enable a leader simply to appoint persons to roles by virtue of his superior position of power or authority. A prime minister or president does this when he selects his cabinet or top administrators. Dictators who have come to power by force or acclamation have presumably the widest discretion in making command appointments. We often picture political bosses as capable of doing so, and many believe that certain power elites can designate who shall govern in the formal sense. In such cases the invisibility of the process makes it difficult to prove or disprove the belief; it is a matter of how much evidence one can put together on each such selection. At this point we shall leave it at that. We are simply identifying 'selection by command' as the exercise of complete discretion over the particular recruitment by some person, position or group. The implicit criterion is most often assumed to be loyalty or prospective obedience, but it could be any other attributes deemed appropriate by the appointer, such as bravery, skill, experience or a variety of such things.

Another selection process is extraordinarily pervasive, but we shall only very briefly treat it here. That is selection by *bargaining*, including both visible and invisible or implicit forms whereby selections are made through exchanges of goods or commitments. Most forms tend to involve building coalitions of support, where legitimating rules leave great leeway for choice, and where political resources must be combined to ensure a victory for any party or group. It is often a subsidiary and complementary process in competitive systems and in cases of regulated conflict such as

---

[5] *Ibid.*, p. 101.

Anderson depicts in Latin America. Since most of the goods, commitments, or even threats that are the media of bargaining have to do with policy promises and performance, we shall discuss them later in that context. But we do want to note its pervasiveness here.

As we intimated above, these various selection, recruitment, or allocative practices are different but they need not be treated as mutually exclusive. No society relies on one to the complete exclusion of the others; all rely upon varying combinations in order to acquire vital political services. The important point concerns the ordering of the combination; in some systems command may be the major method while in another competition may prevail. A wide range of empirical combinations seems possible. What is more important and debatable concerns the consequences of each mode of allocation or selection. What types of leaders will be selected under each set of rules? What effect will it have on the ordinary citizen in each system?

Political Roles and Behavior: Comparative Data on the Supply of Services

Political roles and behavior are but a part of the total social system; other roles and behavior, including the economic, familial, religious, recreational, sexual, etc., demand their due. Each individual has but twenty-four hours each day so he has a problem of allocating his time among his many preferred activities, roles and concerns which he is expected to manage. For some men, economic roles predominate; for others, religious; and for still others, political roles. In Figure 8-8 we have arranged a sample form of possible activities and roles which one can block in with his own time or that of some relative or friend. Try keeping a record of your own time; you may be surprised at the distribution pattern. The point in this exercise is not the fact that we engage in many roles but that we perform most of them intermittently and perhaps one or two in a highly regularized fashion. Outside the family, economic roles would appear to be performed more consistently by more people than any other single type. However, some persons take on highly specialized tasks for particular institutions. Thus some men become priests or ministers while others become professional entertainers or athletes and some, professional politicians or political leaders. Most men perform minor and passive political activities regularly while a much smaller percentage engage in politics as a profession or preoccupation. Occasionally political matters will command massive attention or generate intense political activity, as during major elections, revolutions, wars, or street demonstrations. More typically the citizen pays his taxes, obeys the laws, pays deference to his rulers and consumes public goods and services. Seldom does he 'stand' for elective office, campaign, contribute money, riot, protest, write letters to editors or officials, activities all of which demand a

Figure 8-8
Daily Role and Activity Form

Role and Activity	Monday	Tuesday	Wednesday	Thursday	Friday	Saturday	Sunday	Total Time
Economic Work Consumption								
Religious								
Homemaking								
Recreational								
Political								
Educational								
Other								
Total Time								

greater expenditure of energy and costs. Evidence to support these ideas is plentiful as the following case studies strongly suggest.

Case Study #1   Cross-National Measures of Political Activity (1959-60)

Once more we rely upon the interesting comparative survey of Almond and Verba; this time it is for information on various essentially passive and undramatic forms of political participation or services. The activities which the authors analyzed are a small sample of the many types of activity which can be found in politics but they are probably typical enough for western democracies. We do not believe that the figures which are contained in Table 8-1 would be dramatically altered by a more inclusive set of political roles and actions. But unfortunately the figures do not afford comparative accounts of activity in such other areas as religion or recreation, say, or especially economic and family concerns. The device of the time budget would probably produce a far more relevant assessment of the relative amount of attention and activity devoted to politics. Actual group membership may consist of no more than quite passive identification; political party affiliations, for example, are an especially loose sort of role relationship in such systems as ours. Except for jobs and family life, we do not believe people devote a substantial amount of time to a great variety of relationships and roles with which they identify. The timing or context may therefore affect such responses greatly. Note that the highest percentage indicating politics as the preferred leisure activity is only 3 per cent in Germany. But then we wonder if economic or religious activity would be much more preferred. Three guesses as to the most preferred!

Case Study #2   Political Participation in Great Britain (1960)

Not so long ago, American political scientists were inclined to view Britain as a model democracy, one to be emulated everywhere. Some of the reasoning was sound but much seems questionable now that we have more extensive and precise measures of actual political behavior among the British. We now learn that the ordinary Englishman is no natural-born politician; rather he tends to behave in ways not unlike other mortals. His political concerns are no more exemplary than are those of citizens in many other countries. He prefers other activities and participates in political life primarily through the more passive roles. The more active modes of participation are experienced as costly and uncertain, as elsewhere, so the typical Britisher does not join or participate in many political organizations nor does he indicate intense interest in political information and partisan affairs. All this is clearly stated in Table 8-2, a table compiled by a sympathetic student of British political behavior, Richard Rose.

Table 8-2 indicates that (1) there are a variety of forms of participation, with the amount of participation dependent upon the role; (2) variations in activity are considerable; (3) the more costly the form of behavior,

Table 8-1
Cross-National Measures of Political Activity

Per cent Who	U.S.	U.K.	Germany	Italy	Mexico
Follow Reports of Politics Regularly or from time to time	80%	68%	72%	36%	55%
Politics as Preferred Leisure Activity	2	2	3	1	0
Membership in a Political Party	79	47	31	13	44
Membership in a Voluntary Organization	57	47	44	29	25
Membership in a Political Organization	11	3	3	8	3
Per Cent Voting in National Election (as % of eligible voters)	64	78	87	93	35

Source: Gabriel Almond and Sidney Verba, *The Civic Culture: Political Attitudes and Democracy in Five Nations* (Princeton: Princeton University Press, 1963), pp. 94; 263; 295; 302. Voting data are from Bruce Russett *et al*, *World Handbook of Political and Social Indicators* (New Haven: Yale University Press, 1964), pp. 84-85.

Table 8-2

Political Participation in Great Britain (1960)

Type of Activity	Estimated Per cent of Electorate
Electorate	100% (35,400,000 voters)
Party identifiers	79
Voters (1959 election)	79
Organizational members	49
Party members (all categories)	22
Informed (could name six politicians)	16
Very interested in politics	15
Organizational officers (past or present)	14
Individual party members	9
Local party activists	0.5

Source: Richard Rose, *Politics in England* (Boston: Little, Brown and Company, 1964), p. 89.

the fewer the participants. Actually Table 8-2 does not list all the possible varieties of participation even in Britain; left out are such forms as holding public office (appointive, civil service, or elective), engaging in demonstrations or simply viewing political events on the 'telly.' The first two categories are of course even more passive roles or activities than many of those listed in Table 8-1, and the last might be considerably more demanding. We are sensitized to the fact that political action is, especially in its more professional and costly forms, quite limited for most people, even in democracies where norms permit and strongly encourage active participation.

Case Study #3   Political Participation in the United States

The political activity of Americans has been exhaustively studied by at least a generation of political scientists and opinion pollsters, including Julian Woodward and Elmo Roper in a classic survey study. For an estimate of activities they sampled some 8,000 adult Americans during the late 1940s and asked them to indicate which of a number of actions they had performed during a recent period of time. These activities included such commonplace ones as voting, political discussions, organizational memberships, discussing politics with public officials, working in party politics and contributing money. The more of each activity one performed the greater the number of points he scored. A maximum of 12 points could be scored by an individual. A number of critical comments can be made about the "index of political activity" constructed by Woodward and Roper but the results are still generally consistent with what we know about political participation. Table 8-3 presents some of these results as they were related to the amount of activity found in the United States at the time of the poll (1949-50).

Table 8-3

Distribution of Political Activity Scores

Score of Respondent	Per cent of Total Sample Who Make The Score	Cumulative Per cent	
12	0.1%	0.1%	
11	0.3	0.4	
10	0.7	1.1	Very Active
9	1.2	2.3	(10.3%)
8	1.6	3.9	
7	2.4	6.3	
6	4.0	10.3	
5	6.5	16.8	Active
4	10.3	27.1	(16.8%)
3	15.6	42.7	Inactive
2	19.0	61.7	(34.6%)
1	19.1	80.8	Very Inactive
0	19.2	100.0	(38.3%)
	100.0		

Source: Julian L. Woodward and Elmo Roper, "Political Activity of American Citizens," *American Political Science Review*, 44 (December, 1950), p. 135.

The Woodward and Roper study contains a greater variety of types of participation than the Rose study and is not, therefore, strictly comparable, but it clearly shows that political action is not a 'favorite sport' of most Americans. The 'very actives' include no more than 10.3 per cent of the adult population. In interpreting these figures, recall how really little activity is required to be scored as active. A score of 12 includes little more than voting and occasionally performing each of the aforementioned activities. Too bad we cannot have more continuous data of this sort to indicate trends or fluctuations.

Case Study #4   Political Participation in Newly-Developing Nations

Pages of the daily newspapers offer a somewhat simplified but nevertheless useful portrait of political life in the newly-developing nations. They emphasize the instabilities and dramatic quality of politics. Political behavior in these not so distant lands tends to be less institutionalized, less stabilized, less formalized than in the western nations. The political divisions of labor are not as sharply differentiated and specialized (cf. Figure 8-4). One is apt to read about the more extravagant or unusual forms of political behavior; expressive symbolism and emotional aspects are heavily emphasized. The forms of legitimate behavior include a greater variety than seems permissible in the western democracies. Thus, one reads of political fasts, even self-immolation, rioting and demonstrations as frequent recourses for some of their members. In India the demonstration or riot is a common form for expressing grievances. Indians will lay themselves across government operated railroads to prevent mail service while the Burmese will indulge in the most supine respect for their monarch.[6]

In most new nations recruitment to political roles tends to be erratic, with greater leeway for the roles of the agitator, revolutionist, practitioner of coups, the specialist in violence or intrigue, or impassioned orator before the masses. Since the political role structures of these lands are not as well-defined and stabilized it would seem absurd to conduct studies of the types we have reported on Britain and the United States. Such regularized peaceful modes of participation as voting behavior, membership in interest groups and political parties, keeping informed, contributing to parties, and writing to office holders, have yet to be established in most newly-developing nations. So political behavior can assume many other forms and can often evolve roles and relationships quite different from our familiar procedures. And such practices may spread. The earlier and often greater political activation of students is a case in point. Witness the major role students have played in many systems abroad. American students have been relatively late in their political activism; a few universities experience intense protest over local campus affairs, but few if any students have tried their hand at successful (or aborted) overthrow of a national government, as they have in numerous other systems, such as Japan, South Korea, Turkey, France, Indonesia and Panama, to name but a few. Perhaps the student civil rights movement in the South is the nearest American counterpart. But most political roles and participation in the western democracies are far more routinized and bureaucratic, more predictable, less exciting. Televised events and newspaper reports barely scratch the surface. The countless tasks and roles of politics in this country are for most of us only minutely visible most of the time, and very seldom, if ever, cause a stir sufficient to gain attention through the mass media.

---

[6] Cf. Myron Weiner, *The Politics of Scarcity: Public Pressure and Political Response in India* (Chicago: The University of Chicago Press, 1962); Lucian W. Pye, *Politics, Personality and Nation-Building: Burma's Search for Identity* (New Haven: Yale University Press, 1962); David H. Bayley, "The Pedagogy of Democracy: Coercive Public Protest in India," *The American Political Science Review,* LVI (September, 1962), pp. 663-672.

The Allocation of Roles

This preliminary treatment leads up to a crucial political question: *Who will perform which roles?* From what we have read thus far it would seem that not all men provide political services or have equal access to most political roles. Most people are solely engaged in such mundane and infrequently noticed roles as consumer of public goods and services, or contributor of taxes in rather involuntary fashion, or being just plain citizen. Almost everyone engages in those roles, while very few men become Presidents, Prime Ministers, Kings, Chief Justices, Chancellors. Of the hundreds of millions of Americans who have lived in this land since 1792, only thirty-seven have become President. Calculating the precise probabilities of becoming President hardly seems necessary to make the point: the chances for most men are almost nil. And not all men have the same probabilities. Some do have a greater chance or set of opportunities for achieving high status roles and offices and, as might be expected, those who are higher in the social status hierarchy in most countries have that superior probability. After revolutions, chances may be drastically reversed and new groups come to power, but these too will come to institutionalize certain modes of access to the top.

In the more stable western systems the higher-ranking political positions tend to be filled by persons of higher social status and greater wealth; the middle-ranks by middle-classes; and the lower-ranking offices by the middle- and upper-working classes. In other words, political status tends to be identified with that in the social and economic systems generally. Members of higher social status groups tend not to want the middle and lower ranking political roles, and the lowliest generally do not anticipate higher positions in the political sphere. Yet at some points political roles do offer an opportunity of upward mobility for some groups or persons. In this less than static world we may identify some of the predominant patterns and points of change too. First let us note some of the more obvious or visible criteria for filling political roles in this country.

In the United States we can begin with the legal requirements. For example, to be eligible for the presidency the Constitution specifies that one must be at least thirty-five years of age and a natural-born citizen. There are somewhat lower age requirements for the offices of U.S. Senator or Representative (thirty and twenty-five years, respectively). Yet there are some very strong informal criteria as well. Without even thinking about it, most U.S. citizens would never expect a woman to fill the position of President, nor would they expect to vote very often for a woman senator or representative (there were only twelve in the 89th Congress, which has a full membership of 535). Only one President has been a Catholic, none a Jew, and among congressmen these religions are much less represented than their proportions in the nation at large. At both state and national levels top office holders tend to be far more wealthy than most of their constituents. The number of millionaires who run for the office of President, U.S. Senator or governor is far beyond their relative number in the population. Interestingly, in a country where the norms of geographic representation are very strong, only four Presidents have been born west of the Mississippi (Hoover, Eisenhower, Johnson and Nixon) though more vice-presidents have been from the western areas due to the party norm of 'balancing the ticket.' Some highly specialized political roles have definite educational criteria for eligibility, such as federal judges or justices and many administrative positions. But even for elective positions the number of college degrees far surpasses that considered normal for the relevant age levels.

We might therefore summarize this rather casual treatment by saying that if you aspire to top elective or political office, you had better be a male, past the legal age requirements, and have at least a college degree; your chances will be further enhanced if you are of rather high social status and most propitious if you are a millionaire! But beyond these more obvious 'qualifications' there may be quite distinct and varying recruitment patterns for different national, state and local political roles. There are some good studies of recruitment patterns for the military, for federal executives generally, and for legislators and governors in the United States, to which we shall make reference in the bibliography.

For those concerned with the status of minorities in political roles we think there is much yet to be studied. We have noted in Chapter 5 the incidence of the draft with regard to Negroes and whites. Many have pointed to the public sector as an important alternative avenue of opportunity for minorities, where private employment patterns have been discriminatory. It would be quite useful to check such employment trends in the federal service, and also the subsequent patterns of career tenure and mobility. It may be easier to require 'balanced' hiring in the postal service, for example, than it probably is to ensure further advancement for the more able minority member beyond the initial level. We know that certain ranks of the federal service are filled with women and as you can well guess they are related to such skills as typing and filing; but note in Table 8-4 the dramatic thinning of percentages as one goes up the service grades.

Of course every country or locality may have its own peculiar patterns of filling political roles, and thus the typical requisites and advantages may differ.[7] For example, youth counts for more in many of the newly-developing

---

[7] For an excellent study of recruitment patterns in the state of Oregon, see Lester G. Seligman, "Political Recruitment and Party Structure: A Case Study," *The American Political Science Review*, LV (March, 1961), pp. 77-86. Our own perspectives on role allocation and recruitment have been much influenced by the same author's "Elite Recruitment and Political Development," *Journal of Politics*, 26 (August, 1964), pp. 612-626, and his volume *Political Recruitment* (Boston: Little, Brown and Company, forthcoming).

Table 8-4

Women in the Higher and Lower
Ranks of Federal Government in 1959*

	Number	Women's percentage of total GS employees
Total Women	476,448	49.1%
GS–1	946	27.7
GS–2	23,652	52.4
GS–3	119,276	68.7
GS–4	114,921	70.7
GS–5	68,199	62.2
GS–6	25,248	54.0
GS–7	30,021	33.1
GS–8	5,496	22.1
GS–9	13,825	13.8
GS–10	1,494	10.6
GS–11	5,974	7.5
GS–12	2,634	4.5
GS–13	1,158	3.1
GS–14	351	2.2
GS–15	90	1.2
GS–16	9	1.0
GS–17	7	1.8
GS–18	2	1.3
GS–18+	Not reported	
Grade not specified	63,145	

* Employment Statistics Section, U.S.C.S.C., Washington, D.C. Figures are for October 31, 1959. Included are all women in white-collar positions, employed full time under the General Schedule salary system, both in the United States and abroad. Figures for total employment taken from Table A-6, p. 26, *1960 Annual Report,* U.S.C.S.C.

From: W. Lloyd Warner, Paul P. Van Riper, Norman H. Martin and Orvis F. Collins, *The American Federal Executive* (New Haven: Yale University Press, 1963), p. 179.

nations and being born of the working class or peasantry may be symbolically more useful in communist societies than in capitalist. In most of independent Africa, being black helps; it does not help in South Africa. In most lands being a woman is a definite disadvantage in achieving high elective office although some public duties are traditionally reserved for women (such as positions in welfare and education in the U.S.), and occasionally one achieves a high post as has Mrs. Indira Gandhi in India. Again, we note changes in these typical role allocations, especially for transitional systems. As we noted in the last chapter a very great turnover of leadership takes place after revolutions; in Chapter 3 we had occasion to observe that even in such stable nations as Britain and the U.S. one finds a gradual change in the distributive pattern for governmental positions although not a complete transformation. The same social groups do manage to hold on to the same high-ranking offices for decades and even centuries. Table 8-5 displays the relative proportions of British cabinet positions held by the different social classes. Note the fairly stabilized and low rate of change that took place from 1868 to 1955. On only three occasions has the proportion of aristocrats dropped precipitously (1924; 1929; 1945), i.e., when Labour Governments succeeded to office. On the other hand, we may observe a far greater rate of change taking place in the composition of the French Assembly during roughly the same period (1871-1958). Figure 8-9 depicts these changes for this broader group of elective positions.

Table 8-5

Class Structure of British Cabinets (1868-1955)

Administration	Year	Aristo- crats	Middle Class	Working Class	Total
1. Gladstone	1868	7	8	—	15
2. Disraeli	1874	7	5	—	12
3. Gladstone	1880	8	6	—	14
4. Salisbury	1885	11	5	—	16
5. Gladstone	1886	9	6	—	15
6. Salisbury	1886	10	5	—	15
7. Gladstone	1892	9	8	—	17
8. Salisbury	1895	8	11	—	19
9. Balfour	1902	9	10	—	19
10. Campbell-Bannerman	1906	7	11	1	19
11. Asquith	1914	6	12	1	19
12. Lloyd George	1919	3	17	1	21
13. Bonar Law	1922	8	8	—	16
14. MacDonald	1924	3	5	11	19
15. Baldwin	1925	9	12	—	21
16. MacDonald	1929	2	4	12	18
17. National Ministry	1935	6	10	2	18
18. Baldwin	1935	9	11	2	22
19. Chamberlain	1937	8	13	—	21
20. Churchill	1945	6	9	1	16
21. Attlee	1945	—	8	12	20
22. Churchill	1951	5	11	—	16

* Churchill's wartime government has been left out as the War Cabinet was a very small body.

From *The British Political Elite* by W. L. Guttsman, Basic Books, Inc., Publishers, New York; MacGibbon & Kee, Ltd., London, 1963, p. 78.

We find that the French nobility lost a considerable proportion of the seats and the working-class by 1959 had acquired more than ten times as many as they had in 1871. The losing groups also include the upper-middle and middle-class. It would be most interesting to compare what the trends have been for other national 'representative' bodies.

Figure 8-9

Social Origins of French Deputies (1871-1958)

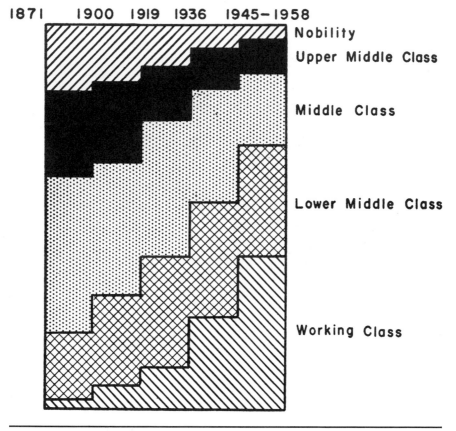

The situation in the newly-developing states, we are told, is one of great change in some roles and incredibly little in others. Access to top political positions has been on the wane for the traditional religious elites, landed nobility, and the local chieftains of tribal groups. One study indicates that the newer elites replacing the older or traditional tend to be of rural or small-town birth, youthful (most attained national prominence during their thirties or late twenties), of middle or upper-middle class origins and are western educated.[8]

Some Explanations of the Level and Distribution of Services

We have a dual problem to resolve: (1) to explain various levels or supplies of service or participation in politics and (2) to account for the fact that so few people attain high office where so many of the important public policies are made. The explanations and the facts which we have already presented are related, just as are some of the data we offered in Chapters 3 and 4 on the public distribution of advantages and statuses. Ideally we should be able to construct a single general theory of political systems which explains all these allocative phenomena but alas we have no such general theory. The ideas you are about to read make a small start, however, and have the additional virtue of being widely accepted partial theories. Perhaps we should begin by attempting to account for the generally low levels of active political participation throughout the world.

Political Participation: The Supply of Services

Like most social scientists we think it convenient and appropriate to classify and to begin with a very simple distinction between the person and his situation. In the present context that means we seek reasons for the levels of participation as they directly relate to the individual person and his environment, i.e., the set of inducements and constraints that assist in shaping his choices and behavior in the political realm. Before we proceed with this line of thought we should like to be very insistent about a point which is often neglected concerning rates of political participation, or how to interpret the level of political activity. In a nation such as ours, it is usually maintained that the level of participation is very low and that people should make more of an effort to be informed and interested in politics. But we insist on this consideration: the levels of participation in all social institutions, except familial and economic, tend to be low. Political participation is probably no lower than that in some other major cultural institutions, whether religious, recreational, educational or other. Each individual has but twenty-four hours each day and he must allocate that

---

[8] Fred R. von der Mehden, *Politics of the Developing Nations* (Englewood Cliffs, N.J.: Prentice-Hall, Inc., 1964), pp. 86-89.

precious resource among many competing uses.[9] For men to increase their
political activity means they must sacrifice other activities. When viewed
this way we believe that the rates that have been observed are not disappointingly low. Churchmen complain because people are not more religious; wives and mothers want the father to devote more time to the home
and less to business; the military wants single-minded dedication on the
part of its members; professors want full not part-time students; so does
every other institution. None of us can satisfy all these conflicting demands
on our time. So the question is: What leads us to allocate our scarce time
and other resources in the ways we do?

Situational Rewards and Costs

Few if any men sit down and determine, at least in detail, what they
will do each minute of each day nor do many of us even know why we
allocated time as we did, say, last week. But if we were to do so we might
very well begin by pointing to a consideration far beyond our own control
(sometimes we try to justify unpopular choices with defensive rationaliza-
tions). In terms of politics we must recognize that some societies—in fact a
great many—do not permit or encourage what we consider typical forms of
political activity. The nation-states which allow people to debate about support of their leaders are probably less than fifty of the more than 120 nations.
And of those fifty, not more than half afford genuinely effective political
opportunities for the citizen to try his hand at influencing top leadership.
Given this situation most of us would not care to make such efforts, at least
not in the more active, aggressive way in which one openly passes critical
judgments and demands to be heard in the making of public policy. The
non-democratic nations, of course, permit and encourage high levels of
certain types of participation, usually the symbolic support roles described
earlier when we were discussing patriotism. *Opportunities to participate*
are therefore a first consideration in any theory of participation. Available
opportunities in most nations are quite restricted and monopolized and this
includes democratic nations as well.

If we assume that opportunities are available for both the passive and
more active forms of participation we are still confronted with the problem
of explaining levels of activity both in the aggregate and as individual
choices. Two or more political systems may have equal opportunities for
participation but different rates of participation among their populations.
These differential rates and levels can be explained in part by continued
reference to the situational factors and more specifically to the inducements
—the rewards or benefits and cost factors. Some systems may provide a more

---

[9] An early investigation of the allocation of time which should interest students because it
is a study of student use of their own time is Pitrim A. Sorokin and C. Q. Berger's *Time
Budgets of Human Behavior*. (Cambridge: Harvard University Press, 1939).

favorable set of inducements than others. When we say 'systems' we mean all the other relevant citizens in the situation who both encourage and discourage one's activities. Political action can afford the promise or expectation of achieving satisfactions. One can feel he derives rewards from it both in symbolic and material form, and even in subconscious benefits. One may also expect to have to pay something for these rewards in some way. The price may be in terms of psychic costs (energy, emotion, disappointments, etc.) or material costs (the value you place on your expenditures of resources, including time, money, property and sacrificed alternative gains). The perfectly 'rational' citizen would calculate his marginal benefits and costs for all alternative forms of activity and make a series of decisions or choices which are presumably optimal for him given his preferences. Ideally, when he has equalized his marginal net returns from all forms of activity, he has reached an optimal set of choices. Of course we rarely do this in any systematic manner. But the logic of the implicit calculus aids us in understanding the degree to which men are political in various societies. In short, we are claiming that the political activity of a person or a group is a function of

1. opportunities to participate and

2. the expectation of net satisfactions or gains.

Politics is perceived by the average individual as having many apparent costs and fewer, less apparent, direct and immediate benefits or satisfactions. Given such a perception of the political system and likely activity in it, is it not readily understandable why people do not devote greater proportions of their time to active mastery of political situations? What if seemingly more profitable uses can be made of one's time by engaging in non-political activities or if it is less costly to perform passively in the more acquiescent or least assertive forms of political activity? Even some of these may be more costly than rewarding for some citizens. Consider the ordinary citizen with a family deciding whether to travel to a congested downtown on the Fourth of July to demonstrate his patriotism by attending a parade. How many more would choose a family picnic, one's favorite pastime, or just plain loafing? Can one believe he is a loyal citizen without going to a parade? It must be so, for relatively few citizens now attend Fourth of July ceremonies. The bulk of the population either stays at home or heads for their own favorite spot. To be utterly consistent in this heresy, consider the typical American's cynical attitude toward the great crowds at Soviet May Day demonstrations: Forced to do it? Fears not to? Nothing better to do?

Note that we have spoken of *expected* benefits and costs. We hedge for a good reason: few persons are in a position to be certain of the outcomes of any set of decisions they might make. They must, accordingly, choose on the basis of their expectations or predictions about uncertain matters. This is especially so for many of the complex and interdependent processes of politics. From all we can observe and read it would seem that costs are more immediately perceived than many of the desired benefits. If this is the case then a good many people who do have an opportunity to participate are still not likely to exploit that possibility as fully as one might expect. Interviews with citizens do not produce carefully reasoned explanations of their own behavior but we do get some rather eloquent and expressive hints about their hopes and fears. The following observations of some Americans are illustrative:

> When politics comes up in conversation, I always say—'Let's talk about something else,' . . . especially when _____ is around. She's a Democrat and gets so riled up.[10]

> . . . I never like to express my political views in public . . . Since I have to deal with so many men, both in the plant and in the buying (of raw materials), there is no sense in making people angry at you over a local election.[11]

> My husband and I talk it over, of course, but I don't talk about it in public because I don't know enough. I wish I knew more. Sometimes I'd like to say something.[12]

> Voting doesn't make much difference. What can an individual do about it? He can't really do much.[13]

> Once they (the politicians) get elected, they don't give a god-damn.[14]

> We'd like to get a higher caliber man to run but it's just impossible. Everybody knows the Republicans will win and nobody wants to waste his time.[15]

> Well, I would say politics is dull in comparison to other news.[16]

> Yes, I think it's better to do something which has direct results. I don't know how party politics go or anything, and maybe I'm wrong, but it seems that you end up doing little things like telephoning or licking

---

[10] Morris Rosenberg, "Some Determinants of Political Apathy," *Public Opinion Quarterly*, 18 (Winter, 1954-55), p. 352.

[11] *Ibid.*, p. 353.

[12] *Ibid.*, p. 354.

[13] *Ibid.*, p. 357.

[14] *Ibid.*, p. 359.

[15] *Ibid.*

[16] *Ibid.*, p. 362.

stamps. You don't have control over things because everything is decided by party leaders, and you don't have much to say about what
goes on. You don't get any direct results. In Girl Scouts, you see these
results; you have a chance to shape the characters of the girls. I think
that's more important.[17]

When I vote, I listen to this fellow and I listen to that fellow and read
this and read that. . . . I say to myself, both these guys are out someplace
to make a buck—there again, you come to corruption. That's the way
I figure it, you know? But who's going to help me most? But (pause)
even though those fellows make a dollar, the way I look at it, I don't
believe that they're going to do anything to hurt this country—any of
them, because no one man could do this thing. It has to be done with a
group of men, and these men are not going to allow it.[18]

Contrast the above feelings and views of Americans with the following from
India, Brazil, Dominican Republic, Philippines and Italy.

I wish that I could get a grant from the government so that I could
buy a number of buffaloes and start a milk route in the nearest city.
Then if I could make a profit I might open a shop for my son and I
would be very happy. (Sixty-seven-year-old farmer, monthly income
$25, India.)[19]

Above all I want a good job. The government should look after us because living in the country today is no joke . . . (thirty-eight-year-old
Brazilian worker).[20]

I requested the government to have this house given me to live in
because I am a victim of Trujillo's tyranny which took my husband's
life for political reasons . . . (forty-three-year-old Dominican woman
who works in domestic employment).[21]

The harvest I get is hardly enough to feed my family. Therefore I wish
that some day I might be able to acquire more government land to
make my farm bigger. (Fifty-three-year-old Philippine farmer.)[22]

---

[17] *Ibid.*

[18] Robert E. Lane, *Political Ideology: Why the American Common Man Believes What He
Does* (New York: The Free Press of Glencoe, 1962), p. 169.

[19] Hadley Cantril, *The Pattern of Human Concerns* (New Brunswick: Rutgers University
Press, 1965), pp. 206-07.

[20] *Ibid.*, p. 211.

[21] *Ibid.*, p. 212.

[22] *Ibid.*, p. 215

No party or organization has ever aided me in my everyday affairs. I have always fought my battles with my own work and strength. (Thirty-one-year-old Italian auto worker.)[23]

I don't think I shall ever be able to realize my aspirations. Maybe if they throw out this government I could still hope for something. Any government would be a gain. But I really know nothing about all these political things. I only think about what could happen to me. (An unskilled Italian worker.)[24]

The above expressions about politics and political participation raise some further intriguing thoughts about political expectations regarding personal benefits and costs. Even though these are very arbitrary selections they can be suggestive. Take the American cases first. On the benefit side we note some expressing a certain futility that anything can be accomplished or that what *is* being accomplished is wrong. In studies of alienation in this country[25] one learns that often what is so frustrating or disappointing to the citizen is that political reality appears to violate the very 'participatory' norms he has been so assiduously taught as good citizenship. The formal democratic doctrines of individual efficacy create enormous psychic costs for those who honor them and yet feel they are not followed. This even denies the possible pleasure for many of engaging in political expressiveness for its own sake. In such cases it is ironic that the more the citizen believes in virtue, the greater his rejection of political reality may be. Now we must note also that there are persons who find politics rewarding and see themselves as efficacious. Note also that the respondents quoted above clearly perceived the nature of the expected costs. There are fears of antagonism, loss of business, ego-deflation, or exposure of ignorance, and the expectation that other activities are more directly rewarding. Not all these expectations are warranted, either on the cost or benefit side, but people in these circumstances are likely to act on their expectations.

Now consider the feelings expressed by citizens of other countries. Whereas Americans express dismay because political participation is not more meaningful and rewarding, these foreign citizens seem less concerned with direct involvement and much more interested in receiving more mate-

---

[23] Hadley Cantril, *The Politics of Despair* (New York: Basic Books, Inc., 1958), p. 155.

[24] *Ibid.*, p. 46.

[25] One of the better studies is Murray B. Levin, *The Alienated Voter: Politics in Boston* (New York: Holt, Rinehart and Winston, Inc., 1960), especially Chapter 4 in which four forms of alienation are defined: powerlessness; meaninglessness; normlessness; and estrangement. How an alienated voter ought to be courted by a rational politician is analyzed in Murray B. Levin and George Blackwood, *The Compleat Politician: Political Strategy in Massachusetts* (Indianapolis: The Bobbs-Merrill Company, Inc., 1962).

rial benefits from the government. Having a more beneficent government is an explicit hope advanced by the Indian, Brazilian, Dominican and Philippine citizen. Perhaps we can best account for these suggestive variations by observing that those who already have a high standard of living, as in the case of the Americans, and who are taught to expect meaningful political participation are more disappointed because their high expectations are not met, while the poorer people of the underdeveloped nations are understandably preoccupied with improving their bleak economic circumstances.

People in non- or less democratic new nations have tended to view government as a distant set of rulers rather than as elected servants of the citizenry. The citizen remains essentially passive but occasionally hopeful that the government will be generous toward him in daily life or, at least, leave him alone. Their orientation toward government is more like that described by Almond and Verba as typical for a "subject" political culture.[26] There is little suggestion that these citizens relate their "subject" role, as recipient of government help, with any normative requirement to be active and informed in what we call 'politics.' The relevant norms or rules for their wishes have to do with making an application, filling out a form, etc., and not with trying to exercise influence over top decision-makers. In other words, as we shall try to explain, the norm of participation as we know it, has not been widely taught in such countries as being appropriate.

The concept of *salience* has been used to designate those role orientations or norms which a person feels or employs as relevant when he reacts to a situation. A person will be politically indifferent if there is nothing in a political situation that is salient, i.e., perceived as relevant, to what he does and cares about. Or the political culture in which he has learned about politics may cause him to apply different norms and expectations from those of another culture. Differences in class, age generations, ethnic and racial groups will thus generate different orientations about what is considered politically appropriate and significant.

For those who like to think in terms of formulas we might say that the amount and kind of political activity a person is likely to engage in are functions of the perceived salience of the matter and his 'calculus' of expected benefits or satisfactions minus expected costs. In situations where there is some choice, the perception of salience will provide the initial guide. Of course, for highly institutionalized roles the activities and performances may be quite automatic and the satisfactions of performance noted only

---

[26] Gabriel A. Almond and Sidney Verba, *The Civic Culture* (Princeton: Princeton University Press, 1963), p. 19. Eric A. Nordlinger, *The Working Class Tories: Authority, Deference and Stable Democracy* (Berkeley: University of California Press, 1967) is an unusually interesting analysis of a considerable number of voters in Britain—the working class Tories who are highly deferential and not alienated from their upper class governors.

when they are disturbed or disrupted. The calculation of burdens and benefits is seldom explicit, but we believe that the choice of political action is
guided by the direction and margin of the differences between expected
returns and costs. The greater the reward-cost discrepancy, the more likely
there will be some emotional feeling about the anticipated action, i.e., hopes
or fears, satisfactions and disappointments, and the likelihood of action.

If there is some political salience but a net return of zero, one should
see more indifference or inaction or turning to non-political activities. If
there is high salience and a balance of either benefits or costs, the person
may feel he "has to do something about it." Several of the quoted American
responses indicate the low salience of political matters. But others indicate
disappointment and frustration, suggesting dissatisfactions which would
more likely lead to negative actions, when there is an opportune time—
whether it be voting out the 'ins' or indulging in expletives when the matter is discussed on television. But note that we cannot suggest the same sorts
of reactions or responses in another culture if the norms and expectations
are not similar. Alienation and bitterness may come from quite different
sources and be directed at quite different targets. We recognize alienation
as it occurs in the western democracies, but what few comparative studies
we have suggest that we have more to learn about the forms it may assume
elsewhere.

Why So Few Are Called

Our approach to political participation has taken us a considerable
way toward an explanation of why so few from among so many are called
for active leadership roles. While the need for leadership is apparent, the
supply of effective leaders tends to be short. While many men would like to
be leaders, few indeed actually receive the call. There are a number of
reasons for this paradox.

First, let us consider the individual. Relatively small proportions of
the population of any society will actually display the requisite motivations
and skills to become leaders. The shortage of these attributes may be partly
a matter of the unequal distribution of inherited talents, but are much more
likely due to socialization experiences and prevailing expectations. The
idea of a free market in leaders is really the heresy of a radical democrat
or utopian. Actually we must rather pessimistically conclude that both
existing leaders and followers tend to have rather strong interests in maintaining less than fully open channels of recruitment. For most persons in
most systems the path to the top does not exist. In spite of log cabin symbols
and the mythical equal chance of every American boy to be President, most
parents do not prepare their sons for that future. If there were nothing

else, the economic barriers alone would exclude a vast number. And as we have mentioned, social barriers make the thought an impossible one for many minorities even if money and resources were available. In other words the *availability of opportunities* is greatly limited by the dominant social and political structures. The rules and norms of existing systems provide formidable channels and outright barriers. These are most obvious in hereditary monarchies, dictatorships and other autocratic systems where the selection processes are strongly controlled.

Electoral procedures also provide a labyrinth of rules and require-ments. Political parties rigorously screen candidates for those offices that count, if indeed the selection is not dictated by some dominant group or interest. Even competitive selection processes within a party will tend to reward those most astute about the rules and possibilities. Opportunities to enter politics may be available, but opportunities to win or succeed may not be consonant. In one-party and even many two-party areas the chances of a minority group winning an election are slim. For example, Uruguay has had a two party system for more than ninety years but the same party has always won every election, while in Mexico one party has won all national elections since the Revolution in 1910. Republican candidates in the South have until recently had little hope of winning anything, while the Demo-crats experienced a similar situation in New England, some midwestern and a few far western states. Willingness to compete can hardly be sustained when the chances of reward are so minimal. To believe one has a chance, in most systems, occurs to the very few.

Even when the opportunity structure is open or barriers are not arti-ficially erected by the more privileged, those having the greater resources and the skills for using them will have the better chance. The *distribution of resources* both flows from and conditions the opportunity structure. Where resources are somewhat dispersed, the problem of pooling them for effective use is also arduous. Few waste their money and time on those with-out a chance of winning, so resources tend to cumulate on behalf of those already showing 'the most promise.' The question of cumulative resources therefore bothers many political analysts, even in competitive or pluralist systems. We will return to this question in Chapter 14.

Case Studies: Political Opportunities and Career Lines

The polity, like an economy, in satisfying general wants also provides opportunities for those with politically relevant concerns entailing current or expected rewards from political effort. In brief, we can view different po-litical structures as affording different types and sets of career opportunities. Our discussion of the modes of recruitment and role allocation is obviously related to the matter of career opportunities. Each polity structures the available opportunities and in so doing patterns the most likely sequences of careers for the typical politician or public servant. In some polities the beginner starts at the local level and progresses up through state and national levels while in other systems he may begin at the national level. Or, the ambitious politician may find it expedient to work his way laterally through a variety of public offices at the same level, acquiring different types of experience and further opportunities with each office.

From the point of view of the young politician, the role structure poses a series of strategic choices as he approaches points where further moves are mandatory. Accordingly, an opportunity structure is also an obstacle course in the sense that a great many givens and uncertainties confront the politician. The offices are given; the dates of elections may be given; the constituencies may be more or less given; the rules of the selection are most often given; the possibilities and constraints of each office are to some extent known. Career choices are normally made under conditions of varying uncertainty concerning the nature of the competition, the nature and timing of issues, and one's own limitations as a candidate. Each of these uncertainties can be somewhat affected by the politician's either improving his own position or affecting adversely his opposition's. How this can be done will be discussed in Chapter 12.

The case studies that follow are meant not to entertain with anecdotes about individual politicians but to illustrate the more typical career opportunities, vicissitudes and patterns found in various political systems. While the paths to political glory may make exciting novels, as well as some bad ones, most political careers are somewhat routinized in the more stable polities. These brief portrayals may be of some value both in understanding the behavior of the politician and even in advising the potential politician on his career possibilities.

Case Study #5   The Road to Power in Britain

Achieving high office in Britain has shown definite historical patterns, although since World War II some changes have developed which may further alter the traditional routes.[27] For the most part, an ambitious politician would stand for the House of Commons directly rather than first enter local or state politics as is so frequently done in the United States. Apparently it is desirable to enter the House of Commons at an early age so that one might acquire experience and establish connections for later advancement. The average politician must spend about fifteen to twenty years in

---

[27] Cf. Austin Ranney, *Pathways to Parliament* (Madison: University of Wisconsin Press, 1965).

Commons before he can be seriously considered for a Cabinet rank. The chances of becoming Prime Minister are very remote (only sixteen of 294 Cabinet members ever became Prime Minister). In short, a top political career in Britain consists, for most men, of two steps—Commons and Cabinet.

Occasionally, when a Labour Government comes into power politicians who have not had previous governmental experience will be appointed to the Cabinet. Some commentators claim that the period of apprenticeships is being reduced and that the 'experts,' including bureaucrats, scientists, and soldiers, are increasingly achieving high office without having pursued the Parliamentary route to important positions. Political careers tend to be lifetime, more like the U.S.S.R. than the United States. Climbing up the ranks in Britain tends to be slower but more assured than in our country. And, unlike the U.S.S.R., careers are seldom terminated by sudden shake-ups, reorganizations, or purges and banishment.

Case Study #6   The U.S.S.R.

The Soviet Union has now been in existence long enough to display fairly definite patterns in political careers. Certain characteristics can be found among office-holders, indicating some typical recruitment steps for Soviet leaders, too. As frequently happens, these patterns and characteristics change over time. A case in point concerns the members of the Soviet Politburo.[28] For example, immediately following the revolution top party members were typically described in the following terms:

Characteristics	*Career*
Born in town or city	Joins party at early age (after 20)
Middle class origins	Does propaganda work
Probably attended a	Arrested and jailed
university	Goes abroad for study
	Probably writes articles
	Becomes member of Central Committee
	Becomes member of government
	Becomes member of Politburo

The early patterns were altered as communism became institutionalized under Lenin and his successors. By the 1950s the typical party leader was being described as follows:

---

[28] This section is based on George K. Schueller, "The Politburo," in *World Revolutionary Elites: Studies in Coercive Ideological Movements*, eds., Harold D. Lasswell and Daniel Lerner (Cambridge: Massachusetts Institute of Technology Press, 1966), Chap. 3.

Characteristics	*Career*
Born in a village	Joins party before age 20
Low social origin	Does party work (also police work)
Little formal education	Becomes member of Central Committee
	Member of Secretariat
	Candidate for Politburo
	High government position
	Member Politburo

The above trends are subject to further change as the nature of Soviet society changes. It is important to point out also that Russian leaders have tended to follow more purely political careers to a far greater extent than have American political leaders. The latter frequently move between private and official positions several times during a career while Russian politicians on the other hand remain in party politics most of their adult lives. But as the nation further industrializes, more leaders will probably pursue a more technical or specialist career ladder, as did Premier Kosygin, an economist by training. Many trained engineers but few lawyers are found in top Russian positions; in the United States, law is the dominant civilian profession among politicians. But political life in the United States may become more professionalized as the rewards of politics increase; conceivably, the political leaders of the two nations could come to resemble one another more.

One aspect of Soviet political careers deserves attention, especially because it was so unusually prominent during the Stalin era. It concerns the role of violence. In western democracies a politician may have his career terminated by failure to win an election, but rarely is he eliminated by execution, murder, or threats of violence. Table 8-6 contains a list of earlier members of the Politburo many of whose careers were terminated by violent means. The list is not complete and does not include all who may have died by suicide or simply disappeared and remain unaccounted for. Fortunately, violent ends are becoming less a possibility; witness the forced but nonviolent retirement of Premier Khrushchev, the demotion of Premier Malenkov and the retirement of V. M. Molotov. Apparently, too, the processes of recruitment, advancement, and succession to high office are showing signs of becoming more regularized.

Case Study #7   Political Opportunities and Careers in the U.S.A.

Aspiring politicians should find the United States a promising system with its more than 530,000 elective offices and many top appointive posts. With short terms of office, ease of entry should be less of a major problem; a handful of votes is all that is necessary to win a great many local and party

Table 8-6

Career Fates of Some
Members of the Politburo (1917-1947)

Members of the Politburo	Date of Accession	Date of Removal	Death
Lenin, Vladimir I.	1917	1924	Died
Stalin, Josef V.	1917	1953	Died
Sverdlov, Yakov M.	1917	1919	Died
Trotsky, Lev D.	1917	1926	Murdered 1940
Bukharin, Nikolai I.	1918	1929	Executed 1938
Kamenev, Lev B.	1919	1926	Executed 1936
Krestinsky, Nikolai N.	1919	1921	Executed 1938
Rykov, Alexei I.	1919	1929	Executed 1938
Tomsky, Mikhail P.	1919	1929	Suicide 1936
Zinoviev, Grigorii	1923	1926	Executed 1936
Molotov, Viacheslav M.	1925		
Voroshilov, Kliment E.	1925		
Kalinin, Mikhail I.	1926	1946	Died 1946
Kuibyshev, Valerian V.	1927	1935	Died 1935
Rudzutak, Jan E.	1927	1931	Disappeared 1938
Kaganovich, Lazar M.	1930		
Kirov, Sergei M.	1930	1934	Murdered 1934
Kossior, Stanislav V.	1930	1938	Disappeared
Ordjonikidze, Grigorii K.	1930	1937	Died 1937
Andreyev, Andrei A.	1932		
Chubar, Vlas Y.	1935	1938	Disappeared
Mikoyan, Anastas I.	1935		
Zhdanov, Andrei A.	1939	1948	Died 1948
Khrushchev, Nikita S.	1939	1964	Removed
Beria, Lavrentii P.	1946	1953	Executed
Malenkov, Georgii M.	1946	1955	Demoted
Voznesensky, Nikolai A.	1947	1949	Dropped

Source: George K. Schueller, "The Politburo," in, *World Revolutionary Elites: Studies in Coercive Ideological Movements,* eds., Harold D. Lasswell and Daniel Lerner (Cambridge: Massachusetts Institute of Technology Press, 1966), p. 103.

offices. Of course the cost of obtaining votes rises as one attempts to win more important positions, but the costs need not be prohibitive at the local levels.

Since there are many more points at which an American can enter politics as a career, the choices can become much more complex and difficult than in Britain where the route is well-defined and leaves few options. Students such as Joseph A. Schlesinger have investigated these career patterns in considerable detail and concluded, among many other things, that:

1. The most typical pattern is one of entering politics at the state level and proceeding to Congress or, in a few cases, the Presidency.

2. More senators come from the House of Representatives than from any other political position.

3. At the state level the typical career is upward from a state legislative or lesser elective post to the governorship.

4. State executive positions such as Governor, Attorney-General and Lieutenant Governor are highly transitory offices which tend to be springboards for achieving higher offices.[29]

To these generalizations we might add that the United States apparently affords a greater opportunity for the amateur politician and the part-time 'politico' who wishes to conduct both private and public careers. A great many men, especially at the national level, move rather easily between high public and private officialdom.They will frequently move among many top appointive positions, as in private business, education and investment or law firms. Of course, the ease of such movement cuts down by that much the upward chances of those relying on other ladders. One wonders if the Soviets have counterparts of our 'Kremlinologists' studying such movements as to policy implications! For those who start in more humble circumstances, loss of an election, at the state and local levels, is not always fatal, for the fortunes of politics may change rapidly. Perhaps the most difficult situation for a budding politician is to be ambitious in a state in which the opposition party has a strong and stable majority. If this is the case, his chances for positions beyond state boundaries are unlikely unless he has remarkable personal resources. With that, we leave you to assess which kinds would help most, and where.

Case Study #8   New Nations

We cannot, in the strict sense of the word, call this a case study since it is not about a particular nation nor does it rest on as much concrete information as have previous case studies.[30] The reason is simple: most new na-

---

[29] See Joseph A. Schlesinger, *Ambition and Politics: Political Careers in the United States* (Chicago: Rand McNally and Company, 1966), pp. 195-98. Chap. 10 contains a detailed and comprehensive summary of generalizations on political careers.

[30] While there are many studies of the social backgrounds of elites in new nations, relatively little has been done on emerging career patterns of the politicians. However, see Frederick W. Frey, *The Turkish Political Elite* (Cambridge: Massachusetts Institute of Technology Press, 1965); S. E. Finer, *The Man on Horseback: The Role of the Military in Politics* (London: Pall Mall Press, 1962); Lester G. Seligman, *Leadership in a New Nation: Political Development in Israel* (New York: Atherton Press, 1964); Marshall R. Singer, *The Emerging Elite: A Study of Political Leadership in Ceylon* (Cambridge: Massachusetts Institute of Technology Press, 1964) and, for military careers as preparations for politics, see John J. Johnson, ed., *The Role of the Military in Underdeveloped Countries* (Princeton: Princeton University Press, 1962).

tions have not existed long enough for distinct career patterns to become established. Politics is less professionalized than in western democracies or the Soviet Union.

Still, it is possible to say some things about the typical experiences of the leadership in these nations although there are many conflicting patterns too. Increasing numbers of the leadership of the new nations are professional military men. Some of them come to power as a result of coups or palace revolts. One military man may oust another, as has frequently happened in Egypt, South Vietnam, several Middle East countries and Latin American states. We estimate that in 1963, for example, some forty-seven new nations had military men holding high public offices and fifteen of them were chief executives. The latter figure has undoubtedly risen since then to about one-fifth of all nations.

A leader of a genuine revolution is likely to be the symbolic hero of the new nation: Lenin, Gandhi, Mao, Ho Chi Minh, Kenyatta, for example. He is very likely to rule until death, so great is the homage he receives. The revolutionary leader, even when he achieves office, is more likely to emphasize the expressive and ideological aspects of leadership than the pragmatic and less colorful skills of bargaining and administration. If the strains of nation building are severe, however, the possibility of a military or forceful coup becomes strong, especially where the leader's personal or nationalist appeal is not strong enough to prohibit such a turn. Some leaders such as Nkrumah and Sukarno have learned this the hard way.

While military training and experience have thus become one important route to political leadership in these nations, we suspect that bureaucratic skills of a civilian sort may provide another increasingly important route to a political career as development proceeds apace and calls for more skilled direction. This has already happened in the Soviet Union as it has industrialized and confronted the need for expertise in running routinized productive systems. To be sure, the newly-developing states have a long way to go before achieving Russia's stage of industrialization. But bureaucrats of various skills will be most needed to assist in that process, and their prestige may more easily rise above that of the military, the more successful the country is in avoiding internal or external crises.

Problems and Applications

1. Imagine a political system in which every citizen participated in every role, more or less continuously—in short, a system without a sharp differentiation of functions and roles. What consequences would you see for the individual citizen, the political process and the content of policies which might flow from such a system?

2. Periodically, political scientists are heard to claim that the American polity is the most complicated ever devised by man. How would you in-

terpret such a claim? Is there much evidence for the statement? How would you go about trying to test such a proposition?

3. Under what conditions are formal political roles accurate indicators or clues to what an individual will do? Under what conditions are such roles of little use in predicting behavior? Why? Provide some illustrations.

4. Consider the problem of political recruitment as one of inducing people to enter political life and serve in political or public offices. What considerations are most apt to encourage such participation? Discourage it? Try your hand at analyzing these factors in the context of some particular country.

5. Analyze your own 'structure of opportunities' for entering a rewarding political career. Indicate the factors which both induce and discourage you from being more active in politics, both at the motivational or incentive level and in the more impersonal features of the political system involved.

6. What do you think of the possibilities of establishing (a) a national academy of politics for aspiring professional politicians somewhat analogous to West Point and the Naval Academy; and/or (b) establishing schools of practical politics at existing universities similar to schools of law, medicine, and business administration? Would such reforms be acceptable to the American people? Would they be an improvement over the present practices of training politicians 'on the job'?

7. How is it possible for the democracies of the world to have such different structural characteristics and still be called democracies? What crucial roles, norms or processes would you identify in defining democracy?

8. Suppose you are concerned about speeding up the decision-making processes within democracies. What kind of role structure would you devise to accomplish that goal? Why?

9. Why are constitutions inadequate as descriptions of what people really do in their political systems?

10. If constitutions are so inadequate as descriptions why do so many countries have them?

11. If you were an aspiring young politician and had a choice of entering politics in the United States, Great Britain, the People's Republic of China, Ghana, or some other new nation, which would you choose? You might need to clarify your own objectives and ask some of the following questions: (a) what are the costs, rewards, and uncertainties? (b) what are the requisite skills or training? (c) what kinds of goals and aspira-

tions are feasible? (d) how likely are the chances of achieving them? (e) what forms of competition or conflict should you expect to contend with? (f) what political advancement can be anticipated in each nation? (g) what happens if one fails to achieve office or major goals?

12. Rank order the desirability or usefulness of the following resources for each of the positions listed:

Resources	Office
money	county sheriff
political skill	Pope
information	civil rights leader (U.S.A.)
social status	Soviet party leader
	college president

13. Can you detect any particular recent career patterns among American Presidents? That is, have they progressed through a similar set of offices and sequences of offices? Explain your findings.

14. Some scholars have claimed that the United States is the land of the common man, yet very few common men have held very high office; in fact, very few working men have entered political life as candidates. How can we explain this paradox? How would you therefore interpret the accolade?

Bibliographical Notes

Role structures are a major concern of sociology as well as political science and are discussed in almost all basic sociology textbooks. We recommend Harry M. Johnson, *Sociology: A Systematic Introduction*, New York: Harcourt, Brace and Company, Inc., 1960, Chapter 2, as a highly readable account of roles. Another text of unusual merit and one which has influenced our own thinking is that of Harry C. Bredemeier and Richard M. Stephenson, *The Analysis of Social Systems*, New York: Holt, Rinehart and Winston, Inc., 1962.

Political role structures have been subject to many simplified classifications since the time of Plato and Aristotle. Modern efforts at reducing complex political structures to manageable analytic proportions have been tried by many political scientists with varying success. One well known effort is that of Gabriel A. Almond and G. Bingham Powell, Jr., *Comparative Politics: A Developmental Approach*, Boston: Little, Brown and Company, 1966, Chapters 9-10. Page 217 contains a summary list of their three major types of systems, nine sub-types, four sub-sub-types and seven sub-sub-sub-types of polities. An earlier work edited by Gabriel A. Almond in collaboration with James S. Coleman, *The Politics of the Developing Areas,* Princeton: Princeton University Press, 1960, pp. 532-576, advanced a typology of system types for the newly-developing nations and attempted to test it on actual systems. Another attempt both to describe role structures and classify actual nations may be found in Austin Ranney, *The Governing of Men,* rev. ed., New York: Holt, Rinehart and Winston, Inc., 1966, Chapter 4. Much of the information on which Ranney drew for his classifications is found in Amos J. Peaslee, ed., *Constitutions of Nations,* 2nd ed., The Hague: Martinus Nijhoff, 1956. Those interested in the history of formal constitutions which attempt to specify role structures with some precision and formality may wish to consult C. F. Strong, *A History of Modern Political Constitutions,* New York: Capricorn Books, 1963.

Public administrators are a professional group which seems to enjoy constructing formal charts of organizations prescribing and describing the behavior of bureaucrats. Almost any volume of administration contains a variety of such attempts. Perhaps the most imaginative may be found in James G. March and Herbert A. Simon, *Organizations,* New York: John Wiley and Sons, Inc., 1958. Besides authority relationships the authors consider such aspects as communication and information processes. Another source is the *United States Government Organization Manual,* issued annually by the U.S. Superintendent of Documents, which contains basic legal prescriptions for all major federal government agencies, and organization charts for many of them. The 1965-66 edition contained forty-five pages of such diagrams. Since they specify formal authority only, they do not impart a sense of the political workings of government, but they do set out the basic legal framework very effectively. A student interested in the greater fabric of legal prescriptions for any subject area or agency should also familiarize himself with the *United States Code* or *U.S. Statutes at Large,* and the *Federal Register.* Browsing through these should lead the student to marvel at the intricacies of codification!

Sociologists and psychologists interested in small groups have done much pioneering work in role analysis. A useful summary of various approaches, including those of Bales, Homans and others, is offered in Clovis R. Sheperd, *Small Groups: Some Sociological Perspectives,* San Francisco: Chandler Publishing Company, 1964. In the actual official setting some implicit use of these small group and role perspectives generally may be detected in Charles L. Clapp, *The Congressman: His Work As He Sees It,* Garden City, N.Y.: Doubleday and Company, Inc., 1963, as well as in Richard E. Neustadt, *Presidential Power: The Politics of Leadership,* New York: John Wiley and Sons, Inc., 1960. Undoubtedly, the most explicit systematic use ever made of role analysis in political science is that of John C. Wahlke, Heinz Eulau, William Buchanan and LeRoy C. Ferguson, *The Legislative System: Explorations in Legislative Behavior,* New York: John Wiley and Sons, Inc., 1962. Informal norms and roles are especially illuminated by this study of legislative perceptions. Biographies of politicians usually proceed to their tasks without a formal framework of analysis; one exception, however, is James MacGregor Burns, *Roosevelt: The Lion and the Fox,* New York: Harcourt, Brace and Company, 1956. Whether such explicit concepts of role improved the study may be debated; in any case, the biography is a good one.

In turning to the allocation of roles among persons, we find ourselves in the rather odd position of having to say that, in one sense, the whole of social science is about role allocation and yet we cannot cite a single volume that deals exclusively with the processes. Much of the more relevant literature in political science goes under the labels of 'political participation,' 'political parties' and 'elections.' Inventories of findings, mostly for the United States, are contained in Robert E. Lane, *Political Life: Why People Get Involved in Politics,* Glencoe, Ill.: The Free Press, 1959, and Lester W. Milbrath, *Political Participation: How and Why Do People Get Involved in Politics?* Chicago: Rand McNally and Company, 1965. Both books contain references to most of the empirical studies made on participation. What is lacking is a systematic cross-national inventory citing the growing number of investigations being conducted in Europe and elsewhere. One issue of the *International Social Science Journal,* Vol. 12, "Citizen Participation in Political Life," 1960, attempted what it could in suggesting comparisons. Unfortunately most of these kinds of studies are published in various professional journals and are not readily accessible to many students.

If cross-national studies were more plentiful, not only would we have better estimates of actual political participation but we would more likely revise our views on what participation consists of for most men. As things stand, our ideas about the forms and meanings of political activity are primarily based upon western democratic considerations. The questions and measures posed by Roper and Woodward, for example, are largely limited to American experiences. How useful are such categories of analysis in studying Gabon, Tibet, North and South Vietnam, and the People's Republic of China?

Of all the processes used to recruit and assign citizens to political roles perhaps the most studied are elections. The volume of writing on elections is out of proportion to their significance since elections are not widely used in many countries. Still, some of the best research and theory in political science is about the electoral process. For those who enjoy formal models of election rules and their significance we suggest James M. Buchanan and Gordon Tullock, *The Calculus of Consent,* Ann Arbor: The University of Michigan Press, 1962, for cogent analyses of such rules as unanimity, simple majorities and extra-majorities. Of the same genre, but restricted to simple majority rules and their political consequences, is the by now classic study of Anthony Downs, *An Economic Theory of Democracy,* New York: Harper and Brothers, Publishers, 1957. A recent critique of Buchanan and Tullock, and somewhat easier to read, is Brian Barry, *Political Argument,* New York:

Humanities Press, Inc., 1965. These three volumes are indicative of a growing concern for choice theory and the use of models in political science.

Less formalistic and more empirical are a number of standard writings in political science about elections including V. O. Key, Jr., *American State Politics: An Introduction*, New York: Alfred A. Knopf, Inc., 1956, a pioneering analysis of state elections. At the national level we suggest Nelson W. Polsby and Aaron B. Wildavsky, *Presidential Elections*, New York: Charles Scribner's Sons, 1968, which speculates about strategies for attaining that office. Peter G. J. Pulzer's *Political Representation and Elections: Parties and Voting in Great Britain*, New York: Frederick A. Praeger, Inc., 1967, is highly informative about that country, as is a broader comparative study by Enid Lakeman and J. D. Lambert, *Voting in Democracies: A Study of Majority and Proportional Electoral Systems*, London: Faber and Faber, Ltd., 1959. Another modern classic, especially interesting for its analysis of electoral systems and their influence on political parties and opinion, is by Maurice Duverger, *Political Parties*, 2nd ed., London: Methuen and Company, Ltd., 1964. A highly useful brief introduction to elections is W. J. M. MacKenzie's *Free Elections: An Elementary Textbook*, New York: Rinehart and Company, Inc., 1958, in which institutional information about elections, voting, etc., is combined with the logic of various types of elections. If you are stimulated by the above volumes and particularly those which present abstract models we suggest you go on to Duncan Black, *The Theory of Committees and Elections*, New York: Cambridge University Press, 1958. This small volume is destined to become a classic for its highly original development of problems involving the order in which propositions are voted upon in elections and the nature of preferences. Finally, we recommend Douglas Rae, *The Political Consequences of Electoral Laws*, New Haven: Yale University Press, 1967, a systematic presentation of just what the title suggests.

In the final section of this chapter we set forth some case studies of career patterns as they are affected by the polity of which they are a part. Although a vast amount of work has been done on the social backgrounds of political leaders, relatively little has been oriented toward their work as a kind of occupational role. Among those which empirically treat of such matters in some degree are Austin Ranney, *Pathways to Parliament: Candidate Selection in Britain*, Madison: The University of Wisconsin Press, 1965, and Lester G. Seligman, *Leadership in a New Nation: Political Development in Israel*, New York: Atherton Press, 1964. Some further material on other countries, including India, France, Germany and the United States, is contained in Dwaine Marvick, ed., *Political Decision-Makers: Recruitment and Performance*, New York: The Free Press of Glencoe, 1961. A book of readings, some of which deal with our problem, is James D. Barber, *Political Leadership in American Government*, Boston: Little, Brown and Company, 1964. A most interesting book by the same author is *The Lawmakers:*

Recruitment and Adaptation to Legislative Life, New Haven: Yale University Press, 1965. Probably the most systematic and thorough analysis to date is that of Joseph A. Schlesinger, *Ambition and Politics: Political Careers in the United States,* Chicago: Rand McNally and Company, 1966.

A somewhat special case of recruitment and career patterns concerns the role of the military in political life and especially their role in the new nations. Americans should not be surprised at this development given the popularity of generals as Presidents in our own history. Nevertheless, we can learn a great deal about the military from Morris Janowitz, *The Professional Soldier: A Social and Political Portrait,* Glencoe, Ill.: The Free Press of Glencoe, 1960. Janowitz has also written about *The Military in the Political Development of New Nations,* Chicago: The University of Chicago Press, 1964. Likewise, William Gutteridge deals with many of the same matters in *Armed Forces in New States,* London: Oxford University Press, 1962. The situation in each newly developing area of the world is analyzed by a specialist in a volume edited by John J. Johnson, *The Role of the Military in Underdeveloped Countries,* Princeton: Princeton University Press, 1962. Of particular significance to the several authors is the problem of why the military promote national modernization in some but not all countries. Finally, for those who are interested in the military in our country we suggest Charles H. Coates and Roland J. Pellegrin, *Military Sociology: A Study of American Military Institutions and Military Life,* University Park, Md.: The Social Science Press, 1965.

Part 2
Politics and Welfare

U.S. Begins Water Problem Stu
The Oregonian, Nov. 22, 1968, Portland, Oregon

Risk in Cuba New Czech Leade
San Francisco Chronicle, Nov. 19, 1968,
San Francisco, California

Britain's Dilemma Back Liberal Poli
Eugene Register-Guard, July 17, 1968, Eugene, Oregon

limbing Unemployment and Surge
f Imports Face the Policy Mappers
The New York Times, May 15, 1967, New York, New York

New Draft Policy Revealed
Eugene Register-Guard, Nov. 19, 1968, Eugene, Oregon

Russia and Czechoslovakia

Moscow Takes 'Decisive Half-Measure
The New York Times, May 12, 1968, New York, New York

raq Retains JOHNSON ORDERS
Old Policies LONG-TERM STUDY
The Oregonian, July 23, 1968,
Portland, Oregon
OF TRADE POLICY
The New York Times,
March 25, 1967,
New York, New York

Rail Dispute Heightens the Pressu
For Legislation to Check Walkou
The New York Times, April 12, 1967, New York, New York

ASTS INCREASING
N A HUNGRY INDIA
Aid Chief Bares
$57,000 Mistake
The Oregonian, July 22, 1968,
Portland, Oregon
Federal Reser
Readopts Easi

rotests a More Immediat New Uncertainties Lending Polici
Problem Than Shortages
The New York Times, Dec. 9, 1967,
New York, New York
The New York Times, May 19, 1968, New York, New York
The Wall Street Journal,
April 21, 1967,
New York, New York

Chapter 9

An Introduction to Public Policy-Making

The methods of deciding public policies are more numerous than we may, perhaps, wish to recognize. Managing this diversity requires us to reduce complex decision-making to simple models and economical categories. Let us analyze public policy-making by reviewing a number of basic considerations generally involved in public policy-making or collective choice. In Chapter 10 specific processes are analyzed in terms of these more general considerations.

Basic Considerations

Public policy involves the deliberative choice of collective goals and the implementation of public decisions. When enacted, such decisions are considered authoritatively binding upon all members of the society. The political system is the vehicle for enacting these decisions.

Analysis of policy-making may be conducted from a variety of perspectives including those which emphasize (1) who makes the decisions; (2) processes of choice and interaction; (3) factual and normative constraints or the framework of choice; (4) the issues or aims of policies; (5) policy innovation; and (6) the consequences of policy efforts. Figure 9-1 presents a graphic summary.

Figure 9-1

The Policy-Making Process

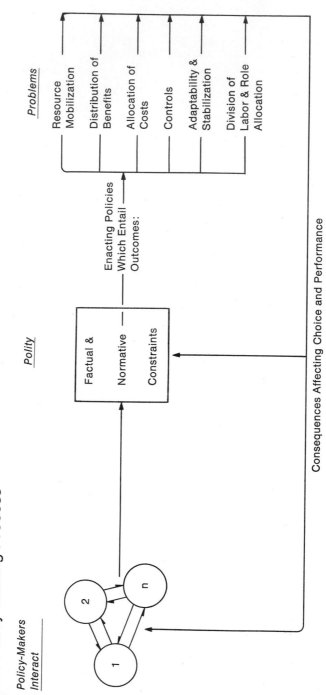

Policy-Makers Interact

Polity

Problems

Factual & Normative Constraints

Enacting Policies Which Entail Outcomes:

Resource Mobilization

Distribution of Benefits

Allocation of Costs

Controls

Adaptability & Stabilization

Division of Labor & Role Allocation

Consequences Affecting Choice and Performance

Public policy-making cannot be fully understood unless each set of elements in the figure is considered. Each element aids in determining who, how, when, and what consequences will flow from the interaction. The exact significance of each component cannot be flatly stated, although in some situations a rough estimate about each can be made. In the abstract *the importance of any one element could be deduced by holding all others constant.* For example, we might want to know what difference it would make in the allocation of resources or the distribution of benefits and burdens if we were to alter one constraint by, say, shifting from a simple majority to a two-thirds voting rule in a decision body. Or, we might perform a mental experiment on the policy effects of a change in the social class or career patterns of policy-makers. Suppose our set of policy-makers consisted in one instance of former workers and in another, of stockholders. Or, suppose we could change the ratio of personalities from an equal number of suspicious and trusting types to one in which the suspicious or conflict-oriented types constituted 75 per cent of the policy-makers. Would this affect policy formation and outcomes? What would be the difference? Why? What evidence is there to support your inferences?

One aspect of the diagram concerns consequences of what policy-makers do. Since consequences have been the subject of special concern in all the preceding chapters, they will not receive much attention here. In systems theory these consequences have been popularly labelled 'feedback,' which suggests that they stimulate the next round of decision-making. However, they are often very diffused and indirect. The dotted line in Figure 9-1 should, therefore, connote the indirectness and the complexity of many kinds of consequences flowing from public decisions. In this text we have chosen to emphasize certain consequences as problems which aid in assessing the performance of political systems.

Policies are made because policy-makers hope and expect that they can alter the human situation in some predictable and desirable direction. Much of the policy-making process, at least in most modern governments, is devoted to understanding the problems about which public action could be taken. Since the nature of the problems themselves is often subject to debate, defining the issues is an important phase of policy-making. Political scientists do not have any particular claim to professional authority in most substantive policy areas because policies concern all facets of human behavior. Thus, for example, if one wants to know how to deter crime he would more likely consult criminologists and psychologists than political scientists. Or if one wishes to know about the economic effects of a particular wage policy on prices, national income and the distribution of income, he would be wise to refer to economists and not psychologists or political scientists. Political science may be of particular value whenever we wish to understand the effects of a policy on the distribution of power among citizens or its effects on political institutions and rules of the game. Presumably, a political scientist could tell us something about the influences on policy formation (initiation, adoption, effectuation) if we alter our political institutions. For example, what effects might be anticipated if our party system changes from a two to a multi-party arrangement? Or, what would be the consequences of a federal rather than a unitary system of distributing power? In short, political scientists have most to say about political relationships and influences within the political system. Curiously, while much of this is available as policy advice, it has not been very well systematized for convenient and ready reference by either political scientists or politicians. In any event, let us consider the various elements of Figure 9-1 as elements in policy-making.

Who Makes the Choices?

Political Actors

Who makes policy is not only an interesting question in itself, but a significant one in terms of the kinds of policies advanced and the ways in which they may be chosen. This is not to claim that if we know certain crucial characteristics of the relevant actors we are then able to predict the precise content of public policies, but such knowledge does provide us with better predictors than none at all. Most citizens share this conviction because they generally try to predict policy outcomes in deciding how to vote. The easiest way is to have the policy-maker reflect the very same values as the voter himself. Southern whites usually predict that they will fare better when whites rather than blacks are in office. Upper-class Englishmen usually rest more secure knowing that one of their own kind is prime minister. Professors appear to prefer intellectuals to businessmen in public office while businessmen feel their concerns are apt to receive a more generous hearing from fellow businessmen rather than from poets, novelists, ballet dancers or, perhaps, even professors.

While members of each group may incorrectly predict the actions of various other groups, the error is considered to rest on factors other than the ascribed characteristics of the actors. It is just not possible for the decision-makers to reflect all elements in the society, or for the voter to expect this. And issues have a way of raising too many kinds of considerations. The prime objective is to find a policy-maker who is generally sympathetic to one's major concerns rather than to one's total policy preferences. Few are in a position to provide complete assurance. The voter or observer is, therefore, moved to assess the more general preferences and orientations of decision-makers.

While the formal division of labor in a political system specifies roles guiding the behavior of politicians and bureaucrats, it remains for the individual officeholder to interpret his role and act; there is typically a range of discretion, often a considerable one. Role definitions or designations about duties, salaries, rights and resources shape the context of choice, but no constitution or set of rules can dictate the precise choices of officeholders who continuously meet new problems as a part of their daily job. The political demands of the job and job-related preferences shape the politician's behavior, experience and outlook; they provide more clues as to his likely orientation or frame of reference. Psychological studies of individual leaders and more general studies of voters have shown the necessity for such information. Students of voting behavior, furthermore, have markedly improved their predictions of electoral outcomes by considering information about the socio-economic characteristics and identifications of voters. In the case of leaders, we know that all have individual and somewhat unique ways of perceiving their situations and, given some information about a leader's role perceptions and typical referents, we can do a decent job of predicting his characteristic ways of meeting situations. We cannot from such data alone make precise estimates or predictions of policies and strategies; few activities of man enable complete and accurate forecasts.

Another consideration having much less to do with the personality and social characteristics of individual decision-makers pertains to the strategic positions held by participants in public policy-making. Citizens and others will want to know, for instance, whether the President or Congress will make the crucial decision. Or will the local or central government be given the prime or sole responsibility? Who makes the decisions at which levels may affect the flow of public goods from the system. Local and state governments in the United States, for example, have worked more easily with more business interests than has the federal government. The latter, on the other hand, has provided more benefits and services to the worker and farmer. The federal government has tended to enact more progressive taxes than have local and state governments. The federal government has tended during recent decades to enact more extensive regulatory legislation than 'have other governments.

Probably the bulk of studies on who makes decisions are restricted to questions of *who* governs, making only inferential statements about the policy outcomes for particular types of leaders. Thus, one crusading venture in community studies was Floyd Hunter's attempt to discern the invisible economic elite making up the *Community Power Structure*.[1] A contending school of thought, using different methods, tended to find a plurality of elites in terms of decisions made. Robert Dahl's *Who Governs?*[2] is the

---

[1] Floyd Hunter, *Community Power Structure: A Study of Decision-Makers* (Chapel Hill: The University of North Carolina Press, 1953).

[2] Robert A. Dahl, *Who Governs?* (New Haven: Yale University Press, 1961).

typically cited work. Efforts to describe who makes the decisions continue: *The Rulers and The Ruled, Community Influentials, Men at the Top*[3] are a few. None of these exemplary studies attempts a systematic correlation of decision-makers with policy outcomes in the broader sense, research which entails difficulties well beyond identifying who participates in various decisions. Still it is easiest to believe that leaders consciously or unconsciously pursue policy alternatives that are reasonably consistent with social and economic premises derived from a lifetime of viewing the world from particular social positions or statuses. Businessmen who enter government posts would be most unusual if they did not continue to view policy alternatives as experienced businessmen. And union leaders might be expected to see the world differently from businessmen and farmers. Of course, the pursuit of a particular policy does not guarantee its acceptance as policy for there may be competitors or other more influential elites. While we need more rigorous research into the relationships of policy-alternatives, outcomes and decision-makers, we do have many isolated and unrelated propositions about such connections. The following propositions are illustrative:

1. "The political type is characterized by an intense and ungratified craving for deference. These cravings, both accentuated and unsatisfied in the primary circle, are displaced upon public objects (persons and practices connected with the power process). The displacement is rationalized in terms of public interest."[4]

2. "In a small group, authoritarian leadership is less effective than democratic leadership in holding the group together and getting its work done."[5]

3. "The higher in an organizational hierarchy a role is located the greater the likelihood that personality factors will have a significant effect on decision-making behavior."[6]

4. "Decision-makers with a high need for achievement and low fear of failure will prefer intermediate risks."[7]

5. ". . . . there appears to be more influence within the U.S. foreign

---

[3] Robert E. Agger, Daniel Goldrich, Bert E. Swanson, *The Rulers and the Ruled* (New York: John Wiley & Sons, Inc., 1964); M. Kent Jennings, *Community Influentials: A Study of Elites* (New York: The Free Press, 1964); Robert Presthus, *Men at the Top* (New York: Oxford University Press, 1964).

[4] Harold D. Lasswell, *Power and Personality* (New York: W. W. Norton and Company, Inc., 1948), p. 38.

[5] Bernard Berelson and Gary A. Steiner, *Human Behavior: An Inventory of Scientific Findings* (New York: Harcourt, Brace and World, Inc., 1964), p. 344.

[6] Richard C. Snyder and James A. Robinson, *National and International Decision-Making* (New York: The Institute for International Order, undated), p. 158.

[7] *Ibid.*, p. 163.

policy-making structure based on role and personality than on either knowledge or ideas. . . ."[8]

6. "Because so much activity in society is related to men who organize working groups, the politician is compelled to understand and be sympathetic to employers and labor union officials who are powerful in determining industrial policy which in turn affects public policy. . . ."[9]

7. [In America during the 1950s:] "The warlords have gained decisive political relevance . . . . virtually all political and economic actions are now judged in terms of military definitions of reality. . ."[10]

It is obvious that more systematic study will qualify and perhaps even contradict many such illustrative findings or assertions. Meanwhile, each succeeding leader, whether a De Gaulle, Kosygin or Brezhnev, Dubcek (Czechoslovakia), Lyndon Johnson, Trudeau, etc., brings unique and interesting qualities to bear on the decisions made during his time in office. Studies of U.S. Presidents in particular are showing increasing sophistication in ferreting out the special influences of the person in the context of rather complicated decision processes. We might therefore summarize some of the major perspectives which can be used in analyzing leadership behavior.

1. *Basic internalized personality traits produce characteristic patterns of perception, choice and behavior.* The psychoanalytic approach has tended to emphasize parental influences and early traumatic relationships or learning experiences; others try to characterize whole personality syndromes, such as 'authoritarian,' 'messianic,' or 'paranoid.'[11]

2. *Special forms of subcultural socialization create characteristic traits and behavior which persons bring to the position in question.* This socialization may be characteristic of a special social strata, as elite studies

---

[8] *Ibid.*, p. 80.

[9] Floyd Hunter, *Top Leadership: U.S.A.* (Chapel Hill: University of North Carolina Press, 1959), pp. 208-209.

[10] C. Wright Mills, *The Power Elite* (New York: Oxford University Press, 1956), p. 275.

[11] The literature on the psychology of politics is enormous. In a single footnote we can provide only a minute sample. The major writings have been those of Harold D. Lasswell, including *World Politics and Personal Insecurity* (Glencoe, Ill.: The Free Press, 1934); *Psychopathology and Politics* (Chicago: University of Chicago Press, 1930); *Power and Personality* (New York: W. W. Norton and Company, Inc., 1948). Cf. G. M. Gilbert, *The Psychology of Dictatorship* (New York: The Ronald Press Company, 1950); M. Brewster Smith, Jerome S. Bruner and Robert W. White, *Opinions and Personality* (New York: John Wiley and Sons, Inc., 1964). Two interesting case studies include Arnold A. Rogow, *James Forrestal: A Study of Personality, Politics and Policy* (New York: The Macmillan Company, 1963), and Alexander and Juliette George, *Woodrow Wilson and Colonel House: A Personality Study* (New York: John Day Company, Inc., 1956).

sometimes emphasize; or they may be communal and regional, as suggested by, for example, American southerners and westerners or 'small town boys,' 'big city politicians,' and the like. Elite theorists have also emphasized the influences of special schooling or social and professional clubs in developing the traits of leadership.[12]

3. *Leadership behavior is affected by the context of choice.* Decision theorists have been exploring the particular effects of certain choice contexts on the responses of persons, such as in highly interactive small group situations (which might apply to congressional committees, city councils, top executive councils and the like) or during times of stress accompanied by high risk, or great uncertainties (as in crisis decision-making or competitive campaigning). These theorists draw upon general theories and experimental studies of human perception and response and attempt to apply them to official decision situations.[13]

4. *Personal or official ideologies of leaders, i.e., their explicit explanations and avowed precepts of public performance, affect their decisions.* The causes of the traits are of less concern here than the ideological patterns and consistencies displayed. However idiosyncratic, the assumption is that whatever is unique to the individual will still be organized by ideologies that provide some degree of predictability and consistency in his behavior. And as officials, most decision-makers are called upon to 'explain themselves' in some form or manner that should provide clues.

There may be new and more insightful perspectives on the unique or highly discretionary aspects of leadership behavior, but these indicate some major possibilities. We hope there will be more inventories of empirical findings in the future or at least more systematic hypotheses than we find at this point in leadership studies.[14]

The Framework of Choice

Framework of Collective Choice: Normative Elements

Public policies are not made in situational vacuums; instead they are formulated within powerful sets of factual and normative constraints, that

---

[12] Two highly stimulating studies of Britain and the United States can serve as good illustrations of this approach to elites: C. Wright Mills, *The Power Elite* (New York: Oxford University Press, 1956) and Anthony Sampson, *The Anatomy of Britain Today* (New York: Harper and Row Publishers, 1965).

[13] Although dated, the best bibliography on these factors is that of Snyder and Robinson, *op. cit.* Those interested in international politics should find Herbert C. Kelman, ed., *International Behavior: A Social-Psychological-Analysis* (New York: Holt, Rinehart and Winston, Inc., 1965) of considerable interest. Each chapter has a selected bibliography.

[14] Cf. Lewis Edinger, *Political Leadership in Industrialized Societies: Studies in Comparative Analysis* (New York: John Wiley and Sons, Inc., 1967).

is, conditions that are not susceptible to much short-run alteration. In sum, men make political decisions within the context of institutionalized rules and expectations, with only limited information, with more or less given distributions of power resources, and mostly with issues or problems not of their own immediate making. The specific situation of choice varies greatly, but all have elements of the enumerated factors. Each of these factors is accompanied by varying degrees of uncertainty and risk, i.e., the actors are ignorant of the situation in varying degrees and cannot, therefore, accurately calculate future outcomes.

Several of these terms refer to normative elements, i.e., the rules or norms by which political action is expected to be conducted. In highly stabilized systems the normative framework is itself widely known and accepted so the predictability of behavior is relatively high. Each actor knows what to expect from others. In primitive and traditional societies, political institutions are very stable; although the norms may be implicit, little uncertainty prevails as to who has how much authority and how it may be employed. In revolutionary situations political institutions are in flux or still being determined so one finds maximal discretion for those in power to make their own rules about how authority will be exercised, or who will make decisions and how. Most of the nation-states of the world, as we have seen, can be ranked according to the amount of political institutionalization constraining their decision-makers.

Normative constraints and rules of the game guide the choices of policy-makers by requiring them to proceed in certain ways and to justify their actions according to the rules. Citizens as well as leaders expect such conduct, and the price for not observing the rules usually means some form of sanction including a diminution of one's influence over others. In highly stabilized processes, decision-makers must employ skilled technicians (often lawyers) who can inform them of the legal requirements. Senior colleagues or superiors may also advise on such other normative considerations as prevailing opinions and informal norms of behavior. Such rules, norms and values must be avowedly honored before the expectant groups. The experienced leader is one who knows these rules so well that they require little deliberation to be honored. Much of a society's resources will, in stabilized systems, be devoted to an inculcation of these generalized norms for leaders and the public alike. Such efforts are collectively termed 'political socialization.'

The institutional norms we have noted thus far usually tend to define the explicit range of permissive official action—the constitutional, legal or bureaucratic sort. There are, however, a variety of other rules, generally informal and stemming from direct or observed experience which not only explain permissible behavior but also sound like strategic maxims. Such 'rules of thumb' are thought by politicians to form sound advice on how to deal with certain types of recurrent situations. These rules then perform two functions: They act as normative constraints on politicians because they are accepted as desirable, and they are of practical value in making decisions to the extent that they do provide a 'pay-off.' Occasionally a perceptive practitioner will call attention to them and even systematize them into explicit statements. The following cases will illustrate.

Case Study #1   Congressional Rules of Thumb

In his study of tariff legislation during 1929-1930, E. E. Schattschneider took account of several rules of thumb which he felt congressmen followed in guiding their decisional choices.

1. "Get a consensus from an industry as to what it needs. Don't listen to any one manufacturer, but make the industry's witnesses tell you what 80 per cent of them would agree to. They know their own business and if they agree they are probably right."[15]
2. "Everyone asks for more than he expects to get, so take the figure asked and discount it some."[16]
3. "Where tariff increases raise someone's cost, raise their protective tariffs accordingly. The solution to injury by tariffs is more tariffs; for example, if you have raised tariffs on wool, raise tariffs on woolen textiles compensatingly."[17]
4. "People in similar situations should be treated equally; if you have given a 30 per cent increase to one textile, give a 30 per cent increase to another."[18]

Case Study #2   Some Rules of the Game in State Legislatures

A recent exhaustive investigation of four state legislatures as role systems turned up a total of forty-two rules of the game as perceived by at least a few state legislators. We list only the more widely known ones.[19]

1. "Performance of obligations: Keep your word; abide by commitments."[20]
2. "Respect for other member's legislative rights: Support another member's local bill if it doesn't affect you or your district; don't railroad bills through; don't appear before another committee

---

[15] E. E. Schattschneider, *Politics, Pressures and the Tariff* (Englewood Cliffs, N.J.: Prentice-Hall, Inc., 1935), pp. 84 ff.; as summarized in Raymond A. Bauer, Ithiel de Sola Pool, and Lewis Anthony Dexter, *American Business and Public Policy* (New York: Atherton Press, 1964), pp. 24-25.

[16] *Ibid.*

[17] *Ibid.*

[18] *Ibid.*

[19] John C. Wahlke, Heinz Eulau, William Buchanan and LeRoy C. Ferguson, *The Legislative System* (New York: John Wiley and Sons, Inc., 1962), Chap. 7.

[20] *Ibid.*, p. 146.

(than your own) to oppose another member's bill; don't steal another member's bill; respect the rights of a bill's author; accept author's amendments to a bill."[21]

3. "Impersonality: Don't deal in personalities; don't make personal attacks on other members; oppose the bill not the man; don't criticize the moral behavior of others; address other members through the Chair; don't refer to another member by name; observe the 'Golden Rule.' "[22]

4. "Self-restraint in debate: Don't talk too much; don't speak about subjects on which you're uninformed."[23]

Case Study #3   The Sixteen Great Maxims of Judicial Self-Restraint

Since rules are of great importance to lawyers and judges we should not be too surprised to learn that the Supreme Court has over its lifetime elaborated a number of self-imposed rules on its own behavior as a Court. These rules have been termed "maxims of judicial self-restraint," by one scholar of the Court.[24] Most of these are culled directly from leading Court opinions which serve as formal precedents or legal dicta, rather than as informal norms derived from interviews. The sixteen great maxims follow:

1. "Before the Court will even glance at a particular issue or dispute officially, a definite 'case' or 'controversy' at law or in equity between bona fide adversaries under the Constitution must exist, involving the protection or enforcement of valuable legal rights, or the punishment, prevention, or redress of wrongs directly concerning the party or parties bringing the justiciable suit."

2. "Closely related to the need for the presence of a case or controversy is the logical demand that the party or parties bringing suit must have 'standing.' "

3. "The Court does not render advisory opinions, i.e. judicial rulings upon the constitutionality of governmental action in the absence of a case or controversy requiring such a ruling for its disposition—nor do the lower federal constitutional courts."

4. "Not only must the complainant in federal court expressly declare that he is invoking the Constitution of the United States—'the ultimate touchstone of constitutionality,' in Mr. Justice Frankfurter's phrase—but a specific live rather than dead constitutional issue citing the particular provision on which he relies in that

---

[21] *Ibid.*

[22] *Ibid.*

[23] *Ibid.*

[24] Abridged from *The Judicial Process* by Henry J. Abraham. Copyright 1962, 1968 by Oxford University Press, Inc. Reprinted by permission.

document must be raised by him; the Court will not entertain generalities."

5. "The Court looks askance at any attempt to have the judicial decision-cake and eat it too. Thus, it will not pass upon the constitutionality of a statute or of an official action at the instance of one who has availed himself of its benefits, but then decides to challenge its legality anyway."

6. "All remedies in the pertinent lower federal and/or state courts must have been exhausted, and prescribed lower court procedure duly followed, before making application to the United States Supreme Court for review."

7. "Assuming it has been properly raised, the federal question at issue must be substantial rather than trivial; it must be the pivotal point of the case; and it must be part of the plaintiff's case rather than a part of his adversary's defense."

8. "Although it would be an oversimplification, if not entirely incorrect, to state that the Supreme Court reviews only questions of law, it is nonetheless generally true that questions of fact—as distinct from questions of law—are not normally accepted as proper bases for review."

9. "While Britain's highest tribunal, the House of Lords, considered itself bound by its own prior decisions until it publicly and expressly renounced that doctrine in 1966, the Supreme Court of the United States has never held itself absolutely bound by its precedents."

10. "The Court has been inclined to defer to certain legislative or executive actions by classifying an issue otherwise quite properly before it as a political question—hence refusing to come to grips with it."

11. "In the event of a validly challenged statute the presumption of its constitutionality is always in its favor."

12. "In the exercise of what some commentators have been fond of styling 'judicial parsimony,' if a case or controversy can be decided upon any other than constitutional grounds—such as by statutory construction, which constitutes the greatest single area of the Court's work, or if it can rest on an independent state ground—the Court will be eager to do so."

13. "The Court will not ordinarily impute illegal motives to the lawmakers."

14. "If the Court does find that it must hold a law unconstitutional, it will usually try hard to confine the holding to that particular section of the statute which was successfully challenged on constitutional grounds—provided such a course of action is at all feasible."

15. "A legislative enactment—or an executive action—may be un-

wise, unjust, unfair, undemocratic, injudicious, '. . . if you like . . . even tyrannical,' or simply stupid, but still be constitutional in eyes of the Court."

16. "The Supreme Court has reiterated time and again that it is not designed to serve as a check against inept, unwise, emotional, unrepresentative legislators."

Case Study #4 The Operational Code of the Politburo

One study of communism in the early 1950s examined the writings of Lenin and Marx to derive the precepts that served as 'correct rules' for the official members of the Politburo at that time. The following will illustrate their normative character.

1. "The Party must at all times have a 'complete set' of 'definite,' 'precise,' 'clear' positions on all matters: '. . . to the devil with all people with 'indeterminate views' . . .'"[25]

2. "The Party's position on any matter must always, in a 'practical', 'business-like' fashion, indicate the correct course of action."[26]

3. "Although the Party leadership need not be concerned with the consistency of the *statements* it makes to the Party and to the rest of the world, it must be sure of the consistency of its *position* on all issues . . ."[27]

4. "The Party must always be oriented to facts, present and future. It must guard against the danger of being 'carried away by phrases,' of being 'deafened by words,' of 'replacing analysis by shouts,' of permitting 'the tongue to dominate thoughts.' "[28]

5. "The Party must arrive at every one of its policy decisions on the basis of an intensive and repeated process of calculation."[29]

6. "The forecasts of the Party must be sober: '. . . revolutionaries will perish . . . only if . . . they lose their sobriety of outlook'; 'Bolsheviks do not believe in miracles.' "[30]

7. " 'We must formulate our programs in such a fashion that we are prepared for the worst; the occurrence of more favorable circumstances will only facilitate our work . . .'; 'we must count on the worst.' "[31]

---

[25] Nathan Leites, *The Operational Code of the Politburo* (New York: McGraw-Hill Book Company, 1951), p. 13.

[26] *Ibid.*

[27] *Ibid.*

[28] *Ibid.*, p. 14.

[29] *Ibid.*

[30] *Ibid.*, p. 17.

[31] *Ibid.*

Other selections of precepts with high normative content have to do with "the control of feelings," "perseverance and flexibility," and "conduct in defeat and victory."[32] Of course strategic rules are strongly mixed with these; they come up for discussion further on.

Framework of Collective Choice: Resource Constraints

Most experienced policy-makers are very aware of, if not always well-informed on, the 'real' world in which they act, i.e., the array of things and people with which they are dealing. Some of these elements may be considered as resources which are 'put to use' in making policy, or serve to bring the intended policy about. While it may seem a rather negative way to put it, resources serve as constraints to the degree they set the definable limits of what and how something can be done. Policy-makers must work with what they have; thus what they do not have to work with represents definite limitations on what they will try to do. The resources used for gaining political results seem to be enormously varied. There are intangible resources such as prestige, trust, likeableness, good reputation, sense of efficacy and so forth; there are technical or skill-type resources such as organization, experience, bargaining abilities, persuasiveness; there are resources of authority, influence, competence; there are the quantities of money, manpower, goods or even information—all of which could be considered useful in producing policy results. Indeed, given the many potential resources, there are those who feel that the greatest sort of constraint on most decision-makers is their lack of awareness of all the possibilities at their command. Thus the ultimate 'factual' constraint may be the policy-maker's own limited perceptions and imagination!

Before blaming any particular policy actor, consider some different situations where resources come into play. First, we must identify those resources immediately at the disposal of the policy actor or actors. In individual decision-making, these may be his highly personal traits which are directly, even automatically, applied to the political activity at hand. Thus, in a committee meeting his resources would include such personality traits as his integrity and trustworthiness, cooperative or dissident qualities, helpfulness, imaginativeness, irritability, etc.

Every decision situation involving different actors, places, and subjects involves unique combinations of personal resources. Thus, we shall not try to describe what they might be but instead pose an important question. To what degree are the immediately applicable resources of the policy actors subject to his own control and use? In highly institutionalized situations many personal resources become a public attribute. Over a period of time many of an individual's personal qualities become known

---

[32] *Ibid.*, Chaps. V, VII and VIII.

as his *reputation* and determine the expectations upon which others act. The more he becomes known in certain roles, the more the actor must live within the confines of his perceived reputation. Machiavelli must be credited with great awareness of the fact that a reputation is a resource which the leader must guard carefully in his public actions. A noted student of the U.S. presidency, Richard Neustadt, devoted two chapters to this resource.[33] Much attention is given to reputation in considering candidates for President, and the reputation of being a 'loser' rests heavily upon a Presidential hopeful. So, too, do such attributes as credibility, honor, confidentiality and so forth. If a reputation becomes the premise upon which others act, then it becomes an important resource which has been created by the actor but which may be beyond his immediate control.

On the other hand, personal *skills* are more directly manipulable by the policy actor. Among such skills may be eloquence, persuasiveness, bargaining talents, or tactical skill in waging conflict or competition in some political arena. These are capabilities at the actor's command to be used as he wishes. Most skills are sharpened by experience but still must be used in ways relevant to each new situation. Thus, skills are limited by the degree of capability and the actor's perception or imagination regarding their use. Which political skills are effective depends very much on the situation and role expectations.

Some political resources are exchangeable and some are not. In policy-making situations which involve competition and bargaining, some resources must be available to promise or trade with those from whom one wants support. In formalized choice situations, as in large-scale democracies, the most common political resource of this sort is the vote. Votes are exchanged for political promises. Delivering what is promised means exchanging or spending resources. The reputation for honoring such commitments in the past or the credibility for doing so in the future are aspects which the policy actor must develop over time. Exchangeable resources are often termed *capabilities* when referring to the physical means of carrying out tasks. The term is most familiar in defense policy where military capability is the resource which backs the promise—i.e., threat—to respond to any attack and, thus hopefully, deter the enemy. Deterrence, therefore, depends upon the credibility of the threatened response.

In defense, as in all policy areas, the reliability of the resource is very important when the resource is beyond the actor's personal possession. If the resources are manpower, money or physical goods, one looks for typical sorts of assurance that these resources are 'deliverable.' One such assurance is that of hierarchical command or legal authority. Richard

---

[33] Richard E. Neustadt, *Presidential Power: The Politics of Leadership* (New York: John Wiley and Sons, Inc., Publishers, 1960). Chapter 4 is titled "Professional Reputation"; Chapter 5 is concerned with "Public Prestige."

Neustadt noted that it was easier for President Truman to fire one of his generals, who belonged to his visible chain of command, than to seize the steel mills where he had to prove his legal power to do so against the contention of others, including those who managed the mills. Where the rules of ownership are clear, wealth can be an important political resource. Control of jobs or a deliverable promise of relevant services and opportunities are also useful resources. Often, however, there is considerable uncertainty as to who controls how much of what.

The likelihood of divergent estimates is considerable in situations where resources cannot be publicly inventoried by disinterested 'accountants.' Even in American presidential conventions experts cannot always determine which candidate has the delegate's vote. Likewise, estimates of popular support or campaign monies and organizational effectiveness are extremely difficult to ascertain with precision and confidence. Much the same problem exists on the international scene with respect to the distribution of power among all nations during any particular incident or crisis situation. Even when one can measure the distribution of resources accurately it may still be difficult to assess the relevance of each resource over time and in specific circumstances. Each resource may be more or less valuable depending on the type of situation in which it is to be employed. Politicians are interested in the specific value of the resource for they confront unique—not general—situations.

Given the uncertainty of resource availability, is it not understandable that men form organizations to increase their collective resources? By joining an organization, one increases his power potential. Organization is, therefore, a major resource in itself, for it can generate and maintain other resources. The man who has organization skills is much in demand in modern political systems, for organization is a complex set of techniques not readily acquired. In Chapter 12, we suggest various means of increasing organizational effectiveness.

Framework of Collective Choice: Uncertainty

Resources are almost always scarce; just how scarce is an open question. In any case, most conditions confronting citizens and politicians as they consider policy are highly uncertain.[34] There are a number of

---

[34] While uncertainty is a pervasive fact of political life, it has not been so explicitly recognized in political theory. However, see Anthony Downs, *An Economic Theory of Democracy* (New York: Harper and Brothers, Publishers, 1957), Part II; James M. Buchanan and Gordon Tullock, *The Calculus of Consent* (Ann Arbor: University of Michigan Press, 1962); Nelson W. Polsby and Aaron B. Wildavsky, *Presidential Elections: Strategies of American Electoral Politics,* 2d. ed. (New York: Charles Scribner's Sons, 1968). The scholar who has done most to bring the concept of uncertainty into social theory is G. L. S. Shackle, *Uncertainty in Economics* (New York: Cambridge University Press, 1961).

reasons for this problematic and unpromising fact of life. The major reason is simply that political life at all levels is subject to continual change. Governments are expected to cope with all facets and variables of human behavior. Likewise, the politician who desires to win and remain in office is confronted by a variety of considerations. Unfortunately, the scientific community, especially social science, is in no position to offer a politician or government a great body of knowledge that will significantly reduce uncertainty. Every known regularity of human behavior is subject to an extraordinary number of possible qualifications. We, therefore, do not know all that is required to make realistic policies and to devise efficient strategies for gaining power.

A major area of policy-making is concerned with economic behavior. Because economic theory has become quite sophisticated about causes and remedies, one might expect that economists could reduce the politicians' uncertainty by a wide margin; but such is not often the case. Consider the following newspaper item about President Johnson's dilemmas and uncertainty in devising taxation policies:

POLITICS AND TAXES

Issues Extend Beyond Economics as Johnson Prepares to Set 1967 Course

By M. J. Rossant

Economic policy-making is always difficult but formulating policy for the coming year looms as an especially difficult task for the Johnson Administration.

The problem is reflected in the sharp division of opinion over the business outlook that now prevails among economic forecasters.

If the Administration takes the advice of economists who predict a continuing rise in business activity accompanied by inflation, it will probably request a rise in taxes for individuals and corporations.

But if it is persuaded by those who think that the pace of activity is already slackening and could go into a retreat, it will postpone tax increases once again.

There has not been so sharp a division since the end of 1962, when some economists, including the Administration's own advisers, felt that a recession was inevitable unless taxes were reduced,

while others predicted a continuation of the expansion even if Congress failed to act on taxes.

A Political Risk

The division now is more critical than it was then because it is much riskier politically to raise taxes than to lower them. Mr. Johnson provided a graphic example of how political considerations influence economic policy in his steadfast refusal to raise taxes this year.

Despite strong evidence that the economy was getting out of hand, and urgent appeals from many of his advisers as well as from the Federal Reserve Board and from private economists and businessmen, Mr. Johnson refrained from acting, presumably because he did not want to risk an unpopular move before the Congressional elections.

Political considerations will again play a part in policy-

making for 1967. But with the election out of the way, the Administration may give greater weight to purely economic developments.

The trouble is that the economic situation is not easy to diagnose. It shows many signs of strengths. It also shows some weaknesses. And there are a number of potential troublespots that could prove very unsettling.

Construction activity is already hard-hit. The National Industrial Conference Board's business trends letter reports that "consumer buying has been gradually losing momentum." And the first important private survey of corporate spending plans for 1967, made by Lionel Edie & Co., suggests an end of the plant-and-equipment boom.

These symptoms do not necessarily mean that the boom is over. The current expansion, after all, has been left for dead before only to rise up stronger than ever.

There are many econo-
mists, moreover, who think
that the danger of a decline is
less real than the danger of
inflation. As the Mellon National Bank and Trust Company observes, continued escalation in Vietnam will
mean an intensification of inflation pressures that "would
argue strongly in favor of
more restrictive fiscal measures including, perhaps, an
increase in both personal and
corporate income taxes."

But the Mellon Bank goes
on to admit that "a number
of prominent economists have
pointed out, with equal persuasion, that to increase tax
rates when demand in key
sectors of the private economy is showing some signs of
slowing down would inevi-
tably run the risk of precipi-
tating a business recession."

Because the economy is
subject to conflicting — and

confusing — diagnosis, it is
not easy to treat. So in making up his mind, President
Johnson may fall back on
his political feel.

Tax Decision Awaited

This year, he put stress on
economic trends that helped
to bolster his position against
raising taxes. Early in the
year, he emphasized that retail sales were declining and
food prices leveling off; a
little later he belittled a private survey of capital spending that indicated that business spending was proceeding
at an unsustainable rate. His
evidence, based on preliminary data, turned out to be
wrong.

It was not until September,
when the Federal Reserve's
singlehanded attempt to cool
things down by tightening
credit brought about a near-
crisis in the money market,

that Mr. Johnson acted. Even
then, he chose to avoid across-
the-board tax increases before
the coming Congressional
elections.

The division among econo-
mists makes it clear that there
is less reason to consider tax
increases now than there was
a year ago. Yet with the election out of the way, the President may now change course.

If he decides to press for
increases in taxes next year,
he is sure to cite economic
justification — the need to
combat inflation and to finance the war in Vietnam.

His real motivation,
though, in taxes may or may
not be the best prescription
for the economy. But the tax
increase in 1967 could pave
the way for tax reductions—
and a new boom — in 1968,
which is when Mr. Johnson
himself will be facing an
election campaign.

The New York Times, Nov. 2, 1966, p. 59.

President Johnson not only had to make estimates of the economic
effects of particular taxes (levels as well as rates) on individual behavior,
on the behavior of firms and on the sum-total of economic activity, but he
had to make estimates of the foreseeable needs of the government he
headed and, above all, the *political impact* of each of these matters. What
were the probabilities of getting various taxes, levels, rates, etc., through
Congress? How would the voters respond to each tax policy? As the article
points out, even the economists were sharply split over the economic consequences and, of course, did not pretend to know the political impacts.
So what was Mr. Johnson to do, confronted as he was with such great
uncertainty about each factor? Imagine, then, the complexity in making
foreign policy where many of the normal 'givens' of domestic issues are
not present. Only with the wisdom of hindsight can we reflect on how
really uncertain President Johnson's—and the country's—future was at
that time!

Politicians resort to a number of practices to reduce uncertainty.
The first response of the more practical person is to acquire more and
better information. Politicians often rely upon their own personal experiences in determining political alternatives and their respective feasibilities;
or they may turn to experienced advisers, pollsters or other analysts. In
substantive policy areas the politician typically relies upon those affected
to estimate political impact and indicate preferences; he may also call in

'outside' experts. American Presidents, for example, consult with a Council of Economic Advisers, composed of highly trained and respected economists, for advice on economic policy. Presidents use the State Department and foreign policy experts for advice on international affairs and a great number of staff and huge departments for advice on domestic affairs—transportation, agriculture, commerce, labor, civil rights, education, etc. The major problem is not so much one of acquiring information, since there is normally more available than is needed, but of assessing its relevance, validity and reliability—not at all an easy task.

Since politicians do not have time to speculate, they often rely on their own experiences and intuitions to develop rules of thumb about events, responses to them and how they can best be handled. Those most likely to operate by these rules are the professionals. The rules may be no better based than are similar rules among other practical persons, but they do provide a guideline for action. It is possible that many of these rules are handed down by those who are successful on the assumption that adherence to them was the cause of success. In any case, newer politicians tend to emulate the rules of the more experienced.

Politicians must often face unusual demands that cannot always be met. It is sometimes quite interesting to see how they handle problems of difficult choice. A few politicians, Hitler, for example, have been known to consult astrologers; some others have consulted medicine men. In the ancient Greek city-states, rulers always consulted the oracles before embarking upon great ventures. In modern-day America, politicians may pray for guidance. American legislatures, including Congress, have chaplains to offer solace, guidance and moral exhortation. President Eisenhower held breakfast prayer-sessions before conducting the daily politics of the nation, while his Secretary of Agriculture (Ezra Taft Benson) is said to have 'got down on his knees' each day to ask for divine guidance on parity, farm prices and crop quotas.

Where uncertainty persists, men are apt to seek emotional security through religious practices; reassurance that one is doing right seems a necessity in our lives. Given the painful dilemmas and enormous tasks of the politicians, the great stakes often involved and the seemingly irreducible uncertainty of decision, the need for reassurance is understandable.

Advice from experts, rules of thumb and emotional reassurances are not the policy-maker's only aids in meeting dilemmas. Policy-makers do attempt to cope intelligently with their problems. One way is for the decision-maker to delay his choice until uncertainty diminishes. Another way is to refuse to commit oneself to any given course of action that may turn out to be premature and embarrassing as the situation clarifies and changes. Politicians prefer to keep their options open as long as possible, especially when opponents are involved. Options are kept open by such techniques as ambiguous statements, no comments, taking vacations or otherwise being unavailable to the press. Trial balloons are sent up to detect and measure possible reactions to contemplated proposals. Opinion polls are followed and, indeed, even commissioned by leaders. Attentive publics and other politicians are sounded to determine sentiment and test the receptivity of the policy proposals. The purpose of all these tactics is to free the politician by reducing his uncertainty concerning citizen opinion and opponent strategies.

One may also note some very distinct personal orientations toward handling uncertainties. Just as Pareto identified different leadership types as lions and foxes, we might posit the cautious and the careless, or the pessimist and the optimist. Or put into more theoretical terms of choice-making, there are those who prefer to maximize gains and those who prefer to minimize losses. Whether these approaches represent basic attitudes toward taking risks or are simply dependent upon the values being risked is open to question. In any case, if outcomes are uncertain and hunches replace hard predictions, then choices may be governed by the weight of one's hopes or fears. For example, a politician's response to the opportunity to run for office may be determined by whether he fears defeat more than he relishes victory, when both are uncertain. After all, what is more rational: to take great risks in the hope of deriving large gains; to reduce losses; to minimize regret that one did not do better; or to assume the worst and then make the best of it? One of the most interesting results of decision theory during recent years has been the discovery that there is no best criterion for selecting a strategy or course of action. Each course can be justified in reasonable terms. In short, the politician's attitudes toward uncertainty are a crucial component of his choices.

Processes of Interaction and Choice

Because it is difficult to determine the exact significance of who makes decisions, it is difficult to assess the exact importance of how decisions are made. Most people think it makes a difference whether decisions are reached through bargaining, competition, conflict, command or cooperation. These different kinds of processes affect the nature of the choice and thereby affect the outcomes. If people did not believe this they would not study, advocate and make so many reforms in decision-making institutions. Generally, those who are disappointed with policy outcomes blame the process and demand a substitute system which is presumed to produce more favorable results. Again, errors may be made in assessing the causal relationships between processes and outcomes. Democratic voting procedures may not produce a happier or better informed citizenry, a stabilized political system or a high degree of participation; on the other hand, dictatorial means may not accomplish these ends any more efficiently. Federalism may produce more conflict than it resolves;

the two-party system may not accomplish its vaunted ends; reapportionment may not change policy; legal edicts may not end political disadvantages. While the social sciences are currently devoting much effort to determining relationships among processes and outcomes under varying conditions, many predictions and generalizations are highly controversial. And worse, many predictions are not likely to be 'scientifically' confirmed in the near future.

Various scholars have observed policy processes and attempted to identify them; some seek to find certain *stages* or *types* of activity in the decision-making of an individual or of an entire political system. Others look at the number of participants. We include a few of these schemes to illustrate alternative, perhaps complementary, ways of structuring complex processes. Table 9-1 lists several attempts at classifying group action and policy-making. They are fairly self-explanatory and need not be elaborated upon for present purposes. Each investigator attempts to identify policy-making in terms of time sequence or types of activity. The purpose is to simplify the complexities and, hopefully, enable us to deduce possible outcomes associated with each stage in the entire sequence of events.

As political scientists, we are beginning to make some progress in predicting the outcomes of decision processes. Drawn from a number of sources, the following propositions characterize processes and outcomes in a variety of systems and circumstances.

1. "Many lesser decisions are continually being made without reference to the power structure at its top levels."[35]

2. "Competition in the Soviet Union tends to magnify policy differences between the contestants; in the United States it tends to moderate them."[36]

3. "In the American system each policy area has a high degree of autonomy."[37]

4. "In any political system centralized power makes innovation more possible although not necessarily more probable."[38]

5. "The foundation of the welfare state is the mutual dependence of people and government."[39]

---

[35] Roscoe C. Martin, Frank J. Munger, and others, *Decisions in Syracuse* (Bloomington: Indiana University Press, 1961), p. 319.

[36] Zbigniew Brzezinski and Samuel P. Huntington, *Political Power: USA/USSR* (New York: The Viking Press, Inc., 1964), p. 193.

[37] *Ibid.*, p. 226.

[38] *Ibid.*, p. 232.

[39] A. F. K. Organski, *The Stages of Political Development* (New York: Alfred A. Knopf, Inc., 1965), p. 200.

Table 9-1

Classifications of Group Action and Policy-Making

Lasswell's Decision Stages	Lindblom's 'Play of Power'	Bales' Types of Small Group Interaction	Froman's Political Processes
1. Intelligence	1. 'Power' to Decide	1. Shows Solidarity	1. Bargaining
2. Recommendation	2. Rules and Authority	2. Shows Tension Release	2. Discussion
3. Prescription	3. Specialization	3. Agrees	3. Democracy
4. Invocation	4. Cooperation	4. Gives Suggestion	4. Hierarchy
5. Application	5. Proximate Policy-Makers in Key Roles	5. Gives Opinion	
6. Appraisal	6. Cooperation among Proximate Policy-Makers	6. Gives Orientation	
7. Termination	7. Organized and Informal Cooperation	7. Asks for Orientation	
		8. Asks for Opinion	
		9. Asks for Suggestion	
		10. Disagrees	
		11. Shows Tension	
		12. Shows Antagonism	

Sources: Harold D. Lasswell, *The Decision Process* (College Park, Md.: Bureau of Governmental Research, 1956); Charles E. Lindblom, *The Policy-Making Process* (Englewood Cliffs, N.J.: Prentice-Hall, Inc., 1968), pp. 116-117; Robert F. Bales, *Interaction Process Analysis* (Reading, Mass.: Addison-Wesley Publishing Company, Inc., 1950); Lewis A. Froman, Jr., *People and Politics* (Englewood Cliffs, N.J.: Prentice-Hall, Inc., 1962), Chap. 4.

6. "In the traditional British system there is no place for the use of the courts to further some evolving purpose of public administration. In America there is."[40]

7. "Neither political party [U.S.A.] can afford to make excessive concessions to any pressure group."[41]

8. "The system [New York City] is more favorable to defenders of the status quo than to innovators."[42]

9. "The making of governmental decisions is not a majestic march of great majorities united upon certain matters of basic policy. It is the steady appeasement of relatively small groups."[43]

10. ". . . it [U.S. polity] does nonetheless provide a high probability that any active and legitimate group will make itself heard effectively at some stage in the process of decision."[44]

These ten illustrative propositions are but a minute sample of the countless statements made about policy processes here and abroad. A complete inventory of such types of assertions would occupy several volumes and most probably would not have the degree of generality desired. Many are only weak hypotheses and others are statements of faith without much evidence. Future students of policy-making must be prepared to develop better generalizations.

Alternative Policies: Conditions of Innovation

In the end, what men want most from public policies are conditions that improve their lives and honor their concepts of the good life. The content of public policy is the object of the struggle. The great debates of legislative bodies, campaigns, speeches of leading political figures, and the complaints and demands of citizens are primarily about the policies of government. Too often political studies focus on activity rather than discussion.

Public policy proposals are intended to affect the lives of people; thus, in democracies discussion often concerns those whose lives will be affected.

---

[40] Andrew Shonfield, *Modern Capitalism* (London: Oxford University Press, 1965), p. 328.

[41] E. E. Schattschneider, *The Semi-Sovereign People* (New York: Holt, Rinehart and Winston, Inc., 1960), p. 41.

[42] Wallace Sayre and Herbert Kaufman, *Governing New York City* (New York: W. W. Norton and Company, Inc., 1960), p. 716.

[43] Robert A. Dahl, *A Preface to Democratic Theory* (Chicago: University of Chicago Press, 1956), p. 146.

[44] *Ibid.*, p. 150.

Much political debate is an exploration of the consequences of alternative policies for dealing with a particular problem. As might be expected, each citizen and politician interprets the consequences in terms of his own values and information. Each proposal may be scrutinized by politicians to see who suffers and who benefits, by administrators to ascertain relative costs and efficiency. And some segments of the population may attempt to persuade others that the effects will not be worth the cost. Both intended and unintended consequences will be predicted and publicized in the effort to mobilize support.

Few public policy alternatives affect all members of a society and still fewer, if any, affect all equally. Most policy disputes are waged by a relatively small proportion of the population. Those whose most important concerns are not touched are indifferent, and it is difficult to mobilize them into action. Unless the obviously affected can translate their concerns into terms salient to others, they are likely to go unassisted. While all men are more or less interdependent, these interdependencies are often indirect and subject to time-lags which prevent consequences from being perceived or felt until months, or perhaps years, have passed. Long-run predictions of promised benefits or burdens are not powerful motivations to immediate action in politics. Present consequences are more easily perceived and, therefore, more powerful goads to action. Besides, most citizens have sufficient common sense to know that long-run prophecy is a dangerous business; the unexpected is usually to be expected!

One of the more interesting, yet little-known, aspects of policy-making concerns the range of available alternatives in various political systems. In the short-run, it would seem that the constraints are quite impressive, i.e., the effective range of choice is very limited. The limit, in terms of number and variety, may expand over longer periods of time. As we have noted, constraints on alternatives are many, including value commitments, beliefs about limited possibilities, resource limitations and the nature of the problems confronting a society. No society—even the most free— grants its citizens a complete choice of all known alternatives. Communist societies do not permit choices of democratic and capitalist solutions to very many citizens, while the democracies of the West do not often permit citizens choices that include fascist and communist solutions. If it were possible to put all contending alternatives on a ballot or agenda of action, it is doubtful that any single choice could be made that would garner the support of other than a small minority. Viewed this way, the limitation of alternatives is one way to 'force' a majority of support. This may seem very undemocratic, but it is logical and workable.

Still, public policies are made and do change. Innovations are introduced and accepted. In Table 9-2 we have summarized major tax revisions since 1945 in the United States as an illustration of but one major area of public policy. Such a table could easily be duplicated for almost any policy area.

Table 9-2

Major Tax Revisions: 1945-1965 (U.S.A.)

1945   Individual income tax rates cut about 5 per cent
       Corporation rates cut to a maximum of 38 per cent
       Excess profits tax repealed

1948   Individual rates reduced
       Personal exemptions increased

1950   The 1946 and 1948 cuts in individual rates rescinded; 1945 rates restored
       Maximum corporation rates raised; excess profits tax reimposed

1951   Individual income tax rates raised by about 11 per cent
       Corporation income tax rates raised to 52 per cent
       Several excise taxes increased (liquor, beer, cigarettes, gasoline, etc.)

1953   The 1951 increase in individual rates and excess profits tax allowed to expire

1954   The 1951 corporation income and excise tax rate increases of 1951, scheduled
       to expire, were extended for one year

1956   Gas tax raised from 2¢ to 3¢ per gallon
       Other excise taxes increased to finance long-range highway program

1958   Excise tax on transportation of freight repealed
       Small business given $260 million in tax relief

1959   Gas tax raised from 3¢ to 4¢ per gallon
       Taxes on life insurance companies raised by $200 million

1962   Investment tax credit, along with depreciation rules, revised, benefiting
       business by $2 billion or more
       Excise tax on rail and bus fares repealed
       Excise tax on air travel cut in half

1964   Most far-reaching postwar tax legislation enacted
       Individual liabilities reduced $9.1 billion
       Corporation liabilities cut $2.4 billion
       Lower minimum standard deduction enacted, removing 1.5 million persons
       from the tax rolls
       Dividend credit repealed
       Deductions tightened for certain state and local excise taxes, but broadened
       in others

1965   First general revision of excise taxes since World War II enacted
       Law provided a $4.7 billion cut in federal excise taxes, eliminating almost
       one-third of existing federal excises

Source: Abridged from *Federal Economic Policy: 1945-1965* (Washington, D.C.: Congressional Quarterly Service, 1966), p. 7.

Innovations in policy or the persistence of the old is undoubtedly one of the more important, yet least understood, areas of political life. We have quite a folklore about the conditions or correlates of such change or the lack of it. It has been said, for example,that 'vested interests' resist new demands and old elites favor their own kind. But we have little knowledge about which systems are most conducive to policy change, nor do we know the specific variety of conditions under which policy alterations will occur or be accepted. In any case, allow us to cite a few propositions—again of an illustrative sort.

1. "In the Soviet Union . . . once a group emerges victorious . . . it not infrequently reverses itself and adopts the policies which had been advocated by its opponents."[45]

2. "Innovation [in the U.S.S.R. and U.S.A.] is easier in times of trouble and crisis."[46]

3. "Whereas the slow process of piecemeal amendment typically alters major policies in the United States, in the Soviet Union policy reversals are often far-reaching, dramatic, and highly visible."[47]

4. "The world of officialdom [in New York City] is often prudent when confronted with recommendations for innovation."[48]

5. "If plans are radical, they seldom survive; if they survive, they seldom work major changes in the system."[49]

6. ". . . every change tends to produce further change in a kind of slow-moving chain-reaction."[50]

7. "The exposé or highly publicized scandal is also a cause of change."[51]

8. ". . . the first reactions to 'pressing' problems [in Latin America] are of a stopgap, remedial character, taken with a minimum of understanding of the problem."[52]

9. ". . . when . . . a policy has proven disappointing, it will be

---

[45] Zbigniew Brzezinski and Samuel P. Huntington, *op. cit.*, p. 193.

[46] *Ibid.*, p. 229.

[47] *Ibid.*, p. 230.

[48] Wallace Sayre and Herbert Kaufman, *op. cit.*, p. 718.

[49] *Ibid.*, p. 719.

[50] *Ibid.*, p. 724.

[51] *Ibid.*

[52] Albert O. Hirschman, *Journeys Toward Progress* (New York: The Twentieth Century Fund, 1963), p. 239.

emphatically cast off, ridiculed, described as an utter failure and abomination . . . [Latin America]."[53]

10. "This pattern of learning [Latin America] makes it likely that policy-making will exhibit wide swings."[54]

11. "Wide swings in policy-making are in fact strongly in evidence [in Latin America]."[55]

12. "Frequently . . . swings in official ideology are far wider than actual swings in policy [Latin America]."[56]

13. "An almost morbid insistence on declaring past policy-making to have been a series of half-hearted, piecemeal efforts, doomed to failure, is one of the most pronounced common characteristics of our three stories [Brazil, Colombia, Chile]."[57]

These propositions may be more or less correct in the light of further experience, but they do serve as convenient examples of the type of propositions future political scientists will need to devise and test on an even wider basis. Hopefully, in the future we will be able to list the conditions of policy changes according to types of policies, forms of change, structures of governments and alternatives of policy processes.

From what we know about the rates of policy change, it would seem that change is constantly taking place but that long periods of fairly low rates are interspersed by sudden rapid changes induced by crises or a sense of urgency. For example, American policies for the advancement of space technology were moderate until the Russians put Sputnik in the sky. One major court decision (Brown vs. Board of Education of Topeka, 1954) seemed to stimulate more persistent demands for civil rights for black Americans. We would be unwise, however, to generalize too much about the patterns of policy change, for each area of policy may be subject to a different configuration of elements. As yet, we have little comparative evidence in sufficient detail to generalize about different nations and governments. On the basis of social science theory we might expect that policy flexibility is a function of political processes and cultural values. Are nations whose culture places a high value upon change more apt to innovate? Are technologically modernized nations more apt to consider change than less scientifically oriented countries? Are nations with modernizing elites more pragmatic than those nations whose leaders are content with the status quo? Social scientists, especially economists and political scientists, are extremely adept at detecting obstacles to change in developing countries. As these in-

---

[53] *Ibid.*, p. 241.

[54] *Ibid.*

[55] *Ibid.*

[56] *Ibid.*

[57] *Ibid.*, p. 243.

quiries proceed, we should learn far more about the possibilities and probabilities of policy innovation in these other contexts. Right now there is much on the agenda of research, not only for the new nations but also for the older ones of the West and East.

Case Studies in Policy-Making

Case Study #5   The Decision-Making Process in Levittown, New Jersey

One of the most famous 'planned towns' in the United States is Levittown, New Jersey. It was one of several suburban communities erected by Levitt during the post World War II period. Our account is based on an excellent analysis presented by Herbert J. Gans,[58] sociologist, who lived in Levittown from 1958 to 1960. Much of his book is about things other than the political, but an unusually perceptive set of chapters (Chapters 6, 12-15) are on political life. We draw especially upon Chapter 13 to quote a few clearly stated propositions which Gans notes as peculiar characteristics of the decision-making process in the various public bodies of Levittown.

1. "Government is normally passive; it waits for issues to come to its attention."[59]

2. "Government avoids or postpones decisions that cannot be resolved without conflict or that expose the gap between the actual and the performing government."[60]

3. "Government gravitates toward decisions with immediate payoffs, avoiding those which produce mainly long-run effects."[61]

4. "The decision-making process is structured so that, whenever possible, every elected official is free—or feels he is free—to reach the decision dictated by his conscience and by his desire to benefit the community."[62]

Through a combination of observation and deduction, Gans describes the outcomes of such decision-making processes.[63] In his judgment:

5. Large or influential blocs of voters which either had constant contact with government or could apply pressure received more of the benefits.

---

[58] *The Levittowners: How People Live and Politic in Suburbia* (New York: Random House, Inc., 1967).

[59] *Ibid.,* p. 333.

[60] *Ibid.,* p. 334.

[61] *Ibid.*

[62] *Ibid.*

[63] These policy outcomes are abridged from Chap. 13 of Gans' *The Levittowners.*

6. Unorganized residents were favored if their demands were modest and not likely to arouse more powerful groups.

7. New businesses were welcomed because they contributed to the taxes.

8. Decision-makers supported each other's pet projects.

9. Decision-making bodies always united to defend their own members.

10. Although responding to the demands of a small number of citizens, many decisions were remarkably responsive to the rest of the citizenry, particularly the lower middle-class majority.

These generalizations about decision processes and outcomes were derived by direct observation, not fancy techniques. Unfortunately, most community studies deal primarily with decision processes and only secondarily with outcomes. Many of these studies offer contrasts to the Gans observations, but more comprehensive generalizations are only beginning to be developed.[64]

Case Study #6   The Situation in Montegrano, Italy

In spite of the obvious or apparent shortcomings of political processes in many American cities, some problems are being considered and many solutions are being proposed and acted upon. This is not the case everywhere in the world. For example, Edward C. Banfield in a study of a small rural community in southern Italy claims that the collective decision-making process in that community is hardly existent.[65] According to Banfield, who lived in the community for nine months during 1954-55, collective decisions were impossible to arrive at because people would simply not cooperate. His inquiry became a search for the reasons why cooperation is so difficult, not only for these rural Italians but for many people throughout the world. His answer was simply if not easily arrived at; he called it a "predictive hypothesis" which people acted upon. The rule is as follows: "Maximize the material, short-run advantage of the nuclear family; assume that all others will do likewise."[66] The person who followed this rule was termed an 'amoral familist,' a label which may carry its own moral connotations. From this basic premise, Banfield deduced seventeen typical kinds of responses on the part of citizens and politicians. We shall not enumerate all of them; a few should serve to stimulate one's curiosity to look into the book.

---

[64] Cf. Terry N. Clark, ed., *Community Structure and Decision-Making: Comparative Analyses* (San Francisco: Chandler Publishing Company, 1968).

[65] *The Moral Basis of a Backward Society* (Glencoe, Ill.: The Free Press, 1958).

[66] *Ibid.*, p. 85.

1. "In a society of amoral familists, no one will further the interest of the group or community except as it is to his private advantage to do so."[67]

2. "In a society of amoral familists only officials will concern themselves with public affairs, for only they are paid to do so. For a private citizen to take a serious interest in a public problem will be regarded as abnormal and even improper."[68]

3. "In a society of amoral familists there will be few checks on officials, for checking on officials will be the business of other officials."[69]

4. "The amoral familist who is an office-holder will take bribes when he can get away with it. But whether he takes bribes or not, it will be assumed by the society of amoral familists that he does."[70]

5. "In a society of amoral familists the weak will favor a regime which will maintain order with a strong hand."[71]

6. "In a society of amoral familists, party workers will sell their services to the highest bidders. Their tendency to change sides will make for sudden shifts in strength of the parties at the polls."[72]

Public life is not very attractive in this Italian town. (Montegrano is a fictitious name.) Apparently, there are many such towns throughout the world. Another town which has been studied is a French village in the commune of Peyrane, in southern France.[73] The author, Laurence Wylie, also finds life there family-centered. Communal life is basically non-cooperative, which makes collective choice extremely difficult. Oscar Lewis, the famous American anthropologist, has observed many of the same features in his classic study of Tepoztlán, Mexico.[74] Public policy-making is inefficient, ridden with graft, exploited by leaders, and the inhabitants generally show a widespread suspicion of politicians, politics, parties and government. Morroe Berger's study of the Arab countries confirms these attitudes for that area of the world.[75] He describes the Arabs as highly egotistical, assertive, rivalrous, intense, secretive, suspicious, formalistic and

---

[67] *Ibid.*

[68] *Ibid.,* p. 87.

[69] *Ibid.,* p. 88.

[70] *Ibid.,* p. 94.

[71] *Ibid.,* p. 96.

[72] *Ibid.,* p. 103.

[73] Laurence Wylie, *Village in the Vaucluse* (Cambridge: Harvard University Press, 1961).

[74] *Life in a Mexican Village* (Urbana: University of Illinois Press, 1963).

[75] *The Arab World Today* (Garden City, N.Y.: Doubleday and Company, Inc., 1962).

polite, and fatalistic. As a result of these cultural traits they want the government to do much for them but remain profoundly suspicious, have little sense of civic pride, have much 'free floating' aggression, little respect for law and are obsequious before officials. They cannot easily cooperate and, in this regard, are much like those in the Mexican, French and Italian communities that Lewis, Wylie, and Banfield observed.

If these various characterizations are at all reliable it becomes clear that public policy-making and cooperative effort are not easily undertaken. Perhaps some special social conditions must be found before widespread cooperation is facilitated. Americans apparently have some of these conditions, for organized cooperative effort is more commonplace in the U.S. Lest we engage in too much self-congratulation, recall some of the generalizations advanced by Gans. American policy processes seldom match our highest ideals; they compare favorably, however, with those found in many parts of the world, including Europe.

Case Study #7   Policy-Making in Latin America

American scholars have rather belatedly begun to study Latin American political processes and, as might be expected, they are making up for lost time. Many of the earlier stereotypes are being abandoned as our cultural biases are confronted by reality. Drastic re-interpretations of Latin American politics and policy-making, in particular, are being made. Perhaps this case study will soon be outdated; in any event, it is based on the very impressive interpretations of Charles W. Anderson.[76]

We have extracted a number of propositions from his study. According to Anderson, Latin American policy-making can be appropriately described as follows:

1. Policy-makers must proceed in highly tentative ways because their legitimacy is not firm, their information about their societies and its problems is very inadequate, and information about citizen demands is limited and generally unreliable.

2. Most of the citizenry do not make demands on the polity and, if they do, such demands are couched in highly ambiguous terms.

3. The political process has a tendency to 'radicalize' citizen demands and proposals.

4. As demands are aggregated and processed they often become totally repugnant to their supporters.

5. The policy-making process tends to obfuscate rather than simplify and reduce policy alternatives.

---

[76] *Politics and Economic Change in Latin America* (Princeton: D. Van Nostrand Company, Inc., 1967).

6. Political discourse tends to be grandiloquent and abstract, rather than directed to practical problem-solving.

7. Policy alternatives tend to be treated as elements of grandiose ideologies: comprehensive, logical, intricate and unrealistic or utopian.

8. Policy responses tend to fluctuate between daring solutions and hopelessness.

9. Governments rarely have the resources and capacity to enact their typically grandiose visions of reform.[77]

These generalizations are hardly a complete inventory of Anderson's conception of Latin American politics, but they are sufficient to convey a feeling about how policy-making is conducted in these political systems. One must remember, however, that nations do change and these generalizations may not hold forever. One must also be aware of the level of generality; these statements are meant to depict a general state of affairs throughout some twenty nations and not the specific processes and outcomes of a single nation. Finally, as in most of our case studies, we remind the reader that a full-scale analysis of the reasons for each state of affairs is not presented in much detail. These policy processes and associated outcomes are functions of culture, specific sets of political institutions, a history of events and the particular groupings of policy-makers. The reader is encouraged to read the original sources and to check these generalizations against other cases and policy situations in comparable or contrasting settings.

Case Study #8   Policy-Making in India

The 470 million population of India is governed by democratic procedures, but the country's economic growth is controlled by a planned economy. The desire to maintain democracy and economic growth has posed some painful dilemmas for Indian policy-planners, politicians and citizenry. The policy-makers want comprehensive, rational plans while most politicians and citizens want government responsive to local, particularistic demands. As Myron Weiner puts it in his interesting study,[78] the local politician makes demands on the government and the government fails to respond. The more active element among the citizens then turns to violence to which the government does respond. As a result, the citizenry is convinced that mass pressures do move conservative governments. On the other hand, planners are often unwilling to listen or unwilling to act if they do listen. As a result, the planner remains uninformed and is unable to assess

---

[77] These generalizations constitute our interpretation of Anderson's discussion in Chap. 5.
[78] *The Politics of Scarcity: Public Pressure and Political Response in India* (Chicago: University of Chicago Press, 1962).

the consequences of his acts and choices. If violence occurs, he is surprised; moreover, the act of violence confirms his view that the political process is an irrational expression of particularistic group demands. As a consequence, many Indian citizens do not vote or participate in ordinary civic activities; instead, they engage in mass activities and violence in the streets.

Weiner describes the situation somewhat as follows.[79] Note that he emphasizes the role of interest groups in his interpretation of policy-making processes:

1. Political parties have attempted to control interest groups, but have not succeeded.
2. Organized interests have only a negative impact on policy, i.e., they can only prevent things from happening, not bring about new policies.
3. Organized interests tend to concern themselves with the administration of programs rather than the formulation of policy goals.
4. Government officials respond readily to some pressures but not to others.
5. Governments respond more readily in policy-making to demands stemming from within the leading party (Congress Party) than to mass demands and petitions.
6. Demand-making procedures have not been highly institutionalized.

These six generalizations about policy-making in India concentrate on the role of interest groups as they affect modernization. Weiner makes no claim of offering a full-scale description. Still, we can detect some variances with policy-making in, say, Levittown, U.S.A., and Montegrano, Italy. In the former, we find government much more responsive to citizen demands, while in Montegrano we find hardly any democratic tendencies in policy-making. For further variations and similarities, the reader should consult the original sources and also more recent cases and studies which may demonstrate other modes of policy change or provide further explanations.

Problems and Applications

1. What are some of the crucial differences between private decision-making in a marketplace and collective decision-making in a political system? How would you evaluate each from the standpoint of:

---

[79] *Ibid.*, Chaps. 1 and 9 contain the analyses from which the six propositions were drawn.

    a. The politician and businessman
    b. The citizen and consumer
    c. The political scientist and economist

2. Under what conditions might knowing the persons who make decisions be of little consequence if one is concerned with predicting policy choices?

3. Why are the *numbers* of alternatives in policy-making important to these political actors: elective officials, radicals, ordinary voters?

4. What consequences might flow from a situation in which a city council, consisting of 100 members, permitted each member to introduce a single bill on every issue and have it voted upon? Are there any other facts or considerations you must know in order to deduce your predictions? Why are they significant?

5. What resources for influencing policy outcomes seem most subject to change generally? In the U.S.A.? In Latin America? In India?

6. Why would some (or many) policy-makers tend to delay making their policy choices? When would they least want to delay?

7. Many critics have argued that there is a power structure in the U.S. which controls policy-making. How could one seek to demonstrate the case in terms of: normative constraints, command of resources, selection of decision-makers, uses of information?

8. Which is easier: to change a conservative public policy to a more liberal one or to alter liberal policies in a conservative direction? When and why? What sorts of policies can you think of to make your case?

9. Comment upon the following propositions:
    a. Politicians prefer policies with short-run or immediate payoffs.
    b. On matters of specific policy, majorities seldom rule or choose.
    c. Policy-making is a process better characterized as muddling through than as rational choice.
    d. The costs of policy innovation tend to be very high.

10. What similarities in policy-making can you detect in the four case studies presented in this chapter? How can one explain these similarities in view of the manifestly different societies and political systems?

Bibliographical Notes

A good volume for this and the next chapter is Charles E. Lindblom's *The Policy-Making Process*, Englewood Cliffs, N.J.: Prentice-Hall, Inc., 1968, which is a brief attempt to organize the subjects of study in policy-making. While it may be hard to find, a pamphlet by Harold D. Lasswell on *The Decision Process; Seven Categories of Functional Analysis,* College Park, Md.: University of Maryland, Bureau of Governmental Research,

1956, should be noted. We list his basic categories in Table 9-1. In a few pages he touches upon many of the themes in this chapter. The political scientist Richard C. Snyder has become identified with a rather detailed conceptual scheme to study decision-making in foreign policy, although few have carried out its ambitious mapping of factors in actual decision studies. It is presented in the chapter, "Decision-Making as an Approach to the Study of International Politics," in *Foreign Policy Decision-Making,* edited by R. C. Snyder, H. W. Bruck and Burton Sapin, New York: The Free Press of Glencoe, 1962. Study the diagrams since they are probably the best means of depicting the conceptual framework. Another very useful classification of policy variables, which presents the most significant propositions about administrative decision-making up to the time of its publicaton, is *Organizations* by Herbert A. Simon and James March, New York: John Wiley and Sons, Inc., 1958. Note especially their chapters on the cognitive limits on rationality and on planning and innovation.

K. W. Deutsch in *The Nerves of Government,* New York: The Free Press of Glencoe, 1963, presents a model of decision-making which very consciously applies modern communication theory, and treats policy as problem-solving involving special forms of information use. On the last page is a very fancy cybernetic-type flow diagram with a detailed appendix explaining the forms of information flow and the decision areas as applied to foreign policy. Chapters 9, 10 and 11 bear most directly on government policy-making, and the comments on learning capacity and creativity in politics offer an interesting perspective on information use. The most thorough attempt to bring together what is known about the role of information in actual policy cases is found in Harold L. Wilensky's *Organizational Intelligence: Knowledge in Government and Industry,* New York: Basic Books, Inc., 1967. Especially useful are his reflections on the influence of hierarchy on intelligence systems and the uses or abuses of secrecy and expertise.

Decision processes can be studied in terms of rational formal models of choice which appear quite removed from the apparent irrationalities of politics. Indeed the contrast between the two is often of greatest interest to analysts. For a simplified version of what scientific decision theory offers, see the very readable introduction by Irwin D. J. Bross entitled *Design for Decision,* New York: The Macmillan Company, 1953. It borrows from mathematical statistics to elucidate the problems of predictions, probability and uncertainty, and the use of models for making choices.

A link with the scientific approach to policy-making can be found in the increasing use of explicit decision models in the operation of administrative organizations. A good sampling of contributions will be found in a volume entitled *The Making of Decisions: A Reader in Administrative Behavior,* New York: The Free Press of Glencoe, 1964, edited by William J. Gore and J. W. Dyson. Even a casual skimming will reveal how often the discussion deals with information and uncertainty in the more rationally oriented treatments, but when political situations are directly treated, the vocabulary changes to actors, values and norms, authority, demands and conflict. For those impatient with the seeming intractabilities of politics, there may be some comfort in Charles Lindblom's famous essay, "The Science of Muddling Through," in that same volume. The more rational possibilities of political strategy are further developed by Charles Lindblom and David Braybrooke in *A Strategy of Decision*, New York: The Free Press of Glencoe, 1963, and by A. O. Hirschman in *Journeys Toward Progress: Studies of Economic Policy-Making in Latin America*, New York: The Twentieth Century Fund, 1963. These studies can be contrasted with the more technical and scientific treatments of policy planning by Jan Tinbergen, *Central Planning*, New Haven: Yale University Press, 1964; Wolfgang F. Stopler, *Planning Without Facts: Lessons in Resource Allocation from Nigeria's Development*, Cambridge: Harvard University Press, 1966; and Charles J. Hitch and Roland N. McKean, *The Economics of Defense in the Nuclear Age*, Cambridge: Harvard University Press, 1960.

The political elements in decision-making are more typically tackled by political analysts who very often possess only the insights of a good journalist. In America this approach has been institutionalized in what is known as the 'case study,' an often detailed yet sometimes exciting account of how some decision was made. Because the complex events are explored at close range, the writer usually concentrates on the idiosyncracies of policy actors, their ambitions and interests. But there have been some more general contributions that we should note. E. E. Schattschneider's *Politics, Pressures, and the Tariff*, Englewood Cliffs, N.J.: Prentice-Hall, Inc., 1935, is a classic of its kind. Schattschneider ingeniously uses what are considered rather dull formal records for impressive theories of activation, directions of interests and successful coalition-building in policy-making. A recent major case study made a comparable contribution using more modern tools to analyze the very same kind of issue, now given the label 'trade' rather than 'tariff.' The impressive modern analysis is *American Business and Public Policy: The Politics of Foreign Trade*, New York: Atherton Press, 1964, authored by Raymond A. Bauer, Ithiel de Sola Pool and Lewis Anthony Dexter. Using the sample survey, attitudinal and communications analysis, these scholars have been able to bring to light the less visible perceptions, expectations and interactions which accompanied the official treatment of recent foreign trade policies. They have very interesting conclusions about the nature and role of general attitudes and ideologies, the popular conceptions of ideologies regarding modern policy issues, the role of economic associations and elected representatives, and the 'poor' lobbyist who apparently has a most frustrating role, whether his side wins or loses. This book must be studied by the policy strategist who wishes to devise a plan of action rising above the level of applied folklore. Few other studies of a major policy decision draw such important generalizations although many add useful insights. Warner Schilling's study of defense budgeting, "The Politics of National Defense: Fiscal 1950," supplies some useful examples of normative and information constraints as felt by officials confronting proposals for greatly increased defense spending. The account appears in *Strategy, Politics, and Defense Budgets,* New York: Columbia University Press, 1962, by Warner R. Schilling, Paul Y. Hammond and Glenn H. Snyder. The role of political leaders in the definition of issues is very well illustrated by Alan K. McAdams in *Power and Politics in Labor Legislation,* New York: Columbia University Press, 1964. The immediate case involved the 'labor racket' hearings of a congressional committee. Coverage by the mass communications media became an important means of crystallizing public support (indignation) on behalf of regulation. Too often the elements of a case study are so complex and special that the conclusion suggests only a conglomerate of reasons why a policy was made. We might call instances such as this 'pluralism by default.' A classic conclusion of this sort was offered in the last chapter of Stephen Bailey's *Congress Makes a Law; the Story Behind the Employment Act of 1946,* New York: Columbia University Press, 1950. Bailey asserts that in legislative systems there are too many participants, so he pleads for a more simplified form of political responsibility.

A more traditional form of policy study in this country centers on the particular institutional setting through which policies are processed. Just as the founding fathers demarcated three branches of government, so does most of this literature treat these governmental bodies separately. But one rather perceptive and now neglected classic did try to justify separate treatments of policy-making on more purely functional grounds: Frank Goodnow, *Politics and Administration,* New York: The Macmillan Company, 1960. This is worth studying for an appreciation of the activities and processes taking place within the institutional setting. More systematic and empirical is Lawrence Chamberlain's study of policy initiatives in *The President, Congress and Legislation,* New York: Columbia University Press, 1946. Recent policy studies, using the institutional perspective, tend to see more politics in administration than the formal organizational boundaries suggest. One of the best examinations of political processes in the administrative branch is the collection of articles by Samuel Huntington in *The Common Defense: Strategic Programs in National Politics,* New York: Columbia University Press, 1961. Those who tend to think that 'politics' is only engaged in by party politicians may be shocked when they realize that even dedicated civilian and military officials in the defense establishment resort to political practices. One should also consider a most interesting study which provides a contrasting case in the legislative branch. *The Government of the Atom* by Harold P. Green and

Alan Rosenthal, New York: Atherton Press, 1963, shows how one relatively young congressional committee has effectively captured administrative functions that tend to be more innovative than the agency it is supposed to be supervising. There are several good recent works which amass much information on the President's many policy roles, but we shall confine ourselves to one which has contributed greatly to our own analytic perspectives —*Presidential Power: The Politics of Leadership,* New York: John Wiley and Sons, Inc., 1960, by Richard E. Neustadt. A very readable discussion of the combative politics taking place in Congress is Bertram Gross' *The Legislative Struggle,* New York: McGraw-Hill Company, Inc., 1953. Gross views the Congress as an arena for 'group struggles,' the kind of combat of which others claim to see too little. One very perceptive contribution on policy processes stands out among what are called the 'organizational behavior' studies. This is Philip Selznick's *TVA and the Grass Roots: A Study in the Sociology of Formal Organization,* Berkeley: University of California Press, 1953, best known for its analysis of how an agency may resort to 'co-optation' as a strategy for saving its policy program. The study is a classic in its contrast of official doctrine with the 'realities' of political power in the organizational environment. Treating the judicial branch in terms of policy processes is an even later departure. Glendon Schubert's *Judicial Policy-Making,* Chicago: Scott, Foresman and Company, 1965, very nicely makes use of the newer techniques of research in formulating this perspective for judicial studies.

We shall mention only very briefly some major works on policy actors, for these are also dealt with in the chapter on the division of labor. David Truman's *The Governmental Process,* New York: Alfred A. Knopf, Inc., 1951, presented the major framework for the 'group' study of policy processes, although Earl Latham's first chapter in *The Group Basis of Politics,* Ithaca, N. Y.: Cornell University Press, 1952, further develops the approach by expanding on the idea that officialdom has special interests and very strategic roles in the processes of group conflict. A contrasting perspective views elites as major policy actors rather than organized groups. *The Comparative Study of Elites* by Harold D. Lasswell, Daniel Lerner and C. Easton Rothwell, Stanford: Stanford University Press, 1952, very briefly outlines this approach and the early literature. Most important for students of American policy-making is Gabriel Almond's assessment of the relation of elites and other publics to foreign policies entitled *The American People and Foreign Policy,* New York: Harcourt, Brace and Company, Inc., 1950. Whereas Almond saw several elites and 'attentive publics,' C. Wright Mills postulates a much more ominous 'power elite' which dominates major foreign and military policy, with command of crucial institutions, resources and, therefore, policy processes. Compare Mills' *The Power Elite,* London: Oxford University Press, 1956, to the contributions of Floyd Hunter, who attempts more systematic evidence to buttress a similar point of view in *Community Power Structure,* Chapel Hill: University of North Carolina Press, 1953, and in *Top Leadership, U.S.A.,* Chapel Hill: University of North Carolina Press, 1959. The 'power study' literature is enormous, and the debate over definitions and methods will most certainly continue so we shall not detail all its phases here.

Little in the way of a systematic treatment of political resources is available except in relation to particular settings. We recommend Robert Dahl's study of New Haven policy-making, *Who Governs?* New Haven: Yale University Press, 1961, especially Book IV, "The Distribution of Political Resources," and Book V, "The Use of Political Resources," where he considers not only the distribution but the non-use of potential resources in relevant policy situations. Less explicit about measuring resources, but very relevant about their use is Edward C. Banfield's *Political Influence,* New York: The Free Press of Glencoe, 1961, especially Chapter 11, "Concerting Action by Influence."

Studies of policy-making in foreign nations are less plentiful. One of the better ones, however, is Zbigniew Brzezinski and Samuel P. Huntington, *Political Power: USA/USSR,* New York: The Viking Press, Inc., 1963-64. Chapters 4-9 are devoted to policy-making in general and comparative case studies of particular policy problems and their solutions. Sidney Ploss in *Conflict and Decision-Making in Soviet Russia,* Princeton: Princeton University Press, 1965, deals with a case study of agricultural policy-making. He concludes that Soviet policy is strongly affected by "whirlpools of vendetta, patronage, opportunism, and rival connections" (p. 278). We have frequently mentioned the paucity of certain types of information about totalitarian societies and again emphasize the difficulty of gathering sound data on policy-making in a land such as the Soviet Union. Much is known about certain aspects of life, but rarely do we learn about actual policy-making. One book which does at least describe the formal framework of policy choice is Derek J. R. Scott's *Russian Political Institutions,* New York: Frederick A. Praeger, Inc., 1961.

Some interesting work on France has been done during recent years. A book by Nathan Leites, *On the Game of Politics in France,* Stanford: Stanford University Press, 1959, recounts certain legislative activities during the 1951-58 period. Leites stresses the role of norms or rules of the game in shaping political behavior and obstructing policy-making. The British have also tried the American approach of group theory with some interesting results. For example, there is Graham Wooton's *The Politics of Influence,* Cambridge: Harvard University Press, 1963, and Allen Potter's *Organized Groups in British National Politics,* London: Faber and Faber, Ltd., 1961. Two American students of British politics who have interpreted the British policy process in terms of interest groups are Samuel H. Beer, *British Politics in the Collectivist Age,* New York: Alfred A. Knopf, Inc.,

1965, and Harry Eckstein, *Pressure Group Politics: The Case of the British Medical Association*, London: Allen and Unwin Ltd., 1960. The former volume is an historical account and wide-ranging interpretation; the Eckstein analysis is a case study of a single interest group. Read the materials on Britain along with a most interesting French study by Charles K. Warner, *The Winegrowers of France and the Government Since 1875*, New York: Columbia University Press, 1960. The Warner book is interesting not only because it deals with a world famous group of farmers, but also because it shows how interest groups in another country participate in policy formation in ways peculiar to the culture and economy of the country.

Kern vs. Occidental

'Power grab' charged, denie

Compromise on Mutual-Fund Bill by SEC,
Palo Alto Times, May 11, 1967, Palo Alto, California

Industry Groups Is Sought by Sparkman

The Wall Street Journal, June 20, 1967, New York, New York

Adamant HHH Decla

U.S. Apparent Winner No Deal With Wallac
The Oregonian, July 23, 1968, Portland, Oregon

In Steel Price Battle

The Oregonian, Aug. 8, 1968, Portland, Oregon

Battling and Barteri
The National Observer, July 22, 1968, Silver Springs, Maryland

Russ-Pakistan Arms Deal

The Oregonian, July 23, 1968, Portland, Oregon

ad Bargain

*The Oregonian,
July 26, 1968,
Portland, Oregon*

NIXON'S 'COALITION CABINET'

Newsweek, Oct. 21, 1968, Washington, D.C.

Just keep in mind one
cardinal rule. The deal you
offer must be profitable.
Americans don't come to your
country because it's a nice
place." *The New York Times, May 19, 1968,*
New York, New York

'Let's Put T
Power-Suck
Against a W

*The National Observer, July 23, 196
Silver Springs, Maryland*

For Every Action a Reaction

The New York Times, May 19, 1968, New York, New York

Receive Benefits In Exchange
The Oregonian, Aug. 6, 1968, Portland, Oregon

The GOP Stra
*The Oregonian, June 6, 1968,
Portland, Oregon*

Negroes Demand Greater Influence

The Oregonian, Aug. 6, 1968, Portland, Oregon

"The market really gets shook
there's a Government-business fi
snapped one stock analyst, expla
last week's steady loss in stock pr
The National Observer, Aug. 5, 1968, Silver Springs, Maryland

"IT WAS JUST like a power play in politics . . . We
ck the knife in the back and kept twisting until it
elded. . ." *Eugene Register-Guard, June 26, 1968, Eugene, Oregon*

'Knock On Head' Seen
Good Way To End Riots

Coalition in the Hous

The Oregonian, July 22, 1968, Portland, Oregon

Czechs Pay A Price

*The Oregonian, Aug. 6, 1968,
Portland, Oregon*

South's Democrats Voting With C
Despite Ford's Rejecting Such T

The New York Times, Aug. 8, 1967, New York, New York

Chapter 10

Policy-Making Processes

How are resources allocated? How are policy choices involving goods and services made? How are tax and financial or revenue choices made? How do systems handle problems of adaptation and change? In short, how are public decisions made which involve such important outcomes? In some ways these are the most interesting questions in political science.

The Problem Oversimplified

The important question of how policies are made may be introduced with a deliberately oversimplified problem. Suppose a public budget is to be decided. Three major questions must be resolved: the overall size of the public budget, allocations or priorities among public goods, and time preferences for expected returns of expenditure. These issues will not come up one at a time, as is often the case when treating them analytically. In order to illustrate some of our main points, we have devised a three-man committee as a miniature political system; each member has his own set of preferences on the alternatives for each issue. The problem is one of attaining agreement, i.e., getting a budget passed.

Suppose you were member A (or choose the member closest to your own typical preferences): How would you proceed to reach agreement with the other two, especially in a manner which would most often

include your own preferences? What would you want to know in order
to proceed? Consider how you could make this a simple 'game' of budget-
making which three actors would actually play to a conclusion.

CHOICE #1   SIZE OF THE PUBLIC BUDGET

Policy Preference Order

	1st	2nd	3rd
Member A	larger	same	smaller
Member B	smaller	same	larger
Member C	same	larger	smaller

CHOICE #2   PRIORITIES AMONG PUBLIC GOODS

Policy Preference Order

	1st	2nd	3rd
Member A	welfare	highways	conservation
Member B	defense	FBI	business subsidy
Member C	conservation	welfare	highways

CHOICE #3   TIME PREFERENCES

Policy Preference Order

	1st	2nd	3rd
Member A	present	immediate future	distant future
Member B	distant future	present	immediate future
Member C	immediate future	distant future	present

Each of these hypothetical situations, or choice problems, illustrates
some important preliminary considerations in public policy-making. First,
it is evident that the members not only have divergent preferences but
also order them in different ways; what may be a first priority for one
member may be the last for another. Indeed, if our models permitted, we
might have included a negative set of preferences, i.e., policies individuals
will *not* accept. These models contain only *acceptable* alternative policies.
Second, the actors in some models (#1 and #3) list the same alternatives
while those in #2 have preferences not found on the lists of the others. Thus,
in some situations, decision-makers may not agree even on alternatives.
When a greater number of alternatives are offered for choice, a different
set of consequences is posed for the individual member, the entire system
and the system's methods of resolving choice dilemmas. Third, these models
presume that members are permitted preferences and are allowed to participate in the resolution of differences. But nothing is mentioned regarding actual rules for decision-making; we do not know how policies will be
decided. Different decisional rules will produce different results. In a
committee which decides on the basis of simple majorities, collective choice

in any of the situations would be impossible because none of the alternatives could gain a simple majority—unless another rule were introduced to permit a weighting of the intensities of the preferences. But that would be a new political system. Maybe the only solution would be to empower a ruler who would impose his own will without regard to committee members' preferences. Or, perhaps rules could be adopted which permit citizens to bargain and trade their votes or support across issue lines, thereby producing coalitions and majorities. Compromise and logrolling, based on varying intensities, could then provide some solutions. Or, citizens could decide to settle their differences through outright conflict, even to the extent of removing one another as participants. Finally, the models are not truly representative of reality because they do not include measures of the respective amounts of political resources held by citizens A, B and C. Citizen A may have twice as many relevant resources as B, and B somewhat more than C; on the other hand, C may be highly motivated whereas A and B are relatively indifferent. Whose choice will prevail? Or, we might further complicate matters by allowing different distributions for different types of resources such as respect, information, wealth and public popularity. Who then would win out?

Despite their simplicity, these models do enable us to visualize the situation of public or collective policy-making, for they suggest the problem of differences over many areas of choice and illustrate the problem of resolution or aggregation of divergent preferences into a *single authoritative policy*. They show the *logic* of the problem but not the processes or dynamics of actual policy-making. They also suggest the utility of having 'rules of the game' or institutionalized processes for resolving differences and making decisions.

Policy-Making Processes

Citizens A, B and C in our model could realize their goals in a variety of ways, but most of the alternatives would be variations on a few basic forms of interaction. We shall label these basic types: (1) bargaining, (2) competition, (3) command, (4) conflict and (5) cooperation.

Consider a situation in which public decisions are made by allowing all interested persons the right to pursue peacefully their own objectives or preferences. Under such a system the interested parties would find it necessary to give and take or *bargain* with one another since no single individual could achieve his ends without the assistance of others. In so doing he must offer inducements to others in the form of benefits, reduced costs or support in exchange for their support. In short, such individuals will exchange desired objects or induce support by offering mutually rewarding promises. In such a system, distributive outcomes are somewhat indeterminate since we cannot automatically predict the substance or terms of the exchanges or bargains.

Differences can also be reduced, if not eliminated, by permitting one person's preferences to predominate over those of all others. Such a system may be highly autocratic or dictatorial, depending on one's view of how it takes place. We choose to label it a *command* system or process. In a command system, one individual or his representatives make the requisite public choices. If regularized, this form of decision-making is not necessarily a forceful or manipulative sort of unilateral rule. It may result from legal delegation, deference, trust and respect, or from absolutely similar values and goals. 'Command' decisions are simply made by one actor and accepted by others in the group or system without any further 'give and take.' Without any assumptions of force or underlying differences it would appeal to many as the simplest form of decision, least costly and most efficient, i.e., *if* there are no differences or costly values at stake.

Where the preferences are incompatible and no actor can prevail at the outset, *conflict* processes may afford the means of settlement. Conflict does not mean just violence, although that is one rather cruel and costly form. Conflict occurs whenever there is interaction which results in one actor prevailing over the other, with the winner requiring direct concession on the point at issue or inflicting costs on the loser. Where the intensity of preferences is great, the normative restraints are weak or the anticipated costs are perceived as low by the actor, violence may be the recourse. Or there may be more subtle, less visible forms of suppressing contenders, or getting them to 'back down.' However, most conflict situations of any duration tend to be regularized in ongoing political systems and are transformed most often into competitive or bargaining processes, where rules are established governing procedures and requirements for winning, and often bringing in third parties as judges, mediators or arbitrators.

Competition, then, refers to regularized situations and processes in which two or more actors strive to win or to acquire the same object without directly imposing costs on the opposition. Like conflict, it is a win or lose situation, but there are 'external' sorts of mediators or criteria by which victory is decided. For example, there are judges and arbitrators who make these decisions in courts and regulatory commissions, or there may be referees selected by the contenders. There are rules about who can vote and how many votes it takes to win in elections, legislatures and other plural bodies. Competition, therefore, tends to result in win-or-lose outcomes, as does conflict, whereas bargained situations usually find the parties agreeing on some middle position or arranging some sort of mutually beneficial outcome. The latter is direct interaction, as with conflict, but moderated by the desire of the parties to come to some mutually helpful agreement. Competition, therefore, involves third parties, or some impersonal criteria of victory. Most readers have competed in games, or for grades or a job. And many readers may have engaged in bargaining over the price of a car, the size of an allowance, or perhaps even over the grade from an instructor. These commonplace activities pervade most local, national and international politics. While the situational context of political competition and bargaining is somewhat different from that of the market or family, the elementary logic of these types of situations is quite similar.

We finally note a most desirable sort of situation, considered by many to be rare, namely, the discovery that the stated initial preferences are identical. If this includes all in the decision-process, only communication is necessary to arrive at agreement. This would be a pure form of *cooperative* process. More typically, initial preferences might differ, but all would share a desire to reach a common set of preferences and, thus, discussion would pursue that purpose. It is still cooperative in the sense that each actor works at adjusting his own preferences relative to others by peaceful, persuasive means. The 'consensus' of the Quakers is arrived at by this sort of cooperative endeavor. Generally cooperative processes take place within groups of actors or decision-makers whose basic goals or values are shared. The concerns held in common ease the need to negotiate or bargain. Without cooperative processes, political life would indeed be cruel and chaotic. Most individuals do not wish to bargain or wage competition and conflict all the time; they would rather join others who are like-minded and can share the costs and rewards of a common cause.

While we have made formal distinctions among these five processes in order to facilitate discussion, we do not wish to imply that policy-making in any society is conducted by one process to the exclusion of others. No society could function in that manner; rather each society will employ all of these means but in quite different combinations or sequences. In assessing a society, one must discover the extent to which each process is used, in which policy areas and with what consequences. This is not an easy task since all processes go on more or less simultaneously and are generally conducted by many of the same persons. Thus, as a citizen plays a variety of social roles, so he plays a variety of policy roles. In one area he may bargain, in another command, in still another cooperate and, finally, engage in some conflicts. A President bargains with foreign leaders, competes with his opposition candidates, commands his staff, cooperates with a variety of people in common endeavors and wages conflict against enemies at home or abroad. Such inconsistent role activities may create problems for each of us but even more for some leaders. But putting aside such problems for awhile, let us consider each of the five basic political processes in some detail.

Political Bargaining

We find it very difficult to talk about bargaining apart from any other process, yet some analytic distinctions are vital. Bargaining is, basically, a matter of making or arriving at mutually profitable exchanges.

In short, each person or group in a quest for benefits or satisfactions finds the sources of these satisfactions controlled by others and can only acquire them by giving or promising something which the other person(s) would like to have. The incentive to trade is to improve or protect one's position; the cost is whatever must be exchanged. Of course, if you wish to bargain, you must find someone who not only has what you want but also who wants something over which you have control.[1]

Direct trades are easier to make than indirect ones unless some medium of exchange, such as money or votes, is available to facilitate the exchange. Exchanges can then take place without bartering. This happens every day in the marketplace when one trades money for a commodity at a fixed price. Exchanges in which the 'prices' are not fixed but are flexible permit bargaining to occur over the terms of the exchanges. The political arena is characterized by bargained exchanges since there is no impersonal and explicit price mechanism at work. Frequently the procedures and negotiation of terms are diffused or implicit—tacit understandings of what is owed and received. The political marketplace would be raucous indeed if it were filled with 'hard bargainers' shrilly advancing their wares and terms. While the cynic may view it as such, in most regularized settings there are many normative constraints mitigating crude behavior. Therefore we need to discuss in explicit terms what is often a diffused and intangible mode of interaction. Normally in economic markets, the range of mutually acceptable terms is somewhat known, i.e., each bargainer has some idea of his own minimal and maximal terms of exchange as well as some idea about the preferences of the other party. In political situations these terms frequently tend to be less well known; often they are vague and only the bargaining process will clarify them. Indeed, political bargainers may not even know what is being bargained, whereas in economic markets the disputed terms are usually very clear: price, quantity, quality and time conditions.

Once an exchange has taken place, a bargainer may still have doubts about whether he acquired the most favorable possible terms. Not knowing the actual minimal and maximal 'offers,' a person can rarely ascertain whether he made a mistake. In any event, exchanges are conducted because each party feels that any agreement is better than no agreement. The impulse to bargain comes from a mutually perceived need to do something

---

[1] The generality of the principles of economic exchange was persuasively put by a great English economist, Philip H. Wicksteed, in *The Common Sense of Political Economy* (London: The Macmillan Company, 1910). Despite the prolix style, it may well be easier to understand than many modern treatments. No doubt the best of the latter is Peter M. Blau's *Exchange and Power in Social Life* (New York: John Wiley and Sons, Inc., 1964). A much more technical analysis of economic exchange is Peter Newman's *The Theory of Exchange* (Englewood Cliffs, N.J.: Prentice-Hall, Inc., 1965).

which is dependent on the cooperation of the other party. Candidates who must look for support or leaders who are expected or required to act—both must achieve their goals by suitable offers or inducements with terms attractive to others. Whether in the economic or political arena, bargainers stand to gain by cooperation or exchange, but they must compete over the terms of the exchange. A good bargainer is a person who can sense or create a strong demand for what he has to offer and can find someone who will give something for it.

Even in the economy, bargaining is viewed more as a necessity than a pleasure. Since each party tries to further his own interests in the interaction, there is some aura of strain, mutual distrust and, of course, an unwillingness to share information fully. In politics this strain is increased to the degree to which differences of interest are considered unjustified or not admirable. Bargaining in the international arena is most accepted because the concept of national interests is well recognized. Bargaining within political systems is less honored, depending on the degree to which political actors are supposed to be seeking some shared value or 'public interest.' In his rhetoric the politician tends to honor such general interests even as he discloses how he 'brought home the bacon' to his following, whether a faction, party, constituency or organized group. Thus, the normative rules for international bargaining tend to be more explicit and the craft of diplomacy to be fairly well professionalized. In more localized political arenas, the rules tend to be more implicit, being taught as informally constraining norms within enduring groups such as legislatures, councils and committees, political party caucuses and conferences, and other administrative or judicial bodies with regular memberships. They are learned through personal political experiences, with trial and error accompanying less understood rewards and costs. Much of the candidate's bargaining with electorates is thus tacitly constrained. In formal bodies, the norms tend to center on the courtesies of interaction: 'excusing' or paying respect to certain values of other members (such as those in the non-bargainable realms of conscience or other binding authority) and developing traits considered desirable in guaranteeing an effective bargaining process (such as confidentiality, keeping one's word, being honest about terms, honoring commitments, etc.).

Most political supporters would prefer that their leaders or agents not 'give anything away' or engage in compromises. But the politician who will not bargain often stands in isolation; usually he and his followers or constituents get less in the short run. In bargaining groups he does not become 'one of the boys.' He desists from engaging in the reciprocities that ease the way for others—the 'give and take' that most bargainers consider the 'fair' way. However, such non-bargainers may be gambling on long run returns. They may be 'tribunes' of new causes or symbolic 'victors over evil.' They may win more immediate gains if their followers believe them to be right and solidify support for them.[2] It is always a matter for conjecture and debate as to which way is right in any ultimate sense, and all must debate the ultimate outcomes in terms of broader values.

Case Study #1   Norms of International Bargaining

One of the commonplaces in politics concerns relations among nations. It is said that nations do not observe law in the same sense that citizens do. While it is true that the world does not have a universal government, nevertheless nations do observe many international rules and agreements. Diplomats who represent nations are governed to a considerable extent by well known norms of behavior. Fred C. Iklé has treated some of these 'rules of accommodation' for furthering agreements among nations; he has also listed some 'hard' and 'soft' rules for maintaining friendly relations. The former refer to those rules which pertain to friendly nations and, if violated, would lead to a termination of the relationship, at least temporarily. The soft rules are those which can be violated but not repeatedly without serious consequences. Examples of each follow:

"Hard Rules" Among Friendly Nations[3]

1. "Unambiguous lies must be avoided."

2. "Explicit promises must be kept."

3. "Invective is never used."

4. "Explicit threats must not be issued."

5. "Agreements in principle must not be blatantly violated in execution of details."

6. "Mutual understandings must not be deliberately misconstrued later on."

"Soft Rules" Among Friendly Nations[4]

1. "Opponent's domestic difficulties must not be exploited in public."

2. "Debts of gratitude should be honored."

3. "Motives should not be impugned."

4. "Discourse ought to be reasonable, i.e., questions answered, arguments to the point, facts not grossly distorted, repetition minimized and technical discussions kept on a factual level."

---

[2] See William White's *The Citadel: The Story of the U.S. Senate.* (New York: Harper and Brothers, Publishers, 1956-57), which has many perceptive insights on the norms of bargaining in the Senate.

[3] From pp. 87, 92-121 in *How Nations Negotiate* by Fred Charles Iklé. Copyright © 1964 by Fred Charles Iklé. Reprinted by permission of Harper and Row, Publishers.

[4] *Ibid.*

Rules for Reaching Accommodation[5]

1. "Never kill a negotiator."
2. "Avoid disputes about status."
3. "Adhere to agreed agenda."
4. "Honor partial agreements."
5. "Maintain flexibility."
6. "Reciprocate concessions."
7. "Return favors."
8. "Refrain from flagrant lies."
9. "Negotiate in good faith."
10. "Avoid emotionalism and rudeness."
11. "Expedite and rationalize the negotiation process."
12. "Encourage community spirit."

Neither Iklé nor the negotiators believe that these rules are always honored. But the conditions under which legitimate bargaining is conducted must be distinguished from those which encourage violation of rules. Bargainers, whether national representatives or local politicians, will usually honor rules if they (1) believe it is expedient to do so; (2) feel others expect it of them regardless of the outcome; (3) believe it is immoral not to observe them or (4) fear the imposition of severe sanctions were the rules not honored.[6]

A bargainer may violate a rule because he does not accept one or more of these reasons for adherence. Those who repeatedly lose out in bargaining are apt to question the neutrality of the rules, believing instead that they were selfishly instituted by more powerful groups or nations. Then, too, the attractiveness of short-run gains may outweigh considerations that are more long-range and uncertain. New revolutionary nations are much more apt to question and ignore the ancient rules of diplomacy formed among imperialist and traditional nations, as has been the case with communist countries since World War I. Note, however, that the Soviet Union does abide by many agreements and, as time passes, may find itself more in league with the West. In short, if rules consistently work against one's interests, one will question and even violate them.

The Outcomes of Exchanges

In bargaining situations compromises are made in the sense that each side ends up with something less than desired. This is typical of

---

[5] *Ibid.*, pp. 92-121.

[6] *Ibid.*, pp. 90-91.

legislatures where final authoritative policies must be made and sanctioned. Each side surrenders more than it wishes and gets less than it ideally prefers. Detecting the outcome of exchanges, i.e., who gets what, is seldom easy, but the content of the legislation, or any formal agreement, should contain some clues.

We may observe that bargaining is pervasive throughout the political universe: citizens bargain with citizens, politicians bargain with politicians, politicians bargain with citizens, interest groups bargain with citizens and politicians, bureaucrats bargain with politicians and interest groups, state bargains with state, and nation bargains with nation. The welter of bargaining is so great that it confuses not only the observer but also the participants. The bargainer has to know his own and others' resources and preferences and when and under what conditions he ought to or can seek a trade. If he is to profit, he must also know the strategies and tactics of effective bargaining. Much of this information is hard to acquire and what is available is often inaccurate, unreliable or untimely.

In systems which permit career longevity among politicians, bargainers become very expert, while in those systems where political careers are short, the relevant skills may be less developed and more haphazardly applied, as in many American city councils, boards and state legislatures. On the other hand, the number of experienced bargainers in many European assemblies and in the United States Congress is very large. Few ordinary citizens in most countries are qualified. Those who are active participants, of course, learn or fail on the job. It would be an interesting quest to detect the poor bargainers and their relative fates.

Since political bargaining generally is indirect and implicit, it is frequently marked by indeterminate solutions or payoffs. The number of explicit and directly bargained-over issues is apt to be few. Since considerable ambiguity and controversy accompany political bargaining, the participants, not to mention onlookers, are frequently confused as to the 'terms' of the bargain. Who gets what from the 'agreement'? In areas involving quantifiable goods, such as numbers of people to be covered by Medicare or amounts of subsidies, taxes, welfare payments, etc., the conditions of a bargain may be settled with a high degree of precision. But where symbolic exchanges are made or implicit promises of future support are offered, the extent of ambiguity increases greatly.

At this point a rather sharp distinction should be made between two different outcomes of bargaining which are brought about in quite distinct ways. The methods are *compromise* and what is typically called *logrolling*. Compromise is usually the product of bargains over a *single isolated issue* when the outcome is one of more or less. Money questions involving budgets and issues of benefits and costs are the most likely and easiest issues to compromise. Logrolling, on the other hand, is a very different type of bargaining which normally is concerned with more than one issue or item of interest. It involves a reciprocity of support for different items of interest to each bargainer. A politician 'rolls logs' whenever he seeks to exchange support across issues. This may be done explicitly or implicitly, but mostly by the latter means. A typically American product of logrolling is the 'omnibus bill' which 'packages' all the particular provisions agreed to in one piece of legislation, thus gaining the support of all involved. Early U.S. tariff legislation, and public works and farm bills have taken this form. A *coalition* is often formed on the basis of reciprocity between two or more groups, involving more continuous exchanges of support on crucial but separate issues. In the U. S. Congress and some state legislatures there are 'conservative coalitions' consisting of occupational, geographic, class or ethnic interests; each derives benefits from reciprocal voting on salient issues. Sometimes a request for support may be explicit on the part of politician A but the promise by politician B to reciprocate is frequently left unstated; it is assumed that another issue will provide an opportunity for repayment.

Much of what has been said can be graphically illustrated; Table 10-1 lists a number of well-known national politicians along with their hypothetical positions and intensities of commitment on four national issues. Assume the intensity of commitment can be measured on a scale of five points, i.e., five being the highest degree of commitment in either the pro or con direction. Thus, President Johnson is depicted as having been deeply committed during 1968 to a higher defense budget (5 points) and only moderately committed on the gun control bill (3 points). On the other

Table 10-1
Political Bargaining: Who Will Bargain with Whom?

	Issues							
	Stronger Civil Rights		Increased Defense Exp.		Increased Income Tax		Stiffer Gun Controls	
	Pro	Con	Pro	Con	Pro	Con	Pro	Con
President Johnson	4		5		5		3	
Senator Dirksen	2		2		2			2
Senator Fulbright		1		4		3		2
Senator Russell		4	4		2			3
Senator McCarthy	3			4	3			1
Senator Morse	5			5		4		4
Senator Eastland		5	3		2			3
Senator Javits	4			4	3		3	

hand Senator Eastland is viewed as strongly opposed to civil rights (5 points).

Given these arbitrarily assigned positions and intensities on the four issues, one can picture how compromises and logrolling might be accomplished. What degrees of commitment do you think would most facilitate a compromise? Where would you search for potential 'logrollers'?

There were many other issues during 1968 which both complicated and simplified matters for the politician and political scientist. But the requirements of bargained agreements can be clarified with this simple table. Any of the bargainers might be able to compromise on an issue isolated from the other issues. The major fight would occur between those who are committed for and against any particular proposal. On stronger civil rights, for example, the chief contenders might have been President Johnson and Senator Morse on the pro side and Senators Eastland and Russell on the con side. They would not like to compromise, but other Senators less committed on both sides (McCarthy; Dirksen; Fulbright) would be in a position to find acceptable common grounds. Whether they would find sufficient inducement to become active is problematic. The intensely committed have little inducement to compromise, while the moderates frequently have no incentive to produce a decision until a more strongly committed side approaches them for support. In the competitive bidding for that support, the moderates are in a better position to extract some concessions, i.e., compromises, in exchange for consolidating a winning vote. The incentive to achieve a decision depends on the perceived need to produce a law rather than no action at all. But if a decision must be made, the 'extremists' will be hard at work to make it more consistent with their own positions.

A number of areas afford opportunities for compromise in civil rights. We will only suggest a few and not discuss them, as space prohibits greater detail. For example, bargainers could compromise on such matters as bussing distances or boundaries, hiring and promotion requirements in public contracts and government employment, amounts of public housing for ghetto areas or low income groups, investment incentives and lending arrangements, types of training programs for adult workers and unemployed, division of responsibilities in administering civil rights and many others. As we have noted above, those areas in which differences can be quantitatively adjusted are most amenable to compromise. And those areas of disagreement which do not entail the surrender of basic values or principles also afford opportunities for compromise. Some of the highly symbolic goods discussed in Chapter 4 do not readily lend themselves to compromise; in that case, the leader who defines the issue may guarantee the results. How many are willing to vote against an 'anti-crime' bill? Or against a crisis resolution? Morality, patriotism and basic statuses are very difficult issues to bargain.

Logrolling is another means of resolving differences. Logrolling, however, has somewhat different requirements. As stated before, a politician engages in logrolling whenever he exchanges votes across issues. You vote for me on issue A and I will vote for you on issue B. Thus, in Table 10-1 each senator with a low intensity of preference on a particular issue will be a likely exchange partner for another senator with a high intensity of commitment on another issue. In short, a legislator who wants something badly will seek out a relatively indifferent or low intensity legislator with the hope of enlisting his support. And the other legislator can grant his support with the expectation of a return favor. There is nothing mysterious about this search and choice of exchange partners; in fact, it is simply an application of the axioms in Chapter 1 which state that men will exchange those goods for which they have less need in return for others which they would like to have in greater amounts. Since the marginal utility of goods decreases as one acquires more goods, it is rational to trade them for goods with higher marginal values. To make an exchange, a bargainer must find someone who places a higher value than he does on a particular policy. If a politician really feels strongly about an issue he may be willing to engage in an 'unequal' exchange, i.e., pledge say three votes for one. Terms of the exchange depend upon the marginal worth of the votes. If a Senator or President needs only one more vote to ensure passage of a bill, he is likely to bid very high for that vote. And the uncommitted are likely to charge an equally high price for their vote. This explains why politicians sometimes hold out in declaring their preferences; by so doing, they hope to enhance the value of their vote. The difficulty in this maneuver is that one may hold out too long and thereby lose or reduce his crucial worth. Politicians must constantly calculate when it is most advantageous to enter the fray and declare their positions. Getting in too early is as bad as coming in too late. The rewards for premature support may be as low as those for some latecomers. Interesting arenas to watch in this connection are the national party conventions in the United States.

No doubt some readers will find this discussion somewhat disturbing. If this is true our prediction is correct—some Americans find vote trading morally reprehensible. According to this view, a legislator should not trade his support; rather, he should have clearly defined positions or principles regarding all possible issues. He should not hesitate to declare these principles. We are inclined to view such a position as highly unrealistic as well as undesirable. First, men—all men—cannot have deep feelings about every conceivable issue. We all place differential value on the various activities and concerns of society simply because some things are more important than others in our lives. The fact that men do not all value similar activities, goods, services and policies alike enables trade. If the requisite conditions are present, these exchanges of differentially valued goods enable more individuals to increase their welfare. Each man trades that which he desires less for that which he desires more. If we assume that it is appropriate that each citizen should have as much of what he wants out of life as he can acquire without inflicting costs on others, then institutions and policies which permit freer and more responsive trading are good and necessary.

Unhappily, compromise and logrolling cannot always be accomplished; even in instances when they can be, the results may not command respect. While bargaining is a search for mutual advantage, it also contains some conflict implications, for each bargainer wants not only to conclude a bargain but to do so on as favorable terms as possible. So let us consider why some men may do better at competitive processes than others.

Political Competition

Recall that competition was defined as an activity in which two or more persons seek the same object. In such situations, the objects being more or less scarce serves effectively to prevent each competitor from acquiring some or all that he wishes. In the marketplace, seller competes against seller(s) for relatively limited numbers of sales among customers, while buyers may compete for scarce supplies or commodities from the sellers. In politics one politician competes with another for the votes of the citizens; one bureaucrat competes with another for the limited resources provided by elected officials; one party competes with another for an electoral victory; one nation competes with another for economic gains, status and power.

Political competition in and among nations may not be any more perfect than economic competition. Types and amounts of competition vary greatly, even within a single nation-state. For example, some nations have competition in which the only contenders are the candidates, while others feature competition over both candidates for office and specific public policies. The number of competing political parties in some nations is two, while in others as many as a dozen may compete in each election. In some societies the balance of competition is close—each party has a reasonably good chance of winning. In others, most elections are won by one party. One estimate of competition in seventy-three new nations during 1960 claimed that only twelve had genuinely competitive party systems, while thirty-six had lesser or semi-competitive systems.[7] Several of the former category have since become semi-competitive, and a number of the originally designated semi-competitive nations have now become dictatorships. So the situation is not promising. At best, the number of nations with strongly competitive party systems seldom exceeds twenty-five. And yet, the stirrings of some competition are beginning to be felt even in the communist world.

---

[7] James S. Coleman, "Conclusion: The Political Systems of Developing Areas," in Gabriel A. Almond and James S. Coleman, eds., *The Politics of the Developing Areas* (Princeton: Princeton University Press, 1960), p. 534.

The most detailed studies of the forms and degrees of competition have been made of the United States. We need not detail these findings except to relate that competition, both in terms of type and extent, is considerably more restricted than many political scientists deem wise. Until recently, most states of the South and New England, for example, were basically one-party systems, while a number of others were only occasionally competitive. Such findings are parallel to those which find reduced competition among business firms in free enterprise economies. Barriers or obstacles to vigorous competition will be considered in Chapter 14; first, let us look at the logic of competition.

Whereas the bargainer seeks out other bargainers and attempts to induce a mutually-profitable exchange, the competitor does not seek out other competitors; in fact, he usually wishes to avoid, eliminate or reduce his competition. Instead of providing incentives for trades, the competitor devises strategies and tactics that will enable him to gain his end without providing benefits for the opposition. The participants' orientations in the two situations are quite distinct. Occasionally competitors will bargain in order to ensure their mutual survival, such as forming government coalitions to avoid deadlock, or two political parties may agree to divide up constituencies or goods rather than contend over all of them. For the most part, competing politicians attempt to outmaneuver one another for a scarce prize, such as an electoral victory or public office which both cannot share.

Concentration is, therefore, upon the choice of optimal strategies and the effective mobilization of resources in order to achieve victory. The situation can be usefully depicted in the form of a 'game matrix' such as displayed in Figure 10-1. The game matrix shows two competitors (they may be politicians, nations, interest groups, bureaucrats, etc.), their alternative strategies and possible payoffs, depending upon individual choices among strategic alternatives. In this particular figure, the total payoff is arbitrarily set at a figure of ten. The first entry in each cell signifies the portion going to Competitor A and the second entry the remainder going to B. Payoffs are then a product of interdependent strategies. If A and B were political parties or candidates competing in an election, the payoffs would be in votes and the distribution of those votes would be a function of the independently derived strategic choices. Thus, if A decided his best strategy was s_1 and B happened to select S_1, A would win all the votes and B would win nothing. On the other hand, if A chose s_3 and B selected S_3, A would receive a single vote and B would receive nine votes.

In real elections one does not know what the total turnout will be so the size of the total payoffs is indeterminant, as is the distribution. As we will learn shortly, the size of the turnout is an important determinant on who will win; some parties prefer large turnouts while others benefit from smaller ones. In any event, the game matrix is a convenient device for simplifying the competitive situation. Formal game theory is an awesome mathematical field with far more complexities and refinements than

Figure 10-1

The Competitive Situation

Competitor B's
Strategies

		S_1	S_2	S_3
	s_1	10,0	8,2	5,5
Competitor A's Strategies	s_2	0,10	2,8	4,6
	s_3	6,4	7,3	1,9

we have shown. Unhappily, this intricate approach to politics is difficult to present realistically; it is best employed simply to depict the logic of competition, not the empirical details.

The competitive situation and its payoffs may be zero-sum—the winnings of one competitor are equalled by the losses of the other—or non-zero-sum—the winnings and the losses are not equal. Competition for elective public office is a zero-sum game, for one either wins or loses. Each competitor knowingly or unknowingly chooses strategies; the interaction of these choices produces an outcome or payoff which has differential benefits and costs. The problem of the competitor seeking office, attempting to win a war or trying to influence a policy is to select that strategy which best enables him to accomplish his ends. Many decision-rules or guides have been devised by game theorists to advise political leaders on how to choose strategies. There is no single rule or norm in this matter. Strategies would vary depending on whether one wished to get as large a payoff as possible, to minimize one's losses or to be content with a highly certain but moderate payoff. We know little about how the actual selection of strategies may vary for different types of people, but there are many politicians whose reputations are made on the basis of tactical successes. In any event, political actors face strategic choices and must make them under more or less uncertain conditions concerning the opponent's choices, his use of resources and the payoffs.

Still, the value of conceptualizing competition in this game form is useful. The game matrix in Figure 10-2 could be used to depict the respective strategic choices of the United States and North Vietnam, or the Arab nations and Israel or two government agencies on matters of budget allocation. But let us use it to consider the following problem in an American election campaign: the Democratic and Republican parties are faced with choices of electoral strategy in their stands on the issue of government spending. Each has but four logical alternatives for gaining votes and victory. The payoff entries would be the distribution of votes between the two parties in terms of net voter gains or losses of each possible stand on the budget, given the position of the other side. There are sixteen possible outcomes confronting the two parties; each outcome depends upon the combination of their respective choices. The trouble is that politicians do not know the exact numbers to insert into the individual cells of the matrix, but they can make informed guesses. For example, in calculations for presidential races, the choices of candidates and issues are analyzed in terms of states which would be won or lost, or where gains would be made among different groups or sections. Estimates are usually based on past experiences.

The dilemma of electoral strategies raises a number of interesting questions about the behavior of politicians as major competitors. Whereas we have learned a great deal about voters, elections and outcomes, we know very little about how politicians behave as competitors. Why this should be is somewhat baffling, but current research is attempting to fill this particular lacuna in political study. For example, we should like to know about such choices as when and how politicians decide to contend for office; how they win party support; how they select or devise campaign strategies; how they actually go about daily campaigning; how they appeal to different groups of voters; how they acquire campaign resources; how

Figure 10-2
Electoral Strategies on Size of Budget

	Republicans' Strategies			
	Increase	Constant	Decrease	No position
Democrats' Strategies Increase				
Constant				
Decrease				
No Position				

they decide to allocate scarce resources among competing uses; how they perceive competition and their competitors. Obviously, the answers to these questions will depend on a great many factors but which factors and under what circumstances? At present we have little in the way of systematic research and theory; for the most part, we must depend on biographies, autobiographies, accounts of various elections (such as Theodore White's *The Making of a President*[8]) and newspaper accounts of daily politics. Confirmed generalizations cannot be easily derived from such scattered sources.

Case Study #2   Some Conditions of Strategic Choice and Victory in the U.S.A.

Politicians are not primarily concerned with general outcomes; they are far more interested in their own situations. Yet their fates are partly shaped by general factors influencing their political chances. In this regard we can point to one of our better confirmed propositions, namely, that incumbents enjoy a much better chance of being reelected than do beginners or challengers. During the years 1924-1956, 90 per cent of the congressmen who ran for reelection were successful.[9] Successful politicians should also be pleased to know that the larger their victory in any particular election, the greater the probabilities of being reelected in the succeeding election. The greatest number of electoral casualties in congressional races occur among those who won their first bid by less than 52 per cent. In short, nothing succeeds like success, and nothing fails like failure. Another interesting phenomenon of American politics, although somewhat more controversial, is the 'coattail effect,' i.e., the tendency for the winning presidential candidate to carry other politicians of his party into public office. Some have claimed that a winning President may be responsible for electing as many as two or three dozen congressmen. Subsequent research into this ambiguous causal nexus has considerably qualified the power of a popular President to influence other elections. We have noted that off-year elections tend to bring out fewer voters; at the same time, the victory chances of the 'outs' appears to increase, perhaps because of growing dissatisfaction with the 'in' party. As a result, rarely has a President been able to increase his support in Congress during the mid-term election.

The chances for a politician to be elected or reelected are affected not only by his own strategic choices but a variety of factors far beyond his immediate control. Depressions, for example, have caused parties to be thrown out of office, whereas prosperity may keep a party in control

---

[8] New York: Atheneum Publishers, 1961 and 1965. (Mr. White is already at work on his third book which will deal with the 1968 presidential campaign.)

[9] David A. Leuthold, *Electioneering in a Democracy* (New York: John Wiley and Sons, Inc., 1968), p. 126.

even though it has had little to do with that state of affairs. Political errors on the part of associates may create serious liabilities for the candidate. Wars may or may not work to assist the 'ins' to remain in office or the 'outs' to replace them. We simply cannot readily predict the direction of impact, but it is clear that wars have affected electoral opportunities. 'In' parties in all democracies have superior resources to lead the public, but at the same time they have the responsibility of making public decisions which inevitably will dissatisfy some elements of the population. The problem is whether in making decisions they create more grateful voters or disgruntled opponents. At best, an 'in' party can only hope to slow down the rate of grievances and keep them at a low intensity.

The 'out' party also has its advantages and dilemmas, as we have implicitly noted. In one sense, all an 'out' party must do is simply wait for the party in power to make poor choices and lose support or incur active opposition. But the strategy cannot be that simple. The 'outs' must criticize effectively and offer something in the nature of an alternative. But if the 'in' party monopolizes the moderate center on major issues, it becomes difficult, especially in a two party system, for the 'outs' to offer an alternative. Opposition for opposition's sake does not make sense. On the other hand, an attempt by the opposition to emulate the 'ins' is subject to the charge of 'me-tooism,' a strategy which may well alienate the party's strongest loyalists. And they are important; for while they may be fewer in number than the moderates, they are usually among the more active members. Whatever strategies the 'ins' and the 'outs' choose, and they are interdependent, both must face the fact that they create benefits and costs for the various members of their parties and the entire electorate. Each strategy has its costs in terms of support lost for gains made. The primary question for the leadership is to have information on voter responses to various strategies and counter-strategies and this is both difficult and costly to attain. All this leads us to the question of devising strategies, a problem we will defer to Chapter 12.

Case Study #3   Further Conventional Wisdom About Electoral Competition, Mainly U.S.A.

As observers have studied and compared electoral processes and experiences, generalizations have been proposed about their outcomes or consequences. Political science literature has proposed its share of generalizations and we shall sample some typical views here.[10]

---

[10] Most of the above generalizations may be found scattered about in texts on political parties. We recommend V. O. Key, Jr., *Politics, Parties, and Pressure Groups,* 5th ed. (New York: Thomas Y. Crowell Company, 1964). Also see Samuel Lubell, *The Future of American Politics* (New York: Harper and Brothers, 1951); Angus Campbell, Philip E. Converse, Warren Miller and Donald E. Stokes, *Elections and the Political Order* (New York: John Wiley and Sons, Inc., 1966).

Influence of electoral laws: Single member districts with plurality rules for winning tend to encourage two-party contests while plural member districts or proportional representation encourage multi-party competition. Genuine multi-party competition, it is said, tends to produce unstable governments, whereas two-party systems increase the sense of voter efficacy, produce more stable governments and policy continuity.

Nature of competition: In two-party systems competition most often occurs between the 'ins' and the 'outs.' The 'ins' have a record of performance and the 'outs' make promises to do better. With time, the 'ins' can please some by what they do but will lose others. There are differential rewards and costs for different groups. The opposition may appeal to a coalition of disparate malcontents or may hope for a catastrophe to turn out the 'in' party. Barring such crises or hard times, the process of cumulating discontents results in a slow, cyclical turnover in office. Because they are competing for support, parties tend to promise similar things. For many, this 'convergence theory' is almost a 'law of competition,' i.e., all competitors (U.S. and U.S.S.R.; Republicans and Democrats; ABC, NBC and CBS; Kennedy and Nixon, for example) tend to copy one another in their eagerness to win. Thus, two-party competition does not tend to produce the instability of great changes.

Size of victory: In real competitive contests the margin of victory tends to be very small. In fact in the United States, a solid majority in such cases would amount to around 55 per cent. Several American Presidents have been elected by less than a majority, and over a period of time the alternations of vote percentages have not been very great.

Voter turnout: The smaller the turnout in a national election (in the U.S., at least) the greater the proportion of highly committed partisans, while the larger the voter turnout the larger the number of independents, indifferents and other less committed voters. These latter groups will then decide the election. Typically, high turnout is associated with bad times and massive discontent. In recent years national elections in the U.S.A. have attracted more voters than local or state elections have attracted. Likewise, off-year elections (between presidential elections) tend to attract fewer voters.

Miscellaneous competitive advantages: Name familiarity helps in all elections—even notoriety may help for less important offices—and incumbents, it is thought, should not mention the names of their opponents and thus give them free publicity.

Policy-Making in Command Systems

We have dealt with some of the complexities involved in policy-making by bargaining and competing. By contrast, command systems would seem simple to define.[11] One person makes the decisions and the rest follow or obey. Because it is the product of one person's intentions, the decision can be quite clearly defined. There are no other bargaining or competing parties, so the person responsible for the decision is obvious. While this is a simplified model of a command system, perhaps it will serve to illustrate some basic comparisons. Perplexities of command decisions and important variations found in the 'real' political world will be noted later.

In formal situations of command, decision-making is supposed to take place according to specified procedures or rules. Some positions are given the right to decide about certain collective activities in specified spheres of jurisdiction. The forms of communication of such decisions, and compliance with them, are also designated—who is to obey whom, when and how. There may be rather elaborate chains of command linking various decisions and compliance procedures in hierarchical form. Bargaining on the other hand emphasizes a kind of simultaneous or sequential decision process among equals who have insufficient capacity to issue unilateral commands. Figure 10-3 may illustrate the contrast. Typically, the relationships in bargaining situations presume some equalities of competence and communication. In command situations the premise is inequality; there are superior-subordinate roles, or exclusive competences not shared by those who must comply. In command systems there must be some explicit differentiation of roles. Leaders are defined or recognized as different, and role expectations conform to these distinctions. In bargaining there can be much more ambiguity about roles, and divisions of labor may often be the subject of bargaining. In an ideal-type command system some behavior is, therefore, quite predictable, because of the leader-follower designations. In bargaining the form of the relationship and mutual activities can be as unpredictable as the outcomes themselves.

But command, even the ideal sort, only reduces some sorts of uncertainty. Even if all decisions presumably emanate from one position at the top, there will be areas of non-predictability for the observer, and even for the decision-maker himself. There will be uncertainties about how he will become aware of or define decision issues, how he will perceive or devise alternatives and how he will guide his choice with premises, values and information. In bargaining systems all bargainers or potential bargainers who discover a problem bring it to the attention of others and seek their support in making it an issue. The issue will not be acted upon until the others acknowledge that it is worthy of action. If only one actor is involved, the question shifts to how he becomes aware of problems that require decisions. There may be many ways, depending upon the kind of

---

[11] For one of the best treatments of command systems see Robert A. Dahl and Charles E. Lindblom, *Politics, Economics, and Welfare* (New York: Harper and Brothers, 1953), Chaps. 8-9.

Figure 10-3

Comparison of Decision Process
in Command and Bargaining Systems

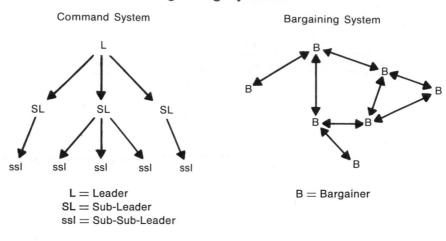

Command System

Bargaining System

L = Leader
SL = Sub-Leader
ssl = Sub-Sub-Leader

B = Bargainer

command leadership and the context. We, thus, move away from any one ideal and predictable case.

Varieties of Command

All of the following are basically command organizations and considering them may reveal some important variations in command decision-making: a prison, a military unit, a business enterprise, a union, a farmers' organization, a Communist Party, a religious cult, a public agency, a dictatorship, a communist state, a presidency, a football team. Without detailing cases, we may posit two general considerations that may tell us more about command decision-making. One is the nature of the goals or tasks of the organization and the other is the degree of compliance or commitment of the membership. The first consideration raises questions about what the leadership must decide in terms of the nature and the context of the task. The adaptation and the uses of information with regard to such problems were discussed in Chapter 7. The question of compliance or commitment is related to the goals of the organization, the internal distribution of positions and tasks, statuses and other resources, and the extent to which commands may or will evoke the expected responses.

A prison system, for example, is expected to exercise strong and exclusive control over most of the social behavior of its inhabitants and at a sustained cost to them. A military unit must be recruited, disciplined and trained to bring highly controlled and organized force to bear against a resistant or aggressive enemy. A business enterprise, a political party and a football team wage competition in different arenas, but they are expected to apply appropriate strategies for the purpose of out-doing a competitor. The leader of a union, farmers' organization or religious cult is supposed to serve the membership, especially in providing security—whether it is against the difficulties of work life, the general insecurities of the market-place, or spiritual uncertainties. Governments and public agencies pre-sumably pursue policies and programs, but the nature of the collective task, the resources and support mobilized, and the likelihood of outcomes are all subject to great variation, as has been stated. The point, then, is to take into account the tasks or goals of leadership and the kinds of command relationship in terms of compliance or commitment in order to appreciate how the command leader engages in appropriate decision-making.

Discretion in Defining Goals

It was common to envy the ease of the dictator's job, until resistances increased; or the warden's control, until prison riots occurred more fre-quently; and one could have thought papal decision-making was rather easy, until doctrinal issues and defections from vows indicated that still an-other command system may be in trouble. The situation of ideal command presumed in each case was the complete autonomy of the top decision-maker. A command decision-maker is most autonomous when (1) his task is highly specified; (2) the appropriate goals are clearly understood by him and his subjects; (3) the definition of problems or issues are directly within his exclusive competence; and (4) the compliance is automatic, once the decision is rendered. A powerful command leader need not demean himself by endlessly bargaining with others; he simply initiates, decides and acts. But few leaders ever achieve such power. More common is the unenviable command decision-maker who either (or variously) doesn't know what to do; finds few who accept his chosen spheres of authority; needs others to help him in diagnosing the situation, considering alternative choices and devising strategies; or has great difficulties in mobilizing and directing those presumably at his command.

In many explicit and formal roles, the norms specify decision criteria and, as long as the problems recur in the expected form, the rules are ex-pected to apply. The tasks of a prison-warden appear to be clearly defined in terms of objectives and prison procedures. Equally clear cut are roles in the more traditional military dictatorships, where the leader engages in a great deal of ritualized performance, or in the institutionalized church, where ritual and dogma are prescribed. This is also the case for many bureaucratic leadership roles which are governed either by automatic legal rules or by scientific and technological criteria. It should be noted, however, that the rules must apply to the *substance of the decision,* and not just to role specifications in terms of expected forms of behavior toward others.

In unstable systems the adaptive problem is one of coping with great uncertainty. In leadership terms, men in top positions who have serious adaptive tasks will cast their decisions with the kind of guidance considered authoritative. Charismatic leaders probably engage in the most discretionary and autonomous command decision-making. Their personal 'magic,' intuitive powers or inspired vision is considered the ultimate base of authority. The spiritual leader is also allowed great discretion on the assumption that he possesses some sort of internal divine guidance (although, as we have noted, the traditional or bureaucratic church imposes considerable limitations). In military history, the heroic commander was often one who disregarded existing rules and, by surprising the enemy, demonstrated his superior powers. A great component of such freedom to command is the form of commitment of the following. When the task is to prevail over a formidable enemy without regard for extraordinary costs, the commitment may be absolute, even sacrificial. Much more puzzling to predict are the decisions of charismatic political leaders, whether they be heads of governments, movements or fighting forces. Part of the magic is to do the unexpected or impossible.

External Authority

Much less autonomous is the command decision-maker who faces situations of change or complexity where he must seek the guidance of external authorities. His discretion becomes limited by the degree to which the external authority exercises its discretion or provides prescriptive sorts of decision rules. This situation frequently occurs in our scientific era where the will of the expert may actually prevail. Seeking the guidance of the holy man or the trained specialist is the same if his guidance is taken as authoritative. Those who wish to command must beware of the institutionalized or highly specialized system which maintains sources of authoritative knowledge which the decision-maker himself cannot learn. If there is an information monopoly, he must decide upon the monopolist's definition of things. If there is a plurality of advice, he may reserve more discretion by encouraging bargaining and competition among the different sources of advice but, of course, that increases the uncertainties and costs of decision again.

Command decisions in competitive organizations call for the strategic considerations discussed in the previous section. If the stakes are high and the resources sufficient, there is a likelihood that some forms of expert guidance will be employed to reduce uncertainty and develop better strategies. In competitive judicial proceedings, the lawyer or team of lawyers practically takes over. The organization frequently involved in judicial processes will develop its own legal staff, as have business firms, interest groups and official bodies. In the case of public bureaucracies, these groups of legal experts become indispensable for guidance and implementation in the command decision process. Recently, specialists in electoral competition have developed their own body of knowledge and precepts or rules of strategy. The advice rendered by public relations firms or campaign organizations using opinion polls, statistical analyses of past elections, and projected electoral counts is now considered critically important for major contestants. The more the candidates follow such advice, the more the locus of command shifts—and the decision criteria as well. However, predictability is enhanced insofar as the ingredients of the newer forms of campaign advice are understood.

Compliance

While every command situation implies relationships of inequality, the basis for compliance to the command may vary considerably. The kind of commitment held by the subordinate prescribes or limits the scope of commands—what the leader can expect from his following and what they are prepared to give. The discussions of the limitations and encouragements to control in Chapter 6 and of the norms and values related to institutional and leadership change in parts of Chapter 7 are relevant here. The most complete command may be found in situations with surprisingly different forms of commitment. Scholars have conceptualized some organizations or systems where the commitment is forced or physically controlled as 'coercive.'[12] Prisons are of this sort, as are (to some degree) totalitarian systems. Highly disciplined armies or militant movements may enhance command by imposing severe sanctions. On the other hand, compliance may be guaranteed not by force but by the whole-hearted devotion of followers. Religious orders rest on this sort of obedience, and charismatic leaders enjoy such devotion from their following. Even ideological movements may evoke ardent loyalty.

Many command systems operate with far more limited commitment. The contractual form of relationship we have discussed in terms of legal authority is typical. Limited spheres of obedience are exchanged for some

---

[12] Cf. Amitai Etzioni, *A Comparative Analysis of Complex Organizations* (New York: The Free Press of Glencoe, Inc., 1961). The author's emphasis upon the compliance factor was most helpful to this discussion and in the treatment of command generally. See also the analysis by Dorwin Cartwright, "Influence, Leadership, Control," in James G. March, ed., *Handbook of Organizations* (Chicago: Rand McNally and Company, 1965), pp. 1-47.

designated reward such as income. The commitment concerns only the work role and the purposes of the enterprise. Many kinds of organizations may have even more limited forms of command. The leadership in clubs and interest groups, for instance, are granted certain authority and duties, with the membership complying in far more limited spheres and times. This mode of compliance has been designated by some as 'normative' in that it is granted for the pursuance of particular values in only certain salient situations. In these kinds of organizations observers may question the precise degree to which the leader actually does lead the following, and when. Do union leaders actually command the votes of working men? Will the members of some association really vote against the recalcitrant legislator? Questions of salience and identification become important in explaining the limits of these forms of command. Command and compliance in these cases are highly fragmented and relationships are often disjointed, cutting across organizations and group affiliations. At different times a person will defer to a great number of different 'authorities' or 'experts' on choices he makes; he may follow the opinion of authorities with whom he identifies strongly, the advice of friends, or 'opinion leaders' such as newspapers, sports heroes or others in whom he has placed trust for certain things. In such cases 'command' must be understood in terms of the situation of the chooser.

Case Study #4   Some Comparisons of Administrative Systems

Lest the reader think the 'ideal type' administrative command system prevails everywhere, let us consider some contrasts in different nations. These systems vary in the degree of command and types of compliance. The following are brief extractions from Ferrel Heady, *Public Administration: Comparative Perspective:*[13]

The U.S.S.R.

"The system aims at monolithic unity under the aegis of the Communist party."

"Control of the state apparatus is the primary means through which the Communist party has established and maintained its power."

"Party control is assured through a network of interlocking directorates at each hierarchical level."

"Under the threat of drastic punishment for failure of performance or loss of confidence, the highly dependent Soviet administrator does

---

[13] Englewood Cliffs, N. J.: Prentice-Hall, Inc., 1966. The above quotations are found on pp. 42-56. The author's references are to Michael Crozier, *The Bureaucratic Phenomenon* (Chicago: University of Chicago Press, 1963).

what he can to minimize the danger. Knowing that as an individual he is expendable and replaceable, he strives to protect himself by having goals assigned that are achievable, by increasing the allocation of resources at his disposal, and by mustering as much political support as he can."

"From the perspective of the Party leadership, multiple control devices must be maintained to insure bureaucratic dependency. The monopolistic nature of state employment is in itself a powerful incentive toward conformity."

"The Soviet system of domination . . . institutionalizes the principle of plebiscitarianism, using a doctrine stressing the equal status of citizens to justify elitist rule by permitting no representative body to intervene between the individual and the supreme authority of the Party."

France and Germany

"In contrast to discontinuity in politics, both France and Germany have had remarkable administrative and bureaucratic continuity."

". . . Public officials are considered members of a corps or cadre representing and closely identified with the state."

"The official who speaks for the state and acts on its behalf tends to consider himself as possessing a bit of sovereignty which entitles him to respectful attention, and this view is at least partly shared by the citizenry. The bureaucrat is considered a public official rather than a public servant."

"In recognition of the preparation required and the career commitment made, members of the service are provided with elaborate and comprehensive guarantees of security and status, backed by legal sanctions."

". . . The tradition is also one of service to the state, whatever masters the state may have. The bureaucratic elite does not lay claim to becoming the political elite as well."

Great Britain and the United States

". . . The British service seems to have a clear advantage over the American in terms of prestige and status. This reflects general patterns of deference toward governmental and other forms of authority in the society . . ."

"Both in Britain and the United States, high ranking bureaucrats play a substantial role in governmental decision-making, but the rules of the game differ decidedly. The British operate under a convention that imposes upon the official and the minister clearly understood mutual obligations based on the principles of impartiality and anonymity. The civil servant is expected to offer his advice to the minister, who has political responsibility, but he is obligated to carry out loyally whatever decision is reached."

"In the American setting, bureaucratic policy-makers must operate much more in the public eye, which gives greater leeway but also involves greater risks. . . . The system is less closed and more competitive. Contesting elements must seek allies not only elsewhere in the government but outside it as well."

"One important general difference pointed out by Crozier is that in Britain administrative organizations 'maintain their effectiveness by relying on the old pattern of deference that binds inferiors and superiors within the limits of the necessary cohesion.' In the United States, on the other hand, organizations 'must use many more impersonal rules in order to achieve the same results.' "

Modernizing Japan

"The transition and the role played in it by the bureaucracy reflected in part the pervasiveness of respect for authority in Japanese society generally. . . . Crozier comments that in Japan a strong authoritarian pattern of hierarchy 'has been internalized, and conflicts are handled more by subservience than by avoidance . . .' In its pattern of stratification, Japanese bureaucracy presents some similarities to the French system; however, 'unlike French bureaucracy, whose main function is to maintain law and order in a rebellious society, Japanese bureaucratic power has a decisive role as prime mover. It is the only way out for an over-controlled society that cannot find other sources of initiative.' "

Conflict Processes

The processes of competition, command and bargaining are essentially peaceful and governed by formal rules and informal normative constraints. Crucial additional elements in the competitive situation are the verdicts of third parties, whether judges, voters or other actors who grant support or award the 'prize.' Conflict on the other hand involves situations where actors pursue goals which are directly incompatible, where the success of one would directly inflict a cost on the other, whether intended or not. There tend to be fewer rules regulating the nature or outcomes of conflict and, in politics especially, the aims and means of conflict may be illegitimate. It has been suggested that competition degenerates into conflict when the competitors forget their striving for a scarce goal and begin instead to concentrate on interfering with or removing the other from the contest. The fears or costs of competition may lead the contenders to inflict damage on the opposition by subverting their reputation or status or otherwise depriving them of the ability to compete. Even our common language reflects different terminology for conflict and competitive situations. For example, in conflict the opposition is viewed as an 'implacable foe'; in competition, as 'a worthy contender.' The outcome of competition can be legitimized more easily: 'we did the best we could,' 'played fair,' 'hope to do better next time.' The outcomes of conflict situations are typically accompanied by ill-will, resentment, bitterness, a thirst for revenge 'to even the score.'

Conflict can be expressed in implicit or covert ways not readily observed by outsiders. Its non-legitimate forms would encourage this. In any case, most forms of conflict seem to be less admirable, less socially useful and more harmful than open competition. But despite the low moral status of most conflict, it is ubiquitous and always has been. As long as incompatabilities of goals and basic values exist, conflict will remain an important means of conducting political life.

We have chosen to discuss two types of conflict—one is a fairly peaceful type frequently waged among organizations or by a private organization and a government, while the other involves situations which end in violence of some form. Processes of intensification of the conflict are stressed in both instances.

Objective Organizational Conflict

A typical organizational conflict occurs whenever a private organization, such as a corporation, engages in an act which the leaders of the government wish to stop. In this country we have witnessed such occasions increasingly during the past twenty years. For example, companies have often raised prices after settling a labor contract, thereby incurring the wrath of a President who wishes to control the price level to prevent or slow down inflation. Typically, the corporation will announce its new price increases and within a day or so the President will issue a statement condemning the action. If the President is serious in his objections, conflict develops as each side moves and countermoves to mobilize support and make the other side back down. Typically, each side will escalate the conflict by introducing more powerful weapons into the fray. The President has the authority of office and enormous communications and administrative resources at his disposal, while the companies have the sanctified tradition of free enterprise and the knowledge that American public officials usually do not wish to press their case too far. Presidents can rally citizen support with cries of patriotism and public interest, can exercise personal suasion, can threaten the companies with loss of government contracts or with anti-trust actions and, generally, can inflict costs the companies do not want to accept.

Case Study #5   ·The Steel Dispute of 1962

President Kennedy's actions in the steel price crisis of 1962 are highly instructive on the resources and strategies a President can bring to bear in a conflict with powerful corporations.[14] Within a period of seventy-two hours, from the time the president of United States Steel Corporation announced price increases and then capitulated before President Kennedy's onslaught, we witnessed an impressive mobilization of resources and escalation of conflict. In brief outline this is what President Kennedy did:

1. Got Senator Kefauver and the Justice Department to announce independent investigations into steel activities, especially possible collusion—a violation of anti-trust laws.
2. Ordered his staff to collect economic information to be used against the companies at a press conference the following day.
3. Asked the Secretary of Commerce to telephone leading businessmen and especially customers of the steel companies to 'explain' the administration view.
4. Investigated the possibility of cutting off some of the steel companies' tax write-offs on new capital investment.
5. Had Congressional leaders denounce the price increases and hint publicly of possible legislation to prohibit such increases.
6. Contacted smaller companies to encourage them not to go along with the big companies; this was induced in part by announcements of steel purchases from them by the government.
7. Had the F.B.I. check into rumors that one steel company president said the price increases were not necessary; this statement was to be cited in an anti-trust case as evidence that the leading company had unduly influenced another corporation to accept price increases.
8. Made implied threats to cancel certain defense contracts.
9. The Democratic National Committee asked Democratic governors to issue statements in support of the President.
10. Two leading Pennsylvania Republicans expressed their opposition to price increases (apparently at Presidential request).

---

[14] A good account of the Kennedy-steel industry confrontation is found in Grant McConnell, *Steel and the Presidency—1962* (New York: W. W. Norton and Company, Inc., 1963). Our listing of events borrows from Arnold M. Rose, *The Power Structure: Political Process in American Society* (New York: Oxford University Press, 1967), pp. 105-107.

In contests of this type one side or the other will prevail in some degree. Prices cannot simultaneously remain constant and be increased. However, astute politicians would generally prefer a bargained outcome in which some prices are raised, but at different rates and, hopefully, the total price increase would be lower than if the government had not interceded. This is what happened a year later.

On occasion such conflicts can become rather emotional and personal. President Kennedy apparently so angered the steel executives by his dramatic reactions and harsh reflections on their motives and ultimate victory, that they never forgave him. President Johnson, however, managed to deal with the same companies in a much more cordial manner. Once a partner to such a conflict commits himself, he must win or suffer 'loss of face,' i.e., his reputation for effectiveness is damaged. Accordingly, each contender normally attempts to control his own responses, to induce acquiescence by covert means, and to escalate in marginal steps only as the other side continues to refuse. If one wishes a bargained (less costly) solution, one must always be prepared to ease up and allow the other side an opportunity to capitulate without serious loss of status. Apparently that principle was applied rather astutely by President Kennedy in the Cuban missile crisis. He made every effort to allow Premier Khrushchev the opportunity to back down by leaving alternative paths open. The Russian leader took advantage of that opportunity and indeed converted it into a victory of sorts among his own supporters. Astute politicians generally try to convert conflict to forms of mutual benefit, if possible, in order to reduce both the possibilities of further conflicts and their own costs of victory. In some cases compensatory advantages cannot be provided and one side or the other suffers a public defeat. Losses in conflict situations are not easily handled and are apt to provide powerful incentives for revenge. Winners of conflict are well advised to handle their own victories with grace and some concern for the loser, if he remains on the scene. Otherwise, he may forever seek opportunities for sweet revenge.

Processes of Intensification

Organizational conflict within political systems is usually non-violent, even though there may be overtones of threat and force. But however peacefully the original issues arise, if the goals are incompatible and threaten high costs, then one cannot rule out the possibility of violent means. Indeed, we see violence as a fact of political life these days, as we noted in our discussion of revolution, coups and instability. Of greatest interest are the ways conflict intensifies as actors persist in trying to win, often to the point of outright violence.

The statics of conflict or of any other form of political interaction are useful beginning points in analysis, but they are not theoretically satisfying. This is why some theorists take a dim view of the potentialities of game theory; it identifies the framework of the action but seldom describes or explains the sequence of events: move, countermove, counter-countermove. A respectable dynamic treatment of conflict cannot be provided here, for there is no single widely-accepted theory. There are, however, partial theories and we shall draw on them.

We are interested in political conflicts which intensify until one or the other side capitulates or a standoff is achieved. We are concerned with an elaboration of the sequences of choices and events, whether deliberately chosen or not. Conflict, after all, may be a rational strategy and the optimal one under some circumstances. Race riots, business-government confrontations and international arms races are examples of such interdependent choices.

We are not as interested here in the rationality of the choices as in the fact that the choices stimulate each contender to react with increasing hostility. In the arms races among nations, for example, each side claims that it had to increase its budgetary allocations for armaments because the other had done so. Further hostile moves (real and symbolic) are then made to maintain honor and defense. These might include belligerent speeches, highly publicized troop movements, meetings with allies, or changes in military expenditures. Imagine the United States and the Soviet Union proceeding as follows:

Initial Move: United States increases its defense expenditures
Countermove: Soviet Union increases its defense expenditures
Countermove: United States flies spy planes over U.S.S.R.
Countermove: Soviet Union shoots down one such U.S.A. plane
Countermove: ?
Countermove: ?

Some of these simple responses could be stated in graphic or mathematical terms, with each actor assigned a 'formula' or decision criteria for reacting to the other's arms level. The formula might include terms which say in effect that if one opponent's strength is greater than the other's, then the other will increase his by so much; or, if mutual conflict situations arise, each opponent will respond similarly in the next round. In Figure 10-4 we have drawn some highly abstract lines to show how two nations' arms disparities may change dramatically as they follow similar decision rules. As disparities change, the kinds and pace of the moves may become so unsettling that ultimately they may lead to war. At least that is what many fear when policy-makers are locked into such a conflict course. Of course, these lines are purely fictitious; most political changes do not take place at rates which can be neatly depicted in straight lines. More than likely

Figure 10-4
Hypothetical Arms Race

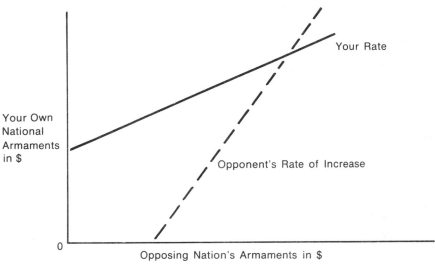

Your Rate

Your Own
National
Armaments
in $

Opponent's Rate of Increase

0

Opposing Nation's Armaments in $

the countermoves will be unequal and will be made in somewhat erratic or discontinuous fashion since time lags between decisions and their implementation are seldom uniform. More realistically, both lines should look like uneven staircases which may or may not meet or cross. The United States and China are in something of an arms race but the United States' line is probably located far above that of China's. How soon the two countries will approximate one another in national military power probably no one, including the C.I.A., knows. All the choices symbolized in these lines are made under some degree of uncertainty which contributes to fears and may intensify reactions.

One may also reason that if there were no conflict premise but instead a mutual concern over costs, the process of disarmament could be equally possible with varying rates of de-escalation. What makes these phenomena so fascinating is the fact that national behavior is partially dependent upon the leader's perceptions of his country's position relative to that of potential opponents, and upon what he thinks or fears these other nations may do. Perceptions are based on a great many only partially understood factors, and nations, like individuals, may misperceive another's actions. Historical studies provide many examples of decisions which produced outcomes contradictory to what was intended because the countermoves could not be controlled. In complex situations, accurate judgments (let alone effective solutions) are extraordinarily difficult to achieve considering the regrettable limitations on information and the secretiveness of one's opponents. General Motors would love knowing Ford's design plans, the Democrats would appreciate knowing Republican Party strategies, and the United States would prefer knowing China's intentions in Southeast Asia. But, intelligence sources are strictly limited for obvious reasons. The anxieties produced by uncertainty often result in reinforcing the premises of the conflict and raising its likely costs because one 'cannot afford to take a chance.' While increased security in international affairs may be wise for the nation in the short-run, in the long-run it may end in the irrational outcome of war. Similarly, the economists have shown how an individual's rational decision to save money may contribute to the unintended collective result of lowering national income and consequently reducing individual savings because there is less income from which to save. Such are the paradoxes of man's choices in an uncertain world.

Spontaneous Violence

Now let us take a different example of conflict processes culminating in violence. Riots, such as those in the Watts District of Los Angeles in 1965 and subsequently in Detroit and elsewhere, have some patterns or sequences that roughly correspond in time and form. Given certain conditions, the sequence may run something as follows:

Step 1 A 'minor' incident occurs in which a black citizen is challenged or wronged by a white, often by a white policeman. The incident may be a traffic violation or some mild disturbance.

Step 2 A fracas takes place between the original parties.

Step 3 Black witnesses spread the word.

Step 4 As the story circulates, the symbolic nature of the event triggers comments which enlarge its meaning. Rumors exaggerate the hostilities involved.

Step 5 Reactions of anger and demonstrations take place; disorder and excitement prevail.

Step 6 Individuals loot and damage property either to get something or to get even.

Step 7 The police are ordered to contain the riot.

Step 8 White officials attempt controls or threats, which confirms their 'enmity' in the eyes of the blacks.

Step 9 Arrests are made and sometimes rough-arm tactics are used by the police as they, too, react with anger, fear or hate.

Step 10 Snipers fire at the police and firemen.

Step 11 The National Guard is brought in to establish 'law and order.'

Step 12   Hostility subsides as the embers die, looters cart home their goods, and the riot leaders and others are jailed.

Step 13   Curfews are in effect; police and soldiers patrol.

Step 14   Order is established and reconstruction begins.

These many stages usually consume hours or, at most, days. Few riots last more than three or four days because energies are expended and the superior force of the government is asserted.

Another way to view riot potential can be seen in Figure 10-5. This diagram relates the levels of 'hostility' or threat perceptions of the two parties. Historically, it would appear that the black man's hostility-threshold for violence has dropped over the years. In other words, more blacks react more aggressively more readily than in the past. White hostility has probably changed in kind and perhaps even has diminished in quantity, although we do not have sufficient evidence on the matter. Figure 10-5 graphically describes what we consider a paradoxical case.

Figure 10-5

Black-White Hostility Trends

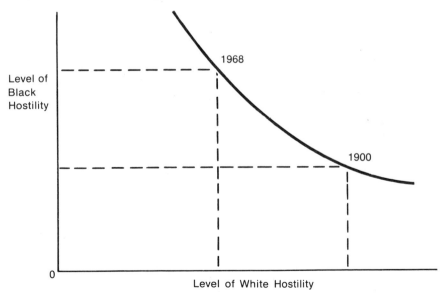

Assuming that hostility can be measured, the following analysis seems reasonable. In 1900, whites expressed more hostility toward blacks than blacks did toward whites. Today, expression of white hostility has probably diminished in intensity while black hostility has increased. This explains the greater willingness of black people to riot and protest. Their 'boiling point' is lower, meaning that a slight that was stoically accepted fifty years ago is considered intolerable today. And so the white man, whether he is conciliatory or indifferent, is confused, for the black man's hostility increases. Thus a reinforcing cycle is established which may be difficult to break, since each side cites the other's failures as reasons for its own behavior. Under such conditions the super-patriots and extremists "who know how to deal with the bastards" become more influential. Increasing hostility encourages extremist reactions. The moderates are branded as 'sellouts' who produced nothing in the past but talk. The 'hotheads' promise action. Eventually peace does come, but at a terrible cost in lives, property and honor. The aftermath of bitterness and the sense of injustice may last for generations.

In this case, polarization of conflict occurs because each side has a different perception of 'progress and harmony'—what it consists of and how much there should be. The decreased feelings of intense hostility on the part of many whites, and their belief that things are improving— perhaps their indifference to disparities—are not shared by most blacks. We hypothesize that the respective thresholds for engaging in overt conflict have shifted but the distance between the two parties, i.e., their lack of information about each other, will contribute to the relevant fears and exaggerations that will continue the destructive spiral.

Are conflict processes always destructive? Yes, if they deny someone's values or goals and are allowed to continue to a violent resolution. Pure conflict means that one side wins only by forcing the other to give in regardless of cost. But obviously cost is a constraining consideration: Is the price of victory worth it? Considering the after-effects of such conflict solutions may encourage a wiser choice of strategies, that is, getting what one wants in ways less destructive or less likely to rebound with future costs. As we shall discuss in later chapters, conflict-resolution may be achieved by restructuring such situations, either by redefining issues so that competition and bargaining can be introduced, by increasing information, or by reducing aggravations (fears, etc.) and the like. But more about that later.

Case Study #6   The Cuban Missile Crisis of 1962

In international affairs the 'confrontation' is a recurring event. Two powers try to 'face each other down' over some issue. The case of Soviet missiles in Cuba has become a famous example, where two great powers appeared to be on a collision course.[15]

---

[15] Our account is based on a special report, "The Cuban Crisis: Fourteen Days that Shook the World," issued by *The New York Times*, November 3, 1962, and on Roger Hilsman's book, *To Move a Nation* (Garden City, N.Y.: Doubleday and Company, Inc., 1967), Part 5.

United States officials had viewed both the communization of Cuba and the Soviet Union's aid to that regime with considerable apprehension. In the summer of 1962 U.S. intelligence began noting suspicious movements of Soviet ships, but determined that the military goods being transported there were 'defensive' in character. "Were it otherwise," President Kennedy stated publicly on September 4, "the gravest issues would arise." There were increasing rumors that it *was* otherwise, rumors which were ultimately confirmed. By October 14, detailed reconnaissance films revealed that there were surface-to-air missile sites being constructed about 100 miles from the U.S. coastline.

Top administration officials held a series of highly secret consultations about what to do: the Soviet challenge was considered intolerable, but the fears of Soviet designs and of aggravating world tensions caused equal concern. Some suspected this was the first step in a clever Soviet move on Berlin, an attempt at nuclear 'blackmail' to force the U.S. to give in to Soviet demands elsewhere. It was agreed that action had to be taken, not only to prevent the threat of nuclear attack but to save U.S. prestige and show that it would not back down on its pledges. Some thought that hostile elements in Latin America would receive great encouragement if the Soviets went unchallenged.

Alternatives were considered. It was decided that diplomatic approaches could prolong matters until it was too late. On the other hand, U.S. bombing of the sites or an invasion of Cuba would shift sympathies, anger NATO allies, and outrage the neutral nations, causing the U.S. to lose morally and giving the Soviets an excuse for countermoves in Berlin or elsewhere. Intermediate measures—various sanctions, a blockade, etc.— were considered, but would they bring results quickly enough, and at what costs? As time pressures increased, there were intensified efforts to obtain further information covertly about the extent of possible Soviet intentions and likely reactions. Until all matters were decided and ready, absolute secrecy and business-as-usual had to be maintained.

On the evening of October 22 the President delivered his dramatic address, documenting the Soviet's "secret, swift, and extraordinary build-up . . . ," protesting their deceitful reassurances, and announcing a "quarantine" by American military forces on further such shipments. The term 'blockade'—considered an act of war—was not used. And an ultimatum was delivered: if the preparation of the missile sites did not cease, "further action" would be taken; Chairmen Khrushchev was specifically requested to remove the weapons already there.

The first Soviet reactions were defensive and accusatory. The U.S. was pictured as violating international law and provoking hostilities; there were protestations of peaceful intent and protective concern toward Cuba. To the President and his advisors it appeared that Khrushchev was caught off guard and playing for time. There were further responses and charges, but the full story of the private communications has not been told. Subsequent accounts indicate there were very real fears of actual hostilities as the Soviets appeared unable to accept the blockade and unwilling to acquiesce. As Soviet ships moved toward Cuba, both countries displayed military preparations, and 'hawks' on both sides were apparently urging harsher actions. Then, on a fateful Sunday morning, Chairman Khrushchev sent a final message to President Kennedy promising to remove the weapons (with U.N. verification) on the assumption that no hostile actions would be taken by the U.S. against Cuba. The crisis was over, to the great relief of all, and apparently such a 'close shave' convinced both leaders to embark on more cooperative means of settlement in the near future.

Confrontation is a war of nerves, really, where threats and moves create such fears that one side finally backs down. Compare this kind of conflict intensification with that of actual military hostilities where the pressure is applied with physical force. Or, think back to the domestic steel conflict presented in Case Study #5, or the intensification of race riots discussed earlier. Are there similarities? Differences? Why?

Cooperation

Conflict, competition and bargaining all rest on the idea that dissimilar goals divide men and that, on public matters, means must be found for achieving divergent ends. Cooperation, on the other hand, assumes that men can share compatible goals without one having to give in or defer to the other.[16] Just as no society and polity can deny the fact of contradictory goals, so no system can deny the fact that men often share aspirations and work together for a common goal or cause. There is no implication, however, that cooperation occurs only for good things, or is less costly in effort or outcome—these depend upon the circumstances. Cooperation can occur for selfish reasons, and it can involve ends that are costly to others, even the participants, depending on what they choose to do and on what unforeseen consequences may occur. Among the forms of cooperation are collusion, conspiracy, collaboration, comradeship, coexistence—any form of joint enterprise for common ends. We can hope that cooperation is used for good ends alone and, if it could replace all conflict, we would indeed have the best of all possible worlds. But this discussion is not an exercise in

---

[16] One of the best analyses of cooperation is contained in Chester I. Barnard's *The Functions of the Executive* (Cambridge: Harvard University Press, 1938), especially Chap. 5. Our view may also be compared with the concept of "discussion" advanced by Lewis A. Froman, Jr., *People and Politics* (Englewood Cliffs, N.J.: Prentice-Hall, Inc., 1962), pp. 58-61, 72-74 and of "integrative bargaining" dealt with by Richard E. Walton and Robert B. McKersie in *A Behavioral Theory of Labor Negotiations* (New York: McGraw-Hill Book Company, 1965), Chap. 5.

utopian philosophy. We merely wish to assert that cooperation is a common political process in many places and for many reasons. Therefore let us look at some of its conditions or requirements, and consider some illustrations.

Although cooperation is possible, it is not always automatic. Except in the most informal or spontaneous circumstances, there must be some recognition by at least one of the actors that there is a mutuality or compatibility of goals. This means that one—or perhaps many, or all—must see that what he wants is something which can be shared or pursued by the other(s), without loss to any of them. In other words, in cooperative endeavors the end is *not* a scarce good so there is no win-or-lose situation. And if it is mutually desired, there need be no command situation involved either.

One of the most appealing aspects of political and social affairs is the abundance of many goods—mostly non-material in form—which are found in political endeavor, namely those symbolic goods which are jointly believed in or shared by many. Many political loyalties and identifications have this potential whether they involve the nation-state or local political clubs, groups or associations. It is fortunate that there are such ends and affiliations which can be shared because if all political endeavor involved bargaining, competition or conflict over scarcities, many would find it intolerably costly.

Instrumental Cooperation

More typically, however, people cooperate at one level in order to compete or bargain more effectively at another. For this reason volunteers will participate in political campaigns during election times when the heat of the contest evokes party loyalty. Within administrative and legislative bodies sub-groups or work associates cooperate to get things done, and often in consultative or collegial meetings more time is spent finding common ground than is spent actually bargaining or competing.

In this sense the most pervasive sort of political cooperation is probably that which takes place informally in the course of almost all political endeavor. This is true whether it is the everyday political discussion between like-minded partisans, the more systematic relationships of political activists or the even more formalized arrangements of bureaucrats, leaders and office-holders, for cooperation is a basic ingredient of all collective endeavor. One might say that cooperation takes place so that the more important issues of public life *can* be communicated and contended. Yet it must be understood that cooperation can also merge into the other kinds of relationships, or alternate with them. It is impossible to separate any of these in real life; we do so only for analysis.

Since so many cooperative processes are quite informal, they are very likely to be unconscious, or habitual; accordingly, the reason for sharing is not directly articulated. It is only when something disrupts the normal state of affairs that the shared goals become articulated. This kind of cooperation would be identified most with the diffused learning processes of informal and immediate associations such as have been found in pre-literate primitive societies or in the more stable and habituated informal groups that persist even in modern life. But we are more interested in the means by which cooperation is achieved in more fluid and complex settings. This is where the 'things in common' must be recognized so that joint endeavor can be arranged and accepted. And this is where one should be clear as to what is shared and what is not, for this will establish the possibilities and limits of cooperation.

Communication of Appeals

The first requisite is some form of communication so that recognition of something in common may take place. One traces cooperative patterns by communication lines although, as we know, not all that is communicated will further that end. It has become a platitude to say that "all people need to do is to communicate"; there are many things which are not agreed upon, no matter how much they are discussed. But communication is at least a first step toward cooperative possibilities, depending upon whether the actors find shared or compatible goals in the process. This is easiest where the initial communication brings an automatic cooperative response. That is, all one has to do is tap a preconditioned response from the other. This is where the socialization of loyalties, feelings, and concerns pays off. The instant recognition of like-mindedness may then easily be transformed into joint political endeavor—provided the shared concerns exceed the expected costs or overcome the obstacles experienced.

Social distance can limit the forms and opportunities for cooperation among groups. Political goals will affect those in different places or positions in divergent ways. Most of the concerns to which persons respond instantly are matters 'close to home'—making a living, personal fears and hopes, private loves and hates, the pleasures and pains of personal existence. Only when these pains cumulate and intensify for some major groups do we see the possibility of a broad and rapid cooperative movement. This is what James Madison would call a "conflagration," and he feared its unstabilizing effect in the American system.[17] But American history discloses few such broad-scale appeals that resulted in sustained cooperative political endeavor. Maybe the pamphleteering and crude propaganda of

---

[17] James Madison, *The Federalist No. 10*. Many editions are available, some under the title of *The Federalist Papers*.

some of the revolutionary leaders caused Madison concern for the new nation. Apparently those appeals did spark a lot of smoldering grievances and new aspirations among the colonists. But the U.S. has seen few movements involving so many people: abolition, perhaps; the agrarian and temperance causes in the late 19th and early 20th century; the unionization of labor; the civil rights movement today, to be sure. More often the general appeals which generate instantaneous response come from established leadership on behalf of patriotic causes, and only rarely is the response massive and purely cooperative. Even in wartime such appeals, while more likely to be effective, could hardly begin to organize a total war effort. Instead, command processes are relied upon extensively. Few peacetime concerns evoke cooperative responses on a wide scale. Conservation campaigns ('Smoky the Bear' is evidently winning considerable cooperation in preventing forest fires) and 'beautification' appeals receive some direct response, and certainly community appeals for one cause or another achieve some measure of local cooperation.

Organized Coordination

More often, however, cooperative processes require more than just communication; there must be additional persuasion and what one scholar calls "mutual adjustment" before joint endeavors are undertaken on any scale in the political realm.[18] And, if cooperation is to be sustained over any length of time, it usually requires organized coordination as well. Few goals are as clearly defined and accepted in a political system as survival in war or in an emergency, or as conservation and beautification, where the shared concern relates so easily to the contribution the individual can and indeed wants to make. More often some persuasion is required for persons to see the value of the common effort, to understand the goal and to relate their efforts to it. In many political issues coordinated cooperation requires time and much consultation, persuasion, clarification and 'adjustment.' There may be a will to agree, but there must also be acceptable ways and means. Much more time is probably spent in party caucuses, club meetings and conferences trying to find agreement than is spent in actually competing and bargaining. Of course, discussion can be argument, i.e., a competition of viewpoints, but this depends on the definition given it by the contenders. A genuine win-or-lose debate is quite different from a discussion starting with initial differences; it has to do with the 'stakes' involved. Compare, for example, the accounts of cabinet meetings during the Eisenhower administration with reports of what took place dur-

---

[18] Charles E. Lindblom, *The Intelligence of Democracy* (New York: The Free Press, 1965).

ing John Adams's administration when Alexander Hamilton apparently
exerted a great influence over many cabinet members contrary to his President's wishes.[19] Accounts of the Eisenhower cabinet meetings suggest a
consensus-oriented endeavor, from opening prayers to organized round-
table discussions of problems. President Eisenhower apparently encouraged
cooperation by emphasizing high-mindedness, courtesy and tact and by
disapproving of adamant differences. During the Adams administration
there were accounts of ill-tempered contention, some exacerbating issues
and a President who angrily resisted the pressures from within his official
family; in other words, confrontation rather than cooperation.

Bureaucratic Devices

In more complex systems cooperation is formally organized and even
institutionalized, whether the participants would have chosen to agree
or not. In a highly bureaucratized public—and private—society such as the
United States's, the conference and committee meeting has become a way
of life. The essential communication on which cooperation depends is
systematized in the form of memoranda, reports, recommendations and
directives which flow across desks and through agencies, guided by route
slips or punched IBM cards. The individual citizen would boggle at the
task of independently selecting the cues for massive cooperative endeavor
but, by systematizing the procedures, the political or public functionary can
perform almost as automatically as primitive man followed tribal custom.

Administrators speak of 'coordination' as the deliberate and rational
sort of magic that keeps an organization running smoothly in the direction
of its designated goals. And more frequently organizations rely on a voluntary cooperative form of division of labor rather than the compulsion so
typically identified with hierarchical bodies. When a division of labor runs
along 'functional' or specialist lines, the communication of information
(rather than commands) becomes the most crucial device for realizing a
collective endeavor. Thus, the kind of non-directive staff relationships
described in Chapter 8 are far more pervasive at the top and middle levels
of bureaucracies than the formal organization chart will show. There are
innumerable forms: the ad hoc consulting group, the advisory committee,
the interdepartmental committee are just a few. Some scholars have tried
to estimate the growth of such consultative bodies in the U.S. federal
bureaucracy. Apparently in 1938 there were about fifty or so bringing
information from outside groups to relevant administrative bodies. Today

---

[19] On the Hamilton-Adams conflict see Leonard D. White, *The Federalists* (New York:
The Macmillan Company, 1956), Chap. 20. For an account of President Eisenhower's
contrasting approach see Robert J. Donovan, *Eisenhower: The Inside Story* (New York:
Harper and Brothers, Publishers, 1956), Chap. 5.

they are estimated well into the hundreds, and some say they run into the thousands.[20]

It must be emphasized that the basic ingredient in cooperative arrangements is the relatively unhampered communication of information to further joint ends. The willingness to share information in this sense depends greatly on trust—some form of mutual identification and expectation of at least some degree of openness. This is what is so often missing in international negotiations and in the relationships between competitors or bargainers. In the latter cases each side furthers its interests by non-disclosure of crucial information, the one to gain the advantages of surprise, the other to reach the best possible 'price.' Trust is a communal sort of thing, best nurtured by mutual and basic identifications or long associations between parties. The stranger and outsider find it harder to come by, unless there are ongoing socialization processes that encourage new forms of identification for particular purposes. Again it is easy to see how such trust is best nurtured in the more intimate or familiar associations of life.

Case Study #7   An Account of the President's Executive Committee During Crisis

Nothing so unites persons as awesome responsibilities during a time of crisis. Much has been speculated and written about that small group of men whom President Kennedy selected to help decide on a course of action during the Cuban missile crisis of 1962. The following are brief excerpts from the account of one participant, Theodore C. Sorensen, as first published in *Look* magazine:

> Shortly thereafter, upon arriving at his office, the President sent for me and told me the news. He asked me to attend the 11:45 a.m. meeting in the Cabinet Room. Those summoned to that session at the personal direction of the President, or taking part in the daily meetings that then followed, were the principal members of what would later be called the Executive Committee of the National Security Council, some 14 or 15 men who had little in common except the President's desire for their judgment. . . .
>
> My recollection of the 96 hours that followed is a blur of meetings and discussions. The proposals varied, our progress varied. . . .
>
> Much misinformation has been written about this series of meetings, about who said what and about such terms as 'hawks and doves,' 'think tank,' 'ExCom' and 'Trollope ploy,' which I never heard used at the time. . . . One of the remarkable aspects of those

---

[20] Norman John Powell, *Responsible Public Bureaucracy in the United States* (Boston: Allyn and Bacon, Inc., 1967), p. 124.

meetings was a sense of complete equality. Protocol mattered little when the nation's life was at stake. Experience mattered little in a crisis that had no precedent. Even rank mattered little when secrecy prevented staff support. We were 15 individuals on our own, representing the President and not different departments. Assistant secretaries differed vigorously with their secretaries; I participated much more freely than I ever had in a National Security Council Meeting; and the absence of the President encouraged everyone to speak his mind.

It was after noting these tendencies in a Wednesday afternoon meeting, held while the President fulfilled a campaign commitment in Connecticut, that I recommended he authorize more such preparatory meetings without his presence. He agreed, and these meetings continued on the State Department's 7th floor. . . . And when he did preside, recognizing that lower-ranking advisers like Llewellyn Thompson would not voluntarily contradict their superiors in front of the President, and that persuasive advisers like McNamara unintentionally silenced less articulate men, he took pains to seek everyone's individual views. In contrast with his first Cuban crisis, when he had conferred with a somewhat different group, he knew his men, we knew each other, and all weighed the consequences of failure.[21]

Problems and Applications

1. Some theorists have maintained that the kind of problems presented for collective choice on page 434 are unrealistic because they do not reflect intensities of preferences or a time period which would presumably permit majorities to form and collective decisions to be made. How would the inclusion of these two factors (intensities and time) in the models permit solutions?
2. Compare and contrast votes with money as a medium of exchange in society. What advantages and disadvantages accompany each medium: For accomplishing what tasks? For realizing people's preferences?
3. Why do so many citizens in western democracies object to the trading and selling of votes? Do you think it is a sound practice? When or why?
4. Do bargaining, competition, command, conflict and cooperative situations require different skills and attitudes on the part of their practioners? If so, why? Why are these skills and attitudes most relevant in each process?
5. Can you formulate any generalizations about the costs of reaching

---

[21] Theodore C. Sorensen, "Kennedy vs. Khrushchev: The Showdown in Cuba," *Look Magazine* (September 7, 1965), pp. 45-46.

decisions using the various choice mechanisms or processes dealt with in this chapter? How might they be tested?

6. Rank-order the following issues in terms of their 'bargainability' in each of these nations: U.S.A., U.S.S.R., Germany, Mexico (or use countries with which you are familiar). Explain your ordering.

   Prayer in public schools
   Property tax
   Nationalization of steel industry (or the reverse)
   Guaranteed annual income for all adults

7. No democracy permits completely free electoral competition in the sense that everyone who wishes may become a competitor. Can you think of some groups in the United States who are prohibited from or discouraged from competition? Why are they denied access? What differences would it make if they were permitted to compete?

8. What kinds of issues permit and encourage bargaining? Which do not? Why? Cite some cases from current newspapers.

9. Why is it that no society finds it possible to rely on a single policy-making process? Could you imagine what such a system would be like?

10. Consider how a legislature might function if both compromise and log-rolling were banned. How would it affect (a) legislators, (b) citizens, (c) the decision costs, (d) policy formation? Are there other considerations you feel are important?

Bibliographical Notes

The problem of collective choice has long preoccupied political scientists, as it should. However, much of the work has been descriptive, anecdoctal, historical and not very analytical. Still, the traditional literature has some gems which we recommend with the highest accolades. For example, E. E. Schattschneider's early writings mentioned in the notes to Chapter 9 come to mind, as does his more recent *The Semi-Sovereign People*, New York: Holt, Rinehart and Winston, Inc., 1960, which is very perceptive about competition and conflict. A less explicitly theoretical work, but one filled with fine insights into American policy-making, is E. Pendleton Herring's *The Politics of Democracy*, New York: W. W. Norton and Company, Inc., 1940. Consistent with the views expressed in these books are two by Edward C. Banfield, *Politics, Planning, and the Public Interest*, New York: The Free Press of Glencoe, 1955, and *Political Influence*, New York: The Free Press of Glencoe, 1961. The former is a case study of policy-making with respect to public housing in Chicago and the latter concerns a number of municipal decisions in Chicago; both are guided by some first-rate theorizing. Case studies of decision or policy-making in other countries have not been abundant. However, we have

managed to locate an interesting set of case studies involving policy-making
in Great Britain, France, West Germany, the Soviet Union and India
under the title of *Cases in Comparative Politics,* edited by James B. Cris-
toph, Boston: Little, Brown and Company, 1965. A similar case book, edited
by John G. Stoessinger and Alan F. Westin, is *Power and Order: Six Cases
in World Politics,* New York: Harcourt, Brace and Company, 1964. Still
another collection on European states is that edited by Gwendolen M.
Carter and Alan F. Westin, *Politics in Europe: Five Cases in European
Government,* New York: Harcourt, Brace and Company, 1965. A fine
collection of research pieces on American local politics, particularly since
the authors attempt to measure outcomes, is found in *City Politics and
Public Policy,* New York: John Wiley and Sons, Inc., 1968, edited by
James Q. Wilson.

Perhaps, of much greater interest in the context of the present chapter
is the rapidly growing volume of more abstract and theoretical work
being done by behavioral scientists on conflict, bargaining and competition. Much of this writing is found in the professional journals and is
often highly technical. We refer to such journals as *The American Economic Review, Conflict Resolution, The Journal of Political Economy,
Behavioral Sciences* and, above all, the new journal, *Public Choice,* which
formerly bore the awkward title of *Papers in Non-Market Decision-Making.* Much of the writing is done by economists and mathematicians, with
sociologists and political scientists gradually working their way into the
scene. As yet, there is no reader or anthology of such research and theory. If we know publishers and fellow academics, several will appear
shortly.

Not all the thinking being done on the basic policy-making processes
is esoteric. We especially recommend the writings of Charles E. Lindblom,
including *The Intelligence of Democracy: Decision-Making through
Mutual Adjustment,* New York: The Free Press, 1965 and, co-authored
with David Braybrooke, *A Strategy of Decision,* New York: The Free Press
of Glencoe, 1963. William A. Gamson, *Power and Discontent,* Homewood,
Ill.: The Dorsey Press, 1968, is a sensitive and yet rigorous attempt to
characterize certain aspects of public policy-making. Neil W. Chamberlain,
A General Theory of Economic Process, New York: Harper and Brothers,
1955, has influenced our thinking. Chapters 6, 14 and 17 on bargaining
are the most relevant for political scientists. Another study of great
import for us and quite easy to read is Richard E. Walton and Robert B.
McKersie's *A Behavioral Theory of Labor Negotiations,* New York: Mc-
Graw-Hill Book Company, 1965. While the book is about labor negotiations, it is highly suggestive on bargaining generally and Chapter 11 has
applications to civil rights and international bargaining. Readers interested
in the latter should also consult the highly readable although less theoretical book by Fred C. Iklé, *How Nations Negotiate,* New York: Harper
and Row, Publishers, 1964. Another highly readable volume, yet sensitive

to both theoretical issues and empirical data, is Albert O. Hirschman's *Journeys Toward Progress: Studies of Economic Policy-Making in Latin America,* New York: The Twentieth Century Fund, 1963, especially Part 2, which deals with such matters as "Problem Solving and Reformmongering." Hirschman is insightful, mature, and writes with ease about technical matters.

Readers more concerned with individual choice or formal model-building might consider a somewhat different type of literature. For example, David W. Miller and Martin K. Starr's *The Structure of Human Decisions,* Englewood Cliffs, N.J.: Prentice-Hall, Inc., 1967, is a good introduction to individual choice theory. Unfortunately most of the examples are from the realm of business, but the imaginative reader can readily see their applicability to the political arena. An excellent collection of classic articles is edited by Ward Edwards and Amos Tversky, *Decision Making,* Harmondsworth, Middlesex, England: Penguin Books, Inc., 1967. Ward Edwards is a distinguished psychologist who has made signal contributions to this rapidly emerging field within psychology. Much of the concern is with choice or decisions under varying conditions of risk and uncertainty. Unlike the economists, psychologists frequently devise interesting laboratory experiments to test their hypotheses. Because students are usually employed as the guinea pigs for the tests, the realism of the results can be limited. One of the rare experiments in political science concerns the making of decisions in small groups such as committees or city councils. James D. Barber, *Power in Committees: An Experiment in the Governmental Process,* Chicago: Rand McNally and Company, 1966, investigates both collective and individual choice, particularly as they pertain to budgetary decisions.

Conflict and its resolution is now an important study for social science; as a consequence, one can turn to many journals and books for first-rate thinking. We suggest you begin with such studies as Lewis Coser, *The Social Functions of Conflict,* Glencoe, Ill.: The Free Press of Glencoe, 1956, a persuasive defense of some of the benefits of conflict, and Kenneth Boulding, *Conflict and Defense,* New York: Harper and Brothers, 1962, a highly stimulating analysis sharpened by the skills of an economist and the concerns of a pacifist. The techniques of economics are used with imagination and skill to elucidate many problems in conflict situations. *The Nature of Conflict,* Paris: UNESCO, 1957, contains four lengthy bibliographic essays by two sociologists, a psychologist and a journalist on different approaches to the analysis of conflict, plus a bibliography of more than 1100 listings. If one seeks to minimize conflict solutions, we suggest a look at Robin M. Williams, Jr., *The Reduction of Intergroup Tensions,* New York: Social Science Research Council, 1947. Williams advances an impressive list of propositions about conflict and its reduction. The approaches to conflict of the several social sciences are also elaborated in *The Nature of Human Conflict,* Englewood Cliffs, N.J.: Prentice-Hall,

Inc., 1965, written by a number of distinguished American social scientists and edited by Elton B. McNeil.

As the following titles strongly suggest, political competition is often treated as a part of conflict theory. Probably the single best introduction to game theory, at least in terms of good writing and wide ranging applications, is Thomas C. Schelling's *The Strategy of Conflict,* Cambridge: Harvard University Press, 1960. Those who might wish a more straightforward exposition on games of strategy should consult J. D. Williams, *The Compleat Strategist,* New York: McGraw-Hill Book Company, 1954. It even has cartoons and exercises. Another readable version of game theory, but one which goes on to analyze critically the typical form of strategic choices in game terms, is Anatol Rapaport, *Strategy and Conscience,* New York: Harper and Row, Publishers, 1964. In particular, Rapaport condemns the basic assumption among many strategic thinkers of zero-sum situations. The tendency to deal exclusively with that type of situation has unfortunate consequences since the person who does so tends to define every situation as a win or lose contest without seeking mutually beneficial outcomes. Another critical analysis of game theory (and of the hard-headed military strategists who might apply it) is Philip Green's *Deadly Logic: The Theory of Nuclear Deterrence,* Columbus: Ohio State University Press, 1966. An object of these critical attacks is Herman Kahn's *On Escalation: Metaphors and Scenarios,* New York: Frederick A. Praeger, Inc., 1965, most famous for its elaboration of some forty-four steps or rungs in the ladder of escalation. A useful summary of escalation as applied to the beginnings of World War II is found on page 29 of Kahn's book in which both German and British countermoves are clearly categorized. Perhaps a less imaginative but a more rigorous analysis of similar intensifications of conflict is Martin C. McGuire's *Secrecy and the Arms Race,* Cambridge: Harvard University Press, 1965. The author examines a number of theories on escalation and evolves his own, largely in economic terms.

As the above titles clearly indicate, much of the work now being done on competition and conflict is being accomplished through the use of rational choice models, generally flavored with economic concepts and theories of behavior. Purely political theories and concepts are difficult to find. It should be noted, however, that much of this same work also focusses, as it never did prior to World War II, on international politics and wars. On the other hand, the famous Kerner Report on race riots, officially known as the *Report of the National Advisory Commission on Civil Disorders,* New York: Bantam Books, 1968, treats a serious domestic problem of conflict and does so with the more general tools of the social sciences. We suggest it not only for its information and insight on this greatest of domestic issues, but also for its valuable example of good social science research written in a style every citizen can understand.

Sihanouk Trusts His Balancing Act
The New York Times, Nov. 14, 1968, New York, New York

60 Per Cent Of Voters Went to Polls
San Francisco Chronicle, Nov. 19, 1968, San Francisco, California

Guatemala City Rated Fir
The Oregonian, Sept. 30, 1968, Portland, Oregon

AKISTAN SEIZES MORE AYUB FOES
The New York Times, Nov. 14, 1968, New York, New York

Voter Faces Tough Choice
Eugene Register-Guard, Sept. 24, 1968, Eugene, Oregon

Bureaucra

SOVIET UNION: Tidy Tyranny
Newsweek, Oct. 21, 1968, Washington, D.C.

Marches (
Eugene Register-Guard, Aug. 16, 1968, Eugene, Oregon

HHH Sees Clear Choice
The Oregonian, Aug. 9, 1968, Portland, Oregon

Police State Atmosphe
The Oregonian, Sept. 30, 1968, Portland, Oregon

Let Conflicting Interests Be Know
Eugene Register-Guard, Sept. 23, 1968, Eugene, Oregon

Final Ballots Alter Nothing
The Oregonian, Sept. 25, 1968, Portland, Oregon

HUNGARY ALTERS ECONOMY TODAY

Cooperation Meet Topic
The Oregonian, Sept. 22, 1968, Portland, Oregon

Rule by the 'Elite'
The National Observer, July 22, 1968, Silver Spring, Maryland

eforms, Long Planned, All Go Into Effect at Once
The New York Times, Jan. 1, 1968, New York, New York

Community Effc
The Oregonian, Aug. 12, 1968, Portland, Oregon

Chapter 11

Assessing Political Processes: Capacities, Achievements and Shortcomings

Few, if any, citizens have an opportunity to choose the political society in which they live, but they can make assessments of what they like or wish to change in the system. While assessments are often made in casual or general terms, they ought to be based on clear-cut criteria. What standards should be applied ought not to be determined until we know what various processes accomplish.

Before beginning the study of processes, let us consider three caveats. The first concerns the need to analyze actual systems rather than abstract conceptions. No idealized or pure process of any kind—command, cooperative, competitive, etc.—has ever existed. While it is desirable to explore the logical implications of various models, the more imperfect and mixed systems of the real world must be studied to ascertain comparative performances and satisfactions. We must choose from among imperfect types, not idealized abstractions.

Second, real-world systems do not fit the contours of the abstract models built by political scientists and others. The models are built with exceedingly restricted sets of variables and not with the full range of human behavior and all its aberrations, confusions, limitations of intelligence, knowledge, integrity, interest and participation. Unforeseen events are likewise excluded. Models are departures from reality; the crucial question concerns their usefulness and that is not easily answered.

Finally, when one type of political activity is said to be *theoretically* superior to another, this cannot be interpreted to mean that it is so in actual practice. We are inclined to follow Aristotle in his preference for the best of the 'practical' systems, admitting beforehand that we are concerned only with a variety of imperfections and less than maximal performances. In this preference we leave a sizeable area for criticism of existing systems and for assessing desirable change. Improvement of man's existence is always possible; being practical is no surrender of the critical faculty. But being practical enables one to detect shortcomings and provide workable solutions for the short run. We do not believe in complete and final solutions, a point we shall elaborate in Chapters 12 and 13. For the moment we claim only that such an attitude is helpful.

Bases for Comparison and Evaluation

The assessment of political activities has been a preoccupation of political scientists but rarely have they been able to formalize or systematize their efforts into a broadly acceptable set of criteria. This lack is due not so much to the shortcomings of the political scientists as to the extraordinary problems raised by such an inquiry. Evaluation depends upon having explicit and realistic criteria, comparable data or evidence about actual performances and, of course, the means of acquiring the data. The first requirement is difficult to meet because men do not value the same things in political life. Accordingly, one man's major criteria are not another's. Still, we ought to make our criteria explicit. While not an easily achieved goal, it should be attempted. Second, acquiring relevant evidence about the workings and achievements or failures of actual systems is costly and often impossible because those possessing the requisite information may be unable or unwilling to provide it. Finding comparable empirical evidence about quite different processes and societies further complicates the problem of assessment because there are many unique combinations of processes. In spite of all these hazards we think it possible to make some progress. If we fail to convince others of our assessments, perhaps we will at least provoke them to a better formulation of their own values, criteria and the necessary evidence for comparison.

Criteria for Evaluation

Since this entire chapter is devoted to evaluations, we should make our basic criteria as specific and explicit as possible. Political systems can be judged from a variety of perspectives other than ours, but naturally we think our criteria are commendable—at least as an initial basis for discussion. In any event, the following standards seem appropriate:

1. A political system ought to provide at least a minimal level of public goods and services, including such generalized goods as order and safety and such symbolic goods as dignity and regard.
2. A political system ought to distribute these goods and services equitably and fairly, and with some concern for effectiveness and efficiency as well.
3. Every system ought to be as adaptable to changing conditions and as responsive to citizen preferences as its resources and basic priorities will allow.
4. Every political system should enhance the opportunities to develop its members' talents, motivations and resources as effectively as possible.
5. Every political system should seek to minimize dissatisfactions and disproportionate costs in its responses to new problems.

We shall not elaborate upon these very broad criteria at this point. However, if the reader is repelled by a particular criterion, he should try defending its opposite. For example, how easily can criterion #2 be dislodged by arguing that every political system should be as inefficient as possible—in short, should produce its public goods and services with the greatest cost or wastage of resources? Similar problems and dilemmas can be found in rejecting the other criteria.

It should also be noted that in establishing criteria one runs the risk of asserting logically incompatible demands, and indeed we have. What may be an efficient use of resources may not protect citizen dignity and vice versa. We cannot provide a generalized means of resolving such dilemmas; one must either choose between incompatibles or attempt to find some combination which will allow a partial achievement of each. Ultimately, each of us must make this decision for himself. As we shall emphasize throughout Part 2, the cost of greater attainment of one value is lesser attainment of some other(s). One cannot have everything, which is why evaluation and advising are so difficult.

One must also understand how each of the five main processes or systems—command, competition, bargaining, cooperation and conflict—relates to the handling of the fundamental problems of politics (such as allocation of resources, distribution of benefits, regulation of behavior, division of labor, stabilization and adaptability, etc.). More specifically, our concern is to link the *processes* and their *outcomes*. One may approve of an outcome without approving of a process, or vice versa, so it is important also to distinguish the two. Figure 11-1 outlines the problem. One must not apply such categories in a rigid mechanical way, but use them as convenient organizers for thought and an indication of questions to come.

Figure 11-1 can be used in two ways. First *empirically based estimates* can be made of the existing and probable capabilities and performances

Figure 11-1

An Outline for Evaluating Political Performance

Problems:	Processes: Bargaining	Competition	Command	Conflict	Cooperation
Resource Mobilization and Allocation					
Distribution of Benefits					
Distribution of Burdens					
Regulation					
Adaptability and Stabilization					
Division of Labor and Allocation of Roles					

for each problem with respect to the particular sets of decision processes; second, these capabilities and performances can be evaluated using our five criteria. To this latter assignment might be added an assessment of goals not attempted. In principle one ought to be able to grade each polity in much the same way that a teacher grades student performances. Such a 'report card' might include grades ranging from an 'A' to 'F' to signify relative achievement. Unhappily, many of the grades would be about as poorly-based as are student grades.

The assessment or evaluation of political performance is bound to be crude; the explicit criteria and precise indicators which economists have for estimating economic performance are lacking in the political arena. Progress is being made, however, and, if widely-accepted criteria cannot be developed, perhaps alternative standards and choices can be found. Thus, one day we may be able to judge the efficiency of a particular process but remain unable to agree on when or whether it should be used in specific instances. Of course, one of the tasks of politics is to provide answers to this latter question. So we shall be political advocates, acknowledging that our positions need not be those of others.

A few more words of caution may be appropriate. In evaluating political systems and policies we must, to quote the distinguished economist Paul Samuelson, "choose among the lesser of evils or among the greater of goods."[1] We might borrow further from his authority to confirm an earlier suggestion: "When we reject a measure on the ground that a better measure is possible, we must be sure that this better measure is in fact being used and that the relevant political choice is not between a half-good measure and no action at all."[2] So we choose in a world of uncertainty among relative imperfections. This is not a counsel of despair, although the impatient are apt to treat it as such. It is the counsel of concerned but qualified hope.

An Overview

In the pages that follow we shall direct most of our discussion to those processes in which differences over preferred goals require strategic choices. We will deal at length with bargaining and competitive processes because they are the most complex and therefore the least understood. We also admit a bias in this emphasis but will try to justify it. First, competition and bargaining are basic decision processes in a democracy and, therefore, in need of more consideration and understanding. Second, the effectiveness

---

[1] "Full Employment versus Progress and Other Economic Goals," in Max F. Millikan, ed., *Income Stabilization for a Developing Democracy* (New Haven: Yale University Press, 1953), p. 562.

[2] *Ibid.,* pp. 562-63.

of each citizen is dependent in great measure on his developing skills for engaging in these democratic processes. Nevertheless, the continuing resort to conflict makes it necessary to appraise its uses as well. We readily admit, however, that an understanding of conflict processes is more difficult and challenging; we can only suggest some possibilities. Somewhat less attention will be given to command and cooperation because their basic attribute—a similar preference for or conformity to one set of goals—makes them more easily understood.

An Assessment of Bargaining and Competition

Modern political theories of democratic systems have come to emphasize the central role of bargaining and competition for the resolution of differences and the rendering of collective choice. Only in recent decades, however, have the intricacies of these processes been studied systematically and, to a degree, sympathetically in the realm of politics. It used to be much more popular to 'expose' such activities as working against democratic ideals. It is still a very popular belief that bargaining and competition involve 'selfish interests' which will bring about outcomes inimical to 'the public good.' This is possible but not necessary. There is no inevitability about what kind of outcomes will result from any form of activity until one considers the nature of the goals and the resources of the parties involved.

In the sections that follow we offer a variety of considerations about bargaining and competition, both pro and con, in terms of the important kinds of outcomes discussed in Part 1. These processes are taken up jointly because, in stable democracies, they tend to influence one another. Indeed, this is quite an important point: that each may contribute some corrective to the less desirable possibilities of the other. Consider, therefore, some of the following pros and cons.

Mobilization of Resources and Division of Labor

Opportunities for Participation—Bargaining and competition work best in systems or situations where there are broadly dispersed resources. In the economy this means many buyers and sellers bringing their resources to the marketplace. In politics this typically means citizens exercising their voting rights. The history of democracies reflects the progressive extension of the franchise until today nearly all adults are granted suffrage. There is a persuasive theory that these extensions of the vote were per se a part of the rising competition of newer social elements with those already in the political establishment. We subscribe to this 'logic of competition' and hope that it will continue to push the actual enjoyment of the franchise to previously deprived groups.

But openness for participation also involves the dispersal of other resources such as the relatively broad distribution of opportunities to exercise influence by running for office, supporting alternative leaders, joining politically salient associations, and assembling openly for the expression of political preferences and demands. Basic to all of this is having relatively easy access to communication; in a complex society that is an especially important resource. Real competitive and bargaining systems cannot tolerate a monopoly of information and it is most crucial that the words of one contestant can be countered by others.

All of these opportunities for participation exist to a greater degree than ever before but they are not consistently exploited by all citizens. For instance, voter turnouts in the United States are generally lower than those in many European democracies. That opportunities are not fully exploited by all is not necessarily a criticism of either the system or the citizenry, for it can represent a 'negative participation' by those who are satisfied with the workings and/or outcomes of the polity. Such satisfied persons may well turn out at the great symbolic occasions for an expression of solidarity and satisfaction. They, too, are participating by giving symbolic support to the system. How else should one interpret the act of millions of Americans who have visited the grave of President Kennedy, or have wept at the death of a beloved political leader?

Most political scientists are inclined to dismiss the supportive forms of participation and measure only those which involve contention. Yet, on these latter grounds the western bargaining systems rank fairly high when compared with other systems. And most of the western democracies are currently experimenting with new methods of participation; for example, Norway has attracted attention and imitators with its ombudsmen who assist citizens in pressing claims against the government. In the United States various experiments are being tried to give the ghetto resident more of a voice in things; these range from the tough-minded approach of Saul Alinsky and some of his more militant black competitors to the controversial government sponsored Community Action Programs. More U.S. legislators are expanding their typical 'errand-boy' services to an active solicitation of citizens' views by questionnaires, roving committee hearings and better publicized office hours in their local constituency.

This active solicitation of voter opinion is important for the development of voluntary participation. In competition and bargaining it is the sense of contest over those issues about which one cares that provides incentives for participating. Electoral studies have shown that the closer the race, the higher the turnout; this is logical since one's sense of efficacy would be correspondingly greater. In bargaining situations it is the desire for the *gain that could be made* which induces people to seek to bargain. If the citizen can identify with one of the contenders or issues in an election, the vicarious excitement can also enhance interest.

Protective Aspects—Finally, the dispersal of resources in bargaining and competitive situations provides guarantees against forced or unpopular means of extracting resources for, or distributing the costs of, running the public sector. Recall the discussion of taxation in Chapter 2 concerning the changes in sources and methods for raising public revenues. Those systems most characterized by widespread bargaining and competition tend to have the broadest tax structures and the most direct forms by which the citizen can measure what he gives to government. Perhaps nothing stimulates participation more than the thought that one may be required to give more than another. Evidence of this can be seen in the taxpayer 'revolts' at the polls. The exchange relationship between government and voter encourages public officials to defend and support the programs which require such resources. Nowhere is this more evident than in the area of school financing. By way of illustration, a Eugene, Oregon, school district's finance proposal was turned down three times by the voters before final approval was given in a fourth balloting. The fierce supporters of 'better' schools found this process very painful but, in the course of it all, the school officials were prompted to hold extensive hearings on complaints and finally conducted a questionnaire survey in the course of the final balloting. This helped to explain in much greater depth what antagonized so many voters (it turned out to be concern over inequitable property taxes). Broadly speaking, therefore, the responsiveness of public agencies is highest where 'public bargaining' opportunities exist.

Inequalities of Resources—One must note, however, some limitations on competition and bargaining as they work in the real world. The very gravest concern is over the inequalities of resources and advantages which not only limit the ability of many to bargain or compete successfully but also may tend to reinforce such inequalities. Do those with the initial advantages always win? If so, then bargaining and competition may serve as devices for the more powerful to cumulate additional resources and command further advantages.

The non-visibility of many bargaining processes makes this more possible. There is a realistic fear about 'deals' in smoke-filled rooms where bargaining may replace competition for office or for policies. We can only say here that the prospective pay-offs of waging competition must be sufficiently promising to forestall such bargaining between would-be competitors. In the long run, at least, it would appear that they do, as our discussion of the 'ins' and 'outs' illustrates. If bargaining can make possible further advantages for the privileged, it can also be expected to cumulate grievances for the have-nots. Political resources, like popularity, reputation and support, may shift *if* there are competitive opportunities for their expression. Without such opportunities, bargaining systems would decline into conflict or enforced command situations.

Bargaining and Competitive Costs—One fact is apparent to anyone who has ever belonged to a club, organization or even a family. The more people one must consult in formulating goals and their implementation, the more time, energy, skills, etc., are 'consumed'—in other words, the higher the real costs. Think of all the time that must be spent requesting, rebutting, persuading; learning the opinions and preferences of others; mediating disputes; correcting false impressions and misunderstandings. Politicians devote most of their time to such activities at the expense of other activities. The costs of their political action are their lost opportunities. We may call these costs 'bargaining costs.'[3]

The positive relationship between the level of bargaining costs and the number of persons to be consulted can be illustrated with a simple graph, as in Figure 11-2.

As we incur real bargaining costs we also pay another cost which seems best described as 'frustration.' The bargaining process is not only time consuming but emotionally disturbing to many. People become frustrated, impatient and irritated at its complexity and their own lack of control and apparent incapacity to begin or conclude any collective decision. In bargaining, one must pay continuous attention to others whether one likes them or not because they have power and may use it in disconcerting ways.

Frustration, or the inability to achieve one's preferences, is a fact of life in all systems but in bargaining it is more difficult to accept because our aspirations tend to be higher when we are active participants. The disappointment of high aspirations is also an inevitable cost of competition—for the losing side. After investing time, energy and often extensive material resources, one can find defeat especially bitter. Was it all worth it? What went wrong? The competitive process must offer considerable promise to make the gamble worth the risk of losing.

Whether winning or losing in competition, both sides pay to wage the contest. American presidential elections, for example, have cost each party over $15 million during recent years. In the 1960 Presidential campaign the cost per vote was estimated to be about 40¢.[4] This does not include the costs of administering the election, a cost borne by the government and ulti-

---

[3] Cf. James M. Buchanan and Gordon Tullock, *The Calculus of Consent* (Ann Arbor: The University of Michigan Press, 1962), Chap. 8.

[4] *Congress and the Nation: 1945-1964* (Washington, D.C.: Congressional Quarterly, Inc., 1965), p. 1536.

Figure 11-2

Bargaining Costs

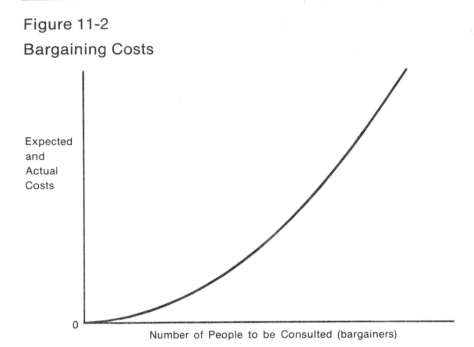

mately the taxpayers. Before a politician can gain the nomination, however, he must spend considerable sums of money. For example, Senator
Eugene McCarthy spent about $2.12 per vote in the 1968 Presidential
primary in the state of Oregon while his opponent, Senator Robert Kennedy, was reported to have spent $1.95 per vote.[5]

Or, consider the money costs of interest groups as they compete for
favorable public policies at the national level. In 1963, for example, some
384 registered interest groups reported a total expenditure of more than
$4 million,[6] the top spender being the United Federation of Postal Clerks
(AFL-CIO) with an expenditure of $202,997.[7] The all-time high in such
reported spending was more than $10 million spent by 430 groups in 1950.
So far as we know, no one has attempted to estimate the total expenditures
on political action by both candidates and interest groups, perhaps because
it is almost impossible to measure. One estimate of the total cash outlay for
all campaigning (electoral competition) during 1960 placed the figure at
approximately $140 million.[8] While this is a huge amount one can argue

---

[5] *Eugene Register-Guard,* June 18, 1968, p. 12A.

[6] *Congress and the Nation: 1945-1964, op. cit.,* p. 1586.

[7] *Ibid.,* p. 1590.

[8] Alexander Heard, *The Costs of Democracy* (Chapel Hill: University of North Carolina
Press, 1960), p. 372.

that it is really a very small price to pay for the advantages of competition. Given the population in 1960, this amounted to approximately 90¢ per person. The national income at that time was about $300 billion, or about $2000 per capita, so in monetary terms the cost was relatively small.

Information Costs—All systems require information, but all do not require the same amounts or kinds of information. Bargaining systems demand an especially great supply of information. Rulers of command systems also require large amounts, but not the citizens. The citizen in bargaining systems, however, has a more important role to play so he too needs information; so do all the lesser politicians. In the United States that means about 523,000 elected public officials plus all their competitors. Information costs tend to be high because the bargainer and competitor require knowledge about one another as well as about the substance of policy alternatives. Each must also acquire information about others regarding their respective preferences, resources, motivations, opportunities, assessments of the situation and strategies. Such information can be difficult to acquire because the actors may have good reason to conceal it. Either party must be prepared to stop the search at the point where it becomes less rewarding to go on, unless one is a lonely scholar. The law of diminishing marginal utility applies to information as well as to other goods.

Figure 11-3 shows the relationship between costs and amounts of information both in terms of actual and expected needs and costs. Note that the total cost is a function of the amount of information sought. The amount of information sought is a function, in turn, of the number of bargainers and/or competitors one must deal with in the system. There are various types of information; we emphasize here those which relate to the contenders themselves. Other kinds include technical knowledge about public policies and information about voter preferences. Political activists spend much money and time gathering such information.[9]

Obviously, in command systems the number of citizens who must pay these high information costs is very limited since the proportion of bargainers and competitors is severely restricted. The ordinary citizen has little need to pay information costs because he is unable to engage in such political processes. Of course, not all members of competitive systems have equal needs for information either. Since many citizens seldom participate, they have little need for information and typically do not acquire much (as the opinion polls consistently demonstrate). So it is up to the elected politicians and higher-ranking appointees to make their case and to do so, they need much information and must, of course, pay more for it. Given its potentials, however, the information is surely

---

[9] See Fritz Machlup, *The Production and Distribution of Knowledge in the United States* (Princeton: Princeton University Press, 1962).

Figure 11-3
Information Costs

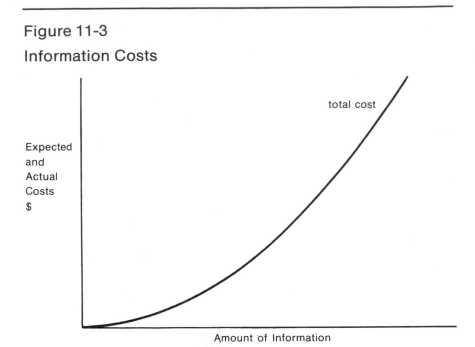

worth the cost, at least up to the point where added costs would equal marginal returns of value.

Allocation of Resources and Distribution of Benefits and Costs

To be discussed here are the policy choices made by nation-states concerning the use of the people's resources. The respective allocations should be judged on the basis of the needs and preferences of the citizenry. As is often the case pertinent data are extremely fragmentary and unreliable but one must make the judgments regardless of the availability of data.

While there is no single allocative standard that can be considered ideal for all nations, it is clear that some criteria are better than others. For example, a nation-state ought to provide its citizens with a basic set of public goods and services, including a reasonably stable money supply, free and universal education, minimum standards of health, a reasonably safe society, and some elementary assurance of a decent standard of living so that private activities of commerce, industry, art and recreation may be facilitated. Nations that are unable to provide these basic requirements are generally not admired. To the extent that the polity is involved in providing whatever levels are available, so it must be judged.

Provision for Alternatives—A recurrent criticism of many western nations has been their failure to provide citizens with 'meaningful' alternatives to existing policies on resource allocation. We reject this wholesale accusation. To be sure not all competitive-bargaining systems provide the same alternatives nor as frequent or clear-cut choices as others. We simply cannot accept the notion that diametrically-opposed alternatives must be offered in all policy areas; such a system would prove unworkable. We do believe, however, that the marketplace of policies and ideas should be sufficiently free to allow discussion of many possibilities so that if some proposals do attract sufficient adherents they may become practical alternatives at some reasonable future date.

Granted that competitive-bargaining systems do not offer extreme alternatives at every election, it should be noted that no other system does either, although occasionally one may do so. An important function of every competitive and bargaining system is to whittle down the number of practical choices so that the costs of collective and individual decision-making are reduced. In this whittling down process a great many policy suggestions are eliminated from effective competition, at least in the short-run. But ideas that seem likely to bring promised payoffs or support usually manage to be considered in competitive processes where the search for better appeals can be rewarded. There is a typical life-history of new issues and proposals, from their support by the few to their acceptance or ultimate rejection by the many, after which they relinquish their place to other concerns. Frequently critical or pressing times will encourage political leaders to seek new ideas and programs. An overwhelming electoral victory provides the most favorable mandate for 'a new start.' After all, politicians who have capitalized on grievances to win office are impelled to do something different to satisfy their supporters. There have been 'critical' elections which have permanently altered the power structure and/or policy commitments of governments. The British election of 1945 and the American election of 1932 are examples of great electoral transformations in both policy and parties.

Marginal Gains—Bargaining systems typically provide voters with an opportunity to inspect and choose among policies and candidates that are only marginally or incrementally different. Choosing between Republicans and Democrats in this country is quite a different thing from having to choose from among Communists, Fascists, Socialists and more middle-of-the-road parties. The same is true in Great Britain; some commentators claim that the differences between the Labour and Conservative Parties are about the same as the Republican-Democratic split in the United States. Such apparently narrow choices may not be very exciting to some, but for those who want some continuity in policies such choices are highly rational. A complete change of governmental performance after every election would so confuse the political demand-maker that he would lose the efficacy of focusing on particular grievances. Behavior and policy would become too unpredictable. Such unsettling changes would probably favor the conservatism of the status quo because too much uncertainty would force most citizens to ask themselves how much they were prepared to risk or lose in order to realize their demands. We believe that most men want some continuity most of the time; we also believe that periodic opportunities to redress inequities that inevitably occur in highly stable systems are also vital. Those who develop favored positions in the distribution of resources and benefits will be opposed to change; opportunities must be available either to persuade them to alter their behavior or to break away crucial support without risking all.

Marginal choices were mentioned as one means of describing the typical situation of alternatives in bargaining and competition. By marginal we mean that the system offers a choice between more or less of a public good rather than a choice between having or not having it. For example, bargaining nations no longer offer voters an opportunity to accept or reject social security but rather offer candidates who support or oppose the particular extent of coverage and/or benefits. Conservatives tend to want to limit such programs while liberals tend toward greater generosity. Likewise, conservative parties tend to protect the interests of the better-off while the less conservative parties tend to advance the interests of the less advantaged. The general social base of their alternative concerns is a useful incentive to continue the competition.

We believe that marginal types of choice situations are produced by the complexities and interdependencies of modern industrialized societies, by the formal political structures, and by the distribution of power. Political considerations do have an independent impact, but only within the limitations posed by the requirements of running industrialized societies. Periodically, marginal changes prove too ineffective and greater policy changes or innovations are initiated and accepted. Such changes may be complete reversals of past policies or lesser innovations. Some cases have been suggested in earlier pages, but as yet the circumstances and rates of innovation require more analysis, both here and abroad.

Electoral Limitations on Choice—The typical voter experiences the limitations on policy alternatives through the special mechanism of elections since the vote is the major means he has of expressing his choices.[10] While it is true that competitive elections are a much prized political achievement, it is equally true that elections are rather imperfect mecha-

[10] For an original and insightful comparison of markets and elections as mechanisms of individual choice see James M. Buchanan, "Individual Choice in Voting and the Market," in the author's *Fiscal Theory and Political Economy* (Chapel Hill: University of North Carolina Press, 1960), pp. 90-104.

nisms for registering individual political preferences. They may be the best available means of aggregating preferences but they are imperfect in varying degrees, depending upon the type of election. We should not deceive ourselves about these shortcomings; if we do, we limit our own capacity to be more effective. Political or collective decisions involving resource allocation and the distribution of goods and costs are very much influenced by the type of election rules that happen to prevail. Both theory and empirical results substantiate this conclusion.

Among the characteristics of elections that define situations for voters and affect their choices are the following: (1) frequency of elections, (2) decision rules, i.e., whether choice is determined by majority rule, 'extra-majority' proportional representation, or plurality rules, etc., (3) type of ballot and order of the candidates or measures on the ballot, (4) nature of the choices—candidates or issues, (5) number of alternatives and (6) the social-political environment of the election.

We will not write in detail about each of these characteristics since every strategic situation needs analysis of its own particulars; we will, however, raise questions about some of the major consequences which ought to be kept in mind. Because elections are generally infrequent they do not allow *continuous* expressions of preferences, not even to the extent of legislative assemblies where voting occurs almost daily. Voting procedures which provide for flexible timing of elections, as is the case in Britain, work to the advantage of the side which controls the initiative for calling them.

The number of electoral alternatives is generally quite limited regarding candidates and still more limited in the case of referenda where the alternatives are restricted to approval or disapproval. Unable to find a more complete array of alternatives the voter becomes increasingly dependent on a candidate or ideology to define his preferences.

In addition to being restricted by the dearth of choice, the voter is also restricted in the degree of choice. Since candidates and issues are seldom divisible, one cannot vote for more or less as one does when buying goods in the marketplace. Because voters cannot divide their vote so as to give fractional support to each candidate, they are unable to express the relative *intensities* of their choices. Proportional representation allows some of this expression in the sense that one may vote for more than one man but that is hardly equivalent to purchasing another pound of butter and giving up a half-pound of sirloin or some other commodity. In other words, marginal choice is not possible because *the alternatives are not divisible*.[11] Effective choice is accordingly reduced.

Indivisibility also applies to referenda issues, i.e., elections in which

---

[11] In all fairness to elections it should also be pointed out that many products in the marketplace are typically not divisible; for example, an automobile, or a house. However, one can buy two cars or two houses if one has the money, whereas the voters cannot have two Presidents.

the voter is permitted to pass approval or disapproval upon substantive issues. Almost any issue can be made into a referendum but most are concerned with governmental expenditure and revenue. Such issues are inherently monetary and therefore can be expressed in terms of more or less expenditures or more or less taxation, yet the issues are seldom if ever stated as such on the ballot. Most often such proposals offer an either/or choice; take it or leave it. The voter cannot express himself in terms of having somewhat more or somewhat less in the way of expenditures or taxation. Furthermore, the voter is usually denied the opportunity to state his preferences on these matters *jointly,* i.e., on costs and benefits together. If he is given a joint choice it is also on an either/or basis. However, costs and returns that cannot be simultaneously evaluated in marginally divisible terms leave the voter in a most difficult choice situation.

        Tendencies Toward Equality—Perhaps the most controversial of our claims for competitive-bargaining systems is the assertion that a tendency toward equality in the distribution of benefits and costs exists in these systems and continues.

        A complete documentation of this claim would entail nothing less than a thorough analysis of practically all policies in the bargaining systems. We are in no position to perform this task and it is hardly appropriate here. However, the data we have dealt with and our own analyses suggest that there is a trend toward equality. It is not rapid enough in our estimation but it proceeds in the right direction.

        Historical evidence strongly indicates that income, status, power and more particularized benefits are being held by larger proportions of the populations in all the competitive bargaining systems. For example, shares of formal power (votes) have been dispersed to the extent that formal universal suffrage now exists in all democratic systems except Switzerland where woman are excluded. And public policies, especially in recent decades, have been directed toward the improvement of traditionally less-advantaged groups. This has been partially accomplished by governmental expenditures on public goods, by income transfers and by taxation policies which have worked to redistribute income. These policies have not been as effective as many reformers would like but they have worked to some extent. This is graphically illustrated in Table 11-1 which depicts the distribution of income over several years in recent American history. The figures show a continuous trend toward greater equality. No one claims that whatever equalization that has taken place is solely the product of governmental policies but few would maintain that such policies had nothing whatsoever to do with this trend.

        Without boring or overwhelming the reader with the obvious statistical facts, we will simply point out that the western democracies with their competitive-bargaining political processes have provided their populations

Table 11-1

Size Distribution of Personal Incomes of
Consumer Units 1929, 1941, 1947, 1963 (Dollars of 1963)

	Per Cent Distribution			
Income	1929	1941	1947	1963
Under $2,000	30	27	16	11
$2,000-$3,999	38	28	28	18
$4,000-$5,999	16	22	26	20
$6,000-$7,999	7	12	14	18
$8,000-$9,999	3	5	7	12
$10,000-$14,999 ⎱	6	6	6	13
$15,000 and over ⎰			3	8
Average (mean) income per consumer unit	$4,300	$4,599*	$5,520	$7,510

* 1962 dollars.

Source: Bernard F. Haley, "Changes in the Distribution of Income in the United States," in Jean Marchal and Bernard Ducros, eds., *The Distribution of National Income* (New York: St. Martin's Press, Inc., 1968), p. 4.

with more (and better) of the basics and amenities of life than have other countries. The standard of living, generally, is considerably higher in western Europe, the United States, Australia, New Zealand and Canada than in the non-democratic states. Even among the so-called democracies, those with the lower achievements tend to be the less stable. Italy and Greece are (or were) cases in point. Among Latin American countries, the greater social achievements are found in the relatively more democratic nations of Mexico, Costa Rica and Uruguay.[12] Standards of health, literacy, housing, inflationary controls, expenditures on development, social security (health insurance, medical and maternity benefits, old age benefits, unemployment insurance)—all seem to be more advanced in the more democratic of the nations the world over, although with some conspicuous exceptions in every area. At one time autocratic Germany, under Bismarck, led the world in social security legislation. Today, one finds dictatorial regimes in many underdeveloped nations making serious efforts to industrialize and improve the standard of living. But on the whole, the record of the democracies is vastly superior even when comparing nations of equivalent

[12] Charles W. Anderson, *Politics and Economic Change in Latin America* (Princeton, N.J.: D. Van Nostrand Company, Inc., 1967), Chap. 11.

natural and other resources. A reason is that the citizenry is able to make legitimate demands upon competing politicians to provide services. In the absence of such demands one must hope that the dictator will either have a social conscience or be rational enough to forestall criticism and revolt by providing more public services.

Policies regarding the allocation of resources are a key to judging the worth of political systems. How a nation allocates its public resources is a good indicator of what its leaders value. The more citizens can participate in the political life of their society, the more likely the leaders will reflect the citizens' values regarding appropriate uses of resources. Of course we speak again of tendencies and not absolute fact. In some nations, including the democratic, many contend that insufficient resources are devoted to public services. In some nations the pattern of allocation among public goods is imbalanced with too much going to military expenditures and not enough to such necessities as adequate police and fire protection, good highways, sufficient recreational areas, beautiful public buildings and extensive libraries. However, one must keep in mind comparative performance. The possibilities are more encouraging when looked at that way.

External Costs—Throughout life each citizen pays costs that are the consequence of the activities and bargains of others; economists label such costs 'external' since they are incurred by other than those who created them. Political systems in which bargaining and competition are practiced tend to keep these costs lower because such systems involve wider participation. In other words, a person who is in a bargaining position can more effectively prevent—or reduce—external costs wherever he becomes aware of them. A unanimity rule would eliminate or seriously reduce external costs because each person could veto any cost imposed on him. Those who are least able to prevent the imposition of an external cost are those who cannot participate in the processes of public choice. Life is so complex that a person cannot entirely avoid such costs, but he may reduce them. Most people seem intuitively to understand this since a great deal of political action and public policy are products of efforts to reduce one's share of external costs. Political scientists have recognized this fact in their development of interest-group theories of political process. When the interaction of certain interest groups results in loss to another interest, those affected are likely to organize to combat the loss. These are the sorts of activities which may broaden the participating electorate.

Whatever the label used to designate these relationships, the factor of external costs is important in accounting for political action. Competitive-bargaining systems do afford opportunities for citizens to reduce or at least exercise some control over their shares by controlling their own political resources. The logic of reduced external costs can be conveyed in the form of a curve which relates costs to the number of participants in choice-making. Other things being equal, the more participants, the lower the potential or expected costs, assuming that individuals generally prefer to reduce their share of the burdens. Likewise, those who are able to participate will prefer to shift their costs onto non-participants. Figure 11-4 states the general shape of the relationship.

Figure 11-4
External Costs and Participation

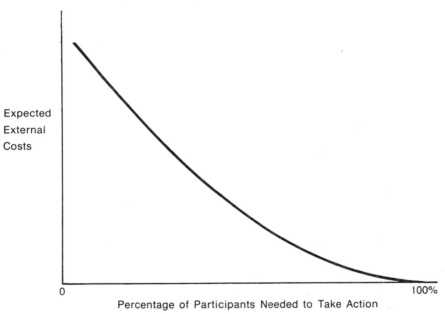

Unpredictable Performance—We should also like to emphasize that policy outcomes can seldom be predicted from the election results of voting for candidates. The policies which are pursued and enacted after an election may have little resemblance to one's actual voting choices. Seldom is the interested voter able to predict the complete policy behavior of winners once they are installed in office. Uncertainty induces politicians to be ambiguous and/or contradictory. The voter who has a strongly ordered set of policy preferences is apt to be disappointed in his quest for information about the long-run policy choices of the various competitors. On the other hand, a vote tells the politicians very little about most citizens' policy preferences. What can a politician infer from an 'X' on a ballot about the dimensions of a voter's substantive concerns and policy choices? Both voter and politician are placed in highly uncertain situations with respect to policy preferences and behavior. The opportunity for some choice leads the voter to assess the more likely probabilities but does not guarantee performance.

'Second-Best' Outcomes—Perhaps this title does not adequately describe what we have in mind. (Anyone who thinks of a better one can send it to us, C.O.D.) What we mean is this: the bargaining process normally ensures that every bargainer will have some say in the determination of the outcome but, by having to bargain, he is forced to accept something less than his most preferred outcome. If a person did not have to bargain, he might maximize his returns; however, since others also want maximized returns, each bargainer normally encounters opposition. Everyone, therefore, ends up with something but no one with everything he prefers. The result: a 'second-best' or minimally acceptable policy and, of course, numerous complaints and frustrations.

Important legislation in bargaining systems may often become a patchwork of compromises, often inconsistent. One of the most famous products of compromise and logrolling is the U.S. Constitution. The founding fathers are highly honored and revered, and they should be—but more for their bargaining skills than for their political vision. We believe that bargained constitutions work; Platonic constitutions do not. The former are hardly ideal, but they do seek out common grounds of acceptability. As the politicians are prone to say, "I can live with that," or "I think they can live with it"—'it' being the 'second-best.' For those who cannot tolerate less than their own most preferred ends, the world of the acceptable, the second-best, is apt to be viewed as an intolerable cost. Such people would have a system in which their ideal becomes the ideal for all others, which is why idealists are so susceptible to totalitarian solutions. For the ideal to be self--evident requires all dissidents to be resocialized or coerced into acceptance. It is true, however, that one cost of bargaining is the fact that one must accept less than one prefers. *But this must be balanced against the costs of no solution.* Failure to agree may have still greater costs. And failures to agree do occur, at least in the short-run. The American Civil War is a prime example. Another is the entire history of the French Third Republic in which agreement came to be regarded as a sign of moral cowardice. Perhaps it was, under the circumstances.

Misallocation of Resources—While competitive-bargaining systems undoubtedly honor more preferences of the ordinary citizen than any other type of political system, they fail to the extent that imperfections are found in the process. Thus, time-lags in adaptation, unequal distributions of political resources, information gaps, misinformation, all contribute to failures in optimal resource allocation and the wider distribution of welfare.

For example, many analysts are convinced that public goods, in general, are sacrificed and that particular public goods are produced in critically short supply. Parks, recreational facilities, welfare services (housing, unemployment insurance, medical protection), beautification, natural resources and education are all minimized in terms of quantity and quality. Since these goods provide little incentive for businessmen to produce them, they are left to political systems and government. In turn, the government, given its dependence on unpopular taxes, is normally confronted with inadequate resources and cannot produce as many of these public goods as are required to complement private consumption. John Kenneth Galbraith claims that public goods are always sacrificed to the private in affluent capitalist societies.[13] He may be right, but it is also true that the amounts devoted to public goods in the poorer societies are disproportionately less than optimal. Recall Chapter 2.

Some students may also argue that bargaining systems emphasize the wrong public goods, i.e., they allocate far too much to such activities as armaments, agricultural subsidies and, indeed, grants to the more well-off generally. The United States Government, for example, enables the shipping industry to remain competitive on the high seas. Domestic airlines are highly subsidized; agriculture outdraws all other groups in terms of subsidies; many non-profit groups such as churches and educational institutions which do not pay taxes are, in effect, subsidized; and the railroads have been traditionally supported by the government in most societies. These groups derive their subsidies not only on the basis of necessary contribution to the society but also on the basis of bargaining power. Activities such as the creative arts and literature (and perhaps the social sciences) are seldom subsidized to the same extent. Even the state of public buildings, parks and grounds is not always admirable.

More importantly, an unequal distribution of political resources enables some groups to have more of their preferred goods than they would have if greater equality in bargaining power prevailed. As we contended in Chapter 3, those who benefit most in bargaining systems are the higher social status citizens with higher incomes and more education. Other groups tend to be underrepresented and therefore underprivileged. The kinds and amounts of public goods that would benefit the less well-off are not produced in sufficient quantities. In fact, the less affluent recognize this themselves. As noted in Chapter 2, various studies have found that lower-status, lower-income voters tend to prefer greater public expenditures and to express approval of greater expenditures on public goods that would benefit themselves, including most social security programs. The higher

---

[13] *The Affluent Society* (Boston: Houghton Mifflin Company, 1960). The same general claim has been made in a rather different way by Anthony Downs, *An Economic Theory of Democracy* (New York: Harper and Brothers, Publishers, 1957), and in "Why the Government Budget Is Too Small in a Democracy," *World Politics*, XII (July, 1960), pp. 541-563.

social status voters tend to support such public expenditures as schools, parks, concert halls, airports, and other public goods that complement their more plentiful private goods and preferences.[14] Furthermore, many of these latter public goods are useless to the lower-income groups or are too expensive to enjoy. The poor travel by bus; the better-off fly first-class, with extensive publicly supported facilities and subsidies easing the costs. The poor do not and often cannot appreciate high culture, and the public parks are usually too inconveniently located for them to enjoy. All public goods are presumably available to all members of society, and they are in a formal sense; but in fact they are less available to certain citizens.

Diffused Responsibility—For whatever reasons, most people want to attribute political responsibility. One reason may be that by distributing rewards and penalties we expect to control actions, i.e., by rewarding some actions we ensure their continuance and by not rewarding others we reduce or prevent their occurrence. In the political system we wish to locate responsibility among public officials and others so as to perpetuate that which we prefer and to discourage that which we dislike. Offering rewards through electoral and budget processes are the major techniques.

Voters in a bargaining system, however, often have trouble locating responsibility. Invisible and/or multiple roles and the interdependence of decision-makers obscure many of those actually involved. Whom are we to credit for the good policies? To whom shall we attribute the bad ones? Since many bargainers participate in the decision-making process, one cannot easily decide which should be credited or discredited. Responsibility is widely if unevenly diffused. Additionally, one must recognize that many events are beyond the immediate control of any public official. In so far as responsibility can be attributed, one must acknowledge that the intricacy of bargaining makes it most difficult for the voter to decide.

How does the multiplication of electoral posts affect this situation? In some ways it helps if the duties and powers are specified. However, this tends to give advantage to particular interests which can mobilize their resources about a given office. Thus some interest groups have benefited more from fragmented state administrations. Yet increased centralization of responsibility offers its dilemmas too. If all outcomes depend upon one contest, how can the citizen selectively express his grievances and his satisfactions? An illustration of this barrier is the 'centralized party' situation in Great Britain which, we think, operates at high cost to the proponents of innovation.

---

[14] Eva Mueller, "Public Attitudes Toward Fiscal Programs,' *The Quarterly Journal of Economics,* 87 (May, 1963), pp. 210-224; and, for contrast, James Q. Wilson and Edward C. Banfield, "Public Regardingness as a Value Premise in Voting Behavior," *American Political Science Review,* LVIII (December, 1964), pp. 876-887.

Concerning Controls

Bargaining and competitive systems are notorious for 'soft' solutions to problems in that they try to find grounds for agreement which are acceptable to all sides. Usually the demand for controls comes from those who feel they have suffered at the hands of others, whether they be the trusts, railroads, labor unions or other elements defined as inimical to society. When reacting to such charges, the accused groups typically try to deflect the anger, protest innocence, redefine the causes of ills, etc. Ultimately, however, if the demands for regulation are substantial, the threatened groups will agree to bargain, and the more effectively if they feel it is a life-and-death matter. Unfortunately for those demanding more controls, the bargaining process usually continues after rulings are made and laws are passed, making the likelihood of continued evasion great. Bargaining and competitive systems typically do not produce 'tough' solutions until the outrage is so general as to provide overwhelming support for stiff control measures.

Soft solutions to control problems do not appear everywhere in bargaining systems; they occur most often where the regulated have disproportionate power. Groups with considerable power will be able to have strong measures enacted on their behalf while those with few resources will be less protected. In this country, tough controls have been exercised against criminals and subversives while little legislation has been enacted on behalf of consumers, small businessmen or even the independent farmers. The larger the enterprise to be regulated, the more likely it is to have resources to spend bargaining for relief; even the underworld seeks ways to buy off forceful regulation. Some commentators have observed that tough sounding but largely symbolic legislation is often passed to pacify radical demands for controls over privileged interests.[15] Once such legislation is enacted, it tends to be administered with diminishing enthusiasm until the regulatory agency is eventually influenced more by those who were originally supposed to be controlled. Many regulatory agencies at the federal level in the United States have thus, in effect, learned to 'live with' the groups they are empowered to regulate. Much the same has happened at the state and local levels in such fields as air and water pollution, control over mining, employers' liabilities, consumer protection, civil rights, etc.

It is not simply bargaining that produces these results but unequal bargaining positions and weak competitive institutions. The solution is not to abandon bargaining but to strengthen the weaker parties.

The competitive mechanism, however, can play a very useful role in maintaining regulations where the costs of violations are borne directly by

---

[15] Murray Edelman, *The Symbolic Uses of Politics* (Urbana, Ill.: The University of Illinois Press, 1964).

the aggrieved parties, thus encouraging them to turn to public authorities for redress. Legal processes provide a highly regularized means of determining violation of controls through the presentation of evidence, with authoritative judgment being rendered by a third party. If there is some benefit to be derived from doing so, the aggrieved parties will initiate the procedure and furnish the relevant information, functions which are typically so costly in directly administered regulatory programs. The expected gains may be awards for damages or the penalties and prohibitions enforced on the violator.

Court procedures are the most pervasive means of turning conflicts between parties into institutionalized competition, but the regulatory commission and public agency have frequently taken on these tasks in more complex and conflicting areas such as marketing or health and safety regulations. In highly competitive sectors, the enterprises may police each other; bringing suit against 'unfair competition' is one such technique. But many regulated enterprises are either natural monopolies (as with certain public utilities) or find advantages in collusion, merger or other means of joining forces. In such cases their customers or suppliers must have the incentive and means to bring relevant charges. More frequently governmental agencies, in their role as purchaser of goods and services, have become major complainants because of their direct concern over costs. For example, the extraordinary 1960 antitrust suits against major electrical companies were instigated by information supplied from a federal government agency which bought electric equipment.[16]

Not to be overlooked is the important role played by the press in publicizing the investigations and stimulating public outrage at violations of the rules of the game. The role of the press in competitive processes can never be underestimated; not only does it dramatize the contest and thus stimulate public interest but it also provides socialization about what the norms of competition should be. There are, of course, great opportunities for the abuse of information, especially in playing upon public emotions by questioning the motives for infractions, abuses, etc. But we think the advantages of such publicly aired contests are still greater. As E. E. Schattschneider points out, the party which can contain the conflict controls the outcomes, and making them public—what he calls 'socializing the conflict'—affords the best means of legitimizing regulatory outcomes where they are most likely to be resisted or otherwise evaded.[17]

---

[16] Clarence C. Walton and Frederick W. Cleveland, Jr., *Corporations on Trial: The Electric Cases* (Belmont, Calif:. Wadsworth Publishing Company, Inc., 1964).

[17] *The Semi-Sovereign People* (New York: Holt, Rinehart and Winston, Inc., 1960), Chap. I.

On Stability and Change

Chapter 7 strongly supported the view that the political scientist cannot, as yet, construct a single index of stability and/or adaptability at the nation-state level. One must employ sets of partial and indirect indicators for the measurement of various dimensions of instability. If we measure stability in terms of 'critical events' (such as the Feierabends' treatment noted in Chapter 7, Problem 11), we see that the competitive-bargaining systems tend to rank very high in stability. New Zealand ranks first; Luxembourg and the Philippines in second place; Iceland and Sweden in third place. The Netherlands, Norway, Costa Rica and Ireland follow, with Saudi Arabia, Cambodia and Romania being the only non-democratic systems among the top twelve nations. Few democracies are found below the median position and few non-democratic systems above it.

Why certain systems should rank high is not fully known; in some cases it may even be the result of effective policies of repression or extreme citizen deference. No doubt several theories could account for the facts and some of the theories would emphasize non-political factors. In any case, the correlation is great and, like doctors, we must recognize that some correlates hold whether the reasons are known or not.

Responsivity to Demands—We suspect that oftentimes conflict is mitigated when there is opportunity for effective expression of demands for change through political channels. Or, it may be that strenuous demands are avoided by political performance which meets most citizens' expectations. Whatever it is—whether 'tame' society or responsive government—if there is a compatibility of citizen aspiration with political performance one must recognize a responsive political system. However, such responsivity seems most likely to occur where bargaining and competitive processes make it positively rewarding for political leaders to build their support by reflecting citizen preferences.

Interestingly, receptivity to changing competitive demands can create both a greater sense of legitimacy and a greater feeling of uncertainty. Where outcomes are in doubt, the citizen feels his vote, or demand, may count; but the competitors—i.e., political leaders—undergo the strain of greater uncertainty. And the outcomes of competitive and bargaining processes are never viewed as permanent solutions to problems and issues but as temporary adjustments subject to some alteration as problems and alignments of political forces change.

Legitimacy and the Public Interest—The fact that outcomes are in doubt in competitive-bargaining systems does intensify problems concerning the legitimacy of solutions. The charge of 'deal' is frequently made about bargained outcomes, suggesting that some parties got together at a cost to others. Democratic ideology rests very strongly on the belief that the acts of political leaders should be unselfish and 'in the public interest,' implying also that there ought to be deference to and respect for superior judgment. The suspicion of self-interest poses difficulties for competitive-bargaining systems because public policies are supposed to be equally applied to all citizens. We may worry more about the consequences of policies than the motives of those who enact or oppose them, but we must also be aware that many other people concern themselves over the legitimacy of the presumed motivation.

Another serious problem of bargaining has to do with the role of secrecy or the nondisclosure of essential information. The bargained agreement can often be exploitive of the interests of others (external costs) because information is lacking and thus the corrective restraints induced by competitive exposure are avoided. This is why we emphasize bargaining *and* competition. Without the restraints of competitive concerns, bargaining may lead to direct conflict processes, especially over the long run, as the cumulation of 'bad' agreements alienates others or induces them to protest in some way.

Orderly Transitions of Authority—One of the most remarkable achievements of bargaining systems has been their capacity to enable orderly and peaceful transfers of power among formal political leaders. This has not been true of many command and conflict systems, especially those found in developing nations. In view of the more uncertain outcomes in bargaining systems, this is a signal achievement. It is remarkable because it means that politicians who lost the elections are willing to accept the leadership of those whom they opposed; frequently this also means accepting policies which they do not want, although in fact, most policy differences tend to be restricted to marginal variations. If more policy differences were sharply drawn, acceptance of change would either not occur or occur at a very high cost. We see evidences of this in the United States where whites find it very difficult to accept a new and higher status for blacks. Earlier, businessmen found it difficult to accept the pro-labor policies of the New Deal in America or the nationalization of industries in European nations.

Great and sudden changes in the direction or purpose of government policies seldom occur within the orderly processes of modern democracies. In few cases has a party been denied its electoral victory by the defeated party in any western democratic nation, and relatively little violence has occurred in transfers of formal power. The day after the election is much the same as the day before for most of these countries.

Conflict: Some Benefits

Conflict, as we have indicated, is ubiquitous. Something so universal could hardly survive as a political and social practice if it did not have some advantages or serve useful purposes. The question, then, is not whether conflict is good or bad, but which forms have what consequences? It must be recognized that conflict is a political process that works and produces results. In some societies it is a major means of attaining certain goals and settling disagreements. In other countries, including our own, it has been a prominent means for achieving some important political goals: national independence, abolition of slavery and re-integration of the nation (Civil War) and, recently, dramatization of the dire grievances of some minority groups. So conflict is, as shown earlier, a fairly common political fact of life.[18] What of its advantages and shortcomings? And also, how shall we evaluate violent means?

Coercive Attainment of Goals

Using forceful threats can provide an advantage in conflict situations which take the form of maneuvering about a conflict-type outcome, i.e., where one side backs down or makes the more costly concessions. Most political actors choose not to place all their hopes for gains by making threats and impelling concessions, but sometimes it appears to be the only tactic to which the other side responds. One cannot blame one party alone for conflict situations; it depends on the merits of the issue.

Thus the use of threats has its advantages when one believes his cause is right and the opposing side is intransigent. This has been the President's position in the recurring disputes with industry over large-scale price increases. This is labor's claim against management when it threatens a strike in order to get concessions at the bargaining table. Many people feel that the Cuban Missile crisis 'cleared the air' in showing both major parties the probable high costs involved in continuing to deal with each other on the basis of conflict premises. It is possible, therefore, to employ conflict tactics in non-violent form with some possible gains when one side is determined and there is no other recourse or when both parties learn by the anticipation of the high costs of failure to work out other means of resolution. At least acting upon the conflict premise makes the crucial points of difference more visible.

On the other hand, threats which are backed up by highly unequal advantages seem an unfair way of winning. Few honor the maxim that

---

[18] See Lewis A. Coser, *The Functions of Social Conflict* (New York: The Free Press, 1956).

'might makes right.' One safeguard is visibility so that external publics or third parties may impose constraints on the conflict. Another is to introduce mediators or arbitrators who can judge the merits of the case or introduce another point of view. All these tend to regularize or constrain conflict by converting it into more of a competitive process.

Effective Signal of Distress

Perhaps the most prominent use of conflict is to call attention to distress and grievances or injustices suffered. Minority groups frequently cannot gain the attention of indifferent majorities. If the majority is aware but opposed, conflict may be the only means of forcing one's views to be considered. History is replete with examples of the use of conflict by embattled minorities: The Dukhobors in Canada, the Afro-Americans, the Irish of an earlier period in this country and in Ireland itself, the peasants of Russia, religious sects in India, language minorities in Belgium, farmers in the United States and France—all are groups that have resorted to conflict to gain attention and better treatment. Furthermore, conflict often works because the majority groups do not wish to have their comfortable advantages continuously disrupted. Threats and the use of violence may not produce immediate attention or all the anticipated advantages, but gains are made in a great many situations when more peaceful means have failed.

Every group faces a strategic problem in the waging of conflict, i.e., whether and when to become violent. All groups confronted with these strategic problems are divided over the employment of violence because it is also a costly tactic. Within the contemporary civil rights movement we have witnessed some of the more established leaders appealing for more peaceful protest, while younger militants are impatient with the daily politics of piecemeal bargaining. The questions confronting these leaders, and all men, is whether violence is morally justified and whether it is effective. There are no universal answers to the former question and only inadequate ones to the second. In any event, violence has succeeded as a means of gaining attention for issues, problems, grievances. Who is to say that is not a considerable advantage in a democracy which prides itself on open communication but where all do not have equally effective means to speak out?

Rewards in Agitation and Violence

Individuals may gain a great deal of satisfaction from successful combat or even from unsuccessful conflict. The excitement of battle gives expression to many otherwise repressed hostilities, even if one is on the sidelines where satisfactions are vicarious. Many commentators have noted the exultant relief that violence affords the militant aggressor, be it in fighting for one's country or engaging in riots and rebellions. Then, too, in institutionalized combat a show of bravery can win the admiration and recognition of others, whether by promotions and medals or the comradeship and esteem of one's brothers. Every nation honors its military; in fact, the military is one of the few occupations which wears its achievements on its uniform for all to see and honor. One's rank and medals are conspicuously displayed. So, too, in highly organized revolutionary movements is great honor heaped upon courageous acts, by accolade, symbol and legend.

Group Solidarity

Few means of integration surpass conflict with a designated enemy. The esprit de corps of elite military units is but an example. The same may be said of union men who have experienced 'combat' with the employers. Some think that a strike now and then is a necessary means of preserving morale and unity in a union. Purely utilitarian organizations cannot enlist the dedication that moral purpose and aggressive militancy elicit from most men. In some societies manliness is defined in aggressive terms and acts of cowardice are apt to produce strong guilt feelings. Tales of heroism become part of the folklore of a people, compelling loyalty and holding the group together in its relationships with the outside world. The extraordinary loyalties and esprit which 'embattled' Israel shows in its dealing with the Arab world is a good example. So the feeling of 'one for all and all for one' is probably renewed and strengthened by periodic reminders of conflict with the 'enemy.'

Social Advances

While a person may concede the above consequences of conflict he may still question its effectiveness in achieving social goals or meeting allocative and distributive problems. In specific instances conflict has not only achieved little but produced costly results. Yet it is a fact that many of man's greatest achievements in social policy have been brought about in response to conflict situations. If national independence be considered an advance, as in most cases it has been, then we must accord conflict with a plus, for that was the way many nations achieved independence. Some of the great revolutions of mankind, including the French, Russian and Chinese, were marked by widespread violence. Few significant public policies in this country have not been at least partly induced by the occurrence of violence. The abolition of formal slavery was accomplished in 1865 because of victory on the battlefield; the civil rights legislation of this decade also acquired its urgency by violence-provoking protest.

Of course, one may argue that all these things might have been accomplished by other means, and so they may; but the fact is they were not. Since we cannot experiment in human affairs on matters of this kind, we shall never really know what the alternatives were or how successful each might have been. What we do know is that delay and resistence were often overcome by conflict. We have the historical evidence and that is that.

Non-Violent Strategies and Moral Victories

A special point must be made about strategies of non-violence. We have seen their most effective moral appeal in Ghandi's leadership of the Indian nationalist movement for independence, and in Martin Luther King's mobilization of Negro demands for civil rights in this country. In a dire conflict situation in which the prevailing powers are adamant, the non-violent demonstration, whether a fast, a peaceful march or other symbolic display, can evoke a great moral response. Such a course can dramatize the plight of the sufferer, those deprived of equality, dignity and rights, to an otherwise indifferent populace. The non-violent strategy is not only a public dramatization but a provocation of the powers that be. The repressive and forceful reactions of the embattled authorities only underscore the charge of oppression. And there is often a crystallizing moment when the use of force against the powerless demonstrator shocks the moral conscience of many even within the establishment. At such points the cause may win victory. Much is dependent upon the immediacy of response. Yet on the other hand, the provocation of violence may prove a risky business.

The Costs of Violence

Many of the costs of violent forms of conflict are, unlike those of competition and bargaining, highly visible and more amenable to quantification. We begin our assessment with the most costly and visible consequences—death, injury and material costs.

Death, Injury and Property Damage

There is a certain finality about death that makes it unpleasant to contemplate and evaluate, for who can fully assess the worth of a human life? Still, we can gain some appreciation of the horrible costs of violence by totalling deaths, injuries, mental disturbances and material costs. In addition, the aftermath of violence often finds economic activity disrupted and the amenities of life reduced. The race riots in the United States are a good case in point. In Figure 11-5, a partial accounting is made for the

Figure 11-5

Tide of Racial Violence

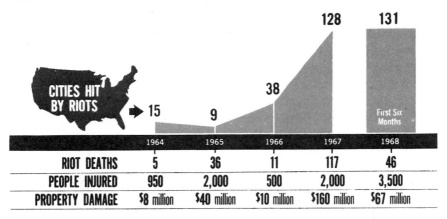

	1964	1965	1966	1967	1968
RIOT DEATHS	5	36	11	117	46
PEOPLE INJURED	950	2,000	500	2,000	3,500
PROPERTY DAMAGE	$8 million	$40 million	$10 million	$160 million	$67 million

NOTE: In addition to 160 million dollars' property damage in 1967, a Senate committee estimated economic losses at 504 million. 1968 property damage includes only insured losses as reported by the American Insurance Association. On top of that were uncounted millions in business losses, tax losses and governmental costs for troops and police required to deal with riots.

Reprinted from *U.S. News & World Report* (July 15, 1968), p. 31. Copyright 1968 U.S. News & World Report, Inc.

years 1964-1968 of the costs resulting from racial riots in the United States. Of course these figures pall into insignificance when contrasted with the costs of international wars, revolutions and civil wars. We need not detail the obvious but merely remind readers that an estimated eighteen million persons lost their lives during World War II alone. Who knows what rich lives these victims might have led? Who knows how they might have enriched our lives?

Bare figures cannot possibly convey the costs of the riots. Over $167 million of property damage was incurred during the riots of 1967 and more than $500 million in business losses, tax losses, and governmental costs for troops and police.[19] In Newark, New Jersey, for example, over 800 business establishments suffered some kind of damage while more than 600 persons were injured, and $200 million of damage was estimated for three days of rioting in Detroit during the same summer. As a consequence many businesses have refused to rebuild and those which have, pay higher insurance premiums as well as other costs of doing business. These costs are unequally distributed among the rioters and the victims, but who pays how much is extremely difficult to determine.

---

[19] "Riot Outlook for '68," *U.S. News and World Report*, July 15, 1968, p. 31.

The following newspaper item contains one estimate of the distributive costs of rioting. Note the wide range of people and activities affected by the riots in a complex industrial system such as this. Whether such costs were inevitable or worth paying cannot now be decided. Sometimes the costs of freedom are incalculable. But each individual must decide how much he is willing to pay for whatever he desires. Unhappily, costs may be levied on innocent persons who have no choice in the matter. But violence is like all political processes in this respect.

ECONOMISTS LOOK AT COST OF RIOTS

Serious Damage Doubted to the Nation's Continuing Productive Capacity

TAXPAYERS HURT MOST

Rise in Insurance Rates Appears Almost Certain Following Surveys

By Robert A. Wright

The economic aftermath of the riots in Newark, Detroit and other cities will be difficult to discern in the customary statistics.

Despite the widespread property damage in the riot areas and the disruption of business operations—to say nothing of the human suffering involved—economists do not expect the national economy to be hurt.

Yet the nation will pay a price. And this cost, unlike the real wounds inflicted in the riots, will be borne largely by Americans outside of the ghettoes—taxpayers.

Whether there are any tax increases specifically related to the riots or not, government will pay the costs of quelling the riots and therefore, indirectly taxpayers.

Purchasers of insurance also will share the cost, as rates are almost certain to be increased, the industry believes.

Lesser Effect

But, while events in Detroit last week may have had much in common with those in Vietnam, the civil commotion is not expected to have much impact on the national economy, as has the Asian war.

A spokesman for the President's Council of Economic Advisers said that, while the council had made no thorough studies of the matter, the gross national product figures would not reflect the rash of riots.

Such periodic economic statistics as average factory work week, personal income and weekly auto production will reflect the riots, but only temporarily, the council spokesman said.

Auto assemblies fell by almost 50 per cent last week because of the closing of plants in riot areas and absenteeism. But the producers' change-

over operations to 1968 models also accounted for some of this decline, and production figures for the year are unlikely to be changed because of last week's closings.

Costs Must Be Set

Before it is determined just who will pay, the cost must be established, a process that will take some time.

Estimates of property loss in Detroit ranged last week between $200-million and $500-million, but those were admittedly "horseback" guesses.

Insurance adjusters began entering the riot areas of Detroit only last Thursday and their assessments will take some time to collate.

In addition to insurance men, businessmen in general, investors and officials of municipal, state and the Federal Government will spend many hours calculating the costs of the riots in the months ahead.

A spokesman for the Michigan Budget Director's office said last week there was yet "nothing like a solid estimate" on the probable losses in taxes and other revenues to the state and the city of Detroit. But the direct cost in extra expenditures by the state connected with the riots, while still incomplete, ranged close to a half a million dollars, the spokesman said.

The state estimates the cost of mobilizing the National Guard at $255,000. This cost ended when the troops were Federalized, but the state calculated that it was costing the national Government $140,000 a day to maintain soldiers in Detroit at $27 a man a day.

It cost the state $175,000-to-$200,000 to provide state troopers in riot work, mostly in overtime. Extra prison costs to the state are running $4,000-to-$5,000 a day.

But in the long term, states and cities hit by riots are likely to find it more costly to borrow money.

Newark decided to postpone a $15.08-million bond issue last week in the wake of its riots. A city spokesman said the move was not related to the riots but to the softness of the market for tax-exempt bonds. Nonetheless, some market observers related the market action to investor wariness of municipal issues of potential riot areas generally.

Two bond rating houses, Standard & Poor's Corporation and Moody's Investors Service, had reduced Newark's credit rating in recent months.

Costs and Quality

An officer of Moody's said last week that he believed any effect on the secondary bond market from the riots would be temporary and that the riots had not led his company to re-examine the credit ratings of any of the cities hit by strife recently.

The reason, he said, was that his Company had anticipated such civil commotion in revising downward the credit standing of cities with large proportions of disadvantaged citizens.

"The riots might affect the primary bond market as specialists come to realize that a few hundred million of ratables (assessed values for real property forming a tax

base) have gone up in some smoke," the Moody's executive said. "It would seem to be a deterrent to investors for the short term, although I haven't seen any evidence of this yet. But the riots have merely re-emphasized the problems of our major core cities."

The bond expert said that two basic things concerned the bond community in assessing credit standings: The increasing costs to cities in taking care of its disadvantaged and the likelihood that, with larger percentages of the undereducated and poor in the population, a deterioration in the quality of local governments.

Much Not Insured

The same kind of reasons are destined to encourage more businesses to move to suburban sites, thus intensifying the problems of the cities.

The small retail merchant is the businessman most directly hurt by riots and the one with the fewest alternatives. Cancellations of extended coverage, which provides insurance from riots, come en masse after a riot.

Congress can expect increasing pressure from these merchants for Federal protection. The Jersey City Merchants Council, for one, wrote President Johnson last week urging passage of Senate bill S1484, which would establish a small-business crime protection insurance corporation that would make extended coverage available to merchants who cannot obtain it elsewhere.

Insurance executives questioned last week said that claims stemming from the riots would be paid. But it was clear that settlements would represent only a frac-

tion of the total property losses because much of this was not insured.

There appeared to be no effort by the insurance industry to avoid payment of claims on the ground that the riots were "insurrections," which would cancel coverage. But it was indicated some claims might be contested.

Many theft claims, for instance, are likely to be rejected because looting in many areas took place long after a store was set on fire. Most policies cover only thefts committed incident to a fire.

H. Clay Johnson, president of the Royal Globe Insurance Companies, noted that it was not possible to lump together claims in New Jersey and Michigan. He pointed out that Michigan law did not provide a legal means of recovering losses from a municipality on the ground that it was negligent in not preventing a riot. In New Jersey, he said, municipalities were liable to such action.

Another long-term effect of the riots was cited by James L. Bentley Jr., Controller General of Georgia and head of the National Association of Insurance Commissioners. Mr. Bentley said he was concerned over the possibility that the insurance industry would withdraw from the market and cease providing insurance in areas with high riot potential.

But Mr. Johnson of Royal Globe said he thought there would be an extension of the so-called Boston plan. Under this setup, local rating bureaus inspect a risk property having trouble obtaining insurance and help in upgrading the property to insurable standards. A surcharge is usually imposed on the coverage.

Source: *The New York Times*, July 30, 1967. © 1967 by The New York Times Company. Reprinted by permission.

High External Costs

The heat of battle also produces victims who are not direct combatants. The war in Vietnam almost daily produces lists of civilians bombed by mistake or murdered without cause by indiscriminate use of weapons or explosives. Their only mistake was being in the wrong place at the wrong time. Where no one is aimed at, anyone may be a casualty. Violence has a tendency to treat people equally and so maims the innocent child as well as the declared enemy. As is to be expected, the greater the scope of the violence, the greater these external costs. Perhaps one fear of nuclear war is the automatic recognition that the bomb is not only terribly powerful but also devastatingly non-discriminatory in its effects.

We are inclined to believe that a political technique should be employed only against those who are directly involved in the dispute. Non-violent conflict is less likely to spread the costs to those who have no choice. Since violence is less easily contained, it is one of the most costly means for the settlement of disputes. Its use not only should be minimized but avoided or institutionalized whenever it is possible to do so without repressing legitimate goals.

Problems of Force: Maladaptive Outcomes

While force, by declaring a winner, may assuredly be used to terminate a dispute, it is not the most appropriate means for making adaptive public choices or decisions. The criteria for forceful solutions relate to comparative strength rather than comparative reasoning among contenders over optimal policies. Disputes over public policy ought to maximize the use of intelligence, reasoning, empathy and peaceful bargaining in settling differences. Force ignores all of these factors. Conflict decisions are the result of quantitative superiority under conditions of fear, intimidation, exhaustion and defeat. We do not believe that producing victors and vanquished is a satisfactory means by which to build a community of citizens who have regard for one another's fate. Force does not legitimate outcomes or provide the long-run rewards or inducements which broaden support for new policies.

Decisions concerning resources and distribution of services and goods provide considerable opportunities for resolution by bargaining and competition rather than by forceful means. The ultimate cost considerations of conflict would deter most bargainers if they have an opportunity to consider them. Distributive issues are often not important enough to be settled by injuring others. Few individuals want to assassinate leaders because of their share of the taxes or to carry a dispute over subsidies or fringe benefits to the barricades. Our lives are not that affected, nor are our fortunes so tied to public policies that we must assume a 'do or die' attitude. As we have pointed out before, most public policies only indirectly affect any single individual citizen and this is reflected in our priorities of concerns. Most issues in stable systems are such that better solutions are produced when men analyze the problem more thoroughly and consider the merits of alternatives.

Violence may call attention to grievances but it does not itself produce effective solutions which will bring about the goals sought; instead it induces the escalatory process whereby all tend to lose. A war decides who dictates the peace terms but it cannot determine the consequences of the settlement. A riot can awaken a nation to an intolerable situation but it does not produce lasting solutions to the problem. Intelligence and information are vital to the diagnosis of any problem, to the invention of alternative solutions and to the choice of programs to reduce or handle the causes and their effects.

And, we might add another preference—some sensitivity and compassion for our fellow man. What policy-makers need are not fears and hatreds but dispassionate analysis and compassionate policies. We hold no brief for ideologies that depend upon perfect men (whatever perfection entails) to implement their designs, but we do believe that a healthy recognition and tolerance of man's emotional tendencies, especially over basic values and identities, offer a firm basis on which to proceed. Such a recognition makes man compassionate, not cynical and violent against those who have legitimate differences of belief, values, norms and policies. The practice of violence encourages further violence, and some rather righteous belief systems encourage more violence than others. Curiously, some of the most idealistic ideologies produce the most violence. More realistic concern for the daily betterment of a man's life may seem mundane but it is more apt to reduce violence and produce the necessary changes. Violence is a *last* resort to be used when there is no alternative. And seldom in politics is there absolutely no other way.

Performance of Command Systems

Organized command processes—bureaucracies, military bodies, and even totalitarian systems—are able to point to very considerable achievements, especially during this century. Exaggerated as they may be, the claims have some basis in fact. What are these achievements?

Administrative Effectiveness

The greatest advantages of command processes are realized where there are singular, high priority goals with specific techniques available for achieving them. The more effective the relevant technologies, both organizational and material, the greater the payoffs for command. This applies whether it involves military action against a hostile enemy, a movement against a government, the construction of an irrigation system, or the exploration of space.

Command is most efficient when every technique or task has a specifiable contribution to make which can be calculated in advance with an overall plan or procedure. Efficiencies are then realized in terms of saving resources or being able to spend them where they will make their greatest contribution. This is the great contribution of bureaucracies which can be organized for complete task performance: the postal service, the engineering team, the exploratory force, the Patent Office. Efficiency is reduced for public endeavors which require 'external' resources for their task completion, whether in terms of compliance or positive cooperation. Even relatively efficient police forces do not stop crime entirely, nor do conservation appeals bring automatic results.

Rapid Rates of Development and Growth

Even the most reactionary of citizenry must recognize that many of the more centralized command systems have astonished the world with their phenomenal rates of development and of economic growth specifically. Nations such as the Soviet Union have industrialized with great speed or are in the process of doing so. In a little over half a century, the Soviet Union has risen from a position of low prestige and power in the post-World War I period to become the second most powerful nation in the world. During that time it has greatly improved the living standards of its people and acquired a vast domain of adherents. Nearly a third of the world's population is found in the communist-dominated orbit. It should not be many years—other things remaining equal—until the Soviet Union has one of the highest standards of living and a general economic productivity second only to the United States.

China seems bent on achieving the same rapid rates of growth and social development, and there is little reason to believe that she could not eventually succeed. If she does, we will have another proof that societies heavily dependent on command processes can achieve rapid change through massive mobilization of their populations' motivations and skills. There are other rapidly developing systems which have used different forms of command effectively, such as Japan and Cuba. And we would do well to remember that all of these societies have made their great strides by incentives other than ours, by methods other than ours and under conditions different from ours. What seems so abnormal to us does not to them. Citizens of Russia, Cuba and Israel love their nations as we do; they can sacrifice—and indeed many have given their lives—with perhaps an even greater sense of dedication than many Americans.

The virtue of command in these situations is that it can cut through the former processes for getting things done. This same impulse is behind the demand for 'strong leaders' in the reform movements of this country—to break through the old tangle of bargains and entrenched interests. But note again, if the demand is based more on wish than capability, the result may be even more costly conflict.

Citizen Involvement in Collective Enterprises

Americans are inclined to feel immense pride in their institutions and achievements. But until recently, one could hardly attribute these to the efficiencies of political command. It is probably most difficult for the typical American citizen to admit or understand the direct rewards that can be found in collective enterprise subject to the direction of a leader. Many command-oriented societies have been able to enlist incredible amounts of voluntary enthusiasm, dedication, self-sacrifice and hard work from their citizens. The passionate loyalty of many Germans to Hitler, the pride of the Russians in their collective achievements and the apparent dedication of the Cubans today to communist ways should make us hesitant to claim that there is any one way to economic and technological achievement. Pride in Sputnik, great athletes and artists is readily apparent among the Russians. Even many Americans tend to accept these achievements as matters of fact, whether particularly welcomed or not.[20] We may also note, from one of the few studies of Russians based on interviews, that they (and even conservative expatriates) have strong bonds of identification with the U.S.S.R. and its socialist institutions. For example, Alex Inkeles and Raymond A. Bauer in their *Soviet Citizen* present interview data which shows powerful support among a wide segment of the population for the welfare features of Soviet life, state ownership of property, social equality and technical advancements.[21] There is little evidence that many citizens wish to reverse these achievements, once the considerable costs of revolutionary strife have subsided.

Some Problems

Let us try to understand clearly the defects of command rather than have simple 'gut reactions.' The command systems of the world are full of imperfections by our standards so we should be highly conscious of the standards we employ. They may not be the standards the citizens and leaders of command polities would use. What, then, are some of the more objectionable features of life under command systems? We have in mind

---

[20] J. Michael Armer, "A Preliminary Analysis and Measurement of National Prestige," *Pacific Sociological Review,* 9 (Spring, 1966), p. 3-8.

[21] *The Soviet Citizen* (Cambridge: Harvard University Press, 1959), Chap. X.

everyday life within both the bureaucracies and the great command societies where public bureaucracies are so prominent.

Limited Forms of Participation—Command processes, by definition, prohibit most meaningful forms of participation in the making of decisions whether one works in the bureaucracy or is a citizen controlled by it. A bureaucrat has his role and work activity carefully and precisely defined, presumably to improve organizational efficiency and to protect the status and authority of the leaders. Thus, a person who labors within a bureaucracy, whether private or public, labors within a specific role defined by others. His freedom to decide is therefore highly limited.

Citizens who are affected by bureaucracies, especially in societies which employ many administrators to run the economy, are apt to have small influence over the bureaucracy itself. Generally neither citizen nor client has much to say about how the organization is to be operated. Criticism of governmental decisions, personnel and ineffectiveness is frequently restricted to grumbling; for example, ordinary citizens in the Soviet Union cannot expect to enter serious public objections about the restrictions on art and literature or the lack of choice as citizens in bargaining and competitive societies can. Apparently, jokes are made about leaders and Soviet institutions among friends, but serious basic indictments in the public media are practically unheard of in Russia.

At another level it is permissible to publish criticism of the performance of industry and product distribution. *Pravda* and *Iszveztia* both carry criticism by citizens, sometimes planted by higher officials against lower officials, for alleged inefficiency. Apparently it has also been possible during recent years for economists to criticize the fundamental tenets of planning in the U.S.S.R.; this has been true on an even more secure basis in Yugoslavia and, until just recently, in Czechoslovakia. Economists obviously now feel sufficiently secure to indulge in some radical thinking. From the reports of tourists and other visitors it would appear that even the most totalitarian societies cannot completely repress grumbling in daily life. As one finds grumbing, cynicism, alienation and the like in western hierarchies, so one may expect to find them in totalitarian states. But the possibilities of aggregating the grumbling and criticism into effective legitimate opposition parties is remote in a totalitarian state. None has existed; none seems probable in the immediate future. Since they lack the strong possibility of forming legitimate dissident political organizations, we cannot score such societies very high on the participation scale. Without participation in actual decisions, genuine competition and bargaining are largely meaningless.

While the bureaucracies of western democratic states are more open to outside criticism, they too rarely provide formal institutions for regularized criticism; in fact, they have a self-interest in protective secrecy for their operations and decisions. Some bureaucracies make an attempt to discover citizen reactions and to provide for some citizen 'feedback,' but few citizens are likely to feel that they are effectively influencing the deliberative processes of bureaucracies.

Grand-Scale Mobilization: Planning Errors and Costs—Large-scale bureaucracies are a necessity because large-scale goals and activities are necessities in the modern state and, perhaps, in the newly-developing states as well. But the effort to achieve these grand goals can be very costly whether pursued in a communist or non-communist nation. Complaints against the inefficiencies of the postal services in this country ought to testify to that point. Then, too, everyone who has ever served in a military unit knows about the efficiency problems of such organizations. Coordinating the activities of thousands of personnel in pursuit of many goals is not likely to be an easy task. Organizational constraints of all sorts, ranging from inept personnel and inadequate divisions of labor to communications problems, incentives, informational difficulties and inadequate resources, all serve to encourage inefficient performances. Nearly every large-scale organization can point to wastage, policy errors and grand goofs. Sometimes they become scandalous.

The history of totalitarian systems in the twentieth century strongly indicates that such societies are extremely goal-oriented—in a perpetual hurry to achieve grandiose goals overnight. Such societies are continuously mobilized for emergencies that must be immediately solved to ward off the enemy or achieve the good life. There is no room for the lazy or indolent; in this limited regard they are much like the villages of our Puritan forebearers.

The tendency is to enact or proclaim extraordinary goals and over-commit limited resources to their achievement. A characteristic approach in the U.S.S.R., China, Nazi Germany and now Cuba is to 'storm' a limited number of objectives, such as building huge dams, greatly increasing agricultural production, collectivizing the peasantry or building a Sputnik. In so doing, decision-makers tend to ignore cost levels and any side-effects, whether good or bad. Running roughshod over obstacles is the height of achievement. The consequences of this approach in solving social and economic problems must be apparent.

For one thing, such haste is bound to produce periodic errors of great magnitude in planning and execution. Some commentators have said that the opening of farm lands in the eastern provinces by Khrushchev was a great mistake in agricultural policy. Certainly this is a constant possibility when leaders attempt to industrialize a backward nation within a generation or two. Alternatives cannot be adequately considered in overnight planning and execution.

Concomitant with the widespread consequences of errors in planning are the costs that any full-scale mobilization entails. Command leaders do not have to be unduly concerned over waste and misallocations of resources because there is no market or election system to check errors and levy costs for their mistakes. Concern for the human costs, especially, is minimized. Labor is coerced, peasants are closely controlled and moral judgment about the means used for revolutionary change is lacking. Success in achieving future goals is paramount; the means of achievement are judged only in terms of effectiveness. Economic expansion and social change have come at very high costs in command societies. Resources, particularly the human, are wasted through overcommitment and misallocation. The latter is a particularly pressing problem in the newly-developing nations striving, as many do, to build symbolic enterprises and investments which may never be able to pay off in effective ways.

Western nations have experienced the same frenetic pursuit of social goals whenever they have suddenly found themselves involved in a major war. The sudden mobilization of the western allies during both World War I and II created many of the same problems which the communist nations and other rapidly mobilizing nations have experienced during peacetime. The coordination of millions of people took time and resources. While command processes were employed with vigor, mistakes were usually justified by the goal—victory.

Red Tape, Inflexibility and Impersonality—Many know from personal experience with bureaucracies or command systems the host of irritations and costs that must be borne as one attempts to 'move' the system and get whatever it is that one wants done. We can summarize these headaches, irritants and costs under the labels heading this section: red tape, inflexibility and impersonality. Most citizens want to reduce the immediate real costs of dealing with governments, but they cannot. They find that relationships with governmental agencies are often unrewarding because impersonal officials are more sensitive to categories of people than to individuals with unique problems. While it is rational for the official to fulfill his duties in this way, it is hard on the citizen; his loyalties to the system may be weakened to that extent. In large-scale systems impersonality is bound to be an ever present factor; how else can one run a society of millions of people?

Just as officials may be impersonal, so may they be required to run offices and fulfill societal objectives with miles of red tape. Anyone who has ever had a problem with the post office, armed forces, police, Internal Revenue Service or almost any other governmental agency must have been required to see more than one official, fill in complex forms in quadruplicate, acquire signatures, consult a lawyer and spend long hours sitting outside offices or standing in line. All this is burdensome in real and psychic terms. Frayed nerves, impatience and time that could have been devoted to more worthy pursuits are commonly experienced costs.

Given the impersonality and red tape, one may also expect command systems, especially the bureaucratic types, to be inflexible since they are run according to highly formalized, generalized rules and regulations that cannot be administered according to personal whim. Very precise prescriptions and proscriptions are constantly encountered by the official and the citizen alike. No one's problem perfectly fits the abstract categories. Yet the bureaucrat is normally unwilling to bend even a little to improve the situation. Bureaucrats respond in rational ways to the complex of rules they must administer and be administered by; to make exceptions might lead to charges of favoritism and would certainly increase the risks of the bureaucrat in carrying out his job. Consequently, bureaucrats are likely to treat or meet most problems with caution, even rigidity. The perceived gains of the bureaucrat are usually outweighed by the costs *he* perceives in innovation and flexibility.

Information Costs—Hierarchies present troublesome and sometimes paradoxical problems of information.[22] The status, social distance and deference enveloping top leaders can hamper the quality of decision-making by erecting barriers to the flow of much relevant and useful information from middle and lower levels. There are all sorts of incentives for subordinates to withhold or distort what they communicate to the top. After all, rewards in hierarchies come from 'looking good' or telling the leader what he wants to hear about operations. Subordinates would most naturally withhold evidence of their poor performance whenever there is opportunity to do so (and in complex hierarchical organizations there may be plenty of opportunity). Or there can be quite a bit of distortion in reporting. Without competitive checks even the most dedicated and mission-oriented agent is liable to selective bias in what he sees, hears and reports. This has been the greatest weakness of secret intelligence agencies where information can travel only through channels. In more loosely organized hierarchies leaders are equally vulnerable to biased gossip, rumor or distorted accounts from those within the ranks who are disgruntled or ambitious.

Paradoxically, the more that a leader or an organization attempts to control, the less effective the control may become. Ultimately a leader would have to supervise all activities and this is clearly an impossibility in a large-scale system. The controller must depend upon others in some division of labor; the more controllers, the greater the chances of mis-understanding and errors among them. A myriad of communications are required for complete control, but the most relevant information may be lost or diverted from the appropriate decision-maker when channels are

---

[22] This has been very aptly treated in the book by Harold L. Wilensky, *Organizational Intelligence* (New York: Basic Books, Inc., 1967).

flooded. Even if communications are not distorted, the total costs of additional controls mount and the marginal cost also rapidly increases, probably beyond the expected returns. At some point, control will even generate its own opposition. We think that societies or organizations which rely heavily on command processes have serious control problems related to the sorts of information they need.

Cooperative Processes

Unlike other major ways of realizing public goals, cooperation cannot be said to operate effectively by itself in any major system. It is certainly a communist ideal, as it was for the utopian socialists and for a variety of democratic and religious movements. But in the real world cooperation seems always to fall short of its full promise, even in the famous kibbutzim of Israel and in the communal settlements in this and other western countries where dedication to the values involved was complete and voluntary. Situations always arise which require some degree of command, bargaining or competition. At best, cooperation is extraordinarily facilitating; but wherever there are divergent collective goals to be achieved, as in every modern polity, cooperation lends its advantages more frequently as complementary to some or all of the other processes. But however diffused or subsidiary an approach to the realization of goals, it can make definite contributions and entail some disadvantages, too. We venture a few considerations.

Harmonies Are Nice

What a pleasant discovery it is when political contenders find they can all agree where before they anticipated conflict, uncertainties, risks and costs. And it does happen in the real political world at special moments: in the recognition of a friend in a cause, an hitherto unknown political ally, the willing joiner of a new political enterprise. In several recent U.S. elections there have been widespread and rather genuine volunteer movements; these volunteers often form political clubs or groups devoted to discussion along cooperative lines, however tentatively achieved. Many observers have noted the degree to which the scientific, technological and service professions have broken down older political barriers by similarly identifying a common mission and being more willing therefore to share information and resources toward their goals. Thus the scientists of the Soviet Union and the United States apparently find it easier to cooperate (as they did in the International Geophysical Year and in the Pugwash movement) than, say, businessmen of two countries or the military establishments. Some analysts have also noted the great cooperative successes of some of the 'functional' agencies of the United Nations where the goal may be shared conveniences, as in postal services, or common enemies, as disease and starvation.

One must be sure, however, that the cooperation *is* a reality; one account of American scientists' efforts to achieve disarmament at the Geneva Conference of Experts indicates that there can be a misleading optimism about technical solutions or shared ideals replacing political differences. The mutual advantages must be acknowledged by all parties, and the analyst must be as realistic as possible about whether cooperative processes are really bringing these advantages or are just providing a facade behind which both parties maintain their differences.[23] That is apparently the great dilemma of the disarmament and arms control talks.

The Gains of Mutual Adjustment

It used to be assumed that the achievement of important collective goals in very complex systems required the elaborate central coordination of command systems. The attempt at overall administrative solutions illustrates this. But more recently there is evidence that Soviet planners have come to realize the information and calculation problems discussed above and have rediscovered the virtues of decentralized decision-making. There are simply too many special sorts of information which have to be considered at the local, factory, regional and even industry-wide level for a central plan to be the effective guide. All the efforts of central planners, even using highly sophisticated economic models and modern computer methods, could not eliminate the critical inefficiencies, waste and errors that defeated overall projected goals. So now, even in the Soviet Union— and paradoxically so—there is a systematic attempt to return to more cooperative forms of adjustment by granting more decision-making discretion to lower levels of operations and relying upon the fuller flow of information to bring more effective decisions. This is the advantage of cooperation, that information is more fully shared where one person's gains do not hurt another's program. If everyone primarily wants to improve his own decisions on behalf of some goal that all believe in, then cooperative sharing of resources promises gains, even in large systems.

The most explicit proponent of the advantages of decentralized cooperative methods in policy-making in this country is an economist, Charles Lindblom.[24] As Lindblom sees it, an important means of achieving decentralized mutual adjustment of differences in policy-making is through what he terms 'partisan discussion,' a term meant to designate those activities in which people attempt to gain their own ends by sharing

---

[23] See Robert Gilpin, *American Scientists and Nuclear Weapons Policy* (Princeton, N.J.: Princeton University Press, 1962), Chap. 7.

[24] *The Intelligence of Democracy* (New York: The Free Press, 1965).

information with others in the hope that such information can be a persuasive inducement to cooperation. Emphasis is placed on talk and persuasion concerning mutually beneficial actions. Presumably others are open-minded on the worth of new information and are willing to be persuaded. The promise of gain should, naturally, encourage such willingness. Of course we should like to know when this works best and when it may not. We know that man is sometimes obstinate because he does not believe new information or suspects that anyone who is anxious to persuade must be distrusted. But not always; a citizen or official can enjoy cooperation just as often, under encouraging conditions.

Size Limitations of Cooperation

Social theorists who have eloquently stated the case for cooperation as a substitute for costly bickering and bargaining, compromise and competition, seem to have in mind a kind of intimate, informal and rather generous group of other-regarding members as their ideal. While we are hardly against such conceptions, they do have some rather powerful limitations. For example, it is very difficult to see how a large-scale political system consisting of millions let alone hundreds of millions of members could make public policy in the same manner as the intimate small group. Impersonal institutions are a necessity when membership exceeds more than a few hundred persons. Even in relatively small systems such as a New England town meeting it would be taxing for everyone to be engaged constantly in energetic conversation over every conceivable issue.

It is also difficult to conceive how appropriate communications are achieved in complex organizations simply by decentralizing and depending upon situational factors to induce agreement. The impersonality and distance created by formal organizations would not necessarily remove all the biases and defenses of positional interests nor be likely to enhance the sense of trust or openness that cooperative processes require. The assumption appears to be that if all decision-makers are specialists in their own particular tasks they will be open to exploring cooperative processes more freely for mutual gains. We feel bound to caution the reader to view this assumption with some skepticism as an apt generalization about most decentralized formal organizations handling questions of policy-making. We are inclined to think this would be most likely in very homogeneous social groups, where shared values are implicit and cooperative action more automatic, rather than in situations of diversity where task-oriented actors must adjust to one another's preferences.

Limitations of Affect

A major assumption of the cooperative ideal is that people can have positive feelings toward one another without their sentiments leading to conflict or hostilities. We question this assumption for many situations. A strong sense of identification and mutuality often entails strong feelings of distrust toward outside elements or third parties. In political situations this appears especially likely where the third party may well be the boss, or the next agent along the decision chain, or anyone who could be viewed as likely to alter decisions or 'readjust' them to other purposes. Furthermore, we seriously doubt whether men can manage their emotions in such a manner as to forget past differences as issues change and new decisions come up. Most of us cannot treat each successive issue as independent of previous ones; we cannot easily and impersonally ally ourselves with past antagonists, especially if they had won. The promise of competitive gains seems always to crop up in larger enterprises, however decentralized or intricate the division of labor. While the appeal of cooperation is everlasting, its limitations must be kept in mind, and conducive circumstances must be rather critically appraised.

Problems and Applications

1. If bargaining costs are a positive function and external costs are a negative function of the number of bargainers, what is one to do in his efforts to control costs? Try reasoning about this first with concrete cases, preferably ones familiar to you, then state the more generalized conclusions.

2. If you are about to become chairman of a committee on campus, for whatever purpose, what size do you think the committee ought to be? Does the job the committee has to do make a difference? Why? Can you imagine other committees which ought to have fewer members? More members? Why?

3. On the basis of what you learned from Chapter 10 and the present one, try evaluating some cases of a presidential candidate's choice of his vice presidential running mate. Consider each competitive choice both in terms of attaining the presidential nomination of the political party in question and the expected role in the election campaign itself.

4. Misallocation of resources is a frequently alleged consequence of bargaining systems. If you really wanted to test this proposition, how could you go about deciding whether optimal or less than optimal allocations have occurred? In short, what sort of evidence is required to test the accusation? Illustrate by examples from bargained political decisions or agreements which you are aware of or find in the daily newspaper.

5. Unanimity rules are said to reduce and even eliminate external costs on decisions which concern highly valued outcomes. If this is so, is it still desirable not to have such rules? Under what conditions might one want a less stringent requirement? Why? Put another way: what are the costs of the unanimity voting rule?

6. A good stiff intra-party battle is said by some politicians to be a good thing for the party before it enters a campaign. Evaluate this generous view of competition and conflict.

7. Competition in the polity is supposed to reduce the range of voter choice among public policies. Do you think this has beneficial results? Under all conditions? Some? Which? Why?

8. Some analysts have claimed that competition is inherently unstable. What could they possibly mean by this assertion? Can you rephrase it to make it less ambiguous? Can you contradict the claim? Or, support it?

9. When are conflict situations least likely to involve high external costs? Where would these most often be found in political situations?

10. Can you think of any political occasions where you have engaged in genuinely cooperative endeavor? Did the outcomes fulfill the cooperative criterion? Can you anticipate the sorts of occasions when you might very well do so in the future?

11. How can the public image of political bargaining be improved? Does it show promise of being so? If so, in what contexts?

Bibliographical Notes

Most of the literature cited in Chapters 9 and 10 are equally relevant in discussions of the worth of various political processes. Perhaps, then, these notes can be put to good advantage by further emphasizing certain themes and authors cited in previous notes as well as introducing some additional useful titles.

A good general evaluation of political bargaining is not yet available. We must build from economic applications and perhaps a good starting point is the book of Neil W. Chamberlain, *A General Theory of Economic Process* (New York: Harper and Brothers, Publishers, 1955); Chapters 6, 7, 8 and 14 are the most important ones for our discussion. Once more we recommend the writing of Richard E. Walton and Robert B. McKersie, cited in the notes to the last chapter. What they call 'integrative bargaining' sounds much like our notion of gaining cooperation. Two other volumes, neither of which are particularly easy to read, deal with bargaining as a means of establishing wage rates but are most germane to our concerns. The first is Jan Pen, *The Wage Rate Under Collective Bargaining* (Cambridge: Harvard University Press, 1959); Chapter VI on the bargaining process is particularly good. The second, a more descriptive attempt at explaining somewhat the same problem, is Carl M. Stevens, *Strategy and Collective Bargaining Negotiation* (New York: McGraw-Hill Book Company, 1963). A much older study, which covers bargaining and other social-economic processes as well, is the now all but forgotten work of John R. Commons, *The Economics of Collective Action* (New York:

The Macmillan Company, 1951); also of interest is his *Institutional Economics* (New York: The Macmillan Company, 1934), especially Chapter X which contains a lengthy and occasionally confusing section on 'collective action.' Still another difficult piece is a report of experiments in bargaining by a psychologist and an economist, Sidney Siegel and Lawrence E. Fouraker, *Bargaining and Group Decision Making* (New York: McGraw-Hill Book Company, 1960). The experiments are of 'bilateral monopoly,' i.e., situations in which two rivals must make an agreement if either is to survive or maintain itself. Politics is not without such situations and particularly so in international relationships. The study is also valuable in that it illustrates how two quite different social sciences can cooperate with benefits for all. On international relations we suggest Kenneth T. Young, *Negotiating With Chinese Communists* (New York: McGraw-Hill Book Company, 1968).

On political competition we should like once again to recommend all the books we have cited by E. E. Schattschneider. Professor Schattschneider has been one of the most provocative thinkers in American political science and especially useful because his work is readable for the novice even though the ideas and theories are quite sophisticated. Another political scientist who has written with originality and ease about competition is Edward C. Banfield, *Political Influence* (New York: The Free Press, 1961). Parts II and III are stimulating treatments of both competition and bargaining. The same can be said of Wallace S. Sayre and Herbert Kaufman, *Governing New York City* (New York: W. W. Norton and Company, Inc., 1965). Both of these books are highly explicit about bargaining and both are good illustrations of the so-called 'pluralist school' of thought about how American politics is conducted and why it is basically a good system.

A little known book which is beautifully written, wise and especially relevant to the analysis of bargaining (compromise solutions) is T. V. Smith's *The Ethics of Compromise* (Boston: Starr King Press, 1956). Of a different genre of writing but equally valuable are, of course, the writings of James M. Buchanan and his former colleague, Gordon Tullock, cited in Chapters 2 and 5. The worth of various political processes may be said to be the chief concern in all their writing. Still a most comprehensive although somewhat dated treatment of a variety of social-political processes is the Dahl-Lindblom volume we have alluded to in several chapters. The discussion of bargaining has been said by Lindblom to be the least satisfying part of the early volume; that is why he went on to do *The Intelligence of Democracy* (New York: The Free Press, 1965).

Some of the problems we discuss in this chapter are considered by David Braybrooke in *Three Tests for Democracy: Personal Rights, Human Welfare, Collective Preference* (New York: Random House, Inc., 1968). Braybrooke, a philosopher and sometimes collaborator of Lindblom, not only knows politics but knows the modern techniques of social science analysis as well. As a result he has written an excellent book. Had this volume been available earlier we suspect our evalutions would be cast in somewhat different terms.

An entire library of writing is available assessing comparative economic systems which include considerations of command and competitive processes in the polity. Among our favorites are two elementary or beginning texts: Harold W. Chase and Paul Dolan, *The Case for Democratic Capitalism* (New York: Thomas Y. Crowell Company, 1964), and Alfred Oxenfeldt and Vsevolod Holubnychy, *Economic Systems in Action*, 3rd. ed. (New York: Holt, Rinehart and Winston, Inc., 1965). Do not ask us how to pronounce the latter author's name. A much more advanced treatment is found in Heinz Kohler, *Welfare and Planning* (New York: John Wiley and Sons, Inc., 1966). A somewhat unique approach to planning (command processes) is taken by Neil W. Chamberlain in *Private and Public Planning* (New York: McGraw-Hill Book Company, 1965). The author is able to make some interesting comparisons between planning in these two sectors which are so often viewed as conflicting in all respects. Discussions of planning inevitably lead to analyses of public bureaucracies and their modes of decision-making and behavior, so we urge the reader to look for such assessments wherever the subject is treated.

Bureaucracy has become a bad word for many, including scholars. Among the better balanced textbook analyses, however, are those of Herbert A. Simon, Donald W. Smithburg and Victor A. Thompson, *Public Administration* (New York: Alfred A. Knopf, Inc., 1954), and John M. Pffiffner and Frank P. Sherwood, *Administrative Organization* (Englewood Cliffs, N. J.: Prentice-Hall, Inc., 1960). Less textbookish, but still comprehensive and certainly stimulating, is Anthony Downs' treatment of administrative bodies in *Inside Bureaucracy* (Boston: Little, Brown and Company, 1967). Downs elaborates on some sixteen laws of bureaucratic behavior. They, plus most of his other basic hypotheses, are conveniently summarized at the end of the book. A less sanguine outlook and more vitriolic condemnation of public bureaucracies is presented by Gordon Tullock in *The Politics of Bureaucracy* (Washington, D.C.: Public Affairs Press, 1965). Although Tullock has a strong distaste for the political he manages to put forth his position with some rigorous analysis.

At the most general level of analysis—and one of the famous tracts of the post World War II period—was Frederick A. Hayek's *The Road to Serfdom* (Chicago: University of Chicago Press, 1944), a bitter indictment of planning, communism, socialism and bureaucracy. All these epithets are closely related, according to Hayek, and give rise to and mutual reinforcement of one another. The case is overstated but remains a useful statement against some of the evils of modern centralization.

A far less polemic analysis of modern uses of bureaucracy and planning and one which is cross-national in scope is the recent publication of Andrew Shonfield, a British economist: *Modern Capitalism: The Changing Balance of Public & Private Power* (London: Oxford University Press, 1965). This book contains a wealth of interpretative materials by a highly informed observer on the subject of the sub-title. Mr. Shonfield is not at all reluctant to express his estimates of planning and public policy in the several western democracies.

For those who like more detailed descriptions and critiques of specific cases of political and economic processes in their national setting we suggest Alec Nove's *The Soviet Economy* (New York: Frederick A. Praeger, Inc., 1961), a balanced perspective on the oldest communist state. C. A. R. Crosland, *The Future of Socialism* (New York: Schocken Books, 1963), is a penetrating analysis of the workings of socialism in Britain. Like many modern socialists, Crosland is not unaware of the real-world shortcomings of the system he advocates, and indeed he suggests new directions for reform which do *not* include further nationalization of industry as a panacea for for all social and personal ills. Warren C. Baum makes some unusually thorough analyses (although now dated) of the working of French national planning in *The French Economy and the State* (Princeton: Princeton University Press, 1958). More up-to-date materials are found in John and Anne-Marie Hackett's *Economic Planning in France* (London: Allen and Unwin Ltd., 1963).

If you are not much interested in national planning and command systems, there are two items of general interest on conflict and competition from the perspectives of a sociologist and a distinguished social psychologist. The sociologist is Hubert M. Blalock, and his *Toward a Theory of Minority-Group Relations* (New York: John Wiley and Sons, Inc., 1967) has a great deal to say about social competition, power and racial discrimination. This study is unusually clear in its statements of propositions about who gets what and why. A convenient list of 97 propositions is appended in pages 204-221. The social psychologist is Kurt Lewin and his book, *Resolving Social Conflict* (New York: Harper and Brothers, Publishers, 1948), is a collection of papers on various aspects of group conflict.

The rarity of books on cooperation, at least as we have defined it, must be an indicator of its rarity in the real world of politics. We have really found very few studies of political cooperation. However, one group of social scientists has done a good deal of thinking and research on the matter and they are the social psychologists interested in small groups. Dorwin Cartwright has edited a useful introduction to such work in *Group Dynamics* (Evanston, Ill.: Row, Peterson and Company, 1956), an anthology of writing and research on small groups. Cooperative activities are among the topics considered. While this work is well done, its political implications are unclear except as they may relate to small groups such as committees. Even that relationship is questionable since the experiments never incorporate party and interest group affiliations as important conditions of action or cooperation.

The philosophically inclined might want to consult P'etr Kropotkin's *Mutual Aid: A Factor of Evolution,* in several editions; this volume has a classic stature among those interested in reducing conflict and competition. Another volume of considerable importance but less philosophical in tone is a work edited by Margaret Mead, *Cooperation and Competition Among Primitive Peoples* (Boston: Beacon Press, 1961). Case studies are the vehicle of analysis, but be sure to read Miss Mead's "Interpretive Statement" at the end which summarizes and comments on what has been learned. This collection ought to be read in conjunction with another collection on primitive conflict: *Law and Conflict,* edited by Paul Bohannan (Garden City, N.Y.: The Natural History Press, 1967).

For those who wish to be practical and improve cooperation we suggest Halbert E. Gulley, *Discussion, Conference and Group Process,* 2nd ed. (New York: Holt, Rinehart and Winston, Inc., 1968). Whether practical or idealistic, much of the contemporary literature of the 'New Left' pertains to establishing a more cooperative way of life in America. Much of this is found in small magazines and titles that are not readily available. We just urge the reader to browse among all magazines offering such political proposals.

U.S. Influence Dwindles
The Oregonian, July 29, 1968, Portland, Oregon

Student Protes

Continually Mou
Oregon Summer Emerald, June 27, 1968,
University of Oregon, Eugene, Oregon

Japanese 'Sleep-in' Strategy

Unlikely to Produce Results
Oregon Emerald, Aug. 21, 1968, University of Oregon, Eugene, Oregon

Goldwater Strategy Use
The Oregonian, Aug. 9, 1968,
Portland, Oregon

Johnson Regime May Offer Job Slash

In Return For Approval Of Surtax
The Oregonian, Nov. 27, 1967, Portland, Oregon

PARLEY IN PAR

ENDS FIRST WE

ON TOUGHER N

Ghetto Feels Riots

ave Aided Blacks
The National Observer, Aug. 5, 1968,
Silver Springs, Maryland

Grubbing for Votes in Arkansas
The National Observer, July 22, 1968, Silver Springs, Maryland

U.S. Says Evasion

of Hanoi, Which (

'Maneuver and
The New York Times
May 19, 196
New York, New Yo

rate Citizens Kill Plan

To Widen Thoroughfare
The Oregonian, Aug. 8, 1968, Portland, Oregon

Double Loss for Wallace
The New York Times, May 12, 1968, New York, New York

Condemns Europe's 'Policy of Blc
The New York Times, Aug. 22, 1968, New York, New York

ruce Soothes Soviet Bloc
The Oregonian, Aug. 6, 1968, Portland, Oregon

hose who protest the income tax, he
ays, should make common cause witl
oung people who protest the draft. He
rgues that there is no difference be-
ween Uncle Sam's taking two years of a
an's life and taking 20 per cent of a
an's income.

Top Nigerian Negotiator Drops H
The Oregonian, Aug. 19, 1968, Portland, Oregon

The Lure of Bargains
The National Observer, July 29, 1968,
Silver Springs, Maryland

July 29, 1968, The Oregonian,
Portland, Oregon

Unlikely Allies

— Nixon promised the S
an acceptable vice pres
tial candidate weeks ago
in meetings here this
sounded a hint that Sup
Court appointees more fa
ble to the South would b
choices. *The Oregonian, Aug. 9, 1968*
Portland, Oregon

It's an amusing idea, this alliance of
e hippies and the little old ladies in
nnis shoes. But it makes a certain
ount of perverse sense.
Eugene Register-Guard, June 26, 1968,
Eugene, Oregon

Maryland Governor Is

All Things to All Men
The Wall Street Journal, Aug. 9, 1968,
New York, New York

Chapter 12

Strategies for Political Competence

As Machiavelli pointed out in his day, one can learn to be more effective and efficient in political life; and this chapter will offer some ways in which this can be accomplished. The proposals are realistic, not grandiose or moralistic generalities with powerful emotional appeal but little practical use. Chapters such as this do not often appear in introductory textbooks to political science.[1] Why this should be we do not know, since presumably most readers will be citizens in a democracy which allows, if not encourages, the pursuit of individual interests and preferences. It seems to be a democratic tradition, however, that citizens should be indoctrinated with something called 'the public interest' and not with norms for the successful pursuit of self-interest. Exception is taken to this civics-book approach; the individual ought to know his own important interests and how to achieve as many of them as possible.

For some unknown reason personal incentives in pursuit of economic interests in one's occupational career are encouraged, while much stricter

---

[1] Rare exceptions are Robert A. Dahl, *Pluralist Democracy in the United States* (Chicago: Rand McNally and Company, 1967), Chap. 17: "Alternative Strategies for Political Activists"; and even earlier, Ivan Hinderaker, *Party Politics* (New York: Henry Holt and Company, 1956), especially Part Four on "Winning Elections: Problems of Strategy."

boundaries are placed on one's concerns in politics. Yet in a highly-complex society it is rather difficult to draw moral boundaries between economic life and the polity (or any other sphere of life), and personal incentives are needed to induce citizens to perform political tasks. Every businessman knows, or should know, that the government and its decisions have an enormous and continuous impact on his private shares of income, power and status. If he is to enhance his business success, he must concern himself with governmental decisions and try to make them as favorable as possible to his situation. Other people should do likewise, at least regarding their most important concerns.

This is not a public-be-damned attitude. On the contrary, the intelligent pursuit of one's interests can lead to mutually beneficial public policies for people with complementary concerns. Most of the great public decisions concerning the civil and economic rights of people have been advanced and won because it was to someone's interest to pay the costs of their achievement. Thus, the civil rights of racial minorities are now being attained and, hopefully, better secured because blacks have a stake in them; these rights serve to facilitate their acquiring a larger share of the benefits of power, income and status. So, too, during earlier stages in American history some colonists found it advantageous to dissociate from the British Empire. Much later American workers strove for gains which would not otherwise have been granted, and they achieved not only rights to organize and bargain collectively, but also benefits in education, health and welfare. Businessmen and farmers are perfectly justified in advocating legislation favoring their perceived interests. The wearer of shoes, as philosophers have claimed, knows better than the cobbler whether the shoe pinches.

How public action and policies affect an individual's self-interest is not always readily apparent, however. One finds considerable uncertainty or ignorance in this matter. Because uncertainty is so prevalent, there exists the continual possibility of developing ritualized non-rational responses rather than more effective adaptation to new circumstances. Thus some businessmen believe that a 'balanced budget' is a sacred state of affairs. Were they less committed to such stereotypes they might concede that at times a balanced budget works against their interests and an unbalanced budget might at other times advance those same concerns. Likewise many Americans, in their confrontation with world communism, have mounted an almost holy crusade to 'defeat' it at *all* costs. This commitment may be so strongly held that even strategic innovations against communism are inadmissible and regarded as treasonable. Hopefully, one can deal even with an enemy in more objective terms.

This chapter is designed to assist the citizen who wishes to participate in political activity in order to affect the allocation of societal resources (including his own), to improve his share of material and symbolic benefits, to limit his share of the burdens, to shape the controls that will be exercised over him, to improve the division of labor, and to influence the rules of the game that, in turn, affect his personal ends in life. While the strategies suggested may be less than optimal and our values and goals rejected, at least a point of view is being proposed. The reader is asked to consider seriously how a democracy might in fact work if every citizen did consciously pursue these suggestions. This kind of inquiry was conducted to some extent by the great political philosophers Locke and Hobbes and more recently, although in different ways, by such theorists as Anthony Downs, James Buchanan and Gordon Tullock, and William Gamson.[2] Game theorists have also made distinct contributions. But first, some notes on typical limitations encountered as one attempts to increase political competence and overcome limitations or barriers to political effectiveness.

Constraints on Rationality

Because the political world has a great many uncertainties one cannot always control and predict behavior and outcomes with any high degree of confidence. Unless he wishes to depend on luck (not a dependable ally), the citizen must improve his individual information in order to achieve more consistently his objectives or preferences. But first he must know what he is up against in attempting to decide how to vote, which rules to adopt, which policies to support, and what actions to take. What he is up against are constraints on rationality.

Rational Behavior

But what is rationality or rational behavior? Many scholars have struggled with the concept and many more have argued whether man is or can be rational, especially in politics. Without answering the unanswerable, let us simply assert that rational behavior denotes to us any activity in which a person keeps an eye on both the satisfactions to be attained and the costs to be paid by pursuing each proposed course of action and attempts to maximize the net rewards. In the more limited sense of the word, rationality applies to any attempt to maximize returns from given means or costs or, alternatively, to minimize costs given the objective. In the broadest sense, rational behavior can be viewed as intelligent behavior concerning the choice of the best means of accomplishing whatever one wishes to accomplish.

---

[2] Cf. Anthony Downs, *An Economic Theory of Democracy* (New York: Harper and Brothers Publishers, 1957); James M. Buchanan and Gordon Tullock, *The Calculus of Consent* (Ann Arbor: The University of Michigan Press, 1962); William Gamson, *Power and Discontent* (Homewood, Ill.: The Dorsey Press, 1968).

Such a view is based on the notion than man is capable of intelligent and disciplined thought. Men do not always act stupidly nor are they the pawns of forces far beyond their control. Achievement of rational behavior is difficult, however, because the circumstances under which men must act, in all walks of life, are demanding and only partially understood. The added fact of opposition makes political life not only more uncertain but perhaps less pleasant and more susceptible to non-rational responses. But the concern is not to make men into computers; rather it is to promote their control over their own condition. Now let us review briefly some of the obstacles to a person's achieving rationality in political life.

Self-Knowledge

One of the hardest things for man to achieve is objectivity about himself as an individual and in relationship to others, especially other interest groups and politicians. One reason is that man is somewhat 'victimized' by an unconscious or sub-conscious emotive life that affects many things he does without his awareness. Accordingly, he tends to think or want to believe that all his decisions are the products of conscious, intelligent decision-making in which he has weighed alternatives and finally chosen an optimal course. But such is rarely the case, especially in political life. If the psychologists are to be believed, man has deeply built-in conceptions of power, authority, identifications, hatreds, etc., that have been learned from a very early age. Political consequences may flow from these recesses of the psyche; an individual may unconsciously identify with a hero-figure or worship a dictatorial type because he needs an authority figure to replace the father. Or, he may rebel out of emotional distress, retreat from imaginary enemies, or get 'hung up' on self-righteousness. Whatever the cause, man frequently engages in actions which are not the resultants of much objective deliberation. Frequently he rationalizes predetermined choices and prides himself on intelligent behavior.

Problems of Learning

One need not be a psychiatrist, however, to appreciate certain other constraints on rational thought. Modern-day studies of learning, perception, and communication also point up the limits of human achievement. Because of limited mental abilities, inadequate education, insufficient sources of factual information, the costs of observing and testing, group influences on perception, as well as emotional needs, the citizen tends to be considerably less informed about governmental policies and their relationships to his interests than may be ideal. He has many lives to lead, and most of them are of far greater significance to him than the political. This being so, he tends to invest less of his resources in becoming a more effective political operative. Even if a citizen wishes to be more rational, he will find distinct limitations which he can little understand or control. Most people do not use their intellectual resources effectively. While the mind can devise and solve many problems in remarkable fashion, the real political world presents a pretty tough puzzle, and the form of analytical skill required is still not well understood. Some of the most brilliant and industrious of thinkers have shown incredible inability to understand politics.

In the learning process as related to political life, man shows an amazing capacity to screen out unpleasant facts, facts that might otherwise assist him in mastering his situation. As human beings, we tend to prefer the harmonies of thought to the discordant, the familiar to the novel, the accepted to the unconventional. Such preferences are not easy to give up and they may be disastrous if pursued at the wrong time. Great errors in strategy and policy have been made by politicians, governments and citizens. 'Collective learning' is apparently more difficult than individual learning but both show distinct and persistent limitations. Unhappily, the psychologists cannot agree on the most effective individual or collective learning processes. Each generation has new theories.

Situational Constraints on Effectiveness

Even if a man were able to achieve a high degree of political rationality, he would still encounter difficulties in applying his calculus to the achievement of his goals. The reason: societies knowingly and thoughtlessly place obstacles before the would-be political activist. The very nature of interdependent living makes the achievement of successful political action very complex and arduous. The following section details a number of these obstacles, including: (a) formal sanctions; (b) informal sanctions; (c) motivational constraints; (d) complexity, interdependence and uncertainty; and (e) costs of political action.

Formal Prohibitions

Meaningful participation in many political systems is simply prohibited; obviously this is the practice in the autocracies of the world. Indeed in many of these lands citizens would never consider participating in the making of public decisions. It is not always realized that prohibitions also exist in democracies: limitations on who votes, who brings court cases, who can petition or lobby, etc. In many nations, including the United States, participation is formally denied various groups such as the illiterate,

the alien, the criminal. In most American states formal registration procedures, lengthy and complex ballots, residence requirements and, at one
time, even property qualifications served to reduce the number of political
participants and/or the frequency and efficiency of their participation.
Many of these legal constraints are being reduced or eliminated in many
countries, but it is not always easy to understand which formal rules serve
more as barriers to participation than encouragements.

Informal Constraints

The citizen who desires to be effective and does not encounter formal
restraints may still face obstacles in the form of informal sanctions or constraints which discourage and reduce his influence. 'Informal' refers to
those practices which are not sanctioned by law or authorized as legitimate
procedures and treatment. Such informal practices can be carried out by
either citizens or public officials. There are many social and economic sanctions against many political activities. The person who chooses to offend
may find his efficacy greatly reduced. For low status groups there are
often intimidations, threats of violence, loss of employment, and the simple
unpleasantness of dealing with hostile officials and more 'secure' citizens.
No law authorizes such treatment but it is still a fact of life.

Motivational Constraints

Even in the absence of formal and informal restraints a political
system which does not encourage its citizenry to participate thereby reduces
their effectiveness. Psychologists and economists have long reported that
men are less apt to act when rewards are absent or denied. Motivation is
surely a partial function of rewards or positive inducements; let the reader
speculate on his own academic performance if he had no possibilities of
achieving higher than a 'C' for a course or were doomed to an 'F.'

Economic systems generally provide for graduated and more or less
continuing rewards for performances to motivate people; but political
systems, including democracies, seldom have such systematic and automatic
reward systems. What does one receive for voting? For paying taxes? For
serving in the military? What does one get for writing his Congressman?
Are citizens honored for not being litter bugs? Contrast the answers to
these questions with the answers to similar questions concerning one's non-
political activities. In nearly all economic activities some kind of graduated
tangible reward is offered as an inducement to perform or make an exchange. But in politics the rewards are seldom as tangible, seldom as
measurable, seldom as immediate, seldom as rewarding, and seldom perceived as connected to specific actions. Programmed learning rewards and

corrects performances almost immediately. In politics, learning is far more ambiguous and less immediately stimulated by pleasing discoveries.

The point is, men will tend to act with less fervor and consistency when the returns are less clear. Political systems must depend upon other inducements than the purely material to move men to action. Such rewards include the psychic ones of serving one's country, of performing one's duty, of participating as an end in itself. These psychic inducements are not equally powerful for all citizens and are all-important for only a few. Statistics on participation presented in Chapter 8 indicate that the number taking part tends to be rather low generally and especially low among certain classes, groups and types of individuals. Because political action is costly to the individual, he must be compensated in some manner for his sacrifices. The number voting in municipal elections would probably increase dramatically if voters were paid to vote. There might even be an increased demand for elections!

Complexity, Interdependence and Uncertainty

Pollsters continually encounter citizens who say they 'don't know' in response to questions on political attitudes. Usually the 'dk's' in the United States number from 12 to 20 per cent of those questioned on even the most familiar political matters. The civic-minded citizen is apt to become a bit impatient with such statistics because he assumes that every good citizen keeps informed about government, has ordered, articulate views, and is willing to announce them. But the political universe is intricate, huge, and indirectly related to most daily activities. Even local politics is baffling to the average citizen; he does not have the necessary time, let alone other resources, to perceive it accurately and meaningfully. If he cannot comprehend local affairs realistically, how can he expect government to perform according to his expectations? Women, especially, have viewed the political system as strange, and few have chosen to seek political office. At the very least politics appears devious and dirty, not the right way of doing things. Issues are too complex, emotions too explosive, activities too strenuous to make politics a rewarding endeavor. Complexity and uncertainty are prime realities for the ordinary citizen; accordingly he becomes less effective.

Complex interdependencies in themselves do not prohibit stable patterns of behavior, but they require more technical information and elaborate theories in order to understand behavior and make predictions. Unless he wishes to become a professional behavioral scientist in order to become a more efficient political actor, the citizen must accept the fact that he will know little about the workings of the system which affects him in such peculiar ways. When decisions must be made under conditions of such great uncertainty, hopes of being more rational are weakened and problems increased. Even presidents and prime ministers, with all their informational resources, are not exempt. Every public official of consequence and humility has at some time sadly observed that he acted on erroneous estimates of situations. President Hoover was not aware of the extent of the impending depression; President Roosevelt did not realize his court-packing plan would fail so miserably; President Truman did not believe the Chinese would enter the Korean War; President Kennedy did not expect his Bay of Pigs invasion in Cuba to be a disaster, and so it goes. Fortunately the decisions of the average citizen are neither so frequently required nor so costly for many. The problems of uncertainty in decision-making affect the government and its organized opposition far more than the ordinary citizen. If you doubt this, try running for public office at the next election.

That uncertainty is pervasive must not be interpreted in tragic terms. Uncertainty can be estimated in terms of risk or probabilities. One might, for example, calculate, estimate or even guess that the chances of serious rioting in a given city are seven in ten, or that the chances of the Chinese directly involving themselves in military action in South Vietnam are about one in ten under present conditions. During general elections there are fairly accurate estimates of probable gains and losses for each party. These illustrations are meant to suggest that not all events in the political world are beyond any form of prediction or practical estimation. A great many elements in every social situation are fairly stable—less susceptible to erratic short-run fluctuations and more prone to orderly long-run trends. Where fluctuations are likely to occur, there are usually warning signs of possible changes; this is especially true of the economy. That is why American Presidents find the Council of Economic Advisors useful in measuring and interpreting the many indicators of economic activity and movements. Political activities apparently are less predictable. Even so, systematic efforts are being made to develop better and more reliable indicators of change, such as conditions under which rioting or revolutions will occur, or the situations that will activate certain groups, etc. Perhaps one day leaders will have a Council of Political Advisors made up of professional political scientists who will try each day or week to predict where wars will erupt, tomorrow's quota of demonstrations, trends in public preferences, the political reactions to regulations, and so forth. In a sense such advisors already exist although they are not so labelled. The Rand Corporation, The American Institute of Public Opinion, and other research groups in and out of government deal with information on which strategic advice is based.

Uncertainty, then, is a fact of life, but it is neither total nor exclusive. Each party in competitive and conflict situations realizes that his uncertainties are matched by the doubts and uncertainties of others. Each party must realize that his own choices rest to some extent on the unknown choices of others. Besides, the complexities of competitive interdependence make life more interesting.

Costs of Participation

Whether or not any of the previous restrictions to participation and effectiveness exist, the citizen still has to pay certain costs to achieve his political ends. The scarcity of most resources guarantees costs. As already noted in Chapters 1 and 7, the resources of time, energy and income can all be used in non-political pursuits which thus compete with political action. No one has more than 24 hours a day at his disposal; no one has more than a certain level of energy to burn at any given time; no one has more than a specific amount of financial resources to spend. To eliminate completely such costs is inconceivable, so the citizen must allocate these precious resources. Curiously, some utopians have constructed or advocated societies in which man would apparently devote all his time to politics because all decisions would, in a sense, be collectively made. However, the cost of all this public life would be the sacrifice of any private pursuits.

While participation costs cannot be eliminated, they undoubtedly could be reduced and/or redistributed. Money costs are particularly high and discourage many aspiring politicians. Enlisting the cooperation and support of others is a most demanding political feat. It is emotionally costly, as anyone who has chaired even a small committee knows, and may produce more anxieties and disturbances than positive outcomes.

A Handbook of Rules

This one-sided concentration on the constraints affecting citizens and politicians has, no doubt, left the feeling that little can be achieved because everything, including one's own deepest feelings, seems to be allied against rational choice. This is not true, of course, but it must be recognized that the political world cannot be remade every day by everyone to achieve his own preferences. The citizen can, however, exercise some control over some variables if he commands the needed information and other resources of action. We intend to assist the reader in trying to master political processes with somewhat more conscious insight so that these constraints weigh less heavily. Remember, therefore, that those who feel defeated or overwhelmed from the beginning will not participate and, by not participating, they make it easier for those who do to achieve their aims. The histories of all nations are replete with instances of citizens being exploited because they either did not act or acted ineffectively. We want to aid in equipping all citizens with some tools and aspirations for effective citizenship.

A person who wishes to be more effective, whether serving as an ordinary voter, politician, member of an organization, government bureaucrat, or party official, is forced to consider his work in terms of the *proximate goals* which he wishes to accomplish and the *available means* to achieve those goals. To accomplish something, one must first understand how one's goals would apply in the actual political situation. Every situation contains certain aspects that cannot be altered; a person must know which ones are beyond his control and which allow for some manipulation. Normally some resources are available, though scarce or costly, which can be employed in *alternative* ways. Accordingly, one must know his *disposable resources* and how they can be used.

Unlike the pure scientist, the politician or citizen desiring to achieve a certain goal usually must expect to encounter *conscious opposition* from others who either do not share his goals or prefer some other order of priority. To be sure there are many situations of shared goals, as indicated in Chapter 10, but the citizen should not be too surprised to discover that others will object and resist what he regards as perfectly reasonable and desirable. Conflict and opposition may be expected when competitors desire the same scarce ends. The challenge, then, is to learn how to enlist cooperation or support from some and wage competition or conflict with others.

Mastery of all these elements of political action is hardly simple or easy. Anyone expecting to achieve anything important politically must be prepared to devote much time and other resources to his work and to develop nearly infinite patience; one cannot expect instant or easy solutions. For the sake of clarification, however, we will try to simplify the tasks involved in political actions as follows: (a) ordering preferences; (b) relating means to goals; (c) taking stock of resources; (d) searching for exchanges; (e) selecting alternatives; and (f) building support.

Ordering Preferences

This odd sounding phrase represents an extremely important aspect of effective political action: the necessity for estimating the relative significance of objectives. If man had but a single objective the problem would not exist because that objective would be first and last, and alternative means could be rated in terms of their comparative efficacy and efficiency. But man is not a single-purpose entity; he seeks multiple goals and, as might be expected, is often confused and inconsistent about what he wants both in private and public life.

The first rule, then, is to attempt to straighten out preferences; what is wanted and how important are these various and often conflicting objectives? Ordering preferences, therefore, means thinking in terms of relative significance, one to the other. Thus a person might prefer A to B and

B to C and, if he is consistent, to prefer A to C. Nothing more is said about
the exact importance of each goal other than its rank. Once this is accomplished (and it is no mean trick), one can better assess the most appropriate
means. Of course, if a person prefers A to B by a magnitude of, say, twice
as much, this helps. If A is preferred only slightly more than B, the choice
of means will be radically affected. For example, during the 1968 elections,
some Democratic voters voted for Republican candidates who were critical
of President Johnson's foreign policies, especially with regard to Vietnam.
They did so because they considered the Vietnam issue of transcendent
importance and were willing, therefore, to accept a candidate whose domestic policies were antithetical to their own. Other voters may well have agreed
about Vietnam, but they ranked other preferences as more crucial and thus
were unable to support that strategy. The way in which white voters, e.g.,
rate racial issues may suggest another strategy of voter choice. Voters and
politicians may unconsciously order their preferences in more or less unsystematic ways. However, in complex choice situations, risks can arise from
automatic selectivity of preferences. The following illustrates the importance of ranking public policies.

Most citizens are interested in the effect governmental polices have
on the state of the economy because they are vitally affected by these
policies. Included among the preferences one might have are price stability,
economic growth, full employment, equitable income distribution, economic efficiency, minimal governmental controls. One need not be a professional economist to realize that these individually admirable goals may
be somewhat inconsistent since to achieve more of one may entail some
sacrifice of one or more of the others. Unless preferences can be rather
strongly ordered, problems will arise in deciding which party will best
achieve one's personal preferences. Political parties in democracies may be
for all these laudatory goals, but they quite typically assign quite different
priorities at any given point in time. Consider these possible preference
orderings:

Democrats	*Republicans*
1. full employment	1. minimal government controls
2. equitable income distribution	2. price stability
3. high rate of economic growth	3. efficiency
4. price stability	4. economic growth
5. efficiency	5. full employment
6. minimal controls	6. equitable income distribution

The above rankings are not scientifically determined but they have a rough
approximation to American political reality; in any event, they suggest
that while the two major parties share the same areas of concern their
order of priorities is in sharp contrast. One cannot vote for either party

expecting them to take the same sorts of actions, i.e., unless they are inconsistent, 'ignorant' and/or cynical. To express an effective voter choice, therefore, the citizen must determine *his* policy priorities as well as those of the political parties and their leaders. Now the importance of ordering preferences, at least in voting, can be seen.

One more dimension might be added. Earlier it was pointed out that goals might be inconsistent, and so they are. The kinds of public policies that will aid in the realization of one goal may work to the detriment of others. For example, the achievement of a stable price level may lead to less than full employment and less than a favorable rate of economic growth. Conversely, if full employment is preferred, one may have to accept some inflationary tendencies and more extensive government control over the economy. Or, growth may be costly in terms of a less equitable income distribution. In other words, every course of action has its costs; the cost of a goal in public policy is the amount sacrificed from another goal. Since some sacrifice is inevitable, the citizen should try to find out what and how much of other alternatives are given up. To do this also requires an ordering of preferences.

In politics the knowledge of feasible alternatives requires some consideration. The more active a person, the more likely he will face situations where his first priorities will not be immediately granted; however, there may be alternatives agreeable to all. One needs a sense of what is being given up or postponed relative to the gains and direct costs involved in accepting substitutes. A candidate needs both a campaign chest and the public support of some notables. In seeking these he would be wise not only to have an estimate of their relative urgency, for the costs of time and search are irreversible, but also to be aware of the kinds of commitments or 'stands' he might be willing to assume or consider as they relate to his major campaign goals. Every political leader implicitly shifts and substitutes preferred ends as he confronts new problems and choices, but the sense of incremental costs and gains is often lost in the process. It may be nice to think that good leaders cite major goals and then persist with unbending vigor. But is there a single leader in history, good or bad, who has done it that way? Yet it is amazing how many people fail to think in marginal terms. It is far better to avoid asking how much one needs and far more important to ask what one is willing to sacrifice in order to gain another unit of whatever is wanted. Asking this question clarifies one's values and preferences under that most realistic situation—that of relative scarcities.

Relating Means and Goals

Once preferences, whether individual or collective, are ordered one can begin to think about effective means for their achievement. The best way of reaching a goal is by no means given in most political situations, or any other for that matter. Occasionally one has no alternative or very limited ones, but generally the imaginative person can concoct new possibilities. Alternative means, of course, have various advantages and disadvantages; the problem is to devise and select the most effective and efficient within the given social and moral order.

The accompanying diagrams (Figures 12-1, 12-2, 12-3) portray a series of increasingly complex means-end staircases or chains. If these figures are studied closely a great deal is learned about choice problems. Note that goals and means are always connected in both direct and indirect ways. Note, too, that alternative means are provided for. Observe that some means will assist in achieving a single goal while others may assist in reaching multiple and complementary goals. There are also a succession of intermediate goals and means before achievement of the final or relatively permanent goals.

Figure 12-1 is a neat and idealized conception. Uncertainty and costs must still be reckoned with. In Figure 12-2 some means are considered inadequate and, at one point, a missing stair is found with the suggestion that a decision be made. Still other means are thought to be vague and in need of clarification, and some means are regarded as subordinate to still other means. Then finally, observe in Figure 12-3 the introduction of a new consideration—the 'premises' that spell out the various wanted and unwanted consequences of each means. It should be emphasized that these diagrams are only aids to more systematic evaluation of means-end problems; *they do not provide solutions* but they suggest systematically the requisite considerations. The diagrams are quite properly limited to sets of connected but empty categories which must be appropriately filled in as one engages in goal-oriented action. They are not easy to fill in. If the reader doubts this, he should try filling in one relating to his role as a student in class. Is the student interested in grades, pleasing the instructor, learning about politics, satisfying his parents, impressing some girl or young man, or 'just getting by'? The student should order his goals and consider possible ways of achieving one or more of them with the means at his disposal. Now try a really difficult problem: Try handling the latest foreign policy crisis of the United States from the perspective of the President, noting the multiple consequences of every step he takes.

As the above diagrams and discussion suggest, one must consider the possible or probable consequences of the alternatives. The blank lines at the bottom of Figure 12-3 are meant to be filled in for any decision-making situation. The various consequences are not easy to detect nor weigh, but some effort must be made if one is to improve his decisions and position. The implications of these choices can be illustrated by analyzing a major contemporary issue, the Vietnam war, and the President's choice of strategies. Here are some possible consequences undoubtedly considered and as-

Figure 12-1

Means-End Staircases and Permanent Goals

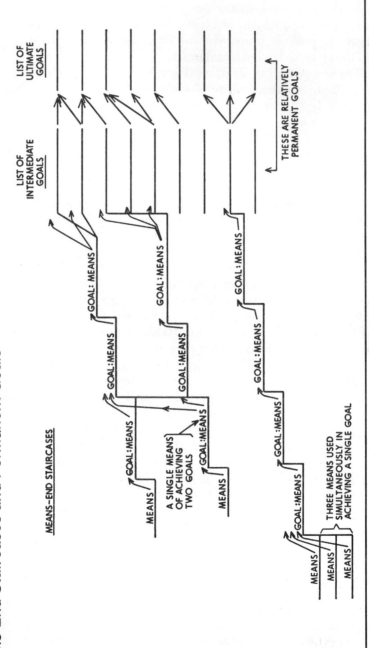

Reprinted with permission from M. H. Jones, *Executive Decision Making* (Rev. Ed.; Homewood, Ill.: Richard D. Irwin, Inc.) p. 19.

Figure 12-2

A Fairly Complex Set of Means-End Staircases
Showing the Points Where Decisions Have to be Made

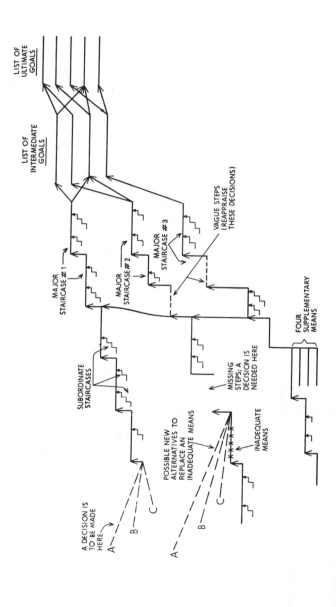

Reprinted with permission from M. H. Jones, *Executive Decision Making* (Rev. Ed.; Homewood, Ill.: Richard D. Irwin, Inc.) p. 21.

Figure 12-3

Simplified Means-End Staircase, Showing Possible Alternative Means and Premises for Each

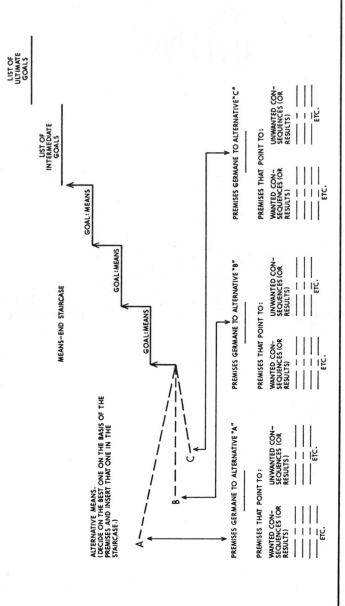

Reprinted with permission from M. H. Jones, *Executive Decision Making* (Rev. Ed.; Homewood, Ill.: Richard D. Irwin, Inc.) p. 58.

sessed in top councils in terms of being either wanted or unwanted. (Their relative importance and probable occurrence are excluded.)

Presumed Unwanted Consequences	*Presumed Preferred Consequences*
1. an interminable war	1. an honorable negotiated settlement
2. higher American casualties	2. continued American influence in Asia
3. higher South Vietnamese casualties	3. independence for the South Vietnamese
4. unbalanced budget	4. prosperity at home
5. higher taxes	5. lower taxes
6. domestic inflation	6. lower interest rates
7. direct war with China	7. increased domestic social benefits
8. military defeat	8. democracy in South Vietnam
9. diminished American prestige	9. re-election of supportive politicians

The above consequences could be stated in different terms and many more could be added either as new consequences or as qualifications of present ones, but they are sufficient to suggest the dilemmas that confront a politician as he attempts to exert control over only partially manageable situations. Each of the above consequences flows from one or more of the various policies that the President could adopt. If he expanded the bombing of North Vietnam, which consequences would follow? If he supported a certain government in South Vietnam, what would happen? And, so it goes. Similar listings could be developed for any policy dilemma of the politician from the most trivial local issue to the most serious and consequential national concern.

Taking Stock of Resources

Before choosing a course of action, the politician had better take stock of available and relevant resources or the possibility of creating them. Knowing what he has to work with ought to shape both his aspirations and the selection of means. So it is imperative that these resources be known in terms of their use value, their quantities and convertibility, and their likely effect as actual political influence.[3]

Earlier discussions in Part 1 have sensitized the reader to the availa-

---

[3] Cf. Edward C. Banfield, *Political Influence* (New York: The Free Press, 1961), Parts II-III; Robert E. Agger, Daniel Goldrich and Bert E. Swanson, *The Rulers and the Ruled* (New York: John Wiley and Sons, Inc., 1964), pp. 51; 55-59; 285-290; and Gamson, *op. cit.,* Chaps. 4-5; 7-8.

bility of a great variety of political resources, including reputation, social status or position, formal office and authority, votes, support, information, and political skills. These resources can be developed and converted into political value if one understands their applicability and how readily they can be employed in a variety of different situations. Effective politicians and activists generally acquire a feel for this. Resources are not appropriate for all occasions, nor are all equally effective even if appropriate. Money, for example, is a powerful resource throughout life and is readily convertible into many uses, but it cannot always be immediately effective in political situations. The crass political bribe is a rather foolish and unrealistic tactic in most situations. Moreover, money alone cannot eliminate non-material problems. If it could, Governor Rockefeller would have been President some time ago. Generalized status in the community usually cannot be converted into instant political influence unless it is relevant to the political situation. A Ph.D. in physics, for example, has a certain status value in American life, but the degree counts for little in political life unless it can be related to a policy problem or issue such as the nuclear bomb and its employment. Knowing the kinds of resources one has command over is a most important step in wielding political power.

Understanding the uses of resources is equally crucial, for the activist can overspend if he is not careful and dissipate his effectiveness. Equally bad is to begin a program and fail because of unanticipated shortages of resources. Unfortunately the politician is not in the enviable position of the businessman who can measure his resources in dollars and cents. True, the politician can say he has so many dollars with which to wage a campaign, but he cannot be equally precise about the amounts of status, support or skills he can mobilize. Whereas money is a precise yet generalized medium of exchange, these other resources are not, and their worth cannot be easily translated into political values. So the politician operates under some uncertainty as to the development and use of his resources. Neither politician nor citizen can go to a bank and borrow such necessary resources as reputation, status, etc., in the same sense that capital can be acquired. Indeed it is even extremely difficult to borrow money for political purposes; few lending agencies will extend credit to finance office seeking or policy changes, particularly if the cause is likely to lose. In brief, some resources are usually in short supply and must be used with care. On the other hand there are other resources which can be used and maintained or even increased as one proceeds. One's status, reputation and credibility are typically not 'used up' and may indeed be enhanced by public exposure. Effective use of resources, therefore, can provide direct returns and expanded resources.

The point has already been made that most resources are not readily convertible into effective political influence. As a result, a great deal of political barter is carried on. The politician trades votes, or support, for jobs, favors, policy promises, changes in goal preferences, etc. Surely, most citizens realize that they cannot visit city hall and acquire whatever they want in the same sense that they can enter the local grocery and purchase whatever they wish by simply exchanging money for goods. Since the political situation is more akin to primitive bartering, it is wise to recognize the possibly severe limitations placed on resource convertibility, particularly the necessity of relating the resource to specific situations and persons. A status resource, for example, is not a generalized resource which will impress everyone; one's status must be salient to the person on whom it is being used. What counts as high status with one citizen may be treated as irrelevant by another. Obviously the latter will not be as impressed as the former and may well resist compliance to any suggestions from the person using the resource. In the United States most politicians are likely to be impressed by the status of bankers, businessmen and the affluent generally, but differ in their regard for the farmer, small businessman, scientist, or even the intellectual. He who would exercise influence is well advised to consider the group and the probable salience of appeals before proceeding.

Calculations about the convertibility of resources are apt not to be very precise or accurate. There is no daily exchange rate which can be checked in the stock pages of a newspaper, nor is there a going price for units of resources. One cannot say that a pound of status currently sells for $10, whereas yesterday it retailed at $9.75. Instead, the politician must translate his resources into votes or potential support. When he wishes to exercise influence, he lets others know how much support he thinks he can command, taking into account the uncertainties and costs of converting resources into actual influence.

Searching for Exchanges

A continual source of skepticism if not cynicism among citizens is the endless capacity of politicians to make deals. There is a theme in the political culture of most democracies that 'principles' are more worthy than 'expediency,' meaning that bargains are a crass form of behavior appropriate in the marketplace but not in the polity. Our political heroes are seldom identified as skilled politicians (although most were, in fact, highly skilled bargainers); but the folklore honors their unbending principles and morality. Washington and Lincoln are the prototypes. Yet Lincoln, the historians tell us, was a consummate politician.[4] Occasionally a politician may believe he is not a bargainer; President Eisenhower apparently was such a person. However, his very ingenuousness added to his bargaining skill and resources. Bargaining in a somewhat ambivalent political

---

[4] The point is well made by David Donald, *Lincoln Reconsidered* (New York: Alfred A. Knopf, Inc., 1956).

culture is likely to produce some odd consequences and styles. But it should be clearly stated that bargaining is a most necessary means of making public policies.

Democracies, of necessity, impose a requirement that men bargain over and across a great number of decisions. They must bargain because they cannot always achieve their objectives solely by command, cooperation or conflict. This also applies at certain levels within command systems since no leader can be omnipotent, omnicompetent, or omniscient; he must depend upon others and, in depending upon them, is forced to bargain with them. In less autocratic or more unstable systems the need to bargain may be even greater, particularly if more forceful solutions are too costly.

In order to consummate a bargain it is necessary that two or more persons have things they are willing to dispose of and acquire. Look at it this way:

I	He
am willing to dispose of	may be willing to acquire
(x)	(x)
and seek to acquire	and might dispose of
(y)	(y)

The problem is to find exchange partners and occasions where exchange is mutually desirable or profitable.

But this simple exchange situation is by no means simple in reality. The most skilled politicians sometimes have only limited insight into what it is they are exchanging. Often the 'agreements' are tacit, i.e., vague promises made in uncertain anticipation of potential benefits. The competent bargainer must be sensitive to the interests of the other participants and, just as importantly, be able to communicate his own views and goals. Nations, in particular, have problems in communication because so much of the bargaining is done indirectly. For example, in 1968 when peace talks were going on between the North Vietnamese and the United States, each side kept demanding some clear-cut sign that the other was de-escalating the war effort. The United States had reduced its bombing in various ways while the North Vietnamese had seemed to disengage itself somewhat in ground actions. But neither side trusted the other; neither believed that the other had in fact de-escalated. Neither knew what sort of sign would be convincing to the opponent. Because of the indirect nature of communications, political misunderstandings are a constant possibility.

Sometimes being too explicit will also be risky because specific commitments may limit the bargainer's range of choice in further moves. Among the various choices are the conditions under which bargaining can take place, the actual processes of bargaining, the terms to be sought, and the terms that would be acceptable. Of course choices will vary, depending on the political context. Hopefully the illustrations added to this chapter will suggest different sorts of strategic possibilities.

In preparing to bargain one must be willing to cooperate and compete; i.e., provide terms attractive to the other party while driving the best possible bargain for oneself. These two aspects make the bargaining situation somewhat contradictory and necessitate almost conflicting talents on the part of the respective bargainers. These divergent needs can be illustrated by a simple diagram such as Figure 12-4.

Figure 12-4

A Bargaining Situation: Minimum Wages

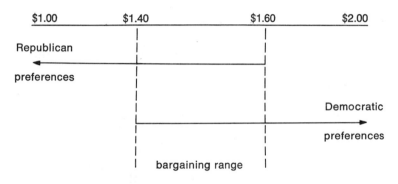

Figure 12-4 depicts a possible bargaining situation involving the level of minimum wages to be legislated, a not uncommon legislative task. The diagram shows a possible range of from $1.00 to $2.00 per hour. The Republicans, it is assumed—not without good historical reasons—are willing to settle for a rate of not less than a dollar but not more than $1.60; the Democrats will accept as little as $1.40 but would prefer something closer to $2.00. The overlap in acceptable rates is 20¢, i.e., from a $1.40 to a $1.60 per hour minimum wage. Assuming that its members are in accord, each party may pursue a strategy of publicly announcing its target or most preferred position while attempting to conceal its least preferred but nevertheless acceptable position. Thus the Republicans will not want the Democrats to know that they will go as high as $1.60, while the Democrats will not want the Republicans to know that they will go as low as $1.40. So each searches for as favorable a settlement as possible within the slowly established bargaining range.

Now consider how this process may work in an actual legislature, such as Congress, where some members of each side may act on their own. Typically those with highest intensities (see Table 10-1) will be most opposed to the opposition's most preferred position, which represents the greatest loss for them. For example, Senator X of the Republicans makes a motion to put the minimum wage at $1.10. In the vote he gains his own party's support but picks up no Democrats. One of his fellow partisans, who prefers a higher figure, may then make his bid in a subsequent motion. If his motion does not quite win the required vote the Democrats may put in a bid, possibly by a member strongly committed to a high minimum wage. Again, it may lose and the 'bidding' will move once more toward the middle of the bargaining range. *When neither side can win without some support from the other (the bargaining situation), the compromise will fall within the bargainable range.* Because Congress frequently faces this sort of voting situation, analysts have actually been able to 'scale' various issues to reveal the relative preference positions of the legislators. Both parties have some mavericks and a wide spread of member preferences, but once these are recognized it is possible to anticipate the future possibilities for this form of competitive bargaining in that legislature.

The shrewd bargainer, then, must know his own and his opposition's likely strategies and potential support and his own resistance capability. He must also be able to estimate what certain opposition members will settle for. Sometimes this is not readily apparent because the opponent may lead from an extreme position or propose a very intensely-held but unacceptable preference. So bargainers constantly search out possible areas of agreement by sending up trial balloons, including some which the other party may never have considered previously. Once the bargainer senses what may appeal to his opposition he is in a better position to test the range of resistance to or acceptance of some of his demands.

This range of resistance is illustrated in Figure 12-5 by curves representing various levels of resistant capacity of liberal Democrats and economy-minded Republicans regarding the size of the budget. The Republicans have considerable power to resist a $200 billion budget while the Democrats have still greater power to resist a budget cut to $100 billion (solid lines). Conversely, each group shows much less desire for and resistance to other budgets above or below their most preferred position. If the bargainers are rational and have the power indicated by the curves, the final budgetary size will be about $160 billion (the intersection of the solid lines).

Now suppose the bargaining power of the liberal Democrats is decreased for some reason—say they didn't have enough votes—to the position illustrated by the dotted line. In this case, the best budget figure they could get would be around $130 billion. In most political situations the power of one side cannot be altered without a corresponding change on the other side. Thus if the Democrats lost seats after an election their power curve would go down and that of the Republicans would rise, shifting the bidding process on the next budget accordingly.

Our nice smooth curves should not be viewed as representing immuta-

Figure 12-5

Budgetary Preferences and Bargaining Power

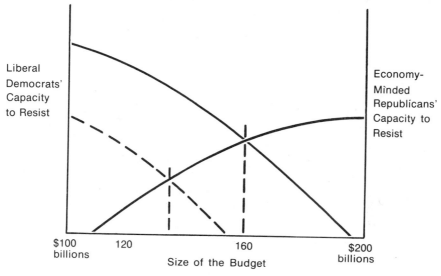

Liberal Democrats' Capacity to Resist

Economy-Minded Republicans' Capacity to Resist

$100 billions   120   160 $200 billions

Size of the Budget

ble natural forces which can pose limitations or possibilities apart from the perceptions of the bargainers. Bargainers may not know their own resources with any precision even though they do know the voting strength of the other party. Much of bargaining is a probing or testing of the other party's intentions and capabilities. There are no formulas to apply, no convenient time-tested rules of thumb available in this search operation. That is why so much of political bargaining is misunderstood and ineffectual.

One can substitute all sorts of issues for the ones illustrated; for example, the groups of citizens to be covered by medicare, the amounts and terms of foreign aid, agricultural subsidies, or the rates of an income tax. Likewise, the United States might bargain in NATO over the number of troops to be deployed in Europe, or with the Soviets over terms in its trade policies. Any situation in which the bargaining objectives may be considered in terms of more or less is an especially good issue over which to make bargains. The Founding Fathers, for example, arranged a compromise scheme of representation to appease both small and large states, and the North and the South as they then existed. Some of these bargains were later to break down, as they did during the Civil War, but by and large they have provided the formal basis of the American polity.

Bargains can also be made with totally different 'commodities' or public goods; in other words, bartered exchanges are possible. One group

may allow another group to have so much of this public good in return
for so much of another public good. In seeking bargains the most rational
approach is to *trade through time and over different issues and public
goods*. It is possible to compromise within a single issue, such as the
minimum wage level illustrated above, but it is also possible to bargain
over several issues simultaneously or with promises of future exchanges.
Thus, a politician who does not feel particularly strong about the minimum wage might consider exchanging his support to one side or the
other for a promise of support on some other issue on which he does feel
strongly, say civil rights. A bargainer ought to be searching constantly for
support and possible exchanges; to do this, however, he must decide what
is most important, less important and least important. And one must search
among people with differing but compatible evaluations. The most committed should look to the less committed for easier exchanges, since there
is no further gain from working only with those who already agree. It can
be seen that bargaining across issues and through time is really a most
complicated and uncertain business. To discover the preferences of others,
the range of their acceptable solutions, the costs of acquiring support, and
to keep one's political books balanced calls for imagination, skill and
knowledge. Be prepared to bargain; be prepared to seek allies; and be
prepared to reward others. The following two cases, one from modern
Senate history and the other from contemporary international dealings,
illustrate all these points well. The first pertains to the competitive maneuvering and bargaining that took place over the filling of a Republican
vacancy on the prestigious Senate Foreign Relations Committee in the
Eighty-second Congress. Note the extraordinary complexity of the dealing
or exchanging.

*Case Study #1   Republican Vacancy on the Senate Foreign Relations
Committee (1951)*

> "Normally the Foreign Relations post would have gone to
> Senator Morse of Oregon, who had urgently requested representation
> for the West Coast and had the explicit backing of Senator Vanden-
> berg. But Vandenberg was ill in Michigan, and Taft and Wherry
> were determined that the liberal and internationalist Morse should
> not be appointed. Since places on major committees are allotted
> strictly according to seniority, the conservatives were able to cook
> Morse's goose by proposing Senator Capehart of Indiana, who out-
> ranks Morse. The liberals countered with Senator Aiken of Vermont,
> who outranks Capehart. The conservatives next advanced Senator
> Brewster of Maine, who outranks Aiken. The liberals came back with
> Senator Tobey of New Hampshire who outranks Brewster. That was
> when the fun really started.
>
> "Tobey already was the ranking Republican on the Banking

and Currency Committee and the Interstate and Foreign Commerce Committee. Brewster did not have any top rank on any committee, although he was second to Tobey on Interstate and Foreign Commerce. Delicate negotiations were now begun, with Brewster trying to obtain an assurance from Tobey that if he went to Foreign Relations, he would withdraw from Interstate and Foreign Commerce, leaving Brewster top Republican there. Tobey for his part offered to renounce Foreign Relations if Brewster would do the same, thus clearing the way for Aiken. Brewster and the conservatives did not like this and redoubled the pressure on Tobey to take the Foreign Relations post if he wanted to, but to retire from the Interstate and Foreign Commerce Committee.

"Refusing to do any favors for Brewster, Tobey quietly retired from the Banking and Currency Committee, applied for the Foreign Relations post and got it, and held on to his ranking position on Interstate and Foreign Commerce."[5]

Case Study #2   The Johnson-Thieu Bargain (July, 1968)

Whereas the previous case illustrated intricate maneuvering within Congress, the present one illustrates a straightforward instance of international bargaining and its outcome. The case is quoted in full from an editorial in a Portland, Oregon, newspaper and should be self-explanatory.

Fair Exchange

"A favor for a favor ('you scratch my back, and I'll scratch yours') is a political practice not limited to legislatures and Congress. Presidents of allied countries do it too.

"President Lyndon Johnson gave President Nguyen Van Thieu of South Vietnam a timely build-up by inviting him—and him alone —to a 'summit' conference in Honolulu. The two issued a long communique which includes a specific promise that South Vietnam would have a leading role in making any peace settlement with the Communist enemy.

"On his flight back to Saigon, President Thieu gave *U.S. News and World Report* an interview in which he said at least one U.S. division of troops can be withdrawn from South Vietnam next year and one or two more in 1970, with the South Vietnamese armed forces taking over.

"This is just the kind of thing the Johnson Administration— now backing Vice President Hubert Humphrey for the nomination—

---

[5] Willard Shelton, "Civil War in the G. O. P.," *The Nation,* Jan. 27, 1951, pp. 75-76, as quoted in Bertram M. Gross, *The Legislative Struggle* (New York: McGraw-Hill Book Company, Inc., 1953), p. 277.

needs as the national conventions and the elections approach. It tends to restore confidence of the American voters in President Johnson's policies. Of course, if the enemy opens another major attack—as has been predicted—and the Paris pre-peace talks continue to stagnate, confidence in an early South Vietnamese take-over of the fighting front may lag some. At the moment, however, the back-scratching may be politically effective in both countries."[6]

Selecting Alternatives

In politics as elsewhere, the whole point is to achieve preferred states, that is, net benefits for one's self and/or others. To do this a person must be able to devise alternatives, then choose among them after assessing their relative costs and the possibilities for deriving gains. This difficult political action must be faced at all levels, from the ordinary citizen deciding how to vote to a national leader deciding whether to declare war.

Business finds it relatively easy to calculate direct money costs of alternatives since the required resources and commodities all have price tags. The average citizen, on the other hand, has great trouble just determining his tax load let alone identifying and measuring policy benefits promised by competing parties. In general, it is easier to identify types and costs of benefits than it is to measure them. Some benefits can be measured in dollars and cents, but many cannot. Still, it is a good exercise to try to estimate comparative values, however qualitative.

A further note of advice: net returns from each alternative should always be thought of in terms of probability, i.e., the chances of their occurrence. Some will be highly probable while others will be highly uncertain. Figure 12-6 suggests a systematic comparison of alternatives in terms of their estimated probabilities for producing desirable and undesirable outcomes. The effective chooser calculates these probabilities not only for what he wants but for other possible consequences as well.

It is not possible to prescribe scientifically what ought to be done when faced with the above types of situations; but it is possible to indicate the nature of the problem and to show how various strategies can have varying outcomes. A government's goals will condition the ranking of desired outcomes in the consideration of strategy choices. An optimal solution in Figure 12-6 is calculated by multiplying the expected payoffs from each alternative strategy by the probability of its occurrence and selecting that strategy which provides the highest expected return. Needless to say, if one can translate the entries of Figure 12-6 into numbers, one's calculations are facilitated and made more precise.

---

[6] *The Oregonian,* July 31, 1968, p. 28.

Perhaps the problem can be further clarified by viewing those situations in which competition prevails—normally the case in most battles over the allocation of resources and distribution of benefits. In such instances one is confronted with a more or less rational opponent who has about the same capacity as one's self to make decisions or choose strategies that will have an impact on one's own choice of strategies.

Figure 12-7 depicts a game matrix showing the expected distribution of 535 Congressional seats between the Republicans and Democrats on the assumption that each party will choose from certain strategies to conduct its campaign. If everything goes as the matrix depicts, it is possible to estimate the number of seats the Democrats will win depending upon which joint strategies are chosen. Each party can pursue a number of strategies provided the probabilities for each set of opposition strategies are taken into account.

To illustrate: Suppose that the Democrats have two strategies (A and B) while the Republicans can choose from among three (C, D and E). Each of the entries indicates the most likely number of seats the Democrats would win given each combination of strategies. For example, if the Democrats select A and the Republicans C, the Democrats will get 300 of the 535 seats in both houses. On the other hand, if the Democrats pursue strategy B and the Republicans strategy C, the Democrats will win only 100 seats. The problem is, which strategy should the Democrats pursue? This will depend on the size of the desired reward and the probability of that reward occurring. Suppose, for example, that the chances of the Republicans adopting strategy C were very low; strategy D, about medium; and strategy E, very high. (This evaluation is made without considering Republican estimates of Democratic counterstrategy.) Under these assumptions the Democrats could opt for strategy A, hoping that the Republicans would pursue C, for that would give them the largest number of seats. The Democrats are least likely to select that strategy, however. If they did, it would be a highly optimistic or 'go for broke' tactic, for were the Republicans to select E, the Democrats would really lose, getting less than a majority of the seats (235). And the chances of Republicans choosing E are high.

A more realistic Democratic strategist might recommend strategy B, reasoning that if the Republicans adopt C, which is very unlikely, the Democrats will have 100 seats; but if they adopt E, which is far more likely, the Democrats will have 245 seats (compared to 235 if the Democrats had chosen strategy A). Which of these strategies should be selected? No one can say without knowing the wants of the party leadership and the expected probabilities of each opposition strategy. Matters would be still more complicated if the Democrats were to develop a third strategy like the Republicans.

This discussion has stressed a basic political fact, that the alternative

Figure 12-6

Expected Probabilities of Outcomes for Strategic Choices (Enter High, Medium or Low): Vietnam, 1968

Hierarchy of Outcomes		Strong & Rapid Escalation	Enclave Defense	Unilateral Withdrawal	Limited War
Highly Desired	Negotiated peace				
	Early withdrawal of U.S. Forces				
	Independent South Vietnam				
	Subsidence of domestic American opposition				
Desirable	Pacified Asia				
	Allied support				
	Tax reduction				

Strategic Alternatives

Least Desirable	Communist unity				
	Coalition government of Vietnam				
	Loss of prestige				
	Endless negotiations				
	Continued Asian instability				
	Election of opposition				
To be Avoided at All Costs	North Vietnam military victory				
	Loss of Asian allies				

Figure 12-7

Probable Democratic Victories on Economic Issues

Republican Strategies

		C	D	E
Democratic Strategies	A	300	295	235
	B	100	200	245

Democratic Strategies:
  A—increase federal spending
  B—promote service programs
Republican Strategies:
  C—reduce federal spending
  D—offer tax breaks for ghetto enterprises
  E—increase incentives to private enterprise
Note: These choices are not mutually exclusive; combining
several strategies is not only possible but highly probable.

possibilities presented by one's opponent, or by some other agent, affect one's own choices of action and outcomes. Nor need these agents be human. Consider the alternatives presented by nature in the form of variable weather conditions. Particularly relevant to the politician are the effects of weather on electoral turnouts, agricultural output and prices, or on riots. The role of information in coping with uncertainty can now be appreciated. Equally to be appreciated are the elements of competition and conflict because they force one to consider actions in terms of winning and losing, and to confront a competent opposition with understanding and intelligence. Case Study #3 illustrates these points.

Case Study #3   Jefferson's Options in 1807: The Chesapeake Incident

This case outlines a strategic choice situation not uncommon to national leaders. Most American presidents have had to define and choose alternatives under crisis conditions in which war or other hostilities have been initiated and/or required some form of response. President Jefferson confronted such a crisis in 1807 after a British attack upon the American frigate *Chesapeake*. His options were not unlike those of subsequent Presidents faced with similar situations. This is how one writer describes the situation:

"When Jefferson was faced, in the fall of 1807, with the accumulated American grievances against the British—impressment, the unprovoked attack upon the U.S. frigate *Chesapeake,* and finally, the Orders in Council forbidding neutral trade with any enemy port—he had three options. He could ask for a declaration of war; he could merely continue to protest, hoping that in time the British would alter their policy; or he could take some sort of drastic measure short of war that might persuade the British to change their policy. War, to Jefferson, was the last and most hated recourse for a people who put their faith in reason. If war was not to be avoided at all costs, it was nevertheless to be avoided at whatever costs could be afforded without loss of national honor and safety. To continue to add protest upon protest was evidently a fatuous policy, since the British had been led to their depredations upon American commerce by what they judged to be their own national interest under the circumstances of their war with Napoleon. They would not alter such a policy simply because the United States objected. Thus some sort of economic sanctions seemed to Jefferson the only sensible alternative. If the behavior of the United States, in matters of vital concern to England, were to alter the circumstances under which England had to conduct the war, she might reconsider her American policy."[7]

Building Support

If the political world is as intricate and interdependent as it appears, the individual is lost if he attempts to move ahead by purely independent or autonomous action. Individuals are least likely to have the necessary resources to define appropriate issues and mobilize sufficient support to achieve favorable decisions. Clearly, allies or coalition partners are needed, but one must first answer some extremely important strategic questions about acquiring and dealing with them. The realistic coalition builder will need and want to decide:

1. How many allies to seek?
2. Who shall they be, providing there is a choice?
3. How can the alliance be maintained?

A common assumption among politicians and lobbyists is that the more supporters and allies the better. This assumption makes sense under conditions of uncertainty, but the coalition-builder still ought to be conscious of what he is doing and why. The more allies one has, the more people there are to share in the winnings, however limited. For example, winning a hard fought electoral contest with a large majority could mean patronage positions would have to be spread more thinly. There are also the costs to be considered. The more people involved, the harder it is to

---

[7] Reprinted with permission of Macmillan Company from *The American Presidency* by Stuart Gerry Brown. Copyright, Stuart Gerry Brown, 1966.

maintain policy consistency and to appease those most intensely concerned about the primary coalition goals. To put it more simply, to please one ally one may have to displease another. Then, too, soliciting supporters consumes time, energy, money and skill which could be spent on alternative opportunities or uses. One must decide when the additional support brings no further net gain.

What, then, is the best or optimal size for an alliance? The answer is really *the smallest size sufficient to win the election, struggle or contest.* At the minimal size one wins the desired goods without having to endure unnecessary costs for recruiting superfluous supporters or having to spread one's gains among unnecessary allies. In many elections the size of the minimal winning combination is defined by the formal rules of the election: for example, a simple majority, or a plurality, or even an extra-majority such as the requirement of a two-thirds vote in particular cases of financial or constitutional referenda. In other cases the minimal size is not defined; in many of the great political battles one can search in vain for some quantitative measure. Street marches, boycotts, sit-ins, etc., were aspects of the tactics to win civil rights legislation, but which and how many allies were needed is not clear.

In stable zero-sum games one can readily calculate a minimal winning combination. But what does one do in uncertain and non-zero sum situations? What politicians typically do is search for as many allies as they can muster. If they get too many, they may incur additional costs and reduced individual or group shares; but at least they have won. Without wide support they risk losing all, perhaps by a single vote. Understandably, the politician attempts to overcome uncertainty by going all out for victory. When he knows he can win, as do Congressmen from safe districts, he seldom attempts to maximize his support or wage an expensive campaign. Why should he? There is little to gain and much to lose. So the principle of minimal winning size is good advice to follow in coalition formation. Furthermore, it aids in clarifying problems of competition as well as providing a norm by which to calculate one's tactics. But it is not a sacred formula to be applied ritualistically to every situation.

Who should be chosen as potential allies must be considered. Who will make the best partners, assuming that one has some choice in the matter? Frequently one finds oneself allied with either strangers or persons whom one might not typically have invited. Politics, it is said, "makes strange bedfellows." And, so it does. During World War II the United States was allied with the Soviet Union; soon after the war she disassociated herself from the U.S.S.R. and became allied with her former enemies— Germany and Japan. Today, the Sino-Soviet alliance seems to be very tenuous while the United States and the Soviet Union are tacitly coalescing. During 1940-1941, even the U.S.S.R. and Nazi Germany were brief partners. Presidential candidates, of course, are almost notorious for selecting former competitors as vice presidential running mates. And certainly one of the most famous and enduring of recent congressional coalitions is the Northern Republican-Southern Democrat alliance. In these instances the coalition was or is produced by necessity, but the 'necessity' is in recognizing that more is to be gained by acceptance than by rejection of the 'unholy' allies.

Suppose, however, that one has a choice of partners? Who should be selected? One consideration grows out of the principle of minimal winning size, i.e., *select a partner who is sufficiently powerful to assist in winning but is unlikely to dominate the coalition and one's self in particular.* A powerful partner will extract a price for his participation and, if his presence makes victory possible, the price is apt to be higher. Selecting less important partners who do not pose threats of domination can still be expensive in terms of the share of the winnings they claim. The greater the number of lesser partners, the greater the interdependence and the higher the bargaining costs. Just how costly is impossible to say, since all the relevant variables have not been identified, but common sense clearly suggests that the more people one must coordinate the more resources will be consumed (cf. Figure 11-2).

Other crucial elements to be considered are the interests and values of potential partners. A coalition is probably most easily formed among those who have either similar values or complementary interests. When political battle lines are drawn, it is relatively simple for political partners who share basic preferences of ways to live, and what to live for, to identify their enemies and friends. But it is not necessary to share basic values in order to form coalitions; indeed, most coalitions are based upon complementary interests which develop in particular situations caused by certain types of political issues. None of the 'unholy' coalitions mentioned earlier was distinguished by commonly-shared basic values (other than the will to win or survive). What, then, caused these antagonistic nations to ally?

The answer must be that they *perceived* themselves to have complementary interests that could be either protected or advanced by coordinated actions. Complementary interests, then, are different goals which can be mutually advanced by concerted efforts. Note that the interests are different but not incompatible in the particular situation, even though the basic values of the partners may be fundamentally incompatible. Neither partner is much concerned about the other's interests but cooperates because it is the price of achieving his own objectives. Because coalitions of complementary interests are particular and situational, they tend to be unstable and last only as long as the interests remain complementary. Coalitions that are based upon shared values are apt to be more enduring because values are more stable than interests. A rational politician is, therefore, sensitive to the changing interests of others and sufficiently flexible and imaginative to find or make interests complementary. On occasion he may even have to identify another's interests and convince him of their importance.

Coalitions are not likely to maintain themselves unless expected gains remain positive. This need not mean that once the original goals have been achieved a coalition will immediately cease to operate; but other complementary interests may be found, including the psychic benefits to be derived from continued mutual association with prospects for future support. In national politics such tentatively satisfying gains may not be as important as continued material payoffs. The long-standing congressional coalition of Northern Republicans and Southern Democrats is a product of reciprocal gains on crucial legislation; it will cease only when these are not forthcoming. This was true for the coalition of John L. Lewis's United Mine Workers with the coal operators and the railroad management and unions. Each benefited from a healthy coal market and was disadvantaged by competing fuels and means of transportation. Finally, of course, a changing technology and competing coalitions defeated the Lewis group. But for at least thirty years it was successful in maintaining itself and providing considerable benefits to the partners. A rational coalition builder does not build coalitions on sentiment alone, and he does not always expect them to continue after their specific objectives are achieved.

Case Study #4   Senator Johnson Puts Together Another Coalition (1959)

The following case study by Russell Baker of *The New York Times* vividly illustrates how a highly skilled politician, Lyndon B. Johnson, then the Majority Leader of the United States Senate, handled a ticklish problem involving the threat of filibusters. Johnson clearly demonstrated his mastery of the situation: the diverse preferences, distribution of resources, possibilities of bargains—all had to be grasped and put together in some form that would achieve Johnson's ends. Note the presence of uncertainties, the complementary interests that Johnson fashioned into a coalition, the hard work required, the need to understand as well as make use of the rules of Senate, the distribution of benefits.

JOHNSON COUP RESULT OF CAREFUL PLANNING

Filibuster Maneuver Shows Strong Mastery of Democratic Forces

By Russell Baker
Special to The New York Times,

WASHINGTON, Jan. 10 —The new Congress was precisely forty-eight hours old this week when Senator Lyndon B. Johnson laid to rest the prophecies that his big new Democratic majority would be an unmanageable affliction for the next two years.

By noon Friday, two days after the new Senate had first assembled, the Democratic floor leader had welded twenty Republican votes to forty from his new majority and crushed a determined bloc of liberals challenging him on the filibuster issue.

The filibuster fight is still unfinished, but it is now clear that Mr. Johnson controls the field and will settle it quickly on his own terms. It is equally clear that Mr. Johnson is now more thoroughly master of the Senate than at any time during the past four years of leadership.

Of the fifteen new Democratic Senators who were supposed to make his conciliatory path so thorny, eight voted with him in a test on proposals for settling the filibuster dispute, potentially one of the most divisive issues facing Democrats in this Congress.

South Is Quiet

The Southern bloc, always eager to lay down its lungs on the barricades against anything smelling vaguely of civil rights, had felt his soothing touch and was in a strange state of peace.

The most ardent anti-filibuster men were, to be sure, nearly apoplectic, but nonetheless isolated.

What distinguished this particular performance was the rapidity, ease and finesse with which it was managed. Much of the time, in fact, Mr. Johnson seemed to be enjoying himself—grinning as he threw the high, hard parliamentary inquiries to his old enemy, Vice President Richard M. Nixon, or needling the frustrated liberals about their reluctance to speed debate and take a look at his votes.

Actually, the performance was a product of several years of Johnsonian labor to change the structure of the Democratic party in the Senate. A typical example of this labor and how it has paid off is the practice he initiated, when he first took the leadership, of getting every Democratic Senator, no matter how junior, at least one good committee assignment.

Mr. Johnson, of course, plays a decisive role in determining who will get what committee. These assignments are not yet made. Thus, as he came up to the filibuster issue, Mr. Johnson already had a powerful bargaining point to use for persuading the new men to follow his lead.

But the groundwork was actually done three months ago, during the campaign. Before the election, Mr. Johnson campaigned for many of the young men now serving under him, thus putting them to some extent under obligation to him after their victories.

Public Pressure

Before election day, public pressure had already begun to build for a change in the rule permitting filibusters.

The election results made it obvious, even to the Southern bloc, that a change was inevitable. The question was: How great will the change be?

It is impossible to document, but there is circumstantial evidence that Mr. Johnson moved quickly in the immediate post-election period. As the new Senators were introduced one by one to the press at the Capitol and asked about the rule change, virtually every one gave the same reply:

"I favor a change, but I want to hear all sides before I say what kind of a change."

The presumption was that Mr. Johnson had been busy telling his new class that he would get them a chance to fulfill their campaign pledges, but to commit themselves to no one until they had heard from him.

The night before the Senate convened he was ready with a three-part plan containing a little something for everybody but not enough to leave anyone really delighted.

It was, in short, a workable compromise.

To win those who had pledged a change in the rule, he proposed a revision under which two-thirds of the members voting—instead of two-thirds of the full membership—could cut off debate.

For those who complained that the old rule—barring cut-off of a filibuster on rule changes—contained an obnoxious self-perpetuating feature, he proposed to make rule-change debate subject to closure by two-thirds of the Senate.

For the Southerners, who feared any proposition that would imply the Senate's right to adopt a new rule by majority vote every two years, he proposed a third section specifying that the Senate was "a continuing body" with "continuing" rules.

The liberal bloc came to the Senate Wednesday morning prepared to start the fight with a motion to establish that the new Senate had a right to adopt new rules by majority vote. This, they insisted, was the essential first step to winning a major revision.

With a surprise maneuver, Mr. Johnson quickly blocked the liberals from shaping the fight on these lines and forced it, instead to center on his compromise.

Skirts Explosion

This he did by getting recognition before the liberals. By tradition, the floor leader must be recognized by the presiding officer whenever there is a choice between him and other Senators seeking recognition.

Once he had the floor Mr. Johnson introduced his compromise, thus putting before the Senate a proposal that would satisfy demand for a rule change while skirting the explosive issue raised by the liberals.

He then refused to yield the floor so that the liberal bloc could move its own proposal that day. Instead, he moved to adjourn—under the rules his own proposal could not be considered until next day—and the liberal bloc

made the tactical error of demanding a roll-call on the adjournment motion.

With no real substantive issue at stake, the adjournment motion was carried by a 73 to 23 majority, thus putting the stigma of failure on the liberal cause before the fight had even begun.

On Thursday Mr. Johnson had his sixty votes. He let the liberals make their motion, then to deepen the psychology of defeat, gathering about them, moved to kill it. Against his sixty votes, the liberals mustered only thirty-six.

Source: *The New York Times* (Jan. 11, 1959), Sec. 4, p. 5.

Justifying Outcomes

Political action and policy in a bargaining society must generally be justified in terms that are consistent with prevailing political symbols, norms, values and beliefs. A politician may follow all the rules advanced thus far and fail to achieve his objectives because he fails to justify his behavior and goals in terms that are familiar and acceptable to the society. We know this in an intuitive sense because we have been thoroughly indoctrinated with a democratic political culture. Politicians, however, must supply the justifications in a more self-conscious manner because it is they who enact the policies.

Whatever course of action one takes, whether in defense of the status quo or to reform it, one must defend his choice in terms such as the 'public interest.' The 'public interest' is a somewhat vague and debatable concept but one which must be invoked because it suggests that one's proposals, while motivated by self-interest, must also be regarded as beneficial to others.

Furthermore, one must justify his policies in terms of the cultural heritage and typical forms of legitimation. These forms make sense to others and set the limits of acceptable behavior and objectives. The basic aspirations of the culture must be honored, and one's position or policies must be shown as reasonable efforts toward their realization and not indefensible breaks in the tradition. In the United States appeals may be made to individual rights and patriotism and to some degree of equality. It is not typical to justify actions in terms of superiority of birth, the power to prevail or noblesse oblige.

Many observers have tended to view efforts at legitimation as rather phony appeals, devised after the action to justify questionable ends. As Machiavelli cautions the Prince (in his famous Chapter 18—"How a Prince Should Keep His Word"—of *The Prince*) *appearing* to be compassionate, faithful, humane, upright, religious is quite useful, for:

". . . men, in general, judge more according to their eyes than their hands; since everyone is in a position to observe, just a few to touch.

Everyone sees what you appear to be, few touch what you are; and those few do not dare oppose the opinions of the many who have the majesty of the state defending them; and with regard to the actions of all men, and especially with princes where there is no court of appeal, we must look at the final result."[8]

This may still be good advice in some totalitarian systems, where leaders monopolize communication, but it is extraordinarily risky business for any major leader in a democratic system where there is a constant glare of publicity, an opposition, and fairly critical publics. Deceitful ploys do not persuade and cannot take the place of substantial reasoning in appealing for public support, without risking exposure from the shrewd appraisals of others who can assess the situation. This was the lesson of the 'credibility gap' issue in this country; President Johnson's credibility became seriously damaged when reporters and analysts noted misstatements, exaggerations and questionable claims in the official versions of 'cold war' policies, especially concerning the war in Vietnam.

The political culture will rule out certain alternatives and will narrow those means considered justifiable in pursuing designated ends, providing the chooser is aware of the broader costs of ignoring or violating the expected norms. As one example, recall the consideration of options in President Kennedy's 'ExCom' meetings during the 1962 Cuban Missile crisis when there was great pressure for the elimination of the missile sites by instant attack: " 'For the United States to attack a small country without warning,' said the Attorney General, 'would irreparably hurt our reputation in the world—and our own conscience.' "[9] As noted in our discussion of reputational resources in Chapter 9, the political actor has to live with what he has done, and with the reasons he gives for those actions. Those who are politically ambitious are well-advised to cherish their reputation as their most valuable resource; and for most, political honor is an exquisite and lasting reward.

Case Study #5   Some Legitimating Appeals

Political leaders spend more time on dealing with the rightness and wrongness of positions and actions than most give them credit for. To cite some great leaders in such moments:

Quotations from Chairman Mao Tse-tung:

"The only way to settle questions of an ideological nature or controversial issues among the people is by the democratic method,

---

[8] Niccolo Machiavelli, *The Prince*, trans. Mark Musa (New York: St. Martin's Press, Inc., 1964), p. 149.

[9] Roger Hilsman, *To Move a Nation* (Garden City, N.Y.: Doubleday and Company, Inc., 1957), p. 203.

the method of discussion, of criticism, of persuasion and education, and not by the method of coercion or repression."[10]

"Our duty is to hold ourselves responsible to the people. Every word, every act and every policy must conform to the people's interests, and if mistakes occur, they must be corrected—that is what being responsible to the people means."[11]

President Eisenhower's veto of a bill freeing natural gas producers from federal controls (1956):

". . . since the passage of this bill a body of evidence has accumulated indicating that private persons, apparently representing only a very great and vital industry, have been seeking to further their own interests by highly questionable activities. These include efforts I deem to be so arrogant and so much in defiance of acceptable standards of propriety as to risk creating doubt among the American people concerning the integrity of governmental processes."[12]

President Roosevelt's early appeals against an intransigent Supreme Court (1935):

Later that month he [President Roosevelt] dictated to George Creel an article to appear under Creel's signature in *Collier's*. The piece, entitled "Looking Ahead with Roosevelt," emphasized the President's "deep conviction" that the Constitution was not meant to be a " 'dead hand,' chilling human aspiration and blocking humanity's advance," but rather "a living force for the expression of the national will with respect to national needs." The President had acted "under the compulsion of terrific necessities," Roosevelt had Creel say, "and never at any time was there a doubt in his mind that such swift action would have had the approval of those great men who put such stress on life, liberty and the pursuit of happiness." (Apparently the President was confusing the Constitution and the Declaration of Independence.) If the Supreme Court continued to hold the present generation "powerless to meet social and economic problems that were not within the knowledge of the founding fathers, and therefore not made the subject of their specific consideration," then, said Roosevelt, he "would have no alternative but to go to the country with a constitutional amendment."[13]

---

[10] *Quotations from Chairman Mao Tse-Tung* (Peking: Foreign Languages Press, 1966), p. 52.

[11] *Ibid.,* p. 173.

[12] *The New York Times,* February 18, 1956, as quoted by Robert Engler, *The Politics of Oil* (New York: The Macmillan Company, 1961), p. 411.

[13] Arthur M. Schlesinger, Jr., *The Age of Roosevelt: The Politics of Upheaval* (Boston: Houghton Mifflin Company, 1960), p. 453.

Special Strategy for Reformers?

The previous section put forth some suggestions on strategy for citizens and politicians, alike, on the assumption that both have need to consider many of the same factors in decision-making. Clearly, one would have to be more concrete about the most effective choices for each of these roles since the specific courses of action open to each are quite different. The citizen tends to have far fewer choice dilemmas and, generally, fewer resources to wield than the politician. But if we were to list all these variations and derive strategies, we would need another volume. For example, determining how to vote most rationally under a variety of conditions is a major task which is now being explored with some theoretical rigor. (We shall recommend some studies in the bibliography for this chapter.) Our considerations are reduced to some very broad rules for the active citizen, office-holder or opposition who would seek gains through the existing processes of a stable democratic system. But in such systems reform impulses occur rather often; and even revolutionary causes are not unknown to this and other countries. Can our advice be relevant to these objectives?

We begin with some hesitation, as indicated by the question mark in the title of this section. Strategies for more extensive change involve more uncertainty and risk; unfortunately, they are seldom studied strategically so as to provide confident generalizations about probable gains. We cannot report a firm consensus about such strategies, for each has worked somewhere and failed somewhere and few studies have made comparative estimations as to which strategies work best under what conditions. All we can do is indicate some alternatives and some of the possible gains and losses or costs.

The major choices facing the reformer revolve about the scope and rate of change which his reforms would introduce. In general, the reformer who wishes a more thoroughgoing change will encounter more resistance, other things being equal; so, too, the more rapid the intended rate of change, the more intense the expected response. Revolutionists may expect to encounter more repressive opposition that ordinary reformers who wish relatively minor alterations in society. These two considerations are expressed graphically in Figure 12-8, with the scope of change charted on the vertical axis and the rate of change on the horizontal axis. The revolutionist wants to change or transform many things very rapidly while the piecemeal reformer desires to change only a few things and usually at a slower rate. No doubt one could draw in many variants on these two basic types. In any event, the more abrupt the preferred transformation, the more likely a more intense opposition will arise.

Likewise, the greater the scope of change, the more persons or groups will be affected in society. Since most men perceive some stake in things as they are, the more one seeks change the more he will impinge on vital interests. There are relatively few in any society who want to see every-

Figure 12-8
Reform: Scope and Rates

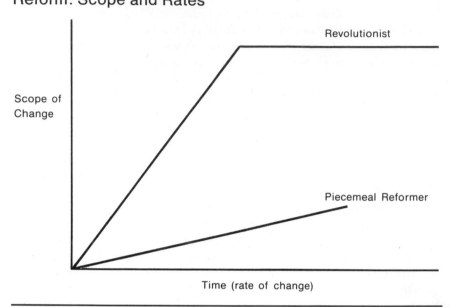

thing shattered and a totally new order imposed. One must therefore be prepared to encounter a great variety of conflicting vested interests as the scope of the proposed alterations is expanded. In some cases affected members will know exactly how reforms will affect them; in other instances the impact of change may not be very clear. Where the effects of change are in doubt, most citizens are more likely to decide that an *uncertain* future cost/benefit ratio is less attractive than the *certain* current ratio. In short, the revolutionist—even the reformer, including the most gentle and accepted types—will encounter the powerful restraining forces of convention and habit, satisfaction with present benefits, and fear of the future. The personal costs of being a reformer or revolutionist are likely to be high under all conditions. The resources of the status quo, under most conditions, are typically superior to those of the reformer. There are situations in which reform will more likely succeed, as suggested in Chapter 7. The problem now is to decide how to translate empirical generalizations about past change into useful and more reliable advice for the present and future.

While there is always a status quo with initial superior resources, one should not commit the error of assuming that all reformers are weak and all revolutions impossible; obviously the facts of history contradict such silly notions. Just as some people profit from the established order, so others are either relatively less well off or actually suffer (pay net costs). Those who are deprived—in whatever sense they may feel deprived—are potential supporters or allies. One should never underestimate the potential resources of such persons, particularly their motivations to amend or improve their situations. The would-be reformer has a potential, however small, in all societies; the problem is to turn potentiality into actuality.

Two strategies immediately suggest themselves for implementing reform: one is, of course, to work for piecemeal changes with patience and without incurring the intense opposition of the status quo. The other is to engage in outright attacks upon the status quo and their favored positions. Those who have labored in the fields of reform have always been torn between these two strategies, just as the status quo is at odds on how best to resist—to exert all out resistance or to appease with piecemeal reforms. Every reform group has partisans of each strategy, and every reform group of any significance has probably gone through different phases using one or the other strategy.

Since we cannot easily prescribe, allow us first to point out some of the considerations stemming from each strategy. Piecemeal reform has the advantage of lowering total costs in the sense that limited objectives generally require but limited applications of resources. Since limited objectives are less likely to offend many people, they are less likely to engender all-out counterattacks in defense of established positions. On the other hand, limited objectives are precisely that—limited. One may become content with small gains when much larger gains might have been possible; in a sense, the reformer settles for a 'second-best' outcome.

Probably most frustrating to the earnest pursuer of reforms are the inevitable exasperations of the persuasive processes for inducing cooperation from those who will have to 'give up' something or adjust. The more intransigent and unwielding the status quo interests look, the more likely the reformers are to look for competitive and conflict strategies. Scandals, shocking publicity, charges of corruption and exploitation are the sort of frontal attacks the crusader utilizes to mobilize an indignant public behind forceful legislation or a 'clean sweep' in elections. But these may be Pyrrhic victories, once the publicity dies, if the new ways have not been effectively institutionalized. If the old interests stay on the scene, the reformer cannot escape the processes of bargaining, competition or effective command for maintaining the gains won. In reform-oriented cultures such as the United States, public exposure can be effective; so, too, 'business as usual.' Without an effective investment in well-devised solutions, the ultimate cost of reform activity may simply be a reversion to the status quo.

The revolutionist, however, goes for the big pay-off, usually at considerable cost and risk. Revolutionists are seldom treated with kid gloves when caught. True, revolutionists attempt the big gains and occasionally win them, but it should also be noted that when they do take over, they usually are forced to wield enormous power to eradicate old enemies and resistors. So the revolutionist may end up being more frustrated than the piecemeal reformer because his resources are diverted into extensive control efforts instead of the positive goals to be pursued. Frustration is a function of both achievements and ideals. So long as the latter remains greater than the former, one is frustrated. The revolutionist soon discovers that the world over which he now has some control remains a product of its lengthy past. The kinds of revolutions most likely to escape such long-run costs are those waged solely for independence. The promise of nationhood is achieved at the point of victory; the opposition, the colonialists, can 'go home' or move on. The American Revolution and more recent struggles for nationhood did enjoy this kind of advantage once victory was won. But revolutionists against an indigenous power or class structure have to anticipate the costs of post-revolutionary resistence and struggles.

The revolutionist does enjoy one kind of gain which the reformer is not apt to experience—the excitement of great change, the direct sense of victory, the exhilaration of achieving a crucial threshold. If a person enjoys the thrills of combat and can sustain himself until that possible moment, then he may be well suited for the revolutionary vanguard. If one prefers a more prosaic life, the role of piecemeal reformer engaged in bargaining over incremental gains with the status quo is recommended. One might even get to enjoy some of the creature comforts of the Establishment with which one deals. Remember, however, that even mild reformers have paid heavy costs for deviance from the conventional wisdom; one can always find members of the status quo who are threatened by the least suggestion of change. The history books are replete with the troubles experienced by reformers. A person may be successful in achieving his reform, but the new generation will hardly know of his contribution and tribulations as the reform becomes institutionalized into a new status quo. Indeed the old reformer may be suspected by younger reformers of being satisfied with his own piecemeal gain. While not every reform becomes part of the existing state of affairs, many elements of the status quo were at one time hard fought reforms.

Most theory and evidence concerning the 'management' of change appears to be confined to small group and organizational changes. Such theory and data may be applicable to change in larger systems, such as nation-states, but we simply do not know the limitations. At the international level there is far more strategic theory on the waging of military warfare than on achieving major political change. Of late, a body of revolutionary precepts on guerrilla warfare is being developed somewhat systematically in the literature, and we shall cite an example in a later section. Undoubtedly more systematic study and comparative analysis is being done on insurgent tactics in official and secret research agencies;

perhaps the student will one day have greater access to their conclusions. The more publicized peaceful theories of national change are also rather tenuous, lending mostly gratuitous advice to developing nations.

The great trouble here, as throughout the social sciences, stems from the relative inability to experiment, to repeat various strategies under controlled conditions to see which work best. As things are, the political scientist can only observe the real world of greatly contrasting but uncontrolled contexts. We are often unable to explain why some strategies worked and others failed, and are left to conjecture on what might have happened if another course had been pursued. In the social sciences it is difficult to eliminate the plausible alternatives.

Some Precepts for Reformers

Those who work for reform, no matter how piecemeal or far-reaching, do have some special problems, as we have noted. Perhaps we can only put together a rule book of precautionary advice, avoiding the worst and most costly endeavors or, at least, citing some advantageous means—if they happen to be available. We admit our indebtedness to several worthy ventures in some greatly varying contexts.[14]

Make the Problem Compelling But Solvable

Many people are resistant to reform because they do not perceive any need for it. Social problems may be experienced by some, but they must also be defined not only for the directly affected but for the potential allies on the sidelines who must be made to feel the need for new solutions. Not all politicians are able to communicate such redefinitions successfully. One must not only persuade about the need, but about the 'solvability' of the problem. The reformer can capitalize on crisis and the sense of urgency if his explanation is relevant. And his explanation must be consistent with the proposed solutions.

But be prepared for great uncertainty, fears and competing claims.

---

[14] Cf. Saul D. Alinsky, *Reveille for Radicals* (Chicago: University of Chicago Press, 1945); Stokely Carmichael and Charles V. Hamilton, *Black Power* (New York: Vintage Books, 1967); Robert A. Dahl, "Patterns of Opposition," *Political Oppositions in Western Democracies,* Robert A. Dahl, ed. (New Haven: Yale University Press, 1966), pp. 332-347; Charles J. Erasmus, *Man Takes Control* (Minneapolis: University of Minnesota Press, 1961), Chap. XIII; Alexander Leighton, *The Governing of Men* (Princeton: Princeton University Press, 1945), Chaps. 17-19; and Herbert J. Spiro, *Government by Constitution* (New York: Random House, Inc., 1959). The latter has a series of recommendations (some strategic) or guides for constitution-makers, found at the ends of Chaps. 14 through 24.

Seeking the causes of crises or deplorable situations may bring on fruitless debate. There may be differences over the nature of the problem and thus, the solutions as well. For example, in the mid-sixties black citizens and their allies were defining their problem as one of conquering poverty caused by racism; more conservative citizens tended to define the situation as one of 'irresponsibility' and a breakdown of 'law and order.' Obviously, policy proposals emanating from each definition will differ considerably, and the strategist must estimate the numbers of people most likely to be comforted by each solution. Efforts at indoctrination on causes may divert resources from effective remedial action. A creative reformer, if we may use the term, had better be armed with some ingenious solutions which cut into the other side's support.

Provide Reassurances for the Insecure

Every change in institutions and policy will affect or impinge unevenly on the different members of a society, and some will be affected adversely. Others will *think* they are about to be unfavorably affected even if there is little supporting evidence for their beliefs. It is good tactical policy to take such possibilities into account and provide reassurances to the insecure, even if they are the 'bad guys.' One of the difficulties with the urban renewal program in recent years has been its failure to provide realistic and meaningful reassurance to those who were being evicted, especially the poor, aged and helpless. Middle-class business-oriented reassurances about the desirability of cleaning up the slums are not reassuring to such people. One cannot expect such a generalized good to compensate for the direct deprivations of specific individuals. What is needed is a means of insuring that the adversely affected will be counselled and that the government will show concern for those from whom it would force compliance.

Huge governmental bureaucracies find this sort of compassionate reform a difficult assignment. But trusted leaders can develop rapport with people, can reassure them and make their transitions easier and hopefully better in the long run. Far less opposition is incurred if one acts on these premises. The most able politicians try to devise some rewards for those who will resist out of insecurity. Such rewards might include incentives for those who would invest in black enterprises, or attractive resettlement for the dispossessed, or reassuring market services for those businesses which must accept further regulation.

Beware of Arrogance and Excessive Righteousness

A not uncommon failing among reformers is arrogance, perhaps because they feel they understand things better than the ordinary people whom they lead or battle. Liberal reformers have been especially prone to view their opponents as uninformed, stupid or simply undersirable, especially when scientific authority can be displayed on behalf of their own position. In recent years we have seen many civic reformers—advocates of fluoridation, slum clearance, control of air and water pollution, birth control, and a variety of other policies—supposedly dedicated to promoting human welfare, who, at the same time, treat their opposition like a bunch of cattle or paranoid fools. This behavior is most undesirable, particularly when it emanates from those who believe themselves to be leaders and friends of the 'people.' No man deserves to be treated as less than an equal human being, especially where public policy is concerned. Furthermore, hard-nosed pragmatic reasoning would indicate that such treatment merely increases unnecessary hostility and opposition; furthering the reformer's long-run self-righteous vindication is a hollow victory if its fruits are bitterness, resentment and hate. And finally, the claim to some kind of authority in matters over which the so-called authorities may themselves differ is really quite inappropriate. The expert on nuclear fission does not necessarily know any more than you or we whether or when to use nuclear weapons. And the man who knows about the chemistry of water or air may know next to nothing about the precious beliefs and values of men.

Unfortunately, the claim to scientific expertise carries great authority in America. Those who feel they are experts about something are strongly tempted to act arrogantly when they are opposed or their authority is questioned. Such behavior merely confirms to the fearful their tyrannical aims and lack of humanity. There are more gracious ways to alleviate fearful resistance, by creating temporary exceptions or optional recourses for those who stand to lose most bitterly or directly, or by just listening for adaptable alternative suggestions from the dissident—sometimes the agreeable compromise is less than shouting distance away. A reformer ought to act humbly in the face of his opposition. Better yet, he ought to be humble if he should be so fortunate as to be on the side of right.

Seek Reciprocal or Mutual Gains

One cannot always neutralize oppositions, although it is always worth some effort (short of extraordinary conflict situations). But a person should always seek to broaden the support for his solutions by demonstrating reciprocal gains, or mutual ones, if there should be such. The expert is a far more useful reformer in this regard if he can employ effective and persuasive analysis about 'what's in it' for other groups when these gains are not obvious. This is part of coalition or support-building discussed earlier, so we need not go on at length; however, it is an important part of the persuasibility of peaceful reform. Richard Neustadt analyzed the President's task of persuading all those with whom he must work as follows: ". . . to induce them to believe that what he wants of them is what their own appraisal of their own responsibilities requires them to do in their interest, not his."[15] One analyst of 'reform-mongering,' Albert O. Hirschman, derived this same type of advice from studies of some rather intransigent reform problems in Latin American economic development.[16] For example, Hirschman noted that the economists, by pointing out the improved balance of payments situation which would flow from better land use, were able to unite financiers and government officials with the peons of the countryside who wanted secured lands to work. In another successful reform—the Kennedy Trade Expansion Act of 1962—not only did the President seek firm business support by the prosperity connotations of the new label (previously labelled 'reciprocal trade measures'), but the most successful appeal was the use of 'cold' information on the direct benefits conferred on certain areas and industries.[17]

Check Out Results

The sole purpose of reform and revolution is to improve life, yet it is amazing how resistant even the dedicated can be to evaluating the results of their reforms. If the change sought is deemed to be an improvement, it ought to be demonstrated as such by the best available testing techniques. Perhaps one reason why reformers and revolutionists are so reluctant to judge their works is the possibility that the ideals may not be as workable as hoped. This is all the more reason for evaluating results, on a continuing basis, to see whether programs have been misconceived or diverted to other ends or have other unanticipated consequences.

Testing social reforms is no easy task, partly because of reporting and analytic difficulties and partly because of the reformer's subjective bias in the maintenance of the change. Few of us enjoy admitting that our pet proposals have not worked out as anticipated. If the latter problem can be overcome, and it usually is contested by opponents, then more realistic evaluation of results can proceed. Fortunately, many social scientists are now actively engaged in improving testing capacities on a more rigorous basis than has heretofore been the case.[18] For example, there have been many recent efforts to define and measure the effects of social welfare

---

[15] *Presidential Power* (New York: John Wiley and Sons, Inc., 1960), p. 46.

[16] *Journeys Toward Progress* (New York: The Twentieth Century Fund, 1963), pp. 265-267.

[17]Raymond A. Bauer, Ithiel de Sola Pool and Lewis Anthony Dexter, *American Business and Public Policy* (New York: Atherton Press, 1964), pp. 347-348; 376-378.

[18] Cf. Raymond A. Bauer, ed., *Social Indicators* (Cambridge: Massachusetts Institute of Technology, 1966); Edward Suchman, *Evaluative Research* (New York: Russell Sage Foundation, 1967 in prep.); Jerome Rothenberg, *The Measurement of Social Welfare* (Englewood Cliffs, N.J.: Prentice-Hall, Inc., 1961); Leslie T. Wilkins, *Social Deviance: Social Policy Action, and Research* (Englewood Cliffs, N.J.: Prentice-Hall, Inc., 1965); Herbert H. Hyman, Charles R. Wright and Terence K. Hopkins, *Applications of Methods of Evaluation* (Berkeley: University of California Press, 1962).

programs and various experimental reforms, both public and private. Many government agencies now conduct research on the effectiveness of their programs. At present, evaluations (often termed cost-benefit analysis) have been made of such diverse activities as water resource utilization, governmental research and development programs, educational reforms, highway investments, urban renewal, the productivity of various governmental agencies such as the Post Office and Veterans' Administration, foreign aid results, administration of justice by courts, economic development programs, crime control, etc.[19] These examples may seem mundane, but the techniques are there for reformers to use, too, and they should have an interest in doing so.

What is much more difficult to assess is the general quality of the civic life. Even here exciting progress is being made. Some recent work has been done on more objective measures of the degree of democracy found in several countries.[20] Other work is being done on the subjective evaluations of citizens with respect to their national political life.[21] This renewed interest in policy among political and other social scientists, makes the future quite promising in this regard. Reform is not only possible and desirable, but a continuing reality. The reformer has available the means for demonstrating results, and he should exploit these in developing and proving his case.

Strategies for Radical Change

When the demands for change are persistently denied and bargaining has failed, then the advocate of change looks for successful conflict tactics.

---

[19] The following titles are but a small sample of the current work: Robert Dorfman, ed., *Measuring Benefits of Government Investments* (Washington, D.C.: The Brookings Institution, 1965); Stephen A. Marglin, *Public Investment Criteria* (Cambridge: Massachusetts Institute of Technology, 1967); Roland McKean, *Efficiency in Government Through Systems Analysis* (New York: John Wiley and Sons, Inc., 1958); Bureau of the Budget, *Measuring Productivity of Federal Government Organizations* (Washington, D.C.: U.S. Government Printing Office, 1964); David Novick, ed., *Program Budgeting* (Cambridge: Harvard University Press, 1965); Martin Anderson, *The Federal Bulldozer* (Cambridge: Massachusetts Institute of Technology, 1964). Of great interest are the more recent efforts to evaluate the various 'poverty' programs. The results are as yet unpublished but reported variously, especially in the Congressional hearings on appropriations for the relevant agencies.

[20] Cf. Philips Cutright, "National Political Development: Its Measurement and Social Correlates," in Nelson Polsby, Robert A. Dentler and Paul A. Smith, eds., *Politics and Social Life* (Boston: Houghton Mifflin Company, 1963), pp. 569-582; and Deane E. Neubauer, "Some Conditions of Democracy," *American Political Science Review*, LXI (December, 1967), pp. 1002-1009.

[21] Gabriel Almond and Sidney Verba, *The Civic Culture* (Princeton: Princeton University Press, 1963); Hadley Cantril, *The Pattern of Human Concerns* (New Brunswick, N.J.: Rutgers University Press, 1965).

Who can deny that strategies of conflict apply even in stable political systems, when today America faces intense demands for the equality and freedom of the black man? And remember the earlier struggle of workers for the right to organize and bargain collectively. Those who resist the demands will call the demanders 'subversive,' 'communist-inspired' and the like, but it appears that intensified demands for change are quite in the American tradition, from abolitionism and women's temperance to farmer populism and today's outspoken militants. Some tactics may be borrowed from abroad, such as the syndicalism of the 'Wobblies' early in this century or the non-violence of the current civil rights movement. Today the question of conflict tactics are hotly debated, and we shall suggest only a few possibilities for you to consider in the light of current issues. And this is not to suggest that militant change-oriented groups pursue only conflict strategies. The civil rights movement has involved everything from self-improvement, legal challenges, welfare activities and electoral strategies, to separatism and violent resistance. We will note here those tactics which directly involve conflict situations, where actual resistance is a fact of life.

Dramatize Injustice

Demonstrations and non-violent provocation should be aimed at exposing the weaknesses, especially the immorality and injustice, of the entrenched opposition in terms of their own basic norms. There will be greater credibility if this provocation is committed by the victimized group and not simply by passionate well-wishers, unless their cause is highly salient (as may be the case with dissenting clergy or other moral guardians). Appeals must be calculated in terms of the relevant audiences. One target is the potential following to be mobilized for active participation. Here there must be direct communication for dramatic impact. Positive appeals should evoke identification with the justness of the cause and with the rewards of solidarity and determination. The opposition will try to isolate and intimidate support, or brand the agitators as outsiders, exploiters and violators of the basic norms. Other target audiences include any responsible or concerned groups of outsiders whose support would not involve direct losses, or whose sympathies stem from strongly shared identifications and values. Persons whose resources may be helpful are often found to be crucial, if unexpected, allies: journalists and the press; articulate members of the theatrical, academic, athletic or business world; economic and political elites, including groups abroad with interests outside those involved in the conflict system. One caution: in direct confrontations it is important to avoid stiffening the back of the resistance without achieving any compensatory gains. Provocation must bring tactical gains, especially publicity, which is needed to reduce the likelihood of costly and tragic repression.

Exploit Dominant Values

Even when fighting for change within the system one must appeal to those higher values which are shared by the active, the acquiescent and the indifferent. This can help neutralize potentially harmful opposition. For example, the black man can point to all sorts of inconsistent treatment in our system which reflects on basic values held by almost all: the black serviceman giving his life for his country, the athlete winning victories for America here and abroad, the cultural contributions of black writers, artists, musicians, etc., all in shocking contrast to situations of discrimination and inequality. If appropriately defined, achievement norms can draw effective allies for struggling groups, and respectable success stories can reassure many who fear that the advocates of change may be 'going too far.'

Isolate the Intransigent

Reformers must spend considerable time on building coalitions, while the radical activist must worry more about limiting repressive or costly counterattacks. Radicals are well-advised not to help broaden the opposition or allow it to take cover in alliances with groups less directly involved. The extreme opposition can often be isolated by the very crudity or brutality of its tactics. The excesses and insensitivities of dominant powers often alienate even those who might stand to gain by the status quo. Thus the most racist Southern opposition have been isolated by identifying them with a 'red-neck' rural or 'backward' culture, or with less than fair and professional law enforcement. Other conservatives have found it difficult to collaborate in opposition across status, regional and cultural differences. Social and economic differences can similarly serve to divide oppositions: the American labor movement could at times count on the contrasting situations of the very wealthy, the factory owner, the small businessman and the farmer to provide insurance against having to face them all at once. In any case, even in peaceful combat the battle cry may be "divide and conquer."

Bargain with Pressure

If concessions are to be gained from conflict situations, then pressure must be applied in peaceful, but coercive, ways. Pressure involves the imposition of costs, short of violence, as inducements to make concessions. Economic means are especially effective here, because the costs can be objectively weighed. The strike was labor's natural means of counteracting the employers' layoff of dissidents; today the boycott is a more generalized method of exploiting economic power. The boycott is an organized withholding of market power, whether directly or indirectly. Here are Kenneth Clark's criteria for an effective boycott, as offered to civil rights activists:

1. It is directed against a product rather than a service.
2. The economic damage or inconvenience is clearly to be borne by the proprietor rather than by the boycotters.
3. The goals and demands are clear and obtainable.
4. The action can be sustained until the demands are met.
5. There is minimum inconvenience to persons who are not responsible for the injustice.[22]

Consider how the boycott could be effectively used by newer type groups who can withdraw resources or support from the market or elsewhere: for instance, the clientele of public welfare, school or other services; the participants in organized endeavors, whether athletic contests, political gatherings or public ceremonies; the donors of services or resources to public agencies (e.g., Armed Forces, draft boards, civil defense groups, etc.) or private (charitable organizations, nonprofit foundations or even political parties). The effective strategist should consider the incidence of costs, the degree of organization, the requisites of effort and solidarity, the visibility and clarity of purposes, and the supplemental inducements that may bring the other side around before hostilities escalate to the point of no return. A pretty intricate business!

Emphasize Rewards

If the antagonists concentrate solely on punitive efforts, conflict situations may turn into miserable 'wars of attrition,' where the costs cumulate for both sides. To be successful, the radical should keep the carrot as visible and credible as the stick. He should use every means to show that the future could be much more rewarding if the opposition would acquiesce or concede. This means, first of all, avoiding the role of 'deadly enemy until death,' and keeping the settlement terms objective—jobs, rights, benefits, even restitution, but not unconditional surrender or total self-effacement. The gains made, such as demonstration projects and experimental solutions which show great promise, should be publicized with this in mind. Promised gains might be economic prosperity for localities, the development of productive human resources, contributions to communal goods, even the blessings of tranquility in an atmosphere of eventual peace and trust. It is not easy for entrenched dominant groups to give up essential advantages (if indeed they do have to give them up), but living a life of ever-increasing guilt and fear may lead them to make the rational choice. At least that is the hope of those radicals who still value peace over a violent victory.

---

[22] Kenneth B. Clark, *Dark Ghetto* (New York: Harper and Row, Publishers, 1965), p. 209.

Case Study #6   National Liberation Strategy

Many feel that the most fascinating developments of strategy in modern times have come from the doctrines of national resistance and guerrilla warfare. What started as military considerations came to be seen even more as political strategies, as these movements sought more to co-ordinate violent and non-violent means toward achieving their goals. Insurgent strategies are sometimes contradictory, as they have been culled from quite different experiences: the French resistance movement, partisan warfare in Greece and Yugoslavia, Mao Tse-tung's protracted conflict against the Nationalist regime in China, the Algerian conflict, Ché Guevara's blueprint for a Latin American take-over and, most painful to Americans, the Vietnamese situation. The Vietnamese National Liberation Front strategy leans heavily upon Mao's analysis, as developed and expanded by their leader in the North, Ho Chi Minh, and his military strategist, Vo Nguyen Giap. A most excellent study by Douglas Pike presents a summary of the strategic criteria of the Viet Minh (League for the Independence of Vietnam). We offer it to show similarities and contrasts in situations where the desired change is system-wide and the choice of means includes violence.

1. Don't try for too much; don't smash the existing social system, use it; don't destroy opposition organizations, take them over.
2. Use the amorphous united front to attack opposition political forces too large or too powerful for you to take over; then fragment their leadership, using terror if necessary, and drown their followers in the front organization.
3. At all times appear outwardly reasonable about the matter of sharing power with rival organizations although secretly working by every means to eliminate them. Don't posture in public.
4. Divide your organization rigidly into overt and covert sections and minimize traffic between the two. The overt group's chief task is to generate broad public support; the covert group seeks to accumulate and manipulate political power.
5. Use communism as dogma, stressing those aspects that are well regarded by the people; don't hesitate to interpret Marxism-Leninism in any way that proves beneficial. Soft-pedal the class-struggle idea except among cadres.
6. Don't antagonize anyone if it can be helped; this forestalls the formation of rival blocs.
7. Bearing in mind that in Vietnam altruism is conspicuous by its absence, blend the proper mixture of the materialistic appeals of communism and the endemic feelings of nationalism. Win small but vital gains through communism, large ones through nationalism. Plan to win in the end not as Communists but as nationalists.

8. Use the countryside as the base and carry the struggle to the cities later; in rural areas political opportunities are greater and risks smaller. Avoid the lure of the teahouse.
9. But forge a city alliance. Mobilization of the farmer must create a strong farmer-worker bond.
10. Work from the small to the large, from the specific to the general; work from small safe areas to large liberated areas and then expand the liberated areas; begin with small struggle movements and work toward a General Uprising during which state power will be seized.[23]

Problems and Applications

1. Assess the possibilities of changing the structure of government in your hometown. For example, if it is now a strong mayor type, consider a weak mayor-strong city council form; if it is partisan-elective system, a non-partisan type. Whatever the direction of the change, consider the possibilities in terms of (a) possible allies; (b) probable opponents; (c) distribution of resources among the actives; (d) legal constraints on changes; (e) alternative strategies of achieving the reforms; (f) likelihood of success.
2. Why do 'third parties' find it so difficult to organize and compete successfully in American elections?
3. The accompanying figure depicts a coalition situation in which you have a choice of one among three possible coalition partners (a, b, c), each of which possesses a different combination of similar or complementary resources (as their positions along the two axes suggest). Other things being equal, which one would you select? Why? What other information would one need, if other things were not equal, to make a good choice?

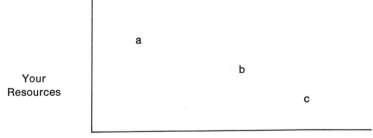

23 Douglas Pike, *Viet Cong* (Cambridge: Massachusetts Institute of Technology, 1966), pp. 41-42.

4. Consider the political feasibility of the various combinations of policies proposed below for a political party of your choice in a presidential election. You might try ranking them from the least to most feasible, given your estimation of resources, preferred goals and likely support. Explain or defend your answer and indicate the kinds of information required to support such advice.
   - (a) Increase in government spending; increase in the tax rate.
   - (b) No change in government spending; decrease in tax rate.
   - (c) Increase in government spending; no change in tax rate.
   - (d) Increase in government spending; increase in tax rate; balanced budget.
   - (e) Decrease in government spending; decrease in tax rate; budget deficit.

   In answering this question it is important to know which voters tend to prefer which policies, and how likely and in what numbers such voters are apt to vote in presidential elections. Try devising a matrix of anticipated gains and costs for each strategy in terms of some crucial voter groups.

5. Consider the following bits of advice from a well-known political strategist of the 1930s, New York's 'boss' and Roosevelt's Postmaster-General, James A. Farley. Do you agree or not? Why?
   ". . . it is both unwise and unlucky to start talking about ambitions too soon."
   "I have always believed that efforts to drag a man down personally are apt to prove more harmful than helpful because sympathy is very often swung over to the person under attack."
   "Another good thing to remember is that nothing is ever gained by trying to seek revenge in politics."
   How are his precepts oriented to the situation of American party politics, as contrasted, say, with the situation in Machiavelli's *The Prince?*

6. Machiavelli had some thoughts on coalition formation which deserve consideration. For example, he counselled that when two opponents are of equal power, the Prince should never remain neutral between them but join one or the other and make him victorious; then the victor will be indebted to him. Do you think this is good advice? Under all conditions? Which and why?

7. "Viable coalitions," claim Stokely Carmichael and Charles V. Hamilton, "stem from four preconditions: (a) the recognition by the parties involved of their respective self-interests; (b) the mutual belief that each party stands to benefit in terms of that self-interest from allying with the other or others; (c) the acceptance of the fact that each party has its own independent base of power and does not depend for ultimate decision-making on a force outside itself; and, (d) the realization that the coalition deals with specific and identifiable—as opposed to

general and vague goals." *Black Power* (New York: Vintage Books, 1967), pp. 79-80. Assess the possibilities of coalitions between black organizations and each of the following groups in terms of the above criteria or preconditions: the AFL-CIO; the American Medical Association; the American Civil Liberties Union; the Democratic Party; a Chamber of Commerce; veterans groups; middle class civic groups such as Kiwanis, Lions, Masons, or the League of Women Voters.

8. Comment on this observation by Thurman Arnold: "The only path of orderly change is through a confusion of principles. Clearcut and logical systems suddenly imposed bring the violence of Russia, Germany, and the French Revolution." Quoted by T. V. Smith, *The Ethics of Compromise* (Boston: Starr King Press, 1956), p. 43.

9. Assess the advantages and disadvantages, from the standpoint of the black movement for equality, of the following targets of boycotts: (a) segregated public schools; (b) Olympic Games; (c) businesses that do not hire enough Negroes; (d) a national party convention.

10. In view of the vulnerability of racial or national conflict tactics for erupting into violence, what would you consider effective strategies for 'cooling off' over-heated situations, consistent with the designated goals of either side you choose?

Bibliographical Notes

There are surprisingly few books which offer generalized advice to politicians and political activists equivalent to, say, a good book in business administration or a consumer's guide. There are in contrast many principles offered to public administrators, which perhaps suggests that most analysts believe it is desirable and possible to teach administration but undesirable and/or impossible to teach politicians how to run for public office or make effective decisions. No school of domestic *realpolitik* has ever really developed in the United States, unless one could cite the now well-known efforts of Saul Alinsky as tending in that direction. See *Reveille for Radicals* (Chicago: University of Chicago Press, 1946) for an earlier statement; look for more recent writings by and about him on the issues of organizational tactics.

Curiously, most political scientists, including those who profess to teach policy and values, rarely instruct citizens and politicians on how to become more effective in their choices beyond the admonition to be well-informed and to participate as a matter of duty or virtue. So it is quite difficult to suggest a lengthy list of obvious reading on strategy and tactics. To be sure, there are many books offering policy advice on such substantive matters as agriculture, war, crime, taxation, etc., but we mean decision-making and strategic advice, such as presented in this chapter. Of course, there is a flood of general information available *about* politics—enough to drown the conscientious reader or at least to divert him from effective action.

Strategic advice must deal with choice in political situations, i.e., how to acquire, use or maintain power for the particular purposes one wishes to achieve in the given situation. We think a prospective politician or activist should develop his or her sensitivities and skills about making choices that will affect others. In addition to a humanist reflection on the values and ethics of choice, we think there are certain skills related to choice and action. We are unaware of any textbooks for the politically oriented which deal with these skills in comprehensive fashion, but there are a good many studies which at least prepare the ground for political applications. We do see more frequent and conscious attention paid to strategic matters, even in the daily columns of rather perceptive political reporters. On the other hand, highly sophisticated academic specalists are developing theories of choice and decision-making through mathematical logic, experiments and complex statistical means. We hope the student will profit from more of this to come.

There is a logic or calculus to strategic choice, and the potential participant should develop his ability to conceptualize the ordered sequences involved in choice-making. One set of explicit guides is presented by formal decision theory. A fine introduction, and one not requiring mathematical training, is Richard C. Jeffrey, *The Logic of Decision* (New York: McGraw-Hill Book Company, Inc., 1965). Preferences and probability are focal points, but do not expect to find political illustrations in these pages. A more advanced treatment may be found in a well-known text by Robert Schlaifer, *Probability and Statistics for Business Decisions* (New York: McGraw-Hill Book Company, Inc., 1959). Much of this text will be of greater use for public administrators than politicians, but the basic ideas of probabilistic decision-making and the use of information are presented in a lucid manner. The bright student should be able to imagine political applications. Another business administration text of considerable value is that of David W. Miller and Martin K. Starr, *Executive Decisions and Operations Research* (Englewood Cliffs, N.J.: Prentice-Hall, Inc., 1960). This volume emphasizes the universality of decision theory and is unusually clear in its presentations of such crucial problems as analysis of payoff matrices, operations research and other tools of contemporary organizational choice. The same authors have written a smaller paperback volume which presents much of the same material in abbreviated fashion: *The Structure of Human Decisions* (Englewood Cliffs, N.J.: Prentice-Hall, Inc., 1967).

Once the individual decision-making process has been grasped in its essentials, it should be possible to make specific applications to unique situations such as are confronted in politics. The business arena is not the political arena! One who is a good businessman does not necessarily make a good politician, or vice versa. So we must learn something about how to act politically. One good place to begin is with William H. Riker's *The Theory of Political Coalitions* (New Haven: Yale University Press, 1962). Riker has propounded the logic of the 'size principle' alluded to in this chapter, namely that it is most rational to seek a coalition of the smallest size possible considering the costs of distributing pay-offs among the components. While the book may sound quite theoretical, its practical lessons should not be overlooked. Another volume we find highly useful is William A. Gamson's *Power and Discontent* (Homewood, Ill.: The Dorsey Press, 1968). Gamson is a sociologist much interested in coalition-formation and political influence, and he is very thoughtful about the problems and choices of the politician working within democracies. Three more specialized volumes dealing with strategies in Congress are also worth perusing: Lewis A. Froman, *The Congressional Process* (Boston: Little, Brown and Company, 1967); Roger H. Davidson, David M. Kovenock and Michael K. O'Leary, *Congress in Crisis: Politics and Congressional Reform* (Belmont, Calif.: Wadsworth Publishing Company, Inc., 1966); and the perceptive earlier work of Bertram Gross, *The Legislative Struggle* (New York: McGraw-Hill Book Company, Inc., 1953). Another highly explicit study of strategies— this time involving federal agencies and Congress—is Aaron Wildavsky, *The Politics of the Budgetary Process* (Boston: Little, Brown and Company, 1964). Wildavsky's treatment probably upset some pious bureaucrats, but its more realistic approach has a firm empirical basis and the reader should enjoy its political relevance. The same author's *Leadership in a Small Town* (Totowa, N.J.: Bedminster Press, Inc., 1964) offers some strategic advice for community politics in the final chapter. Future lawyers ought to be particularly interested in Walter F. Murphy's *Elements of Judicial Strategy* (Chicago: The University of Chicago Press, 1964), in which the writer attempts to show how strategic aspects become important considerations for a justice attempting to achieve his preferred views within the Supreme Court. Bargaining is, says Murphy, a simple fact of life for justices.

We still think it somewhat useful to consult some quickly read books of a journalistic character which nevertheless offer some solid advice on achieving political ends. For example, a famous reporter of the 1920-30s, Frank Kent, did two books that might be characterized as tough-minded journalism: *Political Behavior: The Heretofore Unwritten Laws, Customs and Principles of Politics as Practiced in the United States* (New York: William Morrow and Company, 1928), and *The Great Game of Politics* (Garden City, N.Y.: Doubleday, Doran and Company, Inc., 1935). Each volume attempts to lay bare the way politics was actually practiced in this country, particularly at the local and state levels, although there are plenty of anecdotes about national politics as well. We also think that a student can gain a better insight into American politics from James A. Farley's *Behind the Ballots* (New York: Harcourt, Brace and Company, 1938). Farley is most adept at generalizing about the facts of American political life and how to deal with them. It is a most candid self-portrait of man as a politician.

For amusement and some commentary on an earlier day we suggest that brief classic about big city machines, William L. Riordan's *Plunkitt of Tammany Hall* (New York: E. P. Dutton and Company, Inc., 1963). This small book records the thoughts of a well-known political boss from New York at the turn of the century. His remarks are earthy and cynical. Similar observations of the politicians are made by J. H. Wallis, *The Politician: His Habits, Outcries and Protective Coloring* (New York: Frederick A. Stokes Company, 1935). The book is dedicated to Machiavelli. Along similar lines is a little known volume by Henry Champernowne, *The Boss* (New York: George H. Richmond and Company, 1894). This book is styled after Machiavelli's *The Prince* and extends advice on how to rule American cities

In each Presidential year the market is swamped with 'how to win' campaign books. We do not think most of them are worth their price but occasionally one comes along with some merit. Such a one appears to be Herbert M. Baus and William B. Ross's *Politics Battle Plan* (New York: The Macmillan Company, 1968). As we write these notes a presidential campaign is just beginning and we are reminded of Theodore White's two fine reportorial accounts of the 1960 and 1964 campaigns. The first one—the better—is entitled *The Making of the President—1960* (New York: Atheneum House, Inc., 1961) and dealt with the Kennedy-Nixon race; the second, *The Making of the President—1964* (New York: Antheneum House, Inc., 1965), followed the Johnson-Goldwater contest. Both books are fascinating accounts and have some astute analyses of strategic considerations for the parties involved.

All these tough-minded analyses remind us of some classic efforts at offering strategic advice to those in need of it. In addition to Machiavelli's remarkable classic, *The Prince,* which will continue to amaze readers, there are some less extensively known but enduring attempts: Edward Walsingham's *A Practical Guide to Ambitious Politicians or Walsingham's Manual,* Gordon Tullock, ed., (Columbia, S.C.: University of South Carolina Press, 1961); and the very early Ibn Khaldūn, *The Muqaddimah,* 3 volumes, trans. Franz Rosenthal (New York: Pantheon Books, Inc., 1958). We can hardly fail to mention that little red book, *Quotations from Chairman Mao Tse-tung* (Peking: Foreign Languages Press, 1966), the much-heralded pocket guide for the dedicated Asian communist, culled from Mao's many writings. While there is much of the rhetoric and ideology of communism, many of the precepts are as practical and tame as *Poor Richard's Almanac* by our own Benjamin Franklin.

Working from within institutions to achieve ends in the conventional sense of competing and bargaining is not always possible, as we have learned from the many political movements which have stirred this country. But few have evoked such strategic debate as the civil rights and black power movements of today. Kenneth Clark, black psychologist and a reflective leader, elaborates upon various strategies for his people in *Dark Ghetto: Dilemmas of Social Power* (New York: Harper and Row, Publishers, 1965), Chapters 7-8. With great sensitivity he examines proposed strategies and positions for psychological validity and effectiveness. Another most interesting analysis pertaining both to pacifism and black demands is Richard B. Gregg's *The Power of Nonviolence* (New York: Schocken Books, 1966). If you think being non-violent is some simple-minded activity, read this book; the approach is far from simple and has a rather complex rationale and set of purposes. In fact, the author thinks pacifists and black activists have much in common in conflict situations. One of the more hard-hitting analyses of the racial situation and the necessary strategies to overcome it is made by Stokely Carmichael and Charles V. Hamilton in *Black Power: The Politics of Liberation in America* (New York: Vintage Books, 1967). The authors urge caution about strategies based on coalitions with white groups, even liberal groups such as churches, unions, and the liberal left of the Democratic Party. A book such as this should be read in conjunction with the last few chapters of Robert Dahl's *Who Governs?* (New Haven: Yale University Press, 1961) and the same author's *Pluralist Democracy in the United States: Conflict and Consent* (Chicago: Rand McNally and Company, 1967), particularly Part IV, "How Political Activists Can Exert Influence in a Pluralist Democracy." Chapter 17 delineates four strategies and their respective advantages and disadvantages. Perhaps the reader can fit the Carmichael-Hamilton advocacy into the Dahl categories, or debate the realism and effectiveness of the two approaches.

The emphasis in these notes has mostly been on materials relevant to the domestic American scene. As the latter sections of this chapter indicate, men can also work, intelligently, for massive and even violent political change. A great deal of the past twenty years' history has been a chronicle of precisely such matters. If for no other reason, a realistic American politician ought to know the framework of choice engaged in by his potential allies and enemies. Accordingly, we should like to recommend a small sample of recent work concerning revolutionary strategies.

Probably the most thorough treatment of the National Liberation Front of South Vietnam is contained in Douglas Pike's *Viet Cong* (Cambridge: The Massachusetts Institute of Technology, 1966). Much of the book is concerned with an elaboration of the guerrilla strategies employed over the years by the Viet Cong. If you prefer to learn directly from the opposition, we suggest Vo Nguyen Giap, *People's War: People's Army* (New York: Frederick A. Praeger, Inc., 1962). The book is really an insurrection manual which has obviously been tested and proved to be rather successful. If, on the other hand, you want to know what is considered as effective counter-strategy by U.S. experts you might consult Air Force Major John S. Pustay's summary analysis in *Counter Insurgency Warfare* (New York: The Free Press, 1965), or the more detailed and operations-oriented study by Army Lt. Col. John J. McCuen, *The Art of Counter-Revolutionary War* (Harrisburg, Pa.: Stackpole Books, 1966). And the bookstands are sure to be filled with more recent applications, both domestic and foreign.

Panel on Pollution
Eugene Register-Guard, Nov. 22, 1968, Eugene, Oregon

BUILDING FOR THE FUT
Newsweek, Oct. 21, 1968, Washington, D.C.

Study Shows Integration Benefits
Negro Pupils Without Hurting Wh
The Oregonian, Oct. 16, 1967, Portland, Oregon

Economists Assessing Cost of Riots
The New York Times, July 30, 1967, New York, New York

To Mail For Some
The Oregonian, July 24, 1968, Portland, Oregon

Time for Us to Be Intelligently Selfi
Eugene Register-Guard, June 23, 1968, Eugene, Oregon

Human Beings Of All Nationalities,
Races Insist On Upholding Dignity
The Oregonian, Aug. 11, 1968, Portland, Oregon

The Oregonian, Aug. 8, 1968, Portland, Oregon
Subsidy Limit
Victory For
The Oregonian, Aug. 14, 1968, Portland, Oregon

UGOSLAVS DIFFER
ON STATE SYSTEM
Individual Attitude Conflicts
With Rigid Controls
The New York Times, May 7, 1967, New York, New York

Decision by Default?
McCarthy Aide
Estimates Costs
Eugene Register-Guard, Aug. 15, 1968, Eugene, Oregon

The Wall Street Journal, Aug. 9, 1968, New York, New York
A Peculiar Price Vict

Program Budget.
Tax Review, July, 1968, vol. XXIX, no. 7, Tax Foundation, Inc., New York, New York

The issue is not whether the nation can afford
to spend more at home and abroad but whether the
money is being spent on the right things, at the right
time, and in the right way.
The Oregonian, Jan. 20, 1968, Portland, Oregon

Cost Analysis Method on Arms
Denounced by Admiral Rickover
The New York Times, June 9, 1967, New York, New York

After that, what's left to negot
Eugene Register-Guard, Aug. 12, 1968, Eugene, Oregon

Chapter 13

Policy Guidelines for Human Welfare

Our attention now shifts from strategic considerations to policy choices. In fact, we also shift our perspectives from the individual strategist to a generalized overview of the entire system. What we wish to do in this chapter is make some overall judgments about the kinds of policy outcomes we deem most appropriate in a democracy, if one is concerned with the greater well-being of individual citizens. Analytical aids to further these outcomes will be discussed at the end of the chapter. For the moment we are solely concerned with the formulation of some basic criteria by which to guide policy-makers who have some freedom to choose among alternatives.

First, we must make clear that we are advancing general *policy guide-lines* for resource allocation, distribution of benefits, control, and allocations of burdens, *not* specific policies in specific areas such as agriculture, labor-management relations, or foreign policy. We offer general norms which the reader might accept and apply in assessing specific policy proposals. The rules are general and not easily applied, but they do direct the reader to make appropriate inquiries when he attempts to decide which policies are better and why.

Second, the reader will quickly note that money measures appear rather frequently in these pages; there is a good reason for this occurrence. No matter how idealistic and presumably non-material a policy might be, sooner or later an entry will have to be made in a public budget to implement that policy. The size of that entry is of fundamental concern to those affected by the policy. We do not wish to appear 'hard-nosed' about budgets and money, but the facts of political life in democracies require that some attention be paid to the allocation of scarce resources among competing ends. The several political processes we have discussed all provide means for making such allocations. And, while we have entered some preliminary judgments of their relative worth, it now becomes imperative that more explicit criteria concerning the end-results—public policies—be formulated.

Public Policy Criteria

We cannot provide sound principles on public policy in the sense that a knowledge of such principles will automatically enable society to devise the 'right' policies. All we can do is advocate rules or norms which will make it easier for the individual citizen and politician to achieve his own preferences; that we have done, to some extent. Fortunately, we are not confined to purely individualistic advice; we can make suggestions about the nature of collective outcomes which allow greater numbers of individuals to benefit from the operations of their government. We do this not in the sense of prescribing the contents of particular policies, but in the sense of identifying *criteria of profitable exchanges.* We do not treat society as some kind of organism with known needs nor avow that interpersonal comparisons can be avoided. One person's satisfactions cannot be said to be either inferior or superior to another's. But a political system which tends to treat all more or less alike does enable policy judgments. It is in this conviction that we advance a number of policy criteria.

He who would propose policies for a society confronts some rather formidable obstacles which cannot be ignored. The primary obstacle stems from the fact that modern societies consist of so many individuals and groups with conflicting goals, interests, values and beliefs that cannot be honored to the complete satisfaction of all. It is impossible to produce a single public policy that will satisfy so many divergent individual preferences. Markets allow each consumer to express his own preferences and, to a considerable degree, realize them without impinging upon or denying others their preferences. If we like Fords we can have one without imposing our will on those who like Buicks, and vice versa. Of course, there are limitations in market capacities to achieve complete consumer sovereignty and there are, as we have seen, external costs and benefits which must be confronted. But political systems impose even greater limitations on citizen sovereignty because governments are much more concerned with collective goals than they are with private goods (as would be possible in completely decentralized systems of choice). It is impossible to provide the exact amount of defense each citizen prefers; only a certain aggregate amount can be provided at any given time. Those who prefer other quantities will be frustrated. It cannot be any other way with pure public goods. With quasi-public goods and services it can; consequently, we have advocated policy flexibility in such instances, provided that inequalities of satisfactions are neither enlarged nor intensified.

We have noted how values, norms, and satisfactions are inherently subjective and frequently incompatible. We have also observed that interpersonal utility comparisons are unavoidable yet impossible to measure in any precise manner. Given the necessity and difficulties of making objective value judgments, we are surely in an unenviable spot; but so are the citizenry and politicians in a democracy. Despite formidable obstacles, it does seem possible to render more or less intelligent assessments of policy alternatives. In any case, the more open processes of decision-making require competitors to make reasoned statements of their positions. If this is to be done we ought to have some generalized norms, guidelines or decision-rules by which to assess policies. We will propose such rules. They pertain, first, to some economic-type criteria for the allocation of resources, distribution of benefits and allocation of costs or burdens and controls.[1]

Norms for Resource Allocation

Rule #1   Optimal use of societal resources is achieved when the marginal returns from private and public uses are equalized.

This rule states an obvious condition but we admit it is one that is not very easily converted into practical choices. In brief, the argument is that private and public goods provide satisfactions but that the sum total of satisfactions is dependent upon how we allocate our resources. If we spend too much on one or the other, we encounter the effects of diminishing marginal utilities or satisfactions in our consumption of both private and public goods.

While the logic is indisputable, the techniques for balancing at the margin are extremely crude. The problem results from our inability to measure overall utilities or satisfactions in any direct sense and thereby enable us to say with confidence that an expenditure of 'x' amount on private goods will produce the same satisfactions, in toto, as 'y' amount of public expenditures. We simply do not know what ratios of public/private goods ought to be pursued in any given country. All we know are our own personal values and something about how best to achieve them. If a society can develop a considerable agreement on objectives, the problem of bal-

---

[1] Our prescriptions are heavily dependent on welfare economics. For an excellent survey of the field see Kenneth E. Boulding, "Welfare Economics," in Bernard F. Haley, ed., *A Survey of Contemporary Economics* (Homewood, Ill.: Richard D. Irwin, Inc., 1952), pp. 1-38.

ancing marginal satisfactions is greatly facilitated; however, most objectives are not that widely agreed upon.

Still, the idea of the marginal or incremental adjustment is one which focuses upon the important point and thereby enables intelligent questioning about the allocation of resources. Those who wish to base public policy on some conception of societal needs without consideration for alternative measures and their respective additional benefits and costs mislead public debate and choice. The idea of marginal adjustment is a reminder that choices are seldom either/or, but mostly 'more here' and 'less there.' In short, what difference does it make if the government adds or subtracts a little more of a resource with regard to respective groups in the system? When do the respective utilities of different citizens approach a balance? Fuller resource utilization should attempt approximate comparisons of the relative returns that alternative dispositions of resources bring. Comparing public and private use in terms of comparative returns and satisfactions could be a step toward citizen as well as consumer 'sovereignty.'

Rule #2   Equalize marginal returns among public uses.

All of our rules are abstract and difficult to translate into practical operating guides, but this rule, like the previous one, is most difficult to apply in daily political life, especially in a democracy. What the rule says, in effect, is that a government is wise if it attempts to match marginal returns, payoffs or utilities across all its expenditures. Thus, if a government spends an additional $1,000,000 each on, say, defense, welfare, conservation, police protection, highways, and medical research, it should hope to derive the same amounts of marginal utility from each of these expenditures. If less utility is being returned from any one or more of them, total utilities or benefits would not be maximized. The same point was made in Rule #1 concerning public/private allocations.

The problem, of course, is one of measuring the added utility of each additional expenditure on public goods as well as reductions in utility resulting from shifts in expenditures. We concede these points, but we believe that such a norm, if well-inculcated in the mind of the policy-maker, encourages him to look at a budget and ask how much, if any, redistribution among the items will produce a better outcome. The effort to equate the marginal returns forces the policy-maker to consider alternatives and not just one proposal. The following formula might clarify the matter:

$$\frac{\text{MU of defense}}{\text{MC of defense}} = \frac{\text{MU of conservation}}{\text{MC of conservation}} = \frac{\text{MU of highways}}{\text{MC of highways}} = \frac{\text{MU of education}}{\text{MC of education}}$$

MU = marginal utility
MC = marginal cost or price

In the above formula the MC is the same in all cases: say, an added $1,000 of expenditure by the government. The society is viewed here as a kind of consumer of many public goods and services; as a consumer it should get all the benefits it can from whatever is consumed; to do so means that it must balance returns from each expenditure. The great problem, of course, is that a society is not a single consumer with a single set of preferences but many consumers who, unhappily, cannot maximize some returns without adversely affecting others. In the marketplace it is reasonably possible for one consumer to acquire the things he wants without harming or preventing other consumers from acquiring the things they want which may be vastly different in kind and amount. But political systems do not permit this to the same degree; once a decision has been made it is *binding* on *all* citizens regardless of whether each wants the same budget or set of public goods. One person may want 10 per cent of the budget spent on defense while his friend wants 20 per cent. No matter what per cent is finally agreed upon, some (and perhaps all) citizens will be unhappy. So our rule is not a panacea that resolves such problems, but it does direct attention to the peculiarities of collective allocation of resources and force us to consider alternatives in the quest for an acceptable solution.

Another important qualification deserves mention regarding the equalization of marginal returns among programs: that is, returns cannot be balanced literally in terms of minute amounts of money. One cannot, in other words, equalize expenditures to the last single dollar. When we speak of equalization we are referring to much larger sums, since more precise comparisons are too costly and often impossible to make. Moreover, governments spend astronomical amounts on each activity so these incremental changes may mean tens of thousands of dollars at local levels and even billions at the national level. Finally, many governmental programs are not feasible without initial investments of tens of millions of dollars. In many cases, therefore, the unit of analysis must be a rather large one and the balancing, but a rough approximation.

While we wish again to emphasize that there is no easy formula for the calculation of these marginal returns, we insist on the necessity for asking the question: How much more in benefits will be derived if we spend 'x' amount on A rather than 'x' amount on B? We are strongly opposed to the idea that one should worry only over *total costs* of the budget or simply assert the overall requirements or *needs* of a nation. Everything costs something and most citizens need many things. The problem is how to achieve the most within various possible expenditure levels. The effort should be directed toward getting the most out of public resources. According to Hitch and McKean "there is no budget size or cost that is correct regardless of the payoff, and there is no need that should be met regardless of cost."[2]

---

[2] Charles J. Hitch and Roland N. McKean, *The Economics of Defense in the Nuclear Age* (Cambridge: Harvard University Press, 1961), p. 47.

Rule #3   Support any public outlay or program in which there are very great collective or large-scale economies compared to private outlays.

Once more we advocate a common-sense norm on purely economic or efficiency grounds. We assume that most men, most of the time, prefer to maximize their returns, given certain resources; or, given the objective, they will wish to minimize the amount of resources they have to procure for its achievement. This particular rule suggests that citizens be willing to use public production and/or distribution of goods (including private goods and services) if such means enable them to benefit considerably more. Conversely, private production and/or distribution is to be encouraged if its efficiency can be demonstrated to be higher. The important point is to be flexible and not ideologically committed to either form at all costs. Most likely, flexible persons will advocate a 'mixed' economy since experience has shown that some governments do some things better than private businesses or groups and the private sector does still other things more efficiently. Each project must be assessed on the basis of experience and analytic skills. At some times and in some places and for some activities, it may turn out that the net benefits of having private concerns do the job are greater, while the same activities in another place or at another time may be more effectively performed by government. For example, in many new nations the government must do most of the investing and directing because there are insufficient private resources available for private endeavor. Nothing will be done to advance the country economically unless government accepts the responsibility.

At another time private efforts might work better, even in traditionally public functions. Apparently the Soviet bloc countries are rediscovering some of the virtues of decentralization for certain types of activities. In this country we may find that the post office can be better run as an autonomous enterprise. Most likely there will be more experimentation with newer forms such as the Communications Satellite Corporation—Comsat—where communications are administered by a public-private corporation consisting of private investors and governmental agencies; or the Common Market and Euratom which underscore the possibilities of inter-governmental cooperation. In short, we suggest being very pragmatic about the forms which will best achieve whatever is deemed important.

Rule #4   Support public programs which are widely approved but which private enterprise cannot or will not provide.

The profit motive appears to be a powerful inducement to the production of goods and services, but some activities either do not offer such inducements or do not offer them in sufficient quantities. Where such activities are highly valued, the government should provide them; otherwise, civilized life suffers. We have in mind investments which are too uncertain or too huge for private investors to undertake, such as the provision of national defense which is too costly and unprofitable for private individuals to provide either the initiative or resources, so governments must do the job. General education also falls in this category. Space exploration, vast irrigation and other resource-conservation projects are further typical examples. No doubt some of these activities can be provided for by private agencies but at too high a cost for wide consumption; not everyone can afford to attend Ivy League schools and few can afford private police protection. And the Wright brothers could not themselves have financed a trip to the moon.

A problem, of course, is deciding whether something is widely appreciated or demanded. Hopefully, the institutions for assessing public preferences are sufficiently sensitive to provide good indicators. A personal means of judging the relative desirability of public goods is to deduce what effect the deprivation of services now provided by governments would have on one's life. Consider having to purchase daily highway use, police protection, schooling, weather reports, etc. The inconvenience of arranging for these services is more than most people would care to experience.

Norms for the Distribution of Benefits

The first four general rules have dealt with resource allocations; now we consider the distribution of public goods and services (or benefits) flowing from collective activities. Our point of view throughout this book has been that governments should exist for the advancement of individual welfare. We usually prefer that the individual define his welfare by his own preferences. However, we also believe that no man is an island unto himself; the individual must consider the impact of his actions on others as well as his dependence on what others do or contribute to his state of being. Such is the rationale of processes which enable everyone to participate in advancing their preferences. It is in this hope that we advance the next few norms for public policies regarding the distribution of benefits.

Rule #1   Any policy change which harms no one and which makes some people better off (in their own estimation) must be deemed an improvement (Pareto's doctrine of optimal gain, or 'optimality').

Much has been written about this norm concerning the redistribution of benefits which was advanced by Vilfredo Pareto more than 50 years ago. Most of the writing has been done by 'welfare economists'—economists who are primarily interested in the advancement of public welfare through the use of economic theory.[3] While the subsequent analyses of Pareto's

---

[3] Philosophers have of late been addressing themselves to Pareto's norm. Cf., David Braybrooke, *Three Tests for Democracy: Personal Rights, Human Welfare, Collective Preference* (New York: Random House, Inc., 1968), pp. 121-150; Y. Murakami, *Logic and Social Choice* (New York: Dover Publications, Inc., 1968), especially pp. 130-134.

rule have not directly affected political science, we believe that it is a most fruitful norm with which to begin a discussion of benefits. Even if the norm is rejected as being impractical to implement, we have to admit that, in principle, it forces us to consider relevant issues of policy and their consequences. So much for preliminaries.

In brief, this rule says that income ought to be redistributed so long as someone is being benefited and no one else is being harmed. A simple diagram (Figure 13-1) will aid in clarifying the matter. Pareto's norm indicates that any policy which produces a movement in a northeasterly direction is to be preferred since it advances the welfare of both parties or citizens. But it also says that a policy which adds to one citizen's welfare without harming or diminishing another's is a worthy, though less than optimal, gain. Thus a movement straight north or straight east is an acceptable policy when better ones (northeast) are not feasible. The northeast quadrant contains the most acceptable areas. Obviously the southwestern quadrant is the least acceptable since it diminishes the welfare of both citizens. Unhappily, *most governmental policies are such that for everyone who benefits, there are usually others who gain less or even 'suffer.'* To add

Figure 13-1

Diagrammatic Representation
of Pareto's Doctrine of Optimal Gain

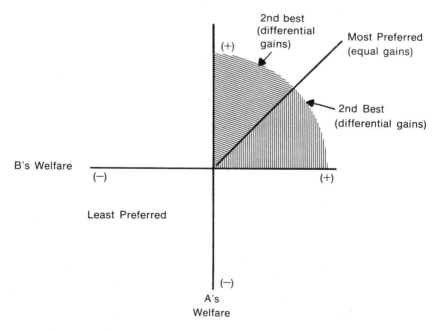

to A's welfare may mean taking away from B (NW quadrant), or adding to B and taking away from A (SE quadrant). Fortunately for the politicians, much of the taking away is done in indirect ways not immediately related to specific gains for anyone, as in the case of general taxation. Indirect taxes and pure public goods are most important in this context. To appreciate this, consider what would happen if each morning all the citizens in a community went down to the city hall and the mayor gave away benefits to some and forced others to pay for them. This is, in effect, what typically happens in the political system, although it is accomplished in less explicit and blatant ways.

There is a qualification to the claim that taking away from both is the least preferred situation. In times when sacrifices are being demanded (wartime, e.g.), many citizens would prefer to suffer equally rather than to see another get away with less sacrifice or with positive gains. We are more likely to feel envy under unequal conditions of either gain or sacrifice. When our neighbor gets a new car we do not pay for his car but we sometimes (and some people all of the time) feel envious. Political scientists must deal with subjective evaluations of welfare as well as objective outcomes. And dealing with subjective evaluations is a troublesome point in assessing public policies.

An example of a public policy which might confer equal benefits on all citizens would be an outright grant of money distributed in equal shares, although even in this instance subjective evaluations might be at sharp variance. For example, for a man earning $1000, a check for $100 would represent a tenth of his income; for a person earning $10,000, the same check would be only 1 per cent of his income. The sum total is the same, but the share is quite different.

Of course, many public goods are indivisible or symbolic so we cannot readily determine who receives how much satisfaction from their presence. A public park probably benefits most people in a community, but all do not benefit equally so we would have to say that such a park would fit either above or below the 45 degree diagonal in Figure 13-1. The children might derive the most gain, their parents next, and those who live within convenient distance more than those who live further away. On the other hand it may be that the park would eventually end up in either the northwest or southeast quadrant if 'transients' move in and frighten away the parents and/or their children. What was a mutual gain is now interpreted as a gain for some (the derelicts) and a direct loss for others who do not like their appearance or behavior.

At first sight Pareto's norm may sound rather impressive and a good solution to the vexing dilemma of producing good public policies. Like everything in social life this norm has its difficulties, too. One difficulty ought to be fairly apparent, namely, that measures of human welfare or benefits are hard to establish, especially when they attempt to relate one man's pleasures to another. In short, it is difficult to say that A is deriving more pleasure or pain than B from policy X. Some theorists would say it is impossible to make interpersonal judgments of this sort. However, we think that it is at least possible to say whether a person or group feels more intensely about some matter at issue one way or the other.

Second, the unequal distribution of resources seldom allows situations in which everyone can benefit; the more typical situation is one in which the 'equal' benefits of pure public goods are more of a comfort to the advantaged. However, the advantaged will resent granting compensatory benefits to the disadvantaged, an action which they view as unequal treatment to them. Thus costs and gains look differently to each. The more frequently encountered policy issues are those located in the northwest and southeast quadrants of Figure 13-1. In fact, a politician may consider himself extremely fortunate if he can deal with issues and policies in which all citizens gain but in different degrees, as suggested by the shaded areas in Figure 13-1. The outer boundary might be viewed as the limits of feasibility; whatever advantages are found beyond it are impossible to attain. In short, the solid line (45 degree diagonal), depicting the most preferred solutions, is the most hoped for but not always the most easily achieved state.

Rule #2   Those whose welfare position is improved by a change in policy should be willing (perhaps required?) to 'compensate' the losers ('compensation' principle).

Here we are advocating that the 'winners' or beneficiaries of a policy be at least generous enough to recognize that they have been made beneficiaries and that, in the interests of equity and reciprocity among members of society, they 'compensate' those who did not gain as much or who may even have 'lost.' A business group which has been granted a tariff concession, e.g., should not be permitted to exploit its position at the expense of the consumers but should pay them some form of 'bribe,' such as a lowered price, market services or the like, for agreeing to support the tariff legislation. The same should hold for any policy changes affecting different groups differently. In a sense we are saying that exchange is generally a good thing wherever possible; more than one party should benefit, and none should lose out entirely. Obviously everyone cannot profit, certainly not equally, in all political situations; zero-sum conditions may prevail, guaranteeing the existence of 'losers.' Nevertheless, we feel that those who make policies should always be sensitive to mutual gain and actively search for means that will enable the losers to gain something from even the worst of situations; in other words, attempt to compensate for the losses of as many citizens as possible.

We think some of this reasoning is implicit in the legislation establishing war veterans' benefits, unemployment policies and utility regulation, and in the claims procedures that have been allowed in connection with many areas of public activity. The pressing of claims where a citizen suffers loss from some government activity is a direct and obvious form of compensation, and repaying the veteran for the service he gives to his country is seldom opposed in principle by the fair-minded. That services and benefits were set up for the unemployed in conjunction with social security seemed equally justifiable in view of the great benefits enjoyed by the worker from social security if he remained employed. And economists have long articulated the compensatory principle that certain public utilities and similar enterprises be legally granted certain monopoly privileges in return for close regulation. We also think this principle should be rigorously applied in conjunction with farm subsidies, urban renewal, and even such programs as space exploration, defense contracting, and research and development, where it would take more intricate reasoning about compensations for external costs. Too often policy evaluation takes the simple form, "If it's good for us, do it," whereas it would be more appropriate to add the compensatory principle, "What do we owe in return?"

Allocation of Burdens: Criteria for Taxation Systems

Because raising revenue is such an important governmental function, we would be remiss if we did not consider it along with norms for public policies on benefits, controls, and the allocation of resources. While governments can and do derive their revenues from a vast number of sources, taxation is unquestionably the major source. Students of public finance have long analyzed and assessed various types and rates of taxation; we do not intend to review that enormous literature for it is highly technical and often the subject of much controversy.[4] We do intend to present a number of very generalized norms for taxation that seem less controversial. These norms ultimately have to do with the base and the rates of taxation and their administration; however, since our purposes are general, we do not advocate specific tax bases or rates, simply general considerations that should apply across the board. These norms pertain to the positions of both citizen and government and, like all norms, are not perfectly consistent or easily adhered to in the real world. We grant that, without at all wishing to give up the endeavor.

Rule #1   Every taxpayer should be treated according to legal rules which apply equally to all taxpayers within the same legal class (formal equity).

Most citizens would agree with the norm that prejudice and caprice should not be a part of the administration of tax laws. These extraneous

---

[4] A useful survey of taxation principles can be found in John F. Due's text, *Government Finance: Economics of the Public Sector* (Homewood, Ill.: Richard D. Irwin, Inc., 1968), Part IV.

considerations are found all too often in many nations, including the most democratic. This norm is based, of course, on the idea that equalization of treatment is a good thing. As an ultimate value we believe it is; as a practical matter in democracies it is even more impressive a position and necessity in political life. The person who claims a privilege has the burden of proof resting on his shoulders in any taxation dispute. Probably the greatest subjects of controversy on this score are the capital gains write-offs and the depletion allowances for some extractive enterprises. Public finance textbooks can provide the details and reasoning involved. Essentially, the argument is over the nature and size of the risk undertaken under conditions of uncertainty of gain. Unfortunately our tax laws permit many loopholes and exceptions, thus violating the rule of formal equity.

Rule #2   Let equals be treated equally, but unequals commensurately (realistic equity).

Aristotle's maxim is not easy to practice, but the idea is worth keeping in mind whenever burdens are being distributed. In brief, we feel that all in similar circumstances should be treated more or less alike (i.e., Rule #1), whether considered in terms of their obligation to contribute or the benefits they may obtain from the government. But actually, all systems must employ both 'benefits' and 'ability to pay' criteria when assessing burdens. The question is, however, how unequally and how often should taxpayers be so treated? What differences are relevant and how much weight should these diverse criteria be accorded? There are no scientific answers, but the analysis of earlier chapters should provide many clues. For some purposes, benefits not only seem appropriate as the basis for taxation but are also administratively feasible. Good examples are license fees for automobiles, drivers, the privilege of doing business, etc., or 'user' fees such as highway and bridge tolls, patent fees and the like. In other cases ability to pay seems more just, but the standards of equity require political as well as economic analysis, for 'ability' in this light may also raise questions about relative opportunities for different groups of citizens. The equality of the vote principle is fairly clear-cut; equality of burdens is a much tougher question to answer. For example, some proponents of the negative income tax justify the proposed transfer of income to very low income groups on the basis that they do not 'enjoy' the income equivalent of the standard exemptions ($600) which the more affluent take before paying taxes. To its critics, the plan seems to be a guaranteed dole; however, proponents have countered that a guaranteed minimum income avoids the psychic costs of a dependency status. How do you feel about this? In all instances, equality of treatment within the more general categories becomes an important point of debate. In our view, it is an imperative for legitimating policy.

Rule #3   Tax bases and rates must be clear and specific (certainty).

When a considerable amount of a person's personal income is subject to taxation, or if he is required to contribute a good share of his resources, he has a right to know about that requirement as clearly and specifically as possible. Both the administrator and the taxpayer are better off if they are relatively certain about the resource contribution so that each can make his own necessary decisions with some degree of predictability. Predictability in private affairs is difficult enough without government increasing the uncertainties of life. Unpredictable exactions are not desirable and tend to generate fear, distrust and conflict. When the burdens are suddenly imposed, the citizen may well feel justified in evading or reducing them; if he was forewarned he may view them as more legitimate. In legal theory this is an important part of the 'due process' concept.

Not only are the impositions of unexpected burdens likely to stimulate countertactics by the citizen, but they tend to generate suspicion of official wrongdoing as well. If the policy does not spell out clearly the formula for the determination of burdens, the official or agency exercising the discretion may become the subject of suspicion. What are the bases for their determination, and why? If there are not standard public rules, what or who actually decides? The possibility of arbitrariness is a constant political fear on the part of distrustful subjects. For example, the property tax in the United States is the subject of much controversy because tax assessors have considerable power to determine taxes and are therefore subject to pressures, corruption and unpredictability in their actions. Such uncertainty ought to be reduced wherever possible.

Rule #4   When costs are being imposed, prime consideration should be given to the taxpayer's convenience or least effort.

Whether acquiring resources or attaining goals, the costs of the effort itself should be minimized wherever possible. In taxation, collection costs ought to be reduced wherever they involve costly inconveniences for either the administrator or taxpayer and where there is a less costly alternative. Of course this is a relative matter, to be weighed and balanced in evaluating policy programs. Payroll deductions, for example, are a convenience for the taxpayer but somewhat costly to the employer, so there are conflicts of interest among the different clientele as well as with the tax collectors. When costs are being imposed, we think it better first to consider the citizen's convenience or least effort, so long as the administrative costs do not soar to uneconomic levels. If the latter occurs, revenues are eaten up on useless activities. Yet if taxes are necessary, their imposition is made more acceptable insofar as the consideration of convenience is added to those of equity and certainty. This is a form of reciprocity similar to those discussed earlier, but it involves also a regard for the clientele, and a reduction of conflict generated by 'adding insult to injury.'

Rule #5   Tax laws must be enforceable.

Laws that cannot be enforced are hardly worth enacting. If tax laws or the distribution of costs are unacceptable, poorly administered or incapable of effective enforcement, they fail in all their purposes. The administration of taxes or the imposition of burdens is demanding on both administrator and taxpayer, and many obvious inducements exist for the latter to minimize his contributions. Citizens cannot be expected to keep intricate records, continuously and accurately, of what they owe and give the system, so the administrative requirements must be as simple as possible to carry out. In some countries tax collection and enforcement of laws may be a maze of confusion and contradiction, and the administrative means often fall short of the task. Tax collection, e.g., is farmed out in some Latin American nations because the governments cannot do the job themselves. In other countries—Italy and France are good examples—income taxes are frequently negotiated between the government and the taxpayer. Needless to say, the higher income groups have the most incentive and resources to bargain successfully. Respect for tax laws is maintained when they are administered with simplicity and effectiveness.

Appropriate Activities of Government

What are the most appropriate activities for government to perform? In some ways this question is the basic question underlying all we have discussed throughout the book. Although we cannot put forth a single set of agreed-upon rules, it is possible to consider a number of such rules as formulated by both liberal and conservative thinkers. Interestingly, the conservatives have probably been more precise in formulating rules because they have been so concerned with delimiting the scope of government. Their rules tend to be stated in negative terms, indicating what they think government ought not or cannot do well. But they do propose some positive conditions under which they believe government ought to perform an activity.

First of all, the conservatives tend to believe that, with the exception of certain activities about to be enumerated, private markets, institutions and agreements ought to handle most activity. They assert that governments should merely facilitate private institutions and perform those functions which cannot be carried out by private persons and resources. What are the most typically accepted government activities? In general, they are:

1. Provide for the common defense.
2. Provide rules of law and order which enable private activity to

take place without one person coercing another or harmfully interfering with his person or property.

3. Enforce private contracts, property rights, private duties and responsibilities.
4. Provide a monetary system to facilitate exchange, and common standards, measures and weights to facilitate commerce.
5. Control monopoly and excessive interference with trade.
6. Overcome external costs, especially the excessively harmful social consequences of private activities.

From the conservative perspective, governments are necessary to control some of the evils and harms that men do. Most obviously, providing for order has been an accepted duty for government, and one that requires centralized power and some or many forms of compulsory support. While traditionally in our capitalistic system the conservative, whether elite-oriented or enamored of a free economy, has honored private institutions, he still recognizes a necessary government role in their preservation. Private activity and commerce, to proceed with maximum effectiveness, need orderly processes and protective services. Government is needed to formulate and administer some rules by which all abide, though only so far as private gains are enhanced. The enforcement of contracts and other legal rights and duties are viewed as necessary toward this end. A monetary system and standard weights and measures are absolutely necessary to carry on intricate exchange and can only be supervised by government. Since several competing monetary and measurement systems would be impractical, one should be adopted which is reasonably stable and convenient.

Those concerned with the health of free enterprise generally acknowledge the existence of some destructive trade practices and constraints, including powerful monopolies. Government then, may be the preferred controller or regulator as the lesser evil. Since government control is relatively direct, visible and subject to citizen objection, public interference may itself be more 'controllable'; but there are no automatic assurances.

These first five areas of governmental activity are the ones most likely to be accepted by liberal and conservative alike, although today we observe the intense demands of radicals of both the right and left to reduce government rules and controls which many of them believe to be inherently evil. Some major alternative to the exercise of centralized power and command is preferred by these people. The more conventional liberal and conservative tend to argue about appropriate tasks beyond those first five. Rule #6, emphasizing 'external costs' or harmful social consequences, reflects much of this controversy and probably relates to more recent governmental activity and demands than any of the others. We introduced the idea in Chapter 5 but did not treat it as a normative or policy matter. Here we do.

The basic idea is simple and readily recognizable even if the concepts are not immediately revealing. Externalities, often labelled 'neighborhood' or 'spillover' effects, refer to those situations in which benefits and/or costs are incurred by people who are not responsible for them in the first place. For example, a fertilizer plant may pollute both the air and water with its fumes and debris, causing discomfort, unsightly conditions and possible ill health for people who live nearby. Prices of fertilizer in the market place do not reflect these added costs imposed on the affected people, nor are the victims typically repaid for their discomfort. On the other hand, a person or group may be the unintended beneficiary of external benefits for which they do not pay. A family who lives next to a beautiful city park derives aesthetic, social and monetary benefits from the added beauty. The value of their house is probably increased, yet they are not responsible for the building and maintenance of the park. In both cases these neighborhood effects (external benefits and costs) pose policy problems: How shall each be treated? Should the creator of costs pay them? How? Should the recipient of external benefits be forced to pay for them? How?

Citizens, politicians, social scientists and political philosophers have debated these questions almost since the beginning of conscious political life and they will continue to do so, so long as the problems continue. We cite here a most perceptive statement of the modern problem from the justifiably honored American philosopher of pragmatism, John Dewey, in his work aptly titled *The Public and Its Problems:*

"The characteristic of the public as a state springs from the fact that all modes of associated behavior may have extensive and enduring consequences which involve others beyond those directly engaged in them. When these consequences are in turn realized in thought and sentiment, recognition of them reacts to remake the conditions out of which they arose. Consequences have to be taken care of, looked out for. This supervision and regulation cannot be affected by the primary groupings themselves. For the essence of the consequences which call a public into being is the fact that they expand beyond those directly engaged in producing them. Consequently special agencies and measures must be formed if they are to be attended to; or else some existing group must take on new functions. . . . Thus the state represents an important although distinctive and restricted social interest."[5]

The point of Dewey's argument, namely, not to elevate the government *per se* as having or being the best solution but to consider it as an approach

---

[5] John Dewey. Pages 27-28, *The Public and Its Problems,* Swallow Press Incorporated, Chicago, Illinois.

to communal problem-solving, is very relevant today. These consequences require the use of knowledge, skill and public debate to determine what the problem is and its best solution—that is the essential 'shared interest' of the polity.

Solutions for externalities are many and varied and often highly technical; they frequently have economic and social consequences which cannot be determined completely. And each situation tends to have some unique characteristics which make catagorization of solutions difficult. Most analysts are prepared to admit that something must be done whenever externalities or serious social consequences are present, but exactly what should be done is open to debate. The more conservative may tend to prefer private collective agreements to governmental solutions because they feel the decision costs and other disadvantages of the political process usually outweigh any gains. Liberals in this country have tended to opt for governmental controls or intervention, although the traditional preferences of both conservatives and liberals are now in the process of being reassessed. Liberals no longer believe that government is the answer to all questions, and conservatives have come to accept far more governmental participation in the economy than seemed conceivable thirty or forty years ago.

Some Rules on Choice of Controls

The previous sets of rules were concerned with specifying criteria for resource allocation, taxes and the distribution of benefits. An elaboration of such criteria is, however, insufficient without some attention being paid to the means of implementation. Many of our policy preferences can be implemented in a variety of ways; because this is so, it poses another set of problems for the administrator and politician. Which instrumental procedures, rules and controls are to be employed? The following list points up a variety of considerations and shows the complexity of control choices.[6] One qualification must be made, however: preface each rule with the highly unrealistic phrase, "Other things being equal . . ."

Rule #1. Choose that control which least impairs individual choice.
Rule #2. Choose that control which maximizes self-administration.
Rule #3. Choose that control which is most clear-cut and explicit.
Rule #4. Choose that control which is most economic.
Rule #5. Choose indirect and impersonal controls.
Rule #6. Choose controls with positive inducements for compliance.
Rule #7. Be prepared to cope with unanticipated consequences.

---

[6] For an excellent analysis of control problems see Victor A. Thompson, *The Regulatory Process in OPA Rationing* (New York: King's Crown Press, 1950).

Rule #1   Minimize controls.

There are a number of reasons why controls should be minimized, i.e., minimized in terms of numbers, scope of coverage, severity. The first relates to the general presumption of democratic values that men ought to be as free as social necessity permits. The burden of proof that another control ought to be instituted should always rest with the person who proposes the control. The presumption ought to be that controls are evil, to be resisted or at least kept under constant surveillance with the hope that they can be improved if not eliminated as soon as possible. In earlier conditions many controls were undertaken directly and forcefully because the state of knowledge did not admit of any easy indirect modes of control. All direct controls are expensive to administer as well as being repugnant to individual respect; for these reasons they ought to be greatly minimized. Moreover, added controls may be deleterious because they cannot be enforced or are unequally enforced. The fewer the number of controls, then, the less chance there is for such consequences as cynicism, poor enforcement, added costs of administration, and the need for rationalization. Minimize controls!

Rule #2   Maximize self-administration.

Other things being equal, we feel that it is best to employ that control which depends upon the controllees' own enforcement or administration. The more obvious reasons for this choice are: (1) public costs of enforcement are apt to be reduced and (2) less resentment is likely to accompany self-imposed and enforced regulations. Not only will costs be reduced but regulation will often be better enforced when each individual checks himself, and expects the self-restraint of others. Self-regulation can become so 'natural' as not to be noticeable and thus, not burdensome. Visible controllers—policemen and bureaucrats—often make citizens uncomfortable and suspicious. Then, too, controlling has unfortunate consequences for the controllers, themselves; they may become insensitive to the plight and perspectives of others; they become power oriented and enjoy domination or they become fearful and defensive, sometimes resulting in over-enforcement of the laws. And they may begin to act in a superior fashion to those whom they are supposed to serve. For these reasons we believe it is wise to depend upon the citizens themselves as much as possible.

Rule #3   Clarify and state exactly what is expected of both controller and controlled.

If controls are deemed necessary they ought to be cast in language that leaves no room for doubt about their meaning or the behavior they are intended to affect. Ambiguity may be desirable in many areas of life but not in governmental controls. Those who are to be controlled as well as those who will do the controlling have a right to have their mutual expectations

specified in the control or rule. Since more adjudication is required to reduce ambiguities and contradictions in the laws, achieving precision
lightens the burden for both citizens and courts.

While there are increased costs in attaining greater precision and
clarity, they seem worth it when compared with the results of ambiguity
and arbitrariness. Among the costs, to be sure, are the time and effort
spent in finding the appropriate way of specifying expected behaviors
and the respective sanctions. But is it not better to use lawyers and analysts
at this stage than later in interpreting the laws? Just as students require
teachers to be clear about their demands and controls, and employees expect the same from employers, so the citizen demands to know what is
expected of him. Generally the instructor or employer, like the administrator, will save himself a great deal of trouble if he makes his demands
and criteria of performance clear at the outset. The high costs of evasion
should provide additional encouragement for making the rules clear and
explicit.

Rule #4   *Equalize marginal costs of administration and marginal returns.*

We come to the most difficult rule to apply: equalization of control
costs and returns at the margin. In other words, the government ought to
administer a regulation in such a way that the compliance to be attained
from spending another dollar will be equalled by that dollar. To some
extent governments try to do this, but problems of measuring the worth of
compliance prevent anything more than a crude approximation. For example, it seems unwise for the Internal Revenue Service to spend two dollars to get one more dollar from a taxpayer. Over the long run there may
be a periodic exception to this rule: that is, in the short run it may be
necessary to lose some money catching a few small taxpayers in order to
make an example of them as a means of discouraging other small taxpayers
from cheating. In effect, marginal costs and benefits are matched over time
periods rather than continuously through time.

We do not pretend that administrators can apply this rule with ease.
We do hope, however, that the statement of the rule sensitizes the administrator to a consideration of some importance so that, once being sensitized,
he will deliberately seek to devise means whereby the rule may be applied.
In any case it seems foolish to support increased costs of rules that do not
produce increased compliance. The administrator might envisage the
situation as we have in Figure 13-2. Increasing expenditures on control
produces increasing returns up to a point, but sooner or later the marginal
returns diminish. Thus one must be aware of what the actual returns are.
The point at which marginal cost = marginal benefits is the level of expenditures on controls which the government should aim for if it is to be
rational. Any expenditure to the right of that juncture costs more than is
returned; any point or expenditure to the left means that the government

Figure 13-2

Cost of Controls

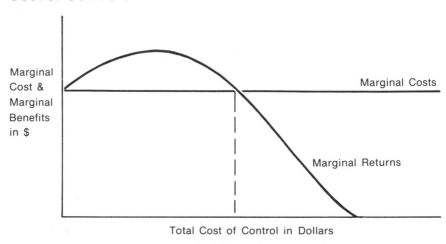

Marginal Cost & Marginal Benefits in $

Marginal Costs

Marginal Returns

Total Cost of Control in Dollars

is not acquiring all the returns it might achieve. Of course, the practical identification of such levels of expenditure is extremely difficult to make, but the basic notion of incremental costs and incremental returns should (as in resource allocation) be a base line for control activities.

Rule #5   Choose indirect and impersonal rather than direct controls.

Indirect or impersonal controls can be more cumbersome and less dependable or predictable in their consequences, but they seem to have some pronounced advantages over direct controls. Direct control generally requires considerable and costly bureaucratic organizations for administration whereas indirect control is typically self-enforcing because it works through the incentives, costs and choices of the citizens. Citizens make their own decisions, but the decisions are selected in response to the changed situational incentives and costs. Such a control enables the citizen to exercise more voluntary behavior. No one is directly telling him what he must and/or must not do. While he regulates his own behavior, the behavior is indirectly conditioned to some extent by the governmentally defined situation. Citizen participation probably also reduces the overhead costs of administration.

There is a problem or danger in indirect controls: they can be looked upon as manipulation, i.e., men suspect that they are being controlled but they do not know how or by whom. Information and explanation is most helpful here. Another problem to which we have already alluded concerns effectiveness and efficiency; indirect controls need not be less effective than direct controls but one should consider the probability of greater time lags and less predictability of and control over all consequences.

Rule #6   Use positive inducements.

As we pointed out in Chapter 6, an administrator normally has a choice of inducements, i.e., whether to employ positive or negative sanctions for compliance. No government, nor anyone in authority, can avoid using negative sanctions, but we believe that the citizenry generally will respond with greater consistency and economy to rewards and expected gains than to negative sanctions and threats. This belief is based upon the axiom that man has concern for his own interests, satisfactions and dignity. He will strive harder to achieve something positive for himself than he will simply to avoid penalties. Obviously, human action involves both rewards and penalties; however, we feel it is more consistent with democratic values to rely on rewards wherever possible and to minimize the fears, anxieties and penalties. No government can afford to reward men with material benefits every time they do what they should do, but material rewards are hardly the only ones available for persuasion. Answering the call to duty may also be a rewarding experience. Honors, conveniences, concessions or privileges, income, status, and power are all positive inducements that are used. As our understanding of social processes increases, even better inducements may be devised or the present ones better employed.

Rule #7   Be prepared to cope with unanticipated consequences.

All regulations, policies and laws have some unintended consequences—in fact, sets of consequences which may be completely opposite to those originally intended. The problem for the administrator and politician is one of prediction; what behavioral consequences will be most and least likely to flow from given courses of action? The behavioral sciences are not so highly developed that leaders can turn to them for precise and confident advice. Regulations may be devised with the intention of altering some behavior and, in the end, stimulate an evasive pursuit of the very behavior that was to be discouraged. A good example is the Prohibition Amendment to the U.S. Constitution. Liquor consumption was to be discouraged; apparently it was increased. Even worse, from the temperance standpoint, some people who never drank before began to drink.

Another good example may be found in economic policy. Herbert Hoover followed the best economic advice of his time in an effort to halt the depression; his efforts were rewarded by a worsening of the cycle. The conventional wisdom of the time involved considerable misunderstanding of economic behavior. Public policies only aggravated the crisis because they were based on the assumption that rational public behavior was simply an extension of rational private behavior in the economy. In other words, what was considered an intelligent thing for a private investor to do was also what a government should do. Few economists make that mistake today, but the example points up the possibility that what seems so logical a set of consequences for one area of activity may not be so in another. Policy advisers are well advised themselves to be cautious about the conventional wisdoms as defined and preached in their own disciplines.

Case Study #1   Some Lessons of Control (Relocation Camps, 1942-44)

We pause here to cite some rules formulated in a remarkable study of one extensive control program undertaken by our government under extreme circumstances. During World War II, Japanese-Americans were compulsorily removed from their homes, had their property confiscated, and were sent to various 'relocation camps' in the western states. It was a shameful episode, based upon fear rather than any evidence of disloyalty, and facilitated by the ease with which the subjects could be differentiated racially from other second-generation Americans and immigrant groups. Out of this stressful situation came a book, *The Governing of Men*,[7] by Alexander Leighton, a psychiatrist who served as an administrator at one of the camps in Arizona. Leighton's book describes the history of that camp with an eye toward learning something about human behavior and its control. In the last five chapters he elaborates a lengthy series of 'principles' and recommendations concerning beliefs, social organization, administration and control. They are worth repeating here for several reasons.

There are many similarities between the situation of these Japanese-Americans and many other human groups suffering social distress and disorganization. We have seen the forceful movement of people by or because of governments at war, and the migration and resettlement of other groups in communities where they are isolated, disadvantaged and typically subject to an intimidating or patronizing government. Thus the situation of Leighton's administration may well be pondered by the occupying force in another land, or by the police and welfare agencies in the American ghetto, the emergency crews in disaster areas, the city official who has received a large refugee population, as well as those who are administering Indian affairs in this country, Vista and other poverty workers, educators seeking to help disadvantaged groups in certain communities, or even the prison official. Whatever the sorry occasion where one is expected to exercise controls over a subject group, these precepts may stimulate comparison and guide policy choices. It is seldom that the tasks of administration have been so sensitively treated with the human understanding and regard that this behavioral scientist conveys. In this perspective these rules may also enlighten a broader set of administrative choices. We wish there were similar efforts in the more mundane areas of official endeavor. The following are sample selections; we urge the interested reader to consult the original set of more extensive considerations.

---

[7] (Princeton: Princeton University Press, 1945).

Individuals Under Stress:

1. "In a disturbed community look for all the specific and all the general types of stress, not one or a few; note which are actually present and try to estimate their intensity."[8]

2. "Never underestimate the deleterious force of circumstances which foster repeated *frustration, incompatible desires* and *uncertainty.*[9]

3. "Never dismiss complaints as trivial; they may be only 'gripes,' but they may also be clear warnings of imminent trouble and one cannot tell which without investigation."[10]

4. "Keep in mind that the strength of an administration rests largely on its ability to meet the needs of people; that relief from the various types of stress comprises a major set of needs; and that complaints are clues to needs."[11]

5. "Cultivate cooperation, but not extremes of compliance and dependence; there are yes-men in all races and creeds and they are usually poor assistants."[12]

6. "Regard extremes of withdrawal, apathy, and indifference as bad signs, but accept mass inertia as characteristic of people and learn to rely on its stability."[13]

7. "Consider aggression as a human reaction to circumstances, not merely as innate cussedness, the work of evil men, or a racial peculiarity."[14]

8. "Recognize rumors, suspicions, scapegoat tendencies, gang activities and crime increase as symptoms of aggression arising out of stress."[15]

9. "Try to guide and control aggression, but do not try to stamp it out; in most instances one cannot destroy it and even if he could, he would lose a force that might be of much value. It is the horse with spirit that is balking."[16]

10. "Remember that it is a common failing of administrators to refuse mild requests they can and should grant, while yielding

---

[8] *Ibid.,* p. 262.
[9] *Ibid.*
[10] *Ibid.*
[11] *Ibid.*
[12] *Ibid.,* p. 275
[13] *Ibid.*
[14] *Ibid.*
[15] *Ibid.*
[16] *Ibid.*

later to aggressive demand that forces itself on their attention; such behavior encourages the destructive aspects of aggression."[17]

11. "Never make threats or pass laws that cannot be enforced; there is no quicker way to undermine the power of an administration."[18]

12. "Never take a strong stand on a weak position."[19]

13. "Capitalize on the feelings of relief and cooperativeness that are likely to occur after an outburst or aggression; do not set the clock back by an ill-placed act of punishment which rouses new aggressions and controls nothing."[20]

14. "Remember that when the administering body is of a different nationality or 'race' from the people being administered, there are particular temptations to make scapegoats out of the people; do everything possible to prevent this, for it can easily destroy all possibility of good administration."[21]

15. "Beware of disordered emotional thinking in administrative officers and the elements of fear that may underlie behavior that is apparently bold, angry, shrewd and determined."[22]

16. "Watch out for administrative officers who give way to fruitless hating under the guise of enforcing discipline; such behavior is a form of self-indulgence and dereliction of duty, and one may become addicted to it as to alcohol."[23]

17. "Give special attention to the distribution of reliable information in an understandable form."[24]

18. "Provide opportunities that will enable the people being administered to develop their constructive tendencies; this not only provides intrinsic satisfactions, but compensates for stresses that cannot be relieved."[25]

19. "Remember that punishment is only one among many useful tools for the control of people. Never use it alone; punishment without relief of underlying stress is like tying down a safety valve and stoking up the fire."[26]

---

[17] *Ibid.*

[18] *Ibid.*

[19] *Ibid.*

[20] *Ibid.*

[21] *Ibid.*, p. 280.

[22] *Ibid.*

[23] *Ibid.*, pp. 280-281.

[24] *Ibid.*, p. 285.

[25] *Ibid.*

[26] *Ibid.*

20. "Keep in mind that to be effective in the long run as an aid to administration, punishments given must be recognized as just by the community."[27]

Systems of Belief Under Stress:

21. "Never forget the strength there may be in a system of belief and the fact that no matter how foreign, useless or destructive it seems it may still be interconnected with those things upon which the security and capacity of the people depend."[28]
22. "Do not ignore complaints that are based on belief rather than fact; people act on what they believe."[29]
23. "Study complaints for the underlying systems of belief they reveal."[30]
24. "Adjust administration to the people's systems of belief as well as to their stresses and needs, and do it as realistically as one would adjust an agricultural program to conditions of soil and climate."[31]
25. "Expect people to respond to the administration in terms of their systems of belief—not the administration's."[32]
26. "In times of stress, be prepared to find rapid changes and increased intensity and conflict in systems of belief."[33]
27. "Realize that systems of belief are as important in administrative function as are policy statements, plans, regulations and organization charts; they can change or cancel all the rest."[34]
28. "Carry out administration in terms of facts as found, not in terms of sweeping, stereotyped beliefs."[35]
29. "Remember that prevention is easier than cure; take care of the basic sources of stress and most of the disruptive systems of belief will take care of themselves."[36]
30. "Granting people some of what they want should not be neglected as a means of establishing rapport with the administra-

---

[27] *Ibid.*
[28] *Ibid.,* p. 294.
[29] *Ibid.*
[30] *Ibid.*
[31] *Ibid.,* p. 295.
[32] *Ibid.*
[33] *Ibid.,* p. 303.
[34] *Ibid.,* p. 313.
[35] *Ibid.*
[36] *Ibid.,* p. 320.

tion and paving the way for modification of inimical systems of belief."[37]

31. "Do not dismiss as irrational everything that does not agree with the administrator's system of belief."[38]

Social Organization Under Stress:

32. "Look on factional struggles in a community under stress as part of the process of breakdown and repair of social organization; be very hesitant to take sides."[39]

33. "Do not back up a minority and force its control on a society simply because that minority is partial to the administration."[40]

34. "Judge leaders not by their ability to curry favor but by their grasp of the people's needs and their capacity to move toward stability."[41]

35. "Be prepared to give the administration's opponents credit for honest motives."[42]

36. "Do not miss opportunities to seek common ground with opponents."[43]

37. "Make sure that no member of the administration is placed unnecessarily in a position where he is exposed to excessive frustration, conflict and uncertainty; have the right man in the right job."[44]

38. "Communication from the people to the administration is no less important than the stream in the opposite direction, although it is even more often neglected. 'I know just how these people think and feel' should be classed among 'famous last words' of administrators."[45]

Analytic Aids for Improving Public Policies

While clear thinking and information are the chief requirements of planning and implementing governmental programs, no intelligent ad-

---

[37] *Ibid.*

[38] *Ibid.*, p. 321.

[39] *Ibid.*, p. 342.

[40] *Ibid.*

[41] *Ibid.*

[42] *Ibid.*

[43] *Ibid.*

[44] *Ibid.*, p. 349.

[45] *Ibid.*, p. 365.

ministrator or politician can do without some effective methods or analytical aids to assist in making his choices. A variety of tools have been devised and are being perfected which enable far better thinking than the simple ends-means planning that has typically been employed.

Some of these tools or aids have been labelled variously as systems analysis, program budgeting, cost-effectiveness or cost-benefit analysis, operations analysis or research. These aids (by whatever name) are quite similar or have much in common; a person who uses one usually knows and works with the others, but for reasons we do not quite know each has been given or acquired a different label. What they have in common is a concern for working out more effective ways of achieving an objective. Each is, therefore, concerned with evaluating alternatives, their costs and benefits, and establishing and applying some criteria, such as our rules, for deciding or settling upon the preferred alternative. A related set of activities may be called formal model-building, in that efforts are made to abstract the major interrelationships that exist among the elements of the situation or programs and to determine how changes in them will affect the final achievements.

Whenever one reads the reports of analysts using these techniques he notes that they make considerable use of economics, statistical data, mathematical expressions, decision-trees and flow charts. Monetary cost figures are found in profusion since assessments of alternatives require some common measure of value. Much of the work is technical and not very exciting reading but is highly valuable to those who must decide on such questions as the best alternative to use in water resources management, highway location, urban renewal, defense strategies and almost every other activity which governments typically perform.

Analytical aids do not offer automatic and perfect answers to complex problems, nor are they substitutes for public debate, politicians, voters and collective choice processes. They are simply analytical tools which enable those who apply them to think more clearly and precisely about the alternative solutions their common sense or practical logic may have conjured up. They remain useful so long as one treats them as convenient tools to be mastered and not to be mastered by. We provide a very brief description of them to illustrate the sort of analytic aids which make policy choice more effective.

Systems Analysis

The basic idea of systems analysis is to conceptualize the performance of policy programs as an interrelated set of steps.[46] Systems analysis starts

---

[46] See Walter Buckley, ed., *Modern Systems Research for the Behavioral Scientist* (Chi-

with what is 'fed into' the policy system, i.e., the inputs, and considers all the flows or processing of those resources and relates them to the level or quality of the product output they would produce. A simplified diagram of the systems framework is pictured in Figure 1-2 (p. 14), the typical 'box with in-and-out arrows' which we employed to conceptualize the political system itself. In policy analysis the approach has both its very complex and very simple applications. Some use it for the broader or more intricate consideration of relevant variables which, thanks to the computer, is now possible. The variables consist of all the measurable units of resources and techniques that are combined into the projected policy operation: manpower, materials, natural energy and such. The techniques are represented by the formulae of computer programs for combining these resources in terms of amounts, uses, timing and so forth. Computer technology promises no end to the kinds of complex processes that can be thus 'simulated' as if they actually took place. The point is to be able to analyze alternatives experimentally, in all their complexity, before having to make costly ventures. The technique enables a laboratory-sort of experimentation for very large-scale enterprises such as one deals with in public policy programs.

Another form of systems analysis tends to emphasize relationships between the inputs of resources for policies and overall levels of outputs in the forms of 'products' or public goods. It is a simpler approach because it ignores the complex 'internal' processes and concentrates on the overall relation of resource levels to output levels. In social science this is often called 'black box' analysis because the inside elements of the system are left out. Figure 1-2 is a 'black box' conception as is Figure 13-3.

Figure 13-3 depicts an array of input resources expected to produce outputs of various sorts—in this case, a water resource project. The problem of the planner, the interested politician or citizen is to measure these inputs and outputs in such a manner as to enable more precise comparisons with alternative uses of the same resources.

The systems analyst attempts to study problems such as pictured in Figure 13-3 in a way that will enable him to recommend the most efficient course of action in producing the given types and levels of output or, what amounts to the same thing in formal terms, maximizing the output from the given inputs. He will view all the elements in the situation or problem as basically interdependent and attempt to measure each element to decide its most appropriate role in the system. If he can attach numerical values to each element he will, since that enables systematic comparisons and

cago: Aldine Publishing Company, 1968) for a collection of important articles on systems theory. With respect to the actual policy use of systems theory, see Edward S. Quade, ed., *Analysis for Military Decisions* (Chicago: Rand McNally and Company, 1964); Stanford L. Optner, *Systems Analysis for Business and Industrial Problem Solving* (Englewood Cliffs, N.J.: Prentice-Hall, Inc., 1965); and Arthur Maass and M. M. Hufschmidt, *et al.*, *Design of Water Resource Systems* (Cambridge: Harvard University Press, 1962).

Figure 13-3

Example of 'Black Box' Analysis: Water Resource Project

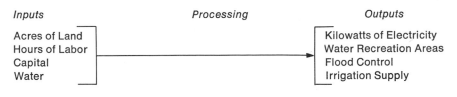

Inputs	Processing	Outputs
Acres of Land		Kilowatts of Electricity
Hours of Labor		Water Recreation Areas
Capital		Flood Control
Water		Irrigation Supply

valuations to be placed on the various components. It is exceedingly difficult to know whether one is being efficient if one does not have this relative measure of value.

Of course, the actual application of systems analysis to large-scale social problems is extremely difficult because common measures cannot be found for incommensurate elements. In our example it seems simple enough to place dollar values on kilowatts of electricity; it is somewhat more difficult to place a value on irrigation supplies and extremely difficult to measure the value of flood control and recreation. There are no convenient market values or prices for these outputs. In such cases, the systems analysts will look for or devise indirect measures. An example might be the fees the government could collect for water and recreational uses of the project. Such values are arbitrary, since no free market decides upon them. But they are the best available measures and one must work with what he has.

The important point to remember about systems analysis is that it is simply organized inquiry into high level problems of economizing or finding the most productive way of doing something. Under this broad rubric many people labor with a variety of skills, including engineering, statistics, mathematics and economics.

Cost-Benefit Analysis

A variant of systems analysis called 'cost-benefit' analysis is another tool designed to assist in making better decisions on ways of accomplishing social goals.[47] While it is difficult to dissociate systems analysis from cost-benefit studies there does seem to be a slightly different focus, with the latter being somewhat more interested in not only identifying benefits but studying their incidence or distribution as well as their costs. Each project or alternative, as we have seen, brings different patterns of costs and bene-

---

[47] See Roland N. McKean, *Efficiency in Government Through Systems Analysis* (New York: John Wiley and Sons, Inc., 1958).

ficial results. An exercise in cost-benefit analysis attempts to specify these results.

One simple device of cost-benefit analysis which promotes clear thinking and thoroughness of estimates consists of no more than a table containing alternative proposals for a policy program and spaces for entering estimates of both costs (as in budgets) and benefits (measured as best as possible) accompanied by estimates of their incidence. Such a table does not provide answers but does permit more systematic consideration of the problems. In Table 13-1 we show a sample policy proposal along with space for hypothetical entries concerning the affected persons and the various impacts of the proposal. Since multiple purpose proposals are normally the case, individual tables would have to be constructed for each and compared in a summary sheet. Space limitations prevent us from doing this, but the example should suffice to make the point. If you try it, the table should also confirm our warning that making estimates of costs and particularly benefits is not simple nor easily accomplished. One has to train his judgment to make good estimates. In fact, a substantial part of the political struggle consists of efforts to discern the costs and benefits of policy proposals (totals and distributions), with each side claiming its estimates to be more realistic than the others.

While cost-benefit analysis is typically applied to domestic policy problems, including water resource development, urban renewal, research and development proposals, highway investments, land use, health control and many other resource-allocative problems, it was most promoted by the Defense Department in its attempt to exercise greater rationality over the vast expenditures of defense preparations and war. War strategists have always, of course, attempted to increase their capacities to outwit and beat an opponent, but they have not always cared about doing so economically or with more sophisticated tools of calculation. Today, with large continuing defense budgets, the concern has turned to 'cost effectiveness,' i.e., either attaining as much defense as possible, given the means, or, given the level of defense, with as few resources as possible. More generally, foreign policy strategists could attempt to select their means with such a rational calculus. That they may not succeed is often likely as foreign policy involves opponents or other countries which cannot be eliminated or removed from consideration and whose own strategies affect our choices. While cost-effectiveness studies cannot be applied to foreign policy problems with the ease and certainty that can be obtained in domestic problem solving, approximations are being attempted. Indeed this is only a refinement of what has always been attempted, although in highly unsystematic ways.

Additional Techniques

'Program budgeting' is an important instrument for enabling the comparison of program costs in terms of what they yield, as well as the

Table 13-1

Cost-Benefit Analysis of Urban Renewal Proposals

Citizen Groups	Number of Citizens	Benefit(s)	Cost	Net	Net Advantage To
Householders Displaced					
Householders Not Displaced					
New Occupiers					
Auto Users					
Park Users					
Shoppers					
Businessmen					
Tourists					
•					
•					
•					

possible alternative yields.[48] It uses the systematic accounting procedures of budgets in a more effective way. Instead of detailing the allocation of costs by the agency which uses the resources, as traditional public budgets did, this method seeks to designate costs or resources applied to the end-missions or objectives of each program. Combining costs with operational goals in this way is often referred to as 'program packaging.' It is not as easy as it sounds, since so many agencies pursue multiple objectives, but assigning specific amounts of resources to those particular goals is a much more effective way of comparing alternatives. It enables the policy-maker to evaluate the marginal costs and returns if he shifts resources to different 'mixes' or policy goals. It can also be an important ingredient for the broader sort of systems and cost-benefit analyses described above. The old government budgets look quaint alongside performance budgets.

'Operations research' applies the systems framework to the concrete activities of particular program operations.[49] It may be one single phase of a program, such as one military sortie within a strategic mission or one typical day's work in the Patent Office, or it may concern the whole complex of interactions required for receiving, routing and delivering the mail in the post office. When one looks at actual operations the focus and measurements become more like engineering: time-phasing the work and specifying resources for various tasks as conditioned by actual constraints or indeterminacies—environmental, motivational and otherwise. In effect, it is a very concrete method of envisaging the dimensions of tasks to be undertaken, an analysis of their sub-procedures, and an effort at rationalizing or optimizing how these are to be performed in achieving goals.

Lest the reader be confused as to how this differs from systems analysis and cost effectiveness, we hasten to say they all have more in common than not. The difference is the level of application; typically in operations research one is not considering broad policy alternatives but merely dealing with the mixture of specific sorts of sub-activities. Thus cost-effectiveness is applied in more detailed and direct form, to more particular operations rather than to the critical evaluation of the costs and merits of entire programs. But each shares techniques with the others, and all take advantage of the more powerful methods of engineering, accounting and computer sciences that have been developed since World War II.

These techniques are not to be worshiped for their own sake but only as ways to achieve policy goals more effectively, if those goals are considered worthwhile. Therein lie some precautions to consider.

---

[48] David Novick, ed., *Program Budgeting: Program Analysis and the Federal Budget* (Washington, D.C.: U.S. Government Printing Office, 1965).

[49] A good brief introduction to operations research as well as several illustrative examples of its use are contained in Philip M. Morse, ed., *Operations Research for Public Systems* (Cambridge: Massachusetts Institute of Technology, 1967).

Some Cautions

In the search for a finer, more rewarding life we believe in a certain amount of stoicism, a sense of the limitations of man and political organization. All men must die and everyone's life will have a certain amount of unhappiness, tragedy, inconvenience and ineffectiveness. Few if any will achieve all they set out to attain. We believe that an appreciation of the ultimate limitations of death and illness, of conflict and hatred should make one a more realistic and humane person. But in stressing these limitations we do not wish to encourage gloating over them as some reactionaries may be inclined to do; we discourage both utopianism and the cynicism resulting from failures. Few persons are less useful than the impatient idealist who has 'seen the light' or the once-disappointed idealist or skeptic who claims no illusions but also no hopes or helpful anticipations either.

All forms of social and political organization have their advantages and costs; none can ever actually perform as the theoretical blueprint suggests. Be sensitive to the great variety of ways of accomplishing both individual and collective choices and values. Let it not be believed that some systems simply cannot work; all manner of systems have worked and all systems undergo changes. We resist 'isms' which declare that some systems are evil and others all good. Only self-justification and little benefit has come from so treating different ways of social organization. A little hard analysis of alternatives is generally a good cure for this tendency. We hope this book has been of some help in considering alternatives.

All-or-nothing solutions that are intended for all time and are imposed on men are, in our estimation, not genuine solutions to any important social problem. We caution the reader to be wary of panaceas. What constituted an adequate solution at one time may fail miserably at another, when new conditions prevail. Flexibility in tackling problems is a virtue and not a sign of weakness. Sensitivity to newly emerging conditions is a vital necessity if one would solve social problems.

We further believe that solutions to social problems cannot be simultaneously maximized. The necessary resources are usually not available and the effects or consequences of solving one problem may produce undesirable consequences for one or more others. For example, adding to the defense of the nation may result in severe dislocations in the economy (inflation, shortages of consumer goods, misallocations of resources), dislocations in family life, concentrated political power, burdensome taxes, the killing and maiming of people, and perhaps many other far reaching consequences of concern. Those who believe that maximal solutions are imperative at any cost ought to reconsider what new problems may be created and old ones aggravated in the process. *The* solution, if there is one to any given problem, will always have multiple implications for others; no solution can be achieved in a vacuum. Systematic analyses, at their best, must incorporate such implications.

One reason for having representatives of as many groups as possible in any policy-making situation is to insure that in the actual policy world such implications will be detected. We cannot rely on ourselves to know all the implications of policies for all walks of life. Those who are affected must speak for themselves, if at all possible.

One should not be at all surprised by the many direct and indirect ramifications each and every policy alternative will foster. We should also be very surprised if the alleged impacts of programs, as stated or predicted by proponents or detractors, have had the consequences predicted. A most recent example is the federal Medicare program. Some doctors and medical associations had predicted all sorts of problems, including overtaxed facilities and malingering by the patients. Thus far, neither has occurred to any marked degree. In an earlier day, critics of the income tax said it would destroy initiative. It was also claimed that welfare payments would keep people from seeking jobs and that subsidies to the farmers would control the farm surplus problem. Others contended that unbalanced national budgets would bankrupt the nation. None of these dire consequences has come about as predicted. From this we should learn that one must be skeptical about the alleged consequences or impacts of policies, especially when someone with a vested interest in bringing them about or defeating them makes the prediction. Many a program has succeeded when some thought it would not and could not. Many a program has failed when its supporters hailed it as a panacea for all ills. The determination of consequences is fraught with bias and uncertainty. It behooves us to be more circumspect and rational about them.

In analyzing the consequences of policies one must also analyze relationships among public goals. We have reiterated the fact that citizens and governments cannot simultaneously maximize all goals and minimize all costs. Indeed, the maximization of one goal may well be the minimization of another. We cannot know this unless we investigate the relationships among goals. Obviously goals may be in conflict (partial or total); they may also be compatible, or complementary, or have no particular relationship, being perfectly independent. If a conflict exists, some way must be found for deciding priorities. If the goals are not in conflict, there are good possibilities, given the resources, to achieve agreement and provide solutions beneficial to all. In order to remember these bits of wisdom we suggest that you arrange goals in lists that will direct your attention to their relationships. Figure 13-4 is intended to stimulate your imagination. Try an actual assessment of several programs which you think significant; see if some third party would come up with similar judgments, and note the kinds of evidence you would most like to have.

The making of public policy in a democracy is a collective enterprise. As such, it depends upon a vast variety of conditions and factors, including

Figure 13-4
Relationships Among Policy Goals

Goals	A	B	C	D
A		conflict	complementary	independent
B	conflict		independent	complementary
C	complementary	independent		conflict
D	independent	complementary	conflict	

political values and beliefs, rules of the game, types of issues, previous experiences, etc. While we may learn and improve our knowledge of these factors we can never make the ultimate choices scientific; we can only make them more intelligent because we possess information on the relationships of means to the ends we desire. Our inquiries have been designed to further that knowledge. While we hope and believe that man can improve his lot, we are also convinced that millennial thinking is of little assistance; better to cope first with the short run and with consideration of the interests and preferences of others.

Problems and Applications

1. Consider the political feasibility and consequences of shifting the production and distribution of one of the following public goods to private enterprise: (a) fire protection, (b) national defense, (c) water supply and (d) local police protection. Would you allow them competitive or monopoly status? Which and why?
2. At least some protagonists have seriously suggested that if a citizen does not like the package of public goods offered in his present locality, he can pack up and go to one which does provide him whatever he wants. How do you view this as a solution to conflicts over public goods?
3. In view of the defeat of many school budgets during the past decade, what would you think of redrawing school districts so that parents and others could voluntarily join the district of their own preference? Thus, presumably, the citizen could receive the type of education he desires and pay accordingly. How would you assess such a policy? Could it work in the real world? What consequences would you anticipate for the citizen, student, school boards and for the financing of education?
4. Some commentators have argued that the average citizen believes government budgets are always too large in relation to the benefits he derives from them. Do you think this is a correct observation? Why?

5. Which of the following activities do you think are best performed by local government? state government? the national government? some combination? Defend your position.

garbage collection	vaccinations
public libraries	highway construction
industrial safety	public utilities
treatment of drug addicts	income redistribution

6. The solution of major social problems by political means usually strains the cohesion needed for a stable society. If this is true, the lesson might be simple: limit the number of issues on which joint action is necessary. Consider this proposition in terms of the irreducible sorts of issues you would permit. What would happen to the disregarded issues?

7. Devise policy solutions for one of the following difficult and controversial issues: (a) bussing black children to schools outside their districts, (b) ending poverty among the rural poor, (c) guaranteeing annual incomes. Have the rules stated in this chapter been of any value in seeking solutions? If not, why?

8. Which of the following activities currently performed by the federal government do you think should be eliminated? Why? Is it politically feasible? What political consequences would you anticipate?
   (a) parity prices for agricultural commodities
   (b) import quotas on oil, sugar, etc.
   (c) legal minimum wages
   (d) public housing
   (e) social security programs, especially old age and retirement insurance
   (f) conscription (military)
   (g) national parks

9. Consider the military draft as a means of providing an army. Are there better alternatives that meet the standards of the military? That satisfy other values? What would be the consequences in terms of costs and benefits?

Bibliographical Notes

Because policy is so important, social scientists have devoted much thought to it, both in terms of elaborating general principles as well as specific applications to such policy areas as defense, agriculture, education, labor, etc. We shall not review the latter types because we cannot presume to be experts about these issues, but we will cite a few exemplary studies with which the reader can familiarize himself. For the most part, we wish to recommend general studies which provide norms for policy-makers.

An excellent starting point is with Wayne A. R. Leys' *Ethics for Policy Decisions* (Englewood Cliffs, N.J.: Prentice-Hall, Inc., 1952), a most sensible approach to the art of asking deliberative questions about policy choices. Leys shows that solutions are highly dependent on the questions put forth. The book has many interesting case studies, most of which are still highly relevant to social problems of today. That most versatile economist, Kenneth Boulding, has also confronted policy questions in *Principles of Economic Policy* (Englewood Cliffs, N.J.: Prentice-Hall, Inc., 1958). The first seven chapters deal with general matters of policy and policy-making while the rest of the book considers specific policy areas such as labor and agriculture. Boulding always surprises the reader with unusual analogies and wise reflections. Chapter 5, on economic freedom, is particularly relevant to problems of conflicting norms and interests and seems a prelude to his book, *Conflict and Defense,* mentioned in the notes to Chapter 10.

An increasingly significant body of writing is being produced that combines the skills of philosophers and social scientists on public policy questions. For example, Nicholas Rescher, *Distributive Justice* (Indianapolis: The Bobbs-Merrill Company, Inc., 1966) attempts to reconsider the utilitarian view of distribution and to formulate some useful rules. The book is fairly easy reading. Another attempt to deal with some of the same problems and many other practical issues of the day is R. W. Baldwin, *Social Justice* (Oxford, England: Pergamon Press, 1966). The author is not only a philosopher but a businessman engaged in the manufacture of textiles in Britain. Richard M. Titmus in *Income Distribution and Social Change* (Toronto: University of Toronto Press, 1962) deals with the question of whether Britain is becoming more equal; he finds that not to be the case. While the study is primarily empirical, it also draws attention to the connection between policy and fact. In a more philosophical work Titmus concerns himself with a variety of questions concerning public policy in Britain; see *Essays on 'The Welfare State'* (London: George Allen and Unwin Ltd., 1958). Health, war and welfare programs are assessed and interpreted. In one of the more imaginative and exciting publications of recent years W. G. Runciman explores attitudes toward social inequality in England: *Relative Deprivation and Social Justice* (Berkeley: University of California Press, 1966). Runciman claims it is possible to assess, in principle, the justice or injustice of inequalities. Knowing attitudes is a part of the test. For just about the first time in social survey work, actual inequalities are compared with perceptions thereof. This book should become a classic analysis.

An area of scholarly inquiry from which we have drawn in a very elementary way is known as 'welfare economics,' a highly recondite area of theory. Since its inception around the turn of the century, welfare economics has been concerned with establishing rules for attaining optimal 'welfare' in a society. The early school of Pareto and Pigou believed that one could establish such rules because (they assumed) the welfare of individuals could be compared. They tended to treat men as equal for such purposes. Later, a number of economists came to challenge the possibility of meaningful interpersonal comparisons and argued that it was all a waste of time. Still, some decided it was possible to salvage welfare doctrines by avoiding some of the inadmissable assumptions. This was done and a new school now labors to do what the old could not. The literature is voluminous, highly repetitive and demanding, but a good introduction may be found in E. J. Mishan, *Welfare Economics* (New York: Random House, Inc., 1964). An extensive bibliography is attached. There is one other volume in welfare economics which deserves mention here; we refer to Jerome Rothenberg's *The Measurement of Social Welfare* (Englewood Cliffs, N.J.: Prentice-Hall, Inc., 1961), valuable because he elucidates welfare economics so well and because he deals with many of the political problems that underlie the treatment in this text. The going may be a bit difficult but is well worth the effort. We do not advise getting into this branch of theory without some preliminary training and a lot of patience, for the debates are highly technical and not about specific concrete policies. But the attempt to conceive of an optimal state of affairs with general rules of application is a worthy endeavor.

As our discussion indicated, the norms of policy-making are quite closely related to various analytical aids that have been developed since World War II. Among the more useful volumes describing and applying these aids are the following: Roland N. McKean, *Efficiency in Government Through Systems Analysis* (New York: John Wiley and Sons, Inc., 1958) and *Public Spending* (New York: McGraw-Hill Book Company, 1968). The former is a technical exposition of what the title indicates, while the latter is a brief and less technical textbook on the subject of its title. Chapters 3 and 8 of that book are particularly useful for policy concerns. McKean does not fill his pages with dry figures on taxes and expenditures. We think it a very good text. If you are interested in governmental program budgeting we suggest David Novick, ed., *Program Budgeting* (Washington, D.C.: U.S. Government Printing Office, 1964). This volume serves to acquaint the reader with the budgetary practices instituted by the Defense Department in 1961 and ordered by President Johnson for use in other government agencies. The book is not a primer but a survey of the rationale for new budgetary conceptions and possible uses. You need not be an accountant to read it.

Readers may at times wonder whether these abstruse writings are ever applied to practical problems of policy; they are, and we should like to recommend just a few examples of applied policy analysis. For a variety of reasons most of these analytic techniques were applied first to national defense and cold war policies by experts employed in such 'think tanks' as Rand Corporation. Their work helped revolutionize management methods, especially for national defense, as well as provide new criteria for policy analysis. A most important influence in this revision was the work of Charles J. Hitch and Roland N. McKean, *The Economics of Defense in the Nuclear Age* (Cambridge: Harvard University Press, 1966). Hitch was in a unique position to implement his ideas since he served as Comptroller of the Department of Defense under President Kennedy. Although a technical work, the book is unusually lucid. We have been much influenced by Hitch and McKean concerning both the uses and limits of economic analysis. Another rigorous policy study concerns foreign aid programs. Charles Wolfe, Jr., *Foreign Aid: Theory and Practice in Southern Asia* (Princeton: Princeton University Press, 1960) advances some ingenious measures of the worth of foreign aid as well as one of the most concrete attempts to measure the vulnerability of nations to communist revolutions. Still in the area of defense and foreign policy, we suggest Seymour J. Deitchman, *Limited War and American Defense Policy* (Cambridge: Massachusetts Institute of Technology, 1964), which strongly reflects an operations research approach.

Americans worry about more peaceful public policies, too. A fine introduction to a major policy area is Wilbur R. Thompson's *A Preface to Urban Economics* (Baltimore: Johns Hopkins Press, 1965) which, despite the title, deals with politics as well as the economic aspects of growing urban crises. Thompson's presentation is an excellent example of theorizing with ease about serious matters. A somewhat less exciting policy area, but an important one because some results can be readily measured, is that of water resource use. John V. Krutilla and Otto Eckstein provide a number of applications of economic analysis in *Multiple Purpose River Development* (Baltimore: Johns Hopkins Press, 1958). Chapter II on the concept of efficiency is also a clear exposition of basic economic analysis. Far less economic in orientation but no less rigorous is the imaginative analysis provided by Leslie T. Wilkins, *Social Deviance* (Englewood Cliffs, N.J.: Prentice-Hall, Inc., 1965). Wilkins does not so much address himself to finding public policy solutions to deviance problems as he does to providing research concepts, questions and measurements for enabling better policies to be enacted. We especially like his consideration of ethical questions as integral to the analytic task, as well as his challenging use of models. We are pleased to recommend this highly thoughtful, systematic and imaginative book to political science readers.

Eugene Register-Guard, Nov. 20, 1968, Eugene, Oregon

Peace Worker Says
Earth Comes First

U.S. Court Upholds
Freedom of Choice
In South's Schools

The New York Times, Nov. 15, 1968,
New York, New York

The Oregonian, Aug. 29, 1968, Portland, Oregon

THIRD PARTIES: Filling the
Newsweek, Oct. 21, 1968, Washington, D.C.

Threat Seen To Freedo

Communism's Failure

leated Arguments

The Oregonian, Sept. 23, 1968, Portland, Oregon

PRAGUE SPEEDING
A FEDERAL SYSTEM

What It Cos

The Oregonian,
Sept. 23, 1968,
Portland, Oregon

The New York Times, May 17, 1968, New York, New York

OSCOW ASSESSING
CONOMIC REFORM

Calm, Watchful Optimism

Day Parley Finds It Falls
Short of Expectations

The New York Times, May 19, 1968, New York, New York

The Oregonian, Sept. 23, 1968, Portland, Oregon

Paranoid Uphea
Newsweek,
Oct. 21, 1968,
Washington, D.C.

The Gallup Poll

olons Pledge Restraint

The Oregonian, Sept. 23, 1968, Portland, Oregon

29 Million Unregister

Eugene Register-Guard, Oct. 10, 1967, Eugene, Oregon

Committee Sifts Ways
To Present Tax Choices

To Cast Vote In Elect

The Oregonian, Aug. 29, 1968, Portland, Oregon

ame Without Rules
The Oregonian,
Sept. 11, 1968,
Portland, Oregon

It is a bad policy to go
and plead with people when
you have no cards in your
hands, no carrot and no
stick," Kennan said in an interview.
The Oregonian, Sept. 23, 1968, Portland, Oregon

The Oregonian, Sept. 23, 1968, Portland, Oregon

Model Law

Expensive Olive Bran

The New York Times, July 31, 1967, New York, New York

Chapter 14

Improving Conditions for
Political Choice

Political scientists ought, like Aristotle, to specify conditions and policies for the optimal operation and maintenance of any type of political process or system. Nevertheless, we favor systems in which competition, bargaining and cooperation are explicit, valued and practiced. In spite of some shortcomings elaborated in Chapter 11, we still prefer the wider use of these processes in the polity. Because of our preferences for broader political choice in democracies, we shall concentrate upon facilitating conditions and optimal policies for the maintenance and encouragement of political competition and bargaining. We suspect it is not simply the absence of certain conditions that promotes bargaining and competition but the positive presence of certain other conditions. In any case, we hope to preserve and improve the workings of competitive-bargaining polities. It order to prescribe wisely it will first be necessary to distinguish those conditions which facilitate democracy from those which do not. At the end of the chapter we prescribe public policies to encourage and protect democracy.

Favorable Conditions

Plato and Aristotle both made profound inquiries into the factors which encourage and discourage different types of polities. This type of political inquiry has intrigued later political theorists; only in recent times, however, has there been extensive political research devoted to the question. At present, social scientists are actively concerned with such matters and with political development more generally, but our knowledge of such matters is still most sketchy and undependable. We have many more hypotheses than confirmed generalizations. It does seem apparent that the conditions which support the establishment and maintenance of competi- tive-bargaining systems must be highly restrictive because there are rela- tively few democracies in the world and the casualty rate has been high. If we really knew these conditions and how to achieve them we would be able to list them in simple tabular form as prerequisites, but the democ- racies, while having much in common, also have distinctive differences and, worse, have far too many non-democratic characteristics.

Our problem, while clear-cut, does not lend itself to neat, precise answers. And, as to be expected, a number of theories have been advanced. In order to illustrate the variety of approaches, we have included a brief summary of factors (Table 14-1) deemed favorable by a number of more or less well-known social scientists during recent years. Instead of discussing these particular theories or list of conditions, we begin with an analysis of

---

Table 14-1

Hypothetical Prerequisites of Democracy

1. Institutionalized Rules
2. Shifting Allegiances
3. Limited Polarization or Conflict
4. Mechanisms of Adjustment
5. Group Memberships
6. Agreement on Basic Issues
7. Social Pluralism
8. High Degree of Psychological Security
9. Limited Disparities of Wealth and Income
10. Considerable Autonomy Among Organizations
11. Open Class Systems
12. Equalitarian Values
13. Industrialization
14. Christianity
15. Respect for Tradition and Authority
16. Willingness to Compromise
17. Religious Tolerance
18. Sympathy for Others
19. Empathy
20. High Levels of Education
21. Individualism
22. Respect for Independence

---

five general types of conditions: (1) social structure, (2) economic factors, (3) culture, (4) personality and, finally, (5) political conditions.

Social Structure

Mass Society

Our information on the most appropriate social structures to sustain democracies is rather weak but we present it, such as it is, for consideration. By social structure is meant the general organization of a society, the patterned relationships and interactions of men. Perhaps the best known attempt to explain the influence of these elements is that of William Kornhauser in his well-known study *The Politics of Mass Society*.[1] His book does not explicitly consider political competition and bargaining but they are implicit and, therefore, useful for our purposes. According to Kornhauser the 'pluralist' or democratic system is best maintained when the following conditions are present:[2]

1. Numerous, strong primary groups, meaning families and local social organizations
2. Numerous, strong intermediary groups, meaning interest organizations with
   (a) overlapping memberships
   (b) diverse interests
   (c) non-inclusive concerns
3. An open-class system

Kornhauser discusses these and several non-social structure factors in detail. We will consider the others later. For the moment the claim is that if the above conditions are present, 'mass society'[3] is avoided and these consequences will follow: Citizens will, under these conditions, have a strong sense of political efficacy and involvement, regard politics as meaningful, and feel secure enough in a political sense to participate. As a further result of these secure feelings the citizens will develop and maintain loyalty to democratic practices, i.e., be willing to engage in peaceful competition and bargaining. It is also claimed that such a social structure will reduce conflict to such dimensions (frequency, scope, intensity) that these attitudes and behaviors can indeed be maintained and practiced. If the opposite type

---

[1] (Glencoe, Ill.: The Free Press of Glencoe, 1959).

[2] Kornhauser actually devotes more time to a consideration of 'unfavorable' conditions which is why, presumably, the book is entitled *The Politics of Mass Society* rather than the politics of democracy.

[3] 'Mass society' is described as a condition in which non-elites, or ordinary citizens, are easily available for mobilization by the elites and the latter are readily accessible to the non-elites.

of social structure prevails, different attitudes and behavior are predicted which will lead either to mass society or totalitarianism. In short, if the following conditions hold, democracy will have a difficult time:

1. Disruption of primary and local associations
2. Prevalence of large-scale bureaucratic organizations
3. High degree of oligarchical control over organizations
4. Rapid mobility rates
5. Centralization of political life

From these conditions flow a series of predicted consequences leading to alienation from political institutions, willingness to violate rules of the game, violence, extremism, dogmatism in debate, and unwillingness to engage in bargaining practices. Men, under conditions of normlessness, powerlessness, apathy, insecurity and alienation seek a charismatic leader and abandon democratic forms for a mass movement. The dissolution of established institutions is a bad omen according to Kornhauser and others who see some continuity with the past as essential to the preservation of democracy.

Although the above 'theory' has been developed or affirmed by several prestigous social theorists, including Robert Nisbet, Philip Selznick, Edward Shils, Erich Fromm, Hannah Arendt, S. M. Lipset[4] and others, and while it is most assuredly highly plausible, it has not been rigorously tested against the realities of the 120 or more nation-states. Part of the problem is that many of the variables are not easily measured and tested with comparable data from many nations and times. Furthermore, an equally plausible case can be made to show that the conditions which are supposed to lead to non-democratic behavior may indeed lead in the opposite direction and sustain democracy.[5] Until better tests are available, we cannot rest assured about relationships between mass society and democracy.

Class Structure

Many commentators, from Aristotle to Kornhauser, have claimed that a more or less open class structure is a prerequisite of democracy. Intuitively the claim seems justified except that 'more or less' open includes

---

[4] Cf. Robert A. Nisbet, *The Quest for Community* (New York: Oxford University Press, 1953); Philip Selznick, "Institutional Vulnerability in Mass Society," *The American Journal of Sociology,* LVI (January, 1951), pp. 320-331; Erich Fromm, *Escape From Freedom* (New York: Farrar and Rinehart, Inc., 1941); Hannah Arendt, *The Origins of Totalitarianism* (New York: Harcourt, Brace and Company, 1951); Seymour Martin Lipset, *Political Man* (Garden City, N.Y.: Doubleday and Company, Inc., 1960).

[5] Joseph R. Gusfield, "Mass Society and Extremist Politics," *American Sociological Review,* 27 (February, 1962), pp. 19-30.

a considerable range of class mobility. India still has a caste-like system even though caste has been formally outlawed; Britain and the continental democracies all have class structures with histories of far greater rigidity than is found in the United States, yet all are now democracies. We simply do not know the acceptable ranges of openness, i.e., mobility among the classes for various types of polities. We know that class stratification has everywhere existed, but we know also that democracies have not taken root in most of the caste based societies.

Most theorists claim that democracies can function with marked social stratification, providing the citizens have some expectation of upward mobility. Also, social distance should be so minimized that belonging to a lower class, in social terms, does not prevent the interests, values and beliefs of that person or group from being effectively considered in the political system. Thus, European democracies operate within highly stratified societies but the lower classes have effective representation within the political life of their respective nations. So class stratification does not prohibit democracy from either emerging or operating fairly effectively.

Many theorists have emphasized still another aspect of class structure, namely, the benefits of a strong and large middle-class. Aristotle was merely the first to advocate the political virtues of the middle-class. Historically, the middle-class can claim credit for assisting mightily in the creation and development of European and other western democracies. As the middle-class rose with and supported capitalism so they worked for political change in making demands for greater participation and more effective representation. They furthered both capitalism and democracy out of self-interest. The record of the middle-classes in the twentieth century has been tarnished somewhat by their greater willingness, under some conditions at least, to support anti-democratic right-wing movements. This was particularly true during the 1920s and 1930s in Germany where extreme social disorganization abetted middle-class abandonment of democratic institutions.

While the fascist movements were in their heyday, many theorists questioned the middle-class commitment to democracy; today, however, we find social theorists rediscovering the middle-class virtues and condemning certain working class anti-democratic 'traits.' The working class, it is said, is particularly vulnerable, given its class position, to anti-democratic appeals and behavior. The interesting thing about these varying observations on the commitments of the several classes to democracy is the fact that each focuses upon some regrettable tendencies and makes them the only logical ones. We think that each class has reasons for being attached and opposed to any given political system; the point is that every polity bestows differential rewards and burdens upon different classes. In some societies the middle-class may do very well, and it should therefore be loyal to whatever system exists; the same may be said of the other classes. For predictive purposes it is necessary for us to know the relative successes of each class in each type of system. Sometimes members of even the more favored classes will become discontent; they may and have become revolutionists.

Perhaps we can clarify the arguments about the anti-democratic tendencies of the two classes—the middle and working-classes—in terms of what has been described as aggravating social situations and some likely perceptual and political responses. Something of a school of thought emerged during the 1950s which attempted to explain the more apparent 'anti-democratic' tendencies of the various classes in terms of sociological and psychological theories. Figures 14-1 and 14-2 attempt to summarize these theories.[6] Figure 14-1 summarizes these for the working-class, while Figure 14-2 does the same for the middle-class. Please note some limitations: the figures do not specify how many members of these classes will experience such situations in the same way nor do they tell us about the opportunities for revolting against democracy. Figures 14-1 and 14-2 merely show diagrams of possible relationships of social structure, culture, individual perceptions and political responses.

The other side of the picture—the possible commitments of the various classes to democratic institutions—is one of the more fascinating yet neglected aspects of political sociology.[7] Thus far we seem to have learned more about why the classes misbehaved as they did during the troublesome events of the past than we have been able to predict about future behaviors. In any case, no class has a monopoly on political virtue so far as the support of democracy is concerned. In the most stable democracies, all classes may lend support and services of one kind or another. In the less stable democracies, anti-democrats are plentiful in all classes. They usually are against democracy for somewhat different reasons but they are 'united' in opposition to a system which they believe does not work effectively for their concerns. So much for social classes.

Group Memberships and Political Consequences

A favorite hypothesis, particularly among political sociologists, concerns the group and organizational structure of a society as a precondition of democratic forms. As we have seen, Kornhauser and the 'group' and

---

[6] In addition to the citations in footnote 4, one must add Daniel Bell, *The Radical Right* (Garden City, N.Y.: Doubleday and Company, Inc., 1963); Robert E. Lane, *Political Ideology* (New York: The Free Press of Glencoe, 1962); Edward A. Shils, *The Torment of Secrecy* (Glencoe, Ill.: The Free Press, 1955); Samuel Stouffer, *Communism, Conformity and Civil Liberties* (New York: Doubleday and Company, Inc., 1955).

[7] However, see the sensitive analysis by Morton Grodzins, *The Loyal and the Disloyal* (Chicago: The University of Chicago Press, 1956); Harry Eckstein, *Division and Cohesion in Democracy* (Princeton: Princeton University Press, 1966); and, Eric A. Nordlinger, *The Working Class Tories* (Berkeley: University of California Press, 1967).

Figure 14-1

Working Class 'Anti-Democratic' Politics

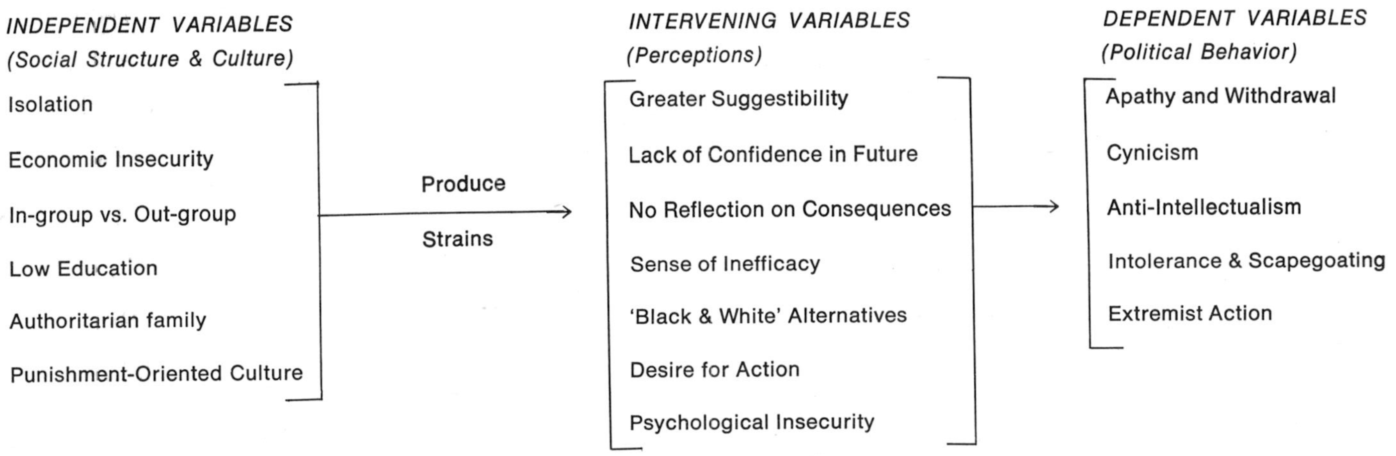

INDEPENDENT VARIABLES
(Social Structure & Culture)

Isolation

Economic Insecurity

In-group vs. Out-group

Low Education

Authoritarian family

Punishment-Oriented Culture

Produce

Strains

INTERVENING VARIABLES
(Perceptions)

Greater Suggestibility

Lack of Confidence in Future

No Reflection on Consequences

Sense of Inefficacy

'Black & White' Alternatives

Desire for Action

Psychological Insecurity

DEPENDENT VARIABLES
(Political Behavior)

Apathy and Withdrawal

Cynicism

Anti-Intellectualism

Intolerance & Scapegoating

Extremist Action

Figure 14-2
Middle-Class 'Anti-Democratic' Politics

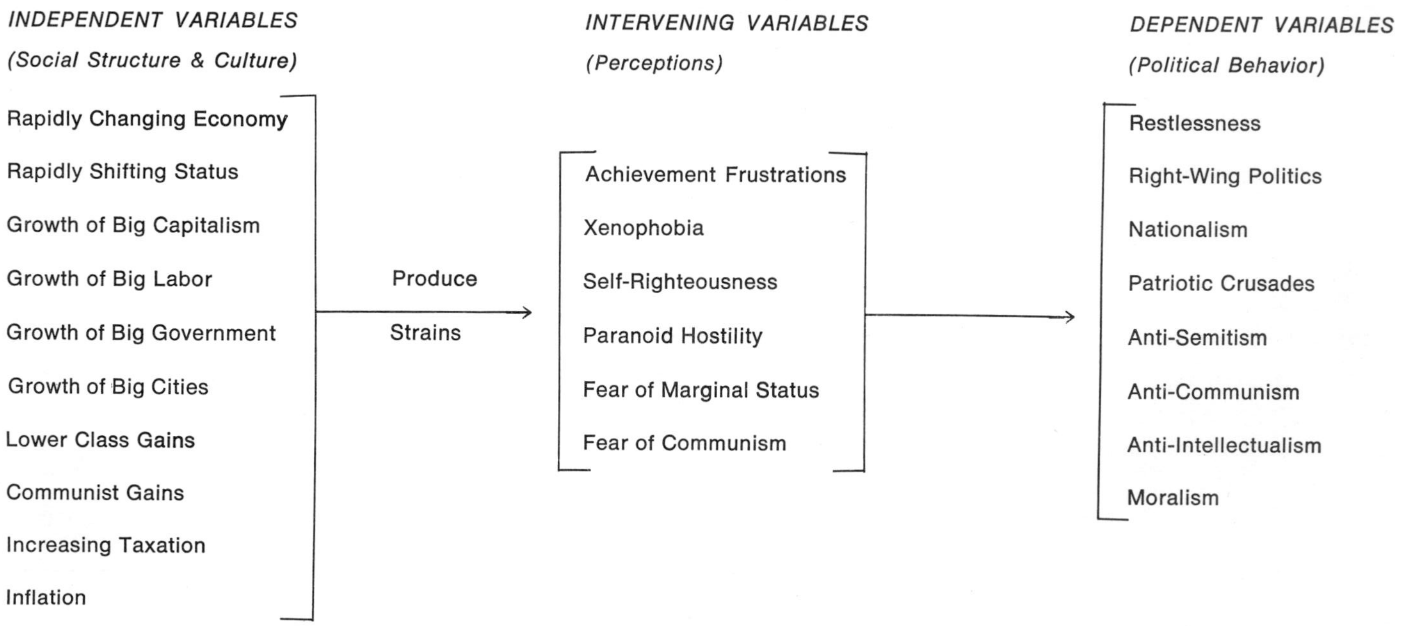

INDEPENDENT VARIABLES
(Social Structure & Culture)

Rapidly Changing Economy

Rapidly Shifting Status

Growth of Big Capitalism

Growth of Big Labor

Growth of Big Government

Growth of Big Cities

Lower Class Gains

Communist Gains

Increasing Taxation

Inflation

Produce

Strains

INTERVENING VARIABLES
(Perceptions)

Achievement Frustrations

Xenophobia

Self-Righteousness

Paranoid Hostility

Fear of Marginal Status

Fear of Communism

DEPENDENT VARIABLES
(Political Behavior)

Restlessness

Right-Wing Politics

Nationalism

Patriotic Crusades

Anti-Semitism

Anti-Communism

Anti-Intellectualism

Moralism

'pluralistic' theorists of political science[8] maintain that the group structure of society must be pervasive, i.e., that many citizens belong to and actively participate in groups and organizations. Extensive group membership, it is claimed, has beneficial consequences for democracy. The basic idea is that such groups give meaning to life in terms of identities and shared values, and serve as buffers between the 'lonely' citizen and the powerful government. Groups are resources of the citizen for effective participation and influence in society and politics. Furthermore, it is believed that 'multiple memberships' (members belonging to two or more groups) on the part of significant proportions of the population tends to reduce the conflict of one group with another, thus facilitating the achievement of bargains and compromises in the polity. The assumption is that too many demands, too often pressed, and with too great intensities by antagonistic groups strains the polity in achieving decisions. If most citizens belong to more than one group, it is assumed, they will constrain each group's demands in the light of their other competing interests and loyalties; and lowered conflict levels are believed to be essential in promoting political effectiveness.

This ingenious set of propositions and beliefs has much logical merit. Unhappily, it does not have much evidence to support it, one way or the other.[9] This is not to say the evidence supports another and contradictory theory, but only that we have little evidence on any aspect of the theory. We know that many people in a democracy do not belong to formal associations. It is not clear, therefore, how many must participate or whether they need to belong to formal organizations as distinct from informal groups or communal institutions. We know that most formal organizations are not democratic in their internal political affairs, whether they be unions, business organizations, professional associations or even most voluntary and civic groups. Most of them confirm Michels' iron law of oligarchy, i.e., run by a small leadership group with a paid bureaucracy. Furthermore, the affiliational ties of membership are quite loose for many of these associations—low levels of participation are the rule, which explains the 'distance' of elites and the discretion they have.[10] We do not know exactly how overlapping memberships reduce conflicting demands on the polity. In fact, membership studies seem to suggest that those who

---

[8] David Truman, *The Governmental Process* (New York: Alfred A. Knopf, Inc., 1951) and Robert A. Dahl, *Pluralist Democracy in the United States* (Chicago: Rand McNally and Company, 1967) are two notable representatives of these views.

[9] For a review of the evidence and the literature see Arend Lijphart, *The Politics of Accommodation: Pluralism and Democracy in the Netherlands* (Berkeley: University of California Press, 1968), Chap. I.

[10] Truman, *op. cit.*, Part II; Henry S. Kariel, *The Decline of American Pluralism* (Stanford: Stanford University Press, 1961); Grant McConnell, *Private Power and American Democracy* (New York: Alfred A. Knopf, Inc., 1966); and H. R. Mahood, *Pressure Groups In American Politics* (New York: Charles Scribner's Sons, 1967).

belong to more than one group or organization belong to those with similar if not identical interests and demands. Members and leaders are not
'cross-pressured' to moderate their demands; rather they are reinforced
in their views. If the typical memberships differ for each social class, more
class stratification is likely. Finally, we have been unable to devise good
tests of the theory on a cross-national basis. There is little doubt that some
of what the theory claims may be true and that, if true, the consequences for
politics will be as stated in the theory. But which parts are correct?

A part of the theory which has much logical appeal is that dealing
with cases of polarized societies which have few mediating political organizations. A society which has few political organizations but persistent
and mutually exclusive alignments appears to increase the likelihood of
strained, conflict-oriented policy-making. Consider the following models
of group alliances or coalitions on three issues.

STABLE COALITION MODEL

Issue	Pro	Con
A	a,b,c	d,e,f
B	a,b,c	d,e,f
C	a,b,c	d,e,f

In the polarized non-overlapping or mutually exclusive group situation
we have the same coalition alignment on all three issues, or whatever other
number of issues may arise. In such a situation each side automatically
knows its opponents and allies. A presumed consequence is that conflict
becomes rigidified and each side becomes increasingly less willing to make
compromises because each issue only reinforces the alliances. The antagonisms of one issue are carried over into subsequent issues that have little
to do with the previous problems. No doubt compromises would be difficult
to achieve under these conditions, but they are somewhat unusual conditions. More likely is the situation, or model thereof, in which groups,
whether they have overlapping memberships or not, form different coalitions on different issues. In such situations one cannot always accurately
predict the composition of coalitions from one issue to the next. Presumably a person must moderate his attacks on today's opponent because tomorrow it may be necessary to work with him.

UNSTABLE COALITION MODEL

Issue	Pro	Con
A	a,b,c	d,e,f
B	a,d,e	b,c,f
C	f,a,b	c,d,e

Reality is reflected in these models insofar as they apply to face-to-face relationships among individuals in daily life, but they are somewhat less persuasive in highly organized national life. Politicians are formal representatives and therefore respond to formalized norms. When an individual plays formal adversary roles he does not have to worry as much about maintaining personal friendships, since the two roles (friend and formal representative) are seldom confused by professional politicians. But more importantly, these two contrasting models could not describe very many, if any, democracies. In other words, we would assert that coalitions are neither permanent nor completely unstable and unpredictable from one issue to the next. Instead, the stability of various coalitions falls somewhere in between. Some coalitions are highly stable while others are less so and a few are purely transitory, coming into existence for a very special issue of short duration.

We would also question whether completely fluctuating coalitions are always a preferable state of affairs. It would seem to reflect a rather unusual condition of society, one in which there are few enduring interests and preferences to align identifiable groups over more than one issue. Like all other change, such unstable coalitions would have their own costs, the costs of establishing new coalitions over every issue. We should think that the politicians would be hard put to keep their score cards, work out agreements and maintain communications among such changing coalitions. The substance of issues might well be lost in the shuffle as the logistics of coalition building assume their place.[11]

We must remain quite tentative about claims concerning the social or structural conditions of democracy. Great variations of structure among the democracies should be a warning that the relationships are not clear; likewise, frequent similarities with non-democratic nations should be a warning. Yet the question is important and most are unwilling to drop these theories; they have no recourse but to persist in finding more effective empirical tests.

Cultural Conditions

Some theorists on democracy have focused on the necessity of having certain 'cultural' conditions, i.e., certain beliefs and values which are con-

---

[11] A fascinating account of a rather persistent case of incessant negotiation, in the worst sense, is contained in Nathan Leites, *On the Game of Politics in France* (Stanford: Stanford University Press, 1959). A more general treatment of what the French call "immo bilisme" resulting from intense conflicts and attempts at coalition building in partisan politics is described by Herbert Luethy in *France Against Herself* (New York: Meridian Books, 1957).

sidered more appropriate or consistent with democracy than with other systems. For example, some have maintained that religious beliefs, especially Christian doctrines, are vital to sustain democratic institutions and behavior.[12] Others have argued that various civic beliefs, concerning equality, liberty, individualism, respect for privacy, belief in man-made law, tolerance, etc., have been most conducive to democratic behavior.[13] Most of this is philosophic speculation posed in theoretic terms. The theorists explore the logical compatibility of these beliefs with 'democratic' forms of behavior as they conceptualize them. But do they occur as logically projected? The empirical question must be answered, too. Even 'illogical' relationships in society may be found to perform quite logical functions. In any case, the theorists do not tell us whether these ideas and ideals are, in fact, found to prevail among the democracies and not to prevail elsewhere. Nor do they inform us about how many people must accept which beliefs, in what order, with what intensities. We have found that there are as many Christian non-democracies as there are democracies and that the Christian democracies range from the stable to the rather unstable. (Check again Table 7-9 on political instability.)

Perhaps the most empirically relevant study yet made on beliefs as related to democracy is that of James W. Prothro and Charles M. Grigg.[14] They confined their study to two cities in the United States (a major shortcoming for our problem) but were able to point up some rather interesting conclusions that probably make sense elsewhere. We will not summarize the detailed survey data but confine ourselves to the major findings. Generally, in the light of their evidence they contend that it is impossible to maintain that consensus on fundamental principles of democracy (as they defined them) is required for the existence of democracy. They did find widespread agreement on the desirability of such highly abstract principles as democracy, majority rule and minority rights when stated only in generalized terms. The principles as stated in general terms were as follows:

Principle of Democracy Itself

Democracy is the best form of government.

---

[12] For a Protestant view see Reinhold Niebuhr, *The Children of Light and the Children of Darkness* (New York: Charles Scribner's Sons, 1945); for a Catholic perspective, Jacques Maritain, *Christianity and Democracy* (New York: Charles Scribner's Sons, 1945).

[13] Cf. Ernest Barker, *Reflections on Government* (New York: Oxford University Press, 1958), Parts I-III; Giovanni Sartori, *Democratic Theory* (New York: Frederick A. Praeger, Inc., 1965); Arne Naess, *Democracy, Ideology and Objectivity* (Oslo, Norway: Oslo University Press, 1956).

[14] "Fundamental Principles of Democracy: Bases of Agreement and Disagreement," *The Journal of Politics,* 22 (May, 1960), pp. 276-294, and reprinted in Nelson W. Polsby, Robert A. Dentler and Paul A. Smith, eds., *Politics and Social Life* (Boston: Houghton Mifflin Company, 1963), pp. 437-446.

Principle of Majority Rule

> Public officials should be chosen by majority vote.
>
> Every citizen should have an equal chance to influence govern-
> ment policy.

Principle of Minority Rights

> The minority should be free to criticize majority decisions.
>
> People in the minority should be free to try to win majority
> support for their opinions.[15]

But when these highly abstract principles were translated into specific
terms, or particular issues close to home, the consensus disappeared. The
specific applications to which the respondents were asked to agree or disagree were as follows (the authors mixed the appropriate 'yes' and 'no'
answers to avoid what is called 'response set' biases):

Principle of Majority Rule in Specific Terms

1. In a city referendum, only people who are well informed about
   the problem being voted upon should be allowed to vote.
2. In a city referendum deciding on tax-supported undertakings,
   only tax-payers should be allowed to vote.
3. If a Negro were legally elected mayor of this city, the white
   people should not allow him to take office.
4. If a Communist were legally elected mayor of this city, the people
   should not allow him to take office.
5. A professional organization like the AMA (the American Medical
   Association) has a right to try to increase the influence of doctors
   by getting them to vote as a bloc in elections.

Principle of Minority Rights in Specific Terms

6. If a person wanted to make a speech in this city against churches
   and religion, he should be allowed to speak.
7. If a person wanted to make a speech in this city favoring government ownership of all the railroads and big industries, he should
   be allowed to speak.
8. If an admitted Communist wanted to make a speech in this city
   favoring Communism, he should be allowed to speak.
9. A Negro should not be allowed to run for mayor of this city.
10. A Communist should not be allowed to run for mayor of this
    city.[16]

---

[15] *Ibid.,* pp. 440-441.

[16] *Ibid.,* p. 441.

Many respondents gave 'non-democratic,' i.e., 'non-logical' responses. Are we to contend, therefore, that democracy does not exist in these communities? Or do democratic practices depend more on the institutionalization of norms rather than the daily opinions of citizenry? Could better research be devised, i.e., better hypotheses or survey questions, to clarify the problem? We leave further reflection on this to the reader.

In any case, studies of cultural factors have tended to be speculative, without much evidence about reality. It has often been said that ordinary men are not up to the great ideals of the theoretical democratic man. We would assert, instead, that democracy, however imperfect, exists and works in various places in the world. But can it work with men who have less than ideal beliefs? We contend that it works with men as they are because effective democracy is based not only on the hoped-for 'virtues' of men but on their 'vices' as well. We question the idea that only specified characteristics of human nature can be related culturally to democracy. Democracies have now taken root in cultures (India and Japan, for example) that are in sharp contrast to those in which western democracies originated. And some western cultures have either failed to produce democracies or have produced only highly unstable ones. The last word has yet to be written on the cultural conditions of democracies and other systems.

Meanwhile, perhaps the best that can be proposed at this time is a much looser relationship between belief and practice, namely: (1) the greater the logical consistency of a culture and its political life, the greater the chances of reinforcing the practices of the system; (2) the greater the commitments of leaders to the belief and value systems of the polity, the better the chances for its maintenance; and (3) the beliefs of ordinary citizens need *not* be highly consistent or articulate to preserve any form of government. In fact, it may be that vague commitments or generalized feelings can be as facilitative of democracy as the opposite case.

Personality Factors

There is another well-known school of thought which asserts that personality properties make a difference in the establishment, performance and maintenance of a democratic political system. Accordingly, a good deal of research and more speculation has been done during recent decades on the political effects of certain personality factors.[17] These psychologically

---

[17] The literature of political psychology is far too voluminous to cite in a single footnote. However, a good beginning for the interested reader can be attained by looking into Robert E. Lane, *Political Life* (Glencoe: The Free Press, 1959); and James C. Davies, *Human Nature in Politics* (New York: John Wiley and Sons, Inc., 1963). Both books have extensive citations to the field.

oriented scholars tend to believe that both 'democratic' and 'non-democratic' personalities can be identified and that their presence in 'sufficient' numbers or in the right roles will make democracy feasible or impossible. The lists of such characteristics are many, sometimes vague and sometimes contradictory, perhaps because the authors themselves disagree about what democracy requires in the way of personalities. Some relate certain character traits to democratic ideals; others posit that, given their definition of democratic processes, there are certain personality requisites for performing effectively in them. The research may describe the personality traits of different groups, or report individual cases of depth analysis or small group experiments, rather than relate the personalities to actual political behaviors in large-scale polities. But what are some of these democratic and non-democratic characteristics?

We will list three representative sets of psychological attributes: the first two (listed in Table 14-2) catalogue alleged undemocratic tendencies; the third (Table 14-3) presents what are considered more favorable personality characteristics. The reader will note it is quite a bit shorter.

The psychological terms in Table 14-2 allude to certain attitudes, ori-

---

Table 14-2

'Undemocratic' Personality Attributes

"The Pathologies of Democratic Personality"	*"The Authoritarian Personality"*
Loss of Identity	Conventional
Self-Alienation	Submissive
Anxiety	Aggressive
Lack of Self-Control	Tough-Minded
Irrationality	Rigid
Anti-Intraceptiveness	Stereotyped
Misanthropy	Power-Oriented
Constricted Empathy	Destructive
Closed Ego	Cynical
'We' and 'They'	Projectional
Conformity	Paranoid
Social Alienation	
Anomie	
Cynicism	
Constricted Uni-Value System	
Traditionalism	
"The World is a Jungle"	

Sources: Robert E. Lane, "The Pathologies of Democratic Personality," *Political Ideology* (Glencoe, Ill.: Free Press, 1962), pp. 400-412; and T. W. Adorno *et al., The Authoritarian Personality* (New York: Harper and Brothers, 1950).

entations and/or behaviors which are regarded by the authors cited as inimical to democracy. It is hard to believe that all men do not experience one or more of them to some degree; even the authors cited do not claim that men are *either* possessed by *or* entirely free of them. The important point must be the degree—and, we would add, whether the social and political institutions encourage or discourage such manifestations. Even more important is comparative confirmation: Is there evidence about the incidence of these apparently bad traits among the populations of the world? If it were possible to measure the distribution of character traits among nations, would we discover that the democracies had less of each than the non-democracies? We do not know, but clearly these psychological theories assert that we would. Furthermore, could it not be that democracies, given the complexity of bargaining and competitive processes, may have a variety of role requirements, so that a more diversified set of character traits is just as appropriate? Psychological studies of many famous leaders in democracies indicate a number of these character traits which the psychologists despair of; these leaders were not all 'normal' by any account. Some had rather severe symptoms of some of the above 'pathologies.'

These first two lists consist solely of the 'bad' traits; they do not specify, except by inference, the needed or desirable traits. Harold Lasswell, a pioneer in political psychology, has done so. Consider his list of democratic traits as found in Table 14-3.

Table 14-3

'Democratic Personality'

Believes in the Worth of the Self
Believes in the Dignity of Others
Questions Authority
Willing to Compromise
Has Multi-values or Goals
Warm and Generous

Source: Harold D. Lasswell, *The Political Writings of Harold D. Lasswell* (Glencoe, Ill.: The Free Press, 1951), pp. 465-525.

Lasswell's list reads like a prescription for small group meetings and face-to-face situations. But there may be some doubt whether these traits would suffice for performance in large-scale democracies where vast numbers of people must have political roles and relationships defined by formal structures rather than through informal and pleasant interactions. Unhappily, neither Lasswell nor Lane inform us on the necessary proportions of democratic and non-democratic personality types throughout a system. How many 'democrats' do we require to function democratically? In which roles? Or, how many pathological types can a democracy tolerate? In which roles? Until we acquire evidence to answer these questions we must remain skeptical about personality requirements. They have a curious ring to them—the virtues of a small, harmonious group transferred to the great nation-state. We think political competition and bargaining are hard-headed activities that may well require some of the opposite traits. Certainly both processes engender some anxiety, constrict empathy and encourage 'we and they' attitudes and even cynicism—and we believe these may be quite realistic in those situations. Certainly both competition and bargaining engender some forms of selfishness, aggressiveness, tough-mindedness and power orientation. Competitors and bargainers who are too warm and generous or too willing to compromise may actually lose out in some strategic situations. While we, too, appreciate some of the attitudes prescribed, we find them more facilitated by certain political processes than the other way around. It just seems too difficult to explain the workings of a political system by personality features alone. The question is, how would a democratic polity function with the following ratios of 'democratic' and 'authoritarian' personality types?

PERSONALITY TYPES

System	'Democratic'	'Authoritarian'
A	90%	10%
B	75%	25%
C	50%	50%
D	25%	75%
E	10%	90%

Clearly we cannot predict processes or policy outcomes from knowing personality types, alone. What can one deduce from this table as it stands? A great deal more in the way of information is required. What kinds of information are needed?

While the relationship between personality and system performance is very tenuous, we do not wish to suggest that knowledge of personalities is irrelevant to many aspects of political life, particularly at the individual level. Much of what we know about individual political activity in the democracies can be understood better by psychological investigations (just as some of what we know about the behavior of dictators must be credited to the psychologists). For example, the motivations for political involvement, for voter choice, and for the perceptual features of decision-making are important subjects of psychological study. But the connection between the functioning of entire systems or policy outcomes and certain psychological traits of individuals is not always convincing; and, fortunately, it is not supported by all psychologists. Many share our view that the psychological factors of political behavior and choice must be related to situational factors in political systems. A great deal of political phenomena can be accounted for in other terms without reference to psychological categories or data, as you may have noted in some of the earlier chapters. Note we said a great deal—not all.

Economic Factors

Superficially, at least, the significance of economic factors seems more readily visible and capable of being tested than is the case with culture, personality and social structure. But, the situation may be deceptive; the fact that many economic factors can be quantified more easily than cultural factors leads to the deception. In general, the concern has been with these sorts of conditions for democratic processes: (1) the type of economy considered most compatible with democracy; (2) the standard of living; (3) the distribution of income and wealth; (4) the rate of growth; and (5) the order of change, i.e., whether democracy and economic growth have occurred simultaneously or in some particular sequence.

Type of Economy

Advocates of capitalism have long argued that democracy cannot be maintained without a capitalist economy; socialism and communism, it is said, will lead to the abandonment of democracy for more autocratic control systems. While insufficient time has passed to determine whether the proposition is correct (it cannot be resolved on grounds of logical compatibility, alone), the evidence does not seem to support the advocates of capitalism. Of the major democracies of the present world, mostly in the West, all have significant amounts of nationalized industry and commerce, and some have almost entirely public-owned basic industries. (See Table 2-4 for some examples.) The United States is among the relatively few which still adhere primarily to capitalism. But who is to say that we do not have increasing public ownership, and who is to claim that the western European countries, with all their substantial mixtures of socialism, are not healthy democracies? While measurement of the degree to which economies are socialized and polities democratized is very difficult, one need not be an economist to realize that a considerable number of nations in Europe have highly socialized economies. Even the United States government controls, owns and administers vast resources of land, labor and capital (Cf. Table 2-4, above). Few commentators would take the position that most of those ten or so European countries are in any dire circumstances and about to collapse as democracies. Political competition and bargaining in many of those nations often seems more rigorous than in the United States.

Still, one must concede some of the long-term possibilities of socialism as predicted by such conservative luminaries as F. A. Hayek, Ludwig von Mises and a host of businessmen less versed in history and theory.[18] Centralized control of an economy can in fact lead to a restriction of human freedom, as we pointed out in Chapter 11. To control a complex economic system may well entail far more pervasive controls over far more people than liberals like to suppose. The problem, of course, is not one of control versus freedom (even a private enterprise system is a control system) but one of optimal types of control, as noted in Chapter 13. A highly monopolized private economy may be just as oppressive a threat to free choice as a government. However, to spell out all the logical possibilities and niceties concerning relationships between types of polities and economies is far beyond the confines of this text. Readers are encouraged to consult the original statements of the debate. We might remind them, however, that much of the previous concern and acrimony over the question has diminished as facts have qualified heretofore untested theories. Planners today are far less contemptuous of capitalist institutions, and businessmen seem less fearful of governmental planners and many types of controls. Socialist theory is being revamped to such an extent that it would not be recognizable to its founders. Actual practices in such nations as Britain and the Soviet Union are not in accord with much of their previous doctrine, nor are contemporary business practices always consistent with conventional economic theory.

Distribution of Income and Standard of Living

One facet of economic conditions has been explored with far less emotive debate: the question of the standard of living as a favorable condition for the establishment and maintenance of democracy. Here we may actually discuss two aspects more or less together: the *level* of personal income and its *distribution*. While it is probably desirable to deal with these matters in purely quantitative terms, it may assist comprehension to be less precise for the present. In short, a major claim is that a high standard of living (as measured by average per capita income) and a wide distribution of personal income are most conducive to democracy. Conversely, low incomes and unequal distributions are serious inhibitors of democratic processes. Figure 14-3 relates the two factors, in preliminary fashion, for testing these propositions. If they are related, most democratic systems should appear in cell (a); the non-democratic should be found in

---

[18] F. A. Hayek, ed., *Collectivist Economic Planning* (London: G. Routledge and Sons, Ltd., 1935) contains the major criticisms of socialism, while the case against the undemocratic tendencies of socialism and communism is most forcefully stated in Hayek's *The Road to Serfdom* (Chicago: University of Chicago Press, 1944).

Figure 14-3
Distribution of Income

Concentration of Income

		Less Unequal	Highly Unequal
Standard of Living	High Per Capita Income	(a)	(b)
	Low Per Capita Income	(c)	(d)

the other cells, especially (d). We do have relevant data for this test in Chapter 2. Table 2-1 would suggest that democracies are most often found in those nations with high per capita income while those with low per capita income tend to have non-democratic polities. Less well known is the relationship between concentration of income and political systems because, as we noted in Chapter 3, income and wealth are everywhere unequally distributed. The more important problem is the degree of inequality. Some studies seem to support the notion that the western democracies do in fact have less unequally distributed incomes and wealth than other countries.[19] Apparently the worst possible set of circumstances is found in cell (d) in which a people find themselves with a low average income and highly unequal distribution. Unfortunately, this is the state of the greater number of nations. We cannot decide which of the two remaining cells is better since relevant evidence is not available. Presumably many communist nations should appear in cell (c); it would be interesting to have the information for checking this. What about cell (b)?

While the relationships between per capita income and democracy are strong, they are not perfect. Germany and Kuwait, for example, are major exceptions, both having high income levels but a poor record so far as democracy is concerned. Kuwait has the highest per capita income in the world, but it is a monarchy. On the other hand, Uruguay has had a per capita income of less than half of the European standard but has practiced democracy for several decades with considerable success. Nevertheless, the direction of the relationship is discernible if not pronounced; it

---

[19] Simon Kuznets, *Modern Economic Growth* (New Haven: Yale University Press, 1966), pp. 206-219; 405; 423-426.

is good to have an affluent nation if one wants a democracy. But it is not necessary to have it from the very beginning; democracies may be established, as in India and elsewhere, with very low per capita incomes and still make political gains.

Distribution of Wealth

While most research and theory have focussed upon income, some has also been directed to the relationship of wealth, or ownership of property, and political systems. The distribution of capital assets and, particularly, of land has been the subject of most interest. Before inspecting some tabular information, let us state the typical generalization. It is believed that democracy thrives most where there is a relatively broad distribution of wealth. Of some forty-seven nations studied in regard to land distribution, thirteen are stable democracies and have above median equality in land ownership, while only three are stable and yet have less than median equality in land distribution. If a nation does have democracy but less than median equality in land distribution it tends to be more unstable. The non-democratic systems are much more likely to have greater inequalities. The evidence is provided in Table 14-4, which categorizes the situation as of a few years ago. The generalization is made still stronger by bringing Table 14-4 up to date. Greece is no longer even an unstable democracy but is a dictatorship. Brazil and Argentina are, likewise, questionable members of the unstable democracy group. Were all present nations included in the analysis it would seem reasonable to assume that many more would be found in the lower-right hand cell. Unfortunately there is little research on other forms of wealth which can be related to political systems, so we do not know whether land is a representative case.

Economic Expectations of Well-Being

Still another aspect of economic conditions for democracy deserves exploration—that of changes in the economic well-being of a people. In general, social scientists are inclined to believe that subjective well-being is, indeed, a partial function of expectations about future economic security as well as about a person's current state. Those who expect their position to improve are more likely to support the institutions which make it possible than are those who do not expect improvement. Tied in with this matter of expectations, of course, is the actual realization of such gains; if expectations are high and realizations low or if there are sudden reversals, frustration is a more likely result. We noted this in Figure 7-5, which illustrated a theory of revolution emphasizing this aspect of disappointed expectations.

Table 14-4

Stable Democracies, Unstable Democracies and Dictatorships by Degree of Inequality in Land Distribution

Gini Index	Stable Democracies	Unstable Democracies	Dictatorships
Greater than Median Equality	Denmark Canada Switzerland India Philippines Sweden Belgium Ireland Netherlands Luxembourg Norway United States United Kingdom	Japan France Finland West Germany	Yugoslavia Poland Taiwan South Vietnam Libya Panama
Median Equality or Less	New Zealand Uruguay Australia	Austria Greece Italy Brazil Colombia Argentina Costa Rica Chile	Egypt Honduras Nicaragua Spain Cuba Dominican Rep. El Salvador Guatemala Ecuador Peru Iraq Venezuela Bolivia

Source: Bruce M. Russett, "Inequality and Instability: The Relation of Land Tenure to Politics," *World Politics,* Vol. XVI (April, 1964), p. 454.

While many social theorists have speculated on the consequences of changes in aspirations and achievements or realizations through time, relatively little is, in fact, known. The logic suggests that the best situation for democracy is one of more or less gradual but steady increases in well-being; a worse alternative would be a sudden downturn after expectations of improvement have been widely instilled and accepted as fact. Impressionistic evidence suggests that the western democracies have all provided their peoples with gradually improving economic welfare. At times the rates have been quite different, as figures on the growth in GNP and per capita income show, and on occasion the upward trends have been reversed or sharply reduced during several depressions, especially the very severe one of the early 1930s. Democracy took its greatest chances during those periods in the sense that the greater the severity and longevity of the depression, the more widespread was the acceptance of non-democratic parties and movements within each nation. Impatience with democratic processes does appear to increase as men grow hungry or face a disturbing economic future. A full stomach may not guarantee an appreciation of democracy but it does seem to help stabilize the system—in fact, any system. This may boil down to saying that prosperity is good for any type of polity. Perhaps those who have at least moderate means and a good chance of improvement are, as Aristotle suggested, more tolerant, less envious, and more willing to seek agreements with others. Why these economic factors should have the political consequences they do is only beginning to be explored. We are not really sure how income levels, distributions and economic growth relate to polities; no doubt we will discover that the connecting linkages are extremely complex. While there is a great body of political theory on these sorts of relationships, we are only now acquiring effective means to study them systematically.

Political Conditions

Social and economic conditions are not the only crucial factors affecting the survival power of democratic institutions. Too many sociologists, psychologists and economists have been inclined to find the conditions of democracy and its failures only in the subjects of their particular disciplines. We not only have our own professional interest in matters political but hope to demonstrate that some favorable conditions of democracy are best described as political and not simply as derivatives of some non-political states of affairs.

Types of Issues

Societies and the behavioral sciences are both confronted with a number of paradoxes that make interesting puzzles for the theorist but pose some unhappy dilemmas for the citizen and politician. One of these paradoxes is the fact that bargaining and competition seem to work best when there are not too many basic issues to compete and bargain over in the polity. The paradox may, however, become less paradoxical or vexing in its significance if we take into account some qualifications of social life.

Competition and bargaining processes do appear to produce more acceptable outcomes and remain legitimate under somewhat restrictive conditions. In this section we delineate these special conditions.

Perhaps the most important single condition relates to the kinds of issues developed in a society. Most analysts would agree that both competition and bargaining work best on policy issues which are not divisive at the level of *fundamental* social values and beliefs. As noted earlier, it is more difficult to handle such absolutely basic moral and ethical matters as religion, marriage and family, or one's survival and status in a system. If large proportions of the population are intensely divided over these basic orientations they will not find it easy to compromise peacefully, trade votes, reciprocate on policy preferences, or bargain over the rules of the game. In time they may succeed, but only as greater agreement and less intense feelings prevail. As we observed in Chapter 4 regarding symbolic goods, most of us find it very difficult to compromise on matters of fundamental principle concerning right and wrong. One does not wish to concede any of his commitments on such matters; that is why we are often well-advised by the popular maxim to avoid 'politics' and 'religion' when making social conversation. An inability to reconcile basic differences about these problems means conflict—and the more intense, the more likely that it will be violent. Peaceful political competition and bargaining are not up to the task of reconciling most fundamental issues.

Issues which involve something less than basic values, especially those which are recurrent, quantifiable and inconclusive, provide excellent issues for competitors and bargainers. Questions of 'more or less', 'now and later,' 'possibly next time' can be resolved through trades, compromises or partial wins and losses. Budgetary battles are often histrionic and exciting but they are always resolved; a budget is produced; resources are allocated and benefits distributed. The politician is at his best on these questions and issues. If they were the only kind of political issue, the bargainers would rule mankind. But great symbolic issues and fundamental dilemmas also find their way into politics. The politician engages in another kind of behavior on these issues.

Distributions and Intensities of Preferences

The type of issue confronting and dividing a people is not the only conditioning factor for effective competition and bargaining. We must also take note of the distribution of positions on the various sides of the issue, particularly along an intensity dimension. Even the profound basic-value issues can be resolved through bargaining under some distributions of opinion. And, conversely, non-basic issues concerning means may prove more or less tractable to bargaining under divergent distributions. Let us consider a few hypothetical distributions: Figure 14-4 portrays three divergent distributions of opinion as well as three divergent sets of intensities of views. Note that a person can only be 'for' or 'against' the policy proposal; the 'don't knows' are not included. As we have seen, the 'don't knows' may be numerous.

Figure 14-4

Hypothetical Distribution of Opinion

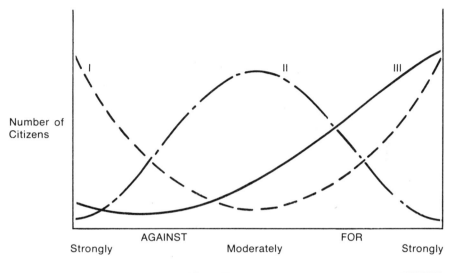

Based on Robert A. Dahl, *Preface to Democratic Theory* (Chicago: University of Chicago Press, 1956), pp. 90-102.

Curve I illustrates an extreme situation of division, one in which most members feel strongly about the issue and are more or less evenly divided on both sides, and few members are characterized by moderate views. Such a distribution reveals a conflict situation and poses severe strains on the political process. Whether bargaining can produce an acceptable compromise or trade is certainly doubtful. It may have been this type and slope of curve on crucial issues which produced the American Civil War. We leave it to you to draw in your own curves or estimates of the situation for recent years regarding civil rights. Draw some curves for different sections of the nation as well as a summary curve for the entire country. Check your estimates against public opinion data.[20] While the

---

[20] Some highly useful data as well as theoretical consideration of the problem of consensus in America is offered by Herbert McClosky, "Consensus and Ideology in American Politics," *American Political Science Review,* 58 (June, 1964), pp. 361-382, and reprinted in Aaron Wildavsky and Nelson W. Polsby, eds., *American Governmental Institutions* (Chicago: Rand McNally and Company, 1968), pp. 385-406.

division on this issue is hardly what it was in 1860, politicians have found it extremely taxing to forge even slight compromises. A considerable amount of violence has also played a part in achieving whatever benefits have resulted for the Negroes. Black Americans have understandably wearied of bargaining tactics, particularly at the local levels. Bargaining has its limitations here.

Curve II, the bell-shaped curve of normal distribution, shows few if any people at the extremes and most arrayed somewhere toward the center of the scale. Moderate views, pro and con, characterize the situation. It is the type of distribution that politicians in democracies can work with effectively. Give and take or trading are possible and desirable under such conditions, for citizens have but moderate commitments to their preferences. To win or lose a bit is regarded as a small price to pay for an acceptable outcome. We would believe that the more stable democracies have a greater number of these types of issues and distributions than they have of the very divisive sort. But we wish there were more extensive opportunity to explore this empirically.[21]

Curve III presents the politician and his followers, at least those aligned with the figure's hypothetical policy, with a rather favorable set of conditions: most citizens are in agreement and most feel strongly about the matter. This is a condition favorable to cooperative political activity. There can be little opposition and therefore very limited opportunity for competition over the issue; bargaining is hardly necessary except, perhaps, to appease the few strongly inclined dissidents. Many believe that the stable democracies encounter this distribution on many matters which once were disputed but are now settled policy and no longer need resolving. Social Security is no longer a divisive issue; over 90 per cent of Americans favor it. If any administration attempted to repeal the Social Security Act, we would probably discover that most of those 90 per cent would even more strongly support it. It would be interesting to see if the bulk of settled domestic policies are supported by some variant of Curve III.[22] Differences are more likely to occur over relatively minor matters of improvement of programs such as the scale of operations, size of benefits or costs, administrative detail, and so forth. Very likely support

---

[21] See Herbert McClosky, Paul J. Hoffman and Rosemary O'Hara, "Issue Conflict and Consensus Among Party Leaders and Followers," *American Political Science Review*, 54 (June, 1960), pp. 406-427, for some highly interesting data on 24 issues and the distributions of policy views among both party leaders and followers. Among other conclusions the authors contend that Republican and Democratic leaders are further apart than are their followers.

[22] For many sensible comments and much data on issues and consensus see V. O. Key, Jr., *Public Opinion and American Democracy* (New York: Alfred A. Knopf, 1961), especially Parts I, II, and III.

for most basic political institutions in the democracies would be characterized in terms of variations of this pattern of distribution. It is a bit difficult to imagine how a democratic system could function effectively without such widespread generalized legitimacy or support. But systematic study might reveal surprises; until they are made we simply speculate about these questions.

Differentiation of Issues

Bargaining and competition work best with variants of Curves II and III. While no society can permanently avoid deeply divisive issues of the Curve I type, we would further suggest, however, that democracies tend to handle most issues separately so that conflicts do not become cumulative and polarized. Insofar as they succeed, the peaceful resolution of conflict issues may be encouraged. Every democracy creates and handles countless issues, problems and crises in which bargaining and competition produce acceptable outcomes. Presumably this enhances both the skills and expectations about the system's capacity to handle the less frequent crises. At least citizens will be more likely to appreciate the formal institutions of decision. Given this stock of dependable residual support, men should be more willing to concede something in order to preserve that which has otherwise made life more comfortable and meaningful. Men seldom choose to withdraw their support from an otherwise rewarding system just because they lose on one issue.

It should also be pointed out in this connection that while we used one set of curves to characterize how many millions of people might align themselves on a single issue, we must conceive a much more complex and often ambiguous or shifting array of preferences in real political systems. There will seldom be a single issue in which all are interested, nor would any one person deal with all the issues that are occurring somewhere in the system. The readers, as concerned citizens, may find themselves located in a different position on the curves for each issue; some may be clear and firm preferences, while others are casual or tentative. As we grow older we may occupy different positions on a single issue and have different concerns and positions in life. People do change their minds and their intensities of commitment. As newer problems capture their concern, they find former positions reduced in importance, and they may become totally indifferent to some issues which were once considered important. We do not know what our views might be about countless other issues because they have so little relevance for us, but who knows as to the future? In short, few citizens have intense views, pro or con, about very many issues; most issues are of little concern to most men most of the time. The fact that this is so would seem to facilitate the decision-making of democracies and not threaten existing allocations of resources and distributions of benefits and burdens to any extensive degree.

We attempted to account for levels of interest and participation on the part of individual persons in Chapters 3 and 8, so further explanation seems unnecessary. But we might add that the citizen who feels intensely about a great variety of issues is a most unusual person. One interesting and instructive project for readers is to construct some models on how a democracy might function, and with what policy outcomes, given different distributions of highly intense citizens. We have started the project in this section but without much detail on individual behavior under each set of conditions.

Finally, let us reiterate that no single distribution of attitudes is unquestionably superior to any other, and that every democracy deals with all sorts of patterns of opinion for different matters. But there may be cumulative divisions which continue to separate the citizens into the same groups. If these are confronted frequently it can make the ordinary political processes of bargaining and competition difficult and highly tenuous.

Distribution of Taxes and Benefits

We have discussed the standard of living and the distribution of both income and wealth; now we consider some matters of the distribution of public benefits and the allocation of burdens. Once more we operate mostly in the dark. We may therefore mistake shadows for substance, as did Plato's characters in the famous Allegory of the Cave. Put in its starkest terms, the choices are but four: more or less widely distributed benefits accompanied by more or less widely distributed burdens, especially taxes. Figure 14-5 describes these four logical combinations.

Of these four possibilities we are inclined to believe that the most popular one in democracies combines widespread distribution of benefits with a narrowly allocated set of burdens (cell c), especially if the burdens can be levied on the high income group. The least popular combination appears to be the precise opposite: narrowly distributed benefits and widespread burdens (cell b), especially if the rich derive the benefits while the less well-off majority pays the bills. The other two cases are difficult to rank, but we suspect that a widely distributed set of benefits and costs would be more acceptable than narrowly distributed costs and benefits, especially if those who benefit are not those who pay. We rely on introspection and logic, not evidence, with respect to these judgments. We suspect that most men do not mind paying a little if they acquire something, but will resist most programs which benefit exclusive minorities.

Impressions accumulated from evidence on policies among the more stable western democracies suggests that overall benefits are widely though unequally distributed and that burdens are also widely though unequally

Figure 14-5

The Distribution of Benefits and Burdens

		Benefits:	
		Widely Distributed	Narrowly Distributed
Burdens:	Widely Distributed	(a)	(b)
	Narrowly Distributed	(c)	(d)

divided. See Chapters 3 and 5. Democratic governments have had to respond to an increasing number of demands for goods and services from an increasingly larger proportion of their populations thus ensuring rather widespread distribution of public goods. On the other hand these same governments have had to find new sources of revenue to finance the increased demand for goods and services. As a result, they have tapped nearly everyone in society who is capable of paying something. To be sure, burdens are unequally allocated but widespread incidence is a fact.

It is our further impression from rather scattered evidence that such choices have not endangered the workings or stability of democracy. The incentive to participate in revenue and expenditure policies is increased when more rather than fewer are directly affected. Since these are monetary matters or issues, they are more easily compromised or used for trading or logrolling purposes. Tax allocation and distribution of benefits are recurrent choices in a polity. Since they are highly suitable bargaining issues for leaders, they expand the opportunities for popular influence and choice in elections. Many may bemoan the actual absence of great 'either-or' choices over the type of system or the structure of society, but we think man's dignity and effectiveness rests far more on the opportunities to influence those choices typical of everyday political decision-making. The grand moments of major political change are much less susceptible to conscious choice-making for the greater segment of any citizenry.

Public Policies

We began with an analysis of conditions—favorable and unfavorable —for democratic competition and bargaining in making collective decisions, as though these conditions existed without intervention on the part of people and governments. But these conditions can also be deliberately altered by political action and public policies. In these remaining pages we make a few modest proposals along such lines. Because the democracies vary in their institutional and cultural settings, we cannot prescribe for each in detail; but we can advance some generalizations about types of reforms to facilitate more effective choice. Readers should be able with further study of particular nations to supply added detail and alternatives.

Encouragement of Competition and Bargaining

Those who have privileged positions do not, as a rule, care to encourage competition, while those who are less privileged may have the incentives but lack the opportunities. Both political and economic competition depend upon those who have to gain by their extension because the privileged will erect barriers to reduce or discourage competitors. Those who wish to protect and facilitate competition must be ever alert in supplying incentives and opportunities for those who have not been winning out recently.

Two general courses of action are open to the reformer: first, he may increase the incentives of the potential competitor to compete and, second, he may improve the opportunities or institutions within which competition takes place. In regard to incentives or inducements, policies which will reduce the costs or increase the probabilities of producing net benefits are very much in order. The costs of competition, especially election campaigning, are usually far too high for most individuals to undertake. We refer to both monetary and psychological costs. It is doubtful that legislation could directly reduce money costs but it could provide funds and other resources which would enable more people to participate. At present, governments do finance elections but not the campaigning itself. The costs run into the millions of dollars in the United States for offices of any significance although, as we observed in Chapter 11, the cost per vote is remarkably small. Governments could easily finance more of the campaigning.

Legislation could be fruitfully employed, and has been to some degree already, to reduce certain non-monetary barriers to competition. Reducing the qualifications to vote has been a major area; the ownership of property, for example, was at one time a requirement. There were other barriers; women are still informally discouraged from active politics in most nations. In other ways minority groups have been effectively removed from competition by legal and informal procedures. Legal requirements, difficult registration procedures, the informal discouragements and sanctions of local elites can all conspire to reduce and minimize voting participation. All are in the process of being effectively if slowly removed by public policy.[23]

Most reforms take the form of improving the institutional environment which conditions competition; few are based upon increasing or altering the incentives of men to engage in politics. Prudence suggests that reform of institutions may be easier than reform of incentives or motivations, but one should not overlook the possibilities. Increasing the probabilities of greater rewards is usually an effective goad to most people. If a citizen can see the chances of bettering his position through political action he is more inclined to view it favorably and be prepared to accept the necessary burdens. A difficulty all democracies face is creating meaningful incentives. Political systems of necessity operate in ways which do not permit individuals the realm of choice afforded in marketplaces, nor many of the possibilities of direct and immediate gratification. Accordingly, we may expect rather pronounced limitations on what can be accomplished.

One incentive insufficiently stressed is that of making politics more rewarding as an activity in itself rather than stressing the possibilities of personal gain through public decisions and their outcomes. Some men do find politics an attractive activity; why not others? One way of providing such encouragement is to make political activity relevant to the newer themes and style of a culture, so that political action maintains an appeal and attractiveness. Competitive leadership can help enhance the appeal of politics by maintaining the legitimacy of their methods, and by the openness and visibility of contesting over important issues.

Present-day democracies afford varying tribute to politics and politicians, with Britain high on the list and the United States somewhat lower. No doubt politics will always be accompanied by an ambivalent status, but it can be improved. A law will not accomplish the change so much as examples set by prestigious persons making political careers interesting and rewarding. This appears to be happening in the United States where ratings of public service continue to climb. A better appreciation of the skills and demands on political competitors and bargainers would also assist in improving their statuses. This can be accomplished through imaginative programs for students and adults: political workshops, simulations of political bargaining and competition, participatory programs of

---

[23] For a realistic assessment and recommendations on voting and other forms of participation, see United States Commission on Civil Rights Reports entitled *Voting* (Washington, D.C.: U.S. Government Printing Office, 1968). Recommendations on improving the quality of political participation are also contained in the report of the U.S. 'riot' commission, *Report of the National Advisory Commission on Civil Disorders* (Washington, D.C.: U.S. Government Printing Office, 1968). The latter is also available in a paperback edition: (New York: Bantam Books, 1968).

many sorts. The rather rare talents of the good politician should not be undervalued.

Acquisition of Political Skills

Few citizens acquire competitive or bargaining skills primarily because these skills are seldom explicitly taught in the school system. We firmly believe that a drastic reorientation must take place in education, particularly at the secondary level since many citizens may not go to college. Such a reorientation would transfer attention from the inculcation of middle-class 'civic responsibility' norms and values to instrumental knowledge about active participation in democracy. More specifically, we believe that young citizens must learn about their rights as well as obligations, about how to protect as well as advance them in political ways. The latter means they must be accorded more access and roles of direct relevance in terms of the issues of the day. They must learn more about the realistic workings of the political processes and about the outcomes of political effort which concern everyone in the ways noted in Part 1. To be efficacious, a person must acquire information that can be 'put to work.' We recommend a problem-solving approach to the workings of politics and the nature of issues such as we have tried to suggest in the problems of each chapter. And, most importantly, the premises of dignity and regard, the considerations and reciprocities of political activity, need emphasis so that young people may make their demands more effectively and efficiently in whatever institutional framework they may find themselves. We firmly believe that young citizens will find this type of instruction far more relevant, interesting and useful; they will, therefore, be more likely to learn it. The abstract principles so typically taught, the ritual and memorization they now undergo have little lasting effect; worse, they discourage certain groups from ever becoming political. Glorified histories of the nation have their roles but they ought to be reduced and supplanted with the kind of approach we have suggested. A politically skilled citizenry is far better off than a naive one which allows the sophisticated to take advantage of them.

Understanding one's stake in political life and policy outcomes, learning how to mobilize intelligence, plan campaigns, gather support, choose strategies and tactics—these should be the goals of our reforms. We see not a collection of highly selfish individuals emerging, but sophisticated, politically minded persons who can engage in fruitful and mutually profitable exchanges enabling more people to enjoy the vast benefits of social life. The number of cynics ought to be diminished considerably by such education and experiences.

Increasing Voter Competence

Improvement of political competition and bargaining requires more sophisticated voters as well as activists. While much attention is paid the general ideal of an informed citizenry, very little of the usual reform suggestions and moralistic preachings get at the basic problem. The basic problem is not one of preaching unrewarding duties to apathetic citizens but one of showing citizens their personal stakes (particularly status and efficacy) in the polity and how they can effectively relate politics to their own situations. Obviously, it will be more difficult to achieve this than it would be to educate for economic competence; we have already shown why this must be the case. But there is room for improvement, and we need not depend upon the schools, alone, to do the job. Every interest group and politician is daily engaged in the task of communicating 'cost-benefit' analyses to their constituents. The pedagogy employed by these interested persons and groups, however, is frequently unrealistic. They, too, tend to preach rather than inform.

We are not demanding the ideal civics-book citizen, perfectly informed, highly interested and motivated and dedicated to an abstract public interest. We are concerned about showing demonstrable stakes and how those who wish to become active can do so in the most efficient manner. While something can be accomplished along these lines after citizens become legal adults, much of the relevant preparation should be done at an earlier age before misconceptions have a chance to form. Once more that means reform of civic education, a task not always easily achieved because both educators and status quo groups in society will resist. Something can be done at the college level where political science and economics can be taught with greater realism than in the high schools. For some peculiar reason it is felt that a person cannot or will not remain loyal if he is taught that political differences require an understanding of competition, bargaining and even conflict. Few who espouse free enterprise regard themselves as disloyal to capitalist institutions because they must engage in economic competition, bargaining and other 'hard-headed' calculations. In fact, such pursuits are highly honored. Still, we manage to cloak the political calculus of our great politicians by calling them statesmen. No doubt some of this approach does rebound to the benefit of society, for no society can be held together solely by rational or selfish considerations; but even the most selfish political concerns do not necessarily produce chaos. After all, support must be earned, agreements arrived at and outcomes legitimated. In any event there is room for a good deal more political objectivity among the citizens.

Improving Competitive Institutions

Increasing the competence of politicians and citizens to compete will not, in itself, notably improve competition if the institutional framework of that activity is not also improved. The most rational of actors can be completely frustrated in terms of their own interests and public policies if the prevailing norms and rules prevent them from achieving their goals. Apparently, the Weimar Republic and the French Fourth Republic imposed such ineffective rules that both systems failed. Great and even minor political issues could not be resolved in mutually acceptable ways in either nation. The problem is not one of extending competition but of providing means whereby competition will produce desirable results, i.e., policies which are acceptable to as many citizens as possible.

A number of specific reforms are in order. First, elections, as the key competitive institution, must be so conducted so that they achieve more of some rather difficult goals: to simplify issues and reduce them to a manageable number, and to produce officials and policies that are a rough reflection of popular preferences. No single set of reforms can be advocated for all democracies since the social structures and histories of each are so divergent, but it is possible to judge the performances of electoral institutions within each nation. We believe there should be as much decentralized choice as possible, relevant to the local or preliminary phases of political decisions, but it should stop short of the point of isolating and excluding minority influences on those public decisions that affect them. We hope better advice and guidance will come from sensitive studies of various forms of issue and area representation—in terms of outcomes and satisfactions. Political institutions probably work best when they are consonant with the cultures of which they are an element. This country offers many such 'sub-cultural' laboratories for study, and comparative research abroad on these questions would be very helpful. The means are currently quite available.[24]

One can maintain that an electoral process should, under most conditions, be as open or free as possible for contenders and electors; that the alternatives be understandable and limited to a few; that elections ought not to be held every day; that electors be treated equally (one man-one vote); that attending elections be made as costless as possible; that alternatives should not be so polarized or extreme that some in fact are ruled out as unacceptable; that whenever possible, expenditure and cost alternatives be presented simultaneously; and that simple majority rules are normally preferable. These suggested guidelines are not absolute or suitable under all conditions. Furthermore, each has its consequences which include some unavoidable burdens. For example, the suggestion that in referenda, expenditure and cost estimates be included will sometimes

---

[24] Two recent volumes on community politics are highly suggestive of the kinds of research that can be done and which ought to prove useful for policy-makers. See Robert E. Agger, Daniel Goldrich and Bert E. Swanson, *The Rulers and the Ruled* (New York: John Wiley and Sons, Inc., 1964), and Terry N. Clark, ed., *Community Structure and Decision-Making: Comparative Analyses* (San Francisco: Chandler Publishing Company, 1968).

reduce public expenditures, especially for projects we may prefer; but that may be the price that must be paid to provide more meaningful choices. On the other hand, we feel the range of positive choices can often be defined more imaginatively. We anticipate continuing efforts at defining progress in the public sector in more realistic and effective ways, which make politics 'worth while' for groups that tend to feel—and are—excluded. We hope the incentives of open political competition work in this direction.

Problems and Applications

1. Compare and comment on the following generalizations in terms of the qualifications or conditions you would apply:

    ". . . democracy works best in small units in which large proportions of the citizenry can observe the operations of their governments."

    "A predominantly immobile agricultural society, which is at the same time very poor, is not very likely to develop a democratic form of government."

    "Democracy can persist only as long as it rests upon a large and powerful middle class."

2. Christian Bay has declared that "coercion, over sane, adult human beings, can be justified only if it in fact serves to reduce coercion or prevent increased coercion." *The Structure of Freedom* (Stanford: Stanford University Press, 1958), p. 133. How do you view this 'principle' as a basis for improving democracy? Why?

3. Which of these rules do you think will best protect deviant minority views: simple majority; plurality; two-thirds majority? Why? Will your choice of rule work under all conditions?

4. Democracy has had a difficult time getting established in the new states of the post World War II period. Does the discussion in this chapter suggest some explanations? What do you see as the most crucial problems?

5. If you were asked to defend the commitment of working or lower classes to democracy in this country, what would you say? What kinds of arguments and evidence can be brought to bear on the issue?

6. The city of Eugene, Oregon, with a population of 68,000, has at least 375 private organizations publicly listed (business, civic, recreational, etc.), while the town of Montegrano, Italy, with 3,400 population, has no organized associations, according to Edward Banfield, *Moral Basis of a Backward Society* (Glencoe, Ill.: The Free Press, 1958), pp. 15-16. Does a fact like this have any relevance to explaining the political life of small towns? Why?

7. Some commentators have suggested that American political institutions cannot be exported to other lands. Is this sound advice? Under

what conditions would it be most possible to transplant the political forms of one nation to another? When is this impossible?

8. "If one wishes to establish and institutionalize bargaining and competitive practices he should adopt a constitution which deals only with basic rules for the procedures, is difficult to amend, observes practices with which the people are already familiar, and is flexible enough to handle new issues." Is this sound advice in view of what has been said in these past fourteen chapters? Try composing a suitable constitution in outline form or come up with some suggested improvements of this country's document.

9. What effective, peaceful sanctions and encouragements are there in either your local or national political system for keeping political competition and bargaining fair and free of abuse? What are the situations where this is least likely to be so? Can you diagnose the contrasting situations in terms of incentives vs. constraints?

10. There are many activist groups today which are demanding change in the form of participatory democracy. What kind of proposals would you suggest to them *to provide realistic incentives* for greater participation on the part of the following groups: the elderly, American Indians, youth, Mexican-Americans, black Americans, women?

Bibliographical Notes

Our footnotes have probably cited most of the crucial research and theory on the conditions for establishing and maintaining democracy. There are, however, a number of items which require citation whether they were used in the preparation of this chapter or not; we should like to proceed by following the major sections of the chapter.

On social structure we would especially recommend these titles: Seymour Martin Lipset, *et al., Union Democracy* (Glencoe, Ill.: The Free Press, 1956), is a landmark in political sociology and a must for anyone concerned with the problems of this chapter. Lipset and his colleagues attempted to study why a 'two party system' was able to develop and function as well as it has in apparently the only trade union in the world with institutionalized competition—The International Typographical Union. The book is highly imaginative and methodologically sophisticated. As a work in theory it should be read along with Roberto Michels, *Political Parties* (many editions), because it tests his theory of oligarchy and offers some qualifications. Michels' thesis about the inherent tendencies of organizations to become oligarchical still stands, as Lipset and his coauthors regretfully agree. Lipset, himself, in his first book, *Agrarian Socialism* (Berkeley: University of California Press, 1950), showed a strong concern for the effects of social structure on politics and more particularly attempted to explain why a rural province in capitalist Canada elected a socialist government in 1946.

Another sociologist with political concerns, Reinhard Bendix, has written with wisdom about social structure and political behavior in *Nation-Building and Citizenship* (New York: John Wiley and Sons, Inc., 1964). Problems of nation-building and democracy, in particular, are focal points. Much the same can be said about the essays of T. H. Marshall, *Class, Citizenship, and Social Development* (New York: Doubleday and Company, Inc., 1964). Parts II and III are most relevant. In a prize winning book, Barrington Moore, Jr., has dealt with the historical problem of the *Social Origins of Dictatorship and Democracy* (Boston: Beacon Press, 1966). Moore advances a number of challenging theses about the growth of different types of polities, including an analysis of the situation in India, a crucial test case, so to speak, of the survival power of democracy in less than perfect conditions. Finally, we suggest a kind of summary or synthesis of explanations on *Why Democracies Fail* (Notre Dame: University of Notre Dame Press, 1957), by Norman L. Stamps. Chapter 7 considers the role of social structure in discouraging democratic rule.

Psychologists and psychologically oriented political scientists have long attempted to unravel politics and explain various forms of political behavior. For the most part they have focussed on the level of individual behavior, although some generalize from this to system and cultural levels. For those wishing a basic introduction to social psychology we strongly recommend Roger Brown's *Social Psychology* (New York: The Free Press, 1965), a model textbook—solid thinking, well-organized, clear and easily read. Chapter 10 is on the 'authoritarian personality' and contains a balanced appraisal of that famous work, *The Authoritarian Personality* (New York: Harper and Brothers, 1950), written by T. W. Adorno, Else Frenkel-Brunswik, Daniel J. Levinson and R. Nevitt Sanford. Those interested in continuities of research ought to consult Richard Christie and Marie Jahoda, eds., *"The Authoritarian Personality,"* a collection of six papers critically assessing the original work. Several works by Erich Fromm take a generalized psychological approach; we shall only mention his most famous of those relevant politically: *Escape from Freedom* (New York: Farrar and Rhinehart, Inc., 1941). In this he develops a psychological theory of the totalitarian movement, writing with the Nazi regime in Germany especially in mind. In the tradition of both Fromm and the Adorno volumes is that of Milton Rokeach, *The Open and Closed Mind* (New York: Basic Books, Inc., 1960). This book is about belief systems and personality, with strong hints about the political consequences of these factors. Obviously, the 'open mind' is viewed as preferable. The last volume we should like to suggest your reading is one with which we do not entirely agree as to approach or conclusions. It may serve to illustrate some of the pitfalls of political theorizing from social-psychological assumptions. The book is entitled *Autocracy and Democracy* by Ralph K. White and Ronald Lippitt (New York: Harper and Brothers, 1960). This reports on experimental studies conducted with small groups of boys; these studies have value in themselves but are used as a basis for advancing political implications in the larger world. We do not think this leap is particularly persuasive. But, you should evaluate it for yourself. The novel, *Lord of the Flies* (many editions), by William Golding provides a more interesting if frightening picture of how political systems might emerge among boys.

Economists, as we have noted, have begun to interest themselves in politics, even with the question at issue in this chapter. One especially intriguing analysis is that of Karl de Schweinitz, Jr., *Industrialization and Democracy* (New York: The Free Press of Glencoe, Inc., 1964). The author's chief contention is that industrialization in the twentieth century no longer encourages the emergence of democracy as it did for the western systems in the nineteenth century. De Schweinitz argues that expectations today outstrip the capacity of governments even to catch up with those western societies. So the demand for extensive controls and government investment is irresistible. Charles Wolfe, Jr., in his volume *Foreign Aid,* a study we have cited several times in different contexts, is again relevant to our problems with his theory of conditions vulnerable to communism; a theory which combines psychological aspirations, expectations, and the events of economic and political change. Mancur Olson, Jr., has put forth an ingenious thesis that rapid economic growth has disquieting political consequences, including revolutions. See "Rapid Growth as a Destabilizing Force" in *Journal of Economic History,* XXIII (December, 1963). The article will be reprinted in a forthcoming volume edited by James C. Davies, *When Men Revolt* (New York: The Free Press, 1969). Similar ideas have been voiced by Alexis de Tocqueville, *The Old Regime and the French Revolution* (New York: Doubleday and Company, 1955), p. 174; Crane Brinton, *The Anatomy of Revolution* (New York: Vintage Books, 1962), p. 64; Eric Hoffer, *The True Believer* (New York: Harper and Brothers, 1952), p. 28. The more general political effects of economic events and programs are ably presented by Charles Wolfe, Jr., in his *United States Policy and the Third World* (Boston: Little, Brown and Company, 1967), Chapters 2 and 6.

Political scientists are not to be outdone in analyzing the condition of, and conditions for, democracy. Our discussion of the importance of issues was based on Robert A. Dahl, *A Preface to Democratic Theory* (Chicago: The University of Chicago Press, 1956) and E. E. Schattschneider's oft-cited work, *The Semi-Sovereign People* (New York: Holt, Rinehart, and Winston, Inc., 1960). Another political scientist who has written at length about these matters of prerequisites is Leslie Lipson, *The Democratic Civilization* (New York: Oxford University Press, 1964), Part II. While the themes of our chapter are indirectly dealt with, Lipson does offer a great deal of information of value for students of democracy. Brief introductory thoughts on democratic preconditions are contained in M. Rejai, ed., *The Contemporary Theories of Democracy* (New York: Atherton Press, 1967), Part II. Some of the selections are a bit too brief, but the major questions and articles are included. Those who may be interested in the actual history of democracy rather than in discovering preconditions may enjoy reading John Simpson Penman's *The Irresistible Movement of Democracy* (New York: The Macmillan Company, 1923). The rise of democracy in America, France and England are recorded in great detail.

What men actually believe and what is necessary to believe to sustain democracy are considered by Gabriel Almond and Sidney Verba in *The Civic Culture* (Princeton: Princeton University Press, 1963). Chapter 15 attempts to elaborate a theory of cultural prerequisites for democratic stability. Most of our generalizations would seem to be reasonably consistent with the theory of Almond and Verba. Their theory, as well as ours, owes a theoretical debt of gratitude to Bernard Berelson, *et al., Voting* (Chicago: University of Chicago Press, 1954); Chapter 14 is a crucial early statement about the most appropriate distributions of attitudes for a 'healthy' democracy. For evidence on the extent of disagreement across class divisions as revealed by election results, see the interesting research of Robert R. Alford, *Party and Society* (Chicago: Rand McNally and Company, 1963). Alford examines the degree of class division of the vote in Great Britain, Australia, United States and Canada. His data range back to 1936, so trends are visible, and he interprets their meaning. The last two chapters offer some 'non-Marxian' speculations about the consequences of class polarization. This book is worth reading for the additional reason that it exemplifies a rapidly growing field of genuinely comparative research on a number of countries.

How to improve democratic processes or to establish them where they are not to be found has been a preoccupation of countless social theorists and practical men. We can only cite but the most minute sample of thinking on the subject. Perhaps we should begin with a general treatment of how best to establish democracy; Herbert J. Spiro, *Government by Constitution* (New York: Random House, Inc., 1959) is a comparative government textbook, but an imaginative one and unique in that the author offers a number of "Guidelines for Constitution-Makers" at the ends of Chapters 14-18; 20-21. Most of them seem sensible, although a bit conventional for this day and age. In any case, we strongly commend the book for making its policy advice explicit.

We shall conclude with some especially sensitive and ethically concerned treatments of the political requirements and guarantees for effective choice and expression in the realm of politics. While there are many general works of political thought which pose the ethical and moral dilemmas of man in society, we are citing these because they are concerned with matters that apply directly to political contexts. We believe there is much to be gained by applying empirical findings to help enlarge the sphere of political choice and by seeking policies which will provide the conditions for doing so. Otto Kirchheimer's *Political Justice* (Princeton, N.J.: Princeton University Press, 1961) provides a most perceptive guide to the uses of judicial processes, reviewing their advantages and costs with both practical and ethical relevance. Alternatively one can consider the content of legal choices and Edmond Cahn does so, combining ethical and political considerations very effectively in *The Moral Decision* (Bloomington: Indiana University Press, 1959).

Another book comes to mind, entitled *The Ethic of Power* (New York: Harper and Brothers, 1962), edited by Harold D. Lasswell and Harlan Cleveland. While many of the selections stray disappointingly from what is implied in the title, we would recommend the contribution of John P. Plamenatz on "What Principles Should Guide Us in Seeking to Influence Foreign Governments and Peoples?" Consider his precepts as applied also to interpersonal political activity; do they sound quite similar to our own proposals? In the realm of public policy, Abraham Kaplan deals with typical moral questions in the American context, and with his characteristic forthrightness and clarity. The work is brief and we commend it highly: *American Ethics and Public Policy* (New York: Oxford University Press, 1963). We also like the imaginative treatment of *The Promise of Politics* (Englewood Cliffs, N.J.: Prentice-Hall, Inc., 1966) by Henry Kariel. The author is especially appreciative of the innovative opportunities afforded by effective political endeavor, and he writes also with an appreciation of political possibilities in the ordinary situations that most citizens experience, especially that of work life. Chapter III on "Conditions for Politics" is especially relevant.

Finally, we would like to close with some very noteworthy ventures in the definition of freedom as it might be realized for individuals in today's political world. For those who want to consider man's personality, his needs and potential in politically relevant terms, we recommend the very thorough and sensitive treatment of Christian Bay, *The Structure of Freedom* (Stanford, Calif.: Stanford University Press, 1958). Part Two considers the political and social implications of personal freedom. And for those who wish to theorize more in terms of the logic of preferences for freedom in the social context and what this implies politically, a most systematic guide is Felix Oppenheim's *Dimensions of Freedom: An Analysis* (New York: St. Martin's Press, Inc., 1961).

NAME INDEX

SUBJECT INDEX